ANGLO-SAXON MONETARY HISTORY

Visby, 1977

Anglo-Saxon Monetary History

Essays in memory of Michael Dolley
edited by M. A. S. Blackburn

LEICESTER UNIVERSITY PRESS 1986

First published in 1986 by Leicester University Press
First published in 1986 in the United States of America
by Humanities Press, Inc., Atlantic Highlands, NJ 07716,
and also distributed by them in North America

Designed by Douglas Martin
Filmset in Linotron 202 Plantin
by Wyvern Typesetting Ltd
Printed and bound in Great Britain by Redwood Burn Ltd,
Trowbridge

The publication of this book has been assisted by a grant from the Twenty-Seven Foundation.
The cost of printing Dr Dolley's bibliography has been met by grants from A. H. Baldwin and Sons Limited, Spink and Son Limited, and B. A. Seaby Limited.

British Library Cataloguing in Publication Data

Anglo-Saxon monetary history: essays in memory of Michael Dolley
1. Coinage–England–History
I. Blackburn, M.A.S. II. Dolley, Michael.
332.4'042'942 HG936

ISBN 0-7185-1239-1

Preface

Anglo-Saxon studies have flourished during the last 35 years, not least in the field of coinage and monetary history. The growing awareness among historians of the need to pursue all forms of primary evidence inspired a post-war generation of numismatists to reassess their material critically and to look for its wider relevance. Significant and rapid advances were made, initially in terms of recording, classification, and chronology, tasks which are fundamental to all numismatic research. This work continues, but building upon it new techniques of analysis and new lines of enquiry have been developed. Increasingly, emphasis is laid upon the economic and administrative aspects of the currency, exploring such features as the relative output of the mints, the degree of over-value of money reflected in variations in weight and fineness, the wastage from currency due to loss, export, and recoinage, the speed of circulation, the production and movement of dies, and the large and closely dated body of personal- and place-name evidence. Many of these topics are still novel and require further exploration to test the preliminary conclusions, yet they indicate the rich potential which lies in the coinage as a source of evidence for the Anglo-Saxon period.

The man who more than any other was in the vanguard of this new wave of research was Dr Michael Dolley. It was originally intended that this volume should be dedicated to him as a *Festschrift* for his sixtieth birthday on 6 July 1985. Sadly he did not live to see its publication or receive the gratitude and warm wishes which it was to have conveyed, although he learnt of its preparation shortly before his death on 29 March 1983.

Michael Dolley's contribution to medieval numismatics was outstanding. His enthusiasm for his subject, his keen historical sense, and his love of writing were major factors in his success. He had an astonishing capacity for work. His career from an Assistant Keeper in the National Maritime Museum and then in the Department of Coins and Medals at the British Museum to Professor of Historical Numismatics at Queen's University Belfast, and finally Associate Professor at Armidale University, New South Wales, has been fully described elsewhere.[1] The bibliography in this volume is a witness to his remarkable productivity, yet he was unstinting of his time in the encouragement of other students in his field, especially the young. Those who heard him lecture or met him briefly will remember his

1. In the following obituaries: *BNJ 52* (1982), 265–71 (C. S. S. Lyon); *The Times*, 4 April 1983, 10; *The Irish Times*, 19 May 1983 (E. Rynne); *The Belfast Telegraph*, 30 March 1983; *AntJ 63* (1983), 541–2 (Anon.); *Mariner's Mirror 69.2* (1983), 113 (H. Wallis and L. Basch); *SCMB* 1983, 121–2 (W. A. Seaby); *NCirc* 1984, 13 (C. E. Blunt); *IN* 1983, 84–5 (D. Young); *NNUM* 1983, 108–9 (T. Talvio); *NNF-Nytt* 1983, 6–7 (K. Skaare); *Mynt Kontakt* 1983, 122 (L. O. Lagerqvist); *Numismatisches Nachrichtenblatt* 1983, 160 (P. Berghaus).

forceful, not to say controversial personality; those who knew him better can testify to the depth and warmth of his humanity.

The papers in this volume reflect but one aspect of Dolley's broad scholarly interests, but they are offered as a mark of respect from all his friends and colleagues, including those precluded by the tight theme of the volume from making their own personal contribution. The editor and contributors would like to thank Leicester University Press for undertaking the publication of this book, and in particular Peter Boulton and Susan Martin who have expertly seen it through the press. The publisher's financial burden has been relieved to some extent by generous grants from the Twenty-Seven Foundation, and Messrs Baldwin, Spink, and Seaby.

M.A.S.B. *Cambridge, February 1985*

Contents

List of plates

List of figures

List of tables

Abbreviations

Note Places of publication are given only for works published outside the United Kingdom. In abbreviating less frequently cited periodicals the commonly accepted usage of *Soc.* for *Society*, *J.* for *Journal*, *Trans.* for *Transactions* etc. has been followed. Other abbreviations are listed below.

AntJ	*Antiquaries Journal*
ArchJ	*Archaeological Journal*
AS Coins	R. H. M. Dolley, ed., *Anglo-Saxon Coins, Studies presented to Sir Frank Stenton* (1961)
ASE	*Anglo-Saxon England*
BAR	British Archaeological Reports
BMC	*British Museum Catalogue* (H. A. Grueber and C. F. Keary, *Catalogue of English Coins in the British Museum. Anglo-Saxon series*, 2 vols., 1887 and 1893)
BMQ	*British Museum Quarterly*
BNJ	*British Numismatic Journal*
CBA	Council for British Archaeology
CH	*Coin Hoards*
CNS	*Corpus nummorum saeculorum* IX-XI *qui in Suecia reperti sunt* (Stockholm)
Commentationes	*Commentationes de nummis saeculorum* IX-XI *in Suecia repertis*, 2 vols. (Stockholm, 1961 and 1968)
DB	*Domesday Book seu liber censualis Willelmi Primi regis Angliae*, ed. A. Farley and H. Ellis, 2 vols. (1783 and 1816)
EcHR	*Economic History Review*
EHD	*English Historical Documents*
EHR	*English Historical Review*
HBNC	*History of Berwickshire Naturalists' Club*
HBN	*Hamburger Beiträge zur Numismatik*
Hild.	B. E. Hildbrand, *Anglosachsiska Mynt*, 2nd edn (Stockholm, 1881)
IN	*Irish Numismatics*
JMP	*Jaarboek voor Munt- en Penningkunde*
JRSAI	*Journal of the Royal Society of Antiquaries of Ireland*
MedArch	*Medieval Archaeology*
MScand	*Mediaeval Scandinavia*
NC	*Numismatic Chronicle*
NCirc	*Numismatic Circular*
NNÅ	*Nordisk Numismatisk Årsskrift*
NNF-Nytt	*Norsk Numismatisk Forening-Nytt*
NNUM	*Nordisk Numismatisk Unions Medlemsblad*

PRIA	*Proceedings of the Royal Irish Academy*
PSAS	*Proceedings of the Society of Antiquaries of Scotland*
PSIA	*Proceedings of the Suffolk Institute of Archaeology*
SCBI	*Sylloge of Coins of the British Isles*
SCMB	*Seaby's Coin and Medal Bulletin*
TRHS	*Transactions of the Royal Historical Society*
YAJ	*Yorkshire Archaeological Journal*
YPSR	*Report of the Yorkshire Philosophical Society*

1 Progress in Anglo-Saxon monetary history

Henry Loyn

More than 20 years ago Michael Dolley edited a volume of studies in honour of Sir Frank Stenton's eightieth birthday under the title *Anglo-Saxon Coins*.[1] Those of us who were privileged to contribute to the volume recognized that this was no ordinary *Festschrift* but a genuine constructive work that with the inspiration of Stenton and the drive of Dolley attempted to indicate the importance of recent numismatic advances to the historical world. Now that such advances can no longer be termed recent it may be useful to ponder again the consequences of the exercise and to discuss the resulting patterns that have emerged after two more decades in relation to two or three of the main fields touched.

My own contribution to that volume concerned boroughs and mints and it is therefore appropriate that I should concentrate on those two institutions for my principal theme. There are, however, two wider fields that demand comment before we turn to specific matters, namely the economic and the administrative. The importance of numismatic investigation for general understanding of the economic background was fully apparent in 1961 and the shades of the Pirenne thesis and consequent discussions lay heavy in the minds of many contributors. It is not without interest that Michael Dolley himself, in his moving farewell speech to the Oxford Symposium on 'Coinage in the Northern Lands' in January 1981, drew special attention to the work of Dr Nils Rasmusson and to Professor Sture Bolin's paper on 'Mohammed, Charlemagne and Ruric' as examples of the range and the depth of thought on economic problems in the 1950s.[2] There has been comparatively little advance on the English side in relation to some of these important general economic aspects, though the work of Stewart Lyon and Michael Metcalf (both incidentally contributors to the Stenton *Festschrift*) has direct bearing on all the major issues.[3] Questions relating to the purpose of currency and to the volume of

1. *AS Coins* (1961).
2. Michael Dolley, 'A summing-up', in *Viking-Age Coinage in the Northern Lands*, ed. M. A. S. Blackburn and D. M. Metcalf (BAR Internat. Ser. 122, 1981), 533–52, at 536; S. Bolin, 'Mohammed, Charlemagne and Ruric', *Scandinavian Economic Hist. Rev. 1* (1953), 5–39.
3. C. S. S. Lyon, most notably in his presidential addresses to the British Numismatic Society: *BNJ 35* (1966), 223–30; *BNJ 36* (1967), 215–21; *BNJ 37* (1968), 216–38; *BNJ 38* (1969), 204–22; and *BNJ 39* (1970), 193–204; and *idem*, 'Some problems in

coins in circulation have been aired vigorously by both scholars, so making better sense of our view of the role of the currency in the economy. But reasons for reticence on some aspects are only too obvious. The visual image is wrong. Gold and silver, bullion, the treasure-hoard of kings, land and the produce of land, other men's labour, cattle, sheep, fish, even eels; these are the things we see initially when we think of media of exchange in the early Middle Ages. Gift-exchange comes as readily to the mind as straight honest trade.[4]

Such images have in the past inevitably led to a degree of distortion but legal historians, archaeologists, and numismatists have united in forcing us to take seriously our late Anglo-Saxon coinage as an important and commonplace means of exchange. The thought of Beowulf, or for that matter Harold Godwinson, fishing in his pockets for small change to pay the coastguard is admittedly incongruous. But serious matter lies here and the social historians, successors of Pirenne and Marc Bloch, some elements in the Annales school, have helped give us new perspective on the workings of what they call a denarial economy, that is to say of an economy used to thinking in terms of large sums of money, gold and silver, pounds, shillings and pence, where the only tangible native-minted coin in general use was the silver penny.[5] Such a denarial economy existed virtually without exception in the more advanced communities of Western Europe from the late seventh to the thirteenth century.

The practical working of such an economy is not easy to envisage, and some of the reasons for reticence on the workings of late Anglo-Saxon currency become apparent. Evidence is scattered and fragmentary and problems of interpretation are huge. Some literary evidence helps. Ælfric Bata, writing in the early eleventh century, describes the purchase of a book costing twelve mancuses and tells us that the purchaser counted out the coins one by one, 360 of them in all.[6] Homilists, sermon-writers, lawyers refer consistently to units of monetary assessment that are part and parcel of an ordered and stable structure, pounds and pence in a standard ratio of 240 pence to the pound and intermediate units, mancuses (30d), shillings (varying from the 12d of the Carolingian scale to 5d in Wessex and 4d in Mercia) and especially but not exclusively in the more Scandinavianized part of Britain the ora (16d–20d). The coins themselves, the pennies, varied in weight and were true coins, tokens of value, reckoned by tale, not value of bullion. Elaborate methods of

interpreting Anglo-Saxon coinage', *ASE* 5 (1976), 173–224. There is much valuable data in H. B. A. Petersson, *Anglo-Saxon Currency* (Lund, 1969), and D. M. Metcalf has more recently brought important ideas and material together in 'The ranking of boroughs: numismatic evidence from the reign of Æthelred II', in *Ethelred the Unready*, ed. D. Hill (BAR 59, 1978), 159–212, and, *idem*, 'Continuity and change in English monetary history, c.973–1086', pt 1, *BNJ 50* (1980), 20–49; pt 2, *BNJ 51* (1981), 52–90.

4. P. Grierson, 'Commerce in the Dark Ages', *TRHS*[5] 9 (1959), 123–40.
5. M. Bloch, *Feudal Society* (tr. L. A. Manyon; 1961), esp. 65–9; R. Latouche, *The Birth of Western Economy* (tr. E. M. Wilkinson; 1961), esp. 143–75.
6. W. H. Stevenson and W. M. Lindsay (eds.), *Early Scholastic Colloquies* (1929), 50.

blanching and testing were generally practised. Domesday Book statistics are only the most prominent reminders that coins were known to all and used by many. There is a revealing entry in the Herefordshire folios relating to Earl Morcar's land at Eardisland which tells us that the steward in 1066 was accustomed to give his lady 18 oras of pence when she visited the estate so that she might be happy. Lady Godiva, Earl Morcar's grandmother, was still alive in 1066 and it is an amusing thought, if she is indeed the *sua domina* the steward had in mind, that her passion for good works relating to hard cash was not exhausted by her experiences at Coventry.[7] We have, of course, to overcome a difficulty that threatens to divorce terminology from reality. A penny sounds small change, but it is not. A few pence only was regarded as a reasonable price for a sheep.[8] Other equivalents suggest a similar range. Ælfric Bata's book must have been in the top class of psalters and service books, worth a substantial flock of sheep.

A basic problem to consider is where and how people kept their money. At the top level this is not too difficult. Kings, great nobles, and churchmen had their treasure hoards from which coins and bullion could be disbursed, 100 mancuses to this bishop, 50 mancuses to that thegn or retainer. They had their treasurers, their strong rooms, their strong men to guard the treasure. In more peaceful times monasteries could be used, one of the reasons incidentally why they were the prime target for Viking attacks. King Eadred when he felt that he was near death ordered Dunstan to bring treasure to him, landbooks as well as cash, which had been entrusted to his care at Glastonbury; and Dunstan duly obliged, transporting the goods on horseback.[9] It is not so easy to discover what happened to the treasures of lesser men. Archaeological evidence occasionally helps. Let me give two examples from opposite ends of the scale in size and for the late Anglo-Saxon period in time. At Cuerdale near Preston in Lancashire there occurred in 1840 one of the greatest finds in the history of Anglo-Saxon numismatics, the discovery of the so called Cuerdale hoard containing more than 7,000 coins in rough proportions 1,000 English, 1,000 Continental and 5,000 Viking. The date of the deposit is c.905 AD. The coins were stored in the last two decades of the ninth century and the first years of the tenth. The hoard represents the treasure-chest of a Viking ruler or army. Men were paid for their services and paid in coins. It may be that we have not emphasized hard enough the simple fact that the coins were current.[10] At the other end of the scale lies the Stockbridge hoard. Dr

7. *DB* i 179b: *praepositus hujus manerie consuetudinem habebat T.R.E. ut veniente domina sua in manerio presentaret ei xviii oras denariorum ut esset ipsa laeto animo.*
8. In Athelstan's reign the compensation price for a sheep was given in a London text as fivepence (VI Athelstan 6.1 and 6.2). At the end of the Anglo-Saxon period the value of a sheep for provender was equated with threepence (*Rectitudines* 9). The Athelstan document places the corresponding value of a pig at tenpence, a cow at 20, an ox at 30, while a good horse was worth the substantial sum of 120 pence.
9. *Memorials of St Dunstan*, ed. W. Stubbs (Rolls Series, 1974), 29–31.
10. The main account of the Cuerdale hoard remains that of Edward Hawkins, 'An account of coins and treasure found at Cuerdale', *NC*[1] *5* (1843), 1–48 and 53–104, with supplementary papers, 105–20. More recent studies include C. E. Blunt and

Gray Hill, a gifted amateur archaeologist working on Stockbridge Down in the mid-1930s, discovered a place of execution clearly in use in the late Old English period. Hidden in the armpit of one of the convicted criminals was a small hoard of six coins wrapped in linen. The coins were of the last type (*Pyramids*) of Edward the Confessor, and the numismatic evidence points to the strong possibility that they were buried with the corpse of a felon executed in the late autumn of 1065.[11] The macabre elements in the Stockbridge find highlight the problem of circulation and protection of coins. We still need a detailed analysis of the evidence from all hoards and considering their many aspects, on the lines of Dolley's masterly survey in his Sylloge volume on the Hiberno-Norse series in the British Museum,[12] and a great leap of imagination on size, distribution, and possible purpose, to reach a satisfactory explanation for the general historian. We might not be far wrong if we thought in terms of silver pennies in the eleventh century being carried about in the possession of ordinary non-official people as frequently, say, as gold sovereigns in the pre-1914 period and £50 notes today.

Coinage was in use, in general use, but the degree of its importance to the general populace is indeed hard to quantify. It is probable that the importance was greater than used to be considered possible, though we all must recognize the existence of a whole economy conducted at the sub-denarial level, gift-exchange, produce, and labour, mechanism strange to an urban twentieth-century population though familiar enough in pre- or early industrial society throughout the world. Recent work has helped in showing us the importance of single-finds for showing patterns of use and circulation.[13] One general observation is perhaps helpful before we turn from the economic side of things and that is to remind ourselves that a denarial economy depended absolutely on local peace if it were to flourish. Stability in local markets was an essential for its success.

The second wider field that demands attention concerns the administrative structure and in this respect the implications of post-war numismatic work have been well exploited, though by no means exhausted. This is especially true at the

R. H. M. Dolley, 'The hoard evidence for the coins of Alfred', *BNJ 29* (1959), 120–47, at 240–6; C. S. S. Lyon and B. H. I. H. Stewart, 'The Northumbrian coins in the Cuerdale hoard', *AS Coins*, 96–121; *eidem*, 'The classification of Northumbrian Viking coins in the Cuerdale hoard', *NC*[7] *4* (1964), 281–2; and R. H. M. Dolley and K. F. Morrison, 'Finds of Carolingian coins from Great Britain and Ireland', *BNJ 32* (1963), 75–87, at 80–1.

11. R. H. M. Dolley, 'The Stockbridge Down find of Anglo-Saxon coins', *BNJ 28* (1956), 283–7.
12. R. H. M. Dolley, *SCBI 8, The Hiberno-Norse Coins in the British Museum* (1966), esp. 48–9.
13. I am grateful to Mark Blackburn for drawing my attention to this point and to the work of Stuart Rigold and D. M. Metcalf in their list of 'sceatta' finds, 'A revised check-list of English finds of sceattas', in *Sceattas in England and on the Continent*, ed. D. Hill and D. M. Metcalf (BAR 128, 1984), 245–68, and Metcalf's list of single-finds c.973–1086 in 'Continuity and change', pt 1, 36–47. There is much of relevance, too, in the papers of Elizabeth Pirie and David Hinton contained below in this volume.

royal level and the association in England of strong monarchic institutions and a managed currency is now firmly fixed in the canon of historical orthodoxy. The essence of Edgar's reform was the institution of a periodic *renovatio monetae* and the complete standardization of the type of silver penny with the head of the king on the obverse and the names of the mint and the moneyer on the reverse. The king took his profits when the currency changed, at intervals of approximately six years for the succeeding 60 years, reduced to perhaps two-yearly and then three-yearly in the reign of the Confessor.[14] There was a multiplicity of mints but control was exercised through the issue of dies, a process that demanded control of men, material, and communications. Complex legal enactments indicate royal concern and the numismatist is able to confirm the substantial success of the currency reform. At the sub-royal level of administration Dolley's clear-sighted pioneering work on stylistic groups, since built upon by others, has established the existence of regional die-cutting centres and under Æthelred their changing pattern has been associated with shifts in balance of power among the ealdormen.[15] As to the moneyers themselves, they were men of substance, public figures. The best way to achieve immortality in the last century of Anglo-Saxon England – and the safest – was not to fight, not to write poetry, not to lead the active or even the holy life, but to strike coins. We know the names of many more moneyers than of any other class of men in the tenth and eleventh centuries, and another advance since the early 1960s has been the expert analysis and arrangement by Dr Veronica Smart and others of this vast body of closely dated name forms, so greatly enhancing our Old English onomasticon.[16] Hints have even been found of something approaching a career open to talents for the ablest of the group. Their skill and standards were high and the continuity of personnel among the moneyers over the crisis of the Norman Conquest has rightly been held as an important indication of the strength and persistence of the Anglo-Saxon administrative infrastructure into the Anglo-Norman world.

There still remain, however, some administrative areas where the role of the coinage is not as clear as it might be. The tax position represents one such area, though it may well be that moneyers were themselves actively involved in the process of tax collection. Harsh things have been said in their day and later about Æthelred and Danegeld. Yet the creation of a tax system capable of raising huge sums was no mean achievement and we may have been a little naive in our failure to give full credit to Edgar's reform in this context. Chronology has accounted in part for our hesitation: reform in 973, Danegeld in 991. But Danegeld in its new manifestation was possible only because of increased efficiency in geld collection and the reform of the silver penny was an important contributory element in such efficiency.

14. R. H. M. Dolley and D. M. Metcalf, 'The reform of the English coinage under Eadgar', *AS Coins*, 136–68, at 152. Dolley refines the evidence for the exact rhythm of the cycles in his later work and there is still controversy over detail: but the fact of periodicity is firmly established.
15. Pauline Stafford, 'Historical implications of the regional production of dies under Ethelred II', *BNJ 48* (1978), 35–51.
16. See Dr Veronica Smart's paper in this volume below and the works there cited.

A second sphere of activity where the coinage was important concerns the Church. Many churchmen had deep and long-lasting interests in the process of coinage and creating a currency. In earlier days archbishops of Canterbury and York issued coins in their own name, and ecclesiastical princes continued to draw profits from moneyers, the Bishop of Hereford at Hereford, the Abbot of Peterborough at Stamford. Domesday Book records show that there were seven moneyers at Hereford, one of whom was the bishop's.[17] There is, however, at vast difference between issuing coins and controlling revenues and rights associated with a mint; and it is the latter, not the former, process that affects churchmen in the later Anglo-Saxon period. Even so, many will continue to ponder the coincidence in time that brings the great Edgar reform into being at the high noon of monastic reform when Saints Dunstan, Æthelwold, and Oswald were changing the face of English ecclesiastical geography and beginning the programme of building and consolidating estates that was a direct consequnce of the Benedictine revival. Work was undertaken and, as we come to know it better (as now in the case of Burton-on-Trent, for example[18]), so do we realise that the dynamic element in the Church demanded among other things stability in the means of exchange at a high level: Edgar's reformed coinage provided part of the means by which such stability could be achieved.

The economic and administrative dimensions of the coinage reorganization begin to converge, and convergence occurs at a point relevant to the last of the themes I wish to present here. Twenty years ago my paper for the Stenton volume was called 'Boroughs and mints', a sensible title, at least in order. For the mint did not create the borough: the borough included the mint. The relationship between the two institutions is relatively straightforward. Of the four principal attributes of a full-formed borough – heterogeneity of tenure, a court, a market, a mint – the mint is the easiest to identify even if not always permanent. Research over the last 20 years has confirmed the picture of between 60 and 80 mints in operation during the last century of Anglo-Saxon England. There has been some refinement in knowledge of the precise number of mints at work at any one time. In the earlier part of the tenth century, before the Edgar reform, there were probably some 30–35 mints. The number rose to 50 in 973 with perhaps a further 20 added as a matter of conscious policy by the end of the century. The number remained stable for the first half of the eleventh century but then there began a slow decline – none of the 9 or so small mints set up by Edward the Confessor were to last beyond the end of his reign. There was some decline during the reign of the first Norman kings, though a dramatic drop did not occur until the reign of Stephen, after which there were never more than 16 mints issuing coins.[19] But for well over a century and a half (973–1135), as a result of a deliberate purposeful policy, the general situation was reached whereby no inhabitant of England south of the Humber would find himself more than a reasonable journey from a mint. This is not to deny that some mints were temporary, not only in terms of long life, that is to say from issue to issue, but also in terms of

17. *DB* i, 179a.
18. P. H. Sawyer (ed.), *The Charters of Burton Abbey* (1979).
19. R. H. M. Dolley, *The Norman Conquest and the English Coinage* (1966), 34–6.

short life, that is to say set up under the direction of a principal moneyer (possibly from a major mint) for a short period, maybe only weeks or even days at a time.[20] Sometimes emergency mints were established for political reasons, as at Cadbury and Cissbury and Salisbury (Old Sarum). Examples of this temporary short-lived quality are slowly accumulating as skilled numismatists examine the die-links carefully, assess the weights and quality of the coins, and help to refine knowledge of sequence and order.[21]

It is now certain, confirmed beyond reasonable doubt, that coins were indeed struck in the localities and this has led to some thoughts about the physical structure of mints and indeed boroughs. Where big mints were established and permanent we look for fortification, church towers and the like, to protect the silver, with the Norman castle offering the final solution. The archaeology does not always conform to the pattern we would like and there is indeed a grey area of uncertainty here. We are beginning to know more about some Anglo-Saxon towns – London, Winchester, York, and Portchester – but it is not always easy to relate fresh topographical information to existing knowledge. The great towns are, however, now beginning to yield some positive evidence. London is as always a special case. Numismatists were initially more cautious than historians in asserting, for example, that London was a major mint in the eighth century or even that London was a Mercian city. In the mid-ninth century it was probably the site of Berhtwulf's and Burgred's substantial mint. There is general and absolute agreement that after Alfred's re-conquest of 886 the importance of London was not in doubt and that from the reign of Athelstan, and even more so after the reform of 973, London was the home of the largest and the most formidable team of moneyers.[22] By 1000 it was the chief die-cutting centre. One piece of evidence helps to bring a touch of topographical reality to the London situation. The so-called Walbrook hoard, the largest by far of the London hoards, contained close on 6,000 coins including one Byzantine, one Danish, and one German coin.[23] There is a strong inference that it was a moneyer's hoard, deposited after the battle of Hastings and before the coronation of William I, and a reminder of the concern shown in so many of our documents with trade, currency, moneyers, and coinage when they relate to London – even to specific reference to bargaining and chaffering at the quayside, and to Billingsgate.

At Winchester recent work based on the more accurate knowledge of the plan of the Norman city that has resulted from archaeological investigation has more direct topographical bearing. This, coupled with a fresh examination of Winton Domesday, has led to the conclusion that there was no special building to house the mint, which consisted of 'quite separate structures and properties, lying more or less

20. These are referred to by D. M. Metcalf, 'Continuity and change', pt 1 32–4. There is room for an up-to-date modern study of this topic.
21. R. H. M. Dolley, 'The relevance of obverse die-links to some problems of the late Anglo-Saxon coinage', *Commentationes 1* (1961), 153–72, remains a classic statement.
22. C. N. L. Brooke and Gillian Keir, *London 800–1216: the Shaping of a City* (1975), especially 377–80.
23. R. H. M. Dolley, 'Coin hoards from the London area', *Trans. London and Middlesex Arch. Soc. 20* (1959–61), 37–50.

together in the same area'.[24] Winchester may yet prove to be exceptional, but it does seem that the moneyers' forges were located in specific industrial areas (including a section of the present High Street), that the moneyers' houses may have been rather storehouses, safe houses, separate from the areas where coins were made, and that the moneyers were indeed responsible and prosperous burgesses. York is another case again, providing parallels and contrasts to Winchester.[25] The Coppergate excavations rank high in importance in the archaeological history of the century, revealing part of the Viking city of saga accounts. Evidence for industrial activity, leather-working, textiles, and metal-working, is accumulating and among the most important of the finds is the discovery of two iron dies, one of the St Peter's coinage and another of Athelstan, and impressions on lead strips, test pieces for the coinage of Athelstan and Eadwig. It seems that the excavators almost literally dropped in at a mint or die-cutters' workshop and that at least one of the four structures examined was used by the moneyers of York to strike the royal coinage. Similar physical evidence is not available for Lincoln, the only major mint to receive a full-length numismatic study in its own right in recent years,[26] but the cumulative material is enough to show that the making, issuing, and regulation of the coinage was indeed an important and active aspect of late Anglo-Saxon social life.

The lesser mints, too, have received attention, sometimes in their own right, sometimes as parts of important regional studies, though more modern research is needed in this area with proper emphasis on die-studies involving as comprehensive a corpus of coins as possible, subjected to critical analysis and full publication with illustrations of every die. Mark Blackburn, for example, in his work on the mint of Watchet in Somerset, has been able to show how sequences in type and regulation of size of issue and nature of weight and silver content within issues coincided with a general national pattern.[27] That mint seems to have been opened c.980 as a direct consequence of Edgar's reform. It was a one-moneyer mint of minor importance, never issuing more than an estimated 1 per cent of the output of any issue. The moneyer Hunewine, who struck coins at Watchet from the beginning of the eleventh century to c.1025, seems to have been very content with his Watchet operation, moving from a position described by Blackburn as 'third moneyer at Totnes' to Exeter and Ilchester and then to Watchet and, in his maturity, holding moneyers' rights concurrently at Axbridge and Lydford with an apparent extra moneyership at Exeter itself. The picture that emerges links with Ian Stewart's perceptive investigation of the phenomenon of 'moving moneyers' and of possible special relationships between major and minor mints.[28] Work on similar studies of mints and coins for

24. Frank Barlow, Martin Biddle, *et al.*, *Winchester in the Early Middle Ages: an edition and discussion of the Winton Domesday* (Winchester Studies 1, 1976), 396–422, especially 406–7.
25. Richard Hall, *The Viking Dig at York* (1984), 60–3 (illus. p. 61).
26. H. R. Mossop, *The Lincoln Mint, c.890–1279*, ed. Veronica Smart (1970), with introduction by Michael Dolley and an analytical note by C. S. S. Lyon.
27. 'The mint of Watchet', *BNJ 44* (1974), 13–38, at 14–18, with extra material in 'Miscellanea', *BNJ 46* (1976), 75–6.
28. Possible alternative *curricula vitae* for Hunewine are suggested *ibid.*, 19–23,

Winchester and the south-west gives hope that we shall soon have a better picture of the men behind the names, and the extension of such studies over the thin line of the Norman Conquest will help again to test Dolley's hypothesis that part of the administrative infrastructure remained intact and strong through at least the first generation of Norman England.[29]

The potential value of exact and detailed study of our coins remains strong. The three general themes that we have discussed – the economic, the administrative, and the urban – touch only the generalized surface of things. It is remarkable to note how new questions are now being asked about the Anglo-Saxon currency which would have been considered impossible a short while ago, and how these questions are receiving solid and valuable discussion if not always exact answers. Michael Metcalf in his paper on 'Continuity and change in English monetary history, c.973–1086', is able to ask how rapidly did the Anglo-Saxon coinage move about, and to indicate that there was in fact an astonishingly rapid and wide-ranging monetary circulation.[30] He is further able to show, following Miss Archibald's work, a strong tendency for coins to move regionally more than nationally. Questions have been put also, by Metcalf and others, concerning the volume of mint output, and reasoned answers suggest a total output of many millions of coins per issue with perhaps half of the total coming from four or five major mints.[31] Others stress the regionalization to be found at different times in the coinage, with Derby emerging as an important centre at one stage, Chester at another, Sandwich at yet a third, and Winchcombe surprisingly but fittingly at the very period when a Winchcombeshire existed (991–1030).[32]

Work on the weights and regulation of weights emphasizes the sophistication of central control. For example, the highest sensible weight for a silver penny (as 1/240th of a pound) was 27 grams, but this weight was rarely achieved and never maintained throughout a complete issue, not even during the first *Reform Small Cross* issue (c.973–9) nor through the *Expanding Cross* issue of the Confessor (c.1050–3) which spanned the abolition of the heregeld. The general tendency was downwards in the course of an issue.[33] Possible attempts to achieve stability under Cnut were not successful and uniformity of weight was not achieved until the reign of William I, associated then with the new tax of *monetagium*. Flexibility and control are

where attention is drawn to B. H. I. H. Stewart, 'The Exeter mint and its moneyers', in the R. P. V. Brettell sale catalogue, Glendining 28 October 1970, 14. Also Stewart on London and Hertford in 'The early coins of Ethelred II's issue with right-facing bust', *NC*[7] *11* (1971), 237–42, developing earlier work of Dolley; and on the Sussex mints in 'The Sussex mints and their moneyers', in *The South Saxons*, ed. P. Brandon (1978), 89–137.

29. R. H. M. Dolley, *The Norman Conquest and the English Coinage* (1966), 12.
30. D. M. Metcalf, 'Continuity and change', esp. pt 1, 25–32, for a tightly-knit and cautious argument pointing to such circulation.
31. *Ibid.*, 32–5.
32. *Ibid.*, 34.
33. Such a tendency, as Mark Blackburn has pointed out privately, is likely to be part of a deliberate policy to maintain the nominal value of the penny throughout the period of a coin-type, more a sign of sophisticated manipulation than of weakness.

the two indices that tell us that economy and society were far out of the primitive stage in late Anglo-Saxon England, underlining the fact that the coinage has the essential marks of a true currency. Indeed the coinage remains the most formidable single piece of testimony to the strength, integrity, and potential of the Anglo-Saxon monarchy.

2 Coins and commercial centres in Anglo-Saxon England

David A. Hinton

Increasing numbers of archaeological excavations, particularly of urban sites, conducted in England during the last two decades are beginning to produce significant new information about coins and the contexts in which they are discovered. Although hoards will always be the main source of information for determining the chronology of a coinage, excavated coins have the potential to advance discussion about circulation and frequency of use. Stray finds are also important, provided that information about their provenance is beyond doubt.

A good example of the increase in data from excavations is provided by the mid-Saxon port at Southampton. When the known coins were listed at the end of the 1960s,[1] some 43 late seventh- and eighth-century 'sceattas' had been recorded from nineteenth-century brick-earth digging, and a further 39, including 23 from a hoard, had been found in more controlled post-1945 excavations. Subsequent excavations have added the very large total of c.93 'sceattas', up to September 1983; of these c.59 have come from the recently completed Six Dials site;[2] ten from the Stoner Motors site in St Mary's Street;[3] and eight (seven 'sceattas' and one Merovingian denier) from the Melbourne Street sites.[4] These numbers should be viewed against the approximate sizes of the sites investigated, and it should be noted that many of the features were sampled rather than completely excavated: Six Dials, 4,400 sq.m; Stoner Motors, 750 sq.m; Melbourne Street, 1,400 sq.m. Another revealing indication of the quantity of material recovered from these Southampton sites is that

Acknowledgments I am very grateful to the many excavators who have supplied me with information, whose names are recorded in the footnotes. I should also like to thank Mark Blackburn and Michael Metcalf for their advice on drafts of this paper.

1. P. V. Addyman and D. H. Hill, 'Saxon Southampton: a review of the evidence', pt 1, *Procs. Hants Field Club Archaeol. Soc. 25* (1968), 61–93, at 85–91; pt 2, *ibid. 26* (1969), 61–96, at 91.
2. Personal communication, M. A. Brisbane, City of Southampton Museums Services, and D. M. Metcalf, Heberden Coin Room, Ashmolean Museum, Oxford.
3. Personal communication, S. M. Davies and J. W. Hawkes, Trust for Wessex Archaeology, Salisbury.
4. M. Archibald, 'The coins, Saxon period,' in P. Holdsworth, *Excavations at Melbourne Street, Southampton, 1971–76* (CBA Res. Rep. 33, 1980), 72–3.

at Melbourne Street 819kg (50,000 pieces) of identifiable animal bone fragments[5] and 364 pottery sherds[6] were found in stratified contexts. Referred to as a '*mercimonia*' by one contemporary writer,[7] mid-Saxon Southampton was certainly a trading port of international importance and a large, if sprawling, centre of human activity.

The 'sceatta' finds at Southampton come from sites throughout the known area of the Saxon town: they are not confined to a particular part, such as a single tax-collection point. Nor are there indications from the other finds that there were zones with particularly wealthy occupants, profligate with their coins. No other precious metal objects are known from 'Hamwih', although the large numbers of broken fragments suggest that there were plenty of drinking-glasses; nor do the food remains indicate anything but a rather monotonous diet, substantial enough but lacking in the delicacies of young, tender meat and hunted game that might be a clue to the existence of a richer elite.[8] A small number of the 'sceattas' comes from graves, but the rest are found with the rubbish which accumulated in the pits and street levels of the town, and are apparently casual losses, as in Ribe.[9]

A surprising contrast to Southampton in terms of the numbers of 'sceattas' found there is Ipswich, another mid-Saxon emporium, where excavations have shown that occupation spread over a large area on both banks of the River Orwell from the early seventh century onwards, with evidence of considerable importing of glass and pottery, and large-scale pottery manufacture.[10] Yet only nine 'sceattas' have been found there, three chance finds and six from recent excavations.[11] This contrast extends to the hinterland, for there is a considerable scatter of the coins throughout East Anglia, and one recently discovered and prolific site, Barham, is only five miles from the port; twelve miles away is another, Burrow Hill, an estuary site.[12] This is quite unlike the Southampton district, in which there are but two 'sceattas' from Winchester and a very thin scatter throughout the rest of Wessex and Sussex.[13]

This difference between the kingdoms may be demonstrating a difference in

5. J. Bourdillon and J. Coy, 'The animal bones', *ibid.*, 79–121.
6. R. Hodges, 'The pottery', *ibid.*, 40–59.
7. A. R. Rumble, 'HAMTUN *alias* HAMWIC (Saxon Southampton): the place-name traditions and their significance', *ibid.*, 7–20.
8. J. Bourdillon, 'Town life and animal husbandry in the Southampton area, as suggested by the excavated bones', *Procs. Hants Field Club Natur. Hist. Soc. 36* (1979), 181–92, at 183–5.
9. K. Bendixen, 'Sceattas and other coin finds', in *Ribe Excavations 1970–76*, I, ed. M. Bencard (Esbjerg, 1981), 63–101.
10. K. Wade, 'Ipswich', in *Recent Archaeological Research in English Towns*, ed. J. Schofield and D. Palliser (1981), 49–50.
11. S. E. Rigold and D. M. Metcalf, 'A revised check-list of English finds of sceattas', in *Sceattas in England and on the Continent*, ed. D. Hill and D. M. Metcalf (BAR 128, 1984), 245–68, at 253.
12. V. Fenwick, 'Excavations at Burrow Hill, Butley, Suffolk 1978–1981', *Anglo-Saxon Studies in Archaeology and History 3* (1984), 35–54.
13. D. M. Metcalf, 'Monetary circulation in southern England in the first half of the eighth century', in *Sceattas in England and on the Continent*, 27–69, esp. 52–5.

trading systems, which geography rather than political or economic development may explain. East Anglia is close to the Rhine, and its trading contacts would therefore be predominantly with Frisian merchants, whereas Wessex has northern France as the natural partner. These connections appear to be demonstrated by the distribution of imported pottery, with French sherds being found principally in the south, Rhenish in the east.[14] Very few French deniers are found in England, in contrast to the 'sceattas' from Frisia and the lower Rhineland, and Metcalf has suggested that this may indicate that Wessex did not have a balance-of-payments surplus in its trade with north France, rather than that Wessex outside Southampton was less coin-using than East Anglia.[15] It remains difficult to see why Ipswich should be such an anomaly in terms of 'sceat' recovery, quite unlike both its most likely main trading partners, Domburg and Dorestad.

There is a sufficiently clear distribution of Series R 'sceattas' to postulate an East Anglian origin. They are mainly found in Norfolk and Suffolk, trailing south-westwards into middle Anglia,[16] a distribution comparable to that of the seventh- to ninth-century Ipswich-type pottery mostly found in Norfolk and Suffolk, with outliers in Northampton, Bedford, London, and a few other centres including Canterbury. There is less of it in Essex:[17] there is some at rural Asheldham and Wicken Bonhunt, at coastal Bradwell, and at estuarine Maldon, a (probable) sherd at Waltham Abbey, but none at Colchester. Although not totally excluded from the neighbouring kingdom, it seems generally to have conformed to the circulation area of the Series R 'sceattas'. The political frontier may well have been a barrier to trade, perhaps by toll impositions, perhaps because commerce followed traditional networks established by kin links in the settlement period.

The absence of Ipswich ware at Colchester may of course be because for a brief period there was very little occupation there. It is, however, a town which has produced evidence of post-Roman use before its capture by Edward the Elder in 917,[18] and a thrymsa and a 'sceat' have been found, though not in the recent archaeological work. If there were inhabitants, they did not proclaim their presence by digging pits: they might, however, have disposed of their rubbish in some other way – dumping it in the river or carting it out as manure to neighbouring fields. This may have been a preferable method in old Roman towns where paved surfaces and collapsed rubble made digging more arduous than in a previously uninhabited site such as Ipswich or 'Hamwih', and could serve to make quite large populations difficult to recognize archaeologically, particularly if their buildings necessitated few post-holes for timber uprights.[19]

14. R. Hodges, *The Hamwih Pottery: the local and imported wares from 30 years' excavations at Middle Saxon Southampton and their European context* (CBA Res. Rep. 37, 1981), 93.
15. Metcalf, 'Monetary circulation', 28, 41–4.
16. *Ibid.*, 37.
17. C. M. Cunningham, 'Medieval and post-medieval pottery', in P. J. Drury, 'Aspects of the origins and development of Colchester Castle', *ArchJ 139* (1982), 302–419, at 360.
18. P. Crummy, *Aspects of Anglo-Saxon and Norman Colchester* (CBA Res. Rep. 39, 1981), ch. 1.
19. The 'Dark Earth' layers in many towns represent another waste-disposal

Problems such as these exacerbate the problem of London, so well located for trade with the Rhineland, and Bede's 'mart of many peoples'. London is the only mint specifically named on the 'sceatta' coinage, yet it has produced only about 25 random (and only vaguely-provenanced) 'sceattas', and one, perhaps two hoards.[20] Current interpretations favour a view of London as a scatter of riverside settlements rather than a single nucleated centre.[21] A similar pattern may be detectable in seventh- and eighth-century York, which is, however, producing a growing number of 'sceattas', now 23 including 14 from recent excavations.[22] It is also interesting to see the volume of north-eastern ninth-century 'styca' finds – 39 from York, 67 or more from Bamburgh, presumably an important trading-station, a remarkable 128 from the minster site at Whitby, and many from other sites.[23] Lincoln, on the other hand, has produced no coins prior to the Viking incursions of the late 860s, even from the site of the church of St Paul-in-the-Bail, which may not, however, have been in use during the period of their currency.[24] Is this a reliable indication that little trading was taking place in eighth-century Lincoln, where it is suggested that a royal centre was developing?[25] Much further inland, Northampton's newly-discovered elite nucleus[26] has produced two 'sceattas': one in the immediate 'palace' area, one from nearby.[27] This is the same number as is known from Winchester, although here recent archaeological excavations have produced only a single 'sceat'.[28] As has already been noted, this is despite its proximity to Southampton: was Winchester really not 'sceatta'-using, or is it another example of differential recovery from Roman sites?

process in some cases, but presumably they would often not have been allowed to build up too close to areas of occupation. See R. MacPhail, 'Soil and botanical studies of the "Dark Earth" ', in *The Environment of Man*, ed. M. Jones and G. Dimbleby (BAR 87, 1981), 309–32.

20. Rigold and Metcalf, 'A revised check-list', 254–5.
21. T. Dyson and J. Schofield, 'Excavations in the City of London: Second interim report, 1974–1978', *Trans. London Middx Archaeol. Soc. 32* (1981), 24–85, at 48–50, but see M. Biddle, 'London on the Strand', *Popular Archaeol. 6.1* (July 1984), 23–7, and A. E. Vince, 'The Aldwych: Saxon London discovered', *Current Archaeol. 93* (Aug. 1984), 310–12, for the view that the early and mid-Saxon centre lay to the west of the Roman city, around Fleet Street and the Strand.
22. E. J. E. Pirie, *Archaeology of York*, XVIII, pt 1 (forthcoming). I am very grateful to Miss Pirie for allowing me to see her lists of coins from both York and Bamburgh in advance of publication.
23. E. J. E. Pirie, 'Finds of "sceattas" and "stycas" of Northumbria', in this volume.
24. B. Gilmour, 'The Anglo-Saxon church at St. Paul-in-the-Bail, Lincoln', *MedArch 23* (1979), 214–18.
25. Lincoln Archaeological Trust, 'Lincoln', in *Recent Archaeological Research in English Towns* (n. 10 above), 54–7, at 55.
26. J. H. Williams and M. Shaw, 'Middle Saxon "Palaces" at Northampton', *Current Archaeol. 85* (Dec. 1982), 38–41.
27. M. M. Archibald, D. M. Metcalf, and S. E. Rigold, 'The coins', in J. H. Williams, *St Peter's Street, Northampton: Excavations 1973–1976* (1979), 243–6.
28. M. Dolley and C. E. Blunt, 'Coins from the Winchester excavations 1961–1973', *BNJ 47* (1977), 135–8.

There are, of course, Roman sites which are prolific of 'sceattas'. These are the shore-forts, principally Reculver, with over 50 coins, and Richborough, with nine 'sceattas'. Non-Kentish sites include Burgh Castle, Suffolk, with four. This results in part from the reuse of these places as minsters, and thus as burial places. There seems to have been a fairly widespread burial rite which involved putting a coin in a grave. The reason for this is not known, for it is undocumented despite its practice during the Christian period. Rigold suggested that the coins are token compensation paid to the dead by the inheritors of their wordly goods.[29] Alternatively, they might be a token to the dead that a wergild compensation owed for an injury to them had been paid – 'if anyone kills a man, he is to pay 20 shillings at the open grave, and within 40 days the whole wergild' (Laws of Ethelbert, clause 22).[30] Whatever the reason, it was a practice with a wide appeal in north-west Europe, being especially common in the Rhine/Meuse area.[31] It should not be assumed, however, that all churchyard finds are from graves, for churches may well have provided convenient foci for marketing activities, so that some of the 'sceattas' recorded as found in burial grounds may be traders' losses, not disturbed grave-goods.[32] This would be in line with their relative frequency as casual finds from route-ways and hill-forts, suggesting droving and fairs.[33] The Continental and insular gold coins of the sixth and seventh centuries are commonly from graves or possible wergild hoards like Crondall,[34] but only a small proportion of 'sceatta' finds can be accounted for in this way; nor do they have inscriptions or designs strongly indicative of political motivation for their issue. It could be that they were symbols of wealth, as has been suggested of Iron Age staters, but none has yet been found set in a mount, as a pendant or brooch, unlike both earlier and later coins, so personal ornamentation does not seem to have created a demand for them. Their recovery at certain types of site most likely to have been places at which commercial transactions took place, and their relative frequency, suggest that they really were used to facilitate trade and exchange in the areas in which they are found.

If this was the role of the majority of the 'sceattas', it is interesting to note how many have been found in comparison to the broad pennies of the late eighth century onwards. Some perspective on the contrast can be demonstrated at Southampton: unfortunately the pre-1946 records of finds of penny coins of the last quarter of the eighth century and later found in the mid-Saxon port are suspect, as they include many from reigns unrepresented in modern excavations.[35] Eleven coins, including

29. S. E. Rigold, 'The two primary series of sceattas', *BNJ 30* (1960), 6–53, at 8.
30. D. Whitelock (ed.), *EHD, I, c.500–1042* (2nd edn, 1979), 392.
31. V. Zedelius, 'Neue Sceattas aus dem Rheinland – Bonn und Xanten', *Zeitschrift f. Archäologie des Mittelalters 8* (1980), 139–52.
32. R. Morris, *The Church in British Archaeology* (CBA Res. Rep. 47, 1983), 76.
33. S. E. Rigold and D. M. Metcalf, 'A check-list of English finds of sceattas', *BNJ 47* (1977), 31–52, at 32.
34. P. Grierson, 'La fonction sociale de la monnaie en Angleterre aux viie–viiie siècles', *Moneta e scambi nell'alto medioevo* (Settimane di studio del centro italiano di studi sull'alto medioevo 8, Spoleto, 1961), 341–62, at 349; repr. in P. Grierson, *Dark Age Numismatics* (1979), art. XI.
35. J. F. Cherry and R. Hodges, 'The

Table 2.1. Boroughs at which post-1960 excavations have produced some ninth-/eleventh-century evidence, including coins (figures = number of coins).
[Boroughs in tables 1–3 are as recorded in the *Burghal Hidage*, *Anglo-Saxon Chronicle*, and Domesday Book (A. Ballard, *The Domesday Boroughs*, Oxford, 1904, 220) where positively identifiable; for summaries and references, see J. Schofield and D. Palliser, *Recent Archaeological Research in English Towns* (CBA, 1981); for a fuller list of late tenth-/eleventh-century coins, including pre-1960 and non-excavation finds, see D. M. Metcalf, *BNJ 50* (1980), 36–46.]

Bristol 1	Ipswich 3	Southampton (late Saxon and post-conquest site) 2 + hoard of 22 deniers	Wallingford 1
Canterbury 2	Leicester 1	Stafford 2	Wareham 1
Chichester 8 (inc. brooch)	Lincoln 32	Stamford 1	Warwick 1
Hereford 2	Northampton 13	Thetford 3	Winchester 19
Huntingdon 1	Norwich 9 (hoard)		Yarmouth 1
Ilchester 1	Oxford 3		York 47 (inc. 4 from hoard)
	Portchester 2		

Table 2.2. Boroughs at which post-1960 excavations have produced some ninth-/eleventh-century evidence, but no published reports of coins.

Axbridge	Colchester	Lewes	Steyning
Bath	Cricklade	Lydford	Tamworth
Bedford	Derby	Lyng	Torksey
Bridport	Dorchester	London	Twineham (Christchurch)
Buckingham	Dover	Maldon	Worcester
Burpham	Exeter	Nottingham	
Cambridge	Gloucester	Shaftesbury	
Chester	Hastings	Shrewsbury	
Chisbury	Hertford	Southwark	

Table 2.3. Boroughs for which there are no post-1960 reports of excavations with late Saxon material.

Barnstaple	Langport	Pevensey	Watchet
Bridgnorth	Malmesbury	Reading	Wilton
Bruton	Marlborough (see *Wiltshire Archaeology Mag. 74/75* (1980), 56–60 for nineteenth-century finds)	Rochester	Winchcombe
Calne	Milborne Port	Romney	
Droitwich		Sandwich	
Dunwich		Sarum	
Fordwich		Seasalter	
Guildford		Sudbury	
Hythe		Totnes	

one, a denier of Charles the Bald, certainly from overseas, the other an imitative *Munus Divinum* gold solidus for Louis the Pious, either English or Frisian,[36] were found between 1946 and 1977: there were none at all from Melbourne Street.

dating of Hamwih: Saxon Southampton reconsidered', *AntJ 58* (1978), 293–309, at 300.

36. H. E. Pagan, 'The coins', in B. Cunliffe, *Excavations at Portchester Castle*, II, *Saxon* (1976), 230–1, at 231.

Subsequent excavations at Six Dials have added c.11, none later than c.900,[37] and there was one early ninth-century penny from Stoner Motors.[38] There is thus a marked difference between the numbers of 'sceattas' lost or deposited at Southampton during the perhaps 50-year currency of those coins, and the numbers of broad pennies from the first 50 years of their issue. Although the precise date of the termination of the port's main activity remains uncertain, no-one would put it earlier than c.830, and the early years of the broad pennies seem to have coincided with one of its generally prosperous periods.

The contrast between the 'sceattas' and the pennies is further emphasized by the numbers from the late Saxon and post-Conquest site of Southampton, a quarter of a mile away. The excavations of the 1950s and 1960s produced a hoard of 22 silver deniers of the eleventh century, but no English pre-Conquest coins: thereafter, only two twelfth-, three thirteenth-, four fourteenth-, and three fifteenth-century English coins (excluding four too corroded to be recognizable) came from one of the busiest ports of medieval England.[39] The citizens of the post-Conquest town were apparently much more careful with their coins. The pennies, though not the fractions, were rather easier to handle, but the nominal value of the penny was the same as that of the 'sceat', so the latter was not like a Roman base-metal coin, to be dropped unregarded: yet their loss-rate seems to have been much greater.

A point to be considered is the risk that particular conditions may cause coins to corrode, preventing their recovery.[40] Various factors will influence this, such as acidity in the soil. The purer the silver in the alloy, the less likelihood there is of corrosion. Consequently coins of different issues may corrode at different rates in the same context. Another factor is stress in the metal: a flan cut and beaten flat before striking is more stressed, and thus more liable to corrode, than a cast flan. This last factor, and their greater thickness, gives the 'sceattas' an advantage over the pennies, an advantage which may often, however, be more than offset by the greater amounts of copper in their alloys. To revert to Saxon Southampton, there does not seem to be any reason why pennies should uniformly corrode and be less recoverable than 'sceattas'.

In very general terms, therefore, loss rates of 'sceattas' and pennies can be validly compared. The custom of burial with a coin seems not to have outlasted the eighth century: no ninth-century pennies have been found in the various excavated cemeteries of the period on which reports are now appearing, so there is probably a bias in favour of 'sceattas' from ecclesiastical sites.[41] There seems to be no reason,

37. M. Brisbane, as n.2 above.
38. S. M. Davies and J. W. Hawkes, as n.3 above.
39. M. Dolley, 'The coins and jettons', in C. Platt and R. Coleman-Smith, *Excavations in Medieval Southampton 1953–1969* II, *The Finds*, 316–30; S. E. Rigold, 'The coins from J. S. Wacher's excavations', in *ibid.*, 330–1.
40. I am very grateful to M. Corfield of the Wiltshire Libraries and Museums Service for his advice on the technical matters discussed in this paragraph.
41. Cf. Richborough, where four ninth-century coins are recorded against seven of Offa and his contemporaries: S. E. Rigold, 'The post-Roman coins', in *Fifth Report on the Excavation of the Roman Fort at Richborough, Kent*, ed. B. W. Cunliffe (1968), 217–23, at 222–3.

however, why greater numbers of casual losses of 'sceattas' should be found than of pennies, unless there were more of them in circulation. A comprehensive list of isolated finds of the earlier broad pennies has yet to be assembled, but Metcalf has gathered together the finds of the post-973 pennies.[42] The casual losses are widely scattered through the south and east, extending rather further westwards than the 'sceattas' had tended to do. The actual numbers of find-spots seem to be broadly comparable, however, when grave goods are discounted. Is the inference to be drawn from this that the numbers of 'sceattas' in everyday use in the eighth century were much the same as the numbers of pennies in the eleventh? If so, the degree of commercial activity in southern and eastern England before the first Viking incursions was considerably greater than is always appreciated. Furthermore, the impression is certainly that the ninth- and tenth-century coins prior to Edgar's reform are, except perhaps in the Burgred/Alfred phase, fewer and further between, suggesting that it took southern England a very long time to regain the volume of coin circulation that pertained in the heyday of the 'sceatta' currency.

Unfortunately it is only at Southampton that 'sceattas' and pennies can be compared in reasonable quantities and over a long time-scale. Nevertheless, an increasing number of published excavation reports is adding to the information about site finds. The incidence of coins at particular types of site was studied some years ago by Rigold with emphasis on later medieval finds and the deductions that could be made from them about the volume of coin in circulation during particular issues.[43] Subsequently published reports show that pre-Conquest pennies are occasionally found on urban sites (see tables 2.1–3), but not in large numbers. To what extent are coin finds a reflection of the scale of the commercial activity on a site, or of the presence of wealthy people? At some places and in some periods, the coins do seem to correlate with other developments: Winchester's rapid growth is mirrored by the increase in coin-finds (table 2.4), but not its thirteenth-century decline, as there are 44 coins of that century from the excavation, albeit half of them from a hoard.[44] The Anglo-Scandinavian epoch at Lincoln is also shown as an era of steady development. At York, however, there is a decline in post-950s coin recovery, which seems to follow no other economic trend. Oxford's recent excavations have so far produced a coin which is either a farthing or an under-weight halfpenny,[45] and two pennies.[46] Similarly Bedford, a mint from at least the mid-tenth century, has produced no coins earlier than the twelfth. In Northampton, discovery of as many as nine St Edmund Memorial pennies has led to the suggestion that some of them were issued there, although other evidence is that a regular mint was established in the

42. D. M. Metcalf, 'Continuity and change in English monetary history, c.973–1086', pt 1, *BNJ 50* (1980), 20–49; pt 2, *BNJ 51* (1981), 52–90; at pt 1, 36–46.
43. S. E. Rigold, 'Small change in the light of medieval site-finds', in *Edwardian Monetary Affairs (1279–1344)*, ed. N. J. Mayhew (BAR 36, 1977), 59–80.
44. Dolley and Blunt, *op. cit.*, 136.
45. D. M. Metcalf, 'A round halfpenny or farthing of King Eadred, found at the Castle and of the Oxford mint', in T. G. Hassall, 'Excavations at Oxford Castle, 1965–1973', *Oxoniensia 41* (1976), 232–308, at 267–70.
46. Metcalf, 'Continuity and change', pt 2, 48.

Table 2.4. Coin-finds from post-1960 excavations with fully published or available coin lists at selected towns, by approximate century. (Question-marks indicate uncertain attributions.)

	'Sceattas'	Pennies, half-pennies, farthings, 'stycas', and foreign coins			
	Late 7th/ 8th cents.	Late 8th/ 9th cents.	10th cent.	11th cent.	12th cent.
Bedford[a]	0	0	0	0	1
Chichester, Sussex[b]	0	2 (inc. one denier)	4?	2? (inc. one brooch mount)	2
Lincoln[c]	0	5	11	18 (inc. one Danish)	not available
Northampton[d]	2	2?	11?	0	3
Oxford[e]	0	0	2	0	2
Winchester, Hants.[f]	1	2 (inc. dirham)	8 (inc. denier)	31 (inc. two foreign)	11 (inc. five from hoard)
York[g]	3 silver 9 base	22 stycas 4 pennies 1 Danish	17 (inc. four from hoard) 1 dirham	4	4

a. D. Baker *et al.*, *Beds. Archaeol. J. 13* (1979).
b. A. Down, *Chichester Excavations*, vols. 1 to 5 (1971–81).
c. M. Blackburn *et al.*, *Early Medieval Coins from Lincoln and its Shire, c.770–1100* (Lincoln Archaeological Trust VI–2, 1983).
d. J.H. Williams, *St Peter's Street, Northampton: Excavations 1973–1976* (1979); F. Williams, *Northants. Archaeol. 14* (1979), 38–79; J.H. Williams and M. Shaw, *ibid.*, *16* (1981), 87–135, and *eidem*, *Current Archaeol. 85* (Dec. 1982), 38–41.
e. T.G. Hassall, *Oxoniensia 41* (1976), 232–308; B. Durham, *ibid. 42* (1977), 83–203.
f. M. Dolley and C.E. Blunt, *BNJ 47* (1977).
g. E.J.E. Pirie, forthcoming.

town only at a later date:[47] the point has also been made that whereas six Edward the Elder coins were found in the nineteenth-century excavations at the castle, none has been found in recent work, on three different sites.[48] As at York, there are many more pre-950 than later coins. With such small numbers of coins, imbalances are inevitable – or were the early citizens really more careless with their pennies?

All the towns mentioned in the last paragraph have had either one or more large excavations, or several small ones, since 1960. Enough has been excavated to get a fair cross-section of data, and in some cases the coin-finds can be compared with other material, such as pottery and animal bones. The stratified sequence at Flaxengate, Lincoln, for instance, yielded over 60,000 fragments of bone giving approximate per-century totals of: ninth century, 6,624; tenth century, 9,064 (plus a

47. M. Archibald, 'The coins', in J. H. Williams and M. Shaw, 'Excavations in Chalk Lane, Northampton, 1975–1978', *Northants Archaeol. 16* (1981), 87–135, at 118.
48. *Ibid.*, 101.

substantial proportion of 4,196 phased c.900–c.1060/70); eleventh century, 24,586; twelfth century (during which the introduction of stone buildings affected recovery rates), 8,885.[49] The increase is broadly in line with the coins (table 2.4). The Flaxengate pottery is not yet published, and it will be very interesting to see if its quantities correspond to those of the bone.

The stratification of the Flaxengate site was exceptionally good, and unfortunately no other published late Saxon sequences can match it. In Northampton, for example, wider phasing bands have to be used, as shown in table 2.5. Such figures are really no more than a very broad indication of increasingly intensive use of a town, an enlarged population having more rubbish to discard. Nevertheless, pottery had to be obtained from a supplier and was not home-made, and the bones came from animals that were not reared by the householders in their back gardens, apart from a few pigs and hens.[50] Both commodities involved trade, and can be as much a record of exchange transactions as can coins. But it could be that many things changed hands without coins being involved: barter and the tally-stick could have helped to prevent the need to involve cash in every piece of dealing. Coin losses do not necessarily directly reflect population growth and the transactions which sustained it.

This pattern can be seen in many towns. For instance, at Bedford 154 sherds of eighth-/ninth-century 'Early Middle Saxon' pottery came from a single site; the next phase produced only 133 sherds, but from a wider spread of sites, indicating increasing activity in the town in the second half of the ninth century. This trend was continued in the tenth to twelfth centuries, the sites producing 4,900 sherds.[51] Yet Bedford, unlike Northampton, has not produced any coins earlier than King John's reign, although its moneyers were active, issuing coins at about half the average estimated for Northampton in Æthelred II's reign, more thereafter.[52] A smaller number of recent sites at Stamford – for a time the fifth largest mint in the country – has also produced no coins, although there is a penny of King Alfred from the site of the castle.[53]

Towns were one of the four categories of sites analysed by Rigold in his paper on coin finds from excavations.[54] Another was the royal, episcopal, and aristocratic residences, and with these also there has been a welcome number of excavation reports published recently. Many, like towns, have produced coins: even the earliest, Yeavering, had a seventh-century gold triens.[55] Comparison between these sites and the urban ones is hampered by the difference in the range of contexts from

49. T. O'Connor, *Animal Bones from Flaxengate, Lincoln c.870–1500* (Lincoln Archaeol. Trust, vol. XVIII–1, 1982), 1 and table 1.
50. *Ibid.* 47.
51. D. Baker, E. Baker, J. Hassall, and A. Simco, 'Excavations in Bedford, 1967–1977', *Beds Archaeol. J. 13* (1979), 148.
52. *Ibid.*, 276; Metcalf, 'Continuity and change', pt 2, 76–7.
53. C. Mahany, A. Burchard, and G. Simpson, *Excavations in Stamford, Lincolnshire 1963–1969* (Soc. for Medieval Archaeol. Mono. Ser. 9, 1982), 10.
54. Rigold, 'Small change'.
55. B. Hope-Taylor, *Yeavering: an Anglo-British centre of early Northumbria* (1977), 182–3.

Table 2.5. Pottery, bone, and coin data from three sites in Northampton

		Early/mid-Saxon pre-c. 900	Tenth/late eleventh cent.
St Peter's Street	sherds[a]	29[b]	1521
	bones[c]	494	2470
	coins[d]	2	6
Marefair	sherds[e]	46	403[f]
	bones[g]	537	567
	coins[h]	?1 or 0	1+?1
Chalk Lane	sherds[i]	1265	9100
	bones[j]	c.150	c.5000
	coins[k]	0	4

a. M.R. McCarthy, in J.H. Williams, *St Peter's Street, Northampton: Excavations 1973–1976* (1979), 167, 179, etc.
b. Excluding 52 from House 2 not attributable to a specific phase.
c. M. Harman, in J.H. Williams, *op. cit.*, tables 38 and 39; D. Bramwell, in *ibid.*, 333.
d. M. Archibald, in *ibid.*, 244–5.
e. M. Gryspeerdt, in F. Williams, 'Excavations at Marefair, Northampton, 1977', *Northants. Archaeol. 14* (1979), table 2.
f. Excludes an unknown proportion of 563 sherds attributed to the late Saxon/early medieval interface.
g. M. Harman, in F. Williams, *op. cit.*, table M 10; D. Bramwell, in *ibid.*, table M 24.
h. M. Archibald, in *ibid.*, 69. The question marks represent an unidentifiable fragment.
i. M. Gryspeerdt, in J.H. Williams and M. Shaw, 'Excavations in Chalk Lane, Northampton, 1975–1978', *Northants. Archaeol. 16* (1981), 108.
j. M. Harman, in *ibid.*, 133.
k. M. Archibald, in *ibid.*, 118.

which the data come. Much urban evidence, for instance, comes from rubbish-pits, which are not always so common in the 'palaces'. Nevertheless, as centres of wealth, and perhaps in some cases at least tax-collection centres, coin-finds might be expected, and table 2.6 shows that this is indeed the case, although without any coherent pattern even between sites of comparable size. Pottery quantities are not always a valid comparison, as some areas were aceramic. Quantities of bone also vary very widely. The large amount from Period I at Cheddar in relation to later periods is caused by the contents of a single prolific ditch. The generally high ratio of teeth: bone on this site indicates that there was a very poor bone survival rate rather than that the small quantities are representative of the original deposition rate.[56] At North Elmham (a site which includes part of the village) and Portchester (in its later phases) the bone totals are substantially fewer than at Flaxengate, Lincoln, or mid-Saxon Southampton. This is a hint that this particular form of archaeological data may sometimes be a valid reflection of the greater density of occupation which would be anticipated from the urban sites, assuming that rubbish disposal patterns were not significantly different (and did not vary from time to time on any particular site, as at

56. E. Higgs and W. Greenwood, 'Faunal report', in *The Saxon and Medieval Palaces at Cheddar*, by P. Rahtz (BAR 65, 1979), 354–62.

Table 2.6. Excavated coin-finds and recorded bone totals from certain residential or similar sites

	'Sceattas'	Pennies etc.			
	Late 7th/ 8th cents.	Late 8th/ 9th cents.	10th cent.	11th cent.	12th cent.
Cheddar, Som.[a]	0	3	4	1	2
Goltho, Lincs.[b]	0	0	1	2	3
Netherton, Hants.[c]	0	1	3	2 (inc. 1 denier)	10 (inc. 2 French)
North Elmham, Norfolk[d]	2	0	0	0	0
Portchester, Hants.[e]	0	2	0	0	2
Sulgrave, Northants.[f]	?0	?0	1	1	?0

a. P. Rahtz, *Palaces at Cheddar* (BAR 65, 1979).
b. G. Beresford, *Procs. Battle Conference IV – 1981* (1982), 13–36, and personal communication.
c. J. Fairbrother, personal communication.
d. P. Wade-Martins, *Excavations in North Elmham Park, 1967–72* (*East Anglian Archaeol. Rep.* 9, 1980).
e. B. Cunliffe, *Excavations at Portchester Castle, II, Saxon*; *idem*, *III, Medieval, the Outer Bailey and its Defences* (Soc. Antiquaries, 1976 and 1979).
f. B.K. Davison, *ArchJ 134* (1977), 105–14.

twelfth-century Flaxengate, Lincoln). The large amount of bone at eighth-/tenth-century Portchester equates interestingly with the coin evidence of two ninth-century pennies from the excavations, and two old finds of a ninth-century penny and an imitation of a ninth-century gold solidus.[57] Were first the bishop, before his exchange of the site in 904, and then perhaps for a time thereafter the king using the place as a port, an experiment for some reason abandoned by 1066, when Portchester was in private ownership?

The archaeological data allow it to be seen that the 'palaces' were more than just residences, but, like some Carolingian 'palaces', might also be centres of artisan activity. Iron was probably smelted as well as smithed at Cheddar, and gold and enamel were worked there,[58] as were gold and silver at Netherton.[59] These activities are not surprising, since the jewellers, perhaps itinerants, probably worked for aristocratic patrons at their residences, and iron was required for various purposes

57. Pagan, *op. cit.*, 230–1.
58. L. Biek, 'Metalworking residues', in Rahtz, *op. cit.*, 252–8.
59. J. Fairbrother, *Excavations at Netherton, Hants.* (forthcoming).

Bones (except Netherton, *sherds*)				Very approx. main area excavated
Pre-930 3,432	Mid-10th/late 11th cents. 962	Late 11th/early 13th cents. 517		76 × 61m
Not yet published				60 × 60m
Sherds: mid-10th/mid-11th cents. 623	Mid-11th/*c*.1200 16,842			75 × 30m (partly × 60m)
8th/late 9th cents. 8,212	Late 9th/10th cents. 3,620	11th/early 12th cents. 1,019		120 × 70m
5th/8th cents. 987	8th/10th cents. 11,271	10th/11th cents. (pit groups only) 2,946	12th cent. 825	85 × 45m
Not yet published				45 × 15m

on the estates. Rather different, however, is the suggestion of mass-production raised by worked bone debris at Portchester[60] and by the concentration of weaving equipment at Goltho which has led its excavator to make parallels with Carolingian capitulary references to specialized *genitum* or *gynaecum* buildings and to deduce large-scale textile production.[61] These are hints that the tradition was continued of the 'efficient estate management' evident at the mid-Saxon *villa regalis* iron-smelting site at Ramsbury, Wilts.,[62] at Tamworth and Old Windsor with their mills,[63] at Hereford with its corn-drying complex,[64] and at Twynham, Hants. (now Christchurch, Dorset), with its oven and evidence of iron-working.[65] A documentary parallel is provided by the description in the Axbridge Chronicle (a fourteenth- or fifteenth-century manuscript, but perhaps drawing on earlier sources) of surplus produce collected at an estate centre being sold in the open market, for cash[66] – another reason for coins to reach such 'palaces', where indeed their weight might

60. A. Grant, 'The animal bones', in Cunliffe, *op. cit.*, 262–87, at 274–5.
61. G. Beresford, 'Goltho Manor, Lincolnshire: the buildings and their surrounding defences, c.850–1150', in *Procs. Battle Conference IV*, ed. R. A. Brown (1982), 13–36, at 25–6.
62. J. Haslam, 'A Middle Saxon iron smelting site at Ramsbury, Wiltshire', *MedArch 24* (1980), 1–68, at 64.
63. P. Rahtz, 'Building and rural settlement', in *The Archaeology of Anglo-Saxon England*, ed. D. M. Wilson (1976), 48–97, at 89.
64. R. Shoesmith, *Excavations on and close to the Defences* (CBA Res. Rep. 46, 1982), 70.
65. K. Jarvis, *Excavations in Christchurch 1969–1980* (Dorset Natur. Hist. Archaeol. Soc. Mono. 5, 1983), 37.
66. F. Neale, 'The relevance of the Axbridge Chronicle', in Rahtz, *op. cit.*, 10–12.

have been checked by the sort of folding balance found at North Elmham and Goltho, a further indication of involvement in exchange transactions.[67]

The estate-centres should therefore be seen as having operated partly in parallel with the new towns, and this role helps to account for their comparable coin-loss rates. It may also explain the emergence of some of them as hundredal market centres after the Conquest,[68] just as some which were administrative or ecclesiastical mid-Saxon centres like Hereford, Northampton, or Winchester emerged as boroughs before it. They were more than the defended residences typical of the Norman and later castles, in which were neither space nor perhaps motive for any unmilitary activity, except for occasional checks on coins as suggested by the tumbrel or coin-balance from Castle Acre Castle, Norfolk.[69]

Excavations at two of the four categories of site defined by Rigold[70] can thus be seen to be yielding a useful number of coins; of the other two categories, religious sites seem to be less fruitful as sources of ninth- to eleventh-century pennies than of 'sceattas' and the pennies of Offa.[71] This may be partly because few major churches have been available for recent work: Glastonbury Abbey produced three pennies in the 1950s, for example,[72] and two are reported from St Augustine's Abbey, Canterbury.[73] In Winchester, the one 'sceatta' and 14 of the other 19 pre-twelfth-century recently excavated coins came from the Cathedral Green, site of the minsters.[74] St Paul-in-the-Bail, Lincoln, yielded nine pre-Conquest pennies.[75] Other religious sites to have produced c.973–1087 coins include Cerne Abbas and Richborough, which have yielded two,[76] and others have yielded single coins; but many of these are old finds, not from recent excavations. Indeed, in Rigold's religious sites category there are no other examples of pre-twelfth-century coins.[77]

Many finds made in churches may result from the misfortunes of those who came to make their offerings, for churches are places to which coins are drawn in some quantity. It would have been easier for a coin's owner who became aware of his loss, or for a sharp-eyed choir-boy, to bend down and pick up the stray if it fell upon a tile

67. G. Oakley, 'Weighing apparatus', in Williams, *op. cit.*, (n.27 above), 258.
68. R. H. Britnell, 'English markets and royal administration before 1200', *EcHR*^{2} *31* (1978), 183–96.
69. S. Margeson, 'Worked bone', in J. G. Coad and A. D. F. Streeten, 'Excavations at Castle Acre Castle, Norfolk, 1972–1977', *ArchJ 139* (1982), 138–301, at 244–5.
70. Rigold, 'Small change'.
71. S. E. Rigold, 'Coins found in Anglo-Saxon burials', in *Coins and the Archaeologist*, ed. J. Casey and R. Reece (BAR 4, 1974), 201–5.
72. D. M. Metcalf and S. C. Minnitt, 'A coin of Æthelræd II from the Ilchester mint, and two of Edward the Confessor, excavated at Glastonbury', *Procs. Somerset Archaeol. Natur. Hist. Soc. 125* (1981), 118–19.
73. Metcalf, 'Continuity and change', pt 1, 39.
74. Dolley and Blunt, *op. cit.*, (n. 28 above).
75. M. Blackburn, C. Colyer, and M. Dolley, *Early Medieval Coins from Lincoln and its Shire, c.770–1100* (Lincoln Archaeol. Trust, vol. VI-2, 1983), 25.
76. Metcalf, 'Continuity and change', pt 1, 36 and 39–40. One of the two from Cerne Abbas is a dirham, and one of the Richborough two is uncertain.
77. Rigold, 'Small change'.

or beaten earth floor. Gaps between floor-boards, or rushes strewn over the ground, would have hampered recovery, however. Such finds cannot be taken as an index of intensive trading, although as with the 'sceattas' some may well have been lost as a result of the Sunday marketing in the churchyard that laws often tried to prevent.

One type of site on which pennies do not seem to be found, unlike earlier 'sceattas', is the hill-fort. Even where they do occur they are often from places of execution.[78] This may imply that the hill-tops were no longer generally in use as fairs, that role having been taken over by the boroughs. But the appearance of such fairs as those at Weybridge, near Andover, and St Giles, near Winchester, after the Conquest, with no very clear statements about their origins or rights, suggests that some at least continued in operation.

Metcalf has shown the potential that the closely dated post-973 pennies with their known points of issue have for studies of trade, internal and overseas,[79] and the Lincolnshire finds have been used to illustrate the relationship between a major town and its hinterland.[80] It is worth pointing out that it is becoming possible to be almost as specific about the source of production of many pot sherds as about coins, through petrological analyses.[81] Pottery may be more direct evidence of local trade, as it was less likely than coinage to be passed through many hands, from producer to user and breaker. Distribution through a local market is potentially as recognizable for late Saxon ceramics as for pennies. Pottery has the great advantage of a much higher survival rate, as the urban sites show. But it was not in use uniformly throughout the country: whereas East Anglia had 'factories' in Ipswich in the seventh century, the west of England and the west Midlands were largely aceramic until the eleventh. Pottery also has a much lower non-excavation recovery rate, as far fewer people will stop to pick up a broken sherd than a silver coin, but the advent of modern field-walking experiments helps to correct this bias. Pottery sequences may never achieve the same refinement of dating[82] as the late Anglo-Saxon coinage, although pots can be reckoned usually to have had only a brief life before being broken and discarded, unlike some coins. Ceramic studies are likely to be of greater use in local than international economic analyses, for pottery did not always follow the world's great trade routes. But the distribution of Stamford-type wares shows an inland range extending as far as Aberdeen up the east coast, though more restricted southwards: concentrations in Derby suggest concern with lead supplies; distance, transport systems, and competition, not political barriers, affected its market dominance: its trade balance shifted southwards in the eleventh century, as though seeking new

78. E.g. Meon Hill, Hampshire: D. M. Liddell, 'Excavations at Meon Hill', *Papers Procs. Hants Field Club Archaeol. Soc. 12* (1934), 127–62, at 132 and 155.
79. Metcalf, 'Continuity and change', pt 2.
80. Blackburn *et al.*, *op. cit.* (n. 75 above).
81. D. P. S. Peacock, 'Ceramics in Roman and medieval archaeology', in *Pottery and Early Commerce*, ed. D. P. S. Peacock (1977), 21–34.
82. E.g. through seriation analysis of pit groups: see one recent attempt by P. Crummy and R. Terry, 'Seriation problems in urban archaeology', in *Pottery and the Archaeologist*, ed. M. Millett (London Inst. Archaeol. Occ. Pub. 4, 1979), 49–60.

outlets.[83] This is evidence about Stamford's trade which can validly be set alongside that provided by the town's coins.

Current results from excavations suggest that coin finds are unlikely to be sufficiently numerous to be a direct measure of the commercial transactions and volume of exchange taking place on a particular site. Coin losses can occur for many reasons, of which trading accidents are only one, and their recovery is influenced by such factors as rubbish disposal practices and soil conditions. Too many anomalies exist – such as the paucity of 'sceattas' at Ipswich and of post-950s coins at Northampton and York – for there to be confidence in them as a mirror of trading activity except at sites where there is a variety of evidence, as at mid-Saxon Southampton with its very large numbers of 'sceattas', pottery sherds, and bones.

Nevertheless, some positive conclusions do seem appropriate from excavation- and stray-find analysis: the 'sceattas' were a large-scale currency, not just gift-exchange tokens; the proportion of late Saxon pennies from urban sites is not so great as to prove that trading was restricted to towns, as the laws might suggest; a simple urban hierarchy had not been established by the Conquest, because estate centres still had a significant economic role. Further work will undoubtedly clarify such points and open new lines of enquiry. It is good to see that the co-operation between archaeologists and numismatists advocated by Michael Dolley[84] is taking place. As this trend continues, so more positive recognition of patterns will emerge: but both archaeology and numismatics require the proper quantification of their data if such patterns are to have any validity.

83. K. Kilmurry, *The Pottery Industry of Stamford, Lincs., c.A.D. 850–1250* (BAR 84, 1980), 150–75. Compare the similar eleventh-century southward trend in Lincoln's trade as evidenced by the coins: Blackburn *et al., op. cit.*, 21.

84. M. Dolley, 'Some thoughts on the manner of publication of coins found in archaeological excavations', in Casey and Reece, *op. cit.*, 224–33.

3 The London mint and the coinage of Offa

Ian Stewart

The first substantive paper on the coinage of King Offa (757–96), published by R. C. Lockett more than 60 years ago, is still useful for the number of coins that it illustrates as well as for some perceptive remarks on their types and stylistic features.[1] But for most purposes it has been superseded by Mr Blunt's classic study, the foundation for all consideration of the subject since it appeared in the *Festschrift* for Sir Frank Stenton in 1961.[2] Soon afterwards the traditional attribution of the bulk of the coins of Offa to the mint of Canterbury was questioned by Dr Metcalf,[3] and arguments were adduced by Mr Blunt, Mr Lyon, and myself for identifying in the coinage of Coenwulf (796–821) a London series which could be traced back into the reign of Offa.[4] There has also in recent years been a developing awareness that minting and monetary circulation were not concentrated in the south-east corner of England in the first half of the eighth century.[5] Publication of a volume in memory of the editor of the Stenton *Festschrift* thus provides a timely occasion to revert to Offa's coinage and the question of where it was minted. My main conclusion is that some moneyers were undoubtedly working for Offa at London before 790. More spe-

1. R. C. Lockett, 'The coinage of Offa', *NC* 1920, 57–89.
2. C. E. Blunt, 'The coinage of Offa', in *AS Coins*, 39–62; references below to coins illustrated in this paper are cited by their number with the prefix 'B'.
3. D. M. Metcalf, 'Offa's pence reconsidered', *Cunobelin* 1963, 37–52.
4. C. E. Blunt, C. S. S. Lyon, and B. H. I. H. Stewart, 'The coinage of southern England, 796–840', *BNJ 32* (1964), 1–74; coins in the corpus are cited below with the prefix 'BLS'. Individual references to this work are not given in the following pages since it deals systematically with the material. The reigns covered are: Coenwulf, Ceolwulf I, Beornwulf, Ludica, and Wiglaf, kings of the Mercians; Eadberht, Cuthred, and Baldred, kings of Kent; Eadwald, king of East Anglia; and Egbert, king of the West Saxons (London coinage). It also treats the Canterbury archiepiscopal coins of Æthelheard (later) and Wulfred.
5. D. M. Metcalf, 'Monetary expansion and recession: interpreting the distribution-patterns of seventh- and eighth-century coins', in *Coins and the Archaeologist*, ed. J. Casey and R. Reece (BAR 4, 1974), is a useful introduction to the literature; for the types and series of the coins see I. Stewart, 'The early English denarial coinage, c.680–c.750', in *Sceattas in England and on the Continent*, ed. D. Hill and D. M. Metcalf (BAR British Ser. 128, 1984), 5–26.

culatively, it is possible that their number and their output may have been as great as, or greater than, those of the royal mint at Canterbury. If correct, this would suggest that the commercial importance of London, which is attested in the first half of the eighth century, was fully maintained under Offa. It may also be of relevance to other historical questions, such as the relationship between Mercia and Canterbury, but I must confine myself here to putting forward the numismatic argument and inviting others to judge its validity and contemplate its implications.[6]

Like those of Pepin the Short and the earlier issues of Charlemagne, before the Frankish types settled down into a standard form, the designs of Offa's coins belong to an experimental phase of the new penny coinage. They are of greater variety than those of subsequent Anglo-Saxon kings and include many of exceptional quality, with a number of splendid portraits and decorative types. The use of portraits may have been prompted by the coinage of Pope Adrian I (772–95), but unlike the pope's Offa's owe nothing to Byzantine models. Indeed, the originality and accomplishment of the best of Offa's coins are unmatched elsewhere in Dark Age Europe. A few years before the end of his reign, probably soon after 790, the weight of the penny was raised above 20gr. (1.3g) and the module was increased. Functional epigraphic types were adopted by all moneyers, with a considerable degree of standardization between them. Prior to the increase in weight, although common features can be found on the coins of small groups of moneyers, there had been relatively little general co-ordination of designs and Offa's earlier and lighter coinage accordingly presents formidable problems of arrangement. In the absence of hoard evidence the lighter coins cannot easily be placed in sequence, nor do they fall readily into discrete series that can be associated with separate mints like those of the first half of the ninth century. There is a particular chronological problem in relation to the coinage at Canterbury, where two Kentish kings apparently used the mint at some stage during the reign of Offa. As Mr Lyon has argued, it is far from clear whether the coinage of Kings Heahberht and Egbert, whose regnal dates are not precisely known, preceded Offa's coinage at Canterbury or interrupted it.[7] This question is of wider interest in considering when and by whom the new eponymous royal coinage, with its broader and thinner fabric, was introduced into southern England, following the example of the reform of the Frankish coinage by Pepin in 755.

The problem is complicated by the difficulty in determining which of the 30 or so

6. I am greatly indebted to Mr Blunt for many constructive comments on this paper and for lending me his card index of coins of Offa while I prepared it. I am also grateful to other friends who have read it in draft and made helpful suggestions: Mr Blackburn, Professor Grierson, Mr Lyon, Dr Metcalf, and Mr Pagan. But the conclusion, like the speculation, is my own. The two plates of illustrations have been selected and mounted by Mr Blackburn, from photographs kindly supplied by Miss Archibald, Mr Blunt, and Professor Grierson.
7. C. S. S. Lyon, 'Historical problems of Anglo-Saxon coinage – (1)', *BNJ 36* (1967), 215–21. No coins are known of King Ealhmund, father of Egbert of Wessex, who in 784 granted land in Kent without reference to Offa (see D. Whitelock, *EHD I, c.500-1042* (2nd edn, 1979), 20, and F. M. Stenton, *Anglo-Saxon England* (3rd edn, 1971), 207).

known moneyers of Offa were operating at Canterbury and which elsewhere. More of them may have worked outside Kent than was previously believed and the main purpose of this paper is to consider which of them might be associated with a mint at London. Provenance is generally of little help in locating the mints of Offa's moneyers, because the single-finds are scattered and do not show a discernible pattern, and there are no concentrated excavation finds. Unfortunately, while there was an adequate supply of coins of Offa for collectors in the eighteenth century, there is no record of the hoard or hoards which supplied them and no Offa hoard has been discovered since. However, the coinage circulated mainly in the south and east of England, with little in the west or north, even though this region included the centre of Offa's original kingdom of Mercia and the areas which he built his dyke to defend.[8] It is clear from coins in the names of local kings that, in addition to the mint at Canterbury, there was at this time a mint situated in East Anglia. The existence of a few coins of Offa's son-in-law, Beorhtric of Wessex (786–802), which are quite unlike anything struck for Offa or Coenwulf, also indicates the operation of a mint in Wessex, although judging by the rarity of Beorhtric's coins its output was very limited and its activity probably short-lived.[9] Apart from York, which continued to produce smaller and thicker coins of pre-Carolingian fabric until the middle of the ninth century, the only other major centre for which a coinage at this period might be postulated is London.

In the seventh century London lay within the kingdom of the East Saxons, but it had come under Mercian control at least from the time of Æthelbald (716–57). In the 730s Bede refers to the city as an important trading centre.[10] Gold shillings and silver (or base) denarii[11] on which its name appears show that a mint was active on occasions during the seventh century and the first half of the eighth. That there was also a mint at London in the ninth century is shown by mint-signed coins of Egbert of Wessex (802–39) and Alfred (871–99). But at some stages in the ninth century its production was apparently very modest and occasional. Of the four mint-series that can be identified during the reign of Coenwulf the (royal) coinage of Canterbury is overwhelmingly the most plentiful, followed by that from East Anglia, while the series attributable to London, like that associated with Rochester, is distinctly rare.

The definition of these series under Coenwulf and Ceolwulf I (821–3) is based on the names of moneyers, the types of their coins and stylistic features of their dies. At

8. R. H. M. Dolley and D. M. Metcalf, 'Two stray finds from St Albans of coins of Offa and of Charlemagne', *BNJ 28* (1957), 459–66.
9. After Beorhtric, who may have been cautious enough to wait until Offa was dead before striking his own coinage, there does not appear to have been any coinage in Wessex until the 830s. In 'The location of the pre-Ælfredian mints of Wessex', *Procs Hampshire Field Club and Archaeol. Soc. 27* (1970), 57–61, M. Dolley suggests that Beorhtric's coins were struck at *Hamwih*; but for such a small issue the capital city of Winchester seems to me a more likely source than the commercial port.
10. C. N. L. Brooke and G. Keir, *London 800–1216: The Shaping of a City* (1975), 15–20.
11. The terms 'shilling' and 'denarius' refer to the early Anglo-Saxon gold and silver coins of Merovingian module which are often erroneously called 'thrymsas' and 'sceattas'.

Canterbury the normal complement of royal moneyers in the 820s and probably earlier appears to have been six. They were generally served by a single engraver at any one time and, although they did not always use identical reverse types, there is a degree of correspondence between them. They can be associated with Canterbury beyond doubt by close affinities with the coinage of Archbishop Wulfred (805–32) and by the use after 821 of several types incorporating the name or monogram of the city. Working backwards, the series of Canterbury moneyers can be traced to the portrait coinage of King Cuthred of Kent before 807; then to earlier (non-portrait) coinages of Coenwulf and Cuthred in the late 790s and early 800s, including an issue in the joint names of Coenwulf and Archbishop Æthelheard (793–805); next to the extremely rare coinage of the Kentish king Eadberht Præn in 796–8; and so back into the coinages of Offa and Kings Heahberht and Egbert of Kent (plate 3.1:7–13). Five moneyers of Offa can be attributed to Canterbury by virtue of having worked also for one or more of the Kentish kings: Babba, Ethelmod, Ethelnoth, Eoba, and Udd (table 3.1).

Table 3.1. Canterbury moneyers of Offa who also worked for Kentish kings*

	Heahberht	Egbert	Offa (light)	Cynethryth	Offa (heavy)	Eadberht	Coenwulf (early)
Babba		4	7		6	3	2
Ethelmod					4	5	9
Ethelnoth			4		9	1	
Eoba	1	2	20	17	5		6[a]
Udd		5	3				

* See n. 16 below.
[a] A moneyer Eaba worked for Coenwulf and Cuthred.

The moneyers of a second Kentish series under Coenwulf are connected with Rochester by the stylistic similarity of their coins to some very rare pennies of Ceolwulf with the name of the city, *Dorobrebia*, and to others of Egbert with the name of St Andrew, its patron saint. One of Coenwulf's two Rochester moneyers, Dunn, was active in succeeding reigns up to Æthelwulf (839–58) and, although the time-span is long, he might be the same man as a king's thegn called Dunn to whom Æthelwulf granted land near Rochester in 855.[12] Dunn's coins begin with the portrait type of Coenwulf, which was introduced at Canterbury c.805 and at Rochester perhaps a few years later. There is nothing to suggest that the Rochester mint was operating in Coenwulf's earlier years or under Offa.

The relative abundance of the East Anglian series of coins from the first quarter of the ninth century is partly due to the discovery in Suffolk of a hoard from the 820s, but the mint seems to have been of some importance since as many as seven moneyers are known of the short reign of Ceolwulf I and at least four seem to have been functioning together at certain other times. Apart from the evidence of the Suffolk hoard, the association of this series with East Anglia is placed beyond doubt by its continuation under the independent kings who obtained control of the region and its mint from the Mercians in 827 and by its origins in the eighth century when it

12. Whitelock, *op. cit.*, 525–6.

also includes coins of local rulers. Prior to the introduction of the new penny there had been extensive issues of the anonymous denarial coinage in East Anglia during the first half of the eighth century. These were followed by some coins with the name of a King Beonna, presumably the king of the East Angles who appears as Beornus in the annals attributed to Florence of Worcester (*s.a.*758) and who in the *Historia Regum* is described as one of the successors to King Ælfwald (d.749).[13] Beonna's coinage comes at the point of transition between the fabric of the pre-Carolingian denarial coinages and the larger module of the new pennies. One of his types, with an interlace design on the reverse, is found on flans broader than any of the anonymous denarii. Examples of another type, bearing the names of moneyers Wilred (plate 3.1:1) and Werheard, were discovered in 1980–3 at Middle Harling in Norfolk.[14] They provide an important link with the new penny coinage since Wilred also coined for Offa (plate 3.1:2). The East Anglian mint again worked for local kings on two later occasions before the end of the century. Three splendid portrait coins are known of King Æthelberht (plate 3.1:4), who was put to death at Offa's command in 794; their reverse type, a she-wolf and twins derived from a Roman model, was an emblem of the East Anglian royal house and played on the name of the Wuffingas.[15] There is also a small group of coins of a King Eadwald (plate 3.1:6), otherwise unknown to history, who appears from the numismatic evidence to have restored the independence of the East Anglian kingdom for a period after Offa's death. The East Anglian moneyers of the second half of the eighth century are listed in table 3.2.[16]

Table 3.2. East Anglian moneyers of the later eighth century

	Beonna	Offa (light)	Æthelberht	Offa (heavy)	Eadwald	Coenwulf	Ceolwulf I
Botred		2				x	x
Eadnoth		0			3		
Efe	x						
Hun..c		1					
Lul			3	3	1	x	
Oethelred		1					
Werheard	x						
Wihtred		3		4	1	x	x
Wilred	x	0					

13. *Ibid.*, 265.
14. A. Rogerson, 'Saxon coin hoard from Middle Harling', *SCMB* 1982, 81; M. M. Archibald, 'Cash credentials of King Beonna', *British Museum Soc. Bull. 42* (March 1983), 34. Wilred's coin of Offa is no. 301 in K. F. Morrison and H. Grunthal, *Carolingian Coinage* (Numismatic Notes and Monographs 158, 1967).
15. J. Campbell, *The Anglo-Saxons* (1982), 67.
16. In the tables the numbers are those of specimens recorded by Blunt, *op. cit.*, (Offa) and Blunt, Lyon, and Stewart, *op. cit.* (post-Offa). I have included the unique coin by Oethelred (B.71) in the table of East Anglian moneyers although no other portraits are known in this series, because of the similarity of its reverse with the reverse of B.113 and the obverse of B.111; it also has a very small o in *Offa* like B.113.

Their coins of Offa are very rare – only Botred (Plate 3.1:3), Lul, and Wihtred are known from more than a single specimen each. The discovery of Eadnoth's unique coin of Offa in 1968 at Wijk bij Duurstede[17] and of the new moneyers of Beonna more recently are further reminders that our picture of the East Anglian coinage in the 780s and 790s may still be incomplete in important respects. For example, so far only Lul (plate 3.1:5) and Wihtred are known in the heavy coinage of Offa, but two light coinage moneyers, Eadnoth and Botred, are both known in later reigns and their heavy coins of Offa may await discovery.

No coins are known in the name of Ecgfrith who, having ruled jointly with Offa since 787, became sole king of the Mercians on his father's death in July 796, but himself died in December of the same year. After a peaceful succession in the Middle Ages a change of ruler's name on the coinage was often delayed for a considerable period, so the absence of coins of Ecgfrith need not necessarily be of historical or numismatic significance. What is relevant, however, is that, while in Kent and East Anglia Offa's coinage was replaced by those in the names of Eadberht and Eadwald respectively, a third series apparently continued from Offa to Coenwulf without interruption. This implies the use by Coenwulf at the beginning of his reign of a Mercian mint only, and the later progress of the series points, as might be expected, to London as its location.

In the portrait coinage of Coenwulf there is a fourth group of moneyers, whose coins cannot be attributed to Canterbury, Rochester, or East Anglia. This includes two names, Ciolhard and Eanmund, also found in the Mercian series of Coenwulf's early non-portrait coinage. Ciolhard and two of the others, Aelhun and Ceolbald, also coined for Ceolwulf I. No coins of this series are known of the next two Mercian kings, Beornwulf (823–5) and Ludica (825–7), whose coinages belong to the East Anglian series,[18] but Aelhun (now spelt Oelhun) reappears under Wiglaf (827–9 and 830–40). In 829 Egbert of Wessex defeated Wiglaf and celebrated his brief occupation of London by issuing a coin on which he styled himself *Rex M(erciorum)* and set out the name of the city, *Lundonia Civit(as)*, in a bold inscription on the reverse. Of comparable style to this piece, and so presumably from the same mint, are coins of both Egbert and Wiglaf by a moneyer Redmudh. Unless, therefore, Redmudh's coins of Wiglaf were struck at a different mint from Oelhun's, which does not seem likely, it is a fair assumption that Oelhun and his colleagues in the reigns of Coenwulf and Ceolwulf were also operating at London. Although there is more diversity of style in this London series than in the other series of the period, a tendency to omit the circle between portrait and obverse inscription and the frequent use of a cross-crosslet for the reverse design are notable features.

Three of Coenwulf's London portrait moneyers, Ciolhard, Eanmund, and Wighard, are known in the early aniconic coinage only by a type with M in the centre

17. C. E. Blunt and G. van der Meer, 'A new coin type for Offa', *Berichten van de Rijksdienst voor het Oudheidkundig Bodemonderzoek Jaargang 19* (1969), 213–4; *eidem*, 'A new type for Offa', *BNJ 28* (1969), 182–3.

18. With the possible exception of a fragment of the London series which could be of either Beornwulf or Beorhtwulf (Blunt, Lyon, and Stewart, *op. cit.*, pl. VII, C).

Table 3.3. Coenwulf's early Mercian moneyers who worked for Offa

	Offa (light)	Offa (heavy)	Coenwulf		
			IA	IB	Later
Ciolheard	9	1		1	x
Eama		1		1	
Ibba	18	1		2	
Ludoman		1	2	2	
Wilhun		3	1	1	

of the obverse and a trirbach on the reverse. On the obverse dies of these moneyers the inscription starts at the bottom of the coin (if the M is placed upright), whereas the dies of those moneyers associated with Canterbury who struck the same type usually have the inscription starting at the top. This feature and other stylistic similarities connect five more moneyers with the London group: Eama,[19] Ibba, Diola, Ludoman (plate 3.1:20) and Wilhun. All of these except Diola are also known in the heavy coinage of Offa. With few exceptions, Offa's heavy coins are distinguished, apart from their weight, by having an obverse type with a horizontal inscription, OFFA in the central line, REX below and M above. Five coins of Coenwulf are known with obverses of comparable type and significantly the moneyers of these coins, Diola, Ludoman (plate 3.1:19), and Wilhun, all belong to the Mercian group. Diola's have on the reverse a trirbach with 'knuckle-bone' ends, but Ludoman's and Wilhun's have reverses with the moneyer's name in two lines within ornamental surrounds, very similar to the types used by the same moneyers in the last coinage of Offa. These very rare coins of Coenwulf with three-line obverses thus provide the only instance of direct continuity between the coinages of Offa and Coenwulf, as would be expected at a mint which remained under Mercian control but not at mints in Kent or East Anglia. On seizing power in those kingdoms, Kings Eadberht (plate 3.1:12) and Eadwald (plate 3.1:6) also used the three-line type, but their longer names took up two of the three lines, leaving REX in the third but no ethnic title. Problems of space may have led to Coenwulf's replacement of the type, on which his name appears either as CENVVLF (the only occurrence on the coinage of this spelling without O, which is more normal in the written sources) or once as COENVVL/F with the last letter dropped to the bottom line. The M/trirbach type was probably in use at London by the time Coenwulf recovered Canterbury, and this is the type used for all except one of his Canterbury aniconic coins. The exception, by the moneyer Seberht, has a 'knuckle-bone' reverse and is perhaps a mule, since the same reverse type had been used at Canterbury under both Offa and Eadberht.

Of the moneyers of the early coinage of Coenwulf who can be associated with London five had been in office under Offa: Ciolhard, Eama, Ibba, Ludoman, and Wilhun (table 3.3). The next question is whether any of the other moneyers of Offa's heavy coinage are connected with them by the style or type of their coins. The

19. Possibly Eama and Eanmund are variants of the same name, but see Blunt, Lyon, and Stewart, *op. cit.*, 8.

reverses of most of the heavy coins of Offa have the moneyer's name written horizontally with various ornaments or a decorative border. Eama and Ibba (plate 3.1:17), however, have a long cross with crosslet ends and one letter of the name in each quarter.[20] Their coins are stylistically similar, with a border of large dots and with pellets loosely distributed in the field on both sides (on coins of Canterbury moneyers the pellets tend to be more tightly grouped). The letter A is large, tall and barred with a horizontal stroke instead of the more usual chevron. Ciolhard (plate 3.1:15) has a lozenge-cross on the reverse[21] and the fact that he also uses a cruciform type serves to confirm that the unique heavy coins of these three moneyers belong together. Ludoman (plate 3.1:18) and Wilhun both have horizontal inscriptions on the reverse, contained within a frame shaped rather like a Boeotian shield.[22] Their coins have thin lettering and the R on the obverse is of distinctive form, with the curved back joining the upright below the top, as found also on the coins of Eama and Ibba.[23] No coin of any undoubted Canterbury moneyer has the R of this form

20. B.90 and 101, each unique.
21. B.87.
22. B.102 and 104. A similar frame is found on a Canterbury coin of Ethelnoth (B.98), but the dies are of different style.
23. I owe this very useful observation about the R to Mr Pagan.

Plate 3.1 1–6 East Anglian mint; 7–13 Canterbury; 14–20 London.

Key to plate 3.1

EAST ANGLIAN MINT

1. Beonna, *Wilred* (BM 1982 4–9.30; *ex* Middle Harling hoard);
2. Offa (light coinage), *Wilred* (*SCBI* Berlin 67: B.-);
3. Offa (light), *Botred* (BMA 30: B.108);
4. Æthelberht, *Lul* (*BMC* 2);
5. Offa (heavy), *Lul* (*BMC* 52: B.114);
6. Eadwald, *Lul* (BM 1925 9–94; found at Richborough; BLS Ea 2).

CANTERBURY

7. Egbert of Kent, *Eoba* (Blunt: B.3);
8. Offa (light), *Eoba* (BMA 20: B.52);
9. Cynethryth, *Eoba* (*BMC* 61: B.119);
10. Offa (heavy), *Eoba* (BMA 36: B.93);
11. Offa (heavy), *Ethelmod* (BMA 38: B.95);
12. Eadberht Præn, *Ethelmod* (Blunt, *ex* Lockett 325: BLS Ep 2(c));
13. Coenwulf, *Ethelmod* (BMA 101: BLS Cn 11(b)).

LONDON

14. Offa (light), *Ciolhard* (BMA 77: B.23);
15. Offa (heavy), *Ciolhard* (B.87);
16. Offa (light), *Ibba* (*BMC* 20: B.64);
17. Offa (heavy), *Ibba* (BMA 42: B.101);
18. Offa (heavy), *Ludoman* (*SCBI* Copenhagen 57: B.102);
19. Coenwulf, *Ludoman* (BMA 102: BLS Cn 1(b));
20. Coenwulf, *Ludoman* (Blunt, *ex* Lockett 3591: BLS Cn 20(a)).

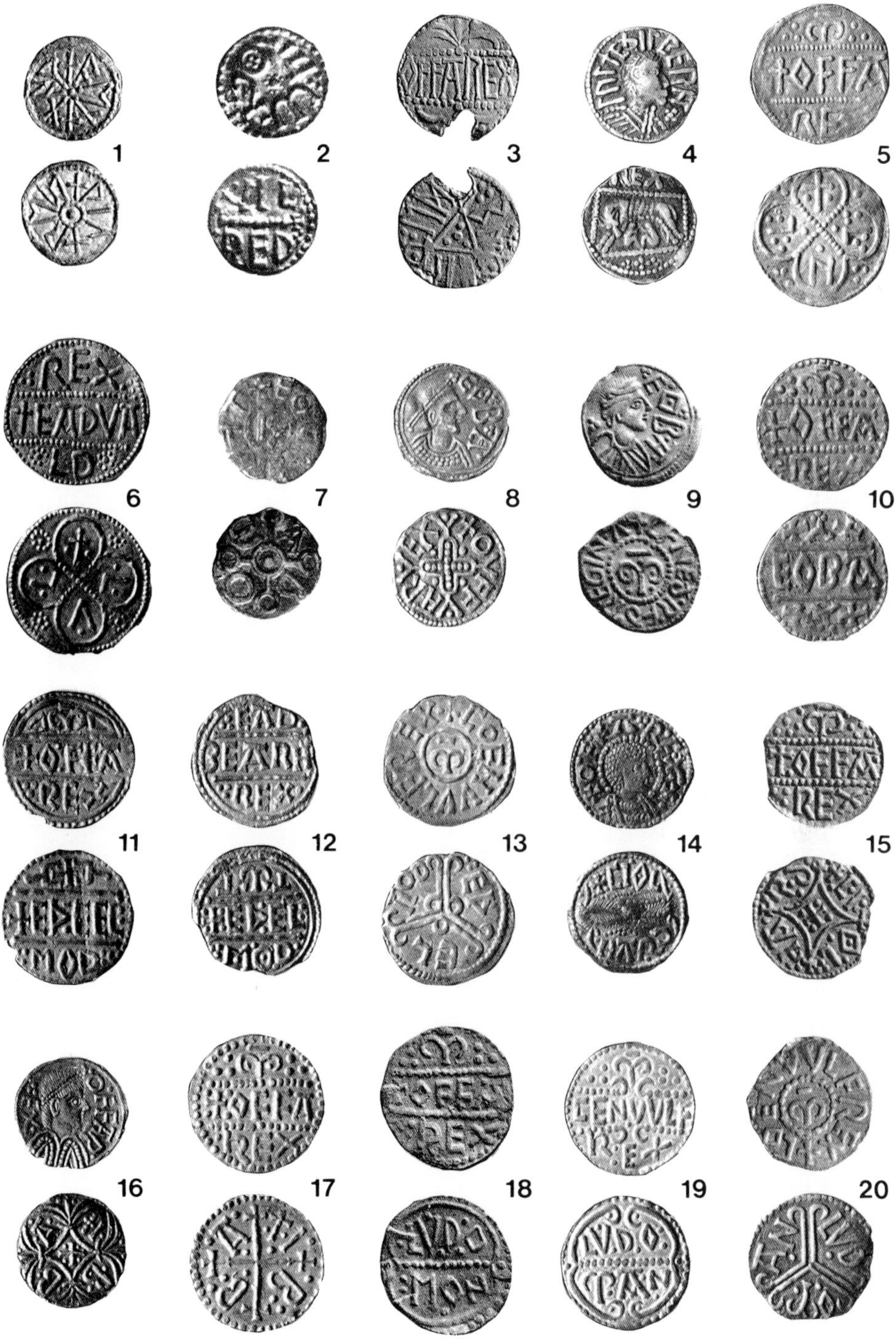
1
2
3
4
5
6
7
8
9
10
11
12
13
14
15
16
17
18
19
20

and, assuming that London-made dies were not supplied to Canterbury in the heavy coinage, it is arguable that the evidential value of this R, as an idiosyncrasy of die-cutting, outweighs the use by some moneyers (e.g. Beagheard and Winoth) of types otherwise associated with Canterbury. The occurrence of common types at separate mints could have resulted either from copying or from gradual moves towards standardization of design.

The moneyers of Offa's heavy coinage who remain to be considered are Beagheard, Deimund, Ealhmund, Osmod, Winoth and Wulfhath. Although Beagheard in both the light and heavy coinages[24] (plate 3.2:38) used a type with oval lunettes resembling that on Canterbury coins of Ethelnoth in the light coinage and of Tidheah under King Eadberht, his heavy coins show the plain A and peculiar R, suggesting that he also should perhaps be regarded as a London moneyer. He spells his name with a runic G (resembling an X) and this is an added reason for not putting him to Canterbury: the distribution of non-numismatic runic inscriptions indicates that they were not much used in Kent[25] and although runes are common on East

24. B.22 and 86.

25. R. I. Page, *An Introduction to English Runes* (1973).

Plate 3.2 Other moneyers of Offa: 21–37 light coinage; 38–40 heavy coinage.

Key to plate 3.2

OFFA, LIGHT COINAGE

21. *Dud* (*BMC* 13: B.27);
22. *Dud* (Lockett 2646: B.25);
23. *Eadberht* (bishop ?), (Lockett 362: B.34);
24. *Eadhun* (*BMC* 14: B.37);
25. *(E)alhmund* (*SCBI* Copenhagen 52: B.41);
26. *(E)alhmund* (*BMC* 32: B.8);
27. *Ealred* (*SCBI* Mack 549: B.9);
28. *Ealraed* (*BMC* 17: B.47);
29. *Ethelvald* (Lockett 3575: B.55);
30. *Ethilvald* (*SCBI* Mack 562: B.58);
31. *Heaber(ht)* (*BMC* 51: B.59);
32. *Lulla* (*SCBI* Edinburgh 57: B.67);
33. *Osmod* (BMA 43: B.72);
34. *Pehtvald* (*BMC* 26: B.75);
35. *Pendred* (RENdREd) (*BMC* 27: B78);
36. *Tirwald* (TIDVVALD) (Blunt, *ex* Ryan 617: B.80);
37. *Winoth* (*SCBI* Oxford 13: B.83).

OFFA, HEAVY COINAGE

38. *Beagheard* (*BMC* 38: B.86);
39. *Ealhmund* (*BMC* 44: B.89);
40. *Winoth* (*BMC* 57: B.105).

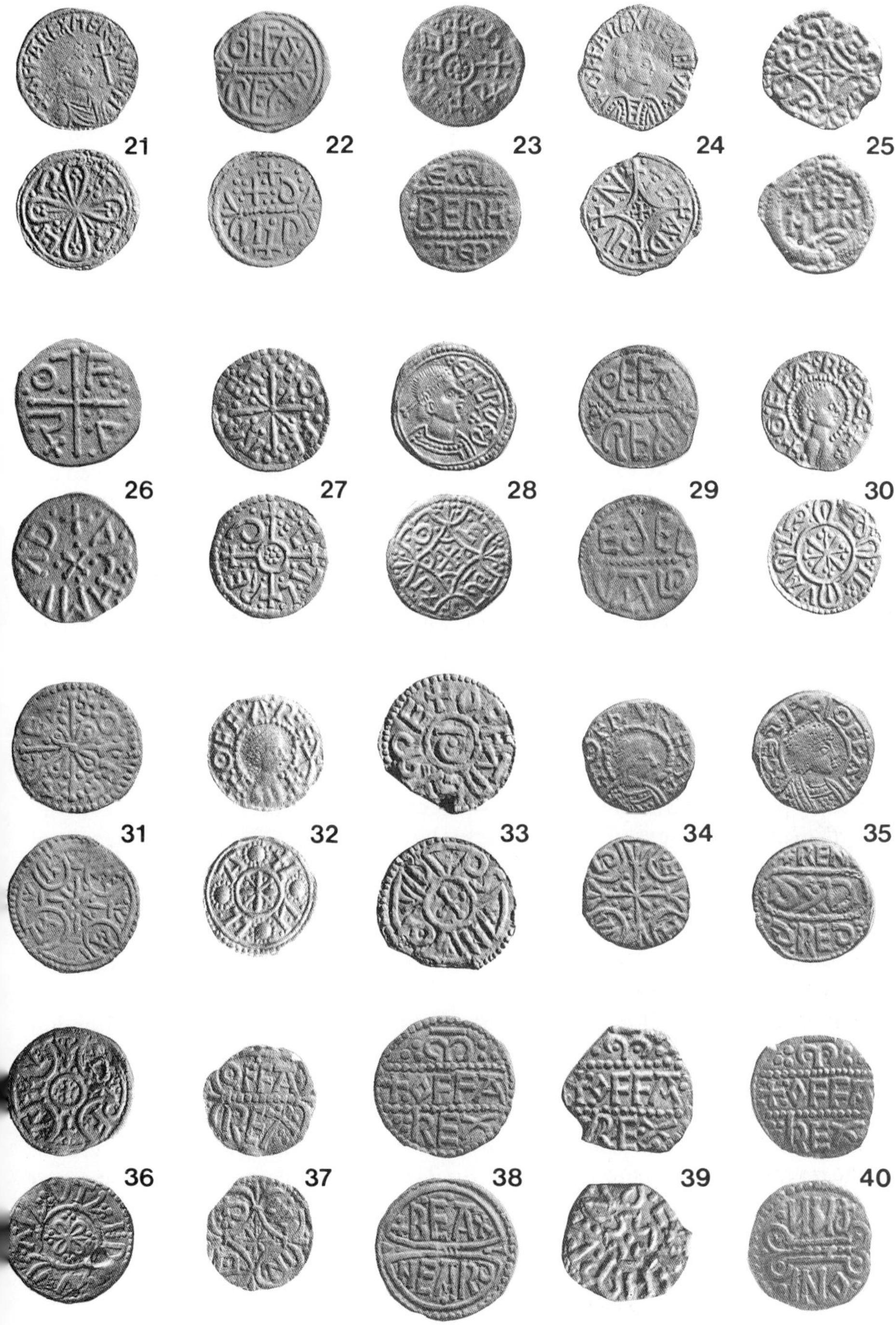
21
22
23
24
25
26
27
28
29
30
31
32
33
34
35
36
37
38
39
40

Anglian coins they do not occur on any that can be attributed to Canterbury. Winoth's coins are mostly of the knuckle-bone type (plate 3.2:40), also used by the Canterbury moneyers Eoba and Ethelnoth, but his use of the peculiar R points to London.[26] So probably does the form of A on the unique coin of Wulfhath, which has a version of the Boeotian shield reverse.[27] No London features are to be found on the unique penny of Deimund or the two of Osmod, who are both likely to be Canterbury moneyers.[28] Osmod's association with Canterbury is strengthened by a coin which has a circular inscription on the obverse (plate 3.2:33) similar to that on some coins of archbishop Æthelheard.[29] The odd case is that of Ealhmund whose three heavy coins (plate 3.2:39) are unlike any others in having the name around a small open cross. But since cross types were also used by Eama, Ibba, and Ciolhard, Ealhmund's coins seem more likely to be associated with London than with Canterbury, and one of them appears to have the peculiar London R.[30]

Leaving aside the East Anglian group, each of the heavy coinage moneyers of Offa may now be associated provisionally with Canterbury or London, and several of the same names are found in the earlier light coinage. The 'London' names involved are Beagheard, Ciolhard, Ealhmund, Ibba and Winoth. It is unfortunate that the number of moneyers known in both the light and heavy coinages is not greater, and this is an area where the discovery of new specimens might be especially useful. But by noting correspondence of design or style or lettering it may be possible to connect further moneyers with the London group. The following remarks must be regarded as somewhat speculative, since the evidence is often equivocal or indecisive. But it seems nevertheless worthwhile indicating some of the possibilities.

Although the light coins of Beaghard, Ciolhard, and Ibba are relatively plentiful, only a single basic type is known of each of them.[31] Beaghard's may date from not long before the heavy coinage since his reverse dies in the two are very similar. The obverse type of his light coins is a cross of lobes which, on specimens of better style, are ornamented with several small points within the outline. The only reverse type of Ciolhard's light coins is a twisted serpent (plate 3.1:14); his obverses have a portrait based on a late Roman bust, enclosed from shoulder to shoulder within a dotted circle. Ibba's light coins all have a portrait in contemporary style, with the letters of his name or Offa's in the field beside it (plate 3.1:16); the reverse type is a lozenge-cross with elaborate floral ends.

Only Winoth and Ealhmund of the moneyers apparently associated with London in the heavy coinage are known from earlier types both with and without portrait. Because of the variety of types that he used Winoth is a key moneyer.[32] Most of his light coins have the same type of obverse as Archbishop Jænberht, with a floral bar dividing OFFA/REX, and a floral lozenge-cross (plate 3.2:37), somewhat like Ibba's, on the reverse. His two other coins have similar reverses, one with a Roman-derived

26. B.105–6. Lockett, *op. cit.*, pl. XII, 12 (*BMC* 57) shows the distinctive R. If Winoth was a London moneyer, his heavy coins are remarkably plentiful.
27. B.107.
28. B.88; B.103.
29. B.72; cf. B.133–4.
30. *SCBI* East Anglia 1068; B.89.
31. B.22; B.23 and B.61–5.
32. B.83, 82, 81.

portrait, the other with a small moulded head and heart-shaped bust, of a kind also used by Ethelwald and Dud.

If the names Alhmund, Ealhmund, and Ealmund all represent the same person, he is a most interesting moneyer who struck types both with and without portrait.[33] Some of his non-portrait obverses[34] read O F RX A (plate 3.2:25–6) instead of the normal O F RX M on his own and other moneyers' coins. If, as it seems, this represents *Rex Anglorum*,[35] one would not expect to find the Anglian title on dies used south of the Thames before the unification of England. One of the RX A coins (plate 3.2:26) is of coarse style and probably comes late in the light coinage since it shares with Ealhmund's heavy coins the unusual feature of a circular inscription around a central cross. His most characteristic reverse type shows his name within a serpent-torque and a comparable type appears to have been used by a moneyer Tirwald.[36]

Serpents also occur on the coins of Pendred (plate 3.2:35) and Ciolhard (plate 3.1:14), both of whom used Roman-derived busts.[37] These two moneyers share the distinction of having produced gold coins that may be identified with the mancuses which figure in texts relating to payments by Offa and Coenwulf to the see of Rome. Ciolhard's gold piece has his name beside a late Roman diademed bust, with a cross-on-steps on the reverse. The types of Pendred are taken from a Lugdunum aureus of Augustus, with his own name added on both sides. Unlike the gold dinar, neither includes the name of the king: the arrangements for producing gold coins must have been less formal than those for the penny coinage.[38]

The use of a long form of *Merciorum* is found on coins of Dud (plate 3.2:21), Eadhun (plate 3.2:24), Ealmund, and Lulla.[39] Enclosed Roman busts like Ciolhard's and Pendred's were also used by Ealmund and Pehtwald (plate 3.2:34).[40] Dud has the greatest variety of portraits and seems to have obtained dies designed for Ealmund, Eadhun, Ethelwald, and Pehtwald.[41] Eadhun and Ealmund struck

33. B.8 and 40–6. Metcalf ('Offa's pence reconsidered', 41) argues for two moneyers, but this does not seem likely to me.
34. B.40, *SCBI* Glasgow 317, and Lockett, *op. cit.*, pl. VIII, 6; B.41; and B.8.
35. Metcalf, 'Offa's pence reconsidered', 41. Lyon, 'Historical problems', 220, suggests O(F)FA RX (RX ligatured) for B.8, but the examples of B.40–1 appear to me to support Metcalf's interpretation.
36. *NC VI*, 1843–4, proceedings pp. 5–6; C. E. Blunt, 'XVII–XIX century manuscript material on Anglo-Saxon coins', *Centennial Publication of the American Numismatic Society* (1958), 125–36, at 134–5.
37. B.76–8 and B.23.
38. H. E. Pagan, 'A third gold coin of Mercia', *BNJ 34* (1965), 8–10; C. E. Blunt and R. H. M. Dolley, 'A gold coin of the time of Offa', *NC* 1968, 151–60; I. Stewart, 'Anglo-Saxon gold coins', in *Scripta Nummaria Romana*, ed. R. A. G. Carson and C. M. Kraay (1978), 143–72. Although originally a Byzantine type, by the eighth century the cross-on-steps would probably have been known to an English moneyer from coins of Beneventum.
39. B.27, 37, 45, and 69. The inscription on the first two of these is very similar.
40. B.44 and 75.
41. B.32, 31, and 29. Metcalf, 'Offa's pence reconsidered', 48. Although Blunt ('The coinage of Offa', 43) identifies Udd with Dud, the types, style, and associations of their coins are so different that I would prefer to

portrait coins with very similar types on both sides and in one case shared an obverse die.[42] Similarities between moneyers are also to be found in the use of some other reverses and non-portrait obverses: for example, a common reverse type was used by Dud, Ethelwald (plate 3.2:30), and Lulla (plate 3.2:32).[43] Dud and Ethelwald both have bar type obverses (plate 3.2:22 and 29);[44] lobe-crosses not unlike Beaghard's occur on reverses of Dud (plate 3.2:21) and Ealmund;[45] and the Celtic cross obverses used by Tirwald (plate 3.2:36) are similar to Heaberht's and Pehtwald's reverse type (plate 3.2:31 and 34).[46]

The ornamented Celtic cross, however, was also used by Archbishop Jænberht (766–92)[47] and this raises the question whether, in the case of some of these moneyers for whom possible London connections have been identified, there may be competing claims from Canterbury. So far six moneyers of the light coinage have been attributed to Canterbury: Babba, Ethelmod, Ethelnoth, Eoba, Osmod, and Udd. The floral bar type was used by Ethelnoth and Archbishop Jænberht (there is a die-link between them),[48] but its use also by Alhmund, Dud, Ethelwald, and Winoth[49] suggests that it was not confined to Canterbury. Heaberht and Pehtwald, the Celtic cross moneyers, have another typological connection with Canterbury in the cross and lobe obverse that they share with Eoba.[50] But against this must be set Pehtwald's affinities with Winoth and Dud and, through them, with other apparently Mercian moneyers. The only moneyer who has connections with Canterbury rather than London seems to be Ealred, who shares a type (plate 3.2:27) with Eoba, Osmod and Udd,[51] and whose portraits (plate 3.2:28)[52] have as much in common with Eoba's (plate 3.1:8–9) as with Ibba's (plate 3.1:16), Eadhun's, or Ealmund's.

The general similarity of some of the portraits of Eadhun, Ealmund, Ealred, Eoba, and Ibba is one of the main pillars of the argument for a single mint-grouping of all Offa's non-East Anglian moneyers.[53] At a later period, as we know was often the case in the tenth century and may well have been sometimes during the ninth, moneyers were liable to work at more than a single mint during their careers. But Eoba and Ibba are among the moneyers of Offa most securely associated with their

regard them as distinct. Most of Dud's coins have fine portraits but Udd's sole portrait (B.33) is exceptionally coarse for Offa's reign.

42. B.38–9 and 46. The rare deuterotheme *-hun* is perhaps a further Mercian link for Eadhun, in view of the London associations of Wilhun and Oelhun. The die-linked coins of Eadhun and Ealmund are *SCBI* Glasgow 309 (B.38) and B.46.
43. B.30–2, 57–8, and 66–7.
44. B.26 and 55–6.
45. B.26–8 and B.43.
46. B.79–80, 59–60, and 73–5. *SCBI* American Collections 188 (B.–) indicates that the moneyer of B.59–60 is correctly read as Heaberht; the obverse of this new type appears to be copied from B.50–1 of Eoba, the reverse from B.66–7 of Lulla.
47. B.132.
48. B.54 and *SCBI* Norweb 83.
49. B.40, 25, 55, and 83.
50. B.59–60, 73, and 50–1.
51. B.9, 12, 19, and 20.
52. B.47–9; also B.21, without moneyer's name, but the portrait die is the same as *SCBI* American Collections 185 (B.49).
53. For stylistic comments see Metcalf, 'Offa's pence reconsidered', 51.

Table 3.4. Other moneyers of Offa
(C = Canterbury; M = Mercian)

	Mint	Offa (light)		Offa (heavy)
		Portrait	Non-portrait	
Beagheard	M?		4	3
Cuthberht	M??		1	
Deimund	C?			1
Dud	M?	11	5	
Eadberht(?)	M?		6	
Eadhun	M?	9		
Ealhmund	M?	20	9	2
Ealred	C?	9	1	
Ethelwald	M?	11	10	
Heaberht	M?		3	
Lulla	M?	12		
Osmod	C		5	2
Pehtwald	M?	5	3	
Pendred	M?	5		
Tirwald	M?		2	
Winoth	M?	2	5	8
Wulfhath	M?			1

respective mints and it would be a large assumption to attribute some of Eoba's coins to London or some of Ibba's to Canterbury.[54] Judging by the undistinguished standard of most Anglo-Saxon coin portraits it may be wondered whether there would have been different engravers of such unusual skill available to Offa at about the same time at both these mints. There is therefore a case for considering the possibility that an exceptional engraver may have been asked to cut dies for the moneyers of more than one mint. The best dies of Eoba, including the Cynethryth portraits, might thus have been the work of the London engraver, perhaps charged with the task of raising the standard of the Canterbury coinage when Offa gained full control of Kent.

Why most of the Canterbury portrait coinage of Eoba was in Cynethryth's name rather than Offa's is a puzzling question, the more so since some of Cynethryth's coins have her husband's portrait. There is no historical evidence to suggest that Offa delegated authority in Kent to his wife, as Coenwulf later did to his brother Cuthred. Cynethryth's coins may therefore have been an honorific issue, following the Roman custom of emperors having part of their coinage struck in the names of their wives and other members of their families. Although Offa was probably conscious of this precedent, there had been no other case of a consort appearing alone on the coins since the end of the fifth century. But Irene (780–802) did have her name and portrait placed conspicuously on the Byzantine coinage at just this time and it may be that word of this had reached Offa and prompted the coinage for Cynethryth.

54. Metcalf, 'Offa's pence reconsidered', 41, suggests the possibility of two Eobas, but I do not think the problem is to be resolved in this way.

In allowing Archbishops Jænberht and Æthelheard of Canterbury to issue coins with their names as well as his, Offa was following the example of Eadberht (737–58) of Northumbria, whose coinage includes a joint issue with his brother Ecgberht as Archbishop of York. It has also been suggested that Offa extended the privilege of coinage to Bishop Eadberht of London, a theory which gains in credibility if there was an important mint in London at this time.[55] On all six coins known with the name Eadberht it is followed by a symbol resembling a rounded M with a bar across one side (plate 3.2:23). Taking this as a monogram of EP, for *Episcopus*, Lockett and Brooke attributed these coins to the Bishop of London in the 780s. Although Pendred's *aureus* has PAENDRAED MVNITARE on the obverse, forms of *Monetarius* or *Moneta* which might be represented by an M with an abbreviation or contraction mark are never found on the light pennies of Offa and there is only one apparent case in the heavy coinage.[56] Bishops of London are not known at any later period to have enjoyed rights of coinage, but Offa was not always on good terms with Jænberht and Eadberht might have been a beneficiary of the king's attempts to diminish the primacy of the see of Canterbury.

If, for the sake of argument, we attribute to the London mint in the light coinage not only the coins of the five apparently London-related moneyers of the heavy coinage, Beagheard, Ciolheard, Ealhmund, Ibba, and Winoth, but also those of a second group, consisting of all or most of Dud, Eadhun, Ethelwald, Heaberht, Lulla, Pehtwald, Pendred, and Tirwald, the implication both from the number of moneyers and from the number of their surviving coins would be that the London mint was at this stage about twice as important as that at Canterbury (table 3.4). This, of course, also assumes that all the moneyers not associated with Canterbury or East Anglia worked in the same place. There is considerable diversity among their coins and there are one or two features (such as Ealhmund's *Rex Anglorum* formula or the style and base metal of the unique coin of Cuthberht)[57] which may not be compatible with a London attribution. The possibility of a further mint or mints cannot therefore be absolutely ruled out. In the heavy coinage the numbers of coins recorded by Blunt for moneyers associated with Canterbury and London respectively are 27 and 21, and in the following period, from 796 to c.805, the relative position of Canterbury is further strengthened, with 9 of Eadberht Præn, 37 of Coenwulf, and 21 of Cuthred, against only 19 of Coenwulf by moneyers associated with London.[58] This is more in line with the dominant position of Canterbury and

55. Lockett, *op. cit.*, 68; G. C. Brooke, *English Coins* (3rd edn, 1950), 22; and cf. Metcalf, 'Offa's pence reconsidered', 39 n.6. Blunt ('The coinage of Offa', 43) notes that there is no (other) recorded instance of a bishop of London enjoying rights of coinage.
56. B.85 of Babba. That the M and O are not simply ornamental shapes is suggested by the same moneyer's coin for Eadberht Præn (Blunt, Lyon, and Stewart, *op. cit.*, pl. I, Ep 1).
57. B.24.
58. Mr Lyon has suggested to me that the number of surviving coins of Æthelheard under Offa (Blunt records 12) might provide a clue to the expected number of royal coins of Canterbury in Offa's heavy coinage; and that a royal: episcopal ratio of between 3 and 4:1, if normal in the time of Coenwulf and Wulfred, might be applied to the last years of Offa,

the limited output of London in the later years of Coenwulf and beyond. But if we look back a generation or two, to the secondary phase of the anonymous denarial coinage earlier in the eighth century, the material does not suggest that the Canterbury mint was of outstanding importance at that time.

Despite the priority of Canterbury in the ninth century, there is thus no intrinsic reason why London should not have been Offa's principal mint before 790, especially if his coinage there began while Heaberht and Egbert ruled in Kent. It is not clear whether the introduction of the new penny coinage in Kent was due to them or to Offa but this question, though still of importance for the arrangement of the Canterbury series, may not have quite the same significance for the chronology of the coinage as a whole if Canterbury is no longer assumed to have been responsible for virtually all of Offa's coins struck outside East Anglia.[59] I emphasize that the number of moneyers, for whom there is direct evidence to connect them with either Canterbury or London, is still small and that the location of most of the others remains uncertain. But if a material part of Offa's coinage was not struck either in Kent or in East Anglia, then I think there is as much of a case for associating most of the unlocated moneyers with London as with Canterbury. I hope that the foregoing paragraphs will be thought to justify further consideration of this hypothesis, and that it may assist in approaching the many unresolved problems of the structure of Offa's coinage.

giving an expected total of Canterbury royal heavy coins of the order of 40–50 rather than 27. The difficulty with this argument is to establish what was a 'normal' ratio of royal to episcopal coinage, since the archbishop's coinage seems frequently to have been suspended. A ratio as low as 2:1 does not seem to me improbable in the light of later practice. For example, the archbishop took three-eighths of the profit in the thirteenth century; and in the anonymous coinage of c.823 surviving examples of the 'episcopal' series actually outnumber those of the 'royal' type.

59. This might enable Lyon's views about the sequence at Canterbury ('Historical problems', 221) to be reconciled with Sir Frank Stenton's suggestion that Offa's coinage began before 770: 'Anglo-Saxon coinage and the historian', in *Preparatory to Anglo-Saxon England*, ed. D. M. Stenton (1971), 371–82.

4 Coinage in southern England, 796–874

Hugh Pagan

During the three-quarters of a century between the death in 796 of King Offa of Mercia and the overthrow by a Viking army in 874 of his successor King Burgred, independent regal authority in England south of the Humber was exercised by three lines of rulers only: Mercian kings ruling from their capital at Tamworth in the north-west Midlands; West Saxon kings based at Winchester or at other royal residences in the belt of country running across from Hampshire to the shores of the Bristol Channel; and a shadowy succession of East Anglian kings whose sphere of operation was limited to the two counties of Norfolk and Suffolk.

During the same period the overwhelming bulk of the coinage was produced at, and circulated from, the three cities of London, Rochester, and Canterbury, lying way to the south-east of the country: London, the last urban community in Mercia at the extremity of its southern frontier; Rochester and Canterbury in the subordinate kingdom of Kent. Control over the coinage from Tamworth or Winchester must thus have been remote, and at times perhaps nominal or nil. Nevertheless, most of the coins carry the names and titles of Mercian and West Saxon kings and at all times the coinage has an official character.

The causes for this lie in the eighth century, for when the new broad flan penny coinage was initiated in the 760s or 770s coin use had not yet spread into the heartland of the Mercian kingdom, or far into Wessex, and the new pennies were primarily intended for use in Kent and the south-east. The fact that most carried the name of the Mercian king Offa simply reflected the political control that he exercised over that part of Anglo-Saxon England, and the occurrence of the names of later Mercian or West Saxon kings on the coinage should not be seen as evidence that coin manufacture moved into Mercia proper or Wessex but as a reflection of changes in political control at Canterbury, Rochester, and London.[1] There was always a small group of moneyers working in East Anglia, either for independent East Anglian kings or for Mercian kings whose rule was recognized there, and on two occasions there may have been a locally manufactured coinage issued from Winchester or

1. Numismatists' traditional arrangement of eighth/ninth-century coins under the principal kingdom of the ruler whose name appears on them, followed even in volumes of the *SCBI* series, leads to such anomalies as the listing of the production of royal moneyers at Canterbury within a four-year period in the 820s under three separate kingdoms, and should now be superseded by an arrangement of the coins by place of production.

Southampton,[2] but it is with the coins struck at the three south-eastern cities that the numismatist is primarily concerned and they will receive extended consideration in what follows.[3]

It will be convenient to give separate treatment to coins struck from 796 to the early 850s and to coins struck from the early 850s onwards, for a Viking attack on south-eastern England in 851 brought minting to a halt throughout the region, and when production of coin in bulk was resumed the basis on which it came to be organized was a new one.

Coinage at Canterbury, Rochester, and London, 796–851

The basic unit of currency in southern England over this period was the silver penny, which by 796 had assumed dimensions and weight that were to remain essentially unaltered right down to the early 870s.[4] It was also a matter of established practice that these pennies should carry on their obverse the name of the ruler whose authority was recognized at their place of manufacture, followed by his royal title, be it *Rex* simply or *Rex M* (for *Merciorum*) or *Rex Cant* (for *Cantuariorum*), and that they should carry on their reverse the name of a moneyer, either on its own or followed by the word *moneta*. The occurrence of the name of the city where the pennies were produced is less frequent, but numismatists have now succeeded in identifying separate series of coins struck at Canterbury, Rochester, and London.

At Canterbury up to 851 coins were struck successively in the names of the independent local ruler Eadberht Præn (796–8); the Mercian king Coenwulf (798–c.801); his brother Cuthred as king of Kent (c.801–7); Coenwulf again after Cuthred's death (807–21); the new Mercian king Ceolwulf (821–3); an independent local ruler Baldred (823–5); the West Saxon king Egbert (825–39); and the West

2. The coinage struck in East Anglia between 796 and 825 is discussed by C. E. Blunt, C. S. S. Lyon, and B. H. I. H. Stewart at pp. 25–30 of their article 'The coinage of southern England 796–840', *BNJ 32* (1963), 1–74, and the later coinage by the present writer in 'The coinage of the East Anglian kingdom from 825 to 870', *BNJ 52* (1982), 41–83. The coinage attributable to moneyers working at Winchester or Southampton comprises a handful of coins in the name of Beorhtric, king of Wessex 786–802, a larger group struck by six moneyers for Egbert of Wessex in the late 820s and 830s, and one single coin of Æthelwulf of Wessex following on directly from the Egbert coins; the older view was that they were struck at Winchester, but Michael Dolley's suggestion that they were struck at Southampton may be preferable (see M. Dolley, 'The location of the pre-Alfredian mint(s) of Wessex', *Procs Hampshire Field Club 27* (1970), 57–61).
3. Many of the issues to be discussed below are touched on in the presidential address delivered to the British Numismatic Society in 1968 by Stewart Lyon and printed in *BNJ 37* (1968), 216–38, under the title 'Historical problems of Anglo-Saxon coinage – (2), The ninth century – Offa to Alfred'.
4. See pp. 183–90 of Lyon's 'Some problems in interpreting Anglo-Saxon coinage', in *ASE 5* (1976), 173–224.

Saxon king Æthelwulf (839–58). There are also coins in the joint names of Coenwulf and of Archbishop Æthelheard (archbishop 792–805), contemporary in date with those struck in Coenwulf's name in 798–c.801; and successive series of coins in the sole names of Archbishop Wulfred (805–32) and of Archbishop Ceolnoth (833–70).

No Rochester coinage is identifiable before c.810, but from then onwards the succession of kings' names on the coins is identical to that found at Canterbury, although it may be that Baldred assumed power at Rochester a little earlier than he did at Canterbury and that the start of Æthelwulf's Rochester coinage also predates the start of his Canterbury coinage.[5]

London was always part of the Mercian kingdom, and the succession of kings' names on coins struck at London more or less mirrors the succession of Mercian kings, except that no London coins exist for the brief reign of Ludica (825–7) and that coinage production at London seems to have lapsed for a decade from the early 830s to the early 840s. The succession of kings' names on the coinage up to c.830 is therefore as follows: Coenwulf (796–821); Ceolwulf (821–3); Beornwulf (823–5); Wiglaf (827–9); and Egbert of Wessex as king of Mercia (829–30). Two surviving coins of Wiglaf of the same appearance as one of those of Egbert and by a shared moneyer may either belong just before Egbert's brief assumption of power over Mercia or to the very early 830s after Wiglaf's restoration to the Mercian throne.[6] Thereafter coinage does not resume until c.843 when a relatively extensive coinage commences in the name of Wiglaf's successor Beorhtwulf (c.840–52).

It is not necessary here to deal in detail with the coinage struck between 796 and c.830, for that is sufficiently discussed in a masterly survey by Blunt, Lyon, and Stewart in a past volume of the *British Numismatic Journal*.[7] The coinage of the latter part of Egbert's reign in Kent awaits considered numismatic analysis, but its Canterbury element is all of one type, and so unlikely to provide many surprises, and its Rochester element is so scanty that its exact arrangement would seem to be of small importance.[8] That leaves only the coins struck in the names of Æthelwulf and Beorhtwulf and Archbishop Ceolnoth in the dozen years before 851 and these will be discussed in their appropriate place below.

It is convenient to begin with some general remarks on the organization and

5. The relative dating of Baldred's coinages at Canterbury and Rochester is discussed by Blunt, Lyon, and Stewart, *op. cit.*, 41–2, and the relative dating of Æthelwulf's coinages by Lyon, 'Historical problems', 223–5. It should be noted that Baldred's Mercian predecessor Ceolwulf received consecration from Archbishop Wulfred of Canterbury as late as 17 September 822 and was still in a position at that date to grant the archbishop an estate near Kemsing in Kent (D. Whitelock (ed.), *EHD* I (2nd edn., 1979), 514–16).

6. These are attributed to Wiglaf's second reign, i.e. to the very early 830s, by Blunt, Lyon, and Stewart, *op. cit.*, 34, but they may just as easily date from the end of his first reign.

7. *Ibid.*

8. C. E. Blunt, 'The coinage of Ecgbeorht, king of Wessex, 802–39', *BNJ 28* (1955–7), 467–76, lists the 21 then known Rochester coins of Egbert's reign as his 'fourth group' on p. 470, while the Canterbury coins of the later part of the reign are discussed, without being listed in full, as his 'third group' on pp. 468–9.

administration of coinage production in the first half of the ninth century. Direct evidence for this is patchy, for there is no surviving documentary material and the coins are more informative at some periods than they are at others, but the evidence is sufficient to reach a number of conclusions about the relationship between kings, moneyers, and coins.

First, the information that the coins provide about their moneyers. It can be established from surviving coins that at Canterbury the number of moneyers striking coins in the king's name remained absolutely steady at five or six right through from the end of the 790s to Æthelwulf's reign, with two further moneyers usually striking coins for the archbishop, making a total of seven or eight moneyers in all at any one time. At Rochester there were probably never more than two moneyers working concurrently in the period between c.810 and c.842, and then, surprisingly, six moneyers for the years c.842–c.851. At London, after an extensive coinage early in Coenwulf's reign which is discussed by Stewart in chapter 3 in this volume, the number of moneyers falls dramatically and between c.805 and c.830 it fluctuates between one and three (three occurring at the end of Coenwulf's reign and in Ceolwulf's reign when London may have been the only south-eastern city permanently loyal to him).[9] When coinage resumed at London c.843 it was on the same scale as at Rochester, with five or six moneyers working concurrently until the early 850s.

The coins also provide evidence for moneyers' careers. It is apparent from a tabulation of moneyers known for Canterbury issues over the period as a whole that a moneyer could continue to operate regardless of changes in ruler or of other external events. This is most vividly illustrated by the fact that the six moneyers among whom coinage production was shared at the end of Coenwulf's reign in 821 were still the six moneyers responsible for coinage production in the early years of Egbert's reign despite the intervening reigns of Ceolwulf and Baldred; indeed, the strength of their position was such that in a period of political confusion at this time they were able to issue coins on which their own names appeared on the obverse in place of that of a king.[10] Moneyers might also remain active for considerable periods of time; it is difficult to compute spans of activity for Canterbury moneyers whose careers began before 796, for the dating of the pre-796 penny coinage is uncertain, but among moneyers whose careers began after 796 Werheard was active c.800–c.827, Diormod and Tidbearht from c.810 to c.830, and Osmund from c.830 to c.851. At London

9. During Ceolwulf's reign the London mint also had the services of a much more competent die-engraver than in other reigns. It has been suggested that the London moneyer Ceolbald, active at the end of Coenwulf's reign and in Ceolwulf's reign but not in later reigns, may conceivably have been the same Ceolbald whose name appears on coins of a Northumbrian king Æthelred which may belong to the late 820s (H. E. Pagan, 'Northumbrian numismatic chronology in the ninth century', *BNJ* 37 (1970), 1–15; the suggestion appears at p. 13), and political difficulties in 823 may have led to the loss both of Ceolbald and of the London mint's die-engraver.
10. The coins are those discussed by Blunt, Lyon, and Stewart, *op. cit.*, 14–15.

Ciolhard was a moneyer from before c.792 to c.823 and at Rochester Dun or Dunun a moneyer from c.810 to perhaps as late as c.845.

All this suggests a considerable degree of stability in the way in which moneyers operated. It can also be deduced that the supply to individual moneyers of dies and of a supply of bullion to turn into coin was governed by recognized principles; it is noticeable that throughout the period there is almost complete uniformity in style between dies used at the same time by different moneyers in the same city, implying that dies were always supplied to them from a common source, and although determining the proportion of any one issue struck by any given moneyer is frankly a matter of guesswork, it is quite apparent from the surviving coins that no one moneyer dominates any given type and hence that bullion was shared out at least relatively equally.

It is less certain whether the numismatist can properly talk of there being 'mints' in Canterbury, London, or Rochester, for die-linkage between coins carrying the names of different moneyers seems to be unknown and that makes it doubtful whether moneyers entered into partnership or worked in shared premises. It is instructive, though, to consider the division of the moneyers at Canterbury into the five or six striking coins in the king's name and the two striking coins in the archbishop's name. The archbishop's participation in the coinage, although very possibly dating from the origins of coinage in Anglo-Saxon Britain, is first evidenced in the 780s, when coins were struck in the joint names of Offa of Mercia and of Archbishop Jænberht.[11] By early in the ninth century this had blossomed into a coinage in the archbishop's name alone with the archbishop's facing bust on the coins' obverses and with reverses distinct in design from those used in the regal series, and although the earliest of these coins simply carry the reverse inscription *Dorovemiae Civitatis* the names of moneyers quickly appear. The relationship between these moneyers and the archbishop may not have been absolutely exclusive, for there were times when archiepiscopal moneyers struck coins for the king, but the mere fact that there were normally specific archiepiscopal moneyers implies that moneyers were not self-employed craftsmen, but subordinate either to secular, or in this instance to ecclesiastical, higher authority. It is natural that this should be so, for in every age coinage was a source of revenue to those who controlled the cities where coin was struck, and one can fairly conclude that although the notion of there having been 'mints' before or after 851 at Canterbury, Rochester, and London may be erroneous, the operations of royal and archiepiscopal moneyers must in practice have been regulated and co-ordinated by higher authority.

The extent of royal or archiepiscopal intervention in the coinage process is not easy to gauge. It was at all times customary for the name on the obverse of the coins to be

11. The best summary of the history of the archbishop's coining privileges at Canterbury is that given by Blunt under the title 'Ecclesiastical coinage in England' in two presidential addresses to the Royal Numismatic Society in *NC* 1960 and 1961. He suggests at p. iii of the 1960 address that prior to the Offa-Jænberht coinage the archbishop had participated in the striking of the uninscribed coinage of the first half of the eighth century, and that still seems a likely hypothesis.

changed on the change of ruler, but this may just as well have stemmed from convention or common prudence as from any specific instruction from above. It does seem quite certain that the coinage reform carried out in the 790s when Offa of Mercia was the dominant figure in southern England, involving as it did an increase in the weight of the coinage and a standardization of coins' obverse and reverse designs on a Carolingian model, stemmed from the direct exercise of royal power, presumably in the form of an edict specifying the designs that the coins should carry and the number of them that were in future to be struck from a pound weight of silver.[12] No such fundamental reform occurred in the following half-century, and it seems unlikely that any general edict of this nature was issued between 796 and the late 840s, for design changes at Canterbury are never quite identical to those at Rochester, still less to those at London.

At the same time there were frequent changes in the appearance of the coins and at times these can be seen to correspond to political change. When Coenwulf's coinage replaces that of Eadberht Præn at Canterbury in 798, the new coins adopt the type of the coinage already being struck in Coenwulf's name at London in clear preference to the type which had been struck at Canterbury continuously since c.792, with the obvious aim of disassociating Coenwulf's coinage from that of his defeated Kentish predecessor. Later in the period, an apparently peaceful transition from the reign of Egbert to that of his son Æthelwulf is marked by an abrupt change in the character of the coinage from Canterbury, Egbert's coins with his portrait on the obverse and a monogram of the letters DOROB C on the reverse being replaced by non-portrait coins with the inscription AEÐELVVLF REX around a cross on the obverse and the word *Saxoniorum* in three lines as the central feature on the reverse, emphasizing the fact that Æthelwulf, who had previously ruled in Kent as his father's deputy, was now king of the West Saxons as well. On a contemporary, or nearly contemporary, issue from Rochester the coins' reverses have the word *Occidentalium* as well as the word *Saxoniorum* and the reference to Æthelwulf's new status is even clearer.

On other occasions changes in coin design seem to be related rather to the requirements of coinage management than to any external factor, but still seem sufficiently deliberate and far-reaching in their effect that royal intervention may have been involved. Into this category may be placed the reversion at Canterbury c.805 to a coinage with the king's profile bust on the obverse, no portrait coins having been struck there since c.790; the introduction at Canterbury c.827 of Egbert's portrait/DOROB C monogram type; and the issue at the end of the 840s both from Canterbury and from Rochester of non-portrait coins with the letters DORIBI as the central feature on the obverse and a monogram of the letters CANT as the central feature on the reverse. Where the coinage of c.805 is concerned it must be relevant that this was a time when Kent had a resident king, Cuthred, to whom the appearance of his portrait, however stylized, on the coinage must have been a matter of consequence; and as for the portrait/DOROB C monogram type the new type was

12. These changes in design and weight seem to have been implemented more or less simultaneously in Kent, at London, and in East Anglia.

obviously different from all preceding regal issues from Canterbury and remained the type of Egbert's Canterbury coinage for the rest of his reign.

The DORIBI/CANT coins of the late 840s are the concluding Kentish issues of the dozen years of coinage which were earlier reserved for separate discussion, and it is now time to embark on the coinage of these years, for the coins struck in the names of Æthelwulf of Wessex, Beorhtwulf of Mercia, and Archbishop Ceolnoth usefully illustrate the various problems that have just been ventilated.

As has been seen, the earliest Canterbury issues in Æthelwulf's name are the non-portrait *Saxoniorum* coins (plate 4.1:1) and the striking of these extends past the deposit c.840 of the sizeable London (Middle Temple) hoard in which this was the only Canterbury type of Æthelwulf represented.[13] They were replaced c.842 by the first of an extensive series of portrait coins, the interpretation of which has been impeded in the past by numismatists' subdivision of it by reverse design, for the real divide within the series is a stylistic one; one group of coins has crudely drawn busts (plate 4.1:2), sometimes rendered without shoulders or with residual shoulders only, contained within a broad but blurred beaded circle, with an outer inscription composed of letters with broad limbs splaying outwards, while the other group of coins (plate 4.1:3) has carefully designed busts with small details of hair and dress shown clearly, a more carefully engraved inner circle, and very much neater lettering.[14] Coins of the moneyer Diar (plate 4.1:4) which combine a reverse die analogous in style to dies of the second group with a DORIBI obverse die provide a bridge from the end of the portrait series to the substantive DORIBI/CANT series. However, they are not literally a mule between the two series, for their style is not quite that of either series and Diar is not recorded as a moneyer either for the DORIBI/CANT series or for the precise variety of the portrait series with the capital letter A as the central feature of the reverse which these coins copy.[15] It seems likely that the portrait series was succeeded c.848 by the third phase of Æthelwulf's Canterbury coinage, the DORIBI/CANT series, and that these coins were struck

13. Only two coins of the type were present in the London (Middle Temple) hoard, but the type was struck on a larger scale than this would suggest and by three moneyers in addition to those documented by the hoard. For the London (Middle Temple) hoard see H. A. Grueber, 'A find of Anglo-Saxon coins,' *NC* 1894, 29–76, and for its find-spot see now *CH 4* (1978), entry no. 342 on p. 104.
14. The discussion of this phase of the coinage by Michael Dolley and Kolbjørn Skaare in their article, 'The coinage of Æthelwulf, king of the West Saxons, 839–58', *AS Coins*, 63–76, correctly groups together as the product of their second *officina* (subsequently identified as Canterbury) coins of no fewer than six apparent types, and it seems clear that provided the coins carried the king's portrait on their obverses considerable latitude was permitted in the design of their reverses.
15. The coins in question are *BMC* 21, *ex* Dorking hoard, and one in the Bibliothèque Nationale, Paris, which is perhaps the coin of this character from the Dorking hoard which passed through the Barclay sale (Sotheby, 21–3 March 1831) lot 38, and the Cuff sale (Sotheby, 8 June 1854, following) lot 435, bought by Curt.

c.848–c.851; the moneyers known for the DORIBI/CANT series do not essentially differ from those who worked earlier, but there are other indications that the DORIBI/CANT series follows, rather than precedes, the portrait series, and a late sub-variety with CANT on the obverse and the cryptic letters C, V (or A), N, and M on the reverse (plate 4.1:5) carries the name of a moneyer Hebeca who enjoyed an extensive career after 851.[16]

Towards the end of the 840s the number of moneyers at Canterbury, which had so

16. Lyon, 'Historical problems', 227, suggests that the DORIBI/CANT issue from Canterbury may have overlapped with the portrait issue, but his grounds for making the suggestion do not seem compelling.

Plate 4.1 Coins of Æthelwulf, Æthelberht, Beorhtwulf, and Archbishop Ceolnoth.

Key to plate 4.1

1. Æthelwulf, *Cross and wedges*/SAXONIORVM, Torhtwald (*BMC* 31, *ex* Dorking hoard)
2. Æthelwulf, *Bust/Cross crosslet*, crude style, Liaba (*BMC* 46, *ex* Dorking hoard)
3. Æthelwulf, *Bust/Cross crosslet*, neat style, Liaba (*BMC* 45, *ex* Dorking hoard)
4. Æthelwulf, DORIBI/*Letter A*, Diar (*BMC* 21, *ex* Dorking hoard)
5. Æthelwulf, CANT/CANM, Hebeca (*BMC* 24, *ex* Gravesend hoard)
6. Ceolnoth, *Bust*/DOROB C *monogram*, Biornmod (BM, *ex* T. G. Barnett, no doubt *ex* C. M. Crompton-Roberts, *ex* J. J. Nunn (sale 1896, lot 54), *ex* Hon. R. Marsham (sale 1888, lot 116), said in Marsham cat. to be *ex* C. W. Loscombe (sale 1855))
7. Ceolnoth, *Bust/Chi-Rho*, crude style, Biornmod (*BMC* 33, *ex* Dorking hoard)
8. Ceolnoth, *Bust/Chi-Rho*, neat style, Biornmod (*BMC* 35, *ex* Rev. T. F. Dymock (sale 1838, lot 39), *ex* R. Barclay (sale 1831, lot 269), *ex* Dorking hoard)
9. Æthelwulf, *Bust/Bar with moline ends and crescents*, Beagmund (BMA 425, *ex* Middle Temple hoard)
10. Æthelwulf, *Cross and wedges*/OCCIDENTALIVM SAXONIORVM, no moneyer (*BMC* 32, *ex* Dorking hoard)
11. Æthelwulf, DORIBI/CANT, Wealheard (*BMC* 15, *ex* Dorking hoard)
12. Beorhtwulf, *Bust/Cross with moline and crosslet ends*, Deneheah (*SCBI* Oxford 22, *ex* R. C. Lockett (sale 1955, lot 390), *ex* T. Bliss (sale 1916, lot 40), *ex* H. Montagu (sale 1895, lot 273), *ex* W. Brice, *ex* W. Lake Price (sale 1880, lot 17), *ex* Capt. R. M. Murchison (sale 1866, lot 99))
13. Ceolnoth, *Bust/Cross*, 'Lil' (*BMC* 46, *ex* Dorking hoard)
14. Æthelwulf, *Bust/Open Cross*, Diar (BM, *ex* L. A. Lawrence, *ex* G. C. Drabble (sale 1939, lot 374))
15. Æthelwulf, *Bust/Open Cross*, Hunbearht (*BMC* 71, *ex* Sir Henry Ellis)
16. Æthelwulf, *Bust/Open Cross*, Hunbearht (*BMC* 69, *ex* Dorking hoard)
17. Æthelberht, *Bust/Open Cross*, Cenweald (*BMC* 11, *ex* Dorking hoard)
18. Æthelberht, *Bust/Floreate Cross*, Cenweald (*BMC* 61, *ex* S. Tyssen, *ex* Rev. R. Southgate)
19. Ceolnoth, *Bust/Cross within lozenge*, Diala (*BMC* 39, *ex* J. D. Cuff (sale 1854, lot 396), *ex* Duke of Devonshire (sale 1844, lot 157)
20. Ceolnoth, *Bust/Cross crosslet, pellets in angles*, Biarnred (*SCBI* Glasgow 403, *ex* T. Coats, *ex* Maj.-Gen. W. Yorke Moore (sale 1879, lot 62))

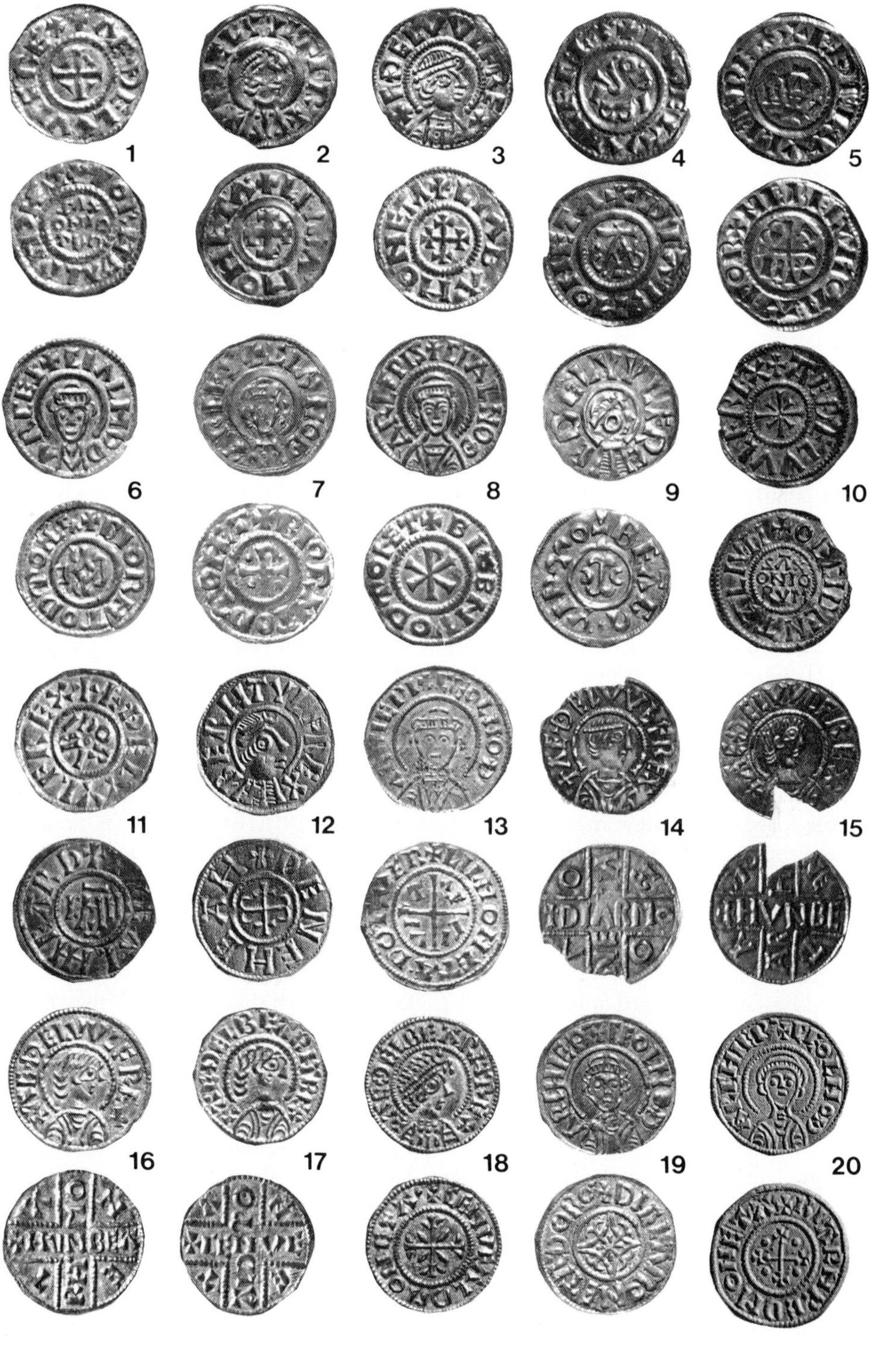
1
2
3
4
5
6
7
8
9
10
11
12
13
14
15
16
17
18
19
20

Table 4.1. Æthelwulf's moneyers at Canterbury, c.839–c.851

Saxoniorum series	*Portrait series*	DORIBI/CANT *series*
Torhtwald		
Diar	Diar	
Herebeald	Herebeald	Herebeald
Manna	Manna	
Osmund	Osmund	Osmund
	Deiheah	Deiheah
	Eanmund	Eanmund
	Hunbearht	Hunbearht
	Liaba	
		Ealgmund
		Ethelmund
		Hebeca

long been static, shows signs of expansion, as table 4.1 indicates. The increase in the number of moneyers may to some extent be more apparent than real, for Liaba is also found as a moneyer of Beorhtwulf of Mercia and his stay at Canterbury may have been brief, while the moneyers recorded for the DORIBI/CANT type and its varieties may include replacements for moneyers disappearing early in its issue; the table includes Herebeald who is only known for a variety where the designs are transposed – CANT on the obverse and DORIBI on the reverse – and Hebeca who is known for the (late?) variety mentioned above. However, it is quite possible that the expansion in coinage production evident at Rochester and London was mirrored at Canterbury. Unexpectedly, although there was a substantial coinage in the archbishop's name early in the reign and for the duration of the regal portrait series, there is no archiepiscopal coinage remotely comparable to the DORIBI/CANT series, and this gives force to the view that the introduction of the DORIBI/CANT type both at Canterbury and at Rochester was a deliberate act of policy, intended to provide a currency of similar appearance throughout Kent and thus necessarily excluding the accustomed facing bust coinage by the archbishop.

At Rochester the earliest coins struck for Æthelwulf were portrait coins in the names of the moneyers Beagmund (plate 4.1:9) and Dun; they occur in the London (Middle Temple) hoard in numbers which have suggested that Æthelwulf may have begun to strike coins there before his father Egbert's death, but all the coins of the moneyer Dun in the hoard were from a single pair of dies and there are also die-duplicates among those of Beagmund, making it unlikely that their striking occupied a period of time proportionate to their number.[17] Alongside them there were non-portrait coins with as obverse type a cross with wedges in the angles and as reverse type the word *Saxoniorum* in three lines surrounded by the word *Occidentalium* (plate 4.1:10), which are the equivalents of the Canterbury *Saxoniorum* coins and which must likewise have been intended to mark Æthelwulf's accession to the

17. Lyon, 'Historical problems', 219–25, sets out the theory that the start of Æthelwulf's coinage from Rochester preceded Egbert's death.

Table 4.2. Æthelwulf's moneyers at Rochester, c.839–c.851

Early issues	*New style issues*	DORIBI/CANT *series*
Beagmund	Beagmund	
Dun	Dun	
Wilheah	Wilheah	Wilheah
	Biarnnoth	Biarnnoth
	Brid	Brid
	Ethelhere	Ethelhere
	Manninc	Manninc
	Wealheard	Wealheard

West Saxon throne.[18] As at Canterbury, the early issues of the reign give way c.842 to an extensive series of coins of new style; they include both portrait and non-portrait coins and it is clear that complete design uniformity was not sought. The moneyers recorded for this period number eight, but Beagmund and Dun disappear early on and it may be assumed that no more than six were at work concurrently. Although the style of the coins is not as neat as that of the neater Canterbury coins of this date, the Rochester coins are boldly designed and well struck on broad flans, and the Rochester DORIBI/CANT series which follows (plate 4.1:11) is actually superior in design to the Canterbury one, the word DORIBI being more clearly set out than on Canterbury coins and the lettering used being distinctly more handsome. As will be seen from table 4.2, the moneyers now remained constant in number and identity.

The London (Middle Temple) hoard contained no coins of Beorhtwulf of Mercia and it looks as if no coins were struck in the names of Mercian kings for the whole of the decade from the early 830s to c.842. It was thus not unnatural that when Beorhtwulf's coinage began the dies for it should have been cut by the same hand as the dies currently being supplied to Æthelwulf's moneyers at Rochester, and that much is obvious from the style of Beorhtwulf's coins (plate 4.1:12). It by no means follows from this that Beorhtwulf's moneyers were themselves Rochester-based, and the presence among them of one known Rochester moneyer of Æthelwulf, Brid, is counterbalanced by the fact that another of Beorhtwulf's moneyers, Liaba, is recorded for Æthelwulf not at Rochester but at Canterbury. There does exist a charter granting the see of Rochester customs privileges at London which carries a later confirmation by Beorhtwulf given by him at *Werburgewic*, a place which it has been suggested was Hoo in the Isle of Sheppey, but this identification is far from certain and the privileges confirmed by Beorhtwulf were in Mercia, not in West Kent.[19] It would be surprising if Æthelwulf were to have allowed moneyers in his

18. This interpretation does not necessarily imply that the *Occidentalium Saxoniorum* issue was the initial issue of Æthelwulf's reign, for Rochester moneyers may only have begun to strike *Occidentalium Saxoniorum* coins when coin users had become familiar with the Canterbury *Saxoniorum* coins. Lyon, 'Historical problems', 224, regards the *Occidentalium Saxoniorum* coins as the production of a moneyer working for the Bishop of Rochester.
19. In her commentary on this charter Professor Whitelock concludes that *Werburgewic* was 'probably in Mercia' (Whitelock (ed.), *op. cit.*, 492, n. 2).

own kingdom to work for Beorhtwulf, and it would also be odd that Rochester should have housed five moneyers – Burnwald, Deneheah, Eanred, Osulf, and Sigeheah – who worked solely for Beorhtwulf and not for Æthelwulf.

The main part of Beorhtwulf's coinage divides into this group of coins of Rochester style and a group of rather different style in which Burnwald, Deneheah, Eanred, and Sigeheah recur and are joined by other moneyers.[20] This second group is quite unrelated to any Rochester coins of Æthelwulf, and the occurrence among its moneyers of Eanred and Wine, moneyers of Beorhtwulf's successor Burgred, points to it being the work of London-based moneyers. The likelihood is that it followed on chronologically from the other group and that despite the Rochester origin of the dies of that group the moneyers were throughout based at London, the presence of Brid and Liaba among them meaning no more than that these moneyers were based at London before or after careers elsewhere. Beorhtwulf's coinage terminates with non-portrait coins by the moneyers Ean..d (Eanbald or Eanred) and Tatel, and Tatel's appearance provides another link with the later production of London moneyers, Tatel striking for Burgred in the 850s and 860s.

The moneyers active for Beorhtwulf are set out in table 4.3. It can be seen from all this that coin production at Rochester and London, which in the 810s, 820s, and 830s had been on a limited scale and served as an adjunct only to coin production at Canterbury, expanded in the 840s to take on a major role in the provision of currency for southern England. How far this was the result of conscious policy is not easy to determine. The fact that in the middle of the 840s dies cut by the same hand were being supplied both to Æthelwulf's Rochester moneyers and to Beorhtwulf's London moneyers might suggest some linkage between the expansion in the number of moneyers at Rochester and the restart of coin production at London, and the existence of a coin struck from a Beorhtwulf obverse die of Rochester style and a reverse die carrying the inscription IAEÐELVVLF REX and of the same approximate type as obverse dies of Æthelwulf's *Occidentalium Saxoniorum* Rochester issue has encouraged numismatists to see Beorhtwulf and Æthelwulf as enjoying friendly monetary relations, whether the coin is an actual Beorhtwulf/Æthelwulf mule or some sort of 'alliance' issue. In fact, as should have been obvious from the fact that the types apparently muled are both obverse types, only the Beorhtwulf die is an official one and the apparent Æthelwulf die is irregular and imitative, and the coin should have no place in the canon of regular issues.[21] It may also be observed that the simultaneous issues of DORIBI/CANT coins from Canterbury and Rochester in the period c.848–c.851, while serving the internal purpose of providing a coinage of similar character throughout Kent, also served to distinguish Æthelwulf's coinage sharply from Beorhtwulf's, and the kings' roles in relation to their coinages are thus more complicated than first appearances suggest. The one proposition that can safely be advanced is that Rochester occupied a position in the monetary history of the 840s that it never enjoyed before or since.

20. These groups were first distinguished by J. J. North, 'The coinage of Berhtwulf', *NCirc* 1961, 213.

21. The irregular nature of the Æthelwulf die was first recognized by Lyon, 'Historical problems', 229.

Table 4.3. Beorhtwulf's moneyers at London, c.843–c.851

Portrait issues Rochester style	*Portrait issues New style*	*Non-portrait issues*
Brid		
Liaba		
Osulf		
Burnwald	Burnwald	
Deneheah	Deneheah	
Eanred	Eanred	
Sigeheah	Sigeheah	
	Eanbald	Ean..d
	Eanna	
	Wine	
		Tatel

Coinage at Canterbury, London, and Rochester after 851

In the immediate aftermath of the Viking raid of 851 the production of coinage seems virtually to have stopped. At Canterbury the only definite grouping of coins likely to have been struck in the early 850s is a small series of coins of Archbishop Ceolnoth with the archbishop's facing bust on the obverse and on the reverse the inscription DOROVERNIA CIVITAS variously set out, sometimes preceded by the name of an apparent (but probably notional) moneyer 'Lil' (plate 4.1:13).[22] It may be that the sub-variety of the regal DORIBI/CANT series struck by the moneyer Hebeca belongs after 851, rather than earlier, but the variety is very rare and the fact that Hebeca's subsequent career is as an archiepiscopal moneyer, not as a royal one, rather confirms that regal participation in the coinage of the early 850s was marginal. The contrast with the situation obtaining immediately before 851 is marked, and it is tempting to see the explanation as a loss of political control in Kent by the West Saxon royal house; Æthelwulf's Kentish sub-king, Æthelstan, is last heard of in 850, and it is not until 855 that Æthelwulf's son Æthelberht is found as king in his place. Loss of political control by the West Saxons would certainly explain the complete cessation of coinage from Rochester.[23] If coinage production continued at London it was at a minimal level, for coins of the moneyer Tatel, the only active moneyer in the early years of the reign of the new king Burgred (852–74), do not survive in great

22. There is no other record of a Canterbury moneyer of this name and the letters LIL may just be intended as space fillers (one die has the obviously meaningless FI in their place).
23. The entry in the Anglo-Saxon Chronicle for 851 records the storming of Canterbury and London by the Vikings but does not refer to Rochester, and the continued appearance of the pre-851 Rochester moneyers Ethelhere and Manninc among Æthelwulf's moneyers in the mid-850s may suggest that Rochester was unscathed by the events of 851.

numbers and were represented by one specimen only in a very large hoard from Dorking, Surrey, deposited c.862.[24]

When the striking of a regal coinage in Kent recommenced it may at first have been on a basis similar to that which had obtained before 851, for although the coins are of a novel design, with a new regal portrait on the obverse and with the reverse occupied by a moneyer's name and the word *Moneta* on the limbs and in the angles of a broad cross, the earliest stages of the coinage include a coin by the Rochester moneyer Ethelhere with all the stylistic characteristics of pre-851 Rochester issues, and coins by the moneyers Diar (plate 4.1:14) and Manna who had been active at Canterbury in the 840s.[25] Gradually, though, the number of moneyers increases and the die-cutting achieves a machine-like precision which makes it impossible to distinguish dies intended for use by Rochester moneyers from dies intended for use at Canterbury. In all, 14 moneyers are recorded for coins of this *Open Cross* type in Æthelwulf's name; leaving the coins of two or three of these aside as dating from early in the type, that leaves 10 or 11 moneyers likely to have been working concurrently towards the end of the reign.

Coins of *Open Cross* design continued to be struck when Æthelberht succeeded his father (plate 4.1:17), but the number of moneyers expands in a very marked manner, as table 4.4 makes clear. It can be calculated from this that even if not all the moneyers recorded for Æthelberht were at work simultaneously the number of moneyers working for the king or archbishop could well have stood at over 40 at the peak of the type's production.

What can have been the cause for so massive an expansion in the number of moneyers? The only realistic explanation is that during the period in which the type was struck those responsible for the coinage intended a *renovatio monetae*, i.e. the calling in and restriking into new coins of as much of the currency of southern England as was feasible. Coin hoards deposited in the early 870s show among other things that pre-851 coins of the south-eastern mints had entirely disappeared from circulation, and the case for supposing that this was due to *renovatio* in the late 850s or early 860s gets powerful indirect support from the fact that these same hoards reveal that the *Open Cross* type itself had disappeared from circulation, presumably as the result of a further *renovatio* carried out in the mid- or late 860s. Unfortunately the evidence of coin hoards deposited in the 860s is less decisive. The Dorking hoard, deposited near the end of the *Open Cross* type, was of a size to have been the

24. The representation of Burgred's coinage in the Dorking hoard by one coin only may owe something to the deliberate exclusion of it from West Saxon territory as part of the monetary policies being pursued by his West Saxon contemporaries.
25. The most accessible coin of Ethelhere is that in the Fitzwilliam Museum, Cambridge (*SCBI* Cambridge 529), which derives from the Dorking hoard via the W. B. Rich sale (Sotheby, 7–9 July 1828) lot 38, and later passed through the Martin, Murchison, Lake Price, Montagu and Murdoch sales. There is a further coin by this moneyer in the Wisbech Museum. Some coins of the moneyer Ethelmod may also be from Rochester dies, but those of Ethelnoth of unusual style seem rather to be imitative of regular Canterbury dies.

Table 4.4. Moneyers of *Open Cross* coins[26]

Æthelwulf only: Diar, Ethelmod, Manna, Tirwald
Æthelwulf and Æthelberht: Degbearht, Dudwine, Ethelgeard, Ethelhere, Ethelnoth, Hunbearht, Hunred, Manninc, Torhtulf, Wermund
Æthelberht only: Bademund, Badenoth, Beagmund, Biarnmod, Biarnwine, Burnwald, Cealeard, Cenred, Cunefreth, Dealla, Deglaf, Denemund, Diarmod, Eadulf, Ealdred, Ethelred, Ethelulf, Heabearht, Herebeald, Herefreth, Heregeard, Heremund, Luceman, Nothulf, Osbearht, Oshere, Sefreth, Sigehere, Torhtmund, Wilnoth, Wiohtmund, Wlanceard, Wulfheard, Wunbearht
Æthelberht and Ceolnoth: Cenweald, Ethelweald, Hebeca, Liabincg
Ceolnoth only: Biarnred, Biarnulf, Cealmod, Herebearht, Heregar(?), Tocga.

hoarded wealth of a royal personage or of a great magnate, and as such it included a reserve of older coin as well as a great sum in current coin, while the Trewhiddle hoard, deposited c.868 and the only other recorded coin hoard from the 860s, seems to have incorporated coins assembled over a long period by a Cornish monastic community in addition to a parcel of recently coined money.[27]

It remains to determine whether *renovatio* commenced under Æthelwulf or whether it was carried out only from the point in Æthelberht's reign when the number of moneyers dramatically increases. Here the political background is relevant. Æthelwulf left England early in 855 to go to Rome to pay his respects at the shrine of St Peter; was in Rome for a year in 855–6; and was still abroad on 1 October 856, when he married Judith, daughter of Charles the Bald, king of the West Franks, in a ceremony at one of Charles's palaces near Senlis in northern France.[28] He cannot

26. It is convenient to note here a number of minor points that will assist in the interpretation of this table. Of Æthelwulf's moneyers, Diar is known only for coins on which the king's bust has a diadem and on which the letters A (alpha) and O (omega) appear in two corners of the reverse (plate 4.1:14), while Manna and Torhtulf are likewise only known for coins with a diademed bust, although their coins are of the normal reverse design for the type. Among Æthelberht's moneyers, Torhtulf is again recorded for coins with a diademed bust, but in this reign he is known for diadem-less coins as well. The listing of Hebeca among those moneyers who worked both for Æthelberht and for Archbishop Ceolnoth is based solely on the listing of one coin of his for Æthelberht in the original publication of the Dorking hoard – the coin itself has not been traced – and he should really be classed as an archiepiscopal moneyer only. Finally, the appearance of Heregar among the moneyers of Archbishop Ceolnoth is based on the occurrence of a coin described as being of this moneyer in the A. S. Napier sale (Sotheby, 3 August 1917) lot 17, and needs verification.
27. The listing of the coins from Trewhiddle in the relevant part of D. M. Wilson and C. E. Blunt, 'The Trewhiddle hoard', *Archaeologia 98* (1961), 75–122, leaves the hoard's date of deposit somewhat uncertain, but a careful study of the very earliest lists of coins from the hoard indicates that it contained no coin of Alfred and only the earliest *Four-line* coins of Æthelred I, and should therefore be dated c.868.
28. For the date of Æthelwulf's marriage see Whitelock (ed.), *op. cit.*, 343 (translation of extract from the *Annals of St Bertin's*).

have reached England much before the end of 856 and that limits the time for *renovatio* in his reign to the year and a bit which elapsed between then and his death in January 858; *renovatio* would have involved recoining money in royal treasuries as well as money held by traders and could scarcely have been carried out while Æthelwulf was abroad. Æthelwulf's kingdom in 856–8 was of diminished size, for he was not recognized as king on his return in Wessex proper, but this was also true of the kingdom ruled by Æthelberht in 858–60, and it is at least possible that the decision to have a *renovatio* was taken under Æthelwulf as a result of knowledge of Carolingian currency management practices acquired when abroad.[29]

The *Open Cross* coins bulked large in the Dorking hoard, which contained at least 105 coins of the type in Æthelwulf's name and at least 249 coins of the type in Æthelberht's name. It is regrettable that the hoard came to light early in the nineteenth century, at a time when numismatics was still an infant discipline, and it is not possible to judge from Dorking coins known today what time-span the Æthelberht coins in the hoard might cover within Æthelberht's reign (858–66). Room must certainly be found within Æthelberht's reign for coins of quite another type, with a different bust on the obverse and a floreate cross on the reverse (plate 4.1:18), which although very uncommon today are known of just sufficient moneyers, seven in all, to show that the type was a substantive one, and to suggest that its present scarcity is simply due to a *renovatio* carried out towards the end of the 860s. On present evidence the date of deposit of the Dorking hoard is best set at c.862 and the *Floreate Cross* coins assigned to the period c.863–c.866.

Æthelberht, recognized from 860 onwards as king in Wessex as well as in Kent and its adjacent counties, was succeeded in the entirety of his kingdom by his brother Æthelred I (866–71) and then by his youngest brother Alfred (871–99). Æthelred's coinage begins with an extremely rare issue with a royal bust on the obverse and the name of a moneyer displayed across the reverse in four lines; only three moneyers are known for it, but as with the *Floreate Cross* coins the issue's present rarity is probably deceptive. It was, however, soon replaced by a much more extensive issue with the moneyer's name shown in three lines, usually with the name itself in the middle line, MON on the top line, and ETA below being contained in lunettes. Coins of Æthelred of this character were well represented in the Gravesend hoard, deposited c.871, and are found alongside similar coins of Alfred in hoards deposited later in the 870s.

The number of moneyers' names on coins of Æthelred and Alfred is substantial,

29. Although no major *renovatio* was under way in Carolingian Europe in 855–6, current concern for the state of the coinage is evidenced by a section of the Capitulary of Attigny, issued in 854, and Æthelwulf's stay at Charles's court was of sufficient duration to achieve familiarity with Charles's coinage. The suggestion by the late Stuart Rigold that the *Open Cross* design derives from that on the lead *bullae* issued in 855 by Pope Benedict III with the Pope's name similarly written *en croix* has some *prima facie* attraction, but the design on the *bullae* is not in fact particularly similar to that on the coins (Rigold's remarks are in his 1974 presidential address to the British Numismatic Society, *BNJ 44* (1974), 100; cf. C. Serafini, *Le monete e le bolle plumbee pontificie del Medagliere Vaticano* (Milan, 1910), I, 10 and pl. E, items 7 and 8).

and the majority of names are those of moneyers associable with Canterbury, or at least with Kent (after the beginning of the *Open Cross* type there is no distinction in style between dies supplied to Canterbury moneyers and dies that may have been supplied to Rochester moneyers if there continued to be such, which is uncertain). Under Æthelred at least 17 evident Canterbury or Kentish moneyers have so far been recorded, in addition to two coining for Archbishop Ceolnoth, and the total of Canterbury or Kentish moneyers recorded for the first five years of Alfred's reign stands at some 30, although here the number is no doubt unnaturally swelled by the pressures of Viking attacks on Alfred's kingdom.[30]

The pattern of Kentish-produced coinage from the mid-850s onwards was thus quite different from that which obtained before 851, and although coin production from London was at first minimal it eventually attained a similar character and volume. Before the mid-860s Burgred's coinage was successively in the hands of the moneyer Tatel alone; then in the hands of Tatel and of a moneyer Dudecil; and then in the hands of the six moneyers Dudecil, Dudda, Dudeman, Eanred, Tata, and Wine. The number of moneyers then expanded rapidly and had reached about 30 by 871.

From the start Burgred's coins had a regal bust on the obverse and the name of a moneyer in three lines across the reverse, foreshadowing the design adopted for Æthelred's coinage c.867, but by the mid-860s four separate ways of setting out the reverse design had evolved and the correct arrangement of Burgred's coinage in the ten years preceding his deposition by the Vikings in 874 is a matter of some intricacy. The composition of the Burgred element in the Trewhiddle hoard, deposited c.868 and therefore highly relevant to the internal chronology of Burgred's coinage, can be partly reconstructed on the basis of lists of the Rashleigh family collection to which the largest part of the hoard passed, and the scale and complexity which Burgred's coinage had already attained in the short period between c.865 and c.868 can at least be glimpsed from a tabulation of the way in which the 39 relevant coins in that collection are divided as regards reverse variety and moneyer (table 4.5).[31] A comparison of this parcel with the composition of hoards deposited in the 870s, taken together with stylistic considerations, suggests that after the initial experimentation with various reverse varieties the order in which the varieties were struck was broadly (1) *BMC* type *c*; (2) *BMC* type *d* (and coins of a related variety *e*); (3)

30. The Kentish moneyers active over the period c.862–c.875 are conveniently listed at p. 17 of H. E. Pagan, 'Coinage in the age of Burgred', *BNJ 34* (1965), 11–27, although the list given there now requires some slight revision.
31. Wilson and Blunt, *op. cit.*, did not attempt a listing of the Burgred element in the Trewhiddle hoard, but the summary of the parcel in the Rashleigh family collection given here provides a fair idea of its character. It should, however, be noted that the Rashleigh collection already contained two coins of Burgred before the discovery of the hoard and that these cannot now be separated from the coins of Burgred deriving from the hoard. Students should also note that in addition to the early manuscript material on the Rashleigh collection utilized by Wilson and Blunt, there is a further late eighteenth-century list of the coins among Ruding's papers in the British Library.

Table 4.5. Parcel of coins of Burgred from Trewhiddle hoard in Rashleigh family collection

BMC type *a* (three line reverse, MON and ETA in lunettes above and below moneyer's name):
Beagstan 2; Berheah 2; Berhthelm 1; Cunehelm 3; Diga 2; Duda 1; Dudecil 1; Dudwine 1; Guthhere 2; Heawulf 2; Hereferth 1; Hugered 3; Hussa 1; Tata 1 — 23 coins

BMC type *c* (three line reverse, MON and ETA in lunettes but the lunettes broken at bottom corners):
Dudecil 1; Liafman 1; Wine 1 — 3 coins

BMC type *d* (three line reverse, moneyer's name between two hooked lines, MON above and ETA below):
Cenred 1; Duda 1; Dudda 1; Dudwine 1; Hugered 2; Liafman 1; Osmund 3; Wine 1; Wulfeard 2 — 13 coins

BMC type *a* (and most coins of the related variety *BMC* type *b*). The hoard evidence also shows that from c.868 to 874 coins being struck for Burgred were chiefly of *BMC* type *a*, the Burgred reverse variety identical in design to the reverses of the mass of coins of Æthelred and Alfred, and hence that between these years there was essential uniformity between coins struck in Kent and coins struck at London.

This makes it more readily explicable that the clear division between a coinage struck in Kent in the names of Æthelred and Alfred and a coinage struck at London in Burgred's name wavers a little c.871 and becomes more blurred as time passes. London-style coins in Æthelred's name exhibit such phenomena as the mis-spelling of the king's name and the erroneous assignment to him of the title *Rex M(erciorum)*, and seem posthumous or imitative or both. Similar coins in Alfred's name include a proportion of imitative specimens but also include coins of good London style with Alfred's name carefully rendered. Happily there are no Canterbury-style coins carrying Burgred's name, and it can be deduced that the existence of London-style coins in the name of the West Saxon kings is a by-product of the intense pressure exerted on coinage operations at London by Burgred's attempts to buy off the Viking invaders of his kingdom.[32]

Alfred's issue of *Lunette* coins extends beyond Burgred's deposition, and in its final stages his Kentish moneyers abandon the reverse design similar to Burgred's *BMC* type *a* for a reverse design similar to Burgred's *BMC* type *b* (three line reverse, MON and ETA in lunettes but the lunettes are broken at the top). Coins of Alfred with reverse designs equivalent to *BMC* types *c* and *d* of Burgred also belong about here in date, but their status and place of manufacture is not self-evident. The coinage had begun to deteriorate in metallic content in the late 860s, and it was now in a very poor state as regards fineness, weight, and even fabric; the exact chronology of the coinage

32. The most probable explanation for the existence of London-style coins in the name of Æthelred is that in their rush to produce new dies in the early 870s London die-engravers copied the name Æthelred from existing coins without bothering about the fact that Æthelred had never ruled in London or Mercia.

of the second half of the 870s is still very uncertain, but by the end of the decade new coins of altogether better weight and fineness were being struck in the names of Alfred and of the Mercian king Ceolwulf II and a new epoch in the history of the coinage was opening.[33]

Any general view of coinage production over the period 851–74 is complicated by the unevenness of the evidence, and it is particularly unsatisfactory that there is so little evidence for the years c.862–c.868 within which both the *Open Cross* coins and the succeeding *Floreate Cross* coins seem to have been withdrawn from circulation. It can be discerned that the *Open Cross* coins, the *Floreate Cross* coins, and the Æthelred coins with the moneyer's name in four lines or three lines across the reverse, would have been visually distinct from previous issues and from each other, and thus all suitable as *renovatio* types, and the existence of what may be examples of rejected designs for *renovatio* types among the post-851 production of Archbishop Ceolnoth's moneyers strengthens the case for supposing that much thought went into the *renovatio* process. Ceolnoth's coinage mostly follows the designs of the regal coinage, but in two instances diverges from it. On the first occasion, two coins struck from a single pair of dies evidence a variety with an obverse broadly similar to those of the archiepiscopal *Open Cross* type and a reverse with a very complex cross and quatrefoil design and the inscription DIALA MONETA DORO (plate 4.1:19), and as these dies can hardly have been cut after the inception of the proper *Open Cross* type, it may well be that they represent a preliminary design for it rejected because of the reverse's complexity and consequent unsuitability for mass reproduction.[34] It will be remembered that the Canterbury coinage of the period c.851–c.855 was essentially archiepiscopal and that it would not have been abnormal for design experimentation prior to the issue of a new type to be evidenced among the production of an archiepiscopal moneyer.

The other exceptional Ceolnoth item is a single coin by the moneyer Biarnred which seems to belong to the mid-860s but has as its reverse design a cross crosslet with a large pellet in each angle (plate 4.1:20); its authenticity has withstood challenge, but no credible explanation for the coin has been offered and it too may

33. The chronology of events in the late 870s is made particularly uncertain by the fact that there are no post-877 documentary references to Ceolwulf II. The present writer's own view is that the division of Ceolwulf's kingdom referred to by the Anglo-Saxon Chronicle under 877 was not of the fundamental character that historians have customarily assumed, and that Ceolwulf retained power in London and even in some parts of the Danelaw until the end of the decade, if not longer still (H. E. Pagan, 'An unpublished fragment of a coin of Ceolwulf II', *BNJ 41* (1972), 14–20).

34. The coins are *SCBI* Glasgow 404 and *BMC* 39. Neither derives from the Dorking hoard and it may be that both derive from some long-forgotten discovery of coins that never truly passed into circulation, for the Glasgow coin was in James West's collection by 1744 and the British Museum coin was part of the collection formed by the 2nd Duke of Devonshire (d.1727), and one of the two must in fact be the specimen which Drs G. van der Meer's researches have shown was once in Sir Robert Cotton's collection.

evidence design experimentation immediately before or after the issue of the *Floreate Cross* coins.[35]

The period is rather too short to draw any very definite conclusions about moneyers' careers either at Canterbury or at London. Among Æthelwulf's moneyers only Manninc seems to survive very long, but among Æthelberht's moneyers Herebeald, Liabincg, Oshere, and Torhtmund strike both for Æthelred and for Alfred, and Hebeca, between 855 and 870 an archiepiscopal moneyer, reappears as a moneyer of Alfred after Archbishop Ceolnoth's death.

What the large number of moneyers recorded for the *Open Cross* type in Æthelberht's reign does very usefully demonstrate is that when a larger volume of coin needed striking it was thought necessary to increase the number of moneyers, rather than simply get the existing moneyers to increase their production. The obvious conclusion from this is that at this date moneyers were still personally involved in striking the coins and not capitalists employing gangs of others to carry out the mechanical side of the coinage process, and it is a conclusion that prompts caution about identifying moneyers among the witnesses of Canterbury or Rochester charters.

It was not necessary in the earlier part of this discussion to deal with the way in which coin was used or circulated in ninth-century Britain, for hoard evidence is scanty almost to the end of the period and it is only in the 870s that hoards provide reliable evidence for the use of coins as currency in counties as remote from the south-east as Staffordshire and Durham. Single finds do something to compensate for the absence of earlier hoard evidence, but most of the recorded single finds fall within the area in which coin had already been used in the eighth century and it is not easy to trace the steps by which coin use spread into the western part of Wessex or into the West Midlands. It is not less ironic to have to record that when there is evidence for the widespread use of coin it comes in the 870s when the coins in circulation were not the typical pennies of fine silver weighing 21 grains which had circulated earlier in the century but the debased and light-weight coinages of Burgred and Alfred. It is remarkable that there was general public acceptance of such coins, and public willingness to take them implies an attachment to the idea of coin as a medium of exchange for which nothing else in the evidence prepares the student. Nor is this the only conundrum which the 870s provide, for whoever might have accepted debased coin it was surely not the great heathen army which sat in London in 872 exacting tribute from the Mercians.[36]

The history of the coinage from 796 to this point in the 870s is one of stability as far as the 840s and then of change aborted first by the Viking raid of 851 and then by

35. *SCBI* Glasgow 403. Its authenticity is vindicated by Lyon, 'Historical problems', 230.
36. The statement in the Anglo-Saxon Chronicle under the year 872 that the Viking army took up winter quarters in London is amplified by a reference in a Worcester charter of 872 to 'the very pressing affliction and immense tribute of the barbarians, in that same year when the pagans stayed in London' (Whitelock (ed.), *op. cit.*, 532). See also the contribution by Brooks and Graham-Campbell, chapter 6 below.

Viking attacks in the 870s. Michael Dolley, both in a pioneer article on Æthelwulf's coinage written in combination with Kolbjørn Skaare and in an article taking as its theme Alfred's abandonment of the *renovatio* system of currency management, recognized the intrinsic interest of the period of coinage beginning in the mid-850s, but he saw Alfred, not Æthelwulf or Æthelberht, as the first major figure after Offa in the history of the Anglo-Saxon coinage, and he was surely right to do so, for the *renovatio* system left no permanent mark on the coinage process and the fact that it might have done so had it operated in a more peaceful age is beside the point; numismatic history has no place for might-have-beens.[37]

37. Dolley and Skaare, *op. cit.*; M. Dolley, 'Ælfred the Great's abandonment of the concept of periodic recoinage', in *Studies in Numismatic Method presented to Philip Grierson*, ed. C. N. L. Brooke *et al.* (1983), 153–60.

5 Finds of 'sceattas' and 'stycas' of Northumbria

Elizabeth J. E. Pirie

No consideration of Anglo-Saxon monetary history may be deemed complete without reference in some form to the coinage of the kings of Northumbria and the archbishops of York – to the coins known, since the days of Archdeacon Nicolson of Carlisle and Thoresby of Leeds (15 June 1695), as 'stycas'. 'Styca' finds have been recorded in some measure since the Ripon discovery in 1695; such coins occur to a greater or lesser extent in many public and private cabinets. The classic collection at York is as yet unpublished and the time has not yet come when one can offer a formal review of the total evidence, at York and elsewhere, and a possible interpretation of monetary developments north of the Humber in the late eighth and ninth centuries. Such a commentary cannot convincingly be divorced from presentation of the York collection in *Sylloge* format when the detail of the various groups can be illustrated.

The present writer is very conscious that it was Michael Dolley who voiced her commission from the British Academy's *Sylloge* committee to prepare for publication the massive collection of 'stycas' in the Yorkshire Museum at York; she is also aware that when, in 1976, she first suggested that the time had come to investigate the possibility of a typological arrangement for the series, it was Michael Dolley who encouraged her to take further her original ideas. Of all Anglo-Saxon numismatists he must have been the least surprised that such an exercise has taken – is taking – a long time to complete.

A full assessment of the coinage cannot be made without taking account of known discoveries of the relevant issues. It is for this reason that the inventory recorded here has been compiled, at a time when the number of finds is increasing steadily. The present lists have been closed in August 1983, with a stop-press notice of the Dacre excavation (101). It is to be hoped that the register, now established, will provide a basis for future discussions; it is to be hoped, too, that the lists will be encouraged to grow, with the filing of information about new recoveries. In both these respects, attention cannot be given to the 'styca' issues alone but must be accorded also to the earlier 'sceattas'. The occurrence of the latter, both in number and in distribution, differs from that of the 'stycas'.

Coins of the two series can be distinguished by the detail of reverse dies. All the authorized 'stycas' depict on their reverse the name of one or other of the officials responsible to the king or to the archbishop for their coinage. Adoption of this practice towards the end of the eighth century must signal some measure of

Table 5.1. Conventional dates for the kings of Northumbria and archbishops of York

Kings	Archbishops
Aldfrith, 685–704	
Eadberht, 737–58	Egberht, 732/4–66
Alhred, 765–774	
Æthelred I, first reign, 774–78	Eanbald I, 780–6
Ælfwald I, 778–88	
Æthelred I, second reign, 790–6	Eanbald II, 796–c.830?
Ælfwald II, c.808	
Eanred, c.810–41	Wulfsige, c.835–7
Æthelred II, first reign, 841–4	Wigmund, 837–54
Redwulf, 844	
Æthelred II, second reign, 844–c.849	
Osberht, c.849–67	
	Wulfhere, 854–900?

It should be noted that the names are in the conventional form, familiar to historians, but such spelling does not in all cases correspond to that used on the coins.

reorganization from the system which allowed its moneyers to remain anonymous. The 'sceattas' themselves have the die with the king's name combined either with one portraying a prancing animal or with one recording the archbishop's name. It must be noted that, apart from joint issues by both Eadberht and Alhred with Archbishop Egberht, there must also have been emissions by Æthelred I and Archbishop Eanbald I together; among examples of the latter are those with the Sancton, Whitby, and Jarrow provenances (11, 18 and 24).

It seems that the eighth-century Northumbrian coinage was far from constant in production; intermittent issues may well have been a feature of the early 'styca' series, too, until the later part of Eanred's reign; coins surviving from this stage (during which silver in various degrees of debasement gave way to copper alloy) show few signs of die-linking either within the work of one man or between the work of several. When the early moneyers gave way to a new team, the output seems to have become reasonably steady and far more prolific, with a pronounced incidence of die-linking. It is in an attempt to distinguish these phases that the entries for finds whose composition overlaps them make use of the rubrics: *Silver and early copper alloy*, and *Later copper alloy*. Space unfortunately does not permit the citation of obverse legend-forms as an indication of further grouping or the detailed specification of the different categories within the irregular issues. It is mainly because the place of these enigmatic imitative coins in the scheme of things is at present a matter of some controversy that the hoard entries lack quotation of a date of deposit. In this, presentation varies from that of other such schedules.

The arrangement of this inventory differs also from previous records in distinguishing more than just hoards and miscellaneous small finds. Rigold has remarked (1967) that hoards composed entirely of Northumbrian 'sceattas' are not known to occur; the 'styca' hoards themselves vary in size, and the smaller among them (of about 20 or 30 coins) are here described as purse-hoards. Further, when so many sites of the period, especially secular sites, are being investigated by archaeologists, it is as well to differentiate excavation-finds of separate coins. Those that have been discovered by chance or, as so often in this day and age, by the metal-detector fraternity's deliberate search, cannot be related to any particular site-context, even at places which are already known to have been occupied in the Anglo-Saxon period. It would seem that the excavation-finds, so many of which await publication, bear out what is apparent from finds at later sites: they include some items not known in the major hoards.

A sense of place has determined the principal divisions in both main sections of the register: that for 'sceattas' and that for 'stycas'. Professor Cramp has briefly commented[1] on the fluctuating extent of the kingdom and its influence: from north Lincolnshire to the Forth in the eighth century; from the Humber in the south to the Tweed region in the north by the ninth century. The Tees has been identified as the eighth-century boundary between the old territories of Deira and Bernicia. The two kingdoms had been united since the mid-seventh century; that there was a boundary in the following century may be seen to imply that the regions developed as separate provinces. This emphasis is on the eastern sector; western finds may be considered separately. There need be no apology for observing the regional basis for the inventory (and topographical rather than alphabetical registration of discoveries) or, indeed, for suggesting that in due course the detailed composition of the hoards, at least, should be considered in relation to their area so that those from south and north of Tees can be compared and contrasted. There is no warrant for considering York as the focus of all activity and the rest of Northumbria as a virtual outback, devoid of potential political or economic developments.

The old adage that Northumbrian coins have not been found outside the kingdom must go by the board, although it may be necessary to consider the status of some of the extra-territorial finds. Some, such as those from Kingscross (109) and Kiloran (110), are clearly Viking souvenirs, as Professor Sawyer once described them in conversation; perhaps those occurring in what was later the southern Danelaw, as well as those overseas, may also legitimately be so identified. Yet to deny that the finds may be indications of contemporary traffic (if not of coin in circulation) from Northumbria is to assume that the men of Deira and Bernicia were interned in the lands north of Humber.

As one can remark that, so far, many of the finds within Northumbria come from places associated with Saxon minsters, so one can note that many of the authenticated finds from beyond the kingdom are coastal in location. In view of this, it may not be too controversial to query whether provenances such as Lindores in the north, Thanet (Reculver), Brighton, and Trewhiddle in the south, are really as unlikely as they may once have seemed to be.

As this paper goes to press in 1985, one is aware that coins in the name of Aldfrith may now be attributed to Aldfrith of Northumbria (685–704). Brief references to

1. R. Cramp, *The Monastic Arts of Northumbria* (1967 Arts Council exhibition handbook).

these issues have been made in relation to Whitby (18) and North Ferriby (see note following 61). All provenanced coins of the reign will be noted in the next instalment of the Inventory.

Abbreviations used in the Inventory are listed on pp. 86–8 and 90.

THE INVENTORY

I. 'SCEATTAS' (Rigold, 1977: Series Y)
A. Humber-Tees
Excavation-finds and strays without site-context; the latter are asterisked.

1.* YORK, Gas Works 1881
1: Eadberht, quadruped right
YM; R and M, 51 with refs.

YORK, 'Roman fortress' *See* 48

2.* YORK, The Mount 1888
1: Eadberht and Egberht
YM (missing); R and M, 51 with ref.

3.* YORK, Walmgate 1892
1: Eadberht, quadruped right
YM; R and M, 51.

4.* YORK, locality not specified before 1893
1: Alhred and Egberht
Leeds, private possession: *ex* Baldwin . . . *ex* Grantley II, Glendining, 27.1.1944, lot 800; *ex* Bateman, 1893. Bateman sale catalogue, Sotheby, 4–6.5.1893, lot 245 for provenance; Grantley (1893), 267–72; R and M,–.Pl.5.1:4.

5. YORK, Minster 1972
1: Eadberht, quadruped left
YoM; R and M,–; site publication forthcoming. *See* 51

Fig. 5.1 Distribution of Northumbrian 'sceattas'.

Sites marked on maps
1. York
2. Naburn
3. Hayton
4. Sancton
5. Beverley
6. Hornsea
7. Driffield
8. Wharram Percy
9. Malton
10. Kirkbymoorside
11. Whitby
12. Bolton Percy
13. Ripon
14. Richmond
15. Malham
16. Malham Moor
17. Settle
18. Ribblehead
19. Piercebridge
20. Monkwearmouth
21. Jarrow
22. Gateshead
23. Tynemouth
24. Newcastle
25. Hexham
26. Jedburgh
27. Bamburgh
28. Lindisfarne
29. Norham
30. Coldingham
31. Otterspool
32. Ribchester
33. Lancaster
34. Grange
35. Dacre
36. Kirkoswald
37. Carlisle
38. Talnotrie
39. Luce
40. Paisley
41. Kingscross
42. Kiloran
43. Wintringham
44. Appleby
45. Epworth
46. Kirmington
47. Caistor-on-the-Wolds
48. Grimsthorpe
49. Peterborough
50. Heacham
51. North Walsham
52. Norwich
53. Caistor-on-Sea
54. Brandon
55. Thetford
56. Hasketon
57. Cadeby
58. Anston
59. Castleton
60. Meols
61. Caernarvon
62. Thanet (Reculver)
63. Richborough
64. Brighton
65. Trewhiddle
66. Lindores

5. *Finds of 'sceattas' and 'stycas' of Northumbria*

6. YORK, Ebor Brewery 1973–4; 1980
5: Eadberht (5): quadruped right, 2; quadruped left, 3
YAT; R and M, 51 (4 only); *AoY 18/1*, forthcoming. *See* 59

7. YORK, Cattle Market, Paragon Street 1973
2: Eadberht (2): quadruped right, 1; quadruped left, 1
YAT; R and M, 51; *AoY 18/1*, forthcoming.

8. YORK, Bishophill I 1975
1: Eadberht, quadruped left
YAT; R and M, 51; *AoY 18/1*, forthcoming.

9. YORK, Rougier Street 1981
1: Eadberht, quadruped right (fragment)
YAT; *AoY 18/1*, forthcoming.

NABURN, near York. Naburn Ings *See* 61

10.* HAYTON, N. Humberside 1982
2: Eadberht, quadruped right, 1; Ælfward I, quadruped left, 1
Metal-detector finds, in private possession; Booth and Blowers (1983).

11.* SANCTON, N. Humberside
I. 1979–82
23: Eadberht (11): quadruped right, 6, and quadruped left, 5; Eadberht and Egberht, 6; Alhred, quadruped right, 2; Ælfwald I, quadruped right, 3. Æthelred I and Eanbald, 1
Metal-detector finds, in private possession; Booth and Blowers (1983).
II. 1983
2: Eadberht, quadruped right, 1; quadruped left, 1
Metal-detector finds, in private possession; unpublished; *see* pl.5.1:1. *See* 62

12. BEVERLEY, N. Humberside. Lurk Lane (minster collegiate buildings) 1980
3: Eadberht, (2); quadruped left, 2; Ælfwald I, quadruped right, 1
Disposition undecided. Site publication forthcoming. *See* 39 and 63

Fig. 5.2 Distribution of Northumbrian 'stycas'.

Sites marked on maps

1. York
2. Naburn
3. Hayton
4. Sancton
5. Beverley
6. Hornsea
7. Driffield
8. Wharram Percy
9. Malton
10. Kirkbymoorside
11. Whitby
12. Bolton Percy
13. Ripon
14. Richmond
15. Malham
16. Malham Moor
17. Settle
18. Ribblehead
19. Piercebridge
20. Monkwearmouth
21. Jarrow
22. Gateshead
23. Tynemouth
24. Newcastle
25. Hexham
26. Jedburgh
27. Bamburgh
28. Lindisfarne
29. Norham
30. Coldingham
31. Otterspool
32. Ribchester
33. Lancaster
34. Grange
35. Dacre
36. Kirkoswald
37. Carlisle
38. Talnotrie
39. Luce
40. Paisley
41. Kingscross
42. Kiloran
43. Wintringham
44. Appleby
45. Epworth
46. Kirmington
47. Caistor-on-the-Wolds
48. Grimsthorpe
49. Peterborough
50. Heacham
51. North Walsham
52. Norwich
53. Caistor-on-Sea
54. Brandon
55. Thetford
56. Hasketon
57. Cadeby
58. Anston
59. Castleton
60. Meols
61. Caernarvon
62. Thanet (Reculver)
63. Richborough
64. Brighton
65. Trewhiddle
66. Lindores

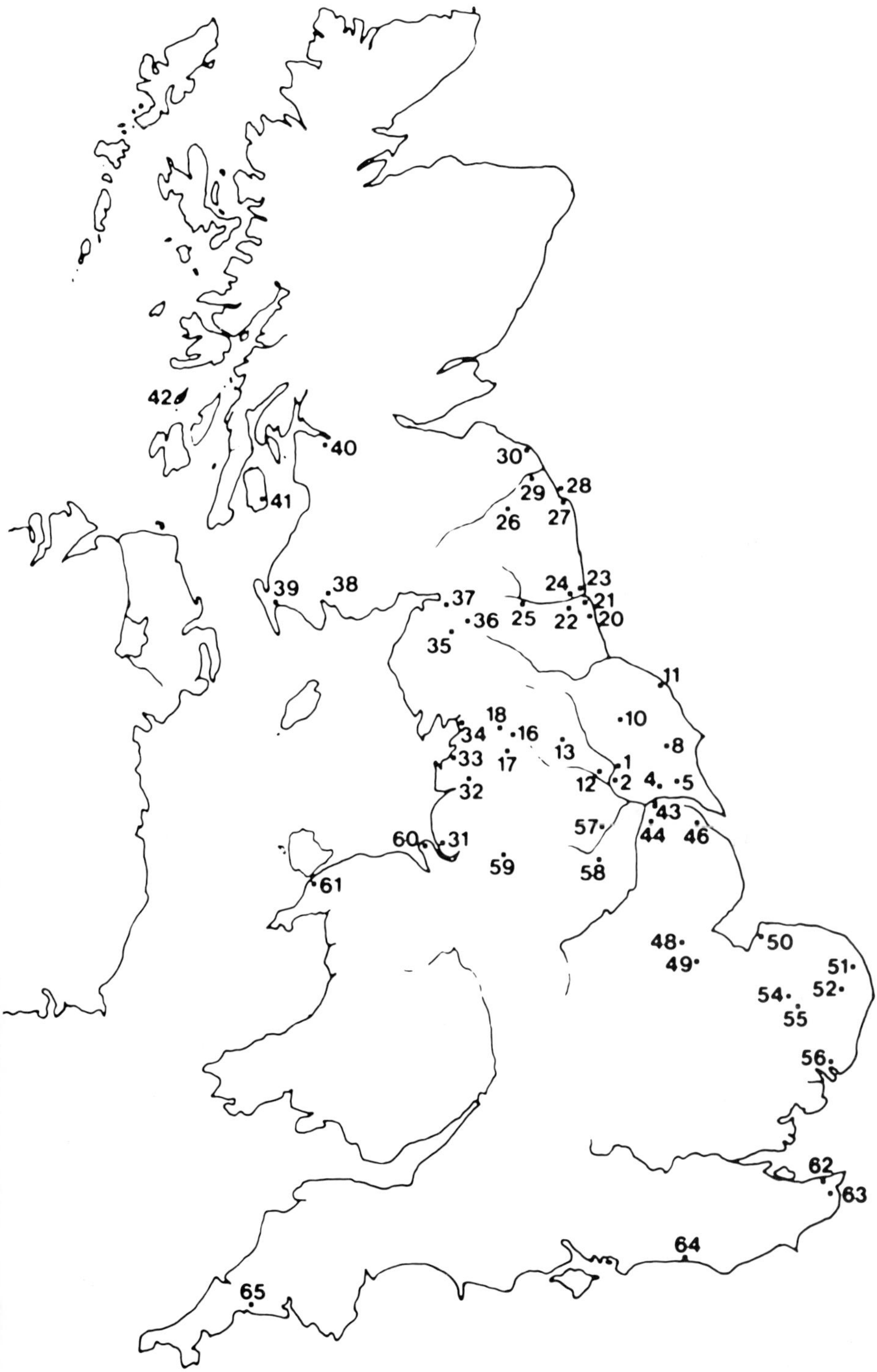

42
40
41
30
29
28
26
27
39
38
37
24
23
21
36
25
22
20
35
11
18
10
34
16
13
8
33
17
1
12
2
4
5
32
43
57
44
46
60
31
59
58
61
48
50
49
51
54
52
55
56
62
63
64
65

13.* HORNSEA, N. Humberside 1875
1: Æthelred I, quadruped right
OAM; Grantley (1892), 87–8; R and M, 40 with ref.

14.* DRIFFIELD, N. Humberside 1981
1: Ælfwald I; no further detail available
Metal-detector find, in private possession; unpublished.

15. WHARRAM PERCY, N. Yorkshire. Churchyard 1964
1: Eadberht: no further detail available
HCM (missing); *MedArch* 9 (1965), 187; R and M, 49. *See* 65

16. WHARRAM PERCY, N. Yorkshire (deserted medieval village) 1975–8
I. (N. manorial enclosure) 1975
1: Eadberht, quadruped right.
R and M, 49.
II. (Site 26) 1978
1: Eadberht, quadruped right
HCM; site publication forthcoming. *See* 64

17.* MALTON, N. Yorkshire 1850
1: Eadberht, quadruped right
BM (*BMC* Northumbria 10); R and M, 42 with ref.

18. WHITBY, N. Yorkshire. Abbey, E. Cliff (A-S minster) 1920s
16: Eadberht, 9 + 1†; Eadberht and Egberht 4; Æthelred I and Eanbald, 1; Ælfwald I, 1; found with two of Aldfrith of Lindsey, c.790 (*recte* of Northumbria, see p. 69 above).
BM: 15; WPPM: 1† (above, presented 1931); R and M, 49 with refs; *see* pl.5.1:2. *See* 44 and 68

19.* RICHMOND, N. Yorkshire. Hospital of St Nicholas 1832
1: Egberht: further detail uncertain
Disposition unknown; R and M, 44 with ref.

20.* MALHAM, N. Yorkshire not dated
1: Eadberht, quadruped right
R and M, –; noted in Sotheby catalogue, 11.6.1980, lot 123 (present disposition unknown).

21. SETTLE, N. Yorkshire. Attemire Cave mid to late 19th cent.
1: Eadberht and Egberht
SPM; R and M, –. *See* 75–76

B. Tees-Forth
Excavation-finds and stray without site-context; the latter is asterisked.

22. PIERCEBRIDGE, Durham (*Magis*, late R. fort) 1977
1: Eadberht, quadruped right
BMBC; R and M, 44; site publication forthcoming.

23.* JARROW, Tyne and Wear. Churchyard c.1850
1: Alhred, quadruped right
BM (*BMC* Northumbria 13); R and M, 41 with ref.

24. JARROW, Tyne and Wear (A-S minster) 1976
2: Eadberht, quadruped left, 1; Æthelred I and Eanbald, 1
JH; R and M, 41; site publication forthcoming; pl.5.1:5. *See* 81

25. LINDISFARNE, Northumberland Priory (A-S minster) 1920–5
1: Æthelred I, quadruped right
LPM, cast (original not known); unpublished.

JEDBURGH, Roxburghshire (A-S minster) c.1834
Miscellaneous coins said to include silver 'sceattas' and copper 'stycas' but now all thought to be from the 'styca' series. *See* 79

C. West Coast
No finds have been recorded.

D. South of Humber
Excavation-finds and stray without site-context; the latter is asterisked.

26.* EPWORTH, Isle of Axholme, Lincolnshire December 1982

1: Eadberht, quadruped right
OAM. J. Booth, 'Sceattas in Northumbria', *Sceattas in England and on the Continent*, ed. D. Hill and D. M. Metcalf (BAR Brit. Ser 128; 1984), 71–111, pl.5, 12.

27. CAISTOR-ON-THE-WOLDS, Lincolnshire. Grammar School (possible minster site) 1967
1: Eadberht, quadruped right
LCCM; R and M, 36 with ref.; Gunstone (1981), no. 1618.

28. CAISTOR-ON-SEA, by Yarmouth, Norfolk (A-S settlement) c.1978
1: Eadberht, quadruped right
NCM; Cf. R and M, 36, for other finds; site publication forthcoming.

THANET (Reculver) *See* 131

E. Overseas
Excavation-finds

29. NETHERLANDS: Dorestadt, Frisia 1968
1: Eadberht, quadruped left
Disposition undecided; site publication forthcoming.

30. NORWAY, Ervik early 19th cent.
1: Eadberht and Egberht
BHM; Skaare (1976), 158, no. 118 with refs.

II. 'STYCAS'
A. Humber-Tees
i. Hoards

31. YORK, Coney Street c.1760
Uncertain number: 'a large lump'
Disposition unknown; Pirie (1975), xxxi, 3 with refs.

32. YORK, Micklegate Bar (?) ? Nov. 1827
Uncertain number – including Æthelred II, 1, and Wigmund, 1. – a purse-hoard?
YM? (not distinguished in cabinet); Pirie (1975), xxxi, 4 with refs.

33. YORK, unnamed site: possibly Bootham, outside barbican, or Marygate 1831
360, Eanred to Osberht: found by some men who were digging near St Mary's Abbey in York. 'The Vase which contains the coins was also dug up with them in the year 1831'.† 322 now partially recorded:
Regular (254): A: *Early copper alloy* (3): EANRED (3): Daegberct, 1; Eadvini, 1; Herred, 1. B: *Later copper alloy* (251): EANRED (31): Aldates, 2, and Gadutes, 1; Brodr, 4; Fordred, 11; Odilo, 1; Monne, 9; Vvlfred, 2; Wihtred, 1. ÆTHELRED II (151): Alghere, 6; Brother, 6; Cunemund, 1; Eanred, 34; Fordred, 23; Leofdegn, 14; Monne, 30; Vendelberht, 3; Vvlfred, 3; Wihtred, 5; Eardvvlf, 25; double obverse, 1. REDWULF (8): Cudberht, 2; Eanred, 2; Hvaetnod, 1; Monne, 1; Vendelberht, 1; Coenred, 1. OSBERHT (9): Viniberht, 1; Vvlfsixt, 1; Eanvvlf, 4; Monne, 1; uncertain moneyer, 2. Abp. WIGMVND (45): Edilveard, 14; Coenred, 7; Hunlaf, 15; Edelhelm, 8; double obverse, 1. Abp. WULFHERE (7): Vvlfred, 7. *Irregular* (68): miscellaneous, 68.
Disposition of container is not known; the 322 coins registered here are now in Stonyhurst College, Lancashire, with annotation quoted above (†), but details of acquisition are not clear. Heywood (1897), 81–99 and (1910), 331–4: the latter claims the coins as a parcel from York, 1842; not as yet formally published. *See* pl.5.1:15.

34. YORK, St Leonard's Place, 1 ('within the rampart, near Bootham Bar') 1833
47 or more; the coins in question were not listed at the time of discovery
YM; 47, presented by Lord Mayor and Corporation of York in 1833; ? others, by R. Davies in 1835 (none

now distinguished in the cabinet). Pirie (1975), xxxi, 5 with refs.

35. YORK, 'Railway' 1840
30 silver (*sic*) 'stycas' (–? a purse-hoard): not listed at time of discovery
YM (none now distinguished in cabinet); Pirie (1975), xxxi, 2 with refs.

36. YORK, St Leonard's Place, 2 1842
c.5,000 of which c.3,000 listed, Eanred to Osberht
YM; a major parcel but total as yet uncertain; Pirie (1975), xxxi–ii, 6 (the list subject to amendment) with refs.; also Pirie (1981), 44, for detail of minor parcel now in private possession.

37. YORK, City Walls (exact location not specified) 1846
Uncertain number: ?a purse-hoard or stray finds; details of two only: Eanred, Fordred, 1; Redwulf, Cudberht, 1.
These are taken from entries in Robert Cook's unfinished manuscript catalogue of 'stycas', registering only Eanred, Wigmund, Redwulf and Wulfhere; it cannot now be known how many other specimens in the Cook collection, unlisted in his notes, may have been from this source.
YM; cf. Pirie (1975), xxix, 1 (unknown site, 1846) with refs.

38. YORK, Exhibition Building (now City Art Gallery) 1879
400: identities not specified
YM (none now distinguished in the cabinet); Pirie (1975), xxxii, 7 with refs.

39. BEVERLEY, N. Humberside. Lurk Lane (minster collegiate buildings) 1981
Excavation find of 23, Eanred-Osberht: a purse-hoard
Regular (8): EANRED (1): Odilo, 1. ÆTHELRED II (6): Eanred, 2; Fordred, 1; Monne, 1; Vendelberht, 1; Eardvvlf, 1. Abp. WIGMVND (1): Edilveard, 1. *Irregular* (15): *temp.* Eanred, 3; *temp.* Æthelred, 6; *temp.* Æthelred–Osberht, 6.
Disposition undecided; site publication forthcoming; *See* pl.5.1:20. *See* 12, 63

40. BOLTON PERCY, 1, N. Yorkshire 1847
Several thousand: Eanred to Osberht
YM: a considerable parcel; Bateman: 620 (dispersed, Sotheby, 4–6.5.1893, lots 249–58); Fennell: 469 (dispersed, Christie's, 14.4.1981, lots 118–34; now in DCM, LCM, and in private possession); others, unknown. Pirie (1981), 32–44 with refs. *See* pl.5.1:19.

41. BOLTON PERCY, 2, N. Yorkshire 1967
1775: Eanred to Osberht (some in a pot, of continental Badorf ware)
Regular (1,335): EANRED, 213; ÆTHELRED II, 598 ('first reign'), 164 ('second reign'); REDWULF, 38; OSBERHT, 75; uncertain regal, 15. Abp. EANBALD, 3; Abp. WIGMVND, 214; Abp. WULFHERE, 15. *Irregular* (397): miscellaneous, 397. *Uncertain* (43): unidentified and fragments, 43.
Dispersed at Sotheby, 23.6.1971: BM: 29; YM: 246, (and the pot); others, uncertain. *MedArch 12* (1968), 163; Pagan (1973), 1–44; *CH 3* (1977), no. 316.

42. RIPON, N. Yorkshire. Ailcey Hill, 1 1695
'A considerable number', Eanred to Osberht
Original parcels to Abp. Sharp of York, Thoresby of Leeds and others: 73 still in the Sharp collection; ?3 in GHM; others now unknown. Pirie (1982b), 93–4, with registers and refs.

43. RIPON, N. Yorkshire, Ailcey Hill, 2 1846
Several 'stycas' of Eanred and Æthelred II, found near Ailcey Hill
Disposition unknown; Pirie (1982b), 100 with refs.

44. WHITBY, N. Yorkshire. Abbey, E. Cliff (A-S minster) 1920s
Excavation find of 22: ?a purse-hoard. The coins in question cannot now be distinguished from the other site-finds. *See* 68
BM; Metcalf, no. 53 with ref.

ii. Excavation-finds and strays without site-context; the latter are asterisked.

YORK, R. Ouse c.1740
There is no indication that the coins recovered included either 'sceattas' or 'stycas'. Pirie (1975), xl, 24 with refs.

45.* YORK, Clifford Street 1884
2: Eanred, Fordred, 1; Æthelred II, Monne, 1. – found with small lead cross, bearing impressions of a 'styca' of Osberht
YM; Pirie (1975), xxxix, 5 with refs., also *BNJ 4* (1907), 235–7.

46.* YORK, Clifford's Tower 1902
1: Æthelred II, Coenred (possibly irregular) Disposition unknown; *YPSR* (1902), 73; Pirie (1975),–.

47.* YORK, Industrial School, Marygate 1920
1: unidentified
YM; Pirie (1975), xxxix, 6 with ref.

YORK, Micklegate Bar (Metcalf, 1960, no. 154). *See* 32

48.* YORK, 'Roman fortress' (E. corner) 1928
1: Ælfwald, Cudheart (AR, base)
YM (missing; illustrated, Lyon, 1957, pl. 18, 7); Pirie (1975), xxxix, 3 with ref. (R and M, 51, include this with 'sceattas').

49.* YORK, Uncertain location c.1755
1: Wigmund, Edelhelm
Disposition unknown; *Gentleman's Magazine* (1756), 64–5, and fig. 5 (note by S. Pegge); Pirie (1975) –. One wonders if the coin in question is properly the second piece, which defied initial identification, from Naburn, 1753 (61).

50.* YORK, Uncertain location c.1840–62
1: Wigmund, Coenred
In private possession; Chalk (1979), 546.

51. YORK, Minster 1970–1
10: *Regular* (6): A. *Early silver* (3): Æthelred I, Ceolbald, 1. Eanred: Eadvini, 1; Vvlfheard, 1. B. *Late copper alloy* (3): Æthelred II: Brother, 1; Eardvvlf, 1. Osberht: Monne, 1. *Irregular* (4): Æthelred II: Odilo, 1; Eanvvlf, 1. Osberht: Herred, 1. Nonsense, 1.
These were found together with a silver penny of Egbert of Wessex, 802–39, by the moneyer Tidbearht, and a Carolingian *denier* of Charles the Bald, 840–77, from Quentovic (Dolley and Morrison (1966), 104).
YoM; Pirie (1975), xl, 25; site publication forthcoming. *See* 5

52. YORK, Aldwark 1971
1: Eanred, Eadvini (Æ)
YM; Pirie (1975), xxxix, 4.

53. YORK, Bedern Chapel 1980
1: Eanred, Tidvini (AR, base)
YAT; *AoY 18/1*, forthcoming.

54. YORK, Bishophill I 1973–4
3: Æthelred II, Vendelberht, 1; Wigmund, Edilveard, 1; Wulfhere, Vvlfred, 1
YAT; *AoY 18/1*, forthcoming.

55. YORK, Cattle Market, Paragon Street 1973
2: Æthelred II: Vvlfred, 1; Eardvvlf, 1
YAT; *AoY 18/1*, forthcoming.

56. YORK, City Garage, Blake St 1975
2: Eanred, Fordred, 1; Æthelred II, Leofdegn, 1
YAT; *AoY 18/1*, forthcoming.

57. YORK, Clementhorpe 1977
1: Osberht, Viniberht (fragment)
YAT; *AoY 18/1*, forthcoming; pl.5.1:16.

58. YORK, Coppergate 1978–81
11: *Regular* (5): Eanred (2): Cudhard, 1; Eadvini, 1. Æthelred II (3): Alghere, 1; Monne, 1; uncertain, 1. *Irregular* (5): miscellaneous, 5. *Unidentified* (1).
YAT; *AoY 18/1*, forthcoming.

59. YORK, Ebor Brewery 1973–4
3: Eanred, Vilheah (AR), 1; Æthelred II, Eardvvlf, 1; Uncertain, 1
YAT; *AoY 18/1*, forthcoming. *See* 6

60. YORK, Old County Hospital 1982
1: Ælfwald, Cudheart (AR, base)
YAT; for inclusion in *AoY 18/2*.

61.* NABURN, near York. R. Ouse at Naburn Ings 1753
2: Ethilred rex, 1; unidentified, 1
Disposition unknown. *Surtees Soc. 80* (1885), 361, quoting Stukeley's *Diary*; R and M, 43 with ref. (there accepted as 'sceattas').

MARKET WEIGHTON and NORTH FERRIBY, N. Humberside
In 1980–2, references (unpublished) were made to these places as the provenances of Northumbrian coins recovered with the aid of metal-detectors; the correct attribution is now accepted as Sancton (62). Finds of other issues from the Redcliffe foreshore at N. Ferriby include two specimens of Aldfrith of Lindsey, c.790 (*recte* of Northumbria, see p. 69 above).

62.* SANCTON, N. Humberside (related settlement not yet investigated).
I. 1979–82
Metal-detector finds: 41 coins, including one mounted in a lead weight (also a Carolingian *denier* of Charlemagne: Dolley and Morrison (1966), 15).
Regular (36): A. *Silver and early copper alloy* (13): ÆTHELRED I (4): 'Cudicils', 1; Tidvvlf, 1; Ceolbald, 1; double obverse, 1 (? Ceolbald's dies). ÆLFWALD (3): Cudheart, 2 + 1‡. EANRED (6): Hvaetred, 1; Eadvini, 4. Daegberct, 1. B. *Later copper alloy* (23): EANRED (3): Fordred, 3. ÆTHELRED II (12): Alghere, 1; Brother, 1; Eanred, 2; Fordred (Eordred), 3; Leofdegn, 1; Monne, 1; Vendelberht, 1. Eardvvlf, 2. (all have obv. in *Edilred* form, with the exception of one Eanred: *Ethflred*). OSBERHT (2): Monne, 2. Abp. WIGMVND (6): Conred, 4; Hunlaf, 2. *Irregular* (4): 'Hexham-style', 1†; others, 3 including one unpublished. *Illegible* (1): in lead weight, 1‡.
LCM; 2 (‡ above), LU; 1 † above): others in private possession. Booth and Blowers (1983). *See* pl.5.1:7.
II. 1983
5: Eanred, Fordred, 1; Æthelred II, Eanred, 1; Abp. Wigmund: Coenred, 1; Edilveard, 1. Irregular, 1‡
LCM: 1 (‡ above); others in private possession. Unpublished.
See 11

63. BEVERLEY, N. Humberside. Lurk Lane (minster collegiate buildings) 1979–81
4: Æthelred I, Tidvvlf, 1 (AR, base); Æthelred II, Eardvvlf, 1; Irregular, 2
Disposition undecided. Site publication forthcoming. *See* 12 and 39

64. WHARRAM PERCY, N. Yorkshire (deserted medieval village) 1966–77
I. (House 6) 1966
1: Eanred, Fordred; Hurst (1979), 132, no. 4.
II. (Site 26) 1977
1: Eanred, Fordred; site publication forthcoming.
HCM. *See* 16

65. WHARRAM PERCY, N. Yorkshire. Church (chancel area) 1973
2: Wigmund, Coenred, 1; Irregular, 1
HCM; site publication forthcoming.

66. KIRKBYMOORSIDE, N. Yorkshire. All Saints' churchyard 1965
1: Æthelred I, 'Cudicils' (AR, base) (found while grave-digging: nearby site later excavated)
RFM; *YAJ 41* (1966), 566–7.

67.* WHITBY, N. Yorkshire. St Mary's churchyard, E. Cliff 1876
1: Eanred, Fordred
WPPM; unpublished.

68. WHITBY, N. Yorkshire. Abbey, E. Cliff (A-S minster) 1920s
127 silver and copper alloy 'stycas' which may be grouped and summarized as follows:
Regular (105): A. *Silver and early copper alloy* (21): ÆTHELRED I (11): Ceolbald, 7; Tidvvlf, 1 + 1†; Cudheart, 2. EANRED (11): Hvaetred, 1; Cunvvlf, 1; Daegberct, 1; Eadvini, 3; Vilheah, 2. Herred, 3. B. *Later copper alloy* (105): EANRED (15): Aldates, 2, and Gadutes, 1; Brodr, 1; Fordred, 4; Monne, 7. ÆTHELRED II (46): Brother, 6; Cunemund, 1; Eanred, 7; Fordred, 4; Leofdegn, 1; Monne, 11; Vvlfred, 1; Vvlfsig, 1; Wihtred, 1; Uncertain, 1. Eardvlf, 11. REDWULF (2): Brother, 1; Monne, 1. OSBERHT (3): Edelhelm, 1; Eanvvlf, 1; Monne, 1. Abp. EANBALD (2): Eadvvlf, 1; Edilveard, 1. Abp. WIGMVND (14): Edilveard, 5; Coenred, 4; Hunlaf, 3; Edelhelm, 2. *Irregular* (9): miscellaneous, 9. *Unidentified* (14).
BM: 127; WPPM: 1 († above).
Allan (1943), 85–6. *See* 18, 44

69.* WHITBY, N. Yorkshire. Spa Ladder, E. Cliff 1931
1: Æthelred I, Ceolbald (AR, base)
WPPM; unpublished.

70.* WHITBY, N. Yorkshire, or vicinity before 1893
1: unidentified
YM; Metcalf, no. 151 with ref.

71.* RIPON, N. Yorkshire. Possible find, no locality specified ?before 1678
5: Eanred: Eadvini, 2; Fordred, 1. Æthelred II: Leofdegn, 1; Monne, 1
Disposition unknown; Pirie (1982 b), 94, with refs.

72.* RIPON, N. Yorkshire. The common (now the race-course) not dated; most probably 18th cent.
Several, not listed.
Disposition unknown; Pirie (1982b), 95 with refs.

73.* RIPON, N. Yorkshire. 'Scots monastery' near Priest Lane before 1875
Uncertain number, not listed
Disposition unknown; Pirie (1982b), 100 with refs.

74. MALHAM MOOR, N. Yorkshire. Prior Rakes c.1960
2: Eanred: Aldates (?), 1; Monne, 1
MTFC; Raistrick and Holmes (1962), 5.

75. SETTLE, N. Yorkshire. Attemire Cave mid-late 19th cent.
4: Eanred, Wihtred, 1; Æthelred II: Fordred, 1; Leofdegn, 1. Eardvvlf, 1
SPM; unpublished; *see* pl.5.1:9. *See* 21, 76. The cave site has been investigated at intervals since at least the middle of the nineteenth century. In addition to the Northumbrian coins, a Carolingian *denier* of Lothaire I (840–55) from the Dorestadt mint (Dolley and Morrison (1966), 84–6) has been found. Apart from coins, other archaeological material which has been recovered represents all periods from late Neolithic to the fourth century AD.

76.* SETTLE, N. Yorkshire. Attemire Cave 1970
1: Æthelred I, Cudheart (AR, base)
Private possession; *YAJ 45* (1973), 203. *See* 21, 75.

77. RIBBLEHEAD, N. Yorkshire (farmstead) 1974–5

4: Wulfhere, Vvlfred, 1. Irregular, *temp.* Æthelred II, 2. Illegible, 1
Disposition undecided; King (1978), 21–5. *See* pl.5.1:17.

B. Tees-Forth
i. Hoards

KIRKOSWALD (marginal) *See* 96

78. HEXHAM, Northumberland. Abbey churchyard October 1832 (residue in Dec. 1841)
About 8,000, early silver and later copper alloy (Æthelred I-Æthelred II and Redwulf) in metal bucket
BM, container and a considerable parcel; NMA, a considerable parcel; MM, another parcel. Pirie (1981), 44, for minor parcel now in private possession; Pirie (1982a), for Newcastle parcel and main inventory: to the bibliography there must be added Hodges and Gibson (1919) 86–7, and – for discussion of the site and the bucket – Bailey (1974), 141–50. *See* pl.5.1:11 and 14.

79. JEDBURGH, Roxburghshire (near Abbey Bridge) c.1834
Miscellaneous coins, including Northumbrian 'stycas'; the latter, unlisted, may have been a purse-hoard.
Disposition unknown; Stevenson (1966), xx with ref.

ii. Excavation-finds and strays without site-context; the latter are asterisked.

80. MONKWEARMOUTH, Tyne and Wear (A-S minster) 1961–6
6: *Regular* (5): A. *Early copper alloy* (2): Eanred: Eadvini, 1; Herred (double rev.), 1. B. *Later copper alloy* (3): Eanred: Fordred, 1; Vvlfred, 1. Uncertain, 1. *Irregular* (1)
SM; site publication forthcoming.

81. JARROW, Tyne and Wear (A-S minster) 1963–78
7: *Regular* (5): A. *Early silver* (2): Æthelred I, Ceolbald, 1. Eanred, Eadvini, 1. B. *Later copper alloy* (3): Æthelred II: Fordred, 2; Leofdegn, 1. *Irregular* (1): Eanbald, Eadvvlf, 1. *Uncertain* (1)
JH; site publication forthcoming; *see* pl.5.1:6 and 10. *See* 24

82.* GATESHEAD MOOR, Tyne and Wear 1757
'three small pieces of very ancient Saxon Coin' – perhaps 'stycas'
Disposition unknown; Pirie (1982a), 5 with ref.

83. TYNEMOUTH, Tyne and Wear (A-S minster) 1963
1: Æthelred II, irregular
NMA; Jobey (1967), 88; (not in Pirie, 1982a).

84. NEWCASTLE, Tyne and Wear. Black Gate (the site includes an A-S cemetery) 1977 and later (continuing)
Apart from coins of other periods, 8: *Regular* (4): Æthelred I: Ceolbald (AR) 1; Eanred: Brodr, 1; Æthelred II: Eanred, 1; Eardvvlf, 1. *Irregular, temp.* Æthelred II (2). *Uncertain* (2)
NMA; site publication forthcoming.

85.* HADRIAN'S WALL, Northumberland (find inferred) c.1599
1: Eanred, Eadvini
'Many memorable Antiquities are found in this Country along the Wall, and in other places: As Peeces of Coyne, Inscriptions, broken and imperfect Altars, &c.' (Speed (1611): Northumberland, 89).
Sir Robert Cotton, whose coins were used to illustrate Speed's *Historie*, is said to have been visiting the Wall in 1599, in company with Camden, in a search for antiquities (Mirrlees (1962), 83–4). It is not altogether impossible that he acquired the 'styca', as a local find, on that occasion.
BM; (*BMC* Northumbria 92); Dolley and Strudwick (1954), 311.

86. BAMBURGH, Northumberland. Castle 1894

1: Eanred, Monne.
BC; Metcalf, no. 69 with refs.

87. BAMBURGH, Northumberland. Castle, West Ward before and after 1971
So far, only the 1971 finds (67 coins) can be listed:
Regular (34): EANRED (4): Brodr, 1; Fordred, 1; Monne, 2. ÆTHELRED II (24): Alghere, 2; Eanred, 3; Leofdegn, 2; Monne, 3; Vendelberht, 2; Coenred, 1. Eardvvlf, 11. Uncertain reign (1): Monne, 1. Abp. WIGMVND (4): Coenred, 2; Hunlaf, 1; Edelhelm, 1. Abp. WULFHERE (1): Vvlfred, 1. *Irregular* (24): *temp.* Eanred, 3; *temp.* Æthelred, 8; *temp.* Æthelred-Osberht, 11; unidentified, 2. *Unidentifiable* (9): fragments or cores, 9.
BC; as yet unpublished; *see* pl.5.1:18.

88. LINDISFARNE, Northumberland 1845
2: Æthelred II, Brother, 1. Abp Wigmund, Edilveard, 1
Disposition unknown. Cartwright (1976), 60 with ref. to *HBNC 2* (1842–9), 159–63.

89.* NORHAM-ON-TWEED, Northumberland (exact provenance not known) before 1891
1: unidentified
1891: in 'Collection of Local Relics', at Birch Hill, Norham. *HBNC 13* (1891–2), 312.

90.* JEDBURGH, Roxburghshire (from river bank) 1859
1: Osberht, Monne
NMAS; Metcalf (1960–1), no. 110 with ref.; Stevenson (1966), no. 42.

91.* COLDINGHAM, Berwickshire. Churchyard c.1882
1: Eanbald, Eadvvlf (AR, base)
NMA; Pirie (1982a), 6 (4), and no. 122.

C. West Coast: Mersey-Clyde (including off-shore islands)
i. Hoards

92. OTTERSPOOL, Merseyside 1863
Uncertain number, unidentified (Æ ?)
Disposition uncertain; a parcel in IM? (see 93). Metcalf (1960–1), no. 38 with refs.; cf. Clough (1980), 106 and 92.

93. LANCASHIRE? Uncertain site 19th cent.
Uncertain number; only one parcel can be summarized: 56: *Regular* (38): A. *Early copper alloy* (1): EANRED, Vvlfheard, 1. B. *Later copper alloy* (37): EANRED (6): Aldates (Gadutes), 1; Fordred, 2; Monne, 2; Odilo, 1. ÆTHELRED II (21): Alghere, 1; Cunemund, 1; Eanred, 3; Leofdegn, 4; Monne, 4; Vvlfred, 1; Wihtred, 1. Eardvvlf, 6. REDWULF (2): Cudberht, 1; Monne, 1. OSBERHT (2): Viniberht, 1; Monne, 1. Abp. WIGMVND (4): Edilveard, 2; Coenred, 1; Hunlaf, 1. Abp. WULFHERE (2): Vvlfred, 2. *Irregular* (18): miscellaneous, 18.
IM; Clough (1980), 106 and cat.

94. LANCASTER, Lancashire. Parish church (vicarage garden) 1914
c.20 (Æ): a purse-hoard?
Disposition unknown; Metcalf (1960–1), no. 28 with refs. *See* 99

95. GRANGE, Lancashire, Castle Head or Atterpile Castle, Penwortham (? hill-fort) 1765
? 95 (Æ): 5 noted by Joseph Priestly
Disposition unknown; Jackson (1909–10), 85; Metcalf (1960–1), no. 16 with other refs.

96. KIRKOSWALD, Cumbria 1808
Uncertain number (Æ) found in a pot; 542 summarized:
Eanred, 99; Æthelred II, 350; Redwulf, 14; Osberht, 15; Abp. Eanbald 1; Abp. Wigmund. 58; Abp. Wulfhere, 5.
It is not clear whether the above figures cover the 39 (including fragments) still in private possession

at Kirkoswald which may be summarized:
Regular (16): Eanred (2): Monne, 1; ?Brodr, 1 (frag.). Æthelred II (14): Alghere, 1; Eanred, 2; Leofdegn, 2; Monne, 3 and frag.; uncertain, 1. Eardvvlf, 4. *Irregular* (23): miscellaneous, 23.
Kirkoswald: 39 (unpublished); NMA: 6 presented in 1814–? others in 1851. Pirie (1982a), 2, 5 (for detail), and cat. (For the brooch found with the coins see Wilson (1964), 139–40, no. 28, with refs.) *See* pl.5.1:12.

97. PAISLEY, Renfrewshire 1782
Many (a considerable number, base AR and Æ): none specifically listed
NMAS, not distinguished in cabinet. Stevenson (1966), xxii with refs.

ii. Excavation-finds and strays without site-context; the latter are asterisked.

98.* RIBCHESTER, Lancashire before 1897
1: Eanred, moneyer unspecified
Disposition unknown; Metcalf, no. 133 with refs.

99.* LANCASTER, Lancashire. Vicarage Fields 1978
1: Wigmund, Coenred
LM; unpublished. *See* 94

RIBBLEHEAD (marginal) *See* 77

100. GRANGE, Lancashire. Merlewood Cave 1892
7: Eanred, 1; Æthelred II, 3; Wigmund, 1; Uncertain, 2
Disposition unknown; Jackson (1909–10), 45–6, 85–9; Metcalf (1960–1), no. 17 with refs.

101. DACRE, near Penrith, Cumbria (? A-S monastery) 1983
This site, in process of excavation, is known to be producing 'stycas' but they are not yet available for identification.
Disposition undecided.

102. CARLISLE (near), Cumbria 1876
2: Eanred, Fordred, 1; Æthelred II, Eanred, 1; found in a tumulus
CFM; Grierson (1958), nos. 282 and 310.

103. CARLISLE, Cumbria. Annetwell Street (*Luguvalium*, R. fort) 1981–
4: Eanred, Cunvvlf, 1; Wigmund, Hunlaf, 1. Irregular, *temp*. Eanred, 2
CTHM; site publication forthcoming.

104. CARLISLE, Cumbria. Blackfriars Street (*Luguvalium*, R. fort) 1977–8
3: Eanred: Herred, 1; Fordred, 1. Wulfhere, Vvlfred, 1
CTHM; McCarthy (1980), 11.

105. CARLISLE, Cumbria. Castle Street (civilian area outside fort) 1981–
6: Wigmund, Coenred, 1; ? Hunlaf, 1 (2 frags). Irregular, *temp*. Æthelred II, 1. Unidentifiable, 1 and 2 frags (? joining separate sliver). Not yet seen, 1.
CTHM; site publication forthcoming.

106. CARLISLE, Cumbria. The Lanes (peripheral to fort)
I. Keays Lane 1979
1: Irregular, *temp*. Eanred, *MedArch 24* (1980), 219.
II. Lewthwaites Lane 1981
1: as yet unavailable for identification
CTHM; site publication forthcoming.

107.* TALNOTRIE, Cairnsmore of Fleet, Kirkcudbrightshire 1912
Miscellaneous jewellery and coins, including 6: Æthelred II, Eanred, 1; Redwulf, Coenred, 1; Osberht, Eanvvlf, 1; Wulfhere, Vvlfred, 1; unidentified, 2
NMAS; Stevenson (1966), xxiii with refs., and nos. 20, 34, 41, 53–55.

108.* LUCE SANDS, Wigtownshire various dates
13: *Regular* (12): A. *Silver and early copper alloy* (4): Æthelred I (2): Ceolbald, 1; Tidvvlf, 1. Eanred (2): Eadvini, 2. B. *Later copper alloy* (8): Eanred (4): Fordred, 2; Monne, 2. Æthelred II (2): Eardvvlf, 2. Abp. Wigmund (2): Edilveard, 1; Coenred,

1. *Irregular* (1): unidentified, 1.
NMAS: 4 (Stevenson, 28, 47, 50, 56); GHM: 4 (Robertson, 147, 154, 225, 253); GKM: 2; DM: 3. Stevenson (1966), xix with refs.

From off-shore islands:

109. KINGSCROSS POINT, Arran (Viking burial) 1909
1: Wigmund, Coenred
NMAS; Stevenson (1966), xx with refs., and no. 44.

110. KILORAN BAY, Colonsay (Viking burial) 1882–3
3: Æthelred II, Fordred, 1; Wigmund, Coenred, 1; illegible, 1
NMAS: (1 missing). Stevenson (1966), xx with refs., and nos. 22, 43: it is noted that both the surviving coins are pierced, as if they had been used as ornaments.
The Viking burials in Arran and Colonsay can be compared with similar sites in the Isle of Man which did not produce 'stycas' (Bersu and Wilson (1966), 85–6).

D. South of Humber-Mersey
East:
i. Hoards, nil.
ii. Excavation-finds and strays without site-context; the latter are asterisked.

111.*WINTRINGHAM, S. Humberside 1750
1: Eanred, Cunvvlf (AR, base)
Private possession; Pirie (1981), 34, 44; *A of L, 6/2* (1983), tb. 2, 6.

112.*APPLEBY, S. Humberside before 1874
1: Æthelred II, Leofdegn
Private possession; Pirie (1981), 34, 44; *A of L, 6/2* (1983), tb. 2, 8.

113.*KIRMINGTON, S. Humberside 1979
1: Eanred, Vilheah (AR, base): metal-detector find
Private possession; Pirie (1981), 34, 49; *A of L, 6/2* (1983), tb. 2, 7. pl.5.1:8.

114.*GRIMSTHORPE, Lincolnshire 1894
1: Æthelred II, Eanred
PCM; *A of L, 6/2* (1983), tb. 2, 9.

115.*PETERBOROUGH, Cambridgeshire. Park Road 1962
1: Æthelred II, Vendelberht
PCM; unpublished.

116.*HEACHAM, Norfolk. 1977–9
7: *Regular* (4): Eanred, Fordred, 1; Æthelred II (2): Monne, 1: ? Leofdegn, 1. Wigmund, Coenred, 1. *Irregular* (3); metal-detector finds
Private possession; casts in NCM; unpublished.

117.*NORTH WALSHAM, Norfolk undated
1: Æthelred II, Monne
NCM; Clough (1980), no. 1030.

118.*NORWICH, Norfolk. Elm Hill undated
1: Æthelred II, Odilo
NCM; Clough (1980), –.

119.*THETFORD, Norfolk. Bury Rd allotment 1975
1: Æthelred II, Eanred
TM; Clough (1980), no. 1020.

120. THETFORD, Norfolk (Saxon defences) (found in an 11th century rubbish-pit) 1977
1: Æthelred I, Hnifula
TM; *MedArch 22* (1977), 148; Clough (1980) –; site publication forthcoming.

121. BRANDON, Suffolk. Staunch Meadow (A-S settlement with cemetery) 1981
1: Æthelred II, Alghere
Disposition undecided; *MedArch 26* (1982), 208; *PSIA 35/2* (1982), 160.

122.*HASKETON, Suffolk 1981
1: Osberht, Viniberht
Private possession; *PSIA 35/2* (1982), 157.

THANET (Reculver) *see* 131

123. RICHBOROUGH, Kent (*Rutupiae*, R. fort)

I.* before 1851
2: Æthelred II: Eanred, 1; Fordred, 1
BM (Eanred – Acquisitions 285); the other, unknown; Roach Smith (1851), 158; *NC*5*4* (1924), 86–95.
II. 1931–8
1: Eanred, Aldates
Disposition uncertain; Rigold (1968), 217–18.

Midland:
i. Hoards, nil.
ii. Excavation-finds, nil; stray finds, without site-context (asterisked).

124.* CADEBY, S. Yorkshire. Pot Ridings Wood 1980–2
3: Æthelred II: Eanred, 1; Leofdegn, 1; Odilo, 1; metal-detector finds
DCM; Dolby (1982). *See* pl.5.1:13.

125.* ANSTON, S. Yorkshire. Moses Seat 1980
1: Æthelred II, Fordred; metal-detector find
Private possession; Dolby (1982).

126.* CASTLETON, Derbyshire. Castle Hill ?various dates
Uncertain number: one only (Æthelred II, Eardvvlf) specifically identified
Bateman collection; present disposition unknown; Metcalf (1960–1), 121–2 with refs.

West:
i. Hoards, nil.

MANCHESTER
R and M, 42, note that 9 coins are more likely to have been 'stycas' than 'sceattas'; the correct provenance is probably Otterspool. *See* 92

ii. Excavation-find and stray without site-context; the latter is asterisked.

127.* MEOLS SANDS, Wirral. Cheshire before 1863
Among coins of many periods, 3: Æthelred, Fordred, 1; Redwulf, Coenred, 1; Uncertain, 1
MCM (2); Warhurst (1982), xx-xxi with refs., and cat. 74, 96.

128. CAERNARVON, Gwynedd (*Segontium*, R. fort) 1922
1: Eanred, Vvlfheard (Æ, early)
NMW; Dykes (1976), 17, 27, and 29 with refs; Boon (1976).

E. Overseas
i. Hoards, nil.
ii. Excavation-find and stray without site-context; the latter is asterisked.

129. NORWAY: Vig (Tumulus) 1876
2, *temp*. Eanred, mounted on lead weights: a) obv.: Eanred Rex; b) rev.: Herred
OU; Skaare (1976), 44–5 and 144, with refs.

130. NETHERLANDS: Dorestadt, Frisia 1958/9
1: Eanred, Monne
Private possession; to be published with Dorestadt site-lists.

III. MISCELLANEOUS RECORDS
A. 'Sceattas'
A. Disputed source

131. ISLE OF THANET, *recte* Reculver, Kent before 1756
1: Eadberht, quadruped left
Disposition unknown. Withy and Ryall (1756); supplementary plate by J. White, 21. R and M, 44–5, with refs., attribute the other 20 pieces illustrated – southern issues – to Reculver on the mainland by Thanet; the omission of the 21st from that Reculver register seems to indicate that such a southern provenance is impossible for a Northumbrian 'sceat'.
The plate published in 1756 exists also as a separate print and has been found together with a second, unfinished plate which shows 12 further coins, numbered 22–33. These include five Northumbrian specimens (22–24, 26–27) which can be listed as

follows: 'Sceatta' – 3: Eadberht, quadruped right, 1; Eadberht and Egberht, 2. 'Stycas' – 2: Æthelred I, Tidvvlf, 1; Eanred, Vvlfheard, 1.

132. LINDORES, Fife. Parkhill, near Abbey 1814
The A-S coins recovered were said by Lindsay to include one of Abp. Egberht, but this identification is noted by Stevenson (1966, xxii with refs.) as incorrect.

B. Non-existent find

133. 'ALTON', Lincolnshire (the place does not exist) 1849
1: Eanred and Egberht
Heywood (1910), 332; reference given in error, presumably for Malton, Yorks., 1850. *See* 17

C. False coins

134. HEWORTH, Tyne and Wear 1812
23 Æ of Ecgfrith of Northumbria, in a pot.
These coins are spurious and this find may now be regarded as a hoax; see Pirie (1982a) for discussion, including results of analysis, and detail of bibliography to which must be added Myres (1977), 21–22 and fig. 111, 340, for the pot.

B. 'Stycas'

A. Disputed source

THANET (Reculver) *See* 131

136. TREWHIDDLE (near St Austell), Cornwall 1774
Gold and silver objects, including coins, among which was a silver penny of Eanred, arguably Eanred of Northumbria; possibly also an unidentified 'styca'.
BM (penny); Wilson and Blunt (1961), 113–16 with refs.

136. BRIGHTON, Sussex before 1940
1: Eanred, Monne
This is said to have been found at or near Brighton together with a half-siliqua of Athalaric (526–34) and a base southern 'sceat'. The associations and provenance may be considered unlikely.
OAM; Sutherland (1941), 87; cf. R and M, 36, for the southern issue.

B. Secondary find

137. BATH, Avon 1867–8
25: Eanred-Osberht 'found in 1867–8 in the foundations of the White Hart Hotel' (now site of Arlington Court).
Regular (21): EANRED (5): Aldates, 1 (248); Fordred, 1 (254); Monne, 2 (268–9); Wihtred, 1 (270). ÆTHELRED II (8): Alghere, 1 (271); Brother, 1 (273); Eanred, 1 (275); Fordred, 1 (287); Leofdegn, 2 (291–2); Vendelberht, 2 (300–1). OSBERHT (2): Eanvvlf, 1 (211); Monne, 1 (212). Abp. WIGMVND (6): Coenred, 1 (325); Edelhelm, 1 (331); Edilveard, 2 (332–3); Hunlaf, 2 (335–6). *Irregular* (4): *temp.* Æthelred II: Eardvvlf, 3 (315–16, 318); Monne, 1 (321).
BPR; Dolley (1965) identified this provenance as spurious, the coins themselves probably having been a parcel from some hoard found earlier in the Northumbrian area. Gunstone (1977), numbers cited above.

C. False coins

138. LONDON, Fore Street 1860
Uncertain number, of Eanred and Æthelred II with other coins
Disposition unknown; Dolley (1960, 38 with ref.) identifies the parcel as one of spurious coins planted on the site.

Index

Carlisle, 102–6; Castleton, 126; Coldingham, 91
Dorestadt, 29, 130; Driffield, 14
Epworth, 26; Ervik, 30
Gateshead Moor, 82; Grange, 95, 100; Grimsthorpe, 114
Hadrian's Wall, 85; Hasketon, 122; Hayton, 10; Heacham, 116; Heworth, 134; Hexham, 78; Hornsea, 13
Jarrow, 23–4, 81; Jedburgh, 79, 90
Kiloran Bay, 110; Kingscross Point, 109; Kirkbymoorside, 66; Kirkoswald, 96; Kirmington, 113
Lancashire, 93; Lancaster, 94, 99; Lindisfarne, 25, 88; Lindores, 132; London, 138; Luce Sands, 108
Malham, 20; Malham Moor, 74; Malton, 17; Manchester, p. 84; Market Weighton, p. 77; Meols Sands, 127; Monkwearmouth, 80
Naburn, 61; Newcastle, 84; Norham, 89; North Ferriby, p. 77; North Walsham, 117; Norwich, 118
Otterspool, 92
Paisley, 97; Peterborough, 115; Piercebridge, 22
Reculver, 131; Ribblehead, 77; Ribchester, 98; Richborough, 123; Richmond, 19; Ripon, 42–3, 71–3
Sancton, 11, 62; Settle, 21, 75–6
Talnotrie, 107; Thanet, 131; Thetford, 119–120; Trewhiddle, 135; Tynemouth, 83
Vig, 130
Wharram Percy, 15–16, 64–5; Whitby, 18, 44, 67–70; Wintringham, 111
York, 1–9, 31–8, 45–60

Institutions at which finds are located: abbreviations used in the text

BC	Bamburgh Castle, Northumberland
BHM	Historical Museum, Bergen, Norway
BM	British Museum, London
BMBC	Bowes Museum, Barnard Castle
BPR	Pump Room, Bath
CFM	Fitzwilliam Museum, Cambridge
CTHM	Tully House Museum, Carlisle
DCM	Doncaster City Museum, S. Yorkshire
DM	Dumfries Museum
GHM	Hunterian Museum, Glasgow
GKM	Kelvingrove Museum, Glasgow
HCM	City Museum, Kingston upon Hull, N. Humberside
IM	Ipswich Museum, Suffolk
JH	Jarrow Hall, Jarrow, Tyne and Wear
LCCM	City and County Museum, Lincoln
LCM	City Museum, Leeds, W. Yorkshire
LM	Lancaster Museum
LPM	Lindisfarne Priory Museum, Northumberland
LU	University of Leeds, W. Yorkshire
MCM	Merseyside County Museums, Liverpool
MM	University Museum, Manchester
MTFC	Malham Tarn Field Centre, Malham, N. Yorks
NCM	Castle Museum, Norwich, Norfolk
NMA	Museum of Antiquities, University of Newcastle upon Tyne
NMAS	National Museum of Antiquities of Scotland, Edinburgh
NMW	National Museum of Wales, Cardiff
OAM	Ashmolean Museum, Oxford
OU	University Museum, Oslo, Norway
PCM	City Museum, Peterborough
RFM	Ryedale Folk Museum, N. Yorkshire
SM	Sunderland Museum, Tyne and Wear
SPM	Pigyard Museum, Settle, N. Yorkshire
TM	Thetford Museum, Norfolk
WPPM	Pannet Park Museum, Whitby, N. Yorkshire
YAT	York Archaeological Trust, York
YM	Yorkshire Museum, York
YoM	York Minster, York

Bibliographical abbreviations

Allan — J. Allan, 'The coins from Whitby', *Archaeologia 89* (1943), 85–6

AoL 6/2 — M. A. S. Blackburn, C. Collyer, and M. Dolley, *Early Medieval Coins from Lincoln and its Shire, c.770–1100* (Archaeology of Lincoln 6/2, 1983)

AoY — *Archaeology of York*

Bailey — R. N. Bailey, 'The Anglo-Saxon metalwork from Hexham', *St Wilfrid at Hexham*, ed. D. P. Kirby (1974), 141–67

Bersu and Wilson — G. Bersu and D. M. Wilson, *Three Viking Graves in the Isle of Man* (Soc. for Med. Archaeology monograph 1, 1966)

Boon — G. C. Boon, 'Segontium fifty years on: II The coins', *Archaeologia Cambrensis 125* (1976), 40–79

Booth and Blowers — J. Booth and I. Blowers, 'Finds of sceattas and stycas from Sancton', *NC 143* (1983), 139–45

Cartwright — R. A. and D. B. Cartwright, *The Holy Island of Lindisfarne and the Farne Islands* (1976)

Chalk — R. S. Chalk (with N. Shiel), 'Some mid nineteenth-century finds from York', *NCirc 87* (1979), 346–7

Clough — T. H. McK. Clough, *SCBI Museums in East Anglia* (1980)

Cramp — R. Cramp, *The Monastic Arts of Northumbria* (1967 Arts Council exhibition hand-book)

Dolby — M. Dolby, 'Northumbrian stycas from South Yorkshire', *NC 142* (1982), 148–51, and pl. 41B

Dolley (1960) — M. Dolley, 'Coin hoards from the London area', *Trans. of the London and Middlesex Archaeol. Soc. 20* (1960), 37–50

Dolley (1965) — *Idem*, 'A spurious hoard of Northumbrian copper coins from Bath', *NC*[7] *5* (1965), 197–200

Dolley and Morrison — M. Dolley and K. F. Morrison, *The Carolingian Coins in the British Museum* (1966)

Dolley and Strudwick — M. Dolley and J. S. Strudwick, 'An early seventeenth-century collection of Anglo-Saxon coins', *BNJ 27* (1952–4), 302–12

Dykes — D. W. Dykes, *Anglo-Saxon Coins in the National Museum of Wales* (1976)

Grantley (1892) — Lord Grantley, 'A unique styca of Ethelred I, King of Northumbria', *NC*[3] *12* (1892), 87–8

Grantley (1893) — *Idem*, 'On a unique styca of Alchred of Northumbria and Archbishop Ecgberht', *NC*[3] *13* (1893), 267–72

Grierson — P. Grierson, *SCBI Fitzwilliam Museum, Cambridge, I* (1958)

Gunstone (1977) — A. J. H. Gunstone, *SCBI* West Country Museums (1977)

Gunstone (1981) — *Idem, SCBI Lincolnshire Collections* (1981)

Heywood (1897) — N. Heywood, 'The stycas of North Humbria'. *Lancashire and Cheshire Antiq. Soc. 15* (1897), 81–99; reprinted in 1899 as a separate booklet

Heywood (1910) — *Idem*, 'A parcel of stycas from the York find, 1842', *BNJ 7* (1910), 331–4

Hodges and Gibson — C. C. Hodges and J. Gibson, *Hexham and its Abbey* (1919)

Hurst — J. G. Hurst, *Wharram, a Study of Settlement on the Yorkshire Wolds, I* (Soc. for Med. Archaeology monograph 8, 1979)

Jackson — J. W. Jackson, 'Notes on the bone-caves of Grange and district', *Lancashire Naturalist 2* (1909–10), 45–6, 85–9

Jobey — G. Jobey, 'Excavations at Tynemouth priory and castle' *Archaeologia Æliana*[4] *45* (1967), 33–104

King — A. King, 'Gauber high pasture, Ribblehead – an interim report', *Viking Age*

York and the North, ed. R. A. Hall (1978)

Lyon — C. S. S. Lyon, 'A reappraisal of the sceatta and styca coinage of Northumbria', *BNJ 28* (1957), 227–42

McCarthy — M. McCarthy, *Carlisle, a Frontier City* (1980)

Metcalf — D. M. Metcalf, 'Some finds of medieval coins from Scotland and the north of England', *BNJ 30* (1960–1), 80–123

Mirrlees — H. Mirrlees, *A Fly in Amber* (1962)

Myres — J. N. L. Myres, *A Corpus of Anglo-Saxon Pottery of the Pagan Period* (1977)

Pagan — H. E. Pagan, 'The Bolton Percy hoard of 1967', *BNJ 43* (1973), 1–44

Pirie (1975) — E. J. E. Pirie, *SCBI Yorkshire Collections* (1975)

Pirie (1981) — *Eadem*, 'Early Northumbrian coins at auction, 1981', *BNJ 51* (1981), 32–51

Pirie (1982a) — *Eadem, Catalogue of the Early Northumbrian Coins in the Museum of Antiquities, Newcastle-upon-Tyne* (1982)

Pirie (1982b) — *Eadem*, 'The Ripon hoard, 1695: contemporary and current interest', *BNJ 52* (1982), 84–103

Raistrick and Holmes — A. Raistrick and P. F. Holmes, *Archaeology of Malham Moor*, repr. from *Field Studies 1* (1962)

Rigold (1967) — S. E. Rigold, on Caistor, in 'Archaeological notes, 1966', *Lincolnshire History and Archaeology 2* (1967), 46–7

Rigold (1968) — *Idem*, 'The Post-Roman coins', in *Excavations at Richborough, 5*, ed. B. W. Cunliffe (1968), 217–23

Rigold (1977) — *Idem*, 'The principal series of English sceattas', *BNJ 47* (1977), 21–30

R and M — S. E. Rigold and D. M. Metcalf, 'A check-list of English finds of sceattas', *BNJ 47* (1977), 31–52

Roach Smith — C. Roach Smith, *The Antiquities of Richborough* (1851)

Robertson — A. S. Robertson, *SCBI Hunterian Museum, Glasgow* (1961)

Skaare — K. Skaare, *Coins and Coinage in Viking-Age Norway* (Oslo, 1976)

Plate 5.1 Northumbrian 'sceattas' and 'stycas' (scale × 1½).

Key to plate 5.1

1–2. *Eadberht*: Sancton, 1983; Whitby
3. *Eadberht and Egberht*: cf. York, 1888
4. *Alhred and Egberht*: York, before 1893
5. *Æthelred I and Eanbald*: Jarrow
6. *Æthelred I*, Ceolbald: Jarrow
7. *Ælfwald II*, Cudheart: Sancton, 1979
8–9. *Eanred*: Vilheah, Kirmington, 1979; Wihtred, Settle
10. *Eanbald II*, Eadvvlf (irregular): Jarrow
11–13. *Æthelred II*: Monne, Hexham, 1832; Alghere, Kirkoswald, 1808; Odilo, Cadeby, 1982
14. *Redwulf*, Hvaetnod: Hexham, 1832
15. *Wigmund*, Hunlaf: York, 1831
16. *Osberht*, Viniberht (fragment): York, 1977
17. *Wulfhere*, Vvlfred: Ribblehead, 1974
18–20. *Irregular*: Bamburgh, 1971; Bolton Percy, 1847; Beverley, 1981

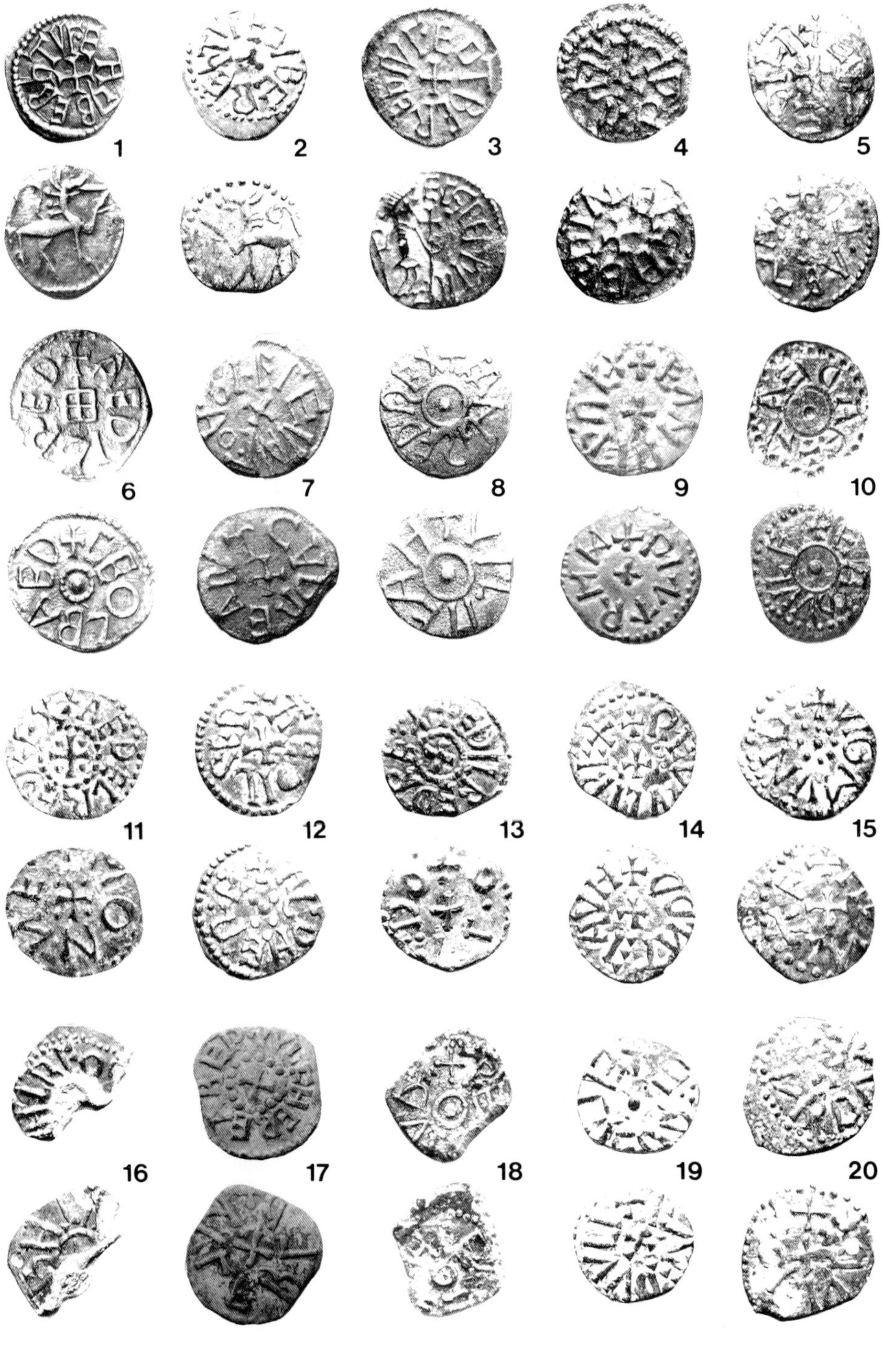
1
2
3
4
5
6
7
8
9
10
11
12
13
14
15
16
17
18
19
20

Speed — J. Speed, *The Theatre of the Empire of Great Britaine* (1611)

Stevenson — R. B. K. Stevenson, *SCBI National Museum of Antiquities of Scotland, Edinburgh* (1966)

Sutherland — C. H. V. Sutherland, 'Post-Roman coins found at Brighton', *NC*[6] *1* (1941), 87

Warhurst — M. Warhurst, *SCBI Merseyside County Museums* (1982)

Wilson — D. M. Wilson, *Anglo-Saxon Ornamental Metalwork 700–1100 in the British Museum* (1964)

Wilson and Blunt — D. M. Wilson and C. E. Blunt, 'The Trewhiddle hoard', *Archaeologia 98* (1961), 75–122

Withy and Ryall — R. Withy and J. Ryall, *Twelve Plates of English Coins* (1756)

Acknowledgments

It is with great pleasure that one records thanks to the following individuals for having helped in the acquisition of material for this inventory. Miss H. Wheeler has confirmed that no Northumbrian coins have yet been recorded in the Trent valley; Dr G. Hatz of Hamburg and Dr P. Ilisch of Munster have given assurance that nothing relevant has been found in Germany. Space permits only the briefest citation of other names: Miss M. M. Archibald, P. Armstrong, R. Bell, S. Bird, I. Blowers, C. E. Blunt, J. Booth, Mrs A. Clark, the late C. Clarke, Professor R. J. Cramp, D. B. Feather, T. Fetherstonehaugh, W. A. van Es, M. A. Gallon, G. Graham, Miss B. Green, the late A. J. H. Gunstone, Miss B. Harbottle, R. H. Hayes, R. J. Hemington, B. K. Hope-Taylor, J. P. C. Kent, A. King, K. Leahy, T. Lord, M. Mc.Carthy, T. Manby, D. M. Metcalf, P. Mitchell, T. Padley, S. Penney, A. Pol, the late S. E. Rigold, G. Robson, J. Rumsby, P. R. Scott, D. J. Smith, D. Sorrenson, A. E. Truckell, the Rev. J. Turner, Mrs E. Tyson, and A. White.

6 Reflections on the Viking-Age silver hoard from Croydon, Surrey

N. P. Brooks and J. A. Graham-Campbell

The ninth-century hoard of coins, ingots, and hack-silver found on the northern edge of the old parish of Croydon, Surrey, in June 1862, remained largely neglected during the twentieth century until Christopher Blunt and Michael Dolley treated it fully in their 1959 paper on 'The hoard evidence for the coins of Alfred'.[1] Their reconstruction of the discovery of the Croydon hoard, its early history and dispersal, and their detailed listing and discussion of its coins, was augmented with an archaeological assessment of the ingots and hack-silver by David Wilson.[2] The authors established beyond doubt that this hoard was deposited c.875 and had 'belonged to – or at least had been recently captured from – a Viking raider' and, in so doing, highlighted some aspects of its importance for numismatists, historians, and archaeologists of the Viking Age. During the last 25 years, however, the hoard has been allowed to relapse into relative obscurity, although it did form part of *The Vikings in England* exhibition in Denmark and then in York during 1981–2.[3] Its wider implications have remained unexplored, but it was to some of these, both archaeological and historical, that the present authors found that they were coincidentally turning their attentions. They have thus combined to offer here their reflections on the Croydon hoard as their tribute to the memory of Michael Dolley, both in recognition of his work on the Viking-Age coin hoards of Britain and Ireland[4] and in gratitude for his personal kindnesses to them.

It is not necessary to repeat here the details of the nineteenth-century evidence

Acknowledgments The authors are indebted to Veronica Smart, Hugh Pagan, and Mark Blackburn for generous guidance *in rebus numismaticis*, but are alone responsible for the views expressed and the errors perpetrated. The photographs in fig. 6.1: 1–6 are reproduced by courtesy of the Visitors of the Ashmolean Museum, Oxford, and those in fig. 6.1: 7–8 by permission of the Merseyside County Museums, Liverpool.

1. C. E. Blunt and R. H. M. Dolley, 'The hoard evidence for the coins of Alfred', *BNJ 29* (1959), 220–47; for the Croydon hoard, see pp. 222–34, superseding the entry in J. D. A. Thompson, *Inventory of British Coin Hoards A.D. 600–1500* (1956), no. 111. See also P. Spufford, 'Some hoard evidence from a nineteenth-century collection', *BNJ 30* (1961), 213–16, at 214–15.
2. Blunt and Dolley, *op. cit.*, 231–2.
3. E. Roesdahl *et al.* (eds), *The Vikings in England* (1981), 66 (D21), where it is confused with the 'Croydon Palace hoard' (see p. 103 below).
4. Notably R. H. M. Dolley, *Hiberno-*

utilized by Blunt and Dolley in their account of the discovery and contents of the Croydon hoard, except to itemize the available sources. These consist of contributions to the *Numismatic Chronicle* by the Rev. Henry Christmas in 1862[5] and by Sir John Evans in 1866,[6] of J. Corbet Anderson's *Saxon Croydon* (privately published in 1877), and of cuttings from the *Croydon Journal* for 6 August and 13 August 1862, preserved in the Croydon Public Library, together with the actual drawings made by Corbet Anderson for his book, and 'an old photograph of the bulk of the hoard as it lay uncleaned and largely intact under an immortelle glass in the window of a Croydon jeweller'.[7]

The hoard appears to have consisted of roughly 250 coins, three ingots, and a cut section of a fourth, and four other pieces of hack-silver (fig. 6.1). These were contained in a coarse linen bag tied with a string which cannot now be traced, although it appears in the above-mentioned photograph and forms the subject of one of Corbet Anderson's drawings.[8] A recently discovered instance of the use of such a linen bag in the concealment of a Viking-Age hoard is provided by the 1972/5 Kirk Michael hoard on the Isle of Man (deposited in the 1060s).[9] At an earlier date, the use of textile bags is deduced for the Cuerdale, Lancashire, treasure deposited c.905, from the presence of some bone pins in the hoard; these had presumably been used for fastening the bags which had been contained in a lead chest.[10] The Croydon hoard is said to have been 'at a depth of about two feet' in a stone 'coffin, or chest' that was 'without a lid', or rather in the debris of this chest which had 'crumbled under the picks and spades' of the navvies working on the new railway line from West Croydon Station to Balham.[11] There is no mention of skeletal remains in any of the sources and it is improbable that the hoard was associated with a human interment, despite Blunt and Dolley's speculation to this effect, not least it would have been most unusual for such a mixed silver hoard to have been deposited *in* a pagan Viking burial, although concealment of hoards in churchyards is a well-known phenomenon at this period.[12]

Norse Coins in the British Museum (*SCBI* 8, 1966) in which the Croydon hoard is listed at p. 49 (no. 40).

5. H. Christmas, 'A discovery of Anglo-Saxon coins at White Horse near Croydon', *NC*² *2* (1862), 302–4.
6. J. Evans, 'The discovery of Anglo-Saxon coins at White Horse near Croydon', *NC*² *6* (1866), 232–40.
7. Blunt and Dolley, *op. cit.*, 223. Photographs of the drawings and of the 1862 photograph are on file in the Department of Medieval and Later Antiquities of the British Museum; these were kindly made available by Mrs Leslie Webster.
8. J. Corbet Anderson, *Saxon Croydon* (1877), 154.
9. A. M. Cubbon and M. Dolley, 'The 1972 Kirk Michael Viking treasure trove', *J. Manx Museum 8.89* (1980), 5–20, at 7–8.
10. B. J. N. Edwards, 'Roman bone pins from the Cuerdale hoard', *AntJ 64* (1984), 365–6. See also J. Graham-Campbell, *Viking Artefacts: a select catalogue* (1980), no. 301, and refs.
11. Corbet Anderson, *op. cit.*, 115; Blunt and Dolley, *op. cit.*, 222–3; see also p. 101 below (and fig. 6.2) for further details of the find-spot.
12. J. Graham-Campbell, 'Viking silver hoards: an introduction', in *The Vikings*, ed. R. T. Farrell (1982), 32–41, at 33; Cubbon and Dolley, *op. cit.*, 10.

Blunt and Dolley were able to list a total of 185 coins as possibly from the Croydon hoard, of which nearly 150 were reasonably certain, thereby establishing 'the composition of at least 60 per cent and very probably of more than 70 per cent' of its contents. These coins consist of 94 from the kingdom of Mercia, all of the reign of Burgred (852–74), 24 from the kingdom of East Anglia, comprising 2 of Æthelstan (c.825–c.845), 4 of Æthelweard (c.845–c.855), and 18 of (St) Edmund (855–69), 1 of Ceolnoth, Archbishop of Canterbury (833–70), and 56 from the kingdom of Wessex, comprising 25 of Æthelred I (866–71), and 31 of Alfred the Great (871–99); in addition to these 175 English coins, there are on record 7 Carolingian deniers, comprising 1 of Louis the Pious (814–40), and 6 of Charles the Bald (840–77) of his *Christiana Religio* issue of 840–64, as well as three Kufic coins in the form of Abbasid dirhams, two being of Hārūn al-Rashīd (786–809), and the other being of Al-Wāthik (842–7).

Blunt and Dolley argued for the Croydon hoard being a Viking treasure on the following numismatic grounds: the English coins were 'not a true cross-section of English currency south of the Thames'; the presence of Kufic dirhams; and the presence of as many as half a dozen Carolingian deniers. This interpretation was fully supported by Wilson on the basis of their being ingots in the hoard, together with fragments cut from objects of Scandinavian origin. The significance of the numismatic composition of the hoard and its date of deposition is discussed further below by one author (N.P.B.), following some consideration of the ingots and hack-silver by the other (J.A.G.-C.).

The ingots and hack-silver

Six items of non-numismatic silver from the Croydon hoard were acquired by Sir John Evans (fig. 6.1:1–6): two complete ingots and the fragment of a third, together with three other pieces of hack-silver. These were presented to the Ashmolean Museum in 1909[13] and are those illustrated by Blunt and Dolley to the accompaniment of Wilson's description and discussion.[14] They failed, however, to trace the other two pieces, an ingot and a piece of hack-silver (fig. 6.1:7–8), known to have formed part of the hoard from the 1862 photograph[15] and Corbet Anderson's publication, although they had since 1953 been in the Liverpool City Museum (now the Merseyside County Museum)[16] and had recently been re-published in the final (1954) volume of *Viking Antiquities*.[17]

The three intact ingots are all small examples of the commonest Viking-Age type with a D-shaped cross-section and rounded ends, but the cut (and hacked) fragment

13. Reg. nos: 1909.556–61.
14. Blunt and Dolley, *op. cit.*, 231–2 and fig. 1.
15. As Blunt and Dolley comment (*ibid.*, 232): 'Reference to the 1862 photograph of the hoard suggests that the eight fragments and ingots account for the bulk, if not the whole, of the non-numismatic element in the hoard'.
16. Reg. nos: 53.114.64 and 65 (*ex* Nelson collection).
17. H. Shetelig (ed.), *Viking Antiquities in Great Britain and Ireland* (6 vols., Oslo, 1940 and 1954), VI, 242–3 and fig. 84.

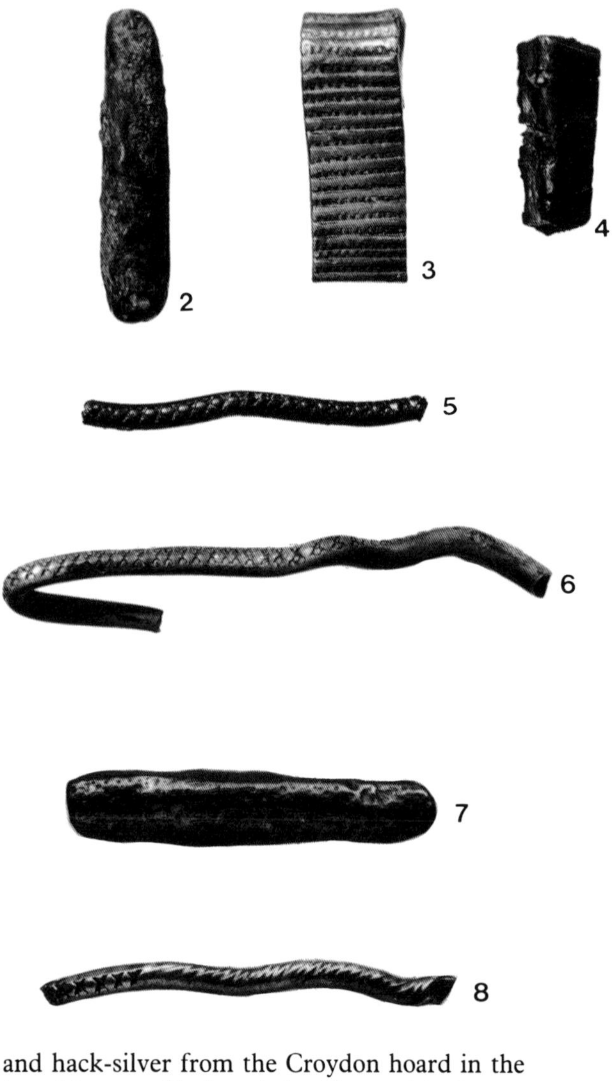

Fig. 6.1 Ingots and hack-silver from the Croydon hoard in the Ashmolean Museum (1–6) and the Merseyside County Museum (7–8) (scale: 1/1).

(fig. 6.1:4) is derived from a larger ingot of sub-rectangular section. There is nothing to add at this stage to Wilson's observation that 'the silver ingots are of a type commonly found in Viking Age hoards in this country and abroad'.[18] However, Blunt and Dolley's enumeration of coin-hoards containing ingots found in the British Isles[19] needs to be augmented as the number of such hoards now known in

18. In Blunt and Dolley, *op. cit.*, 232. 19. *Ibid.*, 232–3.

Ireland has increased from six to ten[20] and in the Scottish Isles from four to five;[21] the Goldsborough (Yorks.) hoard, deposited c.920, must also be added to their list for England and Wales, although its ingots are lost, as well as that from Scotby (Cumbria) of c.935.[22] In addition, it is worth noting that a considerable number of coinless Viking hoards from Ireland and Scotland also contain ingots.[23] The potential for more detailed study of the ingot material from Viking hoards than has hitherto been attempted has been demonstrated by Mrs Jennifer Lewis, working on two parcels from the Cuerdale hoard.[24] A full computer-aided analysis of ingot weights has now become a priority in Viking-hoard studies and work on this subject is now being undertaken by Miss Susan Kruse at University College London, alongside the preparation by one of the present authors (J.A.G-C.) of a catalogue of the Viking silver in the British Museum.

Three out of the four pieces of hack-silver remaining to be discussed are fragments of silver rods, cut at both ends, with stamped ornament along the outer face. The smaller of the two pieces in the Ashmolean is stamped with a row of opposed triangles, each containing a single pellet, as is the fragment in Liverpool, but on the latter this stamped ornament gives way to continuous spiral grooving, giving a corded or rifled effect. The second Ashmolean fragment has a row of opposed triangles containing three pellets. These three pieces are cut from one or more spiral arm-rings of the eastern European type known as 'Permian' rings from their area of densest distribution in the regions of Perm and Kirov (formerly Vjatka),[25] although one variant distinguished by its terminals, found in Danish and Gotlandic hoards, is thought by some to be a Scandinavian imitation of these early Viking-period imports.[26] It is not possible, however, to accept Wilson's claim when writing of these Croydon fragments that such spiral rings represent 'a very common Viking type',[27] for complete examples are not distributed as widely throughout the Viking world as such a statement might lead one to believe.

Only one hoard in Norway (that from Torvik, Volda, Møre, Møre og Romsdal)[28]

20. Nine are listed in Appendix C of J. A. Graham-Campbell, 'The Viking-age silver hoards of Ireland', in *Proceedings of the Seventh Viking Congress*, ed. B. Almqvist and D. Greene (Dublin, 1976), 39–74, at 66–9; the tenth such hoard is Dysart Island (no. 4), Co. Westmeath, dep. c. 910 (see M. Ryan *et al.*, 'Six silver finds of the Viking period from the vicinity of Lough Ennell, Co. Westmeath', *Peritia 3* (1984), 334–81, at 339–56).
21. Listed in Appendix C of J. A. Graham-Campbell, 'The Viking-age silver and gold hoards of Scandinavian character from Scotland', *PSAS 107* (1975–6), 114–35, at 129–30.
22. Unpublished drawing of Goldsborough in the library of the Society of Antiquaries of London; the Scotby hoard has recently been put on display in the Carlisle Museum (see C. E. Blunt, 'The Scotby hoard', *BNJ 42* (special vol. 1974), 156–8).
23. Graham-Campbell, 'Hoards of Ireland', 'Hoards from Scotland'.
24. J. Lewis, 'Silver ingots from the Cuerdale hoard in two northern collections', *Lancs. Archaeol. J. 2* (1982), 47–80.
25. See Graham-Campbell, *Viking Artefacts*, no. 331 and refs.
26. See E. Roesdahl, *Viking Age Denmark* (1982), 200 and refs; for a second variant, see p. 98 below.
27. In Blunt and Dolley, *op. cit.*, 232.
28. J. Bøe, 'Bergens Museums tilvekst av oldsaker 1926 og 1927', *Bergens*

is known to contain such rings and even these are only fragments. There are no complete examples known from Britain or Ireland, but fragments are present in four hoards (listed below in table 6.1);[29] an unprovenanced terminal fragment from Ireland has also been published.[30] Both complete and fragmentary spiral-rings may, however, be described with greater reason as being common in Denmark where they are known from 18 finds.[31] This distribution, notably the single hoard-find of such rings in Norway,[32] raises the question of the route by which the fragments found in insular hoards reached Britain and Ireland; this will be considered further after some discussion of the Croydon hoard's remaining piece of hack-silver.

Table 6.1. The Viking-Age coin hoards from Britain and Ireland containing spiral-ring fragments

Provenance	*Deposition date*	*No. of frags*
Croydon (Surrey)	c.872	3
Cuerdale (Lancs.)	c.905	40+
Co. Dublin	c.935	2
Storr Rock (Skye)	c.935	1

This final piece of hack-silver is included amongst the Ashmolean parcel of non-numismatic material from the Croydon hoard. It is derived from a different type of arm-ring to that discussed above, in this case made from a flat band of silver rather than a rod. Such arm-rings 'are penannular in form, tapering towards the ends; decoration is confined to the outer face and consists of a series of vertical grooves, executed with a variety of stamps, and in most cases with a simple diagonal cross at the centre, sometimes repeated towards the terminals'.[33] On this Croydon fragment the stamping takes the form of plain grooves, one side of which is 'embattled'. Arm-rings of this, the 'Hiberno-Viking' type, were being 'produced by the Scandinavians

Museums Årbok 1927 (Hist.-antik. rekke, no. 2), 1–63, at 24–6 (no. 58) and fig. 4; S. Grieg, 'Vikingetidens skattefund', *Universitetets Oldsaksamlings Skrifter 2* (1929), 177–311, at 250–1 (no. 92).

29. Another feature which these coin-hoards have in common is that they all contain one or more ingots.
30. Shetelig (ed.), *op. cit.*, III, 113 and fig. 75.
31. Seventeen are mapped in E. Munksgaard, 'Skattefundet fra Duesminde', *Aarbøger for Nordisk Oldkyndighed og Historie, 1962*, 94–112, at 98, fig. 3 (including two finds which are from south of the modern Danish/German border in Schleswig), to which must be added the hoard from Kærbyholm, Odense, Fyn (for which see E. Munksgaard, 'To skattefund fra ældre vikingetid: Duesminde og Kærbyholm', *Aarbøger for Nordisk Oldkyndighed og Historie, 1969*, 52–62.
32. Mrs Charlotte Blindheim (Universitetets Oldsaksamlingen, Oslo) kindly indicated that she believes there to be some spiral-ring fragments among the hack-silver from her excavations of the 'Black-Earth' area of Kaupang, but this material has not yet been properly analysed.
33. Graham-Campbell, 'Hoards of Ireland' (n. 20 above), 51.

in Ireland within the period of the second half of the ninth and the first half of the tenth century'.[34] In 1976 one of us even suggested on the basis of this Hiberno-Viking arm-ring fragment, and of the ingots and spiral-ring fragments which were closely paralleled in the Co. Dublin hoard,[35] that the non-numismatic elements in the Croydon hoard might be 'essentially of Hiberno-Viking origin'; it was noted, however, that Croydon was 'an oddity, both on the grounds of its early date and of its location'.[36]

The Croydon hoard is indeed the earliest reliably coin-dated Viking hoard containing non-numismatic silver in not only Britain and Ireland, but also Norway and Denmark;[37] it follows therefore that it is of critical importance in any consideration of the origins of the Hiberno-Viking arm-ring type – a matter which has so far received no discussion in print, for the relevant part of the 1976 paper was concerned only with the definition, distribution, and chronology of the type.[38] It has recently become apparent that the seemingly anomalous nature of the Croydon hoard may hold the key to the solution of this problem. This emerges only when it is appreciated that, in terms of its non-numismatic contents, the Croydon hoard must be seen as a purely *Danish* (rather than a Hiberno-Viking) outlier for reasons which may now be advanced, although they cannot yet be developed in detail.

The first point needing to be brought into consideration is that which has already been introduced above concerning the route by which spiral-ring fragments are likely to have reached Britain and Ireland from the Baltic. The distribution of such rings and fragments in Scandinavia suggests that it is most probable that these passed through Denmark to reach eastern England and also Ireland (and thence, it would seem, north-western England and the Hebrides, for both the Cuerdale and Storr Rock hoards have Hiberno-Viking elements in their hack-silver).[39] The Croydon hoard thus raises the possibility that the origins of the Hiberno-Viking arm-ring type in Ireland (where both its form and ornament are without precedent) might be of Danish inspiration, with the prototypes having travelled the same route as the spiral-ring fragments. What evidence is there then in ninth-century Denmark for the use of arm-rings with the characteristic form of the Hiberno-Viking type, as well as for the use of its characteristic style of ornament?

Six rings and fragments found in four Danish hoards represent a variation on the spiral-ring type by having an expanded band-shaped central part, either unornamen-

34. *Ibid.*, 52.
35. *Idem.*
36. *Ibid.*, 51–2.
37. It is probable, however, that the mixed hoard (including a spiral-ring fragment) from Sønder Kirkeby, Falster, is contemporary with the Croydon hoard, despite Munksgaard's preference for putting its deposition date at c.900, for the two youngest of its 97 Persian and Arabic coins were minted in 839 and 846, whilst all the others were minted in or before 812; the Rantrum (Schleswig) hoard is also coin-dated to the second half of the ninth century, by five Arabic coins of which the youngest is from 848/9, and contains a spiral-ring in the form of a neck-ring (Munksgaard, 'Skattefundet fra Duesminde', 105).
38. Graham-Campbell, 'Hoards of Ireland', 51–3.
39. *Ibid.*, 53–4 (Cuerdale); Graham-Campbell, 'Hoards from Scotland', 119 (Storr Rock).

ted or stamped with transverse grooves; in one instance some of the grooves contain raised pellets.[40] Of even greater interest in connection with the ornament of the Hiberno-Viking arm-rings is the use of diagonal crosses interspersed amongst the vertical grooves on two of the rings (one in the form of a neck-ring) in the Illebølle hoard from Langeland.[41] Given that this particular variant of the spiral-rings has *only* been found in Denmark, it is most probable that it is of Danish manufacture.

Two of the Danish hoards with fragments of standard spiral-rings (from Nørre Alslev and Kærbyholm) also contain two penannular broad-band arm-rings each, ornamented with stamped vertical grooves and a diagonal cross at the expanded centre; a similar arm-ring was found in the Hørdum hoard.[42] The Norwegian hoard from Torvik, mentioned above, consists of the same combination of spiral-ring fragments and two such arm-rings.[43] These associations of spiral-rings and band-shaped arm-rings led Munksgaard to date the latter to the ninth century in Denmark and it should be noted that the Sønder Kirkeby coin hoard (second half of the ninth century)[44] contains an undecorated example of the same form of band-shaped penannular arm-ring with its expanded central portion.[45]

The five classic examples of 'Hiberno-Viking' type arm-rings found in Denmark might very well be of Danish manufacture given the use of related ornament on the band-shaped parts of the apparently Danish variant of the spiral-rings. If so, it is equally possible that the relevant Croydon fragment is of Danish workmanship, for the Danish dating evidence is such that it could well have been made there and still have reached England at the same time as the spiral-ring fragments with which it was found. It is therefore suggested that the origins of the Hiberno-Viking arm-ring type, as developed in Ireland, are to be attributed to ninth-century Danish influence.[46] Detailed comparisons between the Danish and insular spiral-ring and arm-ring material are needed before this interpretation of the evidence can be considered as more than a working hypothesis – but, with the Croydon hoard as the link in the argument, it is one that would have proved both acceptable and of interest to Michael Dolley.[47]

THE COINS AND THE CIRCUMSTANCES OF THEIR BURIAL

It is convenient to consider first those coins that are unusual in an English context. The seven Frankish deniers come into this category, since Carolingian coins seem to

40. Munksgaard, 'To skattefund', 58–9.
41. R. Skovmand, 'De danske skattefund fra vikingetid og den ældste middelalder indtil omkring 1150', *Aarbøger for Nordisk Oldkyndighed og Historie* 1942, 1–275, at 33–4, fig. 4.
42. Munksgaard, 'To skattefund', 59–61, figs. 4–5; Skovmand, *op. cit.*, 29–30, fig. 2.
43. *Loc. cit.* in n. 28 above.
44. See n.37 above for the dating evidence.
45. Munksgaard, 'To skattefund', 59–60, where other related examples of such penannular arm-rings are listed.
46. See now the M.A. thesis of J. Sheehan, 'Viking Age silver arm-rings from Ireland' (University College Galway, 1985); publication forthcoming.
47. The ideas contained in this joint paper were outlined to Michael Dolley in conversation at the 1981 Oxford Symposium when he greeted them with characteristic enthusiasm.

have been excluded from currency in southern and eastern England from the inception of the broad penny coinage under Offa.[48] The Croydon deniers are therefore a testimony not to Anglo-Frankish trade, but rather to the links between Viking activity on the Continent and in England. We cannot know whether they were brought from Denmark, where some 30 ninth-century Frankish coins have been discovered,[49] or directly from the Frankish empire. None of them can be dated later than the mid-860s, a time when a distinct lull in Viking raiding in the Frankish lands began. This lull has prompted the suggestion that many of the Vikings on the Continent then joined the 'great army' (*micel here*) which devasted, terrorized, and ultimately conquered much of England between the autumn of 865 and the late 870s. Such men are likely to have brought Frankish coins of the *Christiana Religio* issue to England with them.

The three Kufic dirhams, known only from Corbet Anderson's drawings, are also likely to have been brought by a Danish Viking, for no coins of the Abbasid caliphs are found in English deposits earlier than Croydon. By contrast well over 100 ninth-century dirhams have been found in Denmark, almost all from the first half of the century – like the Croydon three. It is, however, unlikely that they were all imported into Denmark in the ninth century; as in Norway, many will only have arrived with the main influx of Kufic coins into Scandinavia in the very last years of the ninth and in the first half of the tenth centuries.[50] The relatively well-dated Croydon hoard is therefore a valuable confirmation of the evidence for the spread of Kufic dirhams to be found in Danish hoards, whose ninth-century date, having fewer controls, is inevitably far less securely established. Anderson's drawings also show that one of the Croydon dirhams was mutilated around the edge in a manner typical of Kufic coins from Scandinavian finds – probably to test that it was indeed of silver; apparently it had circulated for a time outside the Moslem world, presumably in Viking hands. Thus both the Carolingian and the Kufic coins in the Croydon hoard agree with the evidence of the hack-silver and the ingots in demonstrating that this is

48. R. H. M. Dolley and K. F. Morrison, 'Finds of Carolingian coins from Great Britain and Ireland', *BNJ 32* (1963), 75–87, at 86–7.
49. K. Randsborg, *The Viking Age in Denmark* (1980), 152. M. Blackburn has kindly pointed out to us that the single Croydon denier now extant (R. H. M. Dolley and K. F. Morrison, *Carolingian Coins in the British Museum* (1966), no. 72) has two fine parallel scratches on the reverse face, which may be Viking test-marks.
50. Randsborg, *op. cit.*, 152; for the absence of dirhams until the 890s in Norway, see K. Skaare, *Coins and Coinage in Viking-Age Norway* (Oslo, 1976), 47–53; on the source and chronology of the spread of dirhams, see T. S. Noonan, 'Pre-970 dirham hoards from Estonia and Latvia', *J. Baltic Studies 8* (1977), 238–59, 312–23, 9 (1978), 7–19, 99–115, and *idem*, 'Ninth-century dirham hoards from European Russia', in *Viking-Age Coinage in the Northern Lands*, ed. M. A. S. Blackburn and D. M. Metcalf (BAR Internat. Ser. 122, 1981), 47–118, and the general discussion in P. H. Sawyer, *Kings and Vikings* (1982), 36, 123–5. There is no adequate analysis of dirham hoards in Denmark; but see Skovmand, 'De danske Skattefund', 14–17, 28–43, and also B. Hårdh, *Wikingerzeitliche Depotfunde aus Sudschweden* (Lund, 1976), 31ff.

a 'Viking' hoard, and more specifically a hoard with Danish rather than Norse connections.

As Blunt and Dolley saw, however, it is the English coins in the hoard that allow its deposition to be dated with some precision. The latest of the East Anglian coins are those of King Edmund, who was martyred on 20 November 869;[51] the Mercian coins are all of King Burgred whose reign was brought to an end in 874 when he was driven out of his kingdom by the Danes and forced to retire to Rome; the latest West Saxon coins are the 31 pennies of King Alfred's *Lunette* type, which belong to the opening three or four years of his reign (871–874×5).[52] The absence from the hoard not only of any of the Viking imitative issues produced in the Danelaw, but also of any coins of the Mercian king, Ceolwulf II (874–879×80), and of any of Alfred's '*Ceolwulf*' type or of his subsequent issues suggests that this assemblage of coins ceased to receive new additions by the end of 874, or within a few months of it. Hence Dolley's date of c.875 for the deposit of the Croydon hoard, which Hugh Pagan has refined as 'probably in the winter of 872–3' on the basis of his chronology of the *Lunette* issues and because of the number of Alfred pennies whose moneyers had not minted for Æthelred I.[53] The certain *terminus post quem* is the accession of Alfred in April 871.

If we consider when, in the period from 871 to 875, a Viking silver hoard might have been buried at Croydon (that is, deep within Alfred's kingdom), there is only one obvious answer – namely during the year from the autumn of 871 until autumn 872, when the 'great army' was based at London. It is always dangerous to suggest a precise historical context for an archaeological find, particularly one that is incompletely recorded. But Dolley taught us how clearly the chronological and geographical pattern of British and Irish silver hoards reflects the known pattern of Viking activities in the ninth and tenth centuries.[54] It must therefore be conceded that many individual hoards must have been directly related to the movements of the major Viking armies. Moreover, the Anglo-Saxon Chronicle provides a nearly contemporary and remarkably detailed account of the movements of these armies in the 870s, particularly in so far as they affected Alfred's kingdom.[55] Whilst we cannot rule out the possibility that there were minor detachments and independent groups of Vikings of whose activities we know nothing, it is clear that the 'great army' was the focus of the Viking effort in England between its arrival in the autumn of 865 and the

51. D. Whitelock, 'Fact and fiction in the legend of St Eadmund', *Procs. Suffolk Inst. Archaeol. 31* (1969), 217–33.
52. R. H. M. Dolley and C. E. Blunt, 'The chronology of the coins of Ælfred the Great 871–99', in *AS Coins*, 78–80.
53. H. Pagan, 'Coinage in the age of Burgred', *BNJ 34* (1965), 14; *idem*, 'The Gainford hoard', *BNJ 35* (1966), 190–1. Mr Pagan has kindly informed us that of the 19 Alfred moneyers represented in Croydon, no less than 12 are not known to have worked for Æthelred. None of the surviving English coins from Croydon in the British Museum or in Corpus Christi College, Cambridge, have any sign of pecking or scratching.
54. Dolley, *Hiberno-Norse Coins* (n. 4 above), 15–40.
55. *The Anglo-Saxon Chronicle*, trans. D. Whitelock, D. C. Douglas, and S. I. Tucker (1965); and for the OE text: *Two of the Saxon Chronicles Parallel*, ed. C. Plummer and J. Earle (2 vols., 1892 and 1895).

settlement of its last section in 880. This army was indeed the main threat to the prosperity and the continued existence of the English kingdoms. In 869–70 it had overrun East Anglia and martyred King Edmund, who had dared to resist rather than pay tribute. In 870–1 it had raided in Berkshire, Hampshire, and Wiltshire, and despite the prolonged resistance of the West Saxons, King Alfred had eventually had to 'make peace' with the army, that is, pay them to move away. In the following year the 'great army' moved to London, and the Mercian king, Burgred, in his turn made peace on terms that seem to have involved collecting 'an immense tribute' of silver from Mercian lords very far distant from London in order to buy off the Danes.[56] It would therefore be no surprise had an individual member of the 'great army' been able to acquire substantial numbers of East Anglian, West Saxon, and Mercian pennies by the year 872 as a supplement to whatever hack-silver, ingots, and Carolingian and Kufic coins he had brought from Denmark with him.

After 872, however, it is very difficult to suggest a context to fit the Croydon hoard. For in the autumn of that year the army moved north and spent successive years in Lindsey (based at Torksey) and in Mercia (Repton). Then in the autumn of 874 the army divided into two separate forces, one going to Northumbria (by the Tyne), the other to East Anglia (Cambridge). It is true that in the autumn of 875 the half from Cambridge did return to Wessex and establish its camp at Wareham (Dorset) for a year, and thereafter at Exeter in 876–7. But that is surely both too late and too distant from Surrey to account for the content and the location of the Croydon hoard. So far as the known movements of Viking armies are concerned, the year 871–2 would seem very much the likeliest time for the hoard's deposition; the numismatic evidence might suggest that it was buried towards the end of that year, in summer of autumn 872.

Having established a possible date, can we learn anything further of the circumstances of the deposit? Here we run into the immediate difficulty that we do not know the precise spot where the Croydon hoard had been buried. The accounts of Rev. H. Christmas and of J. Corbet Anderson do, however, indicate that it was discovered during the construction of the railway line from West Croydon to Balham, and specifically between Thornton Heath and Selhurst stations (fig. 6.2).[57]

56. Bishop Werferth of Worcester leased land at Nuthurst in 872 to a king's thegn in return for a payment of 20 mancuses of gold *pro inmenso tributo barbarorum eodem anno quo pagani sedebant in Lundonia*. See W. de Gray Birch, *Cartularium Saxonicum* (3 vols., 1885–99), no. 533; translated in D. Whitelock, *EHD* I, *500–1042* (2nd edn, 1979), no. 94.
57. Corbet Anderson, *op. cit.* (n.8 above), 115; Christmas, *op. cit.* (n.5 above), 302; Blunt and Dolley, *op. cit.* (n.1 above), 222–3. Anderson and Christmas both agree that the hoard was found 'at White Horse' in the course of constructing, or ballasting, the railway line 'near Collier's Water Lane'. Some idea of the extent of the manor of Whitehorse (alias *Benchesham*) may be gained from the modern streets (Whitehorse Road, Whitehorse Lane, Bensham Lane, and Bensham Manor Road) named after it, and the site of the manor-house can be identified (fig. 6.2) from the first edition of the Ordnance Survey 1″ map. Collier's Water Lane is today the name of a short street from the Brighton Road (A 23) to Brigstock Road, but

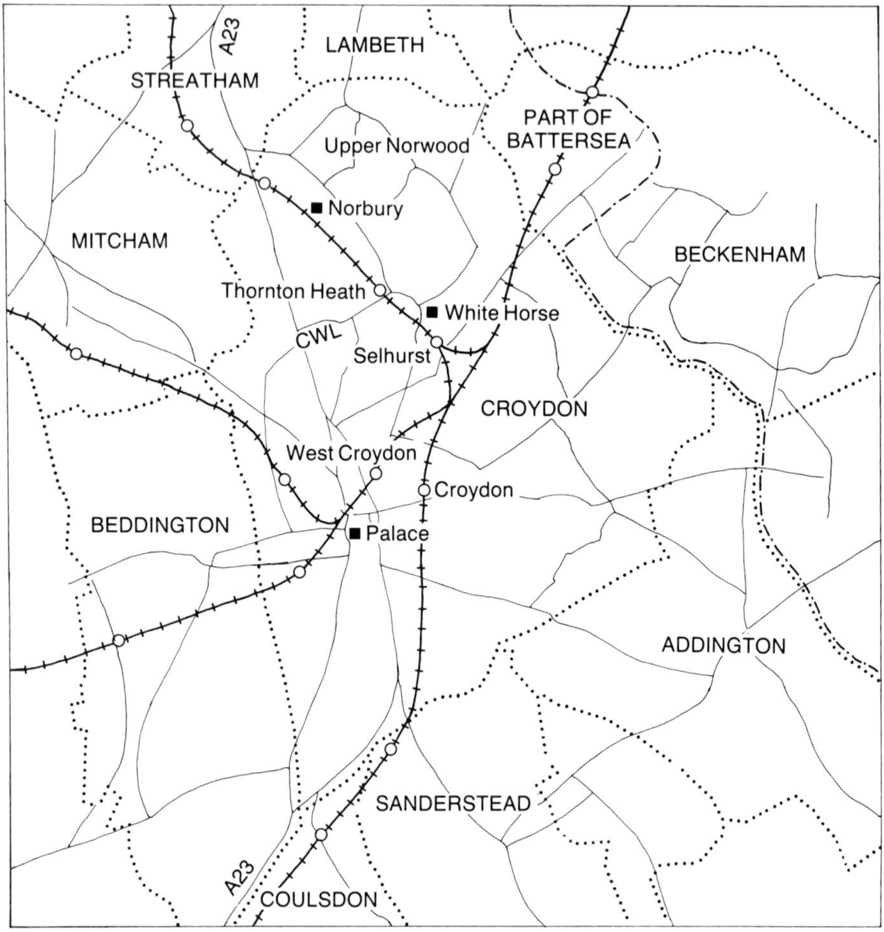

railway line and station
parish boundary of c.1840
Kent-Surrey boundary
roads
CWL Collier's Water Lane
site of medieval manor

0 5 km

Fig. 6.2 The vicinity of the Croydon hoard.

It was therefore within the parish of Croydon, whose nineteenth-century boundaries[58] are likely to have preserved the bounds of the huge medieval manor of Croydon, which was held until the Reformation by the archbishops of Canterbury. Croydon was one of a series of great archiepiscopal estates that lay within easy reach of London. In 1066 it was assessed at 80 hides and was 'worth' £12 per annum.[59] At least from the twelfth century it was also the site of one of the principal archiepiscopal residences or 'palaces'; indeed there may have already been some sort of hall or residence there in the ninth century, for a small assemblage of English pennies (likely to have been buried between c.855 and 860) was recovered in the course of building work on the site of the palace in or shortly before 1907.[60] Known as the 'Croydon Palace hoard' to distinguish it from the subject of this paper, it provides a precious link between the seigneurial *caput* of the manor of Croydon and the era of the Viking raids of the mid-ninth century. We do not know when the archbishops of Canterbury first acquired their manor at Croydon, but we do have evidence that it had belonged to Archbishop Æthelred (870–88). For the cartularies of Christ Church Canterbury have preserved a remarkable vernacular agreement that this archbishop reached with the leading local nobleman – Ealdorman Ælfred of Surrey:[61] Archbishop Æthelred ceded the estate at Croydon to the ealdorman for life, and in return Ealdorman Ælfred granted his own estate of Chartham (Kent) to the community at Christ Church – a bequest, however, that was only to take effect after Ælfred's death. This was clearly a splendid arrangement for the ealdorman. He received the proceeds of the great estate at Croydon at no cost to himself at all. His heirs may well have been less well pleased to find that Chartham was no longer part of their inheritance without any recompense. But in fact we know that Ælfred had no legitimate son to provide for.[62] Moreover, he particularly arranged that after his death Chartham should be held from the archbishop and community for a rent of food or money either by his child (*bearne*) – apparently an illegitimate daughter named Herewyn – or by one of his more distant male kinsmen.

It is at first sight more difficult to understand why the archbishop was willing to forego his revenues from Croydon for the rest of Ælfred's life in return for the expectation of rents from Chartham. In Domesday Book the manor of Chartham is assessed at only four 'sulungs', and since by that time sulungs and hides were

must earlier have also applied to the eastern two-thirds of Brigstock Road, for early maps identify 'Collier's Water' as the site of the present Thornton Heath station. The hoard is therefore likely to have been deposited at approximately TQ 324683.

58. Fig. 6.2 shows the parish boundaries as surveyed in the Tithe Awards of the 1840s and conveniently recorded on the Ordnance Survey's *Index to the Tithe Survey* (1878).
59. *D.B.* I.30b (Croydon), I.5 (Chartham).
60. Thompson, *Inventory*, no. 110; R. H. M. Dolley and K. Skaare, 'The coinage of Æthelwulf, King of the West Saxons, 839–58', in *AS Coins*, 65.
61. F. E. Harmer, *Select English Historical Documents of the 9th and 10th Centuries* (1914), no. VIII; for the manuscripts, see P. H. Sawyer, *Anglo-Saxon Charters: an Annotated List and Bibliography* (1968), no. 1202.
62. See the comments of D. Whitelock on Ælfred's will (Harmer, *Select Documents*, no. IX) in *EHD* I, no. 97.

normally equated for assessment purposes, it might seem that Chartham was a very much smaller and less valuable estate than the 80 hides of Croydon. But in reality the two estates had closely comparable resources. The Domesday survey lists 73 'villeins' and 'bordars' at Croydon, 75 'villeins' and 'cottars' at Chartham; there were twice as many ploughs at Croydon, but this was balanced by Chartham's much greater woodland and its five mills to Croydon's one; both estates were said to be worth £12 in 1066.[63] Archbishop Æthelred therefore seems to have secured the bequest of a valuable estate for his church at the cost of the temporary cession of a comparable estate from his own properties. We cannot tell how long he expected Ælfred to live, or whether his prime concern was rather to cement good relations with a powerful noble who, having no lawful male offspring, could afford to be generous towards the metropolitan church of Canterbury. Certainly Ælfred was to prove to be one of Canterbury's major benefactors.[64]

Unfortunately we cannot date the archbishop's agreement with the ealdorman over Croydon and Chartham more closely than the limits of Æthelred's pontificate (870 × 888). We therefore cannot tell whether the manor of Croydon was in the ealdorman's or the archbishop's hands in c.872 when the Viking hoard was hidden in the ground. Some Christ Church cartularies attribute the agreement to the year 871;[65] that would certainly be a possible date, indeed a convenient one for our purposes. But the dates that the cartularies allocate to undated texts are sometimes highly unreliable, and there must be a suspicion that 871 has been chosen as the first year of the reign of *King* Alfred, on the mistaken assumption that the Ælfred of the agreement was the West Saxon king. Be that as it may, it may help our understanding of how the Croydon hoard could have come to be buried on such an important estate to note that Ealdorman Ælfred is known to have had some contact with the Vikings. One of the most important benefactions that he and his wife, Werburg, made to Christ Church was their gift of a magnificent eighth-century illuminated gospel-book, the so-called 'Golden Gospels' (*Codex Aureus*) now in the Royal Library at Stockholm.[66] For the record of their gift, entered on the first page of the gospel of St Matthew by a contemporary Christ Church scribe, states that Ælfred and Werburg had bought the gospel-book from the 'army of heathens' (*æt hæÞnum herge*) with their pure gold, so that it might not remain any longer in heathen hands but rather be used daily for God's praise by the community at Christ Church. We cannot, of course, be sure which Viking army Ælfred had negotiated with, particularly since he may have become ealdorman as early as 853.[67] The *Codex Aureus* is the product of a Kentish scriptorium and is likely to have belonged to one of

63. *D.B.* I.5, 30b.
64. N. P. Brooks, *The Early History of the Church of Canterbury* (1983), 151–2.
65. Canterbury, Cathedral Lib., Reg. A, f.141; Reg. E, f.42v.
66. Edited in Harmer, *op. cit.*, no. IX, from Stockholm, Kungl. Bibliotek, *Codex Aureus*, f.11. This and other leaves from the manuscript are reproduced and discussed in C. Nordenfalk, *Celtic and Anglo-Saxon Painting* (1977), pls. 33–8.
67. Ealdorman Huda of Surrey died in 853 (Anglo-Saxon Chronicle, *s.a.*). It is uncertain whether Ælfred's authority as ealdorman extended to Kent as well.

the monasteries founded by the kings of Kent. With purple pages and lettering in gold, silver, and white, and with sumptuously illuminated initials, miniatures, and evangelist portraits, the *Codex* must have been the prized possession of whatever church it originally belonged to. But most of the Kentish monasteries had been built in exposed coastal and island sites that were vulnerable to Viking attack. Danish armies are known to have ravaged Sheppey in 835, Thanet in 853, and to have wintered on Thanet in 850–1 and again in 864–5; this last army, which ravaged 'all eastern Kent', may have been the same force as (or may have contributed towards) the 'great army' of the autumn of 865. Any of these Viking forces could have seized the *Codex Aureus*. The leaders of the 'great army' were certainly accustomed to negotiating with English magnates for the payment of tribute or protection-money; they could therefore have had the opportunity to negotiate with Ælfred to sell him the Gospel-book.

It is a curious coincidence that a 'Viking' hoard should have been buried on a property which at much the same time was in the possession of an ealdorman who is independently known to have had dealings with a 'heathen army'. In view of the uncertainties of the dating, both of Ælfred's acquisition of the Croydon estate and of his purchase of the Golden Gospels, there is little point in conjecturing in what way (if at all) these transactions may have been connected with the deposit of the hoard. But if the treasure was still in Viking hands at the time of its burial, the presence of a Viking on this important manor might indicate that the Danes were using the existing English estate organization as the most convenient and effective way of raising food and money for the 'great army'. Certainly the mixture of East Anglian, West Saxon, and Mercian coins in the hoard would not seem to reflect the coinage that was current in the Croydon area, but rather the known movements of the great army in the years from 869 to 872. The absence of Northumbrian coins might therefore have indicated that this particular Viking warrior had not joined the great army until after the years spent in the northern kingdom in 866–7 and 868–9. But unfortunately the evidence of the hoards shows that the Northumbrian copper 'stycas' circulated quite independently of the silver coinage of Midland and southern England,[68] and they would also have been very much less attractive than silver to treasure-seeking Vikings. No argument can therefore be based upon the lack of Northumbrian coins in the Croydon hoard. We must therefore be content with the simple conclusion that the hoard probably represents the accumulated treasure of a member of the great army, hidden in 872, within the boundaries of a manor belonging either to the Archbishop of Canterbury or, more probably, to the ealdorman of Surrey.

Even that limited conclusion has important implications for our understanding of other ninth-century British hoards. Croydon is the earliest to contain ingots, hack-silver, and Kufic coins. With the possible exception of the small hoard from Talnotrie (Kirkcudbrightshire),[69] which had a single dirham, it is the only clearly

68. Dolley, *Hiberno-Norse Coins*, 22–3.
69. Thompson, *Inventory*, no. 349; R. B. K. Stevenson, *National Museum of Antiquities of Scotland: Anglo-Saxon Pennies* (*SCBI* 6, 1966), xii-xiii; Graham-Campbell, 'Hoards from Scotland', 118.

identifiable 'Viking' hoard of the ninth century. But whilst ingots, hack-silver, and dirhams are certainly convenient criteria, it may be dangerous to suppose that we can distinguish clearly between Viking and English hoards. There may have been members of Viking armies who did not bring any silver to England with them and whose treasure might therefore consist entirely of English coins and of English silver ornaments. How, for example, can we determine whether the Gainford or Dunsforth hoards belonged to Vikings or to Englishmen? Gainford had a single penny of Burgred and 3 of Alfred, all of the *Lunette* type; whilst Dunsforth had 14 pennies of the same type, 6 of Burgred, 2 of Æthelred I of Wessex, and 6 of Alfred.[70] Their locations in Durham and Yorkshire respectively are surprising for hoards of pennies rather than of 'stycas', and may be the sole clues that these are Viking hoards, perhaps to be associated with Halfdan's return to Northumbria with half of the great army in the autumn of 874 or with the settlement of the kingdom 'of York' a year later. Even more problematic is the Gravesend (Kent) hoard.[71] With 428 Mercian pennies (all but one of Burgred), 61 of Wessex (the latest a single penny of Alfred's *Lunette* type), and 49 of East Anglia (44 of King Edmund), together with a single denier of Louis the Pious, it has a range that is in some ways very similar to Croydon. Does the single Carolingian coin indicate that this too was a Viking hoard? Does the presence of a silver cross with the coins rather indicate that the hoarder was Christian and English? Or had a semi-pagan Viking acquired it as a talisman or for resale? It is easier to ask such questions than to answer them.

Whether it be deemed a Viking or an English treasure, the contents of the Gravesend hoard suggest that like Croydon it had been deposited during the year 871–2 when the great army was at London. If indeed the hoard originally only had the one penny of Alfred, it may have been marginally earlier than Croydon and therefore have been buried in the autumn of 871 when the army first entered London. Too little is known of the 'Saxon coins' discovered at Barking in 1724 to allow us to attribute their deposit to the same year, for the modern dating of 'c.870' rests upon the single identifiable coin – of Burgred of Mercia.[72] But two other hoards may possibly also belong to the great army's year at London, namely the Waterloo Bridge[73] and Westminster Bridge[74] hoards. Here we seem to meet a different balance of coins, in which Mercian pennies predominate to the exclusion of almost all others. Such hoards may represent the wealth of English inhabitants of London, which at that time was still a Mercian city. Thus Waterloo had 96 Burgred pennies, 1 West Saxon coin of Æthelred I, and perhaps another of Alfred's *Lunette* type. The

70. Gainford: Thompson, *Inventory*, no. 167 and Pagan, 'Gainford hoard', 190–1. Dunsforth: Thompson, *Inventory*, no. 146, and Blunt and Dolley, *op. cit.* 221.
71. Thompson, *Inventory*, no. 176; Blunt and Dolley, *op. cit.*, 221; D. M. Wilson, *Anglo-Saxon Ornamental Metalwork 700–1100 in the British Museum* (1964), 134–5.
72. D. M. Metcalf, '18th-century finds of medieval coins from the records of the Society of Antiquaries', *NC*[6] *18* (1958), 76; Dolley, *Hiberno-Norse Coins*, 49, no. 21.
73. Thompson, *Inventory*, no. 256; Blunt and Dolley, *op. cit.*, 221–2; Dolley, *Hiberno-Norse Coins*, 49, no. 47.
74. Mr Pagan kindly drew our attention to this virtually unpublished hoard. See below, Blackburn and Pagan, no. 68.

Burgred coins compare closely with those from Gravesend, which may indicate that this too was a hoard buried in the autumn of 871. The Westminster Bridge hoard of c.1895 is only known to have contained Burgred pennies, but whilst the handful of coins known today might suggest a date close to that of Croydon, it is too poorly recorded to allow any interpretation of its contents to be more than a conjecture.

We should not be surprised to find that on present evidence, inadequate though it often is, no less than three substantial silver hoards seem likely to belong to the year that the great army was at London – Croydon, Gravesend, and Waterloo Bridge – and that such slight evidence as we have for two others, Westminster Bridge and Barking, would point in the same direction. This does not mean that the Vikings acted with particular brutality or efficiency in that year; rather that the London region was rich in coin in the ninth century and that the chances of accidental discovery have been greater there than elsewhere during the last 200 years because that has been the most intensively developed area of Britain.

Dolley identified 39 hoards as having been buried between c.865 and 879,[75] and it is worth considering how many of these may reflect the known movements of the great army in these years (fig. 6.3). Unfortunately this number has soon to be reduced. We must leave out of the reckoning the 19 hoards of Northumbrian 'stycas', in part because they may reflect Northumbrian civil wars as much as Viking attacks, and in part because of the uncertainties in the dating of the 'styca' series.[76] We must also omit several hoards that are too poorly recorded to permit accurate dating.[77] Inadequacies of record are indeed inherent in the study of hoards, since even in modern finds it is often difficult to be certain that coins that could have been critical for dating have not been removed before any competent numismatist has been able to identify the contents. Few eighteenth- or nineteenth-century finds were as fortunate as Croydon in being studied by active local antiquarians before they had been widely dispersed. The Reading (Berkshire) hoard may serve as a marginal case;[78] though the 11 listed coins – of Burgred, of Edmund of East Anglia, and of Æthelberht (860–5) and Æthelred I of Wessex – may only be a small proportion of those that were originally found, they certainly do nothing to discourage the tempting suggestion that the hoard had been buried in connection with the great army's use of the 'royal vill' of Reading as their annual camp for the year 870–1. But

75. Dolley, *Hiberno-Norse Coins*, 48–9, nos. 12–50.
76. C. S. S. Lyon, 'A reappraisal of the sceatta and styca coinage of Northumbria', *BNJ 28* (1956), 227–47; H. E. Pagan, 'Northumbrian numismatic chronology in the ninth century', *BNJ 38* (1969), 1–15.
77. Of the hoards listed by Dolley, *Hiberno-Norse Coins*, the following have been omitted as too poorly recorded for interpretation: nos. 21 (Barking), 26 (Southampton), 45 (Laxfield), and 48 (Satley). No. 24 (Oakham) must also be excluded as it was misdated; see C. E. Blunt and C. S. S. Lyon, 'The Oakham hoard of 1749 deposited c.980', *NC^7 19* (1979), 111–21. Also omitted is the St Albans hoard (Blackburn and Pagan, below, no. 80), although it has 45 *Lunette* pennies, since the single *London monogram* halfpenny must put the deposit to the late 880s.
78. Thompson, *Inventory*, no. 315; R. J. Sherlock, 'A 19th-century manuscript book on coins', *BNJ 28* (1956), 394–6.

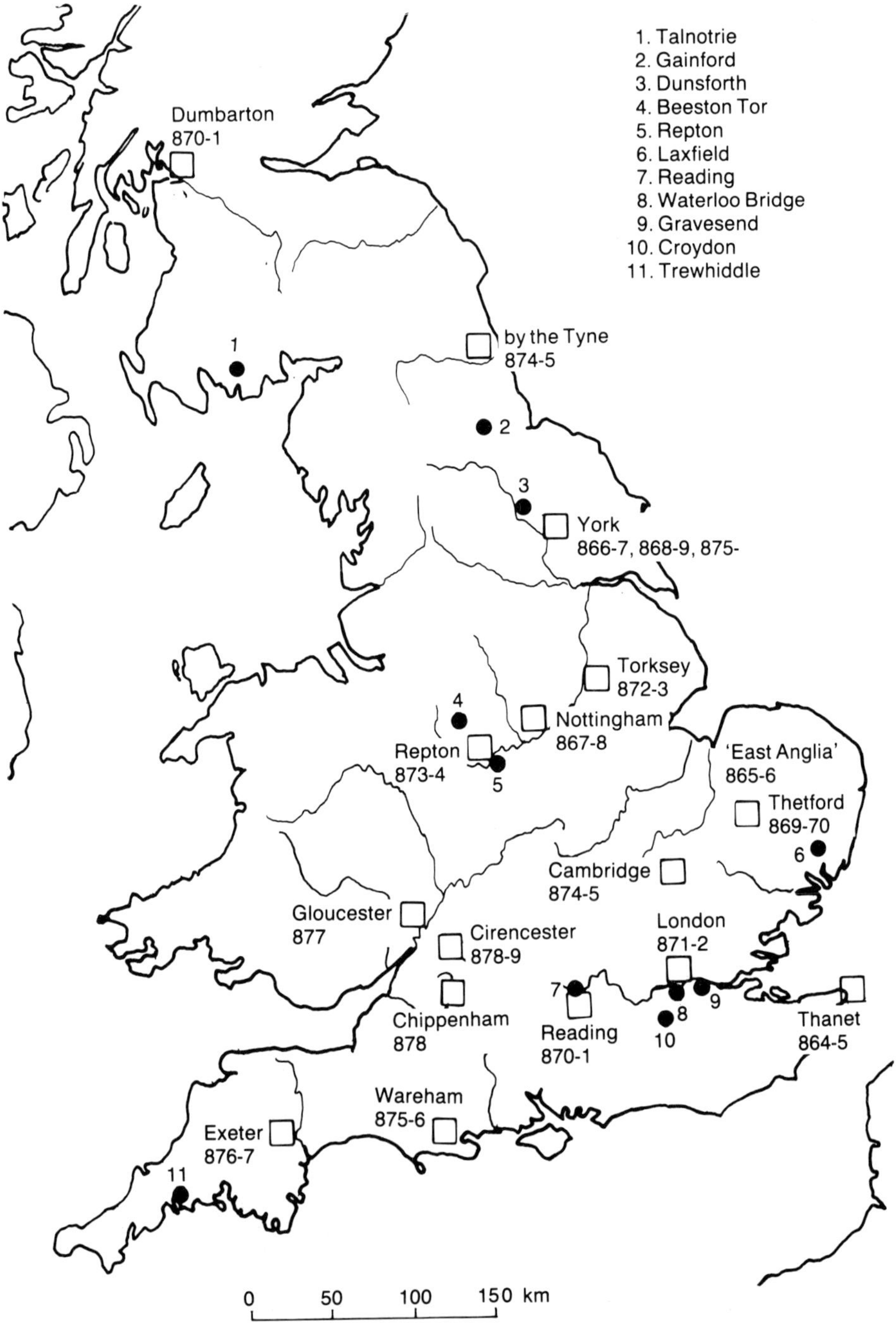

Fig. 6.3 Datable silver-hoards and the movements of the great army, 865–79.

the hypothesis could easily be upset, were a further parcel of coins from the hoard to be identified. Much the same might be said of the hoard from Laxfield (Suffolk);[79] the date of 'c.875' which has been suggested on purely numismatic grounds, rests on too insecure a foundation to allow us to suggest that the hoard was connected with the sojourn of Guthrum's half of the great army in East Anglia in 874–5 when they made their camp at Cambridge.

Small hoards, that is those of less than 20 coins, are almost as dangerous to interpret as those that are poorly recorded; for they too may be unrepresentative of the currency at the time of the deposit. Only when finds are made under conditions of controlled archaeological excavation can their interpretation be well founded. Thus the five coins discovered at Repton in 1982 (2 of Burgred, 1 of Æthelred I, and 2 of Alfred) among the disarticulated bodies of some 250 individuals buried in a room of the earlier 'mausoleum' strongly confirms the association of the dismembered bodies with the great army's year there in 873–4.[80] More typical are the uncertainties that must continue to surround the remarkable hoard from Talnotrie, Kirkcudbrightshire, which uniquely combines 'stycas' (5) with silver pennies (4, all of Burgred) together with a single Carolingian denier and a dirham fragment, alongside insular metalwork and other non-numismatic material including part of a cake of wax. The Burgred coins have been taken to suggest a date of c.870–1,[81] which would allow the hoard to be associated with or a response to the campaigns of Ivar the Boneless amongst the Strathclyde Britons in 870–1 when he captured their stronghold of Dumbarton, but they are surely too few to rule out of consideration Halfdan's ravaging amongst the Picts and Strathclyde Britons in 874–5.[82]

We are left with two substantial hoards: Trewhiddle (Cornwall), and Beeston Tor (Staffordshire). The great Trewhiddle treasure is particularly difficult to date since it is clearly not a currency hoard.[83] It has been reasonably suggested that the coins comprise a number of parcels of different dates, one of which was assembled in the 850s and another in c.868; the estimate of 'c.873–5' for the entire hoard rests upon a single coin of Alfred's *Lunette* issue, but involves the rejection of a much later Alfred penny of the moneyer Franbald (*BMC* xiv) – which seems hazardous in view of the hoard's diverse contents. At all events Trewhiddle is too problematic to be reliably associated with (or separated from) the presence of the great army in Exeter in 876–7. We reach firmer ground with the Beeston Tor hoard, the best recorded large find of

79. Dolley and Morrison, *op. cit.*, 79; Dolley, *Hiberno-Norse Coins*, 49, no. 45.
80. M. Biddle *et al.*, 'A parcel of pennies from a mass-burial associated with the Viking wintering at Repton in 873–4', Chapter 7 below. Small hoards that we have omitted as too small for interpretation are Dolley, *Hiberno-Norse Coins*, 49, nos. 22 (Great Casterton), 23 (Hitchin), 27 (Wandsworth), 44 (Hook Norton), and 46 (Leckhampton).
81. See n.69 above. For the 870–1 dating, see Pagan, 'Gainford hoard', 191b.
82. For Ivar's campaign, see A. P. Smyth, *Scandinavian Kings in the British Isles 850–880* (1979), 154.
83. D. M. Wilson and C. E. Blunt, 'The Trewhiddle hoard', *Archaeologia 98* (1961), 75–122; Wilson, *op. cit.*, 179–91; Dolley, *Hiberno-Norse Coins*, 49, no. 50; Pagan, 'Age of Burgred', 13; C. S. S. Lyon, 'Historical problems of Anglo-Saxon coinage – 2', *BNJ 37* (1968), 235.

all those considered in this paper;[84] there is every reason to think that the 49 known pennies (20 of Burgred, 1 of Archbishop Ceolnoth's *Lunette* issue, 20 of Alfred's *Lunette* type and 8 of earlier West Saxon kings) are all that were ever found. The higher proportion of coins of Alfred, despite the Mercian location, suggests that this is a later hoard than Croydon. But the absence of later Mercian and West Saxon issues provides a *terminus ante quem* of c.875. Willy-nilly we can scarcely avoid concluding that the year 873–4 when the great army was in Mercia and had its base at Repton is the most likely occasion for the deposit of this modest treasure of 49 pennies together with 3 rings (1 of silver, 2 of bronze), 2 silver and niello brooches, and a bronze binding.

It is not likely that any single explanation will serve for all the silver hoards of the 860s and 870s, nor that our sparse records are sufficient to provide a convincing context for them all. We need also to bear in mind not only the unsettled conditions that caused treasure to be hidden in the ground, but also the failure of the hoarder to recover his wealth. But we know that the great army dominated military and political developments in these years, and if we have been right in arguing that the Croydon hoard is characteristically Viking, specifically Danish and datable to c.872, then there seems every reason to accept that it was indeed associated in some way with a Danish soldier of the great army at London in that year. It would also seem that the Danish army's movements gave rise to a significant number of the extant hoards in that and other years (fig. 6.3). Despite the difficulties of handling hoard evidence, which is so often incompletely preserved and recorded, we hope that we have shown that Michael Dolley's pioneering and brilliant insights have provided a base on which historians, archaeologists, and numismatists can and should build. Hoards, indeed, need to be studied in their own right and in all their aspects, not simply from the specialist interests of one particular discipline.

84. Thompson, *Inventory*, no. 40; Wilson, *op. cit.*, 119–22; Dolley, *Hiberno-Norse Coins*, 49, no. 39.

7 Coins of the Anglo-Saxon period from Repton, Derbyshire

Michael Dolley first looked at the medieval coins from the Winchester excavations immediately after the first season in 1961. Every year for the next ten years, latterly in association with Christopher Blunt, he identified and reported on each piece, often commenting by letter or in person on their significance and possible interpretation.[1] His enthusiasm for these discoveries, and his appreciation of their importance, archaeological as well as numismatic, was both an education and an encouragement: the numismatic content of Winchester Studies owes much to his teaching and example.[2] This account of the coins recovered archaeologically from another Anglo-Saxon site is offered as a tribute, perhaps not wholly inappropriate, to a numismatist and a friend who contributed so generously and with such effect to archaeological studies at large.[3]

Martin Biddle

1. A parcel of pennies from a mass-burial associated with the Viking wintering at Repton in 873–4

Martin Biddle, Birthe Kjølbye-Biddle, J. P. Northover, and Hugh Pagan

The Repton mound and the discovery of the coins

On 15 July 1726 Dr Simon Degge[4] recorded in his journal a visit to Repton and the story told to him there by Thomas Walker, a labourer, aged 88, who about

1. Michael Dolley and C. E. Blunt, 'Coins from the Winchester Excavations 1961–1973', *BNJ 47* (1978), 135–8. Their full report will appear in Winchester Studies 8 (see n. 2, below).
2. Martin Biddle (ed.), *Winchester in the Early Middle Ages* (Winchester Studies 1, 1976), 396–422 ('The mint'); Yvonne Harvey *et al.*, *The Winchester Mint and other Medieval Numismatic Studies* (Winchester Studies 8, forthcoming).
3. Warmest thanks are due to Christopher Blunt who has watched over the numismatic interests of the Repton excavations since 1974 and who brought about the collaboration with Hugh Pagan which has made this paper possible.
4. For Simon Degge, M.D., F.R.S., F.S.A. (1694–1729), of Derby, third Director of the Society of Antiquaries and great-grandson of the jurist and antiquary Sir Simon Degge (1612–1703), see Martin Biddle in *AntJ*, forthcoming.

40 years earlier had been 'cutting Hillocks' in a close on the north (*sic*) side of the church:

> near the surface he met with an old Stone Wall, when clearing farther he found it to be a square Enclosure of Fifteen Foot . . . In this he found a Stone Coffin, and with Difficulty removing the Cover, saw a *Skeleton* of a *Humane Body Nine Foot* long, and round it lay *One Hundred* Humane Skeletons, with their Feet pointing to the Stone Coffin. They seem'd to be of the ordinary Size . . . over this Repository grows a Sycamore, planted by the Old Man when he filled in the Earth.[5]

The place was opened again in 1787[6] and briefly explored in 1914 by the antiquary J. C. Cox who 'found that ignorance and folly had entirely destroyed whatever remains there may have been'.[7]

Since 1980 the excavation of a mound in the vicarage garden[8] *west*[9] of St Wystan's church has demonstrated the essential accuracy of Degge's account of Thomas Walker's discovery of c.1686. The mound contains, and in its primary form appears to have been piled over the cut-down remains of, a two-celled masonry building sunk about 0.75 m below the original ground surface. The building is aligned west–east and was entered from the west down a slight ramp and through a narrow doorway in the centre of the west wall. An internal doorway directly opposite leads into a slightly smaller eastern compartment which was found in 1982 to contain the disarticulated remains of at least 249 individuals. The bones were in complete disorder, except for a small group of long bones in the north-east corner which were neatly stacked at right-

5. Simon Degg(e), 'An account of an humane skeleton of an extraordinary size, found in a repository at *Repton* in *Derby-shire* . . .', *Philosophical Trans.* *35* (1727–8), 363–5. Degge's original of this communication is Royal Society, MS. EL. D.2.47 (cf. LBC. 18.340), but his journal has not been found.
6. By the then owner of the close, George Gilbert (c.1756–1831) of Repton: Robert Bigsby, *History of Repton* (1854), 247–8 and 401–2 n. 243, quoting from Gilbert's diary.
7. Only recorded in Alec Macdonald, *A Short History of Repton* (1929), 19. Cox's trench, 34½ft long, but only 15ins wide, was rediscovered during the present excavations (Feature 911).
8. The excavation is part of a project directed by the present writers (M.B. and B.K.B.) and Dr H. M. Taylor to investigate the archaeology and architecture of St Wystan's church, the Anglo-Saxon monastery, and the Viking winter camp of 873–4. The work has been supported by The Society of Antiquaries, The British Academy, The Avenue Trust, The Centre for Field Research ('Earthwatch'), the B.B.C., *The Observer*, J. C. Bamford Ltd, and by Mr Roger Boissier. For permission to excavate in the vicarage garden, we are greatly indebted to the Rev. and Mrs Michael David (1980–1), the Parochial Church Council (1982), and now to the Rev. and Mrs Julian Barker (1983–). Mr Barker has very generously presented the coins and other finds from the mass-burial to the Derby Museum.
9. Degge's reference to the *north* side of the church is an error. The original sycamore planted by Walker c.1686 survived to guide Gilbert's work in 1787 and the site has never been forgotten.

angles to the end wall in typical charnel-house fashion. Fallen stucco below the bones showed that the building was already in decay when the bones were placed there.

An iron axe of early medieval type, a large seax, a series of smaller knives, and other iron objects were found among the bones; together with several fragmentary pieces of precious metalwork, and the five coins which are the subject of this paper.

Preliminary identification of the coins indicated, as Mr Hugh Pagan's detailed consideration here has confirmed, that their deposit should be dated to the years immediately after 871. And this in turn suggested that the great deposit of human remains with which the coins were found was in some way connected with the wintering of the Viking Great Army at Repton in 873–4, and with the overthrow of the Mercian kingdom. These events are succinctly set out in the annal for 874 in the Anglo-Saxon Chronicle:

> In this year the army went from Lindsey to Repton and took up winter quarters there, and drove King Burgred across the sea . . . And they conquered all that land . . . And the same year they gave the kingdom of the Mercians to be held by Ceolwulf, a foolish king's thegn; and he swore oaths to them and gave hostages . . .[10]

The nature of the burial deposit in the Repton mound, and its precise relationship to the events of 873–4, will only be known (if at all) when the excavation has been completed, probably in 1986, and when the scientific examination of the human remains and the associated animal bones, now in progress, has been finished. But it is already clear that in one respect at least there appears to be a discrepancy between Walker's observation and the results of the latest excavation, for there is no sign of a central burial in a stone coffin. Walker also recorded that the feet of the hundred skeletons round the coffin were pointing towards it, while the bones found recently were in total disorder and could not be said to be pointing in any one direction.

The excavation of 1983 showed, however, that Walker had robbed much of the stone from the walls surrounding the burial deposit before filling in the site, and furthermore that he had first thoroughly turned over the bones, leaving only the small pile of regularly stacked long-bones undisturbed in the north-east corner of the room. It seems reasonable to conclude that the long-bones were originally stacked all around the walls in this manner and that therefore, to an untrained observer, the skeletons (actually the disarticulated but tidily stacked leg and arm bones) would appear to be lying 'with their Feet pointing to the Stone Coffin', if such a coffin had originally lain in the centre of the room.

No trace of a coffin was found either recently or in 1787. Perhaps there never was a *monolithic* stone coffin, the weight of which might have left a mark in the floor, and the breakage of which for removal would probably have left stone chips, none of

10. C. Plummer, *Two of the Saxon Chronicles Parallel* (1892), I, 72–3, *s.a.* 874; translated in Dorothy Whitelock (ed.), *The Anglo-Saxon Chronicle* (1961), 48, *s.a.* 874. In this part of the Chronicle, the annals begin in the autumn of the previous year, so that '874' begins in autumn 873 by our reckoning. Thus, the Viking army went to Repton in the autumn of 873 and left, as recorded in the annal for 875, in the autumn of 874.

which was found. But it is entirely possible that Walker saw a coffin the sides of which were formed of a series of upright stone slabs, on which rested the cover, presumably of stone, which he removed 'with Difficulty'. Such 'cist' graves are a common form of early burial. They usually have no stone floor and once dismantled leave no trace behind. Their slabs are small enough to be lifted without breaking, and Walker could have removed them as part of his search for reusable stone, as seen in his robbing of the walls.

Walker's circumstantial account as recorded by Degge includes names and other details which can be verified and which, like his 'archaeological' observations, stand up to scrutiny. He seems to have had considerable curiosity and a good memory, and Degge appears to have been a careful recorder. There are good grounds therefore for suggesting that the east room of the building in the Repton mound did originally contain a central burial in a stone cist, covered with a stone slab or slabs, and surrounded by the bones of at least 249 individuals stacked in tidy piles along the walls, charnel-fashion. The skulls and other bones were probably placed on top of the long-bone stacks.

Many problems remain. The supposed central burial may be primary and the mass deposit secondary, the two may be contemporary, or the central burial may have been placed in a room already partly filled with stacked bones. The mass deposit itself may be the result of long accretion, as bones were disturbed elsewhere (for example, in digging new graves in the monastic cemetery) and collected here, or may reflect a single event either prosaic, such as the clearance of a cemetery or pre-existing charnel-house, or martial, such as a massacre or a battle. Characterization of the population represented and studies of the presence or absence of individual bones and their condition will help to reduce these possibilities, while the circumstances of the deposit as a whole should be clarified by the completion of the excavation of the building, the mound, and its periphery.

The coins, however, provide a date of remarkable precision and suggest that at least one element in this complex may be related to the events at Repton in 873–4. Because the stone coffin seen by Walker has disappeared, and the bones as a whole have been so thoroughly disturbed, we do not know whether the coins were originally separate inclusions among the stacked bones, or whether they were a group deposited in the coffin with the central burial. The major iron objects – the axe and the large seax – the fragments of precious metalwork, and the coins could all have been deposited with the central burial. If this were so, that burial was most likely Viking, since the deposition of grave goods does not seem to have been a feature of Anglo-Saxon burial practice by this date. There are other features of the site which strongly support a Viking interpretation, but it is too early to say what this might imply about the nature and circumstances of deposition of the mass burial around the now vanished central coffin.

During the 1985 season a second parcel of five three-line pennies was discovered in another part of the excavation, in a grave cut down against (and hence later than) the foundations of the east wall of the north porticus of St Wystan's church. These coins (two of Burgred: *BMC* type a, moneyers Cenred and Eadulf; and three of Alfred: *BMC* type 1a, moneyer Biarnwulf, *BMC* type 1b, moneyer Dudda, and *BMC* type

1c, moneyer Diarelm) have been examined by Mr Hugh Pagan and will be published by him in *BNJ* 56 (1986). In Mr Pagan's view the coins could have been deposited between 873 and (say) 876, possibly in the latter part of this period. They are thus virtually contemporary with, and possibly slightly later than, the deposit of the five pennies in the mound.

This second group of five pennies, deposited together with a gold ring beside the head in Grave 529, lying flat on the floor of the grave and originally within the coffin, can only be a deliberate burial deposit. Their discovery provides an immediate parallel for the suggestion made above (written before the 1985 find) that the five pennies from the mound were originally deposited in the coffin with the now vanished central grave.

M.B., B.K-B.

The coins from the mass-burial

A detailed consideration of the five coins concerned both supports the preliminary conclusion of the excavators that the deposit is to be associated with the wintering of the Viking Great Army at Repton in 873–4, and does so in a thoroughly convincing way. It will be convenient to consider each coin in turn, for only one of them is wholly straightforward and they date from rather an obscure period in numismatic history.

The first coin (fig. 7.1:1) may be described as follows:

Obv. BVRGR[Bust r.
Rev. +DYDDA/[MON]/ETA in three lines, the words [MON] and ETA in whole lunettes. 0.64g (half coin). Die-axis 270°. Find no. 3723.

Fig. 7.1 1–5 Pennies from a mass-burial of 873–4.

This is, apparently, the cut half of a coin struck for Burgred of Mercia (852–873/4) by the moneyer Dudda. It is of *BMC* type *a*, the commonest type of the reign, and of a stylistic grouping within the type that can probably be assigned to the late 860s; there were two directly comparable coins, *BMC* 232 and *BMC* 234, in the 1838 Gravesend hoard, deposited c.871.

The second coin (fig. 7.1:2) is also of Burgred of Mercia:

Obv. BVRGRED RE+ Bust r.
Rev. +DVDNN/∴MON∴/∵ETA∵ in three lines, the words MON and ETA in whole lunettes. 0.75g. Die-axis 320°. Find no. 3650.

This is again a coin of *BMC* type *a*, but of a later phase within the type (note the groups of pellets in each corner of the reverse, and the thin, upright lettering used in the reverse inscription). The moneyer's name is not self-evident, and although the die-engraver may have had the name Dudwine in mind, Dudwine's name is spelled DVDPINE in full on other coins of this date, suggesting that DVDNN here may simply be a meaningless collection of letters. The coin belongs relatively late in Burgred's reign and may provisionally be dated to 872 or thereabouts. It is extremely light, as are the remainder of these coins.

The third coin (fig. 7.1:3), carrying the name of Æthelred of Wessex (866–71), may be described thus:

Obv. XAEÐERED REX Bust r.
Rev. LIABINC/.MON./.ETA∴ in three lines, divided by two bars with hooked ends. 0.59g (chipped). Die-axis 270°. Find no. 3395.

This purports to be a coin of Æthelred of Wessex by the well-known Canterbury moneyer Liabinc, but known coins of Æthelred with this reverse design, equivalent to *BMC* type *d* of Burgred, number four only – the present coin; one in the British Museum, *ex* L. A. Lawrence, moneyer Ealhmund; another in the British Museum from the 1924 Beeston Tor hoard, moneyer Ethered; and one in the Somerset County Museum, Taunton, moneyer Heawulf – and the fact that on all four coins Æthelred's name is mis-spelled AEÐERED for the correct AEÐELRED suggests that they are not quite what they appear to be.

There were no coins of this variety in the Gravesend hoard, deposited c.871, or in the Croydon hoard, deposited c.872, in both of which Æthelred's coinage was otherwise well represented, and the clear deduction to be drawn from this, from the mis-spelling of the king's name, from the fact that on all four coins the obverse legend is continuous from left to right rather than broken by the king's bust as is usual, and from their general dissimilarity to Æthelred's coinage proper, is that the variety is posthumous and imitative. Of the four coins in question, that by the moneyer Heawulf is analagous in style to coins struck by the same moneyer in Burgred's name in 871/2, while the remaining ones are more obviously imitative of Æthelred's coinage; the dies of the two coins of the variety in the British Museum are very close to each other in style and were probably engraved by the same die-engraver.

The fourth coin (fig. 7.1:4) carries the name of Alfred of Wessex (871–99):

Obv. AELBRED:/REX Bust r.
Rev. TIÐEHELM/MON/ETA∴ (HE ligatured) in three lines, MON and ETA within whole lunettes. 0.82g. Die-axis 320°. Find no. 3386.

This coin purporting to be of Alfred and of his *BMC* type i, equivalent to *BMC* type *a* of Burgred, combines an Alfred obverse die of normal style for the type with a reverse die of one of the styles found in the coinage struck for Burgred at the London mint c.871–c.873. Although Tidehelm is not otherwise published as a moneyer for Alfred, he is a familiar pre-871 Burgred moneyer, his coins spelling his name TIDHELM, and continued activity by him as a Burgred moneyer after 871 is documented by one coin in the British Museum from the Beeston Tor hoard, on which his name is spelled TIDMELM (*sic*), and by one other coin which recently passed through the Harry Pegg sale (Spink, 8 October 1980, lot 8), and ultimately derived, via the Shand sale (Glendining, 8 March 1949, lot 293), and Sir John Evans's collection, from the Croydon hoard. On the Croydon coin his name is rendered TIDEHELM (HE ligatured), and the bottom right-hand corner of the reverse is occupied by a pyramid of six pellets, as here, so the most likely date for the present coin is c.872 likewise. It appears to be a mule between the coinages of Alfred and Burgred, but appearances may be deceptive and it is odd that the Tidehelm die should mis-spell TIDEHELM as TIÐEHELM with the letter *thorn*.

The fifth and last coin (fig. 7.1:5) also carries the name of Alfred:

Obv. AEL[B]RED RE+ Bust r.
Rev. DVDVI∴/NE MON./ETA [∴?] (NE ligatured) in three lines, divided by two bars with hooked ends and with three pellets in the field above MON and below ETA. 0.71g (chipped). Die-axis 270°. Find no. 3381.

This again purports to be a coin of Alfred, this time of *BMC* i var.c, equivalent to *BMC* type *d* of Burgred. Yet *BMC* i var.c of Alfred is known from seven coins only and it seems unlikely that it was a substantive variety; as well as being absent from the Gravesend and Croydon hoards, it was also absent from the 1968 St Albans hoard, deposited c.873 (or at least withdrawn from circulation then), and whatever its status it must clearly date to c.873/4 or later. Dudwine is only known for Alfred otherwise from one coin in the Beeston Tor hoard, but he is a particularly prolific Burgred moneyer, and the style of the present coin seems to be directly derived from that of coins struck by Dudwine in Burgred's name in the late 860s. It should also be noted that as with the Æthelred coin discussed above the obverse inscription is continuous from left to right instead of being broken by the king's bust as is usual.

It can be discerned from this discussion that although the coins purporting to be of the West Saxon kings are in fact of a somewhat peculiar nature, the excavators' initial supposition that these five coins could be used as evidence to connect the deposit of disarticulated bones with the Viking occupation of Repton in 873–4 is more than vindicated. It can safely be asserted that four out of the five coins were struck no earlier than c.872 and that the latest may belong to 873/4, making 873/4 the earliest possible and indeed the most appropriate time for their deposit. Any oddity involved in three of the five being in the names of Æthelred or Alfred when Repton is so deep in Mercian territory is now readily explicable by the likelihood that these are not truly coins of the West Saxon kings but light weight imitative or Burgred-related strikings which were produced by moneyers working at London or further into Mercia.

It remains odd that the coinages of Æthelred and Alfred should have spawned imitations of this character while Burgred was still in occupation of the Mercian throne, but the Croydon hoard, perhaps deposited as early as the summer of 872, included coins by the moneyers Denewald and Dudd which are stylistically akin to those of Burgred but carry the names of Æthelred or Alfred, and it is apparent that in the early 870s some moneyers in Mercia were producing the occasional die carrying the name of the West Saxon king. By the time the Beeston Tor, Staffordshire, hoard was desposited c.875, a third of the coins of Alfred in it were either of obvious Burgred style, or by known Burgred moneyers, or both, and this cannot simply be because Alfred had obtained temporary control of London in c.874–5 following Burgred's deposition, for the coins are too diverse in character merely to belong to that period.

A further problem is determining how far such coins were the production of Burgred's regular London-based moneyers and how far they might have been the work of moneyers or unauthorised craftsmen working elsewhere in Mercia. A distinction needs to be drawn between Burgred-related coins in the names of Æthelred and Alfred which are of the normal reverse design for these kings, equivalent to *BMC* type *a* of Burgred, and coins such as the two from Repton which have reverse designs equivalent to *BMC* type *d* of Burgred. Coins of the first category could well be the product of London moneyers in 871–3, for during this time they were producing coins of the same design, and in some cases the same style, for Burgred. By contrast, Burgred's *BMC* type *d* was no longer being struck in the 870s – it belongs to the 860s – and London moneyers would have had no obvious cause to produce coins of this design with the names of the West Saxon kings.

Although coins of this nature are extremely rare, the two coins from Repton are not an isolated phenomenon, for there are two of this character in a group of five coins in the Somerset County Museum, Taunton, which seem to be part or the whole of a small hoard deposited c.875 and need a little more attention than they have so far been accorded.[11]

In his introduction to the *SCBI* West Country Museums volume, published in 1977, A. J. H. Gunstone noted the presence in the Somerset County Museum's collection of 'a series of five Mercian and Wessex coins, each in an early Seaby envelope';[12] these were among a number of coins found to be uncatalogued when the collection was checked in the early 1960s, and they are, unhappily, without known provenance. The apparent clue to this provided by the envelopes in which they are

11. Mr Stephen Minett very kindly showed me the coins on an unheralded visit to Taunton, and has subsequently confirmed to me that there is no documentation on them in the Somerset County Museum's archives.
12. A. J. H. Gunstone, *SCB1, Ancient British Anglo-Saxon and Norman coins in West Country Museums* (1977), xxvi.

now contained may itself be deceptive, for W. A. Seaby was briefly Curator of the Somerset County Museum from 1948 to 1951, and although he has no recollection of these particular coins, he has confirmed to me that he usually had a stock of B. A. Seaby Ltd coin envelopes at hand and that these could have been used then or later as receptacles for coins not in fact bought from the family coin firm.

The coins in question are:

1. Burgred. *BMC* type *a*, moneyer Cunehelm. *SCBI* West Country Museums 343.
2. Æthelred. *BMC* type i (= Burgred *BMC* type *a*), moneyer Elbere. *SCBI* West Country Museums 379.
3. Æthelred. *BMC* – (= Burgred *BMC* type *d*), moneyer Heawulf. *SCBI* West Country Museums 381.
4. Alfred. *BMC* type i var.a (= Burgred *BMC* type *b*), moneyer Ethered. *SCBI* West Country Museums 383.
5. Alfred. *BMC* type i var.c (= Burgred *BMC* type *d*), moneyer Cialbred.[13] *SCBI* West Country Museums 382.

It is striking that in so small a group of coins there should again be two coins in the names of Æthelred and Alfred of the same reverse design as Burgred *BMC* type *d*, this time accompanied by a coin of Alfred of *BMC* type i var.a, equivalent to Burgred *BMC* type *b*. This last coin is of proper Alfred style, and it belongs to a group of coins of this type which seem to have been the regular output of Canterbury moneyers for Alfred c.875.

The present writer's own view is that the two Repton coins and the two comparable coins at Taunton evidence the severe pressures exerted on coin production by the Viking occupation of London in 871/2 and its aftermath, and the consequent slackening of official control over the coining process. A full account of the coinage of the 870s is at present very much impeded by the absence of any proper publication of the 1968 hoard from the Abbey Orchard at St Albans, which contained 45 coins struck in the late 860s and early 870s, 23 being of Burgred, 2 of Æthelred, 19 of Alfred, and one of Archbishop Ceolnoth, together with a London monogram halfpenny of Alfred perhaps added to the deposit in the 880s. It is however clear from coins like these that by 873/4 the currency of southern England, as well as deteriorating in weight, fabric, and fineness, was being contaminated by the manufacture of coins carrying the names of kings who did not rule in the place they were made and carrying the names of moneyers who had not made them; and against this background the achievement of Alfred and Ceolwulf II of Mercia in introducing coins of new design and altogether better fineness and physical appearance at the end of the 870s emerges as a major development.[14]

H.E.P.

13. Gunstone catalogues this coin as of the normal variety *BMC* type i, but it is evident both from the illustration in the *SCBI* volume and from the coin itself that it is of *BMC* type i var.c.
14. The chronology of the coinage of the later 870s and 880s remains very uncertain, but it is clear that in its earlier stages moneyers striking coins in Ceolwulf's name played as large a part in the coinage as moneyers working for Alfred, and it should not be assumed that Ceolwulf's role in the reform of the coinage was wholly passive.

Analysis of the coins from the mass-burial

The coins were mounted so that a small area (c.2mm × 1mm) on the edge of each could be ground and polished to metallographic standards, the final polish being with 1 micron diamond paste. The coins were then cleaned with ethanol. They were then analysed using the CAMEBAX automated electron probe microanalyser in the Department of Metallurgy and Science of Materials, University of Oxford.

The routine followed was to analyse over three 50-micron squares on each coin. If the microstructure of a coin had large-scale inhomogeneities of this order of size more squares were required. The elements sought and the limits of detection are:

Fe	0.01%	Sb	0.02%
Co	0.01	Sn	0.02
Ni	0.01	Ag	0.03
Cu	0.01	Pb	0.04
Zn	0.03	Au	0.05
Bi	0.25		

The poor limit of detection for bismuth is a function of the spectral ranges of the spectrometer crystals used and the interference of other lines. As and Cd could also be included but the return in information is not usually sufficient to justify the difficulties involved with this particular apparatus. The results of the analyses are shown in table 7.1.

Table 7.1. Analysis of Anglo-Saxon coins from the excavations at Repton (figures in %)

The coins from the mass-burial

Analysis No.	*King*	*Moneyer*	*Fe*	*Co*	*Ni*	*Cu*	*Zn*	*Bi*	*Sb*	*Sn*	*Ag*	*Pb*	*Au*
3723	Burgred	Dudda	0.12	—	tr	49.92	4.44	0.61	0.04	5.77	37.96	0.86	0.32
3386	Alfred	'Tithehelm'	0.15	0.01	0.07	56.16	0.40	—	0.10	12.97	28.30	1.39	0.48**
3381	Alfred	Dudwine	0.10	0.02	0.03	73.71	0.66	0.40	0.08	6.53	17.92	0.38	0.12
3650	Burgred	DVDNN	0.13	tr	0.06	73.08	1.50	—	0.04	9.09	15.46	0.15	0.19
3395	'Æthelred'	Liabinc	0.17	0.01	0.68	85.57	0.75	—	0.11	6.70	5.54	0.20	0.14
Coin from Trench 10 (see below, p. 130)													
1757	Æthelred II (half-penny)		—	tr	0.05	3.74	0.21	—	0.01	—	94.77	0.97	0.22

** indicates result affected by corrosion

The major point of importance is that all the coins from the mass-burial are severely debased. The debasement of the coinage during the reign of Burgred is currently the subject of an extensive programme of analysis.[15] The range of silver equivalents (Ag+Pb+Au) occurring during this debasement is shown in fig.7.2 with the Repton results indicated (R).

15. D. M. Metcalf and J. P. Northover, 'Debasement of the coinage in southern England in the age of King Alfred', *NC 145* (1985), 150–76.

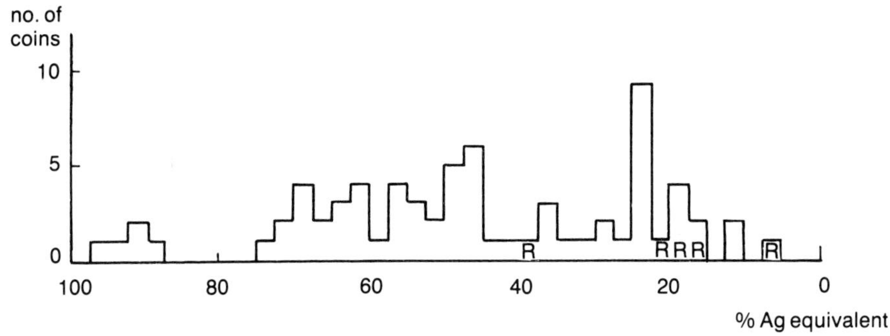

Fig. 7.2 The debasement of the *Lunette* coinage. 'R' indicates coins from Repton.

The earliest coins of Burgred's reign are of a reasonably fine silver, around 93wt% Ag equivalent. However, a progressive debasement started quite early in the reign; as is suggested by fig. 7.2, the first step was to around a 75% Ag standard. This was not well controlled and the Ag content gradually drifted downwards towards a 50% Ag equivalent. One cause of this may have been a practice of debasing whatever silver was available to a nominal 75% standard, irrespective of the metal's initial silver content. In other words the silver was not always refined before debasement. It seems fairly certain that the next step was a debasement to a 50% standard. This was, at least to begin with, much better controlled and it appears that the silver was at least partially refined. However, this control must have been relaxed and there is a tail of intermediate, lower silver contents. The last defined standard to be identified is at 25% silver equivalent, which was, for a time, again well controlled. Beyond this there are several extremely base issues. The possibility has been raised that some of the basest coins have a silver rich surface coating but this point needs further exploration;[16] the Repton coins are too corroded to contribute to the argument. Two other points must be made about the progress of the debasement. The first is that there was a gradual change in the base metal used, from brass, sometimes high zinc brass, to bronze. With the exception of no. 3723 which probably represents a debased 50% Ag issue, the Repton coins, being very base, have high tin contents indicating the use of bronzes in the 7–10wt% tin range. The second is that the intermediate standards, especially those of 50% and 25% where it is probable that the silver was refined first, seem at present to have been much better controlled in the issues of Burgred from the London mint than in the issues of Wessex and the archbishop from the Canterbury mint.

We can now look at the Repton results individually against this background.

Burgred, Dudda (cut-half; no. 3723)
At 39–40% Ag equivalent this is near the end of the long tail of the 50% standard. Compositionally it is entirely consistent with the suggested date in the late 860s.
Alfred, 'Tithehelm' (no. 3386)
In this coin the copper rich phase was completely corroded but the distribution of the

16. Meeks, pers. comm.

remaining silver rich phase suggests a composition at the lower end of the 25% standard range, say 19–22% Ag equivalent. Assuming a firm chronological correlation with the progress of the debasement, the earliest coins of Alfred have Ag equivalents of 28.5% and 24%, clearly around a 25% standard. With Alfred coming to the throne in 871 the suggested date of c.872 for this coin is entirely compatible with this composition, especially as the coins of Æthelred I terminate at the same standard (24.4 and 23.2% Ag equivalent) with the exception of coin no. 3395 from Repton.

Alfred, Dudwine (no. 3381)

With this coin we sink below the 25% standard range to 18.4% Ag equivalent. There are other coins with Alfred's name with fairly similar compositions (Edelstan, 18.1%; Manninc, 18.5%). Interestingly there is a coin of Burgred by the moneyer Tidhelm (22.5%) and another by Heawulf (18.5%) which neatly illustrate the overlap in terms of debasement between the issues of the reigns of Burgred and Alfred.

Burgred, DVDNN (no. 3650)

At 15.80% Ag equivalent this coin is significantly more base than all but one of the coins bearing Burgred's name and even that one has 18.5%. Even allowing for difficulties caused by the effect on analysis of the extremely inhomogeneous microstructures of these coins, this example must be close to the end of the Burgred series if, indeed, it is a genuine Burgred issue.

'Æthelred' 'Liabinc' (no. 3395)

This is the worst coin out of the 73 so far analysed by a long way. Also, the nickel content, at 0.68%, is completely abnormal and can probably be held to derive from copper of a Continental origin. In comparison with other issues bearing Æthelred's name it is very base (5.9% Ag equivalent against a range 48.1% to 23.3%). This composition must be held to give considerable support for the proposition that this coin is posthumous and imitative.

The cut half-pennies

The cut edge of the half-penny of Burgred (no. 3723) and the cut edge of a half-penny of Æthelred II (978–1016), also found at Repton (p. 130 below), were examined under a stereo-optical microscope at magnifications from ×6 to ×50. In both cases there was clear evidence of deliberate cutting. Each coin had been cut from one face with a sharp blade, presumably a narrow chisel, leaving a sloping face to the cut with vertical ridges where separate chisel cuts had overlapped. These cuts did not go all the way through the coin, and the section remaining had been snapped by bending leaving a projecting step. This is sketched in fig. 7.4 (p. 124) and shown in the accompanying photographs (fig. 7.3).

J. P. N.

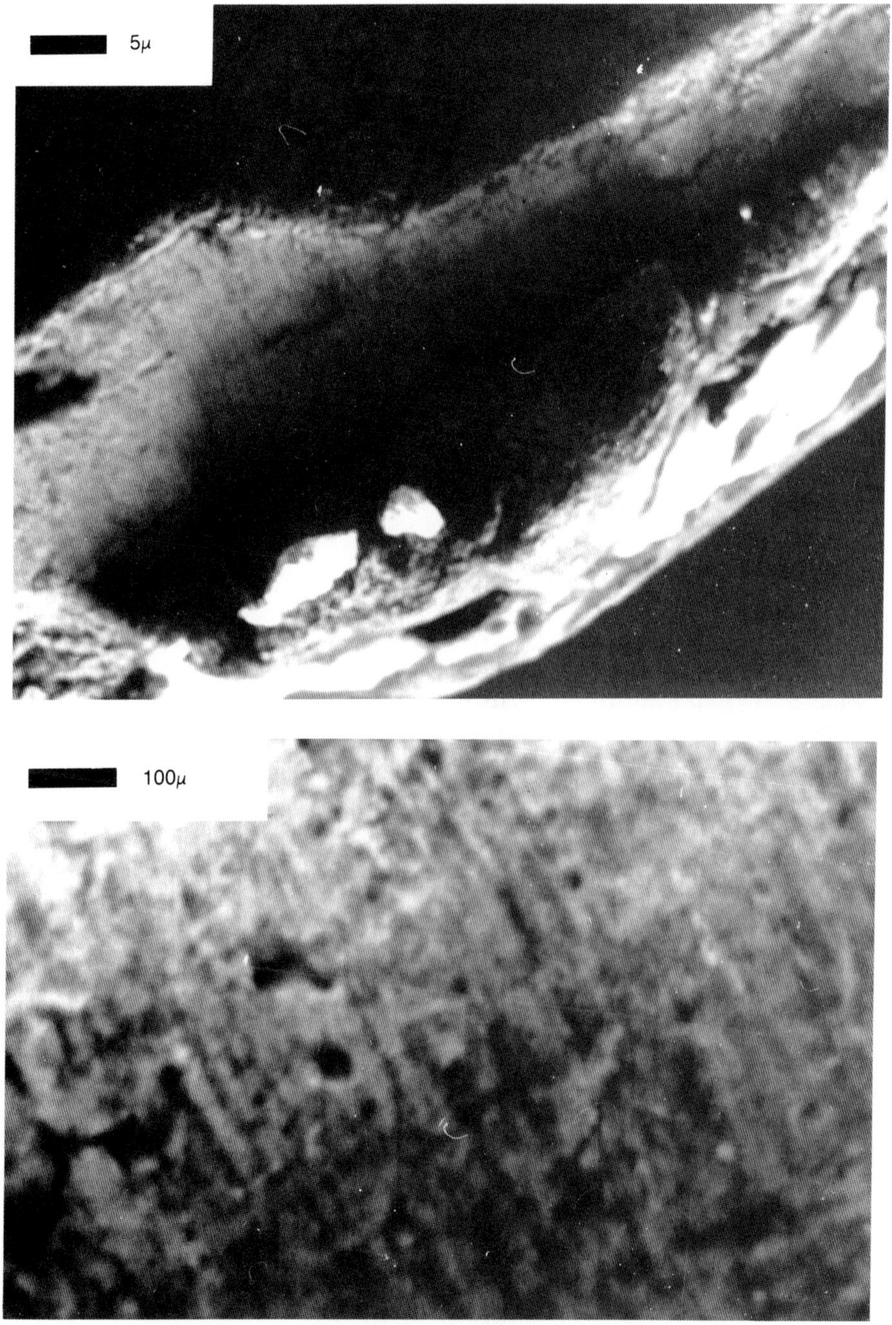

a

b

Fig. 7.3 Cut half-penny of Burgred from Repton (no. 3723): scanning-electron microscope photographs. (a) Cut edge, root of cut. (b) Striations on cut face.

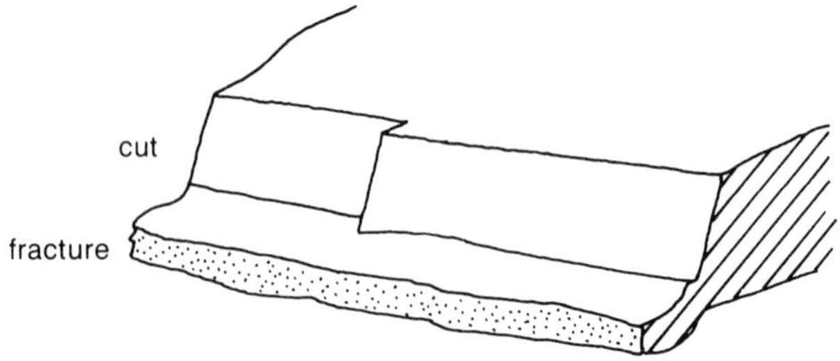

Fig. 7.4 Cut half-penny of Burgred from Repton (no. 3723): diagram showing evidence of deliberate cutting.

2. Other coins of the Anglo-Saxon period from Repton

Philip Grierson, Yvonne Harvey, D. M. Metcalf, and Hugh Pagan

'SCEAT', SERIES J (B IIIB)

A 'sceat' (fig. 7.5:6) was found in 1976, 1.5m south of the south-east angle of the crypt of St Wystan's church, in a layer of construction debris apparently associated with the initial construction of the crypt, and certainly earlier than the growth of a cemetery (Cemetery II) outside its walls (Trench 2, Layer 145; Recorded Find 355). The coin is of Rigold Series J, otherwise classed as B IIIB.[17] Its weight is 0.88g, the die-axis is 225°, and, to judge from its appearance, the coin is of base metal. Since other specimens of the sub-type are of good silver, an assessment of the coin's style is of some importance. The obverse die is very close in style to two other known dies, B IIIB5 and 6, the only difference being that the 'hair' springs from the upper of the double row of dots of the diadem. The reverse matches B IIIB8, (i)a, formerly in the Lockett collection (lot 238/2), in its style and in lacking groups of dots to either side of the cross; and also the reverse of a coin acquired by the Ashmolean since Rigold's paper was written (*ex* Carter). The obverse of this coin is close to a specimen of Hill type 70 (illustrated by Rigold on pl.4). The Carter coin has been analysed, and was found to contain only 40/50% silver.[18] The Repton find similarly may belong late in the sequence of B IIIB, when the issue had suffered debasement. About the absolute, as opposed to the relative, date it is difficult to speak confidently. The numismatic arguments are complicated. As they may have a bearing on the date of construction of the crypt, they need careful consideration. Was Type B IIIB replaced by *BMC* type 37, and if so were all the specimens of B IIIB, including the debased ones, minted before type 37 was introduced? Rigold dated the 'watershed' between the

17. S. E. Rigold, 'The two primary series of sceattas', *BNJ 30* (1960–1), 6–53.
18. D. M. Metcalf, J. M. Merrick, and L. K. Hamblin, *Studies in the Composition of Early Medieval Coins* (1968), 21 and 41.

Fig. 7.5 6–10 Coins of the Anglo-Saxon period from Repton (6 and 7 enlarged ×2).

primary and secondary phases of the denarial coinage to c.730, and by implication put Type B IIIB close to that date. He saw it as the tail-end of Series B.[19] I have called this dating in question by arguing that B IIIB was a Mercian imitation of Type B – and that it may have overlapped it in its date of introduction. I also argued that B IIIA was derivative from B IIIB rather than transitional towards it.[20] Type B IIIA occurs in the Aston Rowant hoard,[21] for which a substantially earlier date (c.710) has been proposed. Between that date and the 750s 'sceattas' of many different types were issued, with progressive debasement. Mercia lay so much on the western fringes of their circulation area that it is, one supposes, possible that Type B IIIB might have continued in vogue there, and might have been re-issued in base metal. The style of the Repton find offers no encouragement to think that it is a later revival of a type from the first quarter of the century. *Prima facie* it is an early 'sceat', even though debased. It may of course have been lost some years after it was minted, but however

19. Rigold, *op. cit.*
20. D. M. Metcalf, 'A coinage for Mercia under Aethelbald', *Cunobelin 12* (1966), 26–39.
21. J. P. C. Kent, 'The Aston Rowant treasure trove', *Oxoniensia 37*, 243–4.

one takes it, it would be no obstacle to the idea that the crypt at Repton was constructed as a mausoleum for Æthelbald, who was buried there in 757.

D.M.M.

'Sceat', Series L

This 'sceat' (fig. 7.5:7) was found in August 1984 in the body of the low earthen mound thrown up in 873–4 to cover the building and mass-burial described in Part I (Trench 8, Layer 72; Feature 904, pebble mound; Recorded Find 5000). The material of the mound contained many Middle Saxon finds – silver and copper alloy pins, fragments of vessel and window glass, and pottery sherds, as well as this 'sceat' – which seems to have been derived from the old ground surface which was scraped up to form the mound. It may be described as follows:

Obv. Diademed bust right, ᛈ + in front
Rev. Standing facing figure, (?) head right, holds long cross to right and (?) similar long cross or bush to left. 0.89g. Die-axis 180°. Bronze with some silver content (15–30%)?

The coin, which is an unrecorded variety, is characteristic of a sub-group within Series L that has been designated Hwiccian.[22] The style of die-cutting, the outline and edges of the flan, the weak striking, and the very base alloy are all consistent with the other known specimens of the sub-group. These issues dominated the currency of Hwiccia in the 740s and thereabouts, which has led to the suggestion that they were minted locally. This interpretation, which is based it must be said on only half a dozen finds from Hwiccia (and the limited occurrence of the style elsewhere) has not met with complete acceptance. Specimens occurred in a hoard from London; and one has recently come to light near Cambridge.[23] The sub-group appears nevertheless to be the work of a moneyer elsewhere than at London, as it copies Series K as well as L.[24] The designs are notably variable, and the appearance of a new variety, such as the Repton find, need not surprise us.

The details of the Repton coin are tantalizingly difficult to make out. What is, fortunately, perfectly clear is that there is an initial cross pommée and a legend on the obverse. Of the legend only one letter can be made out. It was probably intended by the die-cutter to be the same letter as is seen on another Hwiccian coin (found at Badsey), ᑌ.[25] (A third coin, of Series K, in a somewhat similar style, also has a letter

22. D. M. Metcalf, 'Sceattas from the territory of the Hwicce', *NC 136* (1976), 64–74 and pl. 12. The reader will find pl. 12 an essential adjunct to the discussion of the Repton coin.
23. M. Blackburn and D. Sorenson, 'Sceattas from an unidentified site near Cambridge', in *Sceattas in England and on the Continent*, ed. D. Hill and D. M. Metcalf (BAR 128, 1984), 223–7.
24. D. M. Metcalf, 'Monetary circulation in southern England in the first half of the eighth century', in *Sceattas in England and on the Continent*, 27–69, at 36, and see D. M. Metcalf and D. R. Walker, 'The "wolf" sceattas', *BNJ 36* (1967), 11–28. The style there designated 'E–F' is the Hwiccian style, and pl. 7.30 (type 33) is a clear-cut example. If pl.7.29 (from Shakenoak) is correctly identified as Hwiccian in style, pl.7.34 is also, for it is evidently by the same hand.
25. Metcalf, 'Hwicce', pl. 12.10.

ƿ in the same position in the design.[26]) One limb of the Repton coin's V is curved, and overlaps the junction with the other limb. There may possibly have been a second letter in front of the forehead (off the flan). It is fairly certain that there are no letters behind the head. Without more information, it is fruitless to ask what the meaning of the legend might be.

The elongated bust, with its long, modelled neck and long, Roman nose should be compared with the Portishead find.[27] The diadem ties sticking out stiffly are characteristic; and one can see the fine vertical strokes of the hair, and just make out the almond-shaped outline of the eye. The drapery is deceptive. In some lights it seems to be similar to the Portishead coin, in others one can imagine the splaying V-shaped bands of ornament which are characteristic of the Hwiccian sub-group.[28]

The reverse is indistinct, but one can make out the square, flat shoulder-line, the feet breaking the base-line, and the large dot at the back of the helmet. Again, one may compare the Badsey find. The area to the left of the standing figure (and the area on the obverse behind the bust) coincide with the thick end of the wedge-shaped flan, and the design in those places is indistinct presumably because they have received less of the force of the hammer-blow.

D.M.M.

A DENIER OF PEPIN THE SHORT (751–68)

A silver denier of Pepin the Short of the mint of Verdun (fig. 7.5:8) was found in August 1984 immediately west of the low earthen mound thrown up in 873–4 to cover the building and mass burial described in Part 1 (Trench 8, Layer 914; Recorded Find 3841). The denier was found in one of the upper layers covering the western slopes of the mound, but was probably derived from the same rich Middle Saxon deposits which produced the Series L 'sceat' discussed above. The coin may be described as follows:

Obv. RX F (RX ligatured) filling the field, with contraction mark above and pellet to right. Marks to the left are the result of 'ghosting' of the reverse design. Pearl border.

Rev. VIR/ + /DVN in three lines, the N peculiarly formed like an inverted h, with 3 pellets in field left and presumably to right, these being off the flan. Pearl border. 0.76g (fragment). Die-axis 180°. Diam. c.17mm.

Refs.[29] Prou 142 var.; Gariel II, 84, no. 77 var. (pl.iv.77 var.); Morrison and Grunthal 8 var.

The coin shows little sign of wear. Except for the small chip to the left of the obverse,

26. Metcalf and Walker, *op. cit.*, pl.7.34.
27. Metcalf, 'Hwicce', pl.12.4.
28. E.g.*ibid.*, pl.12.1, 2, 5–9, and 11.
29. These are: M. Prou, *Les monnaies carolingiennes* (Cat. des monnaies françaises de la Bibliothèque Nationale) (Paris, 1896); E. Gariel, *Les monnaies royales de France sous la race carolingienne*, 2 vols. (Strasbourg, 1883–4); K. F. Morrison and H. Grunthal, *Carolingian Coinage* (Num. Notes and Monographs no. 158; New York, 1967).

the breaks are old, though we cannot tell whether they were made before the coin entered the ground or as a result of subsequent earth movement.

Pepin the Short succeeded Charles Martel in 741 as joint Mayor of the Palace with his brother Carloman. The latter abdicated in 747, and in 751 Pepin deposed Childeric III, the last Merovingian sovereign, and had himself elected king. Pepin's coins are the first to be struck on a broader, thinner flan than had been customary and most have as obverse type either R F or RX F (for *rex Francorum*) or R P or RX P (for *rex Pepinus*), the X where present being ligatured with the R. It seems likely that the moneyers, on Pepin's accession or soon afterwards, received a general instruction to place on the coins some acknowledgement of his sovereignty and that a reference to the authority *domini nostri Pipini regis Francorum* was variously interpreted, some moneyers regarding *rex Pipinus* and others *rex Francorum* as the operative phrase.

Such an administrative instruction does not survive, but there is a legislative measure relating to the coinage which does, a clause in a capitulary of 754/5 providing that not more than 22 solidi (i.e. 264 deniers) should be struck to the pound weight. On the assumption that the pound in use corresponded more or less to that of Rome, the resulting coins should have weighed about 1.25g, which is a little heavier than many later Merovingian deniers and corresponds fairly well to the average weight of existing coins in good condition. It has been suggested[30] that the RX P form preceded the RX F one in date, since a specimen of the mint of Chartres seems to show traces of an altered die and both forms are known from several mints. An alternative explanation of such duality of type is that at such mints the moneyers who started with one form subsequently went over to the other, either because their neighbours had adopted it or because they came round to believing it was what had been intended, so that even where it occurs one cannot necessarily establish an order of striking. Many mints seem to have used RX P or, as in the case of Verdun, RX F throughout. The pellets in the field have sometimes been taken as some kind of issue marks, but mints were not at this time highly organized and *horror vacui* seems a better explanation.

Like virtually all of Pepin's deniers the Repton coin is very rare, though since seven other specimens of Verdun are known to exist it does not rank amongst the rarest. The deniers of Verdun are of two slightly varying types. Type 1, probably the earlier, has the reverse type in two horizontal lines separated by a bar, with a cross to the left and three pellets to the right. Type 2, that represented by this specimen, has the two parts of the inscription slightly curved to follow the circumference of the coin, with a cross replacing the horizontal bar and two groups of three pellets each to left and right. Type 1 is represented by only three recorded specimens, one at Berlin (*ex* Imphy hoard,[31] illus. Völckers[32] I.29 on pl.M), one at The Hague (*ex* Marie de Man coll., found at Domburg in 1903), and a third in the F. de Saulcy collection in the 1830s when it was illustrated by Combrouse but whose present whereabouts I

30. J. Lafaurie, 'Les monnaies de Pépin le Bref', *Francia 2* (1974), 36–7.
31. A. de Longpérier, 'Cent deniers de Pépin, de Carloman et de Charlemagne, découverts près d'Imphy en Nivernais', *Revue numismatique*[2] *3* (1858), 202–62.
32. H. H. Völckers, *Karolingische Münzfunde der Frühzeit* (Göttingen, 1965), 28–44 and 121–8.

have failed to trace. Of Type 2 there were three specimens known before this one, all from the Imphy hoard. One of these (Longpérier pl. I.13) subsequently appeared in one of the Vogel sales (Hess 16.4.1928, lot 3672) but I do not know what became of it. The others, which Longpérier did not illustrate, are probably those of this type in Paris (Prou 142) and Berlin (illus. Völckers I.30 on pl. N).

Only one other coin of Pepin is known to have been found in Britain. It is a denier of Dorestad (possibly imitative) found at Richborough in Kent in or before 1880, and probably the specimen now in the Fitzwilliam Museum, Cambridge.[33] The interest of this and the Repton coin is that they were probably struck, and may have been imported, before the new penny had been introduced in England and when the currency was largely made up of a dwindling supply of base 'sceattas'.

The earlier coins of Charlemagne (768–814) are only marginally less rare than those of Pepin as English finds. There were two among the many Saxon coins found by brick-earth diggers at Southampton before 1864.[34] Both had the name CAROLVS in two lines and must have been struck before the reform of 793/4, but the mint name could only be deciphered on one, MEDOLVS for Melle, near Poitiers. Another coin of the same period of Dorestad was found in about 1850 near the west entrance to the present abbey church of St Albans.[35] A fourth piece, of uncertain mint (D/MAG/CS), was recently found at Sancton in Yorkshire.[36]

How the Repton coin reached England is of course impossible to say. Verdun was an important trading centre that later acquired a reputation as the main entrepôt for traders importing slaves from the 'Slav' frontier on the Elbe.[37] An Italian writer of the tenth century describes it as the spot where the slaves were castrated before being sent on to Spain as eunuchs.[38] Whether Verdun was already a centre of this ugly commerce in the eighth century we do not know.

As to the route, Verdun lay on the Meuse at the point where this was crossed by the main route from Strasbourg on the Rhine, through Metz, Verdun, Rheims, Soissons, and Amiens, to Quentovic, near the modern Étaples at the mouth of the Canche, the main French port on the Channel between the early seventh and the late ninth century. But traffic from Verdun could equally well go down the Meuse to Huy and Maastricht, and then across the Channel from Dorestadt to East Anglia or

33. D. M. Metcalf, 'A coin of Pepin from Richborough, Kent, struck at (?) Utrecht', *HBN* 6 (1966), 384–7; P. Grierson and M. Blackburn, *Medieval European Coinage* 1 (1986), no. 719.
34. J. B. B(ergne) in *J. British Archaeol. Assoc. 20* (1864), 72.
35. R. H. M. Dolley and D. M. Metcalf, 'Two stray finds from St Albans of coins of Offa and of Charlemagne', *BNJ 28* (1957), 459–66.
36. J. Booth and I. Blowers, 'Finds of sceattas and stycas from Sancton', *NC 143* (1982), 139–45, at 141–2.
37. Miracula S. Bertini, c.4 in *Monumenta Germaniae Historica, Scriptores*, XV.511. Cf. Charles Verlinden, *L'Esclavage dans l'Europe médiévale*, I (Bruges, 1955), 222–4, 715–16, and, on the economic importance of Verdun, F. Rousseau, 'La Meuse et le pays mosan en Belgique: leur importance historique avant le XIIIe siècle', *Annales de la Soc. archéol. de Namur 39* (1930), 72. The *Miracula* were composed between 893 and 900.
38. Liutprand of Cremona, *Antapodosis*, VI.6 in his *Opera*, ed. J. Becker (Hanover-Leipzig, 1915), 156.

Humberside and York. A find-spot in Derbyshire makes this perhaps the more likely route and offers an alternative to the slave trade. The lead mines of Derbyshire, important in Roman times,[39] are known to have been exploited in the ninth century,[40] and it is generally supposed that Abbot Servatus Lupus of Ferrières had Derbyshire supplies in mind when in 852 he wrote to King Æthelwulf (839–58) and his chancellor Felix asking for lead with which to cover the roof of his monastic church.[41]

P.G.

A CUT HALF-PENNY OF ÆTHELRED II

A cut half-penny of Æthelred II (fig. 7.5:9), was found in August 1983 in a late or post-medieval layer immediately east of the burial mound described in Part 1, in an area which formed the westernmost part of the graveyard in the later Anglo-Saxon period (Trench 10, Layer 11; Recorded Find 1757). The coin was struck by Eadsige in the *Second Hand* type (c.985–91) at the Winchester mint. The legends read:

Obv. [+ÆÐEL]RÆD REX Λ[NGLOX]
Rev. +EΛDSIGE[M−O PINTO]
0.60g (cut half). Die-axis 90°.

The coin is from the same dies as a coin in Winchester City Museum (C1261) and another in Stockholm, in the Hildebrand Systematic Collection (Hild. 4211), which allows the readings to be extended and establishes the mint of origin. The cut edge of the coin is discussed by Dr Northover above (p. 122) and his analysis, recorded in table 7.1, shows it to be of very fine silver which is typical of the period.

This is a useful addition to the somewhat meagre corpus of *Second Hand* coins of Winchester known to survive, helping to build up the picture we have of the movement of the coinage in the early years of the reign of Æthelred II. Proportionately, there are far more single-finds from the Winchester mint for this period than in the later years of the reign, which are dominated by the large hoards from Sweden, but, surprisingly, virtually no cut halves from the Winchester mint are known from single-finds from England: almost all the provenanced examples are from Swedish hoards. It is interesting to find a half-penny in an everyday context, in the sense that it was clearly used to provide a coin of a smaller denomination in a working commercial transaction, rather than incorporated with a hoard, when it would possibly be viewed merely as bullion.

Y.H.

39. O. Davies, *Roman Mines in Europe* (1935), 161.
40. P. H. Sawyer, *Anglo-Saxon Charters* (1968), no. 1624 of 835 (annual render of lead from Wirksworth to Archbishop Ceolnoth and Christ Church, Canterbury).
41. Loup de Ferrières, *Correspondance*, ed. L. Levillain, II (Paris, 1935), nos. 84–5.

A BROKEN HALF OF A PENNY OF EDWARD THE CONFESSOR

The one coin of Edward the Confessor (1042–66) produced by the excavations was the broken half of a coin (fig. 7.5:10) of the first issue of his reign, the *Pacx* type, which is dated to the years c.1042–4. It was found in August 1982 folded in half; it was unfolded and repaired by Mr K. A. Howes in the Department of Coins and Medals at the British Museum. The coin was found in a pit immediately east of the north-east angle of the crypt of St Wystan's church (Trench 3, Layer 1143; Feature 1154; Recorded Find 2508). Feature 1154 was cut by twelfth-and thirteenth-century pits and itself cut into at least three 'generations' of Anglo-Saxon graves which were in turn later than the crypt. This coin and the cut-half of Æthelred II described above are among the few indications of Late Saxon activity at Repton. The legends read:

Obv.]DPE[
Rev. +B[]ACH[
0.39g (fragment). Die-axis 135°.

On the obverse there are sufficient traces of a letter E before the letter D and of a letter beginning with a vertical downstroke after the visible letter E for the main part of the king's name to be reconstructed as EDPER. On the reverse the presence of an initial cross makes it clear that the visible letters are to be taken as the initial letters of a moneyer's name and the most obviously acceptable supplement is B[L]ACH[AN], i.e. Blacman.

As the remaining part of the coin is missing, and no die identity has yet been traced, the identification of the mint at which Blacman worked is a matter for conjecture. A moneyer Blacman or Blacaman is recorded for coins of early types of Edward the Confessor's reign at Derby, Dorchester, Nottingham, and probably Leicester. Of these mints Dorchester is very distant geographically from Repton, and the case for the coin being struck at Derby or at Nottingham rather than at Leicester is advanced by the fact that the unique surviving coin of the Leicester moneyer Blacaman, if he is a Leicester moneyer and not a Chester one, is of *Radiate/Small Cross* type and not of *Pacx* type.[42]

It is worth recording that the last word has still to be said in print as to the division of coins of Blacman and Blacaman between Derby and Dorchester. In his catalogue of the Anglo-Saxon coins in the Stockholm collection Bror Emil Hildebrand attributed all four of the relevant coins there to Dorchester,[43] while nearly 80 years later Drs Gay van der Meer attributed the same four coins to Derby.[44] In the light of a coin at Copenhagen with the mint signature DE, which can hardly be of Dorchester,[45] and of a coin now in the Salisbury Museum, with the mint signature

42. *SCBI* Mack 1128. Its attribution is discussed on p. xiii of the introduction to the *SCBI* Mack volume.
43. B. E. Hildebrand, *Anglosachsiska Mynt* (1881) 433, nos. 81–4.
44. G. van der Meer, 'Some corrections to and comments on B. E. Hildebrand's catalogue of the Anglo-Saxon coins in the Swedish Royal Coin Cabinet', in *Anglo-Saxon Coins*, ed. R. H. M. Dolley (1961), 169–87, at foot of 181.
45. *SCBI* Copenhagen IV, 796.

DORC, which can hardly be of Derby,[46] it is evident that there were separate moneyers of this name at Derby and at Dorchester early in Edward's reign; and it seems not unlikely that Hild. 84, with Blacman spelled thus and followed by the mint signature DR, should be assigned to Derby, while Hild. 81 and 82, with the name spelled Blacaman and accompanied by the mint signatures DOR and DO, should be assigned to Dorchester.

H.E.P.

46. *SCBI* West Country Museums 954.

8 The monetary history of England in the tenth century viewed in the perspective of the eleventh century

D. M. Metcalf

The regular renewals of the currency which are so visible an aspect of English monetary history from the time of Edgar's reform (c.973) onwards were accompanied by other features for which the evidence is less easily assembled, but which are perhaps of even greater significance for the general historical interpretation of the period. Continuous heavy wastage from the currency through the export of coin was counterbalanced by inflows of silver in payment for exports. Because foreign coin was not permitted to circulate in England, but was required to be reminted, the English currency has the superficial appearance of a closed system; but this was far from the case. It was heavily dependent on overseas payments and receipts, and the stock of bullion available in England at any particular time was essentially related to the balance of payments over the preceding decades. As well as inflows and outflows across the frontiers there was, necessarily, a complementary movement of coin within the country. Just as the parts of a tree visible above the ground are fed by a branching system of roots below the surface, so England's external transactions were fed by an internal monetary circulation reaching out to each individual purchaser, supplier, or tax-payer. The rapidity with which coins circulated over distances of a hundred or even two hundred miles in the eleventh century can be demonstrated from stray finds.[1]

We enjoy the advantage of having evidence which is logically exceptionally complete and clear-cut about the coinage of the period c.973–c.1086. This has been achieved during the last 30 years by intensive research, with which Michael Dolley's

Acknowledgments I am grateful for expert advice and encouragement from Mr M. A. S. Blackburn, Mr C. E. Blunt, Mr C. S. S. Lyon, and Dr I. Stewart, all of whom read an earlier draft and suggested numerous improvements to the text.

1. This paragraph summarizes the arguments advanced in D. M. Metcalf, 'Continuity and change in English monetary history, c.973–1086', *BNJ* *50* (1980), 20–49; *51* (1981), 52–90. The somewhat hypothetical discussion of outflows in that article is given substance in M. A. S. Blackburn and D. M. Metcalf, 'Five-finger exercises on the List hoard', in *Viking-Age Coinage in the Northern Lands*, ed. M. A. S. Blackburn and D. M. Metcalf (BAR Internat. Ser. 122, 1981), 495–524.

name will always be associated. The question which next arises is this: were the basic patterns of English monetary history in the tenth century (about which our information is by comparison so vague and unfocussed) much the same as in the eleventh? Or did Edgar's reform of the coinage inaugurate shifts in monetary affairs? Either way, the answer should provoke historical reflections. But can we extrapolate back in time – into a period when many of the coins lacked a mint-signature and cannot yet be as closely dated as those of the successive post-reform issues, and when they might remain in circulation for much longer? Can we yet discern the general balance of the monetary system in the period c.880–c.973?

In the time of Burgred (852–74) the striking of coinage in England had been concentrated heavily in the south-east, at London (and/or Rochester) and Canterbury.[2] There had been two other important centres of minting, one somewhere in East Anglia[3] and the other at York,[4] each under independent political control and striking coins of different designs. By the late tenth century this distribution of minting had undergone a dramatic metamorphosis. There were now some 60 mint-towns in England, and the moneyers were producing a national currency of uniform design.[5] The change occurred against a background of the creation of *burhs* in southern England, the emergence of the English monarchy, the progressive re-assimilation of Danelaw territory, and the reconstruction of trading links with the Continent disrupted by the ninth-century Viking assaults.

Because of the radical nature of the developments that occurred in the hundred years to c.973, and because of the rapid pace of change, the interplay of political and monetary considerations is potentially of much interest to the general historian. It should offer many an instructive case. This expectation has until now been disappointed by the relatively large areas of uncertainty in the mint-attributions of the most plentiful types of tenth-century coins. Although there are some outstanding numismatic monographs, hoard-reports, and other articles, little progress has been made in bridging the gap between numismatic minutiae and monetary generalizations. Even the main tendencies of tenth-century monetary history remain to be sketched, and the faithfulness of the outlines tested by discussion and research.

The second half of the tenth century is characterized by the large number of hoards of English money from Ireland and from the Viking west and north,[6] and by unusually active minting in the north-east and the north-west of England, notably at

2. H. E. Pagan, 'Coinage in the age of Burgred', *BNJ 34* (1965), 11–27.
3. H. E. Pagan, 'The coinage of the East Anglian kingdom from 825 to 870', *BNJ 52* (1982), 41–83; C. E. Blunt, 'The St Edmund Memorial coinage', *Procs. of the Suffolk Inst. of Archaeology 31* (1967–9), 234–54.
4. York had been an active mint for more than 100 years before the Viking occupation, producing 'sceattas' and then 'stycas'. After an interval it resumed, late in the ninth century, and thereafter struck silver pennies of the normal fabric.
5. D. M. Metcalf, 'The ranking of the boroughs: numismatic evidence from the reign of Æthelred II', in *Ethelred the Unready: Papers from the Millenary Conference*, ed. D. Hill (BAR 59, 1978), 159–212.
6. The list in R. H. M. Dolley, *The Hiberno-Norse Coins in the British Isles* (*SCBI* 8, 1966), 15–54, is now updated by Blackburn and Pagan in this volume, chapter 15 below.

Chester. At the same time there are very few hoards from England. The foreign hoards have been assumed in general to be buried loot, the fruits of extortion and plunder, rather than evidence of a 'normal' money economy in the regions where they were concealed.[7] Was there a drain of silver out of tenth-century England towards Ireland and the kingdom of Man and the Isles, corresponding in some sense with the eleventh-century drain of silver to Scandinavia? And were the losses replaced by balance-of-payments surpluses earned through trade with the Continent? If England's monetary orientation during much of the tenth century was towards the north, does this mark a complete, or only a partial, turn-about from the normal cross-Channel and Rhinelands orientation discernible from the seventh century onwards and again from the late eleventh? The unusual polarity occurs *after* the Danelaw had been firmly secured under the English crown, and not in the preceding decades, during which the availability of English and Danelaw coin beyond the northern and western frontiers seems to have been on a relatively modest scale. This may suggest that unusual levels of minting at places such as York, Lincoln,[8] Stamford, Tamworth, Stafford, and Chester after the reconquest, were in some way contingent upon free access to and from the south. The activity of the Danelaw mints may have been increased also by the minting of *hacksilber* and other bullion.

What had the pagan Norsemen to sell that the English lacked, or could not obtain better elsewhere? If, in terms of the balance sheet, a large part of the answer were slaves, one could envisage monetary counterflows to an entrepôt trade, by which Irish and perhaps Pictish and Strathclyde slaves were bought in the northern ports, and subsequently sold and shipped to the Continent.

English silver did not, as is well known, begin to accumulate[9] in Scandinavia in any quantities until the 980s, and there are hints that, earlier in the century, the net flow was in the other direction. Thus Sāmānid dirhams (arriving from Scandinavia) occur in Scottish hoards such as Skye and Skaill,[10] and also in the north of England – where they apparently escaped reminting at York while the city remained in Viking control. It is an intriguing question whether dirhams from Scandinavia were

7. In Scotland, for example, there is very little evidence of the use of coin in the Central Lowlands before about 1100, and the hoards from before that date are mostly peripheral and coastal. See D. M. Metcalf, 'The evidence of Scottish coin hoards for monetary history, 1100–1600', in *Coinage in Medieval Scotland (1100–1600)*, ed. D. M. Metcalf (BAR 45, 1977), 1–59 at 8.
8. I. Stewart, 'The St Martin coins of Lincoln', *BNJ 36* (1967), 46–54; and, most recently, C. E. Blunt and B. H. I. H. Stewart, 'The coinage of Regnald I of York and the Bossall hoard', *NC 143* (1983), 146–63, particularly at 153ff. Coins struck at Lincoln, in particular, by the Vikings are very scarce.
9. It has been argued that more may have been carried to Scandinavia than stayed there, and this possibility is of particular concern in the last quarter of the tenth century. See D. M. Metcalf, 'Some twentieth-century runes. Statistical analysis of the Viking-age coin hoards and the interpretation of wastage rates', in *Viking-Age Coinage*, 329–82.
10. *SCBI* Edinburgh, xxii and xxiii, and plates 27–9.

similarly flowing into the port of London, where reminting was rigorously enforced. McKerrell and Stevenson suggested, on the basis of traces of gold (and bismuth) in the coinage, that a great deal of oriental silver was incorporated into the English stock of coinage metal in the second half of the tenth century – enough to change the make-up of the stock radically.[11] If that were correct, it would be a conclusion of major significance for English monetary history, and it would enjoy the benefit of automatically reflecting the balance of the evidence. It is unfortunately (as will be shown below) far from secure.

A programme of monetary research on the tenth century might include the following projects:

1. An attempt to describe the changing composition of the English currency, decade by decade, from the evidence of hoards, and with special reference to the age-structure of the currency. This would be a way of approaching the crucial question of wastage and the balance of payments. For conclusions about wastage, derived from hoard-evidence, to be logically watertight they need, however, to be complemented by:

2. Statistical estimations of mint output, at least for selected mints or periods. These figures would provide a basic statistical series from which to judge (a) the scale of recoinages; (b) inflows of bullion from abroad; and (c) in conjunction with (1) above, the volume of the currency.

3. A topographical analysis in terms of mint of origin, of the coins in (a) hoards from English territory; and (b) stray finds from English territory. This should demonstrate the rapidity or otherwise with which coins mingled in circulation. (The evidence, which is very incomplete, seems to be that in partial contrast with the eleventh century,[12] the currency tended to be compartmented within major regions such as the south, the north-east, or the north-west of England.)

4. A comparison of 'foreign' hoards (other than the Rome hoards) consisting of English money – that is to say, chiefly hoards from Ireland, or from the kingdom of Man and the Isles – with hoards from territory under English control. The eleventh-century Scandinavian hoards have a radically different age-structure from English hoards of the same date.[13] The age-structure and (perhaps even more) the regional derivation – see (3) above – of the tenth-century Irish and Manx hoards, when compared with the English evidence, should offer clues to the nature of the monetary outflows.

5. Reflection upon the weight-standards and metal contents of the coins may lead us to a clearer understanding of the motives of royal policy in altering the intrinsic value of the coinage. Within England the prices of many goods, services, and rents were probably slow to change, in terms of pence, whereas when coins were carried

11. H. McKerrell and R. B. K. Stevenson, 'Some analyses of Anglo-Saxon and associated oriental silver coinage', in *Methods of Chemical and Metallurgical Investigation of Ancient Coinage*, ed. E. T. Hall and D. M. Metcalf (1972), 195–209.
12. Metcalf, 'Continuity and change'.
13. Metcalf, 'Some twentieth-century runes'.

beyond the realm their value would be assessed largely or even entirely in terms of the amount of refined silver they contained.

These various approaches are to different aspects of a coherent system, and evidence on any one aspect would, by itself, be enough to raise pointed questions about the others. But all are needed in order to sketch a description of the English currency: the ebb and flow overseas, the mingling of coins from various mints within England, renewal through reminting, royal policy towards the value of the penny, and the changing orders of magnitude of the country's stock of silver. What follows is inevitably the merest sketch, in which these themes are touched on, and two or three numerical or scientific aspects are explained more carefully. Before a fuller account can be given, there are many coin types for which we still await a competent stylistic analysis and classification. (A great deal of the necessary numismatic work has been done, by C. E. Blunt, C. S. S. Lyon, and I. Stewart, and a volume of studies by them is to be published by the British Academy). We are dependent, also, upon the discovery of new hoards – and on revised accounts of old hoards. The gaps in the evidence for monetary history are at present so large that the answers we can construct are at best fragmentary. One of the chief purposes of this essay is to indicate the shape of the arguments by which we should seek to connect those fragments.

The *Lunette* coins which were hoarded over so large a part of England in the years immediately before the subversion of the kingdom of Mercia were struck in enormous quantities. A meticulous corpus of dies and die-duplicates shows that, of Burgred alone, 592 coins are from 558 reverse dies. An estimate of the original total would be about 5,100 dies or perhaps 50 million coins.[14] As the late *Lunette* coins were at best a quarter fine,[15] their reminting into good-silver pence would have yielded only about a quarter as many. There is unfortunately no evidence of the extent to which the severe debasement of the years around 870 affected prices. Debasement in Northumbria had been even more severe, beginning 30 to 50 years earlier.[16] There too, there was a definitive return to good-silver coins by the 890s.

The promptness of the return to sound money is remarkable, for one must suppose that insecurity on the Continent caused cross-Channel trade to be at maximum risk. When the Vikings were driven out of England in 879, they turned their attention to Flanders. The 880s were a black decade for that province, as the invaders extorted its wealth.[17] One wonders, even, whether Flanders' loss was to

14. Pagan, *op. cit.*; D. M. Metcalf, 'The prosperity of north-western Europe in the eighth and ninth centuries', *EcHR*² *20* (1967), 344–57, at 355 and n.1. Alongside the coins of Burgred there circulated those of Æthelred and Alfred, of the same design. An average output of 10,000 coins per reverse die is assumed here.
15. D. M. Metcalf and J. P. Northover, 'Debasement of the coinage in southern England in the age of King Alfred', *NC 145* (1985), 150–76.
16. Because Northumbria was more remote, and poorer? The debasement became severe during the reign of Eanred, possibly as early as (on the alternative chronology) either the 820s or 830s.
17. A. d'Haenens, *Les invasions normandes en Belgique au IX*ᵉ *siècle* (Louvain, 1967).

some extent Northumbria's gain, for coins of fine silver were minted at York from upwards of 250 obverse dies in the late ninth century.[18]

In the south of England, the *Lunette* coins were replaced first by another convention-coinage, the '*Ceolwulf*' type, minted for the archbishop and for Ceolwulf II as well as for Alfred. Although it was struck by at the very least a score of moneyers, few specimens survive, perhaps because it too was recalled and reminted.[19] Alfred's *London monogram* issue, which seems to have made up the whole of the London (Bucklersbury) hoard and the Erith hoard, also had a short life, but it is of greater significance than this lack of 'success' might suggest, as it is on a new, heavier weight-standard of over 24 grains (1.56g). This is evidence of an intention on Alfred's part to reform the coinage in some way.[20] One's impression – although it is little more than an impression – is that the '*Ceolwulf*' and *London monogram* coinages may not have circulated very freely beyond the south-east (east Kent, London, and the Thames estuary), and that they represent not very successful attempts to restore the traditional pattern of minting and monetary circulation, in which the activity of the moneyers at Canterbury and London in fact depended on an extensive hinterland in eastern and midland England as well as on the prosperity of the Low Countries and the lower Rhineland. The hinterland was now dislocated, and monetary affairs on the Continent were in decline. At Winchester, Exeter, Oxford, and Gloucester, the success of special coinage types minted in the context of urban revival seems to have been minimal,[21] and to have remained local in its influence. From the Danelaw, the Stamford hoard of c.900, which contains imitations of the *Two-line* type, plus singletons from Lincoln, (?) Leicester, and the Continent,[22] points on the one hand to a sense of monetary dependence on the south-east, and an unreadiness to strike out with a clearly independent coinage, while at the same time it hints at the early commercial importance of Stamford,[23] and at an east-coast trade that was by-passing south-eastern England.

In East Anglia, meanwhile, a distinctive regional coinage, the *St Edmund Memorial* type, was struck in considerable quantities,[24] and on the traditional (21-grain) weight-standard. These pence, with a large 'A' as their obverse type, make up a good share of the stray finds that have been recorded from tenth-century England. They

18. Unusually precise figures are available in C. S. S. Lyon and B. H. I. H. Stewart, 'The Northumbrian Viking coins in the Cuerdale hoard', *AS Coins*, 96–121, at 106.
19. Nine of the moneyers are known today from single specimens. Our tally of moneyers is therefore likely to be very incomplete. See R. H. M. Dolley and C. E. Blunt, 'The chronology of the coins of Ælfred the Great', in *A-S Coins*, 77–95. See also Blunt and Dolley, 'The hoard evidence for the coins of Alfred', *BNJ 29* (1958–9), 220–47.
20. Dolley and Blunt, 'Ælfred the Great'.
21. C. S. S. Lyon, 'Some problems in interpreting Anglo-Saxon coinage', *Anglo-Saxon England 5* (1976), 173–224, at 181.
22. Blunt and Dolley, 'Alfred hoards'.
23. There is tantalizingly little evidence about Stamford, either documentary or archaeological, from earlier than the reconquest.
24. Blunt, 'St Edmund Memorial'; C. S. S. Lyon, 'Presidential address', *BNJ 39* (1970), 193–204, at 195.

have also been found in at least two Continental hoards.[25] Again, one wonders whether shipping that had once sailed into the Wantsum channel was now putting into Ipswich.

Alfred's more prosaic and more plentiful *Two-line* types (*BMC* xiv and xv) bear moneyers' names but lack a mint-signature, and set the pattern for the bulk of the coins issued right up to Edgar's reform. They plunge the student into the major drawback of tenth-century monetary research, namely our inability to attribute coins to their particular mints with certainty. What is certain is that some 60 moneyers worked to produce Alfred's *Two-line* coins, and that ten of their names recur (all or nearly all of them presumably the same individuals) in type xvii, which can be firmly attributed to Canterbury.[26] Certain styles of lettering in combination with small variations in the inscription have been used as the basis for a division of the coins between Canterbury, London, Winchester, and Mercia,[27] but it is very difficult to know how one could approach the problem of distinguishing between die-cutting centres and mint places. One may suspect that Winchester, in particular, supplied a number of southern mints. Did the traditional mints produce the bulk of the issue? Or was burghal minting, like the burghal system itself, Alfred's creation? We are close in date here to a moment of great change in the administrative arrangements for the coinage, and judgment is correspondingly more difficult. On the one hand, 60 is a large number of moneyers. On the other hand much of the die-cutting, it must be said, is very uniform. The Leigh-on-Sea grave-find illustrates the work of the Canterbury mint, and shows the range of dies that had been produced at a date possibly as early as 893.[28] The 76 specimens of the *Two-line* types in the (later) Morley St Peter hoard[29] belong mostly to the very end of Alfred's reign at a time when Winchester dominated the supply of dies, and the London and Canterbury mints were temporarily in eclipse. Like other hoards, Morley St Peter shows that the coins struck by different moneyers had become thoroughly mingled together, and thus offers evidence for an intensive monetary circulation. Twenty-one moneyers are represented, mostly by just one or two coins each, the exception being the prolific

25. Apart from Bardwell, Sf, Eriswell, Sf, Thetford, Norwich, Narfond, Nf, and Mursley, Bk, there is a remarkable concentration of finds from Northampton, and there are problematic finds from Cholsey and Long Wittenham, Oxon. Continental finds from Rennes (*RN* 1965, 262) and Denmark (*SCBI* Copenhagen I, no. 153).
26. See *BMC* and J. J. North, *English Hammered Coinage*, I (2nd edn, 1980), 93f.
27. Dolley and Blunt, 'Ælfred the Great', at 84–6; I am much indebted to Mr Stewart Lyon for allowing me to consult unpublished work on Alfred's *Two-line* coins which suggests that the 'Edward the Elder' style, tentatively attributed by Dolley and Blunt to London, was the product of a die-cutting centre in Winchester. The classification of Edward's coinage was revised by him in a paper to the British Numismatic Society in 1977, a version of which is to appear in the forthcoming volume by Blunt, Lyon, and Stewart. Meanwhile, see S. Lyon, 'A significant "Winchester" die-link in the reign of Edward the Elder (899–924)', *NCirc 91* (1983), 261–2.
28. Blunt and Dolley, 'Alfred hoards', 235–7.
29. *SCBI* East Anglia, 40–2, 47–119.

moneyer Wulfred, of whom there is a block of 30 coins in the hoard. If we knew whether coins of different mints were represented, we might be in a position to argue that the hoard gave evidence of the rapidity of monetary circulation. Because of the virtual impossibility of distinguishing between where the dies were cut and where they were used – which seems to be a crucial *impasse* in the historical interpretation of the spread of minting – and because of the unusual character of the Morley St Peter hoard, one may hesitate to draw any very firm conclusions until some other English hoards are available for comparison. But no hesitation is called for in pointing out that there are 70 different reverse dies among the 76, indicating an original total which could well be as high as 500,[30] for these moneyers alone.

How widely did Alfred's *Two-line* types circulate in southern England? Did they make up the whole of the currency, the earlier types having been swept away when the weight of the penny was increased? One must recognize the difficulty of answering even such simple and basic questions as these, when the contemporary evidence consists of one grave-find from Essex.

The southern Danelaw produced its own imitations of the *Two-line* type, with blundered inscriptions and of less reliable weight; but not, so far as one can judge, on any great scale. Further north, one or two again name Lincoln as their mint.[31]

The coinage of Edward the Elder (899–924) continues the *Two-line* type, with matching portrait coins issued on a smaller scale. Over 140 moneyers (cf. Alfred's 60) took part in the issue.[32] Many of the same names are found again on mint-signed coins of Athelstan (924–39).[33] At Southampton, for example, there are just two men who are known to have issued mint-signed coins for Athelstan, namely Eadgild and Frithebriht, both of whom had produced unsigned coins under Edward – presumably at Southampton. As there are very few cases of men of the same name working at widely-separated mints under Athelstan, it is a reasonable assumption that in the time of Edward, moneyers were working at the same mints where they are found under Athelstan. On that basis there were, already in Edward's reign, at least 24 and possibly about 30 mints.

Philip Grierson, following Dorothy Whitelock, has suggested that the often-quoted provisions about mints in the Grateley decrees are from an earlier code, renewed and repeated by Athelstan.[34] The evidence of the moneyers' names allows us to say more specifically that arrangements approximating to those described in the Grateley decrees were already in existence in the reign of Edward. The 11 names we know for London compare with an establishment of 8 – possibly allowing for some replacement as moneyers relinquished office. Canterbury and (already) Winchester have quite large establishments; Southampton has the two names mentioned above, as the code decrees. The places where moneyers may be presumed to have been at work under Edward are:

30. Taking account of the block of coins by Wulfred, because of which an overall estimate will tend to be too low.
31. For the question of lower weight-standards, see Lyon, 'Presidential address', 194f.
32. North, *op. cit.*
33. C. E. Blunt, 'The coinage of Athelstan, 924–939: a survey', *BNJ 42* (special vol., 1974), 35–160.
34. *Ibid.*, 40f.

Wessex, Kent, and London: Canterbury, London, Winchester, Chichester, Southampton, Wareham, Exeter, Shaftesbury, Oxford, Wallingford, Bath, 'Darent', Langport, Lympne
Midlands: Derby, Nottingham, Tamworth, Hereford, Stafford, Shrewsbury, 'Weardburh', Chester
North-east: Unlocated mint or mints, presumably including some or all of Stamford, Leicester, Northampton, and Bedford

To these must be added the East Anglian mint, and probably most of the missing places from the Grateley list.

Only about half Edward's moneyers can be assigned to a mint in this way, and the very awkward question this poses is whether the half we can (tentatively) attribute are typical of the whole, in their regional distribution. There are, alas, no usefully large hoards from English territory from Edward's reign, and relatively few of his coins survive in English hoards from later reigns. The major sources of information are two hoards from Rome – with all the uncertainties that that entails in judging how far they are typical of the currency of England. The magnificent Vatican hoard of c.1928, concealed early in Athelstan's reign, included no fewer than 437 non-portrait and portrait coins of Edward, among which there were apparently only 31 reverse duplicates[35] indicating an original total which may have been between 2,000 and 3,000 reverse dies. The average output of a reverse die is a matter of guesswork. The conventional (but possibly conservative) figure of 10,000 brings us to a total of 20 to 30 million coins. Whatever the margins of uncertainty and error attaching to this estimate, it serves sufficiently to make the point that if a monetary economy was in any way restricted or hampered, it was not for want of coin.

Among the 437 specimens, some 265 can be provisionally attributed, to the following mints:

London	77	Shaftesbury	2	Derby	1
Winchester	59	Oxford or Stafford	2	Mercian (unattrib.)	2
Southampton	11	Langport	2	North-eastern (unattrib.)	24
Canterbury	10	Wareham	1	North-western (unattrib.)	19
Chichester	3	Bath	1		
Exeter	2	Southern (unattrib.)	49		

The contrast between large mints and small mints is a very familiar feature in hoards of the eleventh century, and the Vatican hoard shows the same pattern. (By contrast, the British Museum's holdings from the Rome hoard of 1846[36] for the most part

35. M. A. O'Donovan, 'The Vatican hoard of Anglo-Saxon pennies', *BNJ* *33* (1964), 7–29. Miss O'Donovan's minute listing of the coins and of die-links, on the basis of casts and coins now in the British Museum, and also photographs of some of the coins, signals a number of lacunae, and it is accordingly possible that the total number of reverse duplicates was higher than 31. Mr Lyon has advised me that that is his impression, from his recollection of the first sale. The proposed estimate of 2,000–3,000 which makes some allowance for the coins not fully described in O'Donovan's catalogue, may therefore still be somewhat too high.
36. R. H. M. Dolley and J. S. Strudwick, 'The provenances of the Anglo-Saxon coins recorded in the two volumes of the British Museum Catalogue', *BNJ*

include only one coin of each moneyer or of each variety, and one wonders to what extent they are a selection made on that basis.) Unless the sample of mint-attributable coins is misleading, the Vatican hoard is 80 per cent 'southern'. Midland and northern moneyers are represented by one or two coins each, whereas London moneyers in particular are sometimes represented by ten or more specimens. (This regional imbalance means that the die-estimate is liable to be an under-estimate.)

The exceptional share of minting at Winchester in the 970s and at London in the 980s has been documented from the Scandinavian hoards.[37] For each city it is of some general interest to see that the same is true as early as the first quarter of the tenth century.

One cannot but be impressed by the resilience of the English monetary economy, which recovered within about one generation from the Viking onslaught, or which indeed seems to have emerged richer than it was before. The tally of mints may, so far as we can assert the contrary from the evidence available, have increased mainly in the second half of Edward's reign, but we are entitled to claim a date substantially earlier than 924 as the date by which the arrangements were in place, for the large volume of his issues cannot all have been compressed into his last years. Already in the Cuerdale hoard, concealed c.905, and thus reflecting the currency from the early years of Edward's reign, there is a variety of his issues, about equally divided between the south (predominantly Winchester) and the north-west. This points to a rapid mingling of coins from different regions.[38] The decisive reorganization of English minting arrangements would seem, therefore, to have been put in hand early in the tenth century, and it is possible that the first steps were taken, even, by Alfred himself.

There is an interesting East Anglian series of non-portrait and portrait coins for Edward with – very unusually – blundered and possibly fictitious moneyers' names.[39] This whole coinage, which survives very richly in the Morley St Peter hoard, deposited c.925 (but which is minimally represented in the Vatican hoard) was struck from upwards of 200 pairs of dies. It may represent a hurried effort to sweep away the (lighter) *St Edmund Memorial* coinage and to supply East Anglia with an English royal coinage after the reconquest.

The most intriguing development in Edward's reign, however, is the prominence among the *Two-line* coins of the issues of 'a north-western mint or mints'. For this cautious periphrasis one may, essentially, read Chester – where the walls were repaired by Æthelflæd in 907.[40] It has sometimes been suggested that Welsh silver,

28 (1955–7), 26–59, at 32, etc. See also Mr Blunt's paper below.

37. Metcalf, 'Continuity and change', 72–9.
38. Dolley and Strudwick, *op. cit.*, list 28 specimens by 13 moneyers. I am indebted to Mr Lyon for his assessment of the mint-attributions.
39. Fully published by T. H. McK. Clough in *SCBI* East Anglia.
40. F. M. Stenton, *Anglo-Saxon England* (3rd edn, 1971), 326. This was, of course, only one part of a programme of work designed to secure the north-west against attack. Tamworth, Stafford, and *Weardburh* were also fortified in Edward's time. For a survey of the archaeological evidence, see P. Rahtz, 'The archaeology of West Mercian towns', in *Mercian Studies*, ed. A. Dornier (1977), 107–29. For Chester in the ninth century,

paid in tribute, provided the necessary bullion, and that many of the coins in question might equally have been struck at Shrewsbury.[41] One should be aware that *a priori* assumptions may underlie this idea. True, the amounts of metal involved might plausibly have derived from mining, although they would be rich mines for their output to be sustained for half a century. But there are already six moneyers at work somewhere in north-western Mercia in Alfred's *Two-line* type; and minting activity is in full swing at Chester *before* Athelstan's meeting with the Welsh princes at Hereford (927 × 931), at which hounds and hawks, gold and silver, and oxen were pledged.[42] The meeting-place suggests that this was essentially tribute from south Wales; and the assumption of coining activity arising out of the payment of tribute finds no positive support in the written evidence (unless perhaps in the requirement to work for the king laid on Hereford moneyers in Domesday Book?). Certainly no evidence has been adduced to link the north-western mints with silver mined in Wales. One could probably determine by scientific investigation, whether some or all of the silver was Welsh in origin: it lies well within the art of the possible to discover what the characteristic lead isotope ratio of Welsh silver is and to measure the ratios of a suitable selection of coins, if samples of about one milligramme can be taken from them. No such research has yet been undertaken. Nor is it likely that it would offer simple answers to the more general questions. The dispersion of English coin into the Irish Sea coastlands and beyond, over a period of at least half a century, calls for explanations of a political and economic order, wherever the silver came from. Hiberno-Norse settlement of the Wirral from the beginning of the tenth century[43] points strongly towards trading activity via Chester.

The foreign hoards are by no means exclusively of Chester mintage, and this must lead one to ask whether it is plausible that they reflect the composition of the currency in the region of Chester, or whether the money was more widely gathered. Again, the possibility of a long-distance trade in slaves is in question.

Minting in ports was normally a response to foreign or obsolete silver coming *into* England, and the suggestion, by Dolley, that a late non-portrait type of Edgar (type ii) was struck specially for the export trade should therefore be viewed with some reserve. The evidence which apparently supports this theory, namely that types i.d and ii are of very variable alloy,[44] proves on inspection to be shaky, for if the silver

see A. T. Thacker, 'Chester and Gloucester: early ecclesiastical organization in two Mercian burhs', *Northern History 18* (1982), 199–211.

41. Stenton, *Anglo-Saxon England*, 340. The (exaggerated?) 300 pounds of silver that is mentioned could have been coined with about 10 reverse dies.
42. H. Loyn, 'England and Wales in the tenth century: the context of the Athelstan charters', *Welsh History Review 10* (1980–1), 283–301.
43. Stenton, *Anglo-Saxon England*, 326.
44. The diagram in McKerrell and Stevenson, *op. cit.*, 199, suggests that, although types i.d and ii are *on average* of lower fineness, this is because they were very variable (between 50 and 90 per cent silver); and that the unreliability of the alloy was developing already in Eadred's reign. If the analysis is confined to coins from the Iona hoard, the trend is much less pronounced. Perhaps one could go so far as to say that the authorities recognized that much of the Chester output would go abroad

contents measured by McKerrell are analysed according to the hoards from which the coins come, it appears that low-silver coins are of different provenance from the majority. One must suspect that the history of the coins since their burial may be the major factor. It is difficult to envisage that merchants would ordinarily go to the trouble and expense of having money reminted into new Chester coins merely in order to export it. There may have been special considerations late in Edgar's reign, but the outflows of money through Chester are a phenomenon stretching through most of the tenth century; and the run of Irish hoards do not seem to be selective in their composition, except possibly in their lack of portrait coins.

The activity of the moneyers in tenth-century Chester was nevertheless on an astonishing scale. In numbers, and presumably in output, they even rivalled London, which otherwise, and always after 980, was the premier English mint-place. Chester's position is all the more conspicuous when we note that, after the events of 979/80,[45] it sank back to a modest rank among the mint-towns, rarely accounting for more than 2–3 per cent of the national total in the following hundred years.[46] We may consider that this was its 'natural' level of activity. Its tenth-century apogee began quite suddenly, for there were more than 20 moneyers at the 'north-western mint or mints' already in Edward's reign.[47] A dozen of them were represented in the Vatican hoard, in which their products made up roughly 7 per cent of Edward's coins. The attributions rest mainly on styles of lettering, and on continuity of style and of moneyers' names into the reign of Athelstan. It deserves to be formally demonstrated that there was a contrast between the proportions of coins in the 'north-western' styles in hoards from that region (and the foreign regions to which the Dee and Mersey gave access) and from the south and east of England. Although from Edward's reign there are too few provenanced coins from which to offer any useful statistical evidence, the general conclusion is clear enough. Thus, the Chester hoard of 1862 contained in all eight coins of Edward, of which at least half are of north-western mintage.[48] The Scotby hoard, concealed near Carlisle c.935–40,[49] and the Irish hoards of Glendalough and Killyon Manor, all have a strong north-western flavour.[50]

The pattern of minting which developed in Edward's reign was continued by his successors until c.973. For the reign of Athelstan we are fortunate in having a full-scale monograph on his coinage by Christopher Blunt. For the issues of Edmund, Eadred, Eadwig, and Edgar we await the volume by Blunt, Lyon, and Stewart. The main numismatic handicap remains the same: a substantial proportion of the coins

anyway, and that some laxity was therefore allowed to prevail. But it is very improbable that the recipients, in Ireland or Man, would not become aware of coins of poorer quality.

45. R. H. M. Dolley and E. J. E. Pirie, 'The repercussions on Chester's prosperity of the Viking descent on Cheshire in 980', *BNJ 33* (1964), 39–44.
46. Metcalf, 'Continuity and change', 72–9.
47. North, *op. cit.*, 96–7.
48. R. P. Mack, 'St John's church, Chester, hoard of 1862', *BNJ 36* (1967), 36–9.
49. Blunt, 'Athelstan', at 156–8.
50. *Ibid.*, 54.

lack a mint-signature. Their attribution, even to a broad region, is often a delicate task. There are few hoards from territory controlled by the English kings, and almost all the earlier hoard publications, before they can be of much service to historians, await the attention of a numismatist expert enough to assess the regional balance of their composition. This is the necessary first step towards working out how freely coinage was moving about the country.

As regards movements of bullion into and out of the country there is the evidence,[51] already mentioned, of a pronounced fall in the gold trace levels of the English coinage, implying that the stock of bullion was supplemented or replaced by metal originating from a different mining area. Gold is a noble metal, which is quite unaffected by cupellation. When silver containing small traces of gold is recycled, the ratio of gold to silver is essentially unchanged. Analyses of a large selection of tenth-century coins (in the Edinburgh collection) were published by McKerrell and Stevenson, and as they were all made by the same scientific procedures and on the same occasion, comparisons between them ought to be particularly secure. It has to be said, unfortunately, that some of his scientific colleagues are nervous about the accuracy of McKerrell's figures. Only in so far as they reveal a substantial trend should one be willing to accept their evidence. Some of the very low gold/silver ratios, which are discrepant, are associated with questionably low silver measurements, and these should be treated with considerable reserve for the time being. The historian may, in any case, be more inclined to quibble over the way the results were analysed, namely by dividing them into the two contrasted periods 899–946 and 946–1016. In the later period the gold traces are on the whole much lower. But was the trend gradual, as we are entitled to expect if the suggested interpretation is correct? If we break the results down reign by reign (see fig. 8.1), we may begin to suspect that the incorporation of oriental silver into the English stock of coinage metal was at best a relatively brief process which had ceased by the close of Athelstan's reign; that large proportions of fairly low-gold silver first show up during Edgar's reign (e.g. at Lincoln?), but that high-gold silver is still being re-minted and is retaining its identity; and that the major contrast is not between the first and second halves of the tenth century, but between the stock of coinage metal before and during Æthelred's reign – when the high-gold silver is no longer to be seen at all. Æthelred's coins could reflect Continental rather than oriental silver.

The opportunties for future research are extremely promising. One would like to compare a selection of Edgar's coins from south-eastern mints, for example, with the predominantly north-eastern and north-western specimens analysed at Edinburgh. And the tightly-clustered results from Edmund's reign invite further investigation. There is much more to be said on some other occasion about metal contents, for example about bismuth, about the use of zinc, and about the variability of the silver contents.

Meanwhile, there is one useful aspect of the numismatic evidence from the mid-tenth century where the margins of uncertainty are, fortunately, negligible. The attribution of coins to a particular king rarely presents any problem, and within the

51. See n. 11 above.

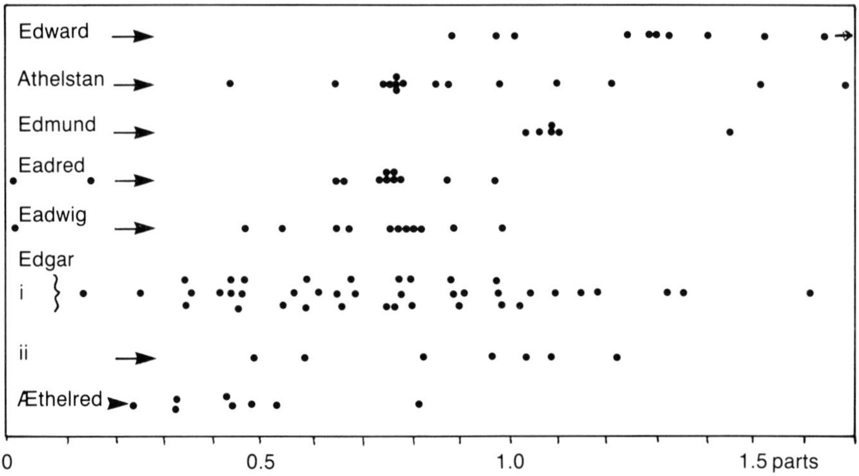

Fig. 8.1 Changes in the pattern of gold traces during the tenth and early eleventh centuries. (Parts of gold per 100 parts of silver. Source: McKerrell and Stevenson.)

periods marked out by their reigns, therefore, the age-structures of the hoards are certain and precise. The histogram (fig. 8.2, of the Chester hoard of 1950[52]) shows a familiar pattern of negative skewness. Reign by reign, that is to say, the later coins are more numerous. Each column in the histogram has an *area* corresponding to the number of coins of a particular king occurring in the hoard. In other words, one may think of the *height* of the column as reflecting 'coins per year'. The negative skewness could be explained in either (or both) of two ways. Mint output may have increased reign by reign, or (altogether more plausibly) old coins may have fallen out of circulation. Estimates of numbers of dies used in later reigns can be derived from the Iona and Chester 1950 hoards. The estimates are not directly comparable, because both those hoards reflect the regional currency of northern England, whereas the Vatican hoard, as mentioned, is predominantly southern. One's impression is that in the third quarter of the century mint-output was on very roughly the same scale as it had been in the first quarter. Nearer than that one cannot say. But even such a vague assessment entitles us to interpret the histogram in terms of a dwindling survival of older coins.

When we remember the very large number of dies used, mainly in the south of England, by Edward the Elder, and see what a trifling proportion of his coins remained in use in the 960s, the scale of the probable losses from the currency begins to appear although obviously we need logically to exclude other possibilities, such as the heavier average weight of Edward's coins resulting in culling, or more particularly a general recoinage, which would have swept most of the older coins away.

52. C. E. Blunt and R. H. M. Dolley, 'The Chester (1950) hoard', *BNJ* 27 (1952–4), 125–60.

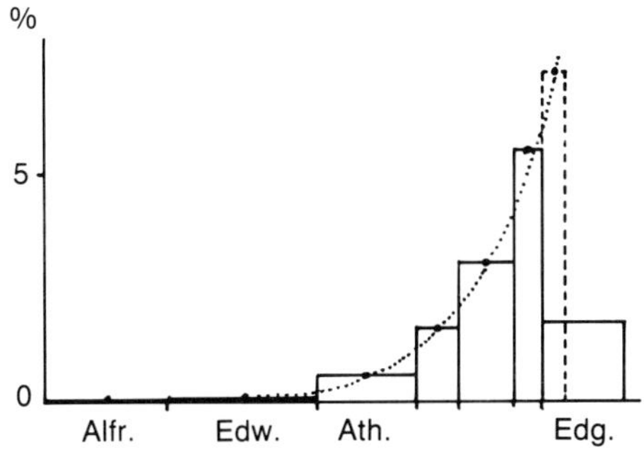

Fig. 8.2 Age-structure of the Chester, 1950 hoard. (The tall column shown by broken lines represents a possible interpretation of the coins of Edgar in the hoard. The dotted line joining the mid-points of the columns can be interpreted as a measure of the wastage rate. Percentage of the coins in the hoard, per year, reign by reign. Source: table 8.2.)

The column for the latest reign in fig. 8.2 is lower than the preceding column, but this is no doubt because Edgar's coins have been assumed in the drawing of the diagram to be spread evenly throughout the period up to c.973. If, as is likely, the hoard was concealed in the mid 960s, the true picture would need a taller and thinner column of the same area – though not as tall as that shown, for example, by the dotted line. Some allowance should in this case be made for the time taken by coins to pass into circulation.

Similar histograms have been constructed for other finds, and in order to make them match each other, they have all been based on the *percentage* composition of the hoard. The total area enclosed by each histogram is therefore the same and their shapes can be compared. Those for the Bath grave-find[53] and the Tetney hoard[54] (figs 8.3, 8.4) show a steeper wastage-rate, as do the Rome (Forum) 1883[55] and the Iona[56] hoards (figs 8.5, 8.6). In each of them the final column may need to be reinterpreted.

Taken in their order of date of deposit the hoards form a sequence (table 8.1) which reveals, so far as one can judge, a steady process of wastage. If there had been a general recoinage at some particular date, one would have expected it to show up as an interruption in the profiles, visible at the same date in more than one hoard. There is no obvious sign of any such cut-off, and on that basis one may suggest that the disappearance of old coins was occurring essentially by a continuous process of wastage. Far more hoard-evidence would be welcome, but already one can suspect

53. C. E. Blunt and H. E. Pagan, 'Three tenth-century hoards: Bath (1755), Kintbury (1761), Threadneedle Street (before 1924)', *BNJ 45* (1975), 19–32.
54. J. Walker, 'A hoard of Anglo-Saxon coins from Tetney, Lincolnshire', *NC*[6] *5* (1945), 81–95.
55. Blunt, 'Athelstan', 141–55.
56. R. B. K. Stevenson, 'The Iona hoard of Anglo-Saxon coins', *NC*[6] *11* (1951), 68–90.

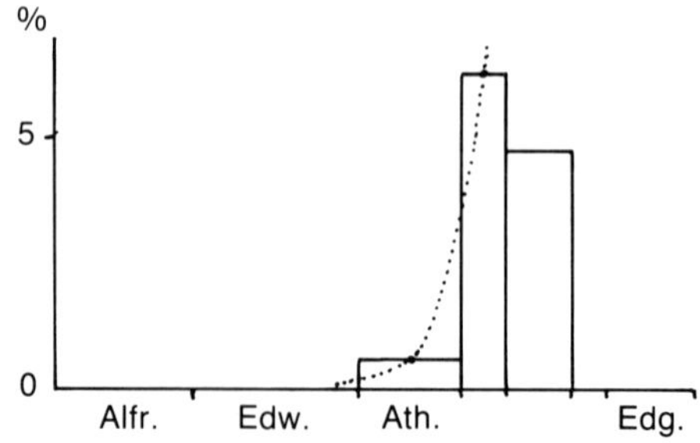

Fig. 8.3 Age-structure of the Bath grave-find. (Source: table 8.1.)

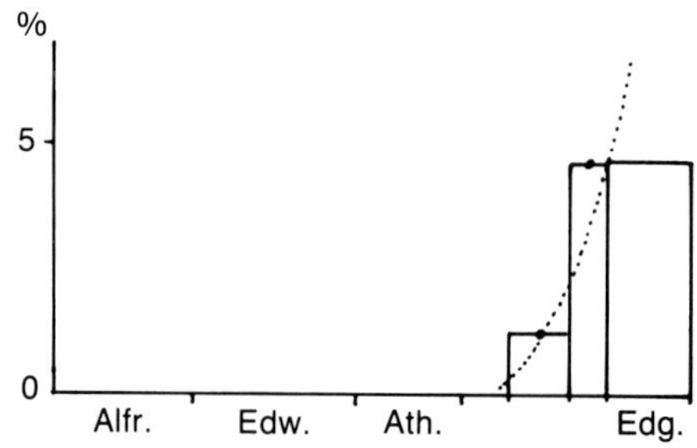

Fig. 8.4 Age-structure of the Tetney hoard. (Source: table 8.1.)

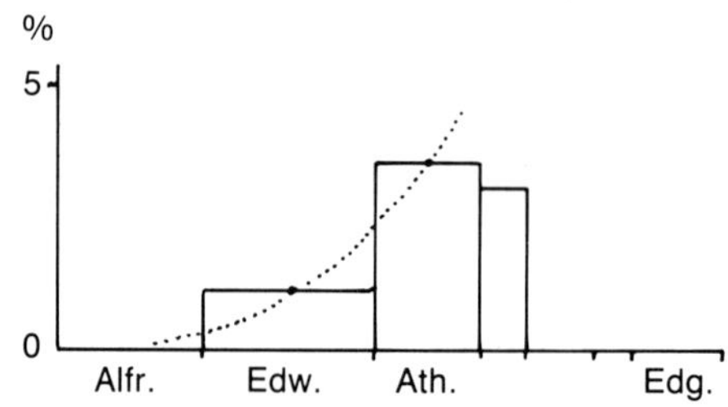

Fig. 8.5 Age-structure of the Rome (Forum) hoard of 1883. (Source: table 8.1.)

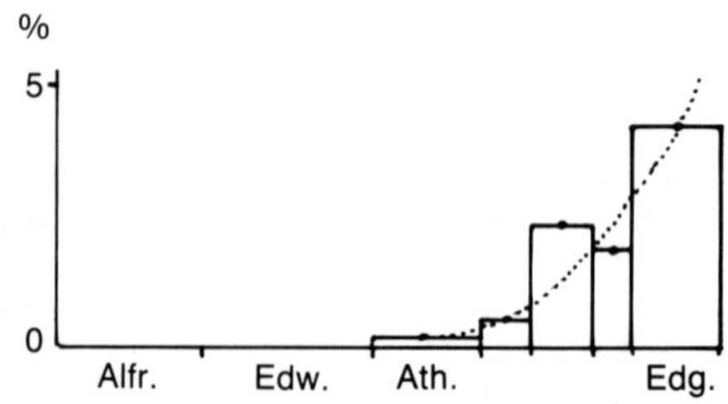

Fig. 8.6 Age-structure of the Iona hoard. (Source: table 8.2.)

Table 8.1. Age-structure of tenth-century finds from England and the Continent: percentage compositions converted into rates per year, reign by reign

	Rome (Vatican)	Rome (Forum)	Bath	Kintbury	Tetney	Chester 1857 (Eastgate)
Alfred (and Plegmund)	0.43	0.04				
Edward the Elder	3.39	1.04				
Athelstan	(0.48)	3.51	0.54	0.64		
Edmund		(3.01)	6.25	1.14		
Eadred			(4.72)	4.04	1.21	1.26
Eadwig				11.36	4.65	2.85
Edgar					(4.70)	5.13
(No. of coins listed)	516	809	40	11	414	35

that there were different wastage-rates in different regions. The Chester 1950 hoard (fig. 8.2) in particular has a more extended age-structure (a savings hoard? – an accumulation of money from beyond English territory brought back into the country? – or just a sample of the currency in the north-western region?), whereas Chester 1857, Tetney (Lincs.) and the more southerly finds from Bath and Kintbury[57] have much steeper profiles.

If for the sake of argument we assumed that mint-output was at a steady level reign by reign, the steepness of the profile would be a direct measure of the wastage-rate. By projecting curves through the mid-points of the steps of the histogram (see the dotted line in fig. 8.2 and similarly in figs 8.3–6) we could quantify the wastage by saying that the currency declined to half its original volume in x years. For the steeper profiles a figure of 10 or 15 years is in question. This is of course only a rough and conjectural estimate, but unless coin production accelerated greatly as the tenth century elapsed, it should be of the right order of magnitude. In the early eleventh century wastage was sometimes at a much higher rate: on occasion the currency had a half-life of as little as two or three years. But a half-life even of ten or fifteen years, it may be suggested, would be a vital clue to the character of tenth-century monetary affairs.

There is a group of foreign hoards,[58] each of which is dominated by pre-reform coins of Edgar, but in which there is a 'tail' of earlier coins, and it is instructive to see (table 8.2) that they are reasonably consistent with each other and (more important) that their age-structures are such as to yield a 'normal' pattern of negative skewness,

57. Blunt and Pagan, *op. cit.* One should mention that the Kintbury coins may not give a fair view of the find's age-structure, for we have only a handful of specimens out of (?) 'some hundreds'.
58. C. E. Blunt, 'The Smarmore hoard of tenth century pennies', *BNJ 27* (1952–4), 161–6; W. A. Seaby, 'Anglo-Saxon hoards and coins found in the north of Ireland', *BNJ 29* (1958–9), 248–50 (Derrykeighan); R. H. M. Dolley, 'The "lost" hoard of tenth-century Anglo-Saxon silver coins from Dalkey', *JRSAI 91/1* (1961), 1–18; and generally as in Dolley, *Hiberno-Norse Coins*.

Table 8.2. Age-structure of tenth-century hoards from Ireland, etc.: percentage compositions converted into rates per year, reign by reign

	Tipperary	Lough Lene	Dalkey	Smarmore	Derrykeighan	Douglas	Machrie	Iona	Chester, 1950
Alfred		0.24							0.01
Edward	1.33	—	0.16	0.17					0.05
Athelstan	3.17	1.70	0.39	0.21	0.12	0.24	0.52	0.20	0.65
Edmund	2.78	1.79	1.03	1.09	0.11	0.28	—	0.54	1.61
Eadred		3.70	1.22	1.29	1.14	1.12	0.67	2.31	3.03
Eadwig		4.76	1.37	3.26	1.71	1.68	0.60	1.99	5.50
Edgar		(0.32)	4.39	3.96	5.36	5.17	5.62	4.16	(1.83)
(No. of coins)	18	21	73	69	117	89	83	327	514

although with a more extended profile than the English hoards and grave-finds (other than the Chester 1950 hoard). Any idea that they are essentially loot, promptly buried intact in a zone where a money economy had scarcely developed, is open to the objection that their age-structure is (almost certainly) different from that of the regional currency in the north-west of England. This difference has a bearing on the question whether there was in any real sense a local currency in Ireland (as there was, arguably, in Scandinavia[59]). The topic deserves fuller consideration, and here I will only observe that the theory of a one-way flow of 'loot' (with a high burial-rate) would not by itself be a sufficient explanation for the probable wastage-rates in England, given the volume of the English currency and its perennial renewal. Nor does it make good sense of the prolific minting at Chester.

Let us turn next to metrology, in order to ask whether there are any tenth-century precedents for the astonishing manipulations of weight-standards which lie at the heart of Æthelred II's monetary policies. Alfred's reform of (?) c.886 marked the decisive change, and under Edward the average weight of the penny remained uniformly high (c.1.58g), but by the time of Edmund the standard had been reduced, apparently, to c.1.52g or a little less. Certainly Edgar's *Two-line* (*BMC* i) and *Circular* (*BMC* iii/iv) types were on different weight-standards from each other, yet they could be hoarded together; and even coins on the same standard varied quite widely above and below the mean. The differences may have been essentially regional, but even so, all the coins were presumably of equal value for payments within England (this may be what the Grateley decrees mean when they speak of '*one coinage* over all the king's dominion'), and we must assume that over-valuation was normal, i.e. there was nothing to be gained, within England, by sorting out the heavy coins and taking them back to a moneyer to be re-minted. There was inevitably an advantage in choosing heavy coins to take out of the country, and it is curious that it seems not to have happened on any great scale – although one should add that the tenth-century evidence has never been laid out. (The theory offered to explain the higher proportion of heavy coins found in eleventh-century Scandinavia is that

59. Metcalf, 'Some twentieth-century runes'.

having been issued early in the validity-period, they had longer in which to be randomly chosen for export. Testing the evidence statistically to distinguish between this and selective export would be a delicate task.[60]) If culling had been prevalent, it would hardly have escaped the attention of the authorities, and one imagines that a sense of annoyance at being obscurely cheated would have provoked some response.

What about weight-variation within types? Do histograms of pre-973 coinages reveal a compact distribution, with a single peak, like those for Edward the Confessor, and unlike Æthelred's more complicated histograms?[61] Although this question is in principle a simple one, the evidence from which an answer can be derived is, as we shall see, by no means straightforward, even at a numerical level.

The histograms that follow have been drawn to the same horizontal/vertical scale and with the same step interval as Bertil Petersson's histograms of the coin types from c.973 to c.1030,[62] and as they are also the same size, they are visually exactly comparable.

Figure 8.7 shows the weights of the *Two-line* type of Edgar in the Tetney hoard – a thoroughly normal-looking distribution, based on nearly 300 coins. Identical coins seem to vary in weight as widely as the whole, but the variability in weight is much greater than under Edward the Confessor: the peak is neither as narrow, nor as tall.[63]

Figure 8.8 shows the same type in the Iona hoard[64] (although this time predominantly of north-western rather than north-eastern mintage), an equally normal histogram, but with a modal value of 1.07g instead of 1.20g. (If in the Tetney histogram the height of the central step were maximized by shifting its position, it would compare more closely in height with Iona.) There may have been regional differences, but the coins of the prolific moneyer Heriger fall very similarly within the histogram. The difference in position between the two histograms would seem therefore to arise from the history of the coins since burial (leaching; modern cleaning) and not from their issue at different weight-standards, nor from selective hoarding.

60. If the Scandinavian currency was 'enriched' with heavy coins, then measuring it against the correspondingly depleted English currency offers an artificial comparison, and the more so the heavier the wastage. Comparisons against the numbers of dies used are not straightforward either, in so far as they may rely on the assumption of equal (average) die-output at the beginning and end of a validity-period. See Blackburn and Metcalf, 'Five-finger exercises', and note the useful case of Edgar's (named) coins, below.

61. H. B. A. Petersson, *Anglo-Saxon Currency, King Eadgar's Reform to the Norman Conquest* (Lund, 1969), 179–94. The reader may also wish to consider the outstandingly good metrological evidence of the Morley St Peter hoard, and Petersson's suggestions (in *SCBI East Anglia*) about variations within a single type.

62. It should be noted that Petersson's histograms are not all on the same vertical scale. His figs. 8 onwards are *not* comparable with those printed here.

63. Mr Lyon has ponted out to me, however, that the York and Lincoln coins respectively are on significantly different weight-standards in the Tetney hoard. It is salutary to note that the histogram conceals this.

64. Data from *SCBI* Edinburgh.

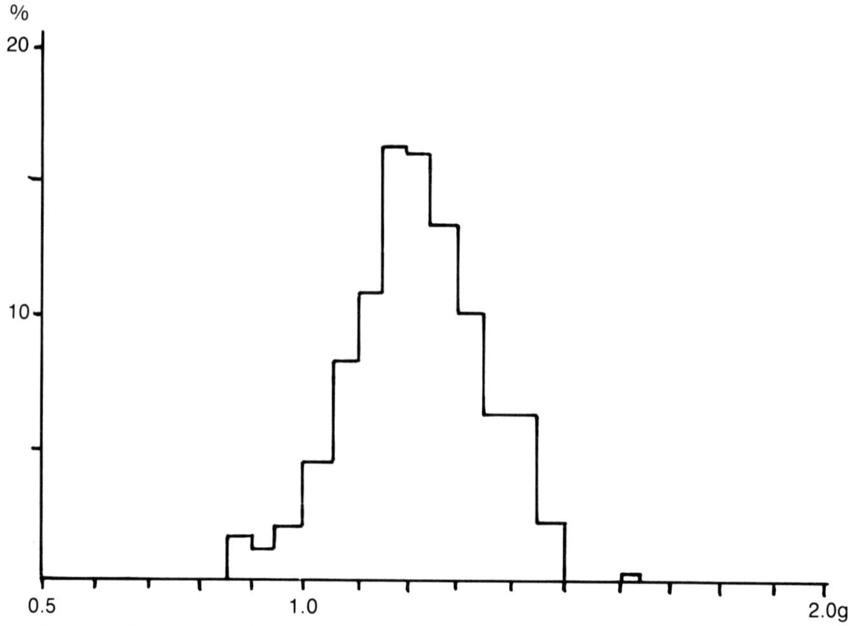

Fig. 8.7 Histogram of the weights of coins of Edgar, *Two-line* type, in the Tetney hoard (to the same scale as Petersson's histograms). No. of coins, 287.

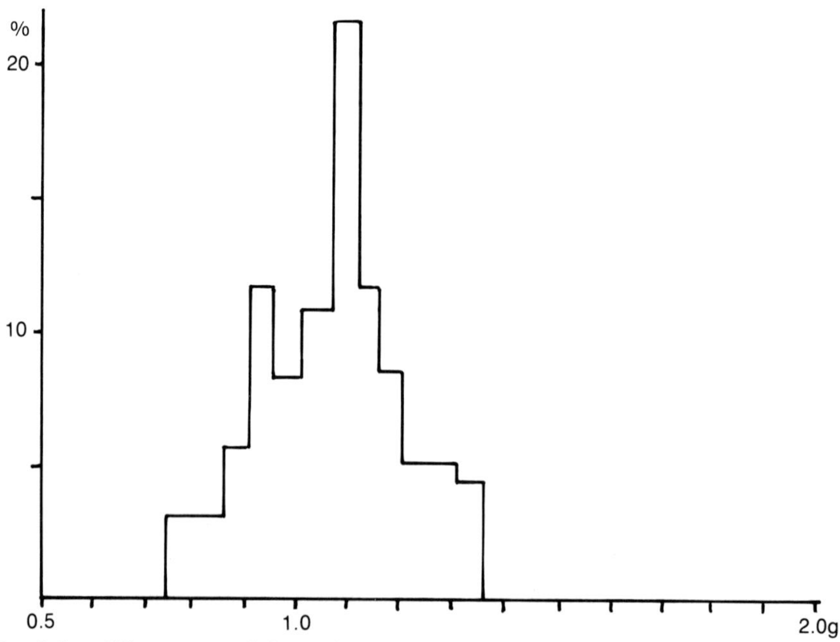

Fig. 8.8 Histogram of the weights of coins of Edgar, *Two-line* type, in the Iona hoard. No. of coins, 119.

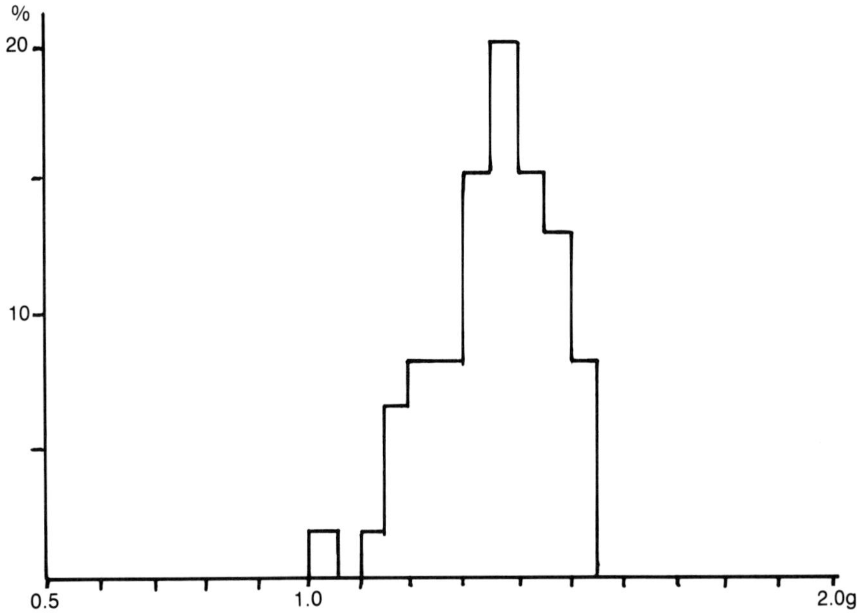

Fig. 8.9 Histogram of the weights of coins of Edgar, *Two-line* type, in the Chester, 1950 hoard. No. of coins, 59.

Figure 8.9, for exactly the same varieties, again, in the Chester hoard of 1950, shows yet another modal point, at c.1.37g or a little higher, but this time with signs of culling of the heaviest coins. The coins of Eadwig in the three hoards vary similarly in their modal weights, with the upper part of the Chester histogram again truncated.

A dreadful warning: if one had followed a procedure similar to Petersson's, and combined the evidence of these three hoards, one would have obtained a superficially very convincing histogram with multiple peaks. It is much safer to keep the evidence of each hoard separate, at least in the first instance. This entails the need for large hoards, fully recorded, and it immediately cuts the available evidence down to less than is needed to answer all our metrological questions. But on the main point, the answer seems to be that weight-variation within an issue was indeed a new instrument of royal policy in c.973.

There are some small hints that in the final years covered by our survey, perhaps the last five or ten years, and in the first five years or so after the reform, monetary activity was depressed in southern England. It is recognized that the *Reform Small Cross* type (c.973–c.979) has had a very low survival-rate in comparison with, for example, Æthelred's issues, and that our knowledge of it is incomplete and quite possibly regionally distorted.[65] The sample of coins is so small that it is entirely

65. Metcalf, 'Continuity and change'.

possible there are mints unrecorded merely because their statistically expected representation would be close to or below one specimen. Even so, these coins of the 970s show the same pattern of export to Scandinavia as has been demonstrated for the *Long Cross* type from the List hoard, namely that the earlier issues of the type (in this case, in Edgar's name) reached Sweden in relatively greater quantities and that conversely they were depleted in England.[66] Die-estimation from a corpus of Edgar's coins based on the Swedish hoards should make matters clearer; meanwhile, one's impression is that the years c.973–5 are genuinely atypical in the regional distribution of minting, and that they saw London in very slack water, whereas business was brisk at York, Lincoln, Stamford, and Northampton. London's fortunes revived swiftly in the 980s; and one ought to ask for how long, before c.973, monetary inflows into the city had been in decline. The answer seems to be, throughout the third quarter of the tenth century.

Elsewhere, however, and specifically in the eastern Danelaw (Stamford, Northampton, Bedford, etc.), minting was active at that time; and the reform may have been devised in response to conditions that had arisen (or been perceived) within the preceding few years rather than gradually over the preceding quarter-century. Thus on the one hand, die-estimates derived from the Iona and the Chester 1950 hoards suggest that the quantities of coinage they reflect were very large, namely the output from upwards of 2,000 and c.6,000 reverse dies respectively;[67] and on the other hand, considerable numbers of moneyers for whom only a single specimen survives hint that work was slack at southern mints.

How should we respond to this apparent conflict of evidence? We must admit that much of the quantifiable information derives from the north Midlands or the north of England and from Ireland or from Man and the Isles. It has little to tell us directly about monetary circulation in southern England, about which we are very ill-informed. Yet economically the south, then as now, was the wealthier part of England, and it was there that the power of the English kings was based. Although the geographical patterns of the money supply were by no means directly related to regional prosperity deriving from agriculture, our ignorance of what was happening to the coinage in the south must be viewed as a serious blind spot.

What little find-evidence we have from the south is in some respects enigmatic. Blunt and Pagan have drawn attention to similarities between the Bath and Kintbury grave-finds – similarities which extend to the occurrence of the same moneyers, and they have shown that many of the coins are from Danelaw mints. The Bath find is coloured by coins from Northampton, more than 80 miles away.

66. This emerges from the statistics printed at 120f. in C. E. Blunt and C. S. S. Lyon, 'The Oakham hoard of 1749, deposited c.980', *NC*[7] *19* (1979), 111–21.
67. D. M. Metcalf, 'How large was the Anglo-Saxon currency?', *EcHR*[2] *18* (1964–5), 475–82, at 479f. Recalculation using the Good/Lyon formula indicates that the known dies reflect 15 per cent and 8.4 per cent of the output respectively. The large discrepancy in the results does not cast doubt on the statistical procedures. The hoards are not drawn from the same populations, and the Iona hoard shows a certain amount of 'clustering', which will have depressed the estimate.

There is a third, similar find from Hundon, in Suffolk, which has been discussed by the same authors. All three finds have been interpreted as hoards, concealed by their owners in consecrated ground as being in a safe place, unlikely to be robbed or disturbed, and together offering us a reasonable cross-section of the currency circulating respectively on the southern borders of Mercia and in East Anglia around the middle of the tenth century.[68] But all three were located in close association with a burial (thus at a sufficient depth, for obvious reasons), and the Bath and Kintbury finds were alleged to have lain *under* the skull. The Hundon find of 1687 was described as having been found near a skull, and, according to some accounts, was a pot hoard, and contained between two and three hundred coins. If this is true, it makes it difficult to believe that it was a grave-find; but numbers are sometimes exaggerated. The question turns on the customary depth of burial. A secretive hoarder excavating a large hole in a churchyard in order to conceal his wealth *under the skull* of a burial would, unlike Hamlet, have been mad more than just north-north-west; accordingly it may be argued that the coins were grave-goods. Their incompatibility with Christian burial makes one wonder whether the Bath and Kintbury burials were of (Danelaw) Danes who had settled in England and whose relations clung, in their grief, to social customs from their past. Paul Robinson, in a recent paper, brings out the distinction between grave-finds from within churchyards, and hoards concealed at the edge of churchyards.[69]

Because they had the money to buy farms and settle in the south, and because they remained 'foreigners', Danish families met with resentment and prejudice: Æthelred spoke of them as having 'sprung up in this island, sprouting like poisonous weeds among the wheat'.[70] Danes were not, of course, the only people who were buying farms. Sawyer reminds us that 'in all parts of England after the ninth century, individuals were acquiring the right to sell, lease, give or bequeath their land'. Indeed, the boot was sometimes on the other foot: there are records of land purchases made in order to settle Englishmen in the Danelaw.[71] Saving, by people of modest rank, in order to buy land may have immobilized a significant proportion of the coins 'in circulation'. Given this possibility, and the source of the coins at mints such as Bedford, Derby, or Northampton, can one after all be confident that the three finds are a cross-section of the *local* currency? Could the coins deposited at Bath and Kintbury have been drawn from savings that had been accumulated while the families were living in the Danelaw? It is, admittedly, improbable that such a chance conjunction would be repeated twice; and the finds do not exhibit the extended age-structure of savings hoards.

If, then, it were to emerge from an analysis of future finds that Danelaw coins were

68. Blunt and Pagan, 'Three tenth-century hoards', at 32. 'The association of all three finds with graves shows that the depositors lived at a time when . . . the sanctity of consecrated ground would be respected.'
69. P. Robinson, 'Saxon coins of Edward the Elder from St Mary's Churchyard, Amesbury', *NC* 1984, 198–201.
70. D. Whitelock (ed.), *EHD I, c.500–1042* (2nd edn, 1979), 591: 'like cockle amongst the wheat'.
71. P. H. Sawyer, *Kings and Vikings, Scandinavia and Europe, AD 700–1100* (1982), 107.

indeed supplying an important fraction of the currency in the south in the third quarter of the tenth century, as the Bath and Kintbury finds might lead one to suppose, there would be further reason to suspect that minting was at a low ebb there. And if Chester coins were prominent, they would again raise the question of long-distance trade – perhaps along a north-west/south-east axis (Watling Street?), which tended to leave the north-eastern and the West Saxon regions a little to one side of the main monetary currents of the tenth century. That thought, at least, is prompted by the tiny Welwyn find of 1912, where two of the three identifiable coins were of Chester.

The picture of tenth-century monetary affairs that has emerged from this survey is of a currency that was as large, probably, as it was during most of the eleventh century, or even larger, and of a wastage-rate high enough to suggest a considerable volume of overseas trade – but not as high as in the eleventh century. Nor was the geographical movement of coin within England as vigorous. If we compare the moneyers represented in the Tetney and the Chester 1950 hoards, for example, for the reigns of Edgar and Eadwig, the greatest similarities are in each case between the two reigns in the same hoard. At Tetney, many of the moneyers found under Eadwig recur under Edgar, while at Chester a broadly different set of moneyers appears. This suggests that the circulation of coin was more compartmented than in the eleventh century. The regionalism of the currency in the time of Athelstan has been well described[72] by Christopher Blunt:

> In the second quarter of the tenth century, the coinage of England was still being organized on a regional basis, and the regions were related to the areas of the former kingdoms and reflect the division of the country following the Treaty of Wedmore. This is clearly shown by the distinctive coinages of Wessex and Kent (combined), Mercia, East Anglia . . ., and Northumbria. The Danish shires south of the Humber (other than Norfolk and Suffolk) equally had an organization of their own, as did the north-midland area round Derby, Nottingham, Tamworth, and Leicester, and there is some evidence of a separate organization for an area on the Welsh border. The distinctive styles, as well often as types, of the coins show that the regions maintained their own die-cutting workshops from which neighbouring mints were supplied.

A rapid circulation of coins within the major regions of England – but not as rapid as in the eleventh century; a monetary system supported by minting in many *burhs* – but not as many as in the eleventh century; a high wastage rate – but not as high as in the eleventh century. By how much is 'not as much'? How could we attempt to measure the difference? The best index, finally, may be that offered by stray finds of single coins, for the size of the currency, as Stuart Rigold demonstrated, is not, beyond a certain point, a good index of the degree of monetization of the economy.[73]

72. Blunt, 'Athelstan', 114.
73. S. E. Rigold, 'Small change in the light of medieval site-finds', in *Edwardian Monetary Affairs (1279–1344)*, ed. N. J. Mayhew (BAR 36, 1977), 59–80.

At Winchester, the excavations have yielded only 5 coins from the tenth century, against 12 from the eleventh.[74] And similarly the Roach Smith collection of stray finds from London included only 3 coins from the tenth century, against 10 from the eleventh.[75] All told, there are over 270 single finds recorded from England in the eleventh century, whereas, for a period of almost the same length, a first sweep has produced fewer than 40 from the tenth century. The list could probably be extended, but the disparity is a real one, and it is almost certainly great enough (five-fold?) to suggest that coins were not passing from hand to hand on such an everyday basis, or not among such a wide section of the population, as they did after Edgar's reform.

We would perhaps be more willing to be impressed, nevertheless, by the vitality of the tenth-century monetary economy, by the speed of its recovery under Alfred and Edward the Elder, and by the activity of moneyers in so many *burhs* – if it were not outshone at almost every turn by the eleventh century.

74. C. E. Blunt and M. Dolley, 'Coins from the Winchester excavations, 1961–1973', *BNJ* 47 (1977), 135–8.
75. BM Accessions Register, 1935, 4–9–19/21; eleventh-century finds, *ibid.*, as listed in Metcalf, 'Continuity and change'.

9 Anglo-Saxon coins found in Italy

C. E. Blunt

In 1961, Michael Dolley and I read a paper at the International Numismatic Congress in Rome on the finds of Anglo-Saxon coins that had been made in Italy. For some reason that I forget we never published this and I suggested to him that the volume that was being prepared in his honour, now, alas, a memorial volume, would be a suitable place to bring up to date what we had jointly written and to this he readily agreed.

These finds are in the aggregate of outstanding importance for the study of our tenth-century coinage, indeed the Forum hoard is our largest recorded source for the coinage of Athelstan and Edmund, as was the Vatican hoard in the case of Edward the Elder until the discovery of the Morley St Peter hoard (and even after that discovery it remained the primary source because the Morley St Peter hoard was so largely confined to the coinage of East Anglia).

The finds on Italian soil consist of five substantial hoards, three of which have been well recorded, a sixth hoard of which very little is known, and a seventh containing just a single Anglo-Saxon coin. In addition, there are a number of isolated finds, some of which are of considerable significance.

Hoard no. 1, Rome 1830

The evidence for this is slight and its composition must remain in some doubt. Giulio di San Quintino writing on coins of the tenth and eleventh centuries found in the neighbourhood of Rome mentions incidentally a hoard found, he believed, in 1830, most of which he said was destroyed. But among the coins that survived he saw pennies of Offa, of two Pippins (of Herestal (*sic*) and of Aquitaine), of several rulers of France and England of the ninth and tenth centuries, and of contemporary papal issues.[1] The publication is dated 1843 and it may well be that a coin of Offa and one of Pippin exhibited at the Numismatic Society in London on 25 May 1843, and stated to have been found at Rome, are from this hoard.[2] Neither coin can unfortunately be identified today. The description of the Offa is limited to the fact

Acknowledgments I am grateful to Mr Mark Blackburn for a number of very helpful suggestions made when editing this article.

1. G. di San Quintino, 'Monete del X e dell' XI Secolo scoperte nei dintorni di Roma nel 1843', *Memorie della Accademia delle Scienze di Torino*[2] *9/10* (1849), 7. We are indebted to Dr Michelini Tocci for this reference.
2. *NC*[1] *6* (1843), proceedings, p. 104.

that it has no portrait, and no description at all is given of the coin of Pippin, nor is it even said of which Pippin it is.

Perhaps to be associated with this hoard, although at least one coin has an earlier provenance, are two clearly defined groups of coins; the one in the Vatican Library consists of one coin of Egbert of Kent, three of Offa, one of Archbishop Æthelheard with Coenwulf, and one (perhaps a contemporary forgery) of Coenwulf;[3] and a comparable group of six coins of Offa and two of Coenwulf which were in the Borghesi sale of 1880.[4] All these coins are in the finest condition, of considerable rarity, and the existence of two parcels of this kind in collections which do not appear to have bought from abroad in these series strongly suggests a local origin.[5]

Hoard no.2, Rome (Vatican) c.1928

This hoard consists of 517 Anglo-Saxon coins, the greater part of which date from the first quarter of the tenth century, six Continental deniers of the same period, and three silver ingots. Its deposit may be dated c.927. It was dispersed in London in two sales in 1929 and 1930,[6] and fortunately Brooke had access to the whole parcel before dispersal and recorded all the weights. As a result of this and of her own investigations Miss O'Donovan has published a full list and reconstruction of the find.[7] The hoard was clearly collected early in the reign of Athelstan and the few coins of his (35 in all) are of considerable importance as providing a sure guide to his

3. C. E. Blunt and R. H. M. Dolley, 'The Anglo-Saxon coins in the Vatican Library', *BNJ 28* (1955–7), 449–58, at 449–53.
4. B. Borghesi II sale (Dura, Rome, 24 April 1880), lots 1362–9. The contents are:
   1362 Offa, moneyer Ibba. BMA no. 21 (C. E. Blunt, 'The coinage of Offa', *AS Coins*, 39–62, no. 61, illus.).
   1363 Offa, moneyer Eoba. Lockett (Glendining, 26 April 1960) lot 3564 (Blunt no. 52).
   1364 Offa, moneyer not stated, but Ryan (Glendining, 22 Jan. 1952) lot 613 is stated to be from this sale. Moneyer Dud (Blunt no. 31).
   1365 Offa, moneyer Ethelnoth. Possibly Lockett lot 3574 (Blunt no. 53).
   1366 Offa, moneyer Ethelwald. Possibly BMA no. 41, bought by Evans in Rome (Blunt no. 56).
   1367 Offa, moneyer Eoba. BMA no. 32 (Blunt no. 11, illus.).
   1368 Coenwulf, moneyer Ludoman. Probably Lockett lot 3591 (C. E. Blunt, C. S. S. Lyon, and B. H. I. H. Stewart, 'The coinage of Southern England, 796–840', *BNJ* 32 (1963), 1–74, no. Cn 20, illus.).
   1369 Coenwulf, moneyer Eama. Drabble (Glendining, 4 July 1939) lot 331, bought by Evans in Rome (Blunt, Lyon, and Stewart no. Cn 15, illus.). Probably the coin illustrated in 1739, see p. 165 below.
5. A note in the Borghesi sale catalogue after lot 1395 suggests that some of the Anglo-Saxon coins came from a hoard, but this comment covers coins from Offa to Edward the Confessor. The possibility that more than one hoard is involved is discussed below.
6. Glendining, 16 May 1929 and 13 Nov. 1930.
7. M. A. O'Donovan, 'The Vatican hoard of Anglo-Saxon pennies', *BNJ 33* (1964), 7–29.

early issues. The find is known to have been made in Rome and understood to have been discovered in the Vatican City during construction of the wireless station there.

Hoard no. 3, near Catania, Sicily, before 1914

In 1962 the British Museum acquired a small parcel of Anglo-Saxon coins of the first half of the tenth century which were said to have been found, corroded into a solid mass, near Catania in Sicily before the First World War. The coins have been much overcleaned and their condition is consistent with the statement that all had been corroded together. There seems, moreover, no reason to doubt the somewhat unexpected provenance. The latest coins in the hoard are two of Edmund and the deposit is likely to have been c.940. The hoard has been fully published by Dolley in the *Numismatic Chronicle*.[8]

Hoard no. 4, Rome (Forum) 1883

This hoard was found in the excavations in the Forum at Rome in 1883, just outside the House of the Vestal Virgins. It consisted of over 800 Anglo-Saxon coins, the bulk of the reigns of Edward the Elder, Athelstan, and Edmund, four Continental deniers of Pavia, Regensburg, and Limoges, and a gold solidus of Theophilus (c.832?–c.839?). With the coins was found a pair of fibulae inscribed +DOMNO MA; +RINO PAPA (Pope Marinus II, 942–6). The hoard provides, as in the case of the Vatican hoard, a valuable source of material on the reigns of Edward the Elder and Edmund and is our most extensive recorded source for the coinage of Athelstan (398 coins). In addition, the few Viking coins struck in Northumbria have proved of vital evidential value, and the papal fibulae, believed to be unique of their kind, are, Dr Plenderleith very kindly informs us, extremely important as an early and closely dated example of niello work. The deposit may be placed c.945.

It is fortunate indeed that this hoard was recorded at the time by Commandante De Rossi,[9] and we are deeply indebted to Professor Panvini Rosati, in whose care at the time it lay, for permitting us to make a complete photographic record of it (a copy of which is deposited in the British Museum) and for offering facilities for some of the more significant coins and the fibulae to be cleaned. For the execution of the first stage of this delicate task we are much indebted to the expertise of Dr Plenderleith.

Hoard no. 5, Rome 1846

The only evidence for this hoard is the entry by Vaux in the British Museum Register of 94 coins bought for £64 4s 0d. from Signor Campanari, a Rome dealer, on 15 September 1846, 'found at Rome'. The entry in the register is sufficiently detailed to

8. R. H. M. Dolley, 'A hoard of Anglo-Saxon pennies from Sicily', *NC*[7] *1* (1961), 151–61.
9. De Rossi, 'A hoard of Anglo-Saxon coins found in Rome', *NC*[3] *4* (1884), 225–55, tr. C. F. Keary. See also C. E. Blunt, 'The coinage of Athelstan, 924–939. A survey', *BNJ 42* (special vol., 1974), 35–158, at 141–55.

enable all but one of the coins to be identified in the collection today. There is nothing to show whether this was the hoard in its entirety. There may well have been Continental coins in it as well as the English. But the fact that there are several near duplicates suggests that the parcel acquired by the British Museum may have been the bulk of the English element, though there is a possibility that a small group of comparable coins in the Borghesi sale of 1880 could have come from the find. The 94 coins acquired by the British Museum were of the following reigns:

Edward the Elder	11
Athelstan	30
Edmund	42
Eadred	8
Norse	2
unlocated	1
Total	94

A detailed list is given as an appendix to this paper, and to this are added details of the ten coins in the Borghesi sale.

The two coins of Eric, both of his first reign, 947–8, provide a *terminus post quem* for the deposit. If this find represents, as it well may, a contribution collected for the Holy See, it would be a current collection rather than a savings hoard. So the fact that there are only eight coins of Eadred out of a total of 94 may be taken as pointing to a date for the loss not too late in his reign – say c.950. There is a distinct East/North-East flavour about the hoard. From that area come 15 coins of Athelstan, 13 of Edmund, 3 of Eadred, and the 2 of Eric, in all 33 coins out of a total of 94.

A silver gilt strap-distributor of trefoil shape presented to the British Museum in 1847 is recorded as being from a hoard of tenth-century coins found in Rome. The likelihood is that this came from the 1846 hoard.[10]

Hoard no.6, near Rome before 1859

A gold ring with legend + AVFRET was found near Rome some years before 1859 and exhibited at the Society of Antiquaries in that year.[11] It was said to have been found with 'a considerable number' of coins of Alfred. The ring is now in the Victoria and Albert Museum;[12] the coins have not been traced and no more details of them have been found, but it is possible that they were the pieces referred to by E. V. Lucas in his *A Traveller in Rome*,[13] where he writes that, on a visit to the Hospital of the S. Spirito in Rome, he was shown 'a few corroded Saxon coins, too defaced to identify,

10. D. M. Wilson, *Anglo-Saxon Ornamental Metalwork 700–1100 in the British Museum* (1964), 161–3, no. 63.
11. *ArchJ 16* (1859), 194.
12. C. C. Oman, *Catalogue of Rings, Victoria and Albert Museum* (1930), 64, no. 228 and frontispiece. See also A. Ward *et al.*, *The Ring from Antiquity to the Twentieth Century* (1981), 45–6, where it is suggested that the ring may be Byzantine.
13. (London, 1957), 350; a reference kindly brought to my attention by Dr Paul Robinson.

all that could be seen and felt of England's long association with this part of Rome'. A tantalisingly vague sentence follows. His guide 'had every Saxon visitor at his finger ends, and how odd it was to hear someone refer to "Alfredo Magno"!' Since the coins were 'too defaced to identify', one cannot link the reference to Alfred with them.

My brother Anthony kindly visited the Hospital on my behalf in November 1980 and was told that it was true that they had had some coins but that they had been sold. It seems unlikely that the problem can be solved unless some numismatist actually saw the coins in the possession of the Hospital and made a note of them.

Hoard no.7, Ariccia, south of Rome between the Alban and Nemi lakes, 1885

This scantily published hoard contained some 213 coins, mostly German of the late tenth century, but it included one said to be of Æthelred II (mint, moneyer, and type unrecorded),[14] although it is possible that this was a Continental derivative, for example, from Bohemia.

Although outside the scope of this article, mention should be made of ten Hiberno-Norse coins of the mid-eleventh century said to have been found in north Italy.[15]

Isolated finds

With the exception of a 'sceat' of the first half of the eighth century said to have been found in Ostia,[16] the isolated finds from Italy fall into three distinct periods: c.775 to 800, shortly before 900 to 965, and 1016 to 1066. If it may be assumed that all the Anglo-Saxon coins in the Vatican Library were found within the patrimony of St Peter, the isolated finds which have been either procured or allegedly found in Italy may be summarized as follows:

Group 1, c.775–800

(a) A unique penny of Heaberht, king of Kent, who was a contemporary of Offa. This is of a similar type and by the same moneyer as a penny of Egbert of Kent in the Vatican Library (of which one other example is known) and may well be the earliest

14. *Notizie degli scavi di antichità comunicate alla R. Accademia dei Lincei*, 1885, 428; 1886, 25–6; J. Lafaurie, 'Le trésor monétaire du Puy (Haute-Loire)', *RN*[5] *14* (1952), 59–169, at 114, no. 16.
15. M. Dolley and S. N. Lane, 'A parcel of late eleventh-century Hiberno-Norse coins found in Northern Italy', *BNJ 37* (1968), 25–8. The coins are nos. 223, 225, 227, 229, 231, 233, 235, 237, 240 and 243 in *SCBI* Copenhagen pt v, where they are dated to the mid-eleventh century. Isolated finds of Hiberno-Norse coins are also recorded from Italy, e.g. one of Dolley's Phase VI from Aosta, north Italy (*NCirc* May 1970, nos. 5683), now in the Fitzwilliam Museum.
16. *BMC* type 48 (Rigold series H); although of unusual style, scientific analysis has apparently confirmed its authenticity. We are grateful to Dr D. M. Metcalf for information about this coin, which will be published in his forthcoming report on the 'sceattas' from the Southampton excavations.

surviving English broad penny. It was procured by Lord Grantley in Rome before 1900.[17]

(b) The celebrated dinar of Offa, now in the British Museum, imitating a gold coin of Caliph Al Mansur, dated 157 AH (= AD 774). The purpose of this coin has been the subject of considerable speculation, some maintaining that it is one of the mancuses which Offa is known to have sent to the Pope, others that it was struck for the purpose of overseas trade.[18] It was procured by the Duc de Blacas in Rome some time before 1841.[19]

(c) Three pennies of Offa, one of the moneyer Lulla, found at Cognento, near Modena, and probably the specimen now in the Berlin Cabinet;[20] a second found at Baggiovara, near Modena, both published in a pamphlet in 1862/3 by F. Calori Cecis of Nonantola, near Modena;[21] a third, an early coin of Offa of the moneyer Eoba procured in northern Italy.[22] The second of these, allegedly reading on the reverse S.PETRVS, has been discussed at some length,[23] and it has tentatively been suggested that, if genuine, the coin might have been struck for the payment of Peter's Pence to Rome. It has still not been traced and there is no evidence that any English numismatist ever saw it, or even a drawing of it. Certainly there is none with Sir John Evans' papers on the subject. Evans never published it, nor has the coin appeared, as far as can be traced, in any collection or sale. Increasingly one is led to the conclusion that Evans decided that the piece was false or a complete fabrication, though one wishes that he had left a note with his final views, even if not for immediate publication.

(d) The celebrated penny of the East Anglian king Æthelberht, who died in 794, said to have been found in 1908 'below the walls of the city of Tivoli'.[24] The reverse type, the wolf and twins, is copied from a Roman bronze coin of Constantine the Great.

(e) Mr Mark Blackburn has very kindly drawn my attention to two coins of Coenwulf and one of Offa described and illustrated (fig. 9.1) in L. A. Muratori, 'De moneta, sive jure condendi nummos. Dissertatio vigesimaseptima', in his *Antiquitates Italicae Medii Ævi*, II (Milan, 1739).[25]

The first coin of Coenwulf is said to have been in the collection of Sabbatini, a collector in Rome whom Mr Blackburn has been unable to trace. The other two were in the collection of the *eruditissimus Eques* Franciscus Victorius, a scholar who published works on numismatics between 1736 and 1749. An Italian provenance for

17. The coin, now in my collection, was lot 878 in the third Grantley sale (Glendining 22 March 1944) and is discussed in C. E. Blunt, 'A coin of Heaberht, king of Kent. Lord Grantley's attribution vindicated', *BNJ* 27 (1952), 52–4.
18. See Blunt, 'Coinage of Offa', 50–1 and references there cited.
19. A. de Longpérier, 'Remarkable gold coin of Offa', *NC*[1] 4 (1841), 232–4.
20. Blunt, 'Coinage of Offa', no. 69.
21. F. C. Cesis, *Di una rara moneta di Offa Re de' Merciani* (Bologna, 1862–3).
22. Blunt, 'Coinage of Offa', no. 10.
23. *Idem*, 44–6.
24. *SCBI* Norweb Collection, 105.
25. Pp. 547–765, at 751 (description) and 760 (illustration); reprinted in P. Argelati, *De monetis Italiae variorum illustrium virorum dissertationes*, I (Milan, 1750), 1–98, at 91 and pl. 79.

Fig. 9.1 Coins illustrated by Muratori (1739)

the coins seems likely. Though the engravings of the two Coenwulf coins differ slightly in detail, the fact that only one specimen of the variety is known today makes it at least possible that the engravings are of the same coin, which must be the one that was later lot 1369 in the Borghesi sale (Blunt, Lyon, and Stewart Cn 15, see n. 4 above).

The coin of Offa is by the moneyer Ethelvald, a variant of Blunt nos. 55–6, if the engraving is accurate. On no. 55 the horizontal dotted line between the two lines of the inscription ends in three branches; on 56 it ends with a cross. On the Italian coin each line is shown as ending in a rosette of pellets. This variant had not been previously recorded and the coin itself has not been traced.

Group 2, c.900–65

In the Vatican Library there are six unprovenanced coins, two of Edward the Elder, one of Edmund, two of Eadred, and one of Edgar.[26] Two are important: Eadred *BMC* v (BC) by a moneyer Hildulf, hitherto unrecorded in the type; Edgar *BMC* iii (CC) without mint-name, but by a moneyer Selewold, who is an Oxford moneyer in Edgar's last (BD) type. This too was not previously known. A pierced coin of Edmund *BMC* vi (BC) by the moneyer Ergimbalt was said in the Wylie sale catalogue to have been 'found in Italy' and may have been an isolated find, if it is not a stray from the Rome (1846) hoard discussed in the Appendix below.

In the British Museum is a brooch made from a tooled coin of Edward the Elder

26. Blunt and Dolley, *op. cit.*, 454–5. The abbreviations for the coin types used here and in the Appendix below are explained in C. E. Blunt, I. H. Stewart, and C. S. S. Lyon, *Coinage in Tenth-Century England* (forthcoming).

which is said to have been dug up at the Villa Wolkonsky in Rome.[27] The coin is an example of the East Anglian issue that formed so large an element in the Morley St Peter hoard. The obverse reads +EADVVEARD RE+: the reverse FRAMV/VIS M-O, both retrograde. The ornaments on the reverse consist, at the top, of a cross with trefoils of pellets either side, and at the bottom, a single trefoil of pellets; three crosses form the middle line. The bust on the obverse has been skilfully tooled to make a very decorative centre to the brooch.[28]

Group 3, 1016–66

Four unprovenanced coins in the Vatican Library, two of Cnut and one each of Edward the Confessor and Harold II, are of this last period of the Anglo-Saxon kingdom. None of these is of special significance. In addition there are five coins in the Vatican Library which were found in excavations under St Peter's, one each of Egbert of Wessex, Æthelwulf, Cnut, Harold I, and Edward the Confessor.[29] The only one of these to call for special mention is the curious one of Harold I's *Jewel Cross* type, an irregular piece of Lincoln by Lefwine, with retrograde obverse legend and right-facing bust.[30]

In the course of excavations in November 1844 at the church of St Paul, *extra muros*, about 400 coins of the tenth to eleventh centuries were found, 'Saxon, Italian, French, Danish, Hungarian and German'. Among the 'Saxon' pieces (number not stated) two are specifically mentioned: Cnut '*Ethric on Rumford*', and Edward the Confessor '*Godfrine on Lund*'. These, 'with other Saxon pieces' were in the possession of the London dealer Mr Curt.[31] Though the group appears to be fairly close in date, it is better to regard the coins as casual offerings of pilgrims rather than a normal hoard.

We have thus the period extending from the introduction of the broad penny to about 800 represented by both a hoard (or hoards) and a significant number of isolated finds, and a second period covering the last years of the ninth century and the first half of the tenth in which occur five hoards and a smaller number of isolated finds, and it may not be without significance that in each of these periods there are known Italian coins (of great rarity) which imitate Anglo-Saxon types. Two coins of Charlemagne, struck at Lucca, are direct imitations of coins of Offa and two more, in the name of a Pope John, derive, the one clearly directly, the other less certainly, from coins of Edward and Athelstan respectively.[32] The only other instance of an imitative type that has been noticed is on a coin of Gaeta that may be dated 978–84 which appears to copy a type introduced in England in 973–5.[33]

27. Illustrated *BNJ 26* (1949–51), pl. B facing p. 234, where it is stated that the brooch was found with the Vatican hoard. This has since proved incorrect.
28. Wilson *op. cit.*, 163, no. 64, pl. 28 (enlarged).
29. Blunt and Dolley, *op. cit.*, 453–7.
30. H. R. Mossop, *The Lincoln Mint c.890–1279* (1970), pl. 58.17.
31. *NC*[1] 7 (1844), 195.
32. C. E. Blunt, 'Four Italian coins imitating Anglo-Saxon types', *BNJ 25* (1945–9), 282–5.
33. J. P. C. Kent, 'A south Italian imitation of an Anglo-Saxon penny', *BNJ 28* (1955–7), 648.

APPENDIX

ROME (1846) HOARD

The following is a list of the 94 coins acquired by the British Museum:[34]

Edward the Elder (899–924)
Horizontal two-line type (BMC ii)

Æthered	*BMC* 10		
—	*BMC* 12	Same obv. die as *SCBI* East Anglia 125, moneyer Wulfred	
Ciolulf	*BMC* 27		
Clip	*BMC* 28		
Ealhstan	*BMC* 39		
Gareard	*BMC* 44		
Pitit	*BMC* 51		
Walter	*BMC* 70		
Wlfheard	*BMC* 65[35]		
Blundered	*BMC* 49		**10**

Diademed bust left (BMC iii)

Dudig	*BMC* 76		**1**

subtotal 11

Athelstan (924–939)
HT 1 (BMC i)

	BMS		
Johann	23		
Mathelwold	26		**2**

IIP 1 (BMC i)

Eclaf	18		**1**

HC 1 var (BMC i)

Sigebrand	31	Cross at top; 5 pellets bottom of rev.	**1**

HT 1, NE I (BMC i)

	BMS		
Are	200	Unusual lettering for *NE I*	
Arnulf	202		
Asulf	204		
Asael	205		
Clac	208		
Dominic	211		
Gislemer	214		
—	215		
Gota	218		
Harger	220		
Nothe	225		
—	226		**12**

HT 1 Irregular (BMC i)

Uncertain	264		**1**

CC (BMC v)

Chester, Wulfgar	69		
Tamworth, Manna	102	Struck from two rev. dies	
York, Regnald	113		**3**

BC (BMC viii)

London, Ælfstan	126		
— Beahred	128		
— Liofhelm	134		
Norwich, Bardel	138		
Wallingford, Beornwald	155	Same rev. die as a coin in the Forum board in the name of Edmund	
— Byrnwald	156		
Wareham, Ælfred	157		
Winchester, Wulfheard	162		**8**

BC var NE II (BMC xii)

Baldric	244		**1**

BC var NE III (BMC x)

Anlaf and Athelmod	256		**1**

subtotal 28

Edmund (939–946)
HT 1 (BMC i)

Abbun	277		

34. In this appendix *BMS*=*SCBI* British Museum, Athelstan-Edgar's Reform.
35. R. H. M. Dolley and J. S. Strudwick, 'The provenances of the Anglo-Saxon coins recorded in the two volumes of the British Museum catalogue,' *BNJ 28* (1955–7), 26–59, identifies the Wulfheard coin of Edward the Elder as *BMC* 113, but the labels in the cabinet make it clear that this should be a coin of the *Two-line* type. *BMC* 64 is, according to Dolley and Strudwick, undated and would be appropriate. But Mr Lyon has pointed out to us that *BMC* 65, which is there attributed to Cuerdale, is of a style too late for that of the hoard and it seems likely that the two coins have got confused. *BMC* 65 seems therefore likely to be the piece from the Rome (1846) hoard.

	BMS		
Ælfric (?)	278		
Ælfstan	279		
Ælfwald	280		
—	283		
Athelmund	286		
Beahired	287		
Diarelm	299		
Dudelet	300		
Manna	320		
Uncertain 'Nono'	322		
Oswald	325		
—	326		
—	327		
Otic	328		
Saxsa	334		
Siademan	335		
Wynnelm	344		
—	345		**19**
HB (BMC i)			
Wigard	351		**1**
HP 1 (BMC i)			
Eadred	353		
Hunsige	354		
Manna	355		**3**
HC 2 (BMC i)			
Eadred	362		**1**
HT 1 York (BMC i)			
Ingelgar	366		
—	371		
—	372		
—	373		**4**
HT 1, NE I (BMC i)			
Clac	383		
Domenc(es)	385		
Dregl	386	reads MOT	
Fugel	390		
Gota	392		
Pitit	400		**6**
HR 1 (BMC i)			
Boiga	407		
Eadmund	421		

	BMS		
Frard	430	Overstruck, obv. on rev., on a CC type, ?reign	
Mann	437	Obv. legend retrograde	**4**
HR 1 irregular (BMC i)			
Ruler and moneyer doubtful	462		**1**
BC (BMC vi)			
Ergimbalt	485		
Fredard	488		
Fugel	489		**3**
		subtotal	*42*[36]
Eadred (946–955)			
HT 1 (BMC i)			
Copoman	513		
Landferth	529		
Rædwine	538		
Warin	542		**4**
HT 1 North-eastern (BMC i)			
Theodmaer	579		
—	586		**2**
HR 1 (BMC i)			
Gislehelm	616		**1**
BC (BMC v)			
No mint, Fredard	702		**1**
		subtotal	*8*
Eric, 1st reign (947–948)			
HT 1 (BMC i)			
Ingelgar	1258		
Wulfelm	1263		**2**
		subtotal	*2*
Unidentified in BM Collection			
A coin at the end of Athelstan's list recorded as reading: IILLLII E			**1**
		subtotal	*1*
		Total	***94***

36. Dolley and Strudwick, *op. cit.*, identifies the following two coins of Edmund as from the hoard: *BMC* 63, Egered, and 91, Liafinc. Neither is listed in the BM register but both are illustrated in R. Ruding, *Annals of the Coinage* (3rd edn, 1840), pls. 18.9 and 19.14, then in the Tyssen collection. Neither therefore can be from the hoard.

LOTS 1372 AND 1378—86 IN THE BORGHESI II SALE OF 1880

Alfred *BMC* xv Æthered
Edward the Elder *BMC* ii Abba
BMC xi (Hand type) Athulf BMA 503
BMC xiii (Church type) Wulfgar
Sihtric *Caoch SCBI*. Copenhagen 627
Edmund *BMC* i (HT 1) Ærnulf
Eand-
BMC vi (BC) No mint, Ergimbalt
Eadred *BMC* i (HT 1) Theodmaer
Warin

There were examples of the two Eadred coins in the BM parcel of the Rome (1846) hoard; also the Edmund, Ergimbalt. Another by Ergimbalt, pierced, was in the Sotheby sale of the Rev. George Wylie, 10 July 1882, lot 257, 'found in Italy'.

10 Scandinavians, Celts, and Germans in Anglo-Saxon England: the evidence of moneyers' names

Veronica Smart

It was more than twenty years ago that Michael Dolley suggested to me that I might find material for research in the personal names appearing on the Anglo-Saxon coinage which designate the 'moneyer' – either the workman who actually struck the coin or the man who was to be held responsible for its quality.[1] These names, recorded on coins from the seventh century until the Conquest (and beyond into the reign of Henry III), had not been entirely neglected hitherto. Leaving aside the early antiquaries for whom everything was grist to the mill, many of the early monographs and collections in Old English onomastics made use of coin-legends, albeit as often from printed lists containing erroneous transcriptions as from first-hand scrutiny of the coins themselves.[2] Most of this early scholarship was concerned with collecting

Acknowledgments In addition to specific assistance acknowledged in the text, I am indebted to Dr N. P. Brooks, Dr Cecily Clark, and the editor of this volume Mr M. A. S. Blackburn, all of whom read an earlier draft of this paper and made many valuable suggestions.

1. For a survey of evidence for the social status of the moneyer see V. J. Smart, 'Moneyers of the late Anglo-Saxon coinage 973–1016', *Commentationes de Nummis Sæculorum IX–XI in Suecia Repertis II*, ed. N. L. Rasmusson and B. Malmer (Stockholm, 1968), 194–276, at 210–15.

   More recent work on the moneyers mentioned in the Winton Domesday is published in M. Biddle and D. J. Keane, 'Winchester in the eleventh and twelfth centuries', in *Winchester Studies* I, ed. M. Biddle (1976), 241–448, at 396–422.

   M. Dolley, L. Lundström, and G. van der Meer, 'A preliminary account of the Anglo-Saxon element in the 1966 find from Tingstäde parish', *BNJ 36* (1967), 62–80, at 70, record a coin of Æthelred II's *Crux* type on which the moneyer's name appears as *Osulf Thein*, and note that it 'sheds new light on the probable status of the Anglo-Saxon moneyer'. *SCBI 21 Yorkshire Collections* contains four York coins of Edward the Confessor reading VLFCTEL ÐEGINC, VLFCTL ÐAGINC (395–6, 492–3) which may have a similar significance, possibly applicable only to York.
2. For example O. von Feilitzen, *Pre-Conquest Personal Names in Domesday Book* (Uppsala, 1937); M. Redin, *Uncompounded Personal Names in Old English* (Uppsala, 1919); W. G. Searle, *Onomasticon Anglosaxonicum* (1894); E.

and interpreting linguistic material to supplement what was available in documentary sources. The novelty lay in trying to discover what might be achieved by applying the finer definitions of time and place which had been made in Anglo-Saxon numismatics largely as a consequence of Michael Dolley's work at the British Museum and in Stockholm. Coins could now be dated much more closely than merely to the regnal years of the ruler who issued them, and attempts had been made at localizing origin where no mint-name appeared on the coin.[3]

The object of studying these personal names is to add to the historical record. The names of the moneyers are by no means all Old English; Scandinavian names are found, and those for which a Continental derivation must be sought. Some Celtic names occur, and also present, though rare, are those biblical and saints' names which, though they play so large a part in name-giving after the Conquest, do not generally seem to have been in use among the Anglo-Saxons, and therefore beg an explanation when they do appear. Why such exotic names of all kinds occur, the time and place where they first appear and are most numerous, may well point to cultural movements, intensities, and influences which are only hinted at or not referred to at all in other records.

We are no longer content to talk of flavour, feel, or tendency. The demand is for quantification, and archaeological and numismatic publications are increasingly taken up by diagrams, graphs, and tables. The personal name material, however, is somewhat intractable to this treatment. The difficulty lies in the impossibility of assigning some names, in the form in which they are recorded, to one category or another. The Celtic names, and biblical and saints' names, are easily distinguished since they stem from a separate tradition and vocabulary, but these form the smallest groups by far to be considered. The bulk of the names belongs to three branches of the Germanic language group: Scandinavian, Continental Germanic, and of course native Old English. All three branches shared to a very large degree the same practice in name-giving and drew on a largely common specialized vocabulary of elements which were considered appropriate for name-formation. The distinctive linguistic characteristics of foreign names deriving from their separate development are frequently obscured in the forms which Anglo-Saxon scribes and die-cutters gave to them. Almost invariably they matched the foreign elements with their Old English cognates; typical of this practice is the annal for 897 in the Anglo-Saxon Chronicle[4] where the names of three Frisians are given as Æbbe, Æthelhere, and Wulfheard. If it were not for the designation *Friesa* suffixed to these names we could not tell that they were not Englishmen. Similarly an *Osbearn*[5]

Björkman, *Nordische Personennamen in England* (Halle, 1910).

3. A pioneer collection of studies on the reigns of, amongst others, Offa, Æthelwulf, Alfred, and Edgar appeared in 1961 in *AS Coins*.
4. *The Anglo-Saxon Chronicle: Two of the Saxon Chronicles Parallel*, ed. C. Plummer and J. Earle (1892–9), *s.a.* 897.
5. Moneyers' names and forms of names found on coins which are given here without other source may be found in *SCBI 28 Cumulative Index 1–20*, Index of Personal Names, 1–84.

on the coins may conceal a Scandinavian *Asbjorn*[6] or a Continental *Esbern*, Osbern.[7]

Occasionally, however, and especially in the coinage where one moneyer's name appears sometimes in several different forms, anglicization may not be so consistent that some tell-tale features may not be discerned in seemingly Old English names. In most cases the direction of change is from exotic into Old English. In some issues, however, where the dominant influence at the mint may have been other than Anglo-Saxon, we cannot entirely rule out the possibility of the reverse process.

Another criterion for the 'nationality' of a name is whether there is a reasonable amount of evidence for its usage in one Germanic folk-area rather than another. This should be formulated perhaps as an indication rather than a criterion, since it often relies on the *argumentum e silentio*, favouring those areas whose names are best documented. There are some items which are seldom or never found as name-elements in Old English even though they exist as words in the Old English lexicon. The Scandinavian name *Thorcetel* illustrates this with both its elements; the name of the Germanic god is found in the form *Thunor* in Old English, and *cietel* in the sense of 'cauldron',[8] but these words are not used in name-formation without Scandinavian influence. Other elements are more controversial. With combinations of elements into whole names there can be even less certainty since if both elements are known and productive in one group's sources it may only be the accident of non-survival that the whole name is not recorded there.

One class of formation seems to have been more popular amongst the Scandinavians than the English. This is the use of what are originally nicknames, possibly first used along with another more conventional name but later accepted as names in their own right.[9]

Having seen how the attribution of moneyers' names may stray all over ruled columns, and how arbitrary decisions on etymologically ambiguous names may, where the sample is small, distort a table to a point where it is misleading, we must further admit that the names cannot be used to plot regional patterns of settlement with mathematical exactness. It is unnecessary here to do more than mention the

6. Scandinavian names cited here without further comment may most easily be traced in G. Fellows Jensen, *Scandinavian Personal Names in Lincolnshire and Yorkshire* (Copenhagen, 1968), alphabetically under the individual names. The original sources have been collected, for West Scandinavian in E. H. Lind, *Norsk-Isländsk Dopnamn* (Uppsala, 1905–15), and for Danish in G. Knudsen and M. Kristensen, *Danmarks gamle Personnavne* (Copenhagen, 1936–48). Early Swedish forms are known mostly from runic inscriptions, which have been published by province, e.g. E. Wessen, *Upplands Runinskrifter* (Stockholm, 1940–58).
7. T. Forssner, *Continental Germanic Personal names in England in Old and Early Middle English Times* (Uppsala, 1916). Names which were current in Frankish territory are collected in M-T. Morlet, *Les Noms de personne sur le territoire de l'ancien Gaule du VI-XII siècle* (Paris, 1968).
8. *An Anglo-Saxon Dictionary Based on the MS Collections of J. Bosworth*, ed. T. N. Toller (1898), supplement and addenda by A. Campbell (1972).
9. Fellows Jensen, *op. cit.*, xxix-xxxi.

effects of fashion and the increasing mixture of names of different ethnic origin even within families as the end of the Anglo-Saxon period approached. Nothing succeeds like success, and an already strong Scandinavian presence in an area may well have popularized Scandinavian names as against English ones amongst the population at large. What must further be advanced is the doubt that has been cast by some recent studies on a simple picture of the moneyers of a borough as a stable part of the population, representative perhaps (though again special factors may have acted in their selection) of the borough and even of the surrounding countryside. Christopher Blunt has shown how in the reign of Athelstan the mint of Derby was probably opened by moneyers seconded from Chester.[10] Pauline Stafford has summarized and added to what is known of moneyer movements in the reign of Æthelred II, though from the nature of the evidence findings can often only be tentative.[11] In a recent paper Pamela Nightingale suggested that a mint could have been staffed in one of two ways: in some cases by a group of local men licensed as moneyers, but in others by royal agents sent into the mint from outside.[12] Her article deals mainly with post-Conquest conditions but considering that there is no visible break in continuity between the Anglo-Saxon and Norman coinages such a model cannot be ignored in our attempts to discover who the moneyers really were.

The inspiration for the beginning of the Anglo-Saxon coinage came from Merovingian Gaul, but there is little evidence that Continental craftsmen were prominent in setting it up.[13] The Continental name *Abbo* which appears on the early gold is probably only imitated from the prolific coinage in his name struck in Aquitaine, though *Eusebius*, the other name of Continental origin found in the gold series, may denote a craftsman who worked in Canterbury at the beginning of the seventh century.[14] The so-called 'sceat' coinage is largely anepigraphic. The few personal names which appear afford only a glimpse at the moneyers of the coinage of this period and suggest that native Anglo-Saxons had mastered the necessary skills since the names, *Pada*, *Æthelræd*, *Epa* and *Tilberht* are Old English. *Wigrd* (if it is to be expanded as *Wigræd*) is also Old English, but *Spi* is enigmatic. Similarly, when large corpora of moneyers' names first emerge in the domain of Offa with the new broad, flat pennies and in Northumbria with the copper 'stycas' of ninth-century kings and archbishops, the names of the moneyers are Old English almost without exception.[15] This appears to be the case with the moneyers of all the English kingdoms during the first half of the ninth century.

10. C. E. Blunt, 'The coinage of Athelstan', *BNJ 42* (1974), 35–158, at 93.
11. P. Stafford, 'Historical implications of the regional production of dies under Æthelred II', *BNJ 48* (1978), 35–51.
12. P. Nightingale, 'Some London moneyers, and reflections on the organisation of English mints in the eleventh and twelfth centuries', *NC 142* (1982), 34–50.
13. *BMC* I, p. xii.
14. C. H. V. Sutherland, *Anglo-Saxon Gold Coinage in the light of the Crondall Hoard* (1948).
15. C. E. Blunt, 'The coinage of Offa' in *AS Coins*, 39–62, at 56–9. Miss E. Pirie, Leeds City Museum, who is working on the Northumbrian 'styca' series, had kindly supplied me with a manuscript list of the moneyers known for this series.

There are, however, rare exceptions which show a tiny but continuous presence of men with Continental connections involved with the coinage. Approximately 30 moneyers strike coins for Offa and one name is probably to be considered as Continental, *Ludoman*;[16] amongst 35 moneyers recorded for the Northumbrian 'stycas' one name, *Odilo*,[17] is of similar origin. In East Anglia under Athelstan I the names *Reghelm* and *Rernher* (for *Regnher*?) may also be Continental in origin.

The group of names which I have termed 'German' in the title of this paper for the sake of succinctness in fact embraces all those names of Germanic structure and vocabulary which are known on the Continent but not among the Anglo-Saxons and Scandinavians, whether they originate from 'Germany', the Low Countries, or Frankish Gaul. Probably the majority of the biblical and saints' names which are found on English coins can also be assigned a Continental origin.

The Scandinavian names which occur amongst the moneyers are easily to be explained in general by a historically documented immigration and settlement. It may well be that there are differences in their concentration amongst moneyers from the population at large, but all the same, large concentrations of Scandinavian moneyers' names are found in just those areas where other sources indicate a heavy Scandinavian settlement. The Continental names are more enigmatic. Certainly there are documentary references to foreigners from the Continent in England, but it is difficult to obtain a clear idea of their strength in numbers and to what extent they were settlers rather than transitory visitors. Few of the place-names which contain Continental names have forms which go back to pre-Conquest times and it is therefore likely that most are Norman introductions, though a few may represent the first recorded instance of an older name. In Forssner's collection of Continental Germanic personal names in England,[18] now more than 60 years old, the number of pre-Conquest instances apart from moneyers is very small. Forssner's sources were limited mainly to the editions of charters available to him and such well-known historical records as the Anglo-Saxon Chronicle, and his collection certainly underestimates the Continental element in the population. Only six such names occur in Forssner for the period 1050–66 and yet no fewer than 120 are found in Domesday relating to the same period.[19] This larger number, however, cannot be taken to imply a consistently numerous presence going further back into the Anglo-Saxon period, since Edward the Confessor is known to have favoured the Norman French amongst whom he grew up.

Although it is not possible to establish figures for the prevalence of Continental Germanic names amongst the populace at large, it is difficult to avoid the conclusion that at certain periods there was some special connection between the occupation of moneyer and Continental origin or descent. An interesting parallel can be drawn from the fact that many of the other bearers of Continental names in Old English

16. E. Förstemann, *Altdeutsches Namenbuch* (Bonn, 1900), 848 and 853.
17. Morlet, *op. cit.*, 176. The name EDILECH which occurs on a few 'stycas', if it is not a mere blundering, may also be of Continental Germanic origin (*Edilicho* or perhaps *Edil-leich*).
18. Forssner, *op. cit.*
19. From a count of names given a Continental Germanic derivation in Feilitzen, *op. cit.*

sources are described as ecclesiastics. In a recent article on Frisians in Anglo-Saxon England,[20] Rolf Bremmer indicated how this group was frequently associated with sailing and shipbuilding. Thus, Continental names may occur in England not as representatives of an expected proportion of the community generally, but because of skills or tradition associated with certain professions.

We have seen how in the eighth and the first half of the ninth century Continental names were almost entirely lacking from the coinage. Alfred's first type conforms to this pattern, but by the end of his reign, in his last type, there are seven out of just over 50 known moneyers whose names are to be considered as Continental. Four are of the hagiological type discussed above: *Chrestien*, *Samson*, *Simon* and *Stefanus*; *Iudelbard*, *Abenel* and *Winiger* are Continental Germanic.[21]

The phenomenon of Continental names on the St Edmund Memorial coinage struck in East Anglia c.890–910 was always too obvious to have gone unremarked.[22] Unfortunately the problems of this issue make numeration difficult, since with the very high proportion of blundered legends one cannot determine the total number of distinct names intended. Here the task is not to identify which names have a Continental etymon but which do not; almost all the identifiable names must be attributed thus, with the possible exceptions of *Arus* (Scand. *Ari*?) and *Sten* (Scand. *Steinn*?), and a few obviously old English names such as *Eadræd*, *Eadwine*, and *Eadwulf*. The control of minting operations by a group of Continental immigrants might, however, have had the effect of obscuring Scandinavian and English names by presenting them in a Continental guise; for example *Semund* could be OE *Sigemund* or Scand. *Sigmundr*, and *Grimo* Scand. *Grímr*.

There seems little reason to believe that the St Edmund moneyers' names do not betoken a large influx of first-generation immigrants from the Continent. But these moneyers themselves seem to have had little connection either with the contemporary coinage in Wessex or with subsequent coinages. Only three of the names occur in other coinages. *Abenel* is found on the coins of Athelstan-Guthrum, *Abonel* on coins of Hertford and Maldon under Athelstan, and various blundered forms which may be attempting the same name on the St Edmunds. The *Winecr*, *Wineir* of the St Edmunds may be attempting a form of the name which appears as *Winigerus* on coins of Alfred's last type and as *Winegear* on coins of Edward the Elder. *BMC* records a *Stephan* amongst the St Edmunds and there is a *Stfamus* in Alfred's last type, possibly a *Stefhan* in Edward the Elder's type ii and a *Stefanus* striking in the north-east for Athelstan.

Although this influx of Continental moneyers into East Anglia in the last few years of the ninth century is separate from the main coinage of the English kings, it nevertheless occurs at the same time as Continental names begin to become significant amongst Anglo-Saxon moneyers. The proportion of these names

20. R. Bremmer, 'Frisians in Anglo-Saxon England: a historical and toponymical investigation', *Fryska Naamen 3* (1981), 45–85.
21. In those reigns for which no detailed surveys of moneyers exist, I have used as a base the lists given in J. J. North, *English Hammered Coinage* I (2nd edn, 1980).
22. *BMC* I, 97. See also V. J. Smart, 'The moneyers of St Edmund', *hikuin 11* (1985), 83–90.

increases under Edward the Elder and Athelstan. In these reigns about a fifth of the moneyers bear Continental names and in the succeeding period of Edmund to Eadwig the proportion rises to between 25 per cent and 30 per cent, but declines steeply after Edgar's death. Once the post-Reform coinage gets fully into its stride in the 990s the proportion of Continental names amongst the moneyers becomes negligible, in the region of 3–4 per cent. Even Edward the Confessor's reign shows no increase of Continental names amongst the moneyers.

From a chronological investigation of the moneyers of Edgar's different coin-types it would appear that the decline in the Continental share of the names occurs within the reign rather suddenly at the end.[23] In the Reform type (after c.973) only about 17 per cent of the moneyers' names are of Continental origin as against about 25 per cent at the beginning of the reign. This accords well with the subsequent gradual decline.

This, then, seems to have been a story of an influx of Continentals who became moneyers in the English coinage towards the end of the ninth and in the first half of the tenth centuries, and it may be significant that the initial increase coincides with the establishment of a substantial number of new mints under Alfred and Edward the Elder. Presumably the same families remained in the business of minting but gradually abandoned their characteristic name-giving in favour of English names.

Because the heyday of the Continental moneyers occurs at a period when mint-signatures were not extensively used it is not always possible to show where the bearers of these names were working, in order to compare their distribution with what emerges from the post-Reform series. At present a study of the pre-Reform coinages of the tenth century is in progress which, whilst founded on such pioneer studies as Dolley and Metcalf, will certainly modify some previous conceptions of regional die provision.[24] A preliminary analysis of the moneyers of Edward the Elder, very kindly made for me by Mr C. S. S. Lyon, suggests that although rather more Continental names are found on coins of the regional die-cutting style he designates as East Mercian than in other styles singly, such names are also well distributed throughout the country in Wessex, Kent, and the West Midlands. The bearers of Continental names which we discover in all areas of England in the consistently mint-signed series after c.973 may well be descendants of these earlier tenth-century moneyers.

For the most part the distribution of Scandinavian names amongst Anglo-Saxon moneyers confirms expectations. They ought to appear after a brief period of assimilation following the first recorded Alfredian settlement, and in fact make an unobtrusive entrance among the moneyers of Edward the Elder. The evidence does not appear sufficient to necessitate a Scandinavian derivation for the name *Brother*

23. O. von Feilitzen and C. E. Blunt, 'Personal names on the coinage of Edgar', in *England before the Conquest, Studies in Primary Sources Presented to Dorothy Whitelock*, ed. P. Clemoes (1971), 183–214.

24. M. Dolley and D. M. Metcalf, 'The reform of the English coinage under Edgar', in *AS Coins*, 136–68. New work by C. E. Blunt, I. H. Stewart and C. S. S. Lyon to appear as *Coinage in Tenth Century England.*

which appears amongst the Northumbrian moneyers of Eanred, Redwulf, and Æthelred II. Though Feilitzen gives a Scandinavian etymon to the name when it appears in Domesday, he cites the ninth-century coins to support the possibility that OE *brothor* may have been used as a personal name.

In Edward the Elder's reign there are four names which can be considered Scandinavian amongst more than 150 known moneyers. None of these four appears in the early types of the reign. *Gunne* is the usual form in England for Scand. *Gunni*; *Irfara* is Scand. *Irfari* ('traveller to Ireland'). The moneyers who bear these names are associated by Lyon with West Mercian dies. *Thurlac* (Scand. *Thorleikr*) is probably a moneyer of the Five Boroughs. *Ellaf* may be Scand. *Eileifr*, though the *ll* makes the form problematical; this name is associated with London in Lyon's study. Thereafter the proportion of Scandinavian moneyers' names increases significantly, climbing from the less than 3 per cent which we saw for Edward the Elder's reign to 5 per cent under Athelstan and then to about 15 per cent under Eadred. From then until the Conquest it remains fairly steady, minor fluctuations being in part caused by changing proportions of coins from various regions, either because of variations in mint output or survival.

Again, before the reform of c.973 it is not possible consistently to analyse the distribution of the Scandinavian names on a regional basis. Christopher Blunt's study of the coinage of Athelstan has, however, allocated all but a few of the moneyers to the region, if not the mint, where they were working. Almost all the Scandinavian and putatively Scandinavian names amongst the moneyers of Athelstan occur in those types he has designated NE I-III. Although these types have sometimes been attributed to York, Blunt finds no place for them in the York series and prefers a location south of the Humber, perhaps Lincoln.

At York under the Scandinavian kings Scandinavian moneyers are by no means dominant (table 10.1). I have remarked elsewhere on the contrast between the tenth-century York mint where Continental names outnumber Scandinavians, and the same mint a century later when all but a quarter of the names are Scandinavian and the remainder Old English.[25] It is not always possible to distinguish York coins in the period after the integration of York into the English kingdom and before c.973, but in Edgar's *Reform* type the Scandinavian names equal the English ones. Of the six Scandinavian names found in this, the last type of Edgar's reign, five are not found in any earlier type, but three other Scandinavian moneyers' names may fairly confidently be associated with York in earlier un-mint-signed types. Thus Scandinavian names seem to have been current at the York mint early in Edgar's reign but show some increase after the Reform.

In my survey of the moneyers' names of Æthelred's reign[26] I noted how the distribution of Scandinavian names was very similar to that known from the study of place-names and of personal names from other sources. At York, Scandinavian names accounted for three-quarters of the names recorded. Four names of Celtic origin occurred there, all early in the reign, and these also are a reflection of Scandinavian settlement, being Irish in derivation and part of the Hiberno-Norse

25. V. J. Smart, 'Moneyers' names on the Anglo-Saxon Coinage', *Nomina 3* (1979), 20–8.
26. Smart, 'Moneyers 973–1016'.

Table 10.1. Moneyers' names under the Norse kings of York

§ Old English	(§) possibly Old English	? obscure
★ Continental Germanic	(★) possibly Continental Germanic	
† Scandinavian	(†) possibly Scandinavian	

Sihtric *Caoch* (921–6)	Possibly at mints S. of the Humber: *Adel..d(md)*§[a], *Are*†, *Eric*†, ?*Hana* (= *Mana*(§†)?), *Sibrant*★
Olaf Guthfrithson (939–41)	York mint: *Athelferth*§[a], *Odeler*★; possibly at mints S. of the Humber: *Arnulf*(★†), *Baciager*(★), *Bleseret*(★), *Hildulf*(★†), *Nothe*(★), *Rodbert*★, *Sigar*(§★), *Sigwold*§
Olaf Sihtricson (1st and 2nd reigns 941–3)	York mint: *Ascolv*★, *Avra*?, *Farman*/*Famlan*(★†), *Rathulf*★
Sihtric II (941–2)	York mint: *Ascolv*★, *Farman*(★†), *Rathulf*★
Rægnald II Guthfrithson (943–4)	York mint: *Avra*?, *Ba[ ]c*(★)
Eric (1st reign 948)	York mint: *Hunred*§, *Ingelgar*★, *Rathulf*★, *Ulfelm*(★§)
Olaf Sihtricson (3rd reign 948–52)	York mint: *Farman*(★†), *Ingelgar*★, *Rathulf*★, *Wadter*★
Eric (2nd reign 952–4)	York mint: *Aculf* (= *Ascolv*★?), *Ingelgar*★, *Leofic*§, *Radulf*★

[a] But form of first vowel suggests Continental influence.

connection with north-western England and York. At Chester only a quarter of the moneyers' names were Scandinavian and one name was Hiberno-Norse, whilst elsewhere in the West Midlands Scandinavian names were rare, *Fastolf* at Tamworth and *Unspac* at Shrewsbury being the only instances. At Lincoln nearly half of the moneyers had Scandinavian names: out of 55 recorded names, 25 were Scandinavian and 4 were Continental Germanic. Derby and Nottingham had a high percentage of Scandinavian names, though overall the numbers were probably too small to be statistically significant. At Stamford the proportion of Scandinavian names was much smaller, only 4 in 33. At Norwich and Thetford Scandinavian names were well represented, but generally the Scandinavian element declined as one moved south. At London there were 7 Scandinavian names in just over 100. Elsewhere in the south Scandinavian names were very few, though they were surprisingly well represented at Exeter by *Cytel*, *Thurgod*, and *Carla*.

According to Sir Frank Stenton,[27] there was a considerable transfer of land to the king's Scandinavian followers in Cnut's reign. Stenton particularly notes, at that level of society, the spread of men with Scandinavian names outside the original areas of Scandinavian settlement. John Insley,[28] on the other hand, draws attention to the fact that this new influx of Scandinavian names was confined to the land-owning classes. We know, mostly from Domesday evidence and particularly from the Winton Domesday which has been investigated with the status of moneyers in

27. F. M. Stenton, *Anglo-Saxon England* (3rd edn, 1971), 413–14.
28. J. Insley, 'Regional variation in Scandinavian personal nomenclature in England', *Nomina 3* (1979), 52–60, at 54.

mind, that moneyers were at the top of the scale amongst the burgess class financially and probably socially.[29] In Winchester at any rate their interests were confined to the borough; there is no evidence of their holding land in the surrounding countryside. If this is general elsewhere it would explain the discrepancy between Stenton's influx of Scandinavians and the lack of any significant increase in Scandinavian names amongst Cnut's moneyers.[30]

Although the proportion of Scandinavian to Old English names in Cnut's reign differs only in detail from that in Æthelred's, I have included a table to illustrate such changes as do appear (table 10.2). Lincoln and Stamford show a fairly noticeable increase in Scandinavian names whilst York and Chester show a slight increase. These are probably the only mints in the table for which the figures can have any real statistical validity since the numbers involved elsewhere are very small. Some of the mints in the southern part of the Danelaw which produced Scandinavian moneyers' names under Æthelred, such as Colchester, Bedford, and Northampton, have none under Cnut, but any pattern of decline in the south would be broken by the increases at Ipswich and Cambridge.

In the west, Shrewsbury retains its moneyer *Grim* into Cnut's first type but has no Scandinavian names thereafter, and Tamworth, which had a possible Scandinavian name *Fastolf* on coins of Æthelred's *Crux* type c.991–7, has no new Scandinavian names under Cnut or later. Elsewhere there is no very visible spread of Scandinavian names into an area not hitherto involved in Scandinavian settlement. In Æthelred's reign London had 7 names of Scandinavian origin amongst a total of 103 moneyers, and 5 out of 95 in the period 1016–42. Canterbury and Dover produce Scandinavian names for the first time in the later period; a moneyer *Cytel* strikes at Canterbury for Harold Harefoot and Harthacnut, whilst at Dover the name *Swartafe* appears on coins of Cnut's second type. This form probably represents Scand. *Svarthofthi*.

In the south-west, Scandinavian names were unexpectedly well represented on Æthelred coins of the Exeter mint, by *Cytel*, *Thurgod*, and *Carla*. Another, *Scula*, joins *Carla* and *Thurgod* in Cnut's reign. The appearance of Scandinavian names at Totnes, Lydford, and 'Gothaburh', a mint of uncertain location but die-linked to Exeter, is thus probably linked with some kind of Scandinavian presence in Exeter. *Thurgod* the Totnes moneyer is likely to be the same man as the Exeter moneyer of the same name. The other Scandinavian name at Totnes is *Farman*, a moneyer of Harthacnut. Again, the 'Gothaburh' moneyer *Carla* may be the same man as the Exeter *Carla*. At Lydford the name *Wicing* is found on coins of Cnut's last, *Short Cross*, issue. Most commentators take this to be Scand. *Vikingr*. A native derivation from OE *wicing*, 'pirate', might seem more appropriate for the name of a West Country moneyer, if it were not for these other examples of Scandinavian names in the area.

Apart from the differences in name-patterns between classes noted above, there is a practical reason why the spread of Scandinavian names found by Stenton in Cnut's England should not apply to moneyers' names. The Danish coinage at the time of

29. Biddle and Keane, *op. cit.*, 421.
30. V. J. Smart, 'Moneyers of the late Anglo-Saxon Coinage 1016–42' (Ph.D.thesis, University of Nottingham, 1981), 243.

Table 10.2. Moneyers' names at York, Chester, and the Danelaw mints

	c.973–1016				1016–42				1042–66		
Mints	Scand.	(+OIr)	OE	CG	Scand.	(+OIr)	OE	CG	Scand.	OE	CG
York	48	(+6)	20	–	35	(+3)	12	–	28	8	–
Chester	6	(+2)	16	–	7	(+3)	16	–	6	13	–
Lincoln	25		32	5	23	(+2)	26	3	17	18	1
Stamford	5		24	3[b]	9		20	3	6	12	2
Leicester	3		7	–	–		8	–	1	9	–
Derby	3(5?)[a]		7(5?)[a]	–	3		3	–	2	4	–
Nottingham	1(2?)[a]		2(1?)[a]	–	2		4	–	3	5	–
Torksey	2		–	–	1		0	–	–	–	–
Caistor[a]	–		1	–	1		1	–	–	–	–
Norwich	3		18	4	4		15	–	4	10	–
Thetford	5		26	1	5		23	–	5	15	1
Huntingdon	1		12	–	1		14	1	1	8	–
Cambridge	1		18	1[c]	3		12	1	1	9	–
Bedford	2		12	1	–		8	1	1	9	–
Sudbury	–		10	–	–		4	–	–	1	–
Ipswich	1		15	1	2		8	2	–	9	–
Colchester	1		17	–	–		6	–	–	8	–
Hertford	–		14	–	–		6	–	1	9[a]	–
Maldon	(1?)[a]		6(5?)[a]	–	–		9	–	–	4	–
Northampton	3		15	2	–		7	1	–	7	–

[a] Doubtful names are: Derby *Osgar*, *Osolf*; Nottingham *Mana*; Maldon *Toga* (? = *Toca* Scand. *Toki*); Hertford reading E7pi)oe *eawig* or *Eadwig*) rather than EPI (OEScand. *Øpi*). The Caistor mint-attribution under Cnut is also in doubt.
[b] Uncertain: Capelin or Cawelin c.1017–29.
[c] Obscure: Clern c.1009–16.

Cnut's accession was in its infancy, imitative of and considerably dependent on dies and probably also on moneyers sent out from England. However much Cnut might have wished to reward a possibly lower rank of his followers with lucrative office, that of moneyer would scarcely have been suitable. Even though most of the men named on the coins at this period probably did not strike those coins with their own hands they would need a knowledge of the working of the mint in order to administer it and perform effective supervision. Thus it would be more reasonable to look for any increase in Scandinavian names amongst moneyers after Cnut's accession only after a time-lag. If we were looking for evidence of new immigration, then this would not be reflected until the incomers had had time to achieve the necessary expertise; if merely for a growth in the fashion of giving Scandinavian names, then long enough for the children so named to grow to maturity.

However, Edward the Confessor's coinage gives little evidence of any great increase in Scandinavian moneyers' names.[31] Table 10.2 gives details of the Danelaw

31. F. Colman, 'Moneyers of Edward the Confessor' (D. Phil. thesis, University of Oxford, 1981). I am indebted to Dr Colman for a summary of the Continental and Scandinavian names in correspondence.

mints. During this reign the York moneyers' names become wholly Scandinavian.[32] The figures given in the table apply to the whole reign, but in fact English names appear only in the first part of the reign. The tiny *Small Flan* type c.1048–50 is the last in which more than one English name appears. Subsequently *Leofnoth* continues alone amongst his Scandinavian-named colleagues until c.1056, and there are no OE names under the two Williams.

Nor is the evidence for Scandinavian moneyers' names outside the Danelaw very impressive. *Colswegn* at Hastings joins the Canterbury moneyer *Cytel* in the south-east, but the group centred on Exeter seems to fade away when *Wicing* leaves it, possibly for Worcester where his name is found on Harold Godwineson's short-lived coinage. But there are mints in the south which begin to show Scandinavian names. *Haldan* at Oxford may be the same man as the Nottingham moneyer. *Thurcil* at Warwick and Wilton is a more common name and probably reflects two different people. *Brand* at Wallingford and *Beorn* at Wareham may also be Scandinavian, though English etyma are not impossible.

The names of the moneyers of the Norman kings have never been systematically investigated and clearly such a study is desirable, to show to what extent this process is continued. From the few single-mint studies in which I have had some part[33] it would appear that Scandinavian names outside the north-west and the Danelaw are negligible until the end of William I's reign and begin to appear in any numbers only under Henry I. By this time, however, we have to reckon with Scandinavian names naturalized in Normandy[34] and brought in with the other Norman-French names that also begin to appear amongst Henry's moneyers.

Little has been said so far of the Celts of the title. The Celtic names on the coins are almost entirely to be considered as a sub-group of the Scandinavian names, since they are mostly of Irish origin and heavily concentrated at Chester and York. The earliest Irish name amongst the moneyers appears to be *Mældomon* at Chester under Athelstan, but the first ascertainable instances for York do not appear until after 975. *Gillys* at Hereford c.973–5 and *Crinan* at Shrewsbury c.1017–23 almost certainly denote the Chester moneyers of the same name. In the east, Irish names appear at Lincoln as well as York, but not until Cnut's reign with *Matathan* and the seemingly ubiquitous *Crinan*. At Stamford their presence is problematical, relying on a Celtic derivation for *Cawelin(?)*[35] and Celtic influence in *Critstign*.[36] *Scot*, though not

32. *SCBI 21 Yorkshire Collections*, pp. xlvii-xlix; *SCBI 29 Merseyside County Museums*, pp. 103–13.
33. L. V. Grinsell, *The Bath Mint* (1973), 40; L. V. Grinsell, C. E. Blunt, and M. Dolley, *SCBI 19, Bristol and Gloucester Museums*, Bristol 36–8, Gloucester 118; and W. Lean's forthcoming study of the Dorset mints.
34. J. Adigard de Gautries, *Les Noms Scandinaves en Normandie de 911–1066* (Lund, 1954).
35. In my thesis, 'Moneyers 1016–42', I suggest that the name is to be read as Capelin and that its derivation is Old French.
36. M. Dolley, 'OE *Christðegn – an unsuspected instance of early Middle Irish influence on OE namegiving', *BNJ 36* (1967), 40–5.

formally a Celtic name, may possibly denote a man of Celtic birth, but may (like *Iri*) refer only to a journey to, or exploits in, Scotland or Ireland.

There are a few possible traces of a disparate Celtic element of the Welsh or Cornish branch, but the instances are all problematical. Feilitzen tentatively offers a Cornish derivation for the Edgar moneyer's name *Hacuf* and suggests Welsh influence in the form *Demence* ‹Lat. *Dominicus*.[37] Neither of these names appears with a mint-signature, though Blunt associates *Demence* with western Mercia and *Hacuf* with the north-east.[38] The obscure *Dilion* appears at Hereford c.997–1003; it is certainly not Germanic but I have yet to find a Celtic scholar who is willing to give it an etymology.

Since phonological data have almost always been obscured by orthographical adaptation, it is possible in only a few cases to identify any more closely the area from which foreign names have been introduced. Feilitzen's analysis of the Edgar moneyers suggests that almost all the Continental names he discusses were current in West Frankish, though many were also, and a few solely, current in Old Saxon and Flemish.[39] Of the Scandinavian names, some are found only in sources for the western branch (Icelandic and Norwegian) and some only in Danish and/or Swedish, although there is an imbalance in surviving sources in favour of West Scandinavian.[40] The majority, however, are known overall and no clear pattern emerges, except perhaps at York where several of the Scandinavian names are now traceable in West Scandinavian sources alone. A significant number of the names are not found in the surviving records from the Scandinavian homelands at all but may have been coined in England from elements of Scandinavian vocabulary;[41] if this were so it would suggest some degree of survival of the language.

To sum up: whilst the distribution of the Scandinavian moneyers' names agrees approximately with what we know of the settlement from other sources, the general lack of reflectors of Danish rule in the years 1016–42 and later is somewhat surprising, though it may well be that if it had not been for continuing Scandinavian involvement in England the influence of the original settlement would have become assimilated and we should have to expect a decrease in Scandinavian names. The progress of Scandinavianization in York is particularly interesting; in a minority under the Norse kings, the Scandinavian-named moneyers are level with the English-named ones in 975 and gradually increase in numbers to take over completely before the Conquest.

Continental involvement as reflected by the moneyers' names is at its strongest throughout the tenth century. Although the annal for 959 complains of Edgar's introduction of foreigners into England his Continental-named moneyers had no larger a share of the business than had those of his predecessors; their decline begins in his reign, although in its latter years, so perhaps he took such criticism to heart. Edward the Confessor was another king who notoriously favoured foreigners and yet

37. Feilitzen and Blunt, *op. cit.*, 193, 198.
38. In correspondence; to appear in *Coinage in Tenth Century England* (see n.24 above).
39. Feilitzen and Blunt, *op. cit.*, 209.
40. Insley, *op. cit.*, 54–6.
41. Fellows Jensen, *op. cit.*, lxiv-lxvi.

there is no increase in Continental names amongst his moneyers over the minimal numbers found under his Scandinavian predecessors. The influence of the Conquest itself does not seem to be reflected amongst the moneyers' names until the early twelfth century. An explanation for such discrepancies between the actual record of the moneyers' names and expectations drawn from the historical record may lie in two factors: differences in naming-patterns and possibly ethnic composition in the land-owning and the merchant classes, and the special skills and experience required by the moneyer who had to oversee minting and exchange.

11 Anglo-Scandinavian trade in the Viking Age and after

Peter Sawyer

Early medieval texts tend only to refer to trade and traders incidentally and there is therefore very little historical evidence for Anglo-Scandinavian commerce before the Norman Conquest. I know of only two contemporary references to it in English sources. The first is in the Old English version of the *Historiae adversos paganos* by Orosius, which was made at the end of the ninth century. This includes some information supplied by a Norwegian – his name is given in the English form Ohthere – who visited Alfred's court.[1] He was by his own account a wealthy man who gathered tribute from the Lapps as well as himself hunting whales and walruses. He described the journey from his home in north Norway to the market places of southern Scandinavia, *Scīringes hēal* and *æt Hǣþum* (Kaupang in Vestfold and Hedeby), where he presumably sold or exchanged the Arctic produce that he had collected. The text does not explain why he came to England; the compiler of the translation was only interested in him as a source of information with which to supplement the very slight and unsatisfactory account of Scandinavia given by Orosius. It is, however, reasonable to assume that he came as a trader to sell, among other things, walrus tusks, some of which he gave to King Alfred. The same text also includes an account of a voyage across the Baltic by a man called Wulfstan who may have been English, although that is not certain.[2] The second text, written about a century later, is the *Vita* of Oswald, archbishop of York from 972 to 992. York is there described as a populous city to which merchants came from all quarters, especially from the Danish people (*maxime e Danorum gentis*).[3]

There are several other references to England's overseas trade before the Conquest but none appears to refer to Scandinavia. The treaty agreed between Æthelred and

Note Many years ago Michael Dolley persuaded me that the Anglo-Saxon coins exported to Scandinavia in the tenth and eleventh centuries had nothing to do with trade. I was therefore astonished to discover when we met for the last time in 1981 that he had changed his mind and greatly regret that we never had an opportunity to discuss the matter fully. The following paper, offered as a tribute to his memory, includes the arguments in defence of his first opinion that I wish could have been put to him personally.

1. J. Bately, *The Old English Orosius* (1980), 13–16; for the date see pp. lxxxvi-xciii.
2. Bately, *op. cit.*, lxxi-ii, 16–18.
3. J. Raine, *The Historians of the Church of York and its Archbishops*, I (Rolls Ser., 1879), 454.

the Vikings in 991 or 994 provides for the safety of English ships landing outside the area of the truce; it does not specify where but it clearly applied to large parts of the British Isles as well as to Continental coasts.[4] There is clearer evidence in *Geþyncðo*, an early eleventh-century text on status according to which a trader who crossed the open sea three times at his own expense was afterwards entitled to the rights of a thegn.[5] There is, however, no warrant for Alexander Bugge's assumption that the North Sea was intended.[6] The London regulations included in the law-code known as IV Æthelred mention traders coming from Rouen, Huy, Liège, and Nivelles as well as more generally from Flanders, Ponthieu, Normandy, *Francia*, and from the Empire.[7] It is possible that provision would also have been made for Danes and Norwegians in normal times and that their omission was due to the renewed Viking raids, but there is no evidence to support that suggestion. The inclusion of both Danes and Norwegians in later versions of these London regulations[8] as privileged visitors is more likely to have been a result of Cnut's conquest than a restoration of rights that had been suspended for the duration of hostilities.

Continental sources may provide some additional clues. Thus, the *Miracula Sancti Trudonis* by Stepelinus has been cited as evidence for English sailors engaged in the Baltic trade in 1050.[9] This may confirm a suspicion that the dearth of historical evidence for Anglo-Scandinavian trade is deceptive, but it is hardly possible to assess the scale of that trade or even to discuss it in any detail on the basis of such scraps of information. Hopes have been raised that archaeological and numismatic evidence may be able to compensate for the lack of written references. The claims made for this evidence merit full discussion but it will be helpful first to consider what can be learned about Anglo-Scandinavian trade from post-Conquest sources.

The earliest reference to Norwegian merchants visiting England is in the *Ecclesiastical History* by Orderic Vitalis. He reports that in 1095 Robert de Mowbray, earl of Northumberland, and his minions attacked and robbed four great ships called *canardes* that were bringing merchants from Norway to England.[10] The merchants appealed to the king and, when Robert disregarded an order to restore the stolen property, full compensation was paid from the royal treasury. This episode suggests that the goodwill of these Norwegian merchants was worth keeping. The term *canardes* appears to derive from the Old Norse for a sea-going ship, *knörr*. A good example of an eleventh-century *knörr* has been recovered from Roskilde Fjord in Denmark.[11] It was probably built in western Norway and had space for over 30 cubic

4. F. Liebermann, *Die Gesetze der Angelsachsen* (3 vols., Halle a.S., 1903–16), I, 220–5; tr. in D. Whitelock, *EHD* I, *c.500–1042* (2nd edn, 1979), 437–9 (no. 42).
5. Liebermann, *op. cit.*, I, 456–9; Whitelock, *EHD* I, 468–9 (no. 51).
6. A. Bugge, 'Handelen mellem England og Norge indtil begyndelsen af det 15de aarhundred', *Historisk Tidsskrift* (Norwegian)[3] *4* (1898), 1–49, at 4.
7. Liebermann, *op. cit.*, I, 232–4; with translation in A. J. Robertson, *The Laws of the Kings of England from Edmund to Henry I* (1925), 70–3.
8. See p. 187 below.
9. P. Grierson, 'The relations between England and Flanders before the Norman Conquest', *TRHS*[4] *23* (1941), 71–112, at 105.
10. *The Ecclesiastical History of Orderic Vitalis*, ed. M. Chibnall (6 vols., 1969–80), IV, 280–1.
11. O. Olsen and O. Crumlin-Pedersen,

metres of cargo. Parts of even larger cargo ships of the early twelfth century have been found inside the entrance of the same fjord, at Lynæs.[12]

Norwegians are later reported in several east coast ports. A writ of Henry II addressed to all the Norwegians who come to the port of Grimsby or to other royal ports of Lincolnshire required them to pay toll and other customs as they did in the time of his grandfather, Henry I (1100–35).[13] Norwegian ships were still landing cargoes at Grimsby in the thirteenth century; ten arrived there in 1230 with deal boards and *oleum*, meaning fish, seal, or whale oil.[14] They also came to many other east coast ports from Newcastle to Ipswich as well as to the south-west of England.[15] Evidence for their presence in London has been sought in William fitz Stephen's panegyric on the city. In a poetic passage describing the exotic goods that arrived from every nation under heaven, he included furs from the Norwegians and Russians.[16] This can hardly be taken as good evidence for visits by either Norwegians or Russians; if so we should also, on the strength of the same poem, have to accept that London was also visited by Arabians, Sabaeans, and Scythians. Rather better evidence is provided by a collection of London customs that was compiled in the reign of John but appears to reflect conditions in the first half of the twelfth century before the reforms of Henry II.[17] Norwegians are there said to be entitled to stay in the city for a year but they were not allowed to go elsewhere. According to the same text, Danes were also allowed to stay for a year but they did not suffer the same limitation as the Norwegians and were entitled to go to fairs and markets anywhere in England. This implies that they were actively trading in England in the twelfth century.

There are several references to contact with Norway, including some trade, in twelfth-century Exchequer records, but none to trade with Denmark. This need not mean that there was any significant difference in the scale of English commerce with those two parts of Scandinavia. The explanation is rather that hawks and gyrfalcons that were highly prized in the English royal court came from Norway and Iceland, not Denmark. Many were given by Norwegian kings and bishops and in 1163 a

Five Viking Ships from Roskilde Fjord (Roskilde, 1978), 118. A model of this boat is illustrated in P. H. Sawyer, *Kings and Vikings* (1982), pl. I.

12. O. Crumlin-Pedersen, 'Skibe på Havbunden: Vragfund i danske farvande fra perioden 600–1400', *Handel og Søfartsmuseets Årbog* (Kronborg, 1981), 28–65, at 52–3.
13. *Calendar of Charter Rolls*, III (1908), 7.
14. *Close Rolls of the Reign of Henry III 1227–31* (1902), 367.
15. In the thirteenth century Lynn was the most important harbour for trade with Norway; K. Helle, 'Anglo-Norwegian relations in the reign of Håkon Håkonson (1217–1263)', *MScand 1* (1968), 101–14, at 103–4. William of Malmesbury, in *Gesta Pontificum*, ed. N. E. S. A. Hamilton (Rolls Ser., 1870), 292, described Bristol as a port to which ships from Ireland, Norway, and elsewhere come. This work was completed in 1125.
16. *Materials for the History of Thomas Becket*, III, ed. J. C. Robertson (Rolls Ser., 1877), 7; cf. C. N. L. Brooke and G. Keir, *London 800–1216: The Shaping of a City* (1975), 258–9.
17. M. Bateson, 'A London municipal collection of the reign of John', *EHR 17* (1902), 480–511, 707–30, at 495–502.

mission was sent to Norway to collect more of these birds.[18] The English king also demanded hawks and gyrfalcons as payment, for example, for licence to export corn to Norway.[19] The merchants were presumably expected to obtain them in Norway, for they do not seem to have been readily available in England. Some debts of these birds are repeated for many years in the Pipe Rolls. A debt of a Norwegian hawk and an Icelandic gyrfalcon, first noted in 1169, was only partly paid eight years later when the gyrfalcon was delivered, but not the hawk.[20]

Falcons and hawks are in fact the only imports from Norway that are mentioned in twelfth-century Exchequer records and the only export to Norway they record is corn. Some loads were sent as gifts and are noted because the cost had to be accounted for,[21] but a few loads taken by merchants appear to be specially noted because licence to export was given in return for hawks or falcons. The character and scale of Anglo-Norwegian trade in the twelfth century cannot be determined from these records and they cast even less light on Anglo-Danish trade, for the Danes did not supply hawks or falcons.

Better evidence for Anglo-Scandinavian trade first appears in the more abundant and varied royal records that are available from the beginning of the thirteenth century.[22] Even then most references were a direct result of the Anglo-French war. Thus in May 1208 royal officials in south-west England were ordered to arrest the ships of all lands except Denmark, Norway, and the foreign islands *que non sint contra nos*, and two months later a merchant from the Danish port of Ribe, called Nicholas *Marinellus*, was licenced to trade freely throughout England.[23] A truce was agreed in 1216, but in May 1224 the war broke out again and on 23 July an order was sent to the bailiffs of Yarmouth to release the ship of Richewin of Ribe that had been arrested.[24] Three days later a general trading licence was granted to Danish merchants for two years.[25] In August of the same year officials at Yarmouth were ordered to permit all fishing boats, except French and Poitevin ones, and merchant ships from Scotland, Norway, Iceland, Frisia, Cologne, and from the lands of the Danish king and further east to leave without hindrance.[26] In December permission was given for corn to be exported to both Denmark and Norway from Lynn.[27] Other incidental references unconnected with the war supplement these glimpses of Anglo-Danish trade. In 1207 the goods of a Danish merchant were seized in Newcastle and in 1220 the bailiffs of the Holland fair in Lincolnshire were ordered to seize Danish goods to the

18. *Rotuli litterarum clausarum*, ed. T. D. Hardy (2 vols., 1833–44), I, 156; *Letters of Henry III*, ed. W. W. Shirley (Rolls Ser., 1862), I, 486; *Close Rolls 1242–47* (1916), 365; *Pipe Roll 9 Henry II*, 28–9.
19. See n. 44 below.
20. *Pipe Roll 15 Henry II*, 16; cf. *Pipe Roll 23 Henry II*, 107.
21. See n. 43 below.
22. Anglo-Norwegian trade is discussed by Bugge, *loc. cit.*, and by Helle, *loc. cit.*, Anglo-Danish by P. Enemark, 'Englandshandel', *Kulturhistorisk Leksikon for nordisk middelalder*, III (København, 1958), cols. 668–74. See also E. Carus-Wilson, 'The medieval trade of the ports of the Wash', *MedArch 6–7* (1962–3), 182–201.
23. *Rotuli litterarum patentium*, ed. T. D. Hardy (1835), 83, 85.
24. *Rot. litt. claus.*, I, 613, 638.
25. *Patent Rolls of the reign of Henry III 1216–25* (1901), 456.
26. *Rot. litt. claus.*, I, 617, 642.
27. *Ibid.*, II, 10.

value of 200 marks in compensation for losses suffered by four London merchants in Denmark.[28]

This evidence shows that in the early thirteenth century Danish and Norwegian merchants might be encountered anywhere along the British coast from the Tyne to Cornwall. The goods they bought and sold are almost never stated. In 1213 the king ordered the purchase of fur from a Norwegian ship at Tynemouth and in 1226 the sheriff of Norfolk was told to buy five or six of the best palfreys from the horses brought to Yarmouth and Lothingland from Denmark.[29] Horses were an important Danish export; in 1231 Ribe was expected to render 350 marks or more annually in horse toll while only 200 marks were owed for other tolls and port dues.[30]

There are, therefore, slight but good reasons for thinking that England had active trade with both Norway and Denmark after the Norman Conquest. There is, however, no hint of any direct trade between England and Sweden before the end of the twelfth century. The west coast of modern Sweden, Bohuslän and Halland, was then controlled by Norwegians and Danes. The only route by which Swedes could reach the North Sea, apart from sailing through the Sound, was by Göta Älv. The market of Gamla Lödöse was established on that river in the eleventh century, but English pottery first appears there at the end of the twelfth.[31] Before that any trade between England and Sweden must have been in the hands of Danes and Norwegians. The earliest record of English contact with Sweden is in 1231 when an otherwise unknown Swedish prince, Andreas *nepos regis de Swathed*', brought goshawks and a hunting dog as gifts.[32] Three years later Gotlandic merchants appear for the first time in English records and were given a safe conduct.[33] In 1235 another group of Gotlanders were given a trading licence for three years, and in 1237 the merchants of Gotland were granted freedom from tolls and customs throughout England.[34] The markets to which notification of this privilege was sent indicate where Gotlanders might be expected; Stamford, Boston, Lynn, St Ives, Huntingdon, St Edmunds, Hertford, Sandwich, Canterbury, and Dover.[35] The main goods they brought were furs and wax which they obtained mainly in Novgorod, and Henry III favoured them because they brought high quality furs which he bought in large quantities.[36] The sudden appearance of Gotlanders in 1234 shows that they were newcomers; had they been regular visitors earlier some mention would certainly have been made in the records that reveal at least some of the activity of Danes and Norwegians. The Gotlanders had been very active in the Baltic in the twelfth century and privileges granted to them by the German king Lothar in about 1130 were confirmed by Henry the Lion in 1161.[37] Their route to England seems to

28. *Ibid.*, I, 81, 419.
29. *Ibid.*, I, 144; II, 133.
30. *Kong Valdemars Jordebog*, ed. S. Aakjær, I. 2 (repr., København, 1980), 8.
31. K. Carlsson, *Importkeramik i Gamla Lödöse* (Stockholm, 1982), 48–9.
32. *Close Rolls 1227–31* (1902), 540.
33. *Calendar of Patent Rolls 1232–47* (1916), 80.
34. *Ibid.*, 131; *Sverges Traktater med Främmande Magter*, ed. O. S. Rydberg, I (Stockholm, 1877), 179–80 (no. 85).
35. *Close Rolls 1234–7* (1909), 426–7.
36. *Calendar of Patent Rolls 1232–47* (1916), 287, 432.
37. Rydberg (ed.), *op. cit.*, 78–80 (no. 42).

have been overland from Lübeck via Hamburg to the ports of the lower Rhine and Flanders.[38] English sources say nothing about the ships in which they came; royal officials were only interested in what interested the king.

Official records reveal at least some of the goods that were traded between Scandinavia and Angevin England. Apart from hawks and falcons, some of which came from Iceland, the Norwegians exported furs, fish oil, and deal boards, the Danes brought horses, and the Gotlanders furs and wax.[39] Another possible Scandinavian export is suggested by the sale in 1198 of an Icelandic ship at Rouen together with its cargo, 17 sacks of wool which fetched £213 6s. 8d.[40] It is likely, but not certain, that this wool came from Iceland. Gifts sent to Norway from time to time included wine, clothing, corn, and jewellery,[41] but the only commercial export to Scandinavia mentioned in official records is corn. A general licence to send corn to both Denmark and Norway was issued in 1224,[42] but the only cargoes that are specifically mentioned went to Norway. Many were gifts. Early in his reign John sent 300 seams of wheat in two ships and a year later at least three times that quantity of corn was sent.[43] It was also sold. In 1180 Arnald *filius Mabilie*, whose name suggests that he was English or German rather than Scandinavian, was licensed to take corn to Norway, and in 1200 the first of several such licences was granted to Robert son of Sunnolf, a leading Lynn merchant.[44] Arnald and Robert were trading on their own account but other merchants acted as agents for important churchmen or secular lords. Gilbert of Sleswig, merchant of Denmark, who was granted licence to trade in England in both 1223 and 1224, was in fact an agent for the duke of Lüneburg,[45] and in 1221 Absalon, count of Sjælland, obtained a safe conduct for his ship and its merchandise.[46] Churchmen also had agents. The archbishop of Trondheim was allowed by Henry II to buy corn and other victuals in England even in times of shortage, and this grant was confirmed by Richard I, John, and Henry III.[47]

Unofficial sources make it possible to enlarge the list of goods traded between Scandinavia and England. The Saga of King Sverre, who died in 1202, was written by a contemporary. It includes a speech attributed to the king in which he thanks the English for bringing wheat and honey, flour and cloth, but complains that the Germans 'who come here in great numbers' impoverish the land by carrying away butter and dried fish, and encourage drunkenness by importing wine.[48] Icelandic

38. H. Yrwing, *Gotland under Aldre Medeltid* (Lund, 1940), 309–10; *idem*, 'Gotlandshandel', *Kulturhist. Leks.*, V (1960), cols. 391–8.
39. See p. 189 above.
40. *Magni Rotuli Scaccarii Normaniae*, ed. T. Stapleton (2 vols., 1840, 1844), II, 306.
41. *Rot. litt. claus.*, I, 138, 168, 231.
42. *Ibid.*, 10.
43. *Pipe Roll 3 John*, 128; *Pipe Roll 4 John*, 104, 131.
44. *Pipe Roll 26 Henry II*, 23; *Rotuli chartarum*, ed. T. D. Hardy (1837), 60; H. G. Leach, *Angevin Britain and Scandinavia* (Harvard, 1921), 63–4.
45. *Pat. R. 1216–25*, 377, 450.
46. *Ibid.*, 289.
47. *Calendar of Patent Rolls 1232–47* (1916), 289. At the beginning of the twelfth century the Norwegian king, Magnus, had a citizen of Lincoln as his agent; *Orderic Vitalis*, ed. Chibnall, VI, 48–51.
48. *Sverris saga*, ed. G. Indrebø (1920), 110; tr. J. Sephton, *The Saga of King Sverri of Norway* (1899), 129–30.

sagas about the Viking age contain many references to traders, trading ships, and markets but these are more valuable as evidence for the time in which they were written, the twelfth and thirteenth centuries, than for the tenth and eleventh. Thus, in Egils Saga, written in the thirteenth century, Thorolf Kveldulfsson is said to have taken a ship loaded with dried fish, skins, furs, and the coarse woollen cloth known as *wadmal*, to England and returned with wheat, honey, wine, and cloth.[49] Some of these goods may have been traded in the tenth century but we cannot rely on Egils Saga to prove it.

Apart from falcons, the most valuable Scandinavian export was fur. Adam of Bremen emphasized the importance of Scandinavia as a source of high-quality furs at the end of the eleventh century, and complained that Germans coveted a marten-skin robe more than eternal life.[50] There was probably a demand for fine furs among rulers and aristocrats of the Viking Age but the fashion seems to have spread in the eleventh and twelfth centuries. An elaborate terminology was developed then to describe different types of fur;[51] the English had been content with the word *fell* which they used for all types of animal skins, even dragon skins. In the early twelfth century some churchmen protested against the fashion for furs. In 1127 an English church council ruled that abbesses and nuns were not to wear garments more precious than those of lambs' wool or black cats' fur, and in 1138 the prohibition was made more explicit: 'We forbid that nuns wear fur of vair, gris, sable, marten, ermine, or beaver, put on gold rings or twist or make up their hair.'[52] Domesday Book does provide one clue that marten skins were highly prized before the Conquest. The customs of Chester include a rule that the king's reeve had the right to pre-empt any marten skins that arrived in the port.[53] It is not possible to say whether these were expected to come from Ireland or Scandinavia, but the high value implied by the rule suggests that the better quality skins from Scandinavia were meant.

Evidence from London indicates that Scandinavians were well established there before the Conquest and it seems likely that some were engaged in trade. The possibility that the privileged position of the Danes may date back to the time of Cnut has already been mentioned. Other signs of an early Scandinavian presence in the city relate to a slightly later date. The clearest is the group of six churches dedicated to St Olaf, who was killed in 1030. We cannot prove that any of these dedications is pre-Conquest, but a church of St Olaf certainly existed in York in 1051 and it is likely that at least some of the London dedications are similarly early. The cult was well established in England before 1066 and was naturally most popular in

49. *Egils Saga Skalla-Grímssonar*, ed. S. Nordal (Íslensk Fornrit 2, Reykjavík, 1933), 41–2; tr. C. Fell, *Egils Saga* (1975), 22.
50. Adam of Bremen, *Gesta Hammaburgensis ecclesiae pontificum*, ed. B. Schmeidler (Scriptores rerum germanicarum, Hannover, 1917), 245, 251, 267 (lib. iv, 18, 21, 32); Adam of Bremen, *History of the Archbishops of Hamburg-Bremen*, tr. F. J. Tschan (New York, 1959), 199, 203, 213.
51. E. M. Veale, *The English Fur Trade in the Later Middle Ages* (1966), 215–29.
52. Brooke and Keir, *op. cit.* (n.16 above), 259.
53. *Domesday Book*, I, f. 262b.

areas of Scandinavian settlement, and in Chester and York.[54] The many Olaf churches in London suggests that Scandinavians were already numerous and important there before the Conquest. The traditional association of the church of St Clement with the Danes, even though the church was taken over by the Germans early in the thirteenth century, may also be early.[55] The Haakon who seems to have given his name to the church of St Nicholas Acon is unlikely to have lived before Cnut's time; dedications to St Nicholas became popular in the middle of the century.[56] It has been claimed that a Scandinavian presence in London before Cnut's time is revealed by the name of the weekly court, the husting, which is said to be a Scandinavian word. It first occurs in a Latin translation of a late tenth-century will.[57] Sir Frank Stenton considered this to be good evidence for the importance of Scandinavians in the city before the Danish conquest, although he admitted that 'we have no direct evidence of any Scandinavian immigration into London so considerable as of itself to produce a new form of public assembly.'[58] One may, however, wonder whether the word is indeed a Scandinavian loan; Old English had both its component words, *hūs* and *thing*.

Hopes that archaeology would compensate for the slightness of the historical evidence for Anglo-Scandinavian commerce in the Viking Age have not so far been fulfilled. Very few of the goods that may have been traded are normally likely to have left traces for an excavator to discover and the Scandinavian provenance of some of the material that does survive is not always certain. Norway was not the only source of soap-stone and German hones cannot always be readily distinguished from Norwegian ones.[59] The soap-stone vessels, generally with signs of wear, that have been found in both Lincoln and York were probably personal possessions.[60] Hones are a more convincing commercial export and some were undoubtedly exported from Norway, but the numbers so far reported are not large. The site at Flaxengate in Lincoln, which was occupied from the end of the ninth century, has produced only 36 hones that may have come from Norway from levels that can be dated before 1100.[61] This is hardly good evidence for lively commerce. Another recognizable Norwegian import is walrus ivory which came from northern seas. English Romanesque ivories are normally made from walrus rather than elephant tusks. Very little has, however, been found or identified that can be dated earlier than the tenth century. The two pieces found at Flaxengate were in post-Conquest levels and the seal matrix of Snarr the toll collector from York is also later.[62]

54. B. Dickins, 'The cult of S. Olave in the British Isles', *Saga-Book of the Viking Society 12* (1937–45), 53–80.
55. Brooke and Keir, *op. cit.*, 267–8.
56. *Ibid.*, 138.
57. *Chronicon Abbatiae Ramesiensis*, ed. W. D. Macray (Rolls Ser., 1886), 58.
58. F. M. Stenton, *Preparatory to Anglo-Saxon England*, ed. D. M. Stenton (1970), 30.
59. A. MacGregor, *Anglo-Scandinavian Finds from Lloyds Bank, Pavement, and other Sites* (1982), 73–4; D. T. Moore, 'The petrography and archaeology of English honestone', *J. Archaeol. Science 5* (1978), 61–73, at 68.
60. J. E. Mann, *Early Medieval Finds from Flaxengate, I: Objects of antler, bone, stone, horn, ivory, amber, and jet* (1982), 20–1, 42, 47.
61. *Ibid.*, 27–31.
62. *Ibid.*, 38; A. MacGregor, 'Industry and commerce in Anglo-Scandinavian York', in *Viking Age York and the*

The excavations in Lincoln and York have confirmed the historical evidence that they were large and flourishing towns in the eleventh century. Both apparently grew rapidly in size in the late ninth and early tenth centuries, probably as a direct result of the settlement in their neighbourhoods of relatively wealthy Scandinavian immigrants.[63] Despite the lack of direct evidence it is difficult to believe that such large towns could have existed without a substantial overseas trade before the Conquest, as they certainly had later. York was in close touch with other Scandinavian colonies in the British Isles in the tenth century; the last king of York, Erik Bloodaxe, was in fact an exiled Norwegian king.[64] It is therefore most probable that York had some commerce with Scandinavia and the same was probably true of Lincoln and other Danelaw towns such as Stamford and Norwich.

Several Scandinavian ports of the period have also been excavated.[65] The most readily identifiable English export found in them is pottery. Much of this, like the soap-stone vessels, was probably personal equipment rather than a traded commodity, which would explain why there is such a marked contrast between the large quantities of imported pottery found in some ports and its rarity inland. The pottery can nevertheless provide a useful guide to the provenance of the ships visiting a port. The very large quantities that have been found at Bryggen and Gamla Lödöse give some hope of determining the relative importance of the overseas contacts of those ports. Thus, among some 24,000 sherds from Bryggen that have been investigated by Ian Reed, 2,158 came from deposits earlier than the fire of 1248.[66] About a quarter of these were English, 92 from Stamford and 403 from the London area. Most of the sherds were German (1565) and a few (92) came from the Low Countries while a mere six were identified as Baltic or south Scandinavian. These figures help put the Anglo-Norwegian trade in perspective, and show that Sverre did not exaggerate the scale of German activity. Excavations at Kaupang have yielded some 2,000 pottery sherds from the eight and ninth centuries.[67] The absence of any English pottery means presumably that Kaupang was not visited by English ships. Some imports from the British Isles were found there in the form of bronze jewellery, and similar ornaments have been found in Norwegian graves of the Viking

North, ed. R. A. Hall (1978), 37–57, at 39.

63. P. H. Sawyer, *From Roman Britain to Norman England* (1978), 204, 230.
64. A. P. Smyth, *Scandinavian York and Dublin*, II (Dublin, 1979).
65. A. Andrén, *Lund* (Medeltidsstaden 26, Stockholm, 1980); K. Carlsson and R. Ekre, *Gamla Lödöse* (Medeltidsstaden 21, Stockholm, 1980); *Archaeological Contributions to the Early History of Urban Communities in Norway*, ed. A. Herteig, H.-E. Lidén, C. Blindheim (Instituttet for sammenlignende Kulturforskning, Oslo, 1975); O. Olsen, 'The Medieval Town – a historical-archaeological project initiated by the Danish Research Council for the Humanities', *Danish Medieval History New Currents*, ed. N. Skyum-Nielsen and N. Lund (Copenhagen, 1981), 137–52.
66. I wish to thank John Hurst for kindly making the results of this investigation available to me.
67. E. K. Hougen, 'Leirkarmaterialet fra Kaupang', *Viking 33* (1969), 97–118; English summary, 113–16.

period.[68] Some of these objects may have been traded but other methods of distribution, including robbery and gift, cannot be excluded.

One English export that certainly reached Scandinavia in large quantities in the tenth and eleventh centuries was coin. Well over 50,000 English coins, mostly minted between 980 and 1051 have been found in hoards or separate finds in Scandinavia and in the lands south and east of the Baltic, and the coins that have been recovered can only be a tiny part of the total that reached Scandinavia.[69] There is general agreement that most of these coins were either extorted as tribute in the course of the Viking raids that began in 980, or were paid to Scandinavians who, until 1051, helped defend England. Several scholars, including Michael Dolley himself, have, however, argued that at least some of these coins were exported by way of trade.[70] This view has recently been restated by Mark Blackburn and Kenneth Jonsson who have concluded that they represent 'a period of increased money-oriented trade, overlaid and emphasised by the fruits of raiding and payments of tribute and *heregeld*'.[71] They draw a comparison with the larger German element in the Scandinavian hoards, which they say arrived principally by trade and shows a similar decline in the second quarter of the eleventh century. The increased flow of both English and German coins to Scandinavia commenced in the early 970s and the decline continued after 1051, representing, they suggest, the beginning and end of a period in which trading produced a balance of payments surplus in the northern lands. The scale of this surplus cannot be estimated because it is masked by the payments of tribute and *heregeld*, but, they argue, it is likely to have been substantially greater in the middle than at the beginning or end. The reduction may also have been exaggerated after the mid-eleventh century by the development of national currencies in Denmark and Norway. Michael Metcalf puts forward a similar argument. After referring to the large German element in the Scandinavian hoards which he also believes was mainly the product of trade, he says: 'If that is true of the German coins, could it be partly true also of the Anglo-Saxon?'[72] He emphasizes the importance of the east coast ports in England and, using a theoretical model of the currency, suggests that the outflows were often greater than the

68. C. Blindheim, 'Trade problems in the Viking Age. Some reflections on insular metalwork found in Norwegian graves of the Viking Age', in *The Vikings*, ed. T. Andersson and K. I. Sandred (Uppsala, 1978), 166–76.
69. M. Blackburn and K. Jonsson, 'The Anglo-Saxon and Anglo-Norman element of north European coin finds', in *Viking-Age Coinage in the Northern Lands*, ed. M. A. S. Blackburn and D. M. Metcalf (BAR Internat. ser. 122, 1981), 147–255, at 149.
70. Grierson, *op. cit.* (n.9 above), 105; F. M. Stenton, *Anglo-Saxon England* (3rd edn, 1971), 542–3; H. R. Loyn, *Anglo-Saxon England and the Norman Conquest* (1962), 95; D. M. Metcalf, 'Some twentieth-century runes. Statistical analysis of the Viking-age hoards and the interpretation of wastage rated', in *Viking-Age Coinage in the Northern Lands*, 329–79; M. Blackburn and M. Dolley, 'The Hiberno-Norse element of the List hoard from Sylt', *BNJ 49* (1979), 17–25.
71. Blackburn and Jonsson, *op. cit.*, 184.
72. Metcalf, 'Some twentieth-century runes', 330.

recorded sums of tribute and *heregeld*.[73] Some of this, he suggests, passed in trade to Scandinavia rather than to the Rhineland which is thought to have had a balance of payments deficit with England.[74] There have also been attempts to distinguish hoards or parts of hoards that were gathered by merchants from those that were accumulated by warriors.

The analogy which is drawn with the German coins in the Scandinavian hoards relies on the assumption that they were the product of trade, but I have argued elsewhere that these and the Islamic coins found in Scandinavia were more probably the fruits of tributes and raiding.[75] A few English coins clearly did reach Scandinavia before 980. Blackburn and Jonsson have noted some 50 tenth-century English pennies earlier than Edgar's Reform coinage of c.973 in Scandinavian collections.[76] There is also a substantial increase with the Reform issue, and the hoards suggest that some of these reached Scandinavia before 980 when the renewed raids on England began.[77] It can hardly be claimed that these represent a significant trade balance, even on the assumption that they were all taken from England by traders. There is, however, no justification for any such assumption. Edgar was criticized in the Anglo-Saxon Chronicle soon after his death for favouring and attracting foreigners to England.[78] William of Malmesbury interpreted that as meaning Saxons, Flemings, and Danes.[79] That may have been William's invention, but there is contemporary evidence to show that Edgar asserted his overlordship over other rulers of the British Isles and entertained them. They included two men with Scandinavian names, one of whom ruled 'a kingdom of many isles'; presumably he was king of the Isles.[80] Part of the gifts that Edgar must have presented to these men and their followers could possibly have reached Scandinavia sooner or later.

In 1051 Edward the Confessor disbanded his Scandinavian fleet and the flow of English coins was greatly reduced. The change can be illustrated from Henry Mossop's catalogue of Lincoln coins.[81] This shows that Scandinavian collections contain 241 coins minted between 1042 and 1051, and only 44 for the period 1051 to 1066.[82] The number for William I's reign is only 16. There is a general decline during the Confessor's reign, but the most significant and enduring reduction comes between the *Expanding Cross* (c.1050–3) and *Pointed Helmet* (c.1053–6) types. Furthermore, these figures minimize the change because for about 20 years after

73. D. M. Metcalf, 'Continuity and change in English monetary history *c*.973–1086', pt 2, *BNJ 51* (1981), 52–90, at 63–5.
74. *Ibid.*, 57–8; *idem*, 'Some twentieth-century runes', 340.
75. Sawyer, *Kings and Vikings* (n.11 above), 124–9.
76. Blackburn and Jonsson, *op. cit.*, 151.
77. *Ibid.*, 154.
78. Whitelock, *EHD* I, 225 (*s.a.* 959); *Two of the Saxon Chronicles Parallel*, ed. C. Plummer and J. Earle (2 vols., 1892, 1899), I, 115.
79. William of Malmesbury, *Gesta Regum*, ed. W. Stubbs, I (Rolls Ser., 1887), 165.
80. Stenton, *Anglo-Saxon England*, 369–70.
81. H. R. Mossop, *et al.*, *The Lincoln Mint c.890–1279* (1970).
82. The number of coins per type are: *Pacx* 66; *Radiate/Small Cross* 77; *Trefoil Quadrilateral* 40; *Small Flan* 27; *Expanding Cross* 42 (light 31, heavy 11); *Pointed Helmet* 14; *Sovereign/Eagles* 6; *Hammer Cross* 6; *Facing Bust* 2; *Pyramids* 5; Harold II *Pax* –.

1051 the proportion of Lincoln coins reaching Scandinavia was unusually high. There are far more Lincoln than London coins for that period in the Systematic Collection in Stockholm, which is surprising for London was a much more productive mint.[83] This means that the evidence of the Lincoln coins tends to obscure the scale of the change that occurred after 1051.

Neither the continued flow of English coins nor the preponderance of Lincoln coins among English exports to Scandinavia necessarily indicates a balance of trade; there are other, more likely, explanations. Apart from any coins that may have been taken by English exiles after the Conquest or by the English churchmen who were active in Scandinavia thoughout the century, some must have been taken home by the Danish fleet that came to England in 1069. After seizing York, the Danes moved to the south bank of the Humber where the people of Lindsey welcomed them, even entertaining them at village feasts.[84] They were eventually bought off by William and there is no reason to suppose that he was careful only to use his own coinage when paying these raiders.[85] In these circumstances, the discovery in Scandinavia of Edward's later coins, especially from the Lincoln mint, might be expected. Another occasion on which English coins could have found their way to Scandinavia arose six years later, when a large Danish fleet was recruited by rebels against William.[86] It is also worth noting that one of the main pre-Conquest landowners in Lincolnshire was a Dane, Ulf Fenisc, that is, of Fyn.[87] If that name means that he was a recent arrival, he might be expected to have had rather closer links with his homeland than earlier Danish settlers.

The second argument in support of the claim that there was a commercial outflow of English coins depends on the identification of hoards, or parts of hoards, that reflect trade. This was attempted by Mark Blackburn and Michael Dolley in the course of a discussion of a hoard from List on the island of Sylt.[88] They pointed out that the hoard had two components. The first included 66 heavily bent and pecked coins, some fragmentary, of the *First Hand*, *Second Hand*, and *Crux* issues that were minted c.979–c.997. They suggested that 'these had passed through the Baltic where they had been used for trade, as presumably had the Hedeby, German, Byzantine,

83. Blackburn and Jonsson, *op. cit.*, 187 n.27.
84. D. C. Douglas, *William the Conqueror* (1964), 218–22.
85. It may be objected that the four York hoards associated with the rebellion of 1069 contain no coins of Edward the Confessor (Elizabeth Pirie, *SCBI Yorkshire Collections*, xxxiv-xxxvi) and that other payments made in that year are unlikely to have included such coins. Pre-Conquest coins were, however, still available for hoarding after the Conquest. See, for example, the hoards from St Mary Hill Church and Walbrook in London, Rotherham, Soberton in Hampshire and, perhaps, Whitchurch in Oxfordshire (*Inventory* nos. 250, 255, 318, 334, 376). If, as seems likely, the York hoards belonged to William's own men who were killed or driven from the city, the absence of his predecessor's coins is not surprising.
86. C. Clark, *The Peterborough Chronicle 1070–1154* (1970), 5.
87. F. M. Stenton, 'Introduction' to *The Lincolnshire Domesday and the Lindsey Survey*, ed. C. W. Foster and T. Longley (1924), xxxvii.
88. Blackburn and Dolley, *op. cit.*

and Oriental coins [these numbered 95 in all]. Viewed as a separate group, the proportions (50 per cent German and 42 per cent English) are much as one would expect of a hoard from Gotland or southern Scandinavia, and they probably represent thc purse of a Viking trader.' We do not, however, know under what circumstances coins were pecked and bent, and it should not be assumed that this only occurred during trading transactions. Moreover, coins once traded could become the accumulated wealth of others, so that we cannot assume that all the hoards found in southern Scandinavia and Sweden were traders' purses, and no good reason has been offered for identifying this parcel from the List hoard as one.

The second part of the List hoard is more important for the present discussion. It consists of 29 Hiberno-Norse coins and 580 *Long Cross* coins that were, with one exception, fresh and flat. Blackburn and Dolley say that 'the presence of both English and Hiberno-Norse coins suggests that the parcel is the proceeds of a successful trading expedition, rather than part of a Danegeld payment', and that 'the composition of the English element also bears out this conclusion'. The mints of Stamford, London, Exeter, and Lydford are said to be over-represented, nine mints are named as being significantly under-represented (including three that are in fact absent), while some 24 mints are not represented at all. From this they conclude that it was the deposit of a man who 'crossed the North Sea to trade principally with York, Lincoln, London, and Exeter, as well as taking the Irish Sea by the southern route to sell goods to the Ostmen of Dublin'.

A similar approach has been adopted by Mark Blackburn and Kenneth Jonsson in discussing the Lübeck hoard.[89] They report that it contained 1,854 ascertainable English coins, 1,607 of which were of Cnut's last two issues, and they argue that in these two issues the mints of south-east England are over-represented. They conclude that these coins 'certainly do not give the impression of being part of a mercenary's payment derived from a nationally collected *heregeld*' and that 'the presence of the two issues in almost equal numbers and with a similar regional bias may represent continuing trade over a period of years or may indicate that already by the early 1030s old coin remained in circulation after demonetization and was used in payments to foreign traders.'

If one examines the so-called special features which are said to distinguish these hoards as traders' hoards, one finds that they are far from conclusive. In the case of the List hoard there is no good reason to assume that the Hiberno-Norse coins were only acquired by Scandinavians by means of peaceful trading; raids on Ireland or on Dublin merchants, as well as payments to Scandinavian warriors, are only two of many possibilities. As for the equal representation of two types at Lübeck, it is difficult to see why that should indicate a traders' hoard; it is just as likely, indeed more likely, to be the pay of a member of the *here* who served over a decade or so, or a payment made from a sum of money accumulated in England over several years.

The authors take support for their views that these hoards were gathered by merchants by finding that the coins from one or more regions are over-represented.

89. Blackburn and Jonsson, *op. cit.*, 157–60.

There is, of course, the problem of choosing a standard against which the representativeness of each mint in each issue can be measured. Obviously no single hoard can serve this purpose and the Systematic Collection in Stockholm offers no more than an arbitrary basis for comparison. Blackburn and Dolley in their discussion of the List hoard accept that although the Systematic Collection in Stockholm and the Danish National Collection are 'not wholly representative of Scandinavian hoards, and still less of English production, the sample is large enough to form a basis for comparison sufficient for the present purpose'.[90] What is more, the *Long Cross* coins in the Igelösa hoard are said to have a remarkably good correlation with those in the two Scandinavian collections, despite some divergences that are dismissed as random. Blackburn and Jonsson have also accepted that the majority of the *Crux* and *Long Cross* coins in the Igelösa hoard represent two or more parcels of tribute.[91] Eleven mints are in fact not represented in the *Long Cross* coins from Igelösa and 13 others are only represented by a single coin each. These were admittedly minor mints whose presence or absence need not be particularly significant in determining the bias of a hoard. It is perhaps more significant that several important mints, including Exeter, Lincoln, London, and Winchester, are better represented in Igelösa than in the two Scandinavian collections.[92] Such variations must make the description of a mint or region as under- or over-represented a somewhat subjective process. This method of distinguishing trader's hoards depends too much on impressions.

We cannot assume that all hoards drawn from a nationally collected tribute or *heregeld* would have a similar composition. We can have no idea how thoroughly or in what ways the coins collected in different shires were mixed before payments were made. Some might be distributed straight from the tax on one shire, others might come from a group of shires that were not necessarily in the same region. Many factors must have affected the composition of individual payments. One shire might pay early, another late, and advance or early payments might be made from a different pool of coins than later payments. As we cannot know how these administrative processes worked, or whether they always worked in the same way, the differences between hoards are an unsatisfactory basis for distinguishing money gathered by a merchant from that paid to a warrior.

The main objection to the theory that a significant proportion of the English coins that reached Scandinavia in the tenth and eleventh centuries did so by way of trade is simply that the export dropped suddenly after 1051 when the Scandinavian fleet was disbanded. This difficulty has been countered by the suggestion that there was then a shortage of silver which is also reflected in a decline of German exports of coin to

90. Blackburn and Dolley, *op. cit.*, 18.
91. Blackburn and Jonsson, *op. cit.*, 160.
92. The percentages of *Long Cross* coins from the following mints in the List and Igelösa hoards and in the Systematic Collection at Stockholm and the Danish National Collection are, according to Blackburn and Dolley, *op. cit.*, 19–20:

	List (537 coins)	Igelösa (538 coins)	Stockholm and Copenhagen (1215 coins)
Exeter	8.6	5.0	3.9
Lincoln	13.8	15.3	11.9
London	38.0	28.8	22.7
Winchester	0.4	7.7	4.2

Scandinavia.[93] There was, however, enough silver in circulation in England after the Conquest to make it worth William the Conqueror's while to levy regular gelds, including at least one at the high rate of six shillings on the hide.[94]

English coins reached Scandinavia in many ways; as gifts, pay, tribute, and loot as well as in the purses of churchmen and exiles. Some must have been taken by traders but we are not entitled to assume that all the English coins that were exported to Scandinavia before 980 or after 1051 came from a trading balance. Nor can we hope to estimate how many, if any, of the coins found in Scandinavia between those dates were exported by traders. We cannot therefore hope to determine the scale of Anglo-Scandinavian commerce on the basis of numismatic evidence.

The fact that there is very little evidence for Anglo-Scandinavian trade before the Norman Conquest does not mean that there was no such trade. In the twelfth and thirteenth centuries there is little positive evidence for overseas trade but enough hints are given to show that the historical sources are deceptive. Of the foreign merchants who came to Lincolnshire in the time of Henry I only the Norwegians are mentioned by name,[95] and the Gotlanders who came to Boston and Lynn in the reign of Henry III travelled in ships about which the sources are silent. It is only by chance that we hear of the shipment of horses from Ribe to Yarmouth or that in 1220 four London merchants were robbed in Denmark. We may therefore suppose that there was some trade between England and Scandinavia in the tenth and eleventh centuries despite the virtual silence of our sources.

There were certainly many contacts; we hear of the movement of exiles, missionaries, ambassadors, as well as raiders and mercenaries. It would have been very strange if there were no traders. The remarkable size of some east coast towns in the eleventh century and earlier is more easily understood if we assume that there was a significant volume of overseas trade, some of which must have been with Scandinavia. The Scandinavians had suitable ships, exports that the English welcomed and a demand for English goods. Contact with Norway was probably direct; the four *canardes* that came in 1095 cannot have been the first. Much of the trade with Denmark, and the Baltic beyond it, on the other hand, was probably indirect. There is rather better evidence in the eleventh century for German trade with Scandinavia and England separately than for direct Anglo-Danish trade and it is likely that much of the Scandinavian produce that did reach England before the Norman Conquest came, as later, through ports on the lower Rhine, such as Tiel, or the towns of Flanders.[96] The Gotlanders who were welcome newcomers in thirteenth-century England were using a route that was already well established in the eleventh century and probably long before that.

93. Blackburn and Jonsson, *op. cit.*, 156–7, 192.
94. P. H. Sawyer, 'The wealth of England in the eleventh century', *TRHS*[5] *15* (1965), 145–64.
95. A. Ballard, *British Borough Charters 1042–1216* (1913), 168.
96. G. Hatz, *Handel und Werkehr zwischen dem Deutschen Reich und Schweden in der späten Wikingerzeit. Die deutschen Münzen des 10. und 11. Jahrhunderts in Schweden* (Stockholm, 1974); J. de Sturler, *Les relations politiques et les échanges commerciaux entre le Duché de Brabant et l'Angleterre au Moyen Age* (Paris, 1936).

12 The English presence in Viking Dublin

Patrick F. Wallace

The late Michael Dolley was a generous and inspiring scholar whose knowledge of the history and numismatics of what he used to call 'the Anglo-Celtic Isles' was second to none. He could make newly discovered coins 'talk' even in the discomfort of excavation huts. I was introduced to him by Breandán Ó'Ríordáin whose discoveries of coins, bracteates, and tokens over years of excavation in Viking and Anglo-Norman Dublin had engaged his attention and intuition. Fortunately, the focus of his attention on our Dublin discoveries remained as concerted and productive during my excavations at Wood Quay/Fishamble Street from 1974 to 1981. Except for a nummular brooch about which he had enthused but upon which he had not yet pronounced, and three coins from Fishamble Street, he had seen and identified all the coins from the Dublin excavations before his untimely death. The three exceptions have been identified by my colleague Michael Kenny to whom I am most grateful. Mark Blackburn has also given me much help with this paper.

Rather than here present detailed descriptions of the Dublin coins based on Michael Dolley's reports which will be included in the final site publication, I hope instead to assess the overall impact of the English on Norse Dublin, using his identifications of the coins as a substantial plank of my platform of belief that this impact was greater than has hitherto been recognized, at least in the archaeological literature. It is hoped that this essay and its concern are appropriate to the memory of an Englishman who laboured long and spectacularly in the service of Irish numismatics, not least the coins of our Viking Age.

Students of history have long recognized the relative closeness of the links which existed between Dublin and England in the period from the late ninth to the late eleventh century[1] and will hopefully suffer a fresh summary[2] of the historical

1. Many of the historical facts and dates which are cited and used in the course of this article have been gleaned from secondary works and not by recourse to the original documents (except for some of the Irish Annals). Therefore, references will be made only in respect of opinions and interpretations rather than to support dates or facts. Among the most comprehensive histories of the ninth- /tenth-century links between Dublin and York are A. P. Smyth, *Scandinavian York and Dublin* (vol. I, Dublin, 1975, and vol. II, New Jersey and Dublin, 1979); *idem*, *Scandinavian Kings in the British Isles 850–880* (1977); F. T. Wainwright, *Scandinavian England* (1975); and C. Haliday, *The Scandinavian Kingdom of Dublin*, 2nd edn (Dublin, 1884; repr. Shannon, 1969). Modern general historical surveys of the period include D. O Corráin, *Ireland before the Normans* (Dublin, 1972) and M. Richter, *Irland im Mittelalter* (Stuttgart, 1983).
2. See also P. F. Wallace, 'Viking Age in Dublin', *British Heritage* 1983 (Harrisburg, PA), 37–41, 54–5.

connections before my principal concern, the archaeological evidence. It suffices to say that shortly after Dublin was established as a *longphort* or proto-urban trading base by the Norse in 841, it continued to expand and to have ambitious rulers who took an interest in Scotland and the Southern Hebrides in the 863–76 period and later in York and Northumbria. A combination of emigration, the absence of a strong leader, and the emergence of native military strength led to the temporary dislodgement of the Dublin Vikings from 902 to about 917, when circumstances arose which were favourable for their return to Ireland from exile in northern England, where, since the resurgence of Saxons (especially in Mercia), matters were going against them. Of the two great leaders to emerge in the second decade of the tenth century, Sihtric *Caoch* took over the Dublin interest of the dynasty, and presumably set about the establishment of an urban settlement on or (more probably) near the site of the previous Viking *longphort*, while Rægnald took over York, initiating 35 years of close political contact between Dublin and York.

It became usual that when a king of York died or was killed, the reigning king of Dublin moved to York to be succeeded in Dublin by a junior member of the dynasty who could be promoted to York as the need arose. In this way Sihtric *Caoch* succeeded Rægnald at York in c.920, but on his death in 927 Athelstan seized the opportunity to capture York, temporarily ousting the Viking leaders. In 937 the new king of Dublin, Olaf Guthfrithson, led an army of Irish-Norse, Scots, and North Britons to defeat by Athelstan at the Battle of Brunanburh, a major turning-point for Dublin and Irish-Norse interests at York. Olaf was back in York by 940, having taken advantage of the transfer of English power to Edmund, but died in the following year, being succeeded by his Dublin cousin Olaf *Cuarán* Sihtricson who was in turn driven out of Northumbria by Edmund in 944. Although this Olaf also returned to rule York in 948, he was soon banished back to Dublin. Finally with Eadred's expulsion of the Norwegian prince Eric Bloodaxe from York in 954, the Viking Age in York may be said to have come to an end. Thenceforth, Dublin would be the principal Viking town in the west. It continued to be ruled by local Norse kings for two centuries more until the arrival of the Anglo-Normans in 1171.

The sea-borne monarchy connecting Dublin and York failed to endure for a variety of reasons: the physical barriers between Dublin and York, the English resurgence, the unexpected death of able leaders like Sihtric *Caoch* and Olaf Guthfrithson, the probable difference in religion between the Danes and the Irish-Norse, and the drain on Dublin's resources due to continuous fighting with the Uí Néill. It is important to realize that York/Northumbria was not the only interest of the Irish-Norse in early tenth-century England. One of their exiled leaders, Hingamund, was militarily active in the Wirral/Chester area where, as in adjoining areas of Lancashire, many of the Norse exiles from the east coast of Ireland settled, no doubt with population injections from other Norse colonies.

The foregoing historical background has to be kept in mind in any study of the origins, development, and character of tenth-century Dublin, rather as Professor Gwynn remarked in relation to Bristol's earliest links with Dublin: 'We fail to grasp the influences that must have moulded the city's earliest history if we lose sight of these far-distant battles and sea-raids.'[3] A case has already been made[4] for the importance to the understanding of the origins of tenth-century Dublin of the economic and military resurgence of late ninth- /early tenth-century England and the 'urban revolution' it underwent with the establishment of newly defended *byrig* as well as the re-defending of older urban centres. It can hardly be a coincidence that all this was going on in England just when the Dublin Norse were exiled there. They would have had first-hand experience of some of the freshly defended towns like Chester and Viking York, and were probably inspired to re-establish Dublin within defensive embankments on their return. This may not have happened immediately after 917 but could have followed the 927 expulsion of the Irish-Norse from York, after which there was a flurry of Viking activity in Ireland.[5]

While the re-foundation of Dublin in or about 917 seems not unrelated to political developments and interests at the other side of the Irish Sea, it is important to realize that there was also a strong English connection with Dublin in the eleventh century. This was to have enormous consequences for subsequent Dublin and Irish history, as it seems to have inspired Leinster kings to discover the economic importance of towns and indirectly to have paved the way for the coming of the Normans to Ireland. In contrast to the connections of the early tenth century, which were mainly related to Norse Dublin's political interests in northern England, the relations of the later tenth and eleventh centuries reflect growing English political, ecclesiastical, and commercial interest in Dublin. It is also important to remember that Dublin was involved in the political affairs of Norway, the Scottish Islands, the Isle of Man, and Wales during the eleventh century, especially during the Ua Briain supremacy at the end of that century.

Among the strongest links between Dublin and England in the eleventh century were those forged by the Church. Arising from Cnut's great influence on the king of Dublin and following the English king's agreement with the German Emperor Conrad whereby the safe passage of pilgrims to Rome was guaranteed, Sihtric Silkbeard followed Cnut's footsteps to Rome in 1028 and on his return to Dublin established a bishopric in the town.[6] At least five Irish royal pilgrimages to Rome are recorded between 1028 and 1064, of these three or possibly four had a direct Norse Dublin connection, and they all probably originated from the port of Dublin. Sihtric's son, Amlaim, was actually killed by the English *en route* to Rome in 1034. Although Gwynn[7] believed that the 1066 Norman conquest of England had a

3. A. Gwynn, 'Medieval Bristol and Dublin', *Irish Historical Studies 5* (1947), 275–86, esp.278.
4. P. F. Wallace, 'The origins of Dublin', in *Studies on Early Ireland*, ed. B. G. Scott (Belfast, 1982), 129–43.
5. R. H. M. Dolley, *The Hiberno-Norse Coins in the British Museum* (1966), 28; K. Hughes in A. J. Otway-Ruthven, *A History of Medieval Ireland* (1968), 25.
6. A. Gwynn, 'Ireland and Rome in the eleventh century', *Irish Ecclesiastical Record* 57 (1941), 213–32, esp. 223, and M. Richter, 'The first century of Anglo-Irish relations', *History* 59 (1974), 195–210.
7. Gwynn, 'Ireland and Rome'; M. Richter, 'The European dimension of eleventh- and twelfth-century Ireland', (A. Gwynn Memorial lecture, University College Dublin, 8 December 1983).

negative effect on Irish pilgrim traffic to the Continent, this may not have been totally negative if the 1072 death notices of Diarmait mac Máel-na-mBó, the *de facto* king of Dublin and Leinster, as 'gentle towards pilgrims' can be relied on as evidence for the survival of pilgrimages from Dublin after 1066.

Dublin's earliest bishops were consecrated at Canterbury and not in the Irish church.[8] It was not until the Synod of Ráith Breasail and Muirchertach Ua Briain's Hibernicization of the Dublin see in the 1120s that Canterbury's grip was finally broken. Lanfranc himself consecrated Patrick as second bishop of Dublin in 1074 and Archbishop Ralph of Canterbury consecrated Bishop Gregory for the Dublin see as late as 1121. Before the end of the eleventh century Limerick and Waterford, the other great Norse towns, also gave obedience to Canterbury, with Gilbert of Limerick once reminding the archbishop how they had met at Rouen. The influence of Cnut on Sihtric and the possible submission to Cnut of Echmarcach, the king who deputized for Sihtric during his absence (1028–9) in Rome when Amlaim, Sihtric's son, was in temporary captivity, are important in the sequence of events which led to the strong influence of Canterbury in Dublin. Gwynn suggests that the Peter's Pence which was paid from Dublin was due to 'the influence of Anglo-Saxon custom at a time when it was almost certainly unknown in the rest of Ireland'.[9] Apart from the Dublin-Canterbury connection there appears also to have been a level of English involvement in Irish church reform. Until 1066 'English and Irish monks shared a common cultural world', while abroad 'both Irish and English looked to the German Empire' and went to Rome 'under the patronage of the German emperor'.[10]

Aside from Dublin's control of Man and Ireland's interests in Wales in the later eleventh century, and apart from the unfortunately poorly documented submission to Cnut in 1028–9, Dublin's main English political links centre on the activities of the Godwine family.[11] Harold and his brother Leofwine, sons of Earl Godwine, fled to Ireland probably principally to hire a fleet to assist in their campaign against Edward the Confessor. They came late in 1051 and stayed well into 1052, the year their host Diarmait mac Máel-na-mBó, Uí Cheinselaig king of Leinster (1042–72), captured and occupied Dublin and left his son, Murchad, in charge of the Viking town. It is possible that they came to Dublin because of the local king Echmarcach's probable acquaintance with Godwine, who had been given charge of Bristol in 1018 and who would be well acquainted with Irish affairs, not least the value of Dublin's fleet in warfare. It was to the rising star of Diarmait that they hitched their wagon of fortune in Ireland and began an alliance that was to last even after the Battle of Hastings, 15 years later. The arrival and stay in Ireland of English nobles versed in the value of controlling towns coincided with the taking of Dublin by Diarmait, who like other contemporary Irish kings would not yet have lived in nor perhaps fully

8. A. Gwynn, 'The first bishops of Dublin', *Reportorum Novum 1* (1955), 1–26; M. Richter (ed.), *Canterbury Professions* (Canterbury and York Society 140, 1973).
9. Gwynn, 'Ireland and Rome', 232.
10. D. Bethell, 'English monks and Irish reform in the eleventh and twelfth centuries', *Historical Studies 8* (1971), 111–35, esp. 125.
11. B. Hudson, 'The family of Harold Godwineson and the Irish Sea Province', *JRSAI 109* (1979), 92–100.

realized the potential value of towns, and it has been suggested that Diarmait was inspired to conquer Dublin by his royal guests. While Diarmait's strong rule of Dublin from 1052 to 1072 and the appointment of his son to administer the town until his death in 1070 undoubtedly show that this great king of Leinster quickly learned the potential of controlling a rich fortified port with its fleet, its fighting men, and its trade and industry, it is likely that he already knew the value of such towns since he had taken over Waterford as early as 1037 and probably Wexford even earlier. Irish kings may not have been as ignorant of the value of Norse towns as might at first have been thought, although Diarmait's burning of Waterford in 1037 could suggest otherwise. It should be remembered that the Uí Briain had controlled Limerick since the tenth century, and that Dublin had been visited rather than attacked by the king of Leinster in 1018, the king of Brega in 1023, and the king of Waterford in 1035, and Donnchad mac Briain spent three days there in 1026. Diarmait's growing consciousness of the value of taking rather than destroying a town may be implicit in his not burning it and specifically in not taking any cattle from its hinterland. This is in contrast to his burning of Waterford in 1037 and Máelsechnaill's burning of Dublin as recently as 1025. The rarity of annalistic references to Dublin after 1052 as to Waterford after 1037 probably shows the extent to which Diarmait controlled them while Donnchad mac Briain's attack on Fingal in 1053 may be seen as a retaliation for Diarmait's taking of Dublin, a symbol of how important possession of Dublin had already become.

The sons of Godwine sailed to England with nine ships in 1052 and presumably the relationship with Diarmait continued after Godwine's restoration in 1052 and Harold's accession to the earldom of Wessex in 1053. In 1055 Ælfgar, son of Leofric of Mercia, fled to Ireland – presumably to hire ships from Diarmait and Murchad in Dublin – and returned for further help in 1058. Harold's sons came to Ireland with their cousin Tostig Sweinson after their defeat at Hastings, and almost certainly came to Diarmait in Dublin as their father had in 1051. It was probably they and not Harold who gave Diarmait the present of 'the standard of the king of the Saxons' (i.e. Edward the Confessor), which he was later to give as a present to his protégé Toirrdelbach Ua Briain. Harold's sons Godwine and Edmund launched two attacks on England from Ireland in 1068 – one against Bristol in which Godwine was successful and the other against Exeter in which he was repulsed. After this the royal brothers may have returned to Ireland and to Diarmait. The principal lasting result of this was to cause William the Conqueror to fortify successfully his south-west coasts against Hiberno-Norse fleets and to pave the way for an alliance between William and the Uí Briain. It is even possible that, as with Echmarcach and Cnut in 1028, Toirrdelbach may have submitted to William in 1074. William is reputed to have been interested in the conquest of Ireland and to have been prevented from attempting it only by his death. Building on his father Toirrdelbach's friendship with the Normans, Muirchertach developed an understanding with Henry I, who on one occasion had to place an embargo on Irish goods and on all trade between England and Ireland to bring the Irish king to heel, causing William of Malmesbury to ask: 'For of what value would Ireland be, if goods were not brought to her by sea from England?'.

Toirrdelbach Ua Briain surpassed his patron Diarmait in power and took over Dublin after Diarmait's death in 1072 when his grandson, Domnall, was taken prisoner. While it is possible that Diarmait lived in Dublin in his last years, and although he controlled three of the four Norse towns of Ireland and possession of Dublin was so highly rated by the various Irish 'kings with opposition' that it may be regarded as the capital of Ireland from the time of his reign, it was the Uí Briain, Toirrdelbach and Muirchertach, who were Ireland's first true urban-based monarchs. Along with their role in church reform and their alliance with the Normans, their use of and residence in towns may be regarded as innovative, although based on beginnings made by Diarmait mac Máel-na-mBó, whose descendants temporarily broke the long late-eleventh-century Munster domination of Dublin briefly in 1078 and 1089.

Before leaving the historical evidence it is important to consider briefly the English towns for which there is most contact with later Viking-Age Dublin. York resurfaces as late as 1014 when Brodar of York is the only foreign leader at Clontarf to have his place of origin mentioned so precisely. As late as 1032 the Irish annals record a fire at York and according to William of Malmesbury Irish ships met German ships at York. Chester too continued to be of importance and even in the reign of Henry I there is a reminder of the special privileges which the merchants of Chester enjoyed in Dublin.[12] Bristol was the English town with which Dublin traders and fleets of mercenaries seem to have had most dealings from the eleventh century until well after the close of the Middle Ages. Wulfstan refers to the slave trade with Dublin. Other documents describe Irish cloth merchants in tenth-century Cambridge and Viking attacks on English cloth ships sailing to Dublin in the eleventh century.

There are references to Irish cloth merchants in Bristol in the twelfth century, to the fact that Diarmait mac Murchada remained in the port of Bristol 'on account of the ships which made frequent voyages from Ireland to that port', and to the rights enjoyed by the men of Bristol in Dublin in the time of Henry I. Bristol's importance to the Godwine family probably also linked it politically with Dublin. Diarmait mac Murchada's reception in Bristol in 1146 and 1166 may be seen as part of a common Bristol-Dublin trade pattern and a common patronage of the Arrossians which was introduced to Dublin by Diarmait.

Gwynn poses two important possibilities of early English contact with Dublin;[13] first, and more easy to answer, the possibility of an early English-style borough court like that at pre-Conquest Bristol having governed Dublin. There is historical and now also archaeological evidence to refute the necessity of such a borrowing, though whether or not Saxon models were used is impossible to say. As early as 1023 the king of Brega was met by 'the foreigners in their own *aireachtus*' or assembly in Dublin. Presumably this was the Viking *Thing* for which there is other literary evidence. The existence of kings in Dublin throughout its Viking history, the survival of the local dynasty (Ivarson) even after the Irish take-over of the town from 1052, and reference to the office of mormaor in the twelfth century, suggest the existence of a Dublin

12. J. H. Round, 'Early Irish trade with Chester and Rouen', *Feudal England* (1895), 465–7, esp. 466.

13. Gwynn, 'Medieval Bristol and Dublin', 277.

assembly or government from an early date. The discovery of over 250 lead weights[14] which come in multiples or fractions of the Carolingian ounce of 26.6g gives archaeological support to the existence of an ordered society. So does the establishment of a mint c.997 and the discovery of rigidly adhered-to property boundaries built in succession of one another over the generations.[15]

Gwynn's other question[16] raises the possibility of an actual English settlement in Dublin 'prior to Strongbow's invasion'. He cites the strong religious and economic links of Chester and Bristol with Dublin and holds that 'close trading relations . . . make it probable that English settlers from both Chester and Bristol, perhaps also from other ports, had settled in Dublin during the twelfth century before the Norman invasion, but do not suffice to prove that there were such settlements.' No less than with the suggested Irish enclave in tenth-century Chester,[17] an actual English settlement in Dublin cannot be proved. Archaeologically, as will be seen, the case for a strong English presence in Fishamble Street is greater than for the Irish at Chester, but the relative strength of both arguments may be in proportion to the relative amounts of excavation which has been carried out at both cities.

Turning to the archaeological evidence for the English presence in Dublin and prior to considering particular items of influence, it is important to repeat that the origins of Dublin as a tenth-century town must be studied against the background of the 'urban revolution' which the returning Irish-Norse had experienced in England. The new Irish towns of Dublin, Limerick, and Waterford were probably styled more on English than any other models. This had to be so in view of the absence of towns in the Norse homelands and colonies and the rather different role of the native Irish monastic centres.[18] In fairness, the native secular and monastic centres probably played a greater role in determining the character, buildings, and layout than did any Scandinavian models. It is possible that the banks which enclosed Dublin were based on Irish *rath*-type fortifications and were built to the dictates of local military experience. It is also possible that Dublin's street network, which appears to consist of the free accommodation of streets to a natural crest, derives to some extent from the street system employed in native Irish settlements. Dublin's buildings seem to be close to native houses and to have been built in a local tradition. The problem is that there is such a lack of hard archaeological evidence for the layout of domestic buildings of native secular and ecclesiastical settlements that it is impossible to say where the most immediate source of inspiration lay. The gridded layout of English towns and *byrig* seems to have played little part in determining the

14. P. F. Wallace, 'A catalogue of Dublin's tenth to thirteenth century weights with an account of their production and use' (forthcoming).
15. P. F. Wallace, 'The archaeology of Viking Dublin', in *Comparative History of Urban Origins in Non-Roman Europe*, ed. H. B. Clarke and A. Simms (BAR Internat. Ser. 255, 1985), 103–45.
16. Gwynn, 'Medieval Bristol and Dublin', 278–9.
17. R. H. M. Dolley, 'The mint of Chester', *J. Chester and N. Wales Archit. Archaeol. and Hist. Soc. 42* (1955), 1–20; J. D. Bu'Lock, *Pre-Conquest Cheshire* (1972), 58–65.
18. C. Doherty, 'The monastic towns in Early Medieval Ireland', in Clarke and Simms (ed.), *op. cit.*, 45–75.

layout of Dublin. Interestingly, York with its organic street layout[19] comes closest of the English towns in its street plan as well as in the scale and position of its defensive embankments. However, the idea of enclosing towns within such banks was anyway so widespread all over late ninth- /early tenth-century England that its lesson can hardly have gone unnoticed by the Irish-Norse in England. The Dublin buildings[20] seem very different from those in contemporary English towns, although there is a unique later eleventh-century building in Fishamble Street which has a roof-support system consisting of two pairs of sloping blades or crucks which find better parallels in English vernacular contexts[21] than they do in the Irish archaeological or vernacular architectural record and might be an English introduction to Dublin. Therefore, while the character and layout of tenth- /eleventh-century Dublin cannot be said to be borrowed from England, the parallel at York for the layout and enclosing embankments raises the possibility of Scandinavian originality and the possible idea of a Viking response derived from a variety of sources, Irish, English, and Scandinavian. This is not to deny the immediacy of English urban political/military and economic influences to the origins and timing of the foundations of the tenth-century *dún* at Dublin.

Archaeological proof for commercial contact between Dublin and England in the Viking Age ranges from the importation of raw materials to finished articles – brooches, weapons, and souvenirs. It is also likely that both raw materials like amber and silver as well as finished products like silks and other textiles were not always shipped directly from ports in their countries of origin but were often trans-shipped to Dublin from English ports and markets.

The best tangible proof of commercial contact between Dublin and England in the tenth and eleventh centuries must be the coins which have been recovered from the excavations. When Dublin's own mint was eventually established c.997, it was English prototypes of Æthelred II which were copied by the Dublin moneyers, a development which in Cronne's words[22] must be 'suggestive of Anglo-Irish trade'. It soon became usual for new English issues to be copied in Dublin within a few months of their appearance in England.[23] It would seem that Dublin's coins were intended for use in the Viking communities in Ireland and for overseas trade. Many hundreds of Hiberno-Norse coins of the period c.997–c.1030 have been found in Scandinavia where they circulated and were imitated;[24] thereafter their decline in the hoards is in

19. R. A. Hall, 'The topography of Anglo-Scandinavian York', in *Viking Age York and the North*, ed. R. A. Hall (CBA Res. Rep. 27, 1978), 31–6.
20. P. F. Wallace, 'Carpentry in Ireland AD 900–1300 – the Wood Quay evidence', in *Woodworking Techniques before AD 1500*, ed. S. McGrail (BAR Internat. Ser. 129, 1982), 263–99, esp. 266–75; *idem*, 'Viking Age in Dublin', 40 and 54; *idem*, 'The archaeology of Viking Dublin'; *idem*, 'Irish early Christian "wooden" oratories – a suggestion', *N. Munster Antiq. J.* (1982), 19–28.
21. E.g. at Midhope, Yorkshire, *q.v.* C. F. Innocent, *The Development of English Building Construction* (1916).
22. Quoted in Gwynn, 'Medieval Bristol and Dublin', 276.
23. R. H. M. Dolley, 'Neglected evidence from Ireland for periodicity of type in the English coinage of Æthelræd II', *Irish Numismatics 11.6* (1978), 278–81.
24. M. Blackburn and M. Dolley, 'The Hiberno-Norse element of the List

line with that of the German and English coins and is presumably attributable to internal factors in Scandinavia.[25] The virtual absence of Hiberno-Norse coins from English finds does not indicate that they were not used in trade with English merchants, for most foreign coin was rigorously reminted on entry to the country and one would not expect to find their use in external trade reflected in coin-finds. Among the Viking communities English and Hiberno-Norse coins were probably regarded as of similar value, at least until c.1020 when the Dublin mint raised its weight standard and started striking its own distinctive type (Dolley Phase II), albeit based on an earlier Irish and ultimately English design.

English coins continue to figure prominently in Dublin archaeological contexts until the late 1020s/1030s when after the close alliance of Sihtric of Dublin and King Cnut political contacts tailed off with the death of Cnut and were not activated again until Harold and Leofwine, the sons of Earl Godwine, fled to Ireland in 1051. While Dublin continued to mint coins in this period, that is, Dolley Phases III (c.1035–55) and IV (c.1055–65), it was not until about 1065 (or the beginning of Dolley Phase V) that imitation of contemporary English models was resumed. It is important to realize that although numismatic evidence indicates an absence of English influence in the mid-eleventh century, the political/historical, ecclesiastical, and possibly the ceramic and art-historical information does not, although eventual analysis of the Fishamble Street tree-ring samples should substantially clarify this impression.

Dolley's as yet unpublished reports on Ó Ríordáin's High Street (1962–3, 1967–72) and Winetavern Street (1968–72) excavations identifies three Anglo-Saxon pennies, a Hiberno-Danish penny probably struck at York c.942 in the reign of Olaf *Cuaran*, as well as eight Hiberno-Norse coins and several later English and Continental coins and two certain Roman coins which originated in Köln and Trier (table 12.1). Dolley thought that the Trier *follis* could have come to Dublin from a Chester ballast quarry, a possibility which also has interesting implications for the numerous sherds of *terra sigillata* which have turned up in tenth- and especially eleventh-century Dublin contexts.[26] Apart from the Alfred the Great penny which was struck in London in 886 and probably lost before the end of the ninth century, the other two High Street English pennies are of Æthelred's *Crux* type (c.991–7), one being minted at Barnstaple, Devon, and the other at London, and possibly connected with the 997 Viking raid on the British Channel in which the Dubliners joined. The c.942 York coin found in a boulder clay level at High Street is paralleled

hoard from Sylt', *BNJ 49* (1980), 17–25; M. Dolley, 'Imitation and imitation of imitation: some problems posed by the non-English *Helmet* pennies with the name of Æthelræd II', in *Studies in Northern Coinages of the Eleventh Century*, ed. C. J. Becker (Copenhagen, 1981), 89–111.

25. M. Blackburn and K. Jonsson, 'The Anglo-Saxon and Anglo-Norman element of North European coin finds', in *Viking-Age Coinage in the Northern Lands*, ed. M. A. S. Blackburn and D. M. Metcalf (BAR Internat. Ser. 122, 1981), 147–255, esp. 153–7.

26. A-C. Bélier, 'A sherd of terra sigillata from Wood Quay, Dublin', *Ulster J. Archaeol.*, 3rd ser. *44–5* (1981–2), 192–4.

Table 12.1. Coins of the Anglo-Saxon period from the High Street, Winetavern Street, and Christchurch Place, Dublin, excavations

Ruler	Issue	Mint	Moneyer
High Street			
1. Alfred	*London Monogram*	London	–
2. Olaf *Cuaran* Sihtricson	*Two-line*	– (York?)	Bleseret
3. Æthelred II	*Crux*	Barnstaple	Ælfsige
4. Æthelred II	*Crux*	London	Byrhtlaf

There were also 3 Hiberno-Norse coins (1 Phase II, 2 Phase III) and 19 Irish bracteates of the twelfth century.

Winetavern Street

No Anglo-Saxon coins were found, but there were 5 Hiberno-Norse coins (all of Phase V) from the second half of the eleventh century.

Christchurch Place

Ruler	Issue	Mint	Moneyer
1. Edmund	*Two-line*	–	Eferulf
2. Edgar	*Circumscription* (cross)	Warwick	O(swerd)
3. Æthelred II	*Last Small Cross*	Shaftesbury	Ægelric
4. Cnut	*Pointed Helmet*	Gloucester	Sired

There were also 23 Hiberno-Norse coins (4 Phase II, 8 Phase III, 1 Phase IV, 10 Phase V) and 9 Irish bracteates of the twelfth century.

by an Edmund penny which was found in association with an Edgar coin of Warwick in a boulder clay pit on the Christchurch Place site. Dolley's report on the coins from the latter site, which produced a considerable number of Hiberno-Norse coins, is not yet as coherent as that for the other sites directed by Ó Ríordáin. His general conclusion[27] that the discovery of coins in Dublin and its neighbourhood mirrors Dublin's obsession with York in the first half of the tenth century will have to be radically revised in the light of the Fishamble Street coins, the identifications of which were the subject of his last lecture in Ireland (February 1981).

Seventeen of the 23 pre-Norman coins in the remarkable Fishamble Street/Wood Quay series are of English origin (table 12.2). Although the relevant coins were recovered from different levels and from different plots and span about a century, there is a consistently English complexion about the whole series. The series comprises three pennies from the reign of Athelstan (924–39), none from that of Edmund (939–46), three of Eadred (946–55), three of Edgar (957–75), seven of Æthelred II (978–1016), and one of Cnut (1016–35), as well as seven Hiberno-Norse coins, one bracteate, and three post-Norman specimens. The earliest of the Athelstans was probably minted at Oxford about 925 or slightly later, another at

27. M. Dolley and C. J. Lynn, 'A provisional note on the incidence of coin-hoarding in Viking Age Ireland', *Irish Archaeol. Research Forum 3.2* (1976), 1–6.

Table 12.2. Coins of the Anglo-Saxon period from the Fishamble Street/Wood Quay, Dublin, excavations

	Ruler	Issue	Mint	Moneyer
1.	Athelstan	*Two-line*	– (Oxford?)	Sigeland
2.	Athelstan	*Circular*	Derby?	Ma[ ]
3.	Athelstan	*Crowned Bust*	Canterbury	Ælfric
4.	Eadred	*Two-line* (rosettes above and below)	– (north-west)	Agtardes
5.	Eadred	*Two-line* (rosettes above and below)	– (north-west)	Rægtheres
6.	Eadred	*Crowned Bust*	Norwich	Hrodgar
7.	Edgar	*Circumscription* (rosette)	– (north-west)	Siferth
8.	Edgar	*Two-line*	– (north-east?)	Ive
9.	Edgar	*Two-line*	–	En[ ]e?
10.	Æthelred II	*First Hand*	Barnstaple	Ælfem
11.	Æthelred II	*First Hand*	London	Ælfgar
12.	Æthelred II	*First Hand*	London	Ælfgar
13.	Æthelred II	*Second Hand*	London	Cynsige
14.	Æthelred II	*Crux*	London	Ægnulf
15.	Æthelred II	*Long Cross*	Exeter	Wynsige
16.	Æthelred II	*Helmet*	Exeter	Wulfsige
17.	Cnut	*Pointed Helmet*	Gloucester	Godricc

There were also 7 Hiberno-Norse coins (2 Phase I, 4 Phase II, 1 Phase V) and 1 Irish bracteate.

Derby about 930, and a third at Canterbury about 935. Two of the Eadred pennies appear to have been minted in north-west England and one at Norwich in East Anglia; they were given a 'horizon for loss' of 950–75 by Dolley. One of the Edgar pennies appears to have originated in north-east England and, while Dolley believed that stylistically it resembled products of the York mint, he did not rule out Lincoln as its possible source. He thought it was minted earlier rather than late in Edgar's reign. Another Edgar penny is a well-preserved Mercian coin which was probably struck at Chester between 965 and 970. The third is in fragmentary condition and does not bear the name of its mint. Michael Kenny kindly reports that it is a *Two-line* coin of Edgar's pre-Reform coinage (i.e. pre-973) and feels that it may possibly be from a north-eastern mint (the absence of rosettes precludes the north-west).

The Fishamble Street Æthelred series is most remarkable for containing three coins from the Devonshire mints of Barnstaple and Exeter. It also contains four pennies from London, which is less significant, for whereas London then probably produced c.30 per cent of all coins minted, the mints of Devon and Cornwall only accounted for about 6 per cent. The London pennies in question consist of two *First Hand* coins (c.979–95), one *Second Hand* (c.985–91), and one *Crux* (c.991–7). The Barnstaple penny is of the *First Hand* type and the Exeter coins are of *Long Cross* (c.997–1003) and *Helmet* (c.1003–9) types. The discovery of the latter three coins in Fishamble Street and of a *Crux* from Barnstaple at High Street could be related to the importation of tin from south-west England. However, although considerable evidence for copper-alloy and other non-ferrous metalworking has been unearthed at Dublin, especially in the Christchurch Place area where Ó Ríordáin uncovered a metalworking quarter,[28] the relative paucity of copper-alloy artefacts and the absence of large-scale metalworking evidence at Fishamble Street cautions against the ready acceptance of such an explanation.

The Cnut penny found at Fishamble Street was minted c.1024–30 at Gloucester, an area of growing importance in Dublin's trading network, given the gradual swing of the axis of this trade away from Chester and towards Bristol. It is closely paralleled by another Cnut coin of the same type from Gloucester, but of a different moneyer (Sired), found in the Christchurch Place excavations in 1974. Dolley's demonstration[29] that one sixth of the Kildare Hoard (deposited c.991) was made up of Devonshire minted coins and the knowledge that some of Dublin's earliest coins were based on those of West Country mints like Bath, Watchet, and Lydford has been seen as related to the commercial decline of the Chester-Dee monopoly of trade with Dublin and the concomitant gradual rise of Bristol.[30]

The markedly English content of the Fishamble Street series appears to be in contrast to the other Dublin sites which have relatively higher proportions of Hiberno-Norse coins. It is perhaps not coincidental that unlike Fishamble Street, which is on the waterfront side of the natural crest on which Viking Dublin was located, the other sites were on the south or landward side of the crest. In this way, it can be argued that the preponderance of English coins in the Fishamble Street area need not come as a surprise as this area fronted on to the dockside where so much international trade would have gone on and where foreign (especially English) merchants might be expected to have congregated. Areas of industrial activity such as bone, comb, and metalworking have been identified at sites some distance from the waterfront, but at Fishamble Street, apart from one amber-working plot, no definite industrial activity can be ascribed to the other dozen plots which have been excavated. It is impossible as yet to prove that all or any of these plots were occupied by merchants, although given their location and the absence of concentrated industrial debris this is a likely possibility. Put another way, if English coins were used (and lost to be found by archaeologists) anywhere in Dublin, the most likely place would have been in the Fishamble Street/Wood Quay area. Some of the other artefacts to be discussed presently confirm the relatively greater English contact on this than on other Dublin sites, although the only possible topographical and structural indicator of this is the probable late eleventh-century building with the cruck blade roof-support system which by analogy with later ethnological traditions has a possible English derivation.

A number of other implications also arise from the Viking-Age coin evidence from the excavations. The relatively earlier English coins of Fishamble Street are not so clearly in evidence in the more landward sites and the later Hiberno-Norse series is not as commonly represented in Fishamble Street as on the other sites. This is difficult to understand, since all sites seem to span the same tenth- /eleventh-century range. The greater number of Chester rather than York coins from the tenth century

28. *Viking and Medieval Dublin: Catalogue of Exhibition* (Dublin, 1976), 15.
29. Dolley, *Hiberno-Norse Coins*, 36.
30. L. V. Grinsell, *The Bristol Mint – An Historical Outline* (1972), 2.

seems to be in reverse proportion to the degree of Dublin's dynastic and political interests in York and Chester and serves to illustrate the danger of relying on political/historical references as a barometer of relative commercial contact. It has to be remembered that Dublin's urban and commercial life seems only really to be getting under way in the 930s – or just at the time when its political interest in York was waning. The importance of Chester as the great English port for Ireland in the 930s–80s is certainly well borne out by the relative frequency of the Mercian coins both in Dublin and its hinterland[31] and, as will be seen, by the amount of pottery which was brought to Dublin from the same port. Although it is impossible to sustain a tempting argument for the possibly tenth-century cemetery at Castleknock being the successor of the graveyard of the ninth-century *longphort* at Islandbridge/ Kilmainham on the basis of the association on a solitary coin, it may not be without significance that the coin in question has a mid-tenth century Chester mint-signature. The prevalence of many different mints among the English coins from the excavations must be a significant indicator of the disparate rather than concentrated nature of Dublin's commercial links with England. Not all the contact appears to have been with Chester or later with Bristol, although the likelihood of coins of many different mints having accumulated in the way of ordinary business at great ports like Chester and Bristol has also to be kept in mind.

Coins apart, pottery produces the greatest body of artefactual evidence for Dublin's tenth- /eleventh-century trade contact with England. It must be remembered that unlike the great Viking towns of England or Denmark which produced their own wares, Norse Dublin – like much of contemporary Ireland, Norway, and the Norse colonies – does not appear to have produced pottery, although to judge from the numbers of potsherds in Viking-Age Dublin[32] the demand for imported pottery was enormous. There are glazed pots as well as unglazed cooking pots (sometimes soot-encrusted) from tenth- and eleventh-century levels. Among the English kilns represented are pots which have been identified by John Hurst as of Stamford, Chester, and possibly Winchester, as well as many Crowland bowl sherds. These are typical wheel-stamped bowls with a characteristic crazed brown glaze. Janet Rutter has kindly identified fabric types similar to those at Chester, an impressed design paralleled there at Crook Street and examples of her rim types 1a, 1b(iii), 1c(i), and 1d(ii).[33] The comparatively early date at which Chester ware was coming to Dublin is indicated by its contemporaneity with an Athelstan coin. Many as yet unidentified glazed wares may be attributable to other English kilns. There is also a great influx of what appear to be northern French pottery imports in the later eleventh and twelfth centuries. Glazed Andennes wares and red-painted and Normandy gritted wares are

31. Dolley, *Hiberno-Norse Coins*; Dolley and Lynn, *op. cit.* 1–6.
32. P. F. Wallace, 'North European pottery imported into Dublin 1200–1500', in *Ceramics and Trade*, ed. R. Hodges and P. J. Davey (1983), 275–30.
33. P. Carrington, 'Some types of late Saxon pottery from Chester', *Cheshire Archaeol. Bull. 3* (1975), 3–9; *idem*, 'Chester: Crook Street pit group', in *Medieval Pottery from Excavations in the North-West*, ed. P. J. Davey (1977), 14–17.

also conspicuous but not as common as the grey wares,[34] and it is presumed tha much of this material came by way of England in the wake of the Norman Conques of England or by Dublin's contact with the English trading network. Significan among this material are parts of a rare pair of lidded and spouted jugs of possibl north French or English origin.

It is not clear how the sherds of *terra sigillata* which have turned up in eleventh century Dublin actually came here. It may have been as souvenirs, as part of ballast or even as material for medicinal compounds.[35] Again, the possibility of their being mediated through English maritime contact cannot be discounted.

The Anglo-Saxon disc brooches which have come from the excavations constitut one of the most sizeable surviving bodies of evidence for Dublin's English trad contact and fashion imitation, although only a short account of them is necessar here as it is intended to treat them in full elsewhere. Thirty specimens have beer identified to date – ten from High Street, eight each from Christchurch Place anc Fishamble Street, three from Winetavern Street, and one from Wood Quay. Som are of silver or copper-alloy, but most are of lead-alloy, and while the majority ar cast, there are stamped and hammered varieties in lead-alloy and some of the copper alloy specimens are made from sheet metal. The decoration is usually of beaded wir in actual or skeuomorphic form, 'C' curves set back-to-back, pellets, and occasion ally iconographic motifs. A number of different groups can be distinguished. Th largest includes specimens in which a decorated central circular area is surroundec by one or more rings of beaded wire and a typological progression can be discerned Another group includes discs with raised pyramidal and dome-shaped bosses o combinations of both, while a third incorporates stamped star and cinquefoil motifs There are also a number of individual brooches which although related to the genera series have to be regarded separately.

Although finds of similar disc brooches have been made in other parts of th Viking world, the early dates and best parallels are from England. One of the silve specimens from Coppergate, York,[36] resembles two of the Dublin brooches although the others, while clearly of the same general type, appear to have differen decorative motifs[37] from those in Dublin. There is no doubt that these brooche were made in England[38] and that they were brought to Dublin mainly in the tent century.

34. J. Hurst, 'The pottery', in *The Archaeology of Anglo-Saxon England*, ed. D. M. Wilson (1976), 283–348; R. Hodges, 'Some early medieval imported wares in the British Isles; an archaeological assessment of the French wine trade', in *Pottery and Early Commerce*, ed. D. P. S. Peacock (1977), 239–55.
35. A-C. Bélier, 'A sherd of terra sigillata from Wood Quay, Dublin', *Ulster J. Arch.*, 192–4; 3rd ser., *44–5* (1981–2); J. Bradley, ' "Medieval" Samian ware – a suggestion', *Ulster J. Arch.*, 3rd ser., *44–5*, 196–7.
36. D. Tweddle, 'Discussion', *Interim 8:2* (1982), 26–9.
37. R. A. Hall, 'Coppergate', *Interim 5:4* (1978), 28; *idem*, 'News from Coppergate', *Interim 7:1* (1980), 15–17 E. Roesdahl *et al.* (ed.), *The Vikings in England* (1981), 50, 105–6.
38. D. M. Wilson, *Anglo-Saxon Ornamental Metalwork 700–1100 (in the British Museum)* (1964), 36.

In contrast to the disc brooches which appear to be pure English imports, the numerous copper-alloy, antler, and even bone strap-tags or strap-ends which have been found in Dublin appear to be more local in origin. Their characteristic tips are treated 'as stylised animal-masks' and while paralleled in Viking contexts in Scotland,[39] they are quite different from the more bow-sided English series now known from sites like York.[40] Given the likely popularity of prototype strap-ends in Saxon rather than Irish contexts, the Dublin strap-end type probably has its origins in ninth-century English fashion from which it was brought westwards by the Vikings who eventually produced the distinctive interpretation of it that we find in Dublin and the Udal.

Apart from the importation of raw materials such as jet (from Whitby in Yorkshire) from which luxury items were manufactured in Dublin, a number of finished products also came from England. Conspicuous among these was a late Saxon sword of which the hilt survived to be found in Fishamble Street. This iron hilt was decorated in a bronze inlay and is of Evison's Wallingford type which is characterized by having a slightly drooped hilt plate and a pommel comprised of three fused spheres.[41] Other finished luxury items brought from England probably include some of the worsteds represented among the numerous textile fragments.[42] A gold ring with a red garnet set in a cloison may also be of English or Germanic origin.

Two carved walrus ivory pieces of English origin which were found in the Dublin excavations have recently been studied.[43] One of these is a lentoid plaque bearing a rampant griffin carved in relief with a dark glass inset in the eye. This plaque 'is a high quality piece of ivory carving which probably comes from an ecclesiastical object such as a book-cover or reliquary rather than a secular source'.[44] The object was excavated from late tenth-century urban habitation levels at Fishamble Street. An Anglo-Saxon origin has also been suggested[45] for two further carved objects

39. J. A. Graham-Campbell, 'A preliminary note on certain small finds of Viking-age date from the Udal excavations, North Uist', *Scottish Archaeol. Forum 6* (1974), 17–22.
40. D. M. Waterman, 'Late Saxon, Viking and early medieval finds from York', *Archaeologia 97* (1959), 59–105, esp. 76–7; Rosedahl *et al.*, *The Vikings in England*, 40; Wilson, *Anglo-Saxon Ornamental Metalwork 700–1100*, esp. nos. 18, cata. 24, 29, 71, and 114; D. A. Hinton, *Catalogue of the Anglo-Saxon Ornamental Metalwork 700–1100 (in the Department of Antiquities, Ashmolean Museum)* (1974), esp. cat. nos. 5, 31, 33, 34, and 37.
41. V. I. Evison, 'A sword from the Thames at Wallingford', *ArchJ 124* (1968), 160–89.
42. Information from Ms Frances Pritchard, Department of Urban Archaeology, Museum of London, who is the textile consultant for the Dublin material.
43. L. Webster, 'Two Anglo-Saxon carved zoomorphic mounts from Dublin', in *Keimelia; Studies in Archaeology and History in Memory of Tom Delaney*, ed. G. MacNiocaill and P. F. Wallace (Galway, forthcoming).
44. L. Webster, 'Plaque with griffin', in *The Golden Age of Anglo-Saxon Art 966–1066*, ed. J. Backhouse, D. H. Turner, and L. Webster (1984), 126, no. 130 and fig. 130.
45. By James T. Lang (pers. comm. 1984).

found at Fishamble Street. These are a perforated crook-shaped ivory piece, which features a beaked quadruped with a herringbone motif in two adjoining panels on its only decorated side, and a perforated bone plaque with a terminal incised to resemble a rat's head in profile with a glass (?) sphere set into the eye socket.

The two main periods of Dublin's later Viking-Age contact with England – the early tenth and mid-eleventh centuries – each seems to be reflected in the art-historical record. It would appear that there was something of a cross-fertilization of art traditions between northern England and Leinster in the earlier tenth century and that the Dublin Vikings were the catalysts in this mutual transfer of influence. The Irish High Cross and its ringed head may be seen as ancestral to the Northumbrian crosses,[46] and there are iconographic parallels as well as similar measurement and carving systems employed in the Castledermot and Old Kilcullen crosses on the one hand and some of the Northumbrian stone carvings on the other.[47] An English inspiration for one of the Clonmore, Co. Carlow, crosses has also recently been posed.[48] It is also significant in the context of early tenth-century north English influence that the only known possible Irish 'hogback' grave cover is located at Castledermot.[49] There are references to the activities of the Dublin Vikings at both Castledermot and Old Kilcullen.

The second period of what might be described as Dublin's rather than Leinster's Viking-Age artistic relationship with England dates to the second half of the eleventh century. In this period a close stylistic association appears to have existed between the Dublin interpretation of the ultimately Scandinavian inspired *Ringerike* style and its southern English counterpart which finds probably its best known expression in a carved slab in St Paul's graveyard in London. It should be noted that in contrast to the earlier art relationship which appears to have had a Leinster-Northumbrian axis, the later connection seems to have been Dublin-southern England in direction. This resemblance of *Ringerike* styles between the two places has given rise to the suggestion[50] that the production of Ireland's *Ringerike* can be attributed to Scandinavians who, having settled in southern England during Danish rule, found a safe haven in Ireland's Norse towns in the years following the Norman Conquest of England when commerce with Scandinavia may have stopped. Fuglesang suggests an influx of 'merchants, soldiers, and possibly artisans' into Ireland as well as 'of new merchants with direct ties with Scandinavia', all of which culminates in 'a strongly increased application of Scandinavian ornament in the workshops of Irish towns'. While such a theory fits neatly with the general proposition of this paper, not least with the connections between the king of Leinster and the Godwinesons before and after the Battle of Hastings, the art-historical and archaeological evidence raise a number of objections to its acceptance.

The abundance of the Dublin *Ringerike* and its non-Scandinavian character

46. R. N. Bailey, *Viking Age Sculpture* (1980), 71.
47. J. T. Lang, lecture to Royal Soc. Antiq. Ireland 1983 and in *Keimelia*, *op. cit.*
48. P. Harbison, in *Keimelia*, *op. cit.*
49. J. T. Lang, 'The Castledermot Hogback', *JRSAI 101* (1971), 154–8.
50. S. H. Fuglesang, 'Some aspects of the Ringerike style' (*a Phase of 11th century Scandinavian Art*) (Odense, 1980), 78.

suggest that the style was introduced to Ireland not by those people whose 'direct ties with Scandinavia' have been emphasised but by some whose experience was of a modified insular version, and present indications are that it was already established in Dublin before 1066. This possible early date and its insular rather than Scandinavian character seem to fit the development of *Ringerike* in Dublin more with Henry's view[51] of the gradual onset of Scandinavian art influence from the time of Clontarf (1014) onwards, and especially with her suggestion[52] of the possible involvement of the Danish kingdom in England in the transmission of ideas to Ireland. While the gradual assimilation of Scandinavian derived styles in Dublin were probably transmitted through trading contacts,[53] the English dimension should not be overlooked. It would seem that it is to the time of Cnut and his period of influence on Dublin (its king, church, and economy) that we should look for the period of the introduction of *Ringerike* to Ireland.

While the runic inscriptions from the Dublin excavations all appear to belong to a Scandinavian tradition there is also evidence of Anglo-Saxon epigraphy. Okasha[54] has found that the inscription on a Christchurch Place comb was in a script which 'fits well into the context of late Anglo-Saxon inscriptions' (i.e. those of tenth-/ eleventh-century date), and there is a suggestion that even the comb itself is best paralleled by a bone specimen from Wallingford, now in the British Museum. An incised leather scabbard from the eleventh-century Christchurch Place stave-built house also accords with Anglo-Saxon inscriptions, as does an inscribed iron sword from Christchurch Place. Recently, a similar suggestion[55] has been made for the origin of the first five letters of the Latin alphabet which were incised on a leather fragment found in late eleventh- /early twelfth-century levels in the John's Lane part of the Wood Quay site. It is hoped that future research may elucidate the meaning of the characters 'BSα' on the Fishamble Street nummular brooch (fig. 12.1), which is probably also of Anglo-Saxon origin.

Dolley's study[56] of the forms of the proper names which appeared on the earliest coins struck in Dublin produced 32 versions of eight personal names which he concluded gave 'perhaps our first hint that the population of Dublin at the end of the tenth century included men with English blood'. He is perhaps being over-cautious in his remark that it would be curious 'if intermarriage had not brought the odd English name to the Viking settlements in Ireland'. The discoveries of so many English coins in Fishamble Street in the years after Dolley wrote this and the

51. F. Henry, 'The effects of the Viking invasions on Irish art' in *Procs of the Internat. Congress of Celtic Studies 1959*, ed. B. O'Cuiv (Dublin, 1962), 61–72, esp. 66.
52. *Ibid.*, 72.
53. M. and L. de Paor, *Early Christian Ireland* (1964), 165–72.
54. E. Okasha, 'Three inscribed objects from Christchurch Place, Dublin' in *Proc. of the Eighth Viking Congress*, ed. H. Bekker-Nielsen, P. Foote, and O. Olsen (Odense, 1981), 45–50.
55. J. Bradley, 'An inscribed stone axehead from Gurteen, Co. Clare', *N. Munster Antiq. J. 21* (1979), 11–14, esp. 13–14.
56. M. Dolley, 'The forms of the proper names appearing on the earliest coins struck in Ireland', in *Otium et Negotium*, ed. F. Sandgren (Stockholm, 1973), 49–65.

Fig. 12.1 Nummular brooch from Fishamble Street, Dublin.

conjunction of other suggestions of English presence in Dublin would probably have reduced his caution if he were writing now.

It is probably time that linguists questioned Greene's remark[57] that 'English speaking communities were first established in Ireland in 1169', especially as by his own admission 'there is solid linguistic evidence that a small number (of words) were taken from Old English into Irish before the arrival of the Anglo-Normans'. One is entitled to question whether 'the possibilities of cultural contact were *so* [my italics] much greater' with the Scandinavians than with the English, especially as Greene himself admits that the linguistic evidence shows that the Irish and Scandinavian communities 'had remarkably little influence on one another'. The discovery of runic inscriptions at relatively late levels in our excavations indicates the probable survival of old Norse into the twelfth century,[58] a remarkable phenomenon considering that the Vikings had already been over three centuries in Dublin, that they had been politically dominated by the Irish, that their church and trade was linked with England, that much of their earlier contact with the original homelands and Atlantic colonies had probably declined, and that they had long intermarried with

57. D. Greene, 'The evidence of language and place-names in Ireland', in *The Vikings*, ed. T. Andersen and K. I. Sandred (Uppsala, 1978), 119–23, esp. 119.
58. This seems to accord fully with D. Greene, 'The influence of Scandinavian on Irish', in *Procs. of the Seventh Viking Congress*, ed. B. Almqvist and D. Greene (Dublin, 1976), 75–82, esp. 81 where Greene writes: 'Norse must have survived as a spoken language in Dublin . . . up to 1169 at least' because certain place-names 'were received directly from Norse into English'.

the native population. Nevertheless, outside of Dublin and the few other towns their lasting impact seems to have been very small. There is little evidence of Scandinavian influence on Irish place names.[59] The time has come for a reassessment of Lucas's reappraisal[60] of the Viking impact and to ask whether the Vikings were so important in bringing about the passing of what Binchy[61] termed 'the old order'. Any reassessment will have to recognize the possibility of a sizeable English contribution.

It is doubtful if many indisputably Irish objects exported through the port of Dublin will ever be recognized in the English archaeological record. Fanning has already surveyed the Hiberno-Norse ringed pins of Scotland and the Isle of Man.[62] His survey of the English material will probably multiply the numbers already known from urban sites like York and Chester.[63] His earlier caution[64] that such artefacts are to be regarded more as indicators of Irish-Norse trade contact rather than themselves as imports from Ireland probably also applies to the specimens found in England, in spite of the interpretation of the York pins as imports from 'the Celtic West'.[65] While the great silver hoard from Cuerdale in Lancashire was probably deposited during the troubled years of the Irish-Norse exile in north England, and even though it is likely that this hoard was amassed in Ireland[66] and probably in Dublin, such opinions are impossible to prove conclusively at present. The main items of export from Dublin to England (i.e. after the decline of the slave trade) were probably perishable organic products like hides and fleeces, which in the present state of archaeological science cannot be equated to place of origin even when rarely they survive to be found in urban excavations. Our almost total dependence on historical sources and on the inferences of what must be regarded as logistics (such as provisioning ships) has to be maintained for any estimate of the bulk and content of Dublin's trade with England and elsewhere in the Viking Age. Our dependence on history is total in respect of some of Dublin's exports and imports (such as wine) as well as on its sizeable income from the hire of its fleet in contemporary warfare.

In general the archaeological and numismatic evidence seems to accord reasonably well with the historical picture with regard to the closeness of commercial contact

59. M. Oftedal, 'Scandinavian place-names in Ireland', in *Procs of the Seventh Viking Congress*, 125–33.
60. A. T. Lucas, 'Irish-Norse relations: time for a reappraisal?' *J. Cork Hist. and Archaeol. Soc. 71* (1966), 62–75.
61. D. A. Binchy, 'The passing of the old order', in *Procs. of the Internat. Congress of Celtic Studies 1959*, 119–32.
62. T. Fanning, 'Some aspects of the bronze ringed pin in Scotland', in *From the Stone Age to the 'forty-five'*, ed. A. O'Connor and D. Clarke (1983), 324–42; *idem*, 'The Hiberno-Norse pins from the Isle of Man', in *The Viking Age in the Isle of Man*, ed. C. Fell *et al.* (1983), 27–36.
63. Waterman, *op. cit.*, esp. 78–9; J. D. Bu'Lock, 'The Celtic, Saxon and Scandinavian settlement at Meols in Wirral', *Trans. Hist. Soc. Lancs. and Ches. 112* (1960), 1–28, esp. 14–21 and fig. 5 p. 16.
64. T. Fanning, 'Some aspects of the bronze ringed-pin in Scotland', in *From the Stone Age to the 'forty-five'*, ed. A. O'Connor and D. Clarke (1983), 324–42.
65. R. A. Hall, *The Viking Dig* (1984), 91, 104.
66. J. A. Graham-Campbell, 'The Viking-Age silver hoards of Ireland', in *Procs. of the Seventh Viking Congress*, 39–74, esp. 54; Smyth, *op. cit.*, II, 244–5.

between Dublin and the English towns in the tenth and eleventh centuries. Apart from ecclesiastical contacts, there appear to have been four major waves of political contact – the early tenth-century contact with York and north Britain, the Sihtric/Cnut contact from the end of the first quarter of the eleventh century, the Uí Cheinselaig/Godwineson alliance of the mid-eleventh century, and the Uí Briain/Norman relationship of the late eleventh century. In the absence of a refined chronology from our excavations, it is impossible to gauge the extent to which any of these waves were mirrored commercially. Given the varying time taken for fashions and other influences to catch on and the uncertain influence which political developments have on commercial contacts, it is unlikely that such equations can ever be made. Coins appear to be the most promising indication of measurable contact and even then selective hoarding, accidental loss and discovery can distort what in the reality of the Viking Age might have been a different picture.

It is significant that it is artefacts – coins, *objets d'art*, pottery, luxury items, and souvenirs – which are the indicators of contact with England and *not* the building types, construction methods, and town layout. Any argument for extensive and/or ongoing English settlement in Viking Dublin should include evidence for English influence on the character and layout of the physical landscape, even allowing that it was usual for Viking-dominated towns to use the prevailing local building types and methods of the territory in which the town was located.[67] Apart from a single late eleventh-century house in Fishamble Street, from the idea rather than scale of the embankments, and from the un-English layout and street plan which Dublin shares with York presumably because of their common domination by Scandinavian overlords, there are no markedly English influences in the physical make-up of Viking-Age Dublin as we know it from our excavations. This is true even in the Wood Quay/Fishamble Street waterfront area where such influences on logistical and artefactual grounds ought to be most obviously manifested. In contrast with the topographical evidence which points away from England, many of the artefacts (especially those derived from trade) point very definitely in that direction. Perhaps in this apparent contradiction lies the answer to Gwynn's speculation about an English settlement at Dublin. In a full settlement a greater similarity of topographical and architectural evidence between Dublin and contemporary English towns would be expected, whereas with trading and other business contacts, no matter how frequent, only the portable artefacts would suggest foreign origin, just as the imported fashions and gadgetry of modern Europe are used by communities in the Middle East, Africa, and Asia where European traditions have little impact on indigenous buildings, urban layout, language, etc.

Our conclusion must be that rather than an English settlement in Viking-Age Dublin we are witnessing strong English commercial influence and related presence. The coins and artefacts bear witness to the closeness of the commercial ties between Dublin and England and are a useful detailed and tangible witness for an impression

67. D. M. Wilson, 'Scandinavian settlement in the north and west of the British Isles: an archaeological point of view', *TRHS 26* (1976), 95–113; *idem*, *The Vikings in the West: Economic aspects of the archaeological evidence* (Felix Newburgh Lecture; Odense, 1980).

until now derived from historical sources alone. This is not, however, to reduce the importance of the inspiration for urbanization which the English had on the Irish-Norse in the early tenth century, nor to deny the possible influence visiting English noblemen had in bringing Irish kings to realize the potential for wealth and power which would accrue from domination rather than destruction of Norse towns.

The archaeological evidence from the Dublin excavations is also a useful barometer of the wealth and importance of eleventh-century Dublin. It tallies with the impression gained from the historical sources that by then Dublin was a great commercial centre which had networked itself to an expanding Norman empire which would eventually spread to Ireland along sea-routes opened up by the Hiberno-Norse towns. The eleventh century had witnessed the emergence of Dublin as the capital of Ireland in both commercial and political terms. Its location on the Irish Sea and its links with England were very significant factors in its commercial rise. Although in the eleventh century much of Dublin's contact with England was commercial rather than political, such links probably paved the way for the coming to Dublin and Ireland of the Normans in the following century. Thereafter the direction of the contact was reversed and its main thrust was political rather than commercial. Eventually, and probably over several successive rebuildings of the city, Dublin's street plan and architecture would take on the strong English influences it retains to this day – in marked contrast to the Viking Age when its merchant captains only sought commercial links with England. Nevertheless, it has to be realized that many of the seeds of Dublin's and Ireland's later history were sown in the course of the eleventh century.

13 Regional die-production in Cnut's *Quatrefoil* issue

Mark Blackburn and Stewart Lyon

During the eighth and ninth centuries it appears to have been the normal practice for each mint to supply its own moneyers with dies.[1] The first system of regional die-production, with a limited number of centres producing dies for the mints in their localities, was probably introduced by Alfred (871–99) and extended by Edward the Elder (899–924) as mints were established throughout Wessex and Mercia and in the reconquered Danelaw. Most of the 35 mints named on Athelstan's coinage are thought to have been established before the end of Edward's reign, and the majority of their dies were obtained from eight main centres: Winchester, London, Canterbury, two in the west Midlands (Chester and one further south), two in the east Midlands, and York. This practice was continued during the next half century with some additional centres opening and some closing, although the absence of mint-signatures makes it hard to follow the pattern in detail.[2]

One of the achievements of Edgar's reform of the coinage c.973 was to centralize die-production – with very few exceptions his *Reform Small Cross* coins are consistently of one style. Yet if this was intended to be an enduring policy it soon failed, for already under Edward the Martyr (975–8) Lincoln and York had begun cutting dies again, and there were at least six centres in operation by the beginning of Æthelred II's reign (978–1016). Towards the end of Æthelred's *First Hand* type

1. There are occasional exceptions, such as the Rochester moneyer, Dun, who in Coenwulf's reign used a pair of dies probably made by a Canterbury die-cutter: C. E. Blunt, C. S. S. Lyon, and B. H. I. H. Stewart, 'The coinage of southern England, 796–840', *BNJ 32* (1963), 1–74, at 23. The absence of mint names, particularly in the mid-ninth century, may be obscuring more complex arrangements for die distribution. Thus Berhtwulf's earlier dies were produced by the Rochester die-cutter, but there is some uncertainty as to whether his coinage was struck at Rochester or London: C. S. S. Lyon, 'Historical problems of Anglo-Saxon coinage (2)', *BNJ 37* (1968), 216–38, at 228–9, and H. E. Pagan, 'Coinage in southern England, 796–874', above. From early in Æthelwulf's *Inscribed Cross* issue a single style of die-cutting is found on the coinage of Wessex, but it is possible that there were several mints operating with dies obtained centrally, from Canterbury.
2. The coinage of this period will be discussed in C. E. Blunt, C. S. S. Lyon, and I. H. Stewart, *Coinage in Tenth-Century England* (forthcoming).

there was a move towards central die-production.[3] In *Second Hand* the majority of dies appear to be of one style, although some of the later dies, notably at eastern and south-western mints, were locally produced, and the type was scarcely struck in the north-east and in western Mercia. A similar arrangement was followed in the next three issues – *Crux, Long Cross*, and *Helmet* – whereby the initial dies were produced at one or two southern centres (London and Winchester), with a number of regional centres coming into operation to supply mints with additional or replacement dies.[4]

In Æthelred's last issue, *Last Small Cross*, there was a greater degree of decentralization from the start. Four centres appear to have participated in the initial distribution of dies. Winchester supplied dies of Dolley's 'Southern B' style[5] to mints in southern and central England as far north as Lincoln. Its later 'Southern A' dies were restricted essentially to central Wessex. Exeter supplied 'Southwestern' dies to west Wessex and at the beginning of the issue to several mints in eastern England. A 'West Mercian' die-cutter, probably based at Gloucester, supplied western mints from Chester to Somerset and Oxford, and he also provided many of the London moneyers with their earliest dies. York supplied its own moneyers with dies of 'Northern A' style throughout the issue. Significantly, London does not appear to have been producing dies at the inception of the issue, and the three southern and western centres had to be organized to cover the mints in eastern England which would normally have looked to London for their dies. The cause of London's temporary failure may be that which led to the aborting of the *Agnus Dei* issue – possibly the approach of Thorkell's great army in summer 1009? But within a short time the London centre was again in operation and serving mints in the east and south-east. Lincoln also soon began cutting its own dies, initially of the 'Northern B' style, copying the Winchester-style dies it had been using originally. Its later dies resemble those of York.[6] During the course of the issue further centres

3. M. Dolley and T. Talvio, 'The regional pattern of die-cutting exhibited by the *First Hand* pennies of Æthelræd II preserved in the British Museum', *BNJ 47* (1977), 53–65.
4. A full stylistic analysis of these issues has not been published, but see I. Stewart, 'The Small Crux issue of Æthelred II', *BNJ 28* (1957), 509–17; M. Blackburn, 'A York die-cutting centre in the Crux issue of Æthelræd II', *NCirc* 1982, 336–8; V. J. Smart, 'A subsidiary issue of Æthelred II's *Long Cross*', *BNJ 34* (1965), 37–41 (an eastern die-cutting style), and P. Stafford, 'Historical implications of the regional production of dies under Æthelred II', *BNJ 48* (1978), 34–51, at 45–8.
5. R. H. M. Dolley, *Some Reflections on Hildebrand type A of Æthelræd II* (Antikvariskt Arkiv 9, Stockholm, 1958). This pioneering study, based on the form of bust, demonstrated the decentralized nature of die production in the issue. But an analysis of the epigraphy and the declining weight pattern, unknown in 1958, has suggested further refinements and explained certain anomalies in Dolley's original scheme; cf. C. S. S. Lyon, 'The significance of the sack of Oxford in 1009/1010 for the chronology of the coinage of Æthelred II', *BNJ 35* (1966), 34–7, at 36.
6. Dolley termed both the York and later Lincoln dies 'Northern A'. They are most readily distinguished by the first letter of the king's name – Lincoln-cut dies normally commence with Æ, while York dies have E.

were opened in East Anglia (at Norwich or Thetford) and in Kent (at Canterbury), both imitating London styles. Small distinctive groups of dies are also found at Sussex mints, at Ipswich, and possibly at Chester towards the end of the issue.

Thus in *Last Small Cross* there were six major die-cutting centres active virtually throughout the issue, supplemented by a further five or so which supplied their own localities. This is the system which Cnut found in operation when he took control of the country in 1016, and as we shall see he adopted it without significant change at the introduction of his first type, *Quatrefoil*, although allowing a number of additional centres to open during the course of it. For the two subsequent issues, *Pointed Helmet* and *Short Cross*, die-cutting arrangements were radically reviewed and the number of centres was reduced probably to six or less.[7] In the *Jewel Cross* issue of Harold I and Harthacnut, Talvio has identified four centres, reducing to three towards the end of the type.[8] No studies have been made of subsequent issues of Harold and Harthacnut or of Edward the Confessor, although it is clear that there is some degree of local die production. Pagan has shown that most of Harold II's dies were produced centrally at London, but some locally produced dies were used at York, Chester, and in the east Midlands.[9]

The above sketch of the pattern of die-cutting before the Conquest, broad and tentative as it is, could not have been contemplated some 30 years ago. The concept of regional die-production did not exist until Michael Dolley made the acute observation that certain styles were common to particular groups of mints and saw the significance of this for the late Saxon coinage generally. Most of the published work on regional styles has been carried out by Dolley personally. *Quatrefoil* was the first type for which he published a stylistic analysis – an interim report limited to mints in the West Country.[10] He intended to follow it with studies covering other parts of the country, and a manuscript dated 1957 exists listing the coins in Hildebrand's catalogue divided into 13 regional styles.[11] Unfortunately this work was never published, except as line drawings of the principal styles in North's *English Hammered Coinage*.[12] He also used stylistic criteria in various short notes discussing individual specimens, and Elmore Jones, with whom he collaborated, provided comments on many of the *Quatrefoil* coins in the sale catalogue of his own collection.[13]

The analysis presented below has been developed independently, although it owes much to Dolley's personal inspiration and encouragement, and inevitably it has benefited from many exchanges of ideas with him. It is in broad agreement with his

7. R. H. M. Dolley and J. Ingold, 'Some thoughts on the engraving of the dies for the English coinage c.1025', *Commentationes* I (Stockholm, 1961), 189–222; and see the review by C. S. S. Lyon, *BNJ 30* (1960), 197–8.
8. T. Talvio, 'Harold I and Harthacnut's *Jewel Cross* type reconsidered', below.
9. H. E. Pagan, 'The coinage of Harold II', *Numismatiska meddelanden* (forthcoming).
10. R. H. M. Dolley, 'The regional distribution of dies in the West Country, c.1017–1023', *NCirc* 1956, 321–5, 373–4.
11. Copy in the possession of C. S. S. Lyon.
12. J. J. North, *English Hammered Coinage*, I (1st edn, 1963), 118.
13. Glendining & Co., 12 May 1971.

1957 classification, although it is more detailed. The work for this study began in the early 1960s when one of us (C.S.S.L.) photographed and weighed the 1,500 *Quatrefoil* coins in the Stockholm Systematic Collection and arranged photographs of the obverses into stylistic groups. This formed one of the subjects of a paper read to the British Numismatic Society in October 1963. A systematic search for inter-mint die-links was also made. Unfortunately other work intervened and the research lay dormant for many years, until the other of us gladly accepted an invitation to complete the analysis and prepare it for publication. The opportunity was also taken to include the 1,500 coins in the Copenhagen collection published in the *Sylloge* series and to provide a metrological analysis of the issue.

At the beginning of an issue each main die-cutting centre must have been sent a common model to copy, but provided the essentials of the design were present the die-cutter was permitted considerable latitude in the detail of composition. The form of the letters was partly dependent upon the dimensions of the punches available, and the legends could vary, especially in the use of abbreviations and ligatures, provided the meaning was clear. Such differences help one to recognize the work of particular die-cutters and support the more subjective impressions of style. Many die-cutters achieved a remarkable consistency in their products, but some, usually the less productive ones, were capable of considerable variation. We have therefore illustrated each style by at least two examples, to give an indication of the range of composition.

THE *QUATREFOIL* STYLES

We have identified 19 die-centres in the *Quatrefoil* issue, producing 42 different styles or sub-styles. Most centres employed only one die-cutter and the sub-styles usually represent significant developments in his work, but occasionally there is a complete change of style (e.g. at Thetford) when a new man seems to have taken over the die-cutting. London is the only centre where two die-cutters appear to have been working simultaneously. An indication of the duration and sequence of the styles and sub-styles can be gained from their weight distributions, since the weight standard fell progressively during the issue, from c.1.40g (22gr.) to c.1.00g (15½gr.) or less.[14]

We have named the styles after their likely place of origin, as we consider this more convenient than the alternative practice of describing them by the region in which they are generally found. In most cases it is reasonably clear where the dies were cut, but in a few instances we have had to choose between two or more plausible candidates and then the alternatives are considered in the text below. The die-cutting centres are discussed in a geographical sequence starting with Winchester, moving clockwise around the country, and ending with London. Appendix 1 tabulates the coins in the Stockholm Systematic and Copenhagen collections by mint and style, while Appendix 2 gives weight distributions for each style and Appendix 4 lists the coins, by reference to Hildebrand's catalogue and *SCBI* Copenhagen, according to their styles. These analyses are based on the styles of the obverse dies.

14. See p. 254 below.

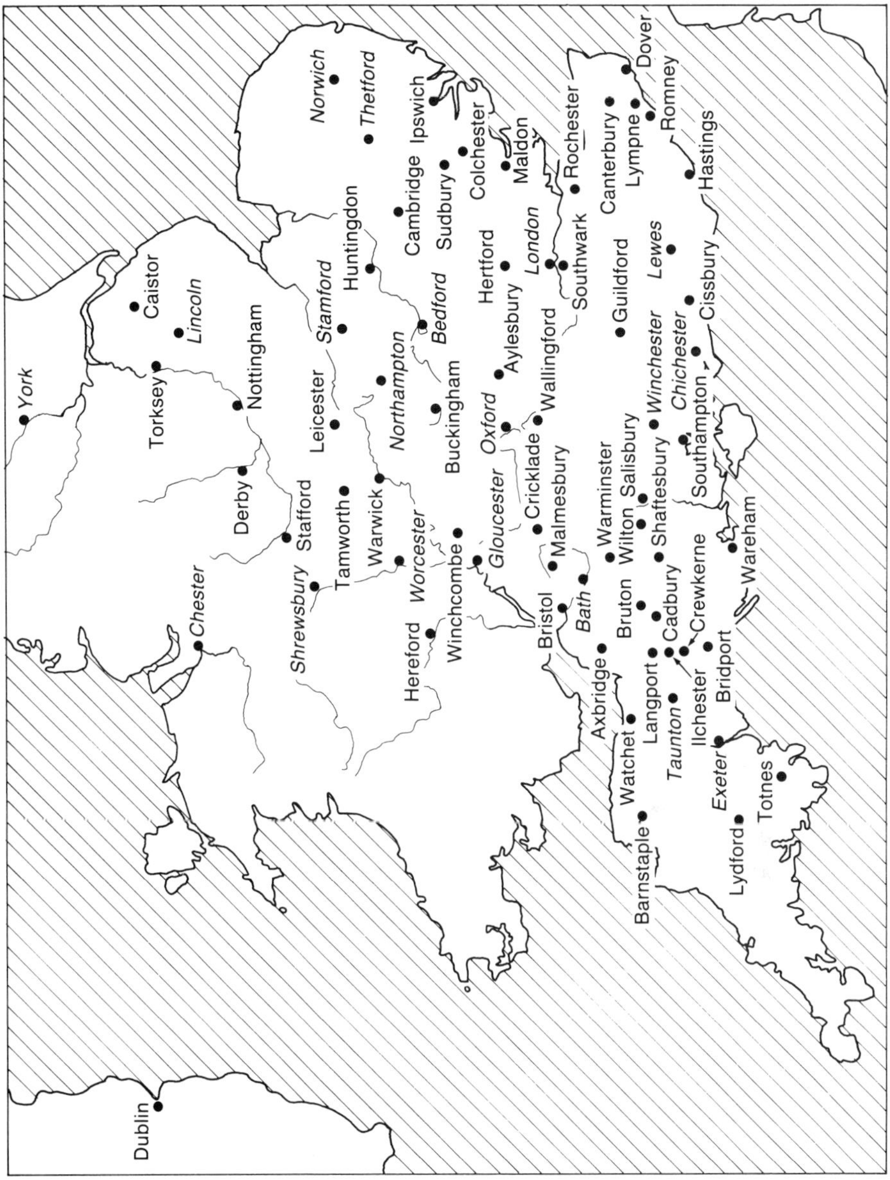

London mint and die-cutting centre
Cambridge mint only

Fig. 13.1 Mints and die-cutting centres in the *Quatrefoil* issue (two mints have not been located: 'Eanbryi' near Dorchester, and 'Gothabyrig' in the extreme south-west).

Winchester style (Win. e, m, and l)

The dies are loosely cut with naturalistic drapery curling round behind the neck. They have a prominent nose and cheek; the width of the latter is exaggerated by the eye being set close to the forehead. The band of the crown, which is often double, turns down around the ear. The obverse legends tend to be full (ANGLORVM–ANGLOR, the shorter forms becoming more common later in the issue), and almost invariably start at 12 o'clock. The continuity of style suggests that one person was responsible for all the dies, and this was probably the same individual who cut the later *Last Small Cross* dies at Winchester (Dolley's 'Southern A'). However, there is a progressive stylistic development which enables one to distinguish early, middle, and late products of the centre. The *earliest dies* have a rather narrow and upright bust, with drapery often taking the form of three or four parallel curving lines projecting down from a neck band. On the *middle dies* the nose and cheek become more prominent and the drapery is often formed of pairs of parallel lines radiating from the brooch. This is the largest group. The *later dies* are similar, but the workmanship is cruder, the bust smaller, and errors occasionally creep into the legends.

There can be no doubt that these dies were cut at Winchester. The centre was operating throughout the *Quatrefoil* period, to judge from the full weight range and the fact that it satisfied virtually all the die requirements of the Winchester mint. Initially it supplied mints in Hampshire, Berkshire, Wiltshire, Dorset, and Somerset, as well as the first dies for the Oxford mint, but as other die-cutting centres were established its service area was reduced to the half dozen mints nearest to Winchester (Chichester excepted). A notable anomaly is the provision of a number of middle and later dies to the Leicester mint.

Obverse legends commence: 12 o'clock
Ethnic: *Win. e.* ANGLORVMX 4%; ANGLORVMΩ 3%; ANGLORVM 85%; ANGLORVI 1%; ANGLORV 7%; stops (: or ∴) 40%
Win. m. ANGLORVMΩ 4%; ANGLORVM 46%; ANGLORVI 2%; ANGLORV 44%; ANGLOR 3%; stops (· or :) 16%
Win. l. ANGLORVM 35%; ANGLORVI 6%; ANGLORV 55%; ANGLOR 4%; stops (:) 6%
Reverse: ON

Chichester style (Chi.)

This is a small but distinctive group of dies. The drapery is divided at the front by a Λ with double lines, and the curved back intersects the separate line of the neck. The crown band follows the curve of the brow and on earlier dies it contains pellets. At the back of the crown there is usually a pair of ties. The obverse legend commences at 12 o'clock; the Os are pelleted and the As topped and usually barred. The earlier dies have deeper quatrefoils on the obverse and reverse. The centre supplied virtually all the *Quatrefoil* dies used at the Chichester mint, and the style is also found at Winchester, Salisbury, Guildford, Lewes, and Cissbury; in the latter case the die was subsequently used at Chichester (p. 250 below). The die-cutter apparently operated throughout the issue.

Obverse legends commence: 12 o'clock
Ethnic: ANGLORVM 27%; ANGLORV 51%; ANGLOR 10%; ANGLO 10%; stops (:) 6%
Reverse: ON

Oxford style (Ox. e and l)

This minor die-cutting centre opened mid-way through the issue to supply the Oxford mint, which had received its dies initially from Winchester. The style reflects certain features of Winchester-cut dies, notably the lines of the drapery curling behind the back of the neck, but they have been accentuated so that they fly out irrelevantly behind the bust. The *earlier dies*

Plate 13.1 Winchester, Chichester, and Oxford styles (× 1·4).

have two such lines terminating in pellets, small fleurs to the crown, and obverse legends ending ANGLORVM (or occasionally ANGLORI or ANGLORV). There can be variations in the size of the letters even within one legend. One apparently early Oxford style die has a right-facing bust (*SCBI* Copenhagen 2707, attributed to London, but probably of the Buckingham mint). On *later dies* the bust is more irregular, with two or three folds of drapery projecting horizontally beyond the back, and on some an extra line flies out from the point where the hair intersects the back of the neck. The crown has larger fleurs and the crown band terminates in a pellet at the rear. The obverse legends usually end in ANGLORV. The quatrefoils on the reverse are looser than on early dies. A coin of anomalous style, of the Oxford moneyer Wulfwine (*SCBI* Oxford 667), is perhaps an experimental product of this die-cutting centre. The bust imitates London A style, but there are some features, particularly in the epigraphy, which are similar to Oxford-cut dies.

Besides Oxford, the style is found at London (? *SCBI* Copenhagen 2322), Aylesbury, Buckingham, Northampton, Winchcombe, and Cricklade; in the last case an obverse die-link (pl. 13.9: 3–4) shows that the die was transferred from the Oxford mint.

Obverse legends commence: 12 o'clock
Ethnic: *Ox. e.* ANGLORVM 71%; ANGLORVI 6%; ANGLORV 24%; stops (∵ , : , or ·) 18%
Ox. l. ANGLORVM 6%; ANGLORV 87%; ANGLOR 6%; stops (·) 6%
Reverse: ON

Exeter style (Ex.)

The style is readily recognized by the folds of drapery in parallel hoops around the neck and the ample hair filled with dots (or hatched lines on earlier dies) and protruding at the front as if to form a peak to the crown. The very earliest dies are distinctive for their unconventional busts and deep quatrefoils (these are few and have not been singled out in the analysis below), but we have found no satisfactory division of the main series. Generally, the looser the quatrefoils the later the dies; the inner border is almost a circle on the lightest coins. On some dies the drapery is split at the front by a Λ, but there appears to be no chronological significance in this. A few dies have symbols in the obverse field the meaning of which is unknown; S (Exeter), star (Exeter), cross (Bristol), pellet and cross (Ilchester), pellet (Barnstaple and Ilchester). Some earlier dies have trefoils in the reverse quarters (Barnstaple, Exeter, Gothabyrig, and Ilchester). One pair of Exeter dies (pl. 13.9:17 = Hild. 419) with a star in the obverse field has a pelleted annulet in each reverse quarter and appears to anticipate the *Pointed Helmet* issue. The coin is a puzzle, particularly coming from Exeter where one would not expect new designs to have been originated, but it is not obviously a mule, nor does it appear to be struck from an altered reverse die (no quatrefoil is evident from our photograph). Its weight, 1.10g, suggests that it was struck either during the first half of the *Quatrefoil* issue or early in *Pointed Helmet*.

The centre was in operation throughout the issue and supplied virtually all the dies used at Exeter. Continuity with the Exeter-cut *Last Small Cross* dies (Dolley's 'Southwestern' style) is suggested by the similar treatment of the drapery. As in that issue, Exeter was the exclusive supplier of dies to the four Devon mints, and until the establishment of the Taunton die-cutting centre it was a major supplier to mints in Somerset. Otherwise the area of distribution was more limited than in *Last Small Cross*, although the Salisbury moneyer Sæman continued to obtain his dies from Exeter, and an occasional die reached Bristol and Bath.

Obverse legends commence: 12 o'clock
Ethnic: ANGLORVMI 3% (1 die); ANGLORVI 2%; ANGLORV 18%; ANGLORI 1%; ANGLOR 51%; ANGLOI 15%; ANGLO 12%; ANGL 11%; stops (: or ·) 17%
Reverse: ON or occasionally O

Ex.e

Ex.main

Taun.A

Taun.B

Bath A

Bath B

Plate 13.2 Exeter, Taunton, and Bath styles (× 1·4).

Taunton styles (Taun. A and B)

These styles are apparently successive products of one centre, for long thought to have been Ilchester, but for reasons given below Taunton is perhaps more likely. Both styles have a small dumpy bust with a rather flat face, yet despite the superficial similarity they are probably the work of different people. *Taunton A* shows influences of the Exeter style in the shape of the hair behind the head and the treatment of the drapery, two or three fairly straight folds coming from the front of the neck or Λ, if present, rather than the brooch. This is the only group of dies in which the king's name is often spelt CNVD. The workmanship is generally crude and the letters not carefully formed; X in *rex* is sometimes rendered as +.

Taunton B dies are more plentiful and more skilfully produced. The drapery flows as smooth pairs of lines from the brooch below the chin, seemingly influenced by the Winchester style. There is a double line to the crown band and the three fleurs each have a neat central wedge. Perhaps the most distinctive feature is the arc below the eye which on many dies gives an impression that the king is wearing spectacles. The quatrefoils on obverse and reverse are very loose, often appearing almost as a circular border.

Both styles have similar distributions, namely the west Somerset mints of Axbridge, Ilchester, Langport, Taunton, and Watchet, and Lydford in Devon, with an occasional die reaching Exeter and London (see Appendix 1). The greatest number occur at Ilchester, which had been a relatively minor mint during the latter part of Æthelred's reign and was not apparently operating during *Last Small Cross*. Its production was modest during the earlier part of the issue when it obtained its dies from Exeter and Winchester. But its output soared later in the issue and for the only time in its history it became the most important mint in the West Country. Of other mints in the region only Taunton showed a significant increase at this time, although on a much smaller scale than Ilchester. We do not know why these mints should have been called upon to increase their production, or over what period it occurred, but it spanned at least one weight change and most of the coins were struck to a very light, presumably late, weight standard. The operation of the die-cutting centre seems broadly to have coincided with the period of increased production, and it is not unreasonable to assume that it was opened to facilitate this. Ilchester would be the obvious site, but the fact that it continued to obtain a significant proportion of its dies from elsewhere suggests that the centre was not at Ilchester. Mints which had their own die-cutting facilities normally supplied virtually all their own dies, but of the 85 Ilchester coins in our sample, 48 per cent are of Taunton A and B styles, 26 per cent are of Bath B style, and 2 per cent are of late London C style (the remaining 18 per cent are from dies of Exeter or Winchester style, probably acquired before the local centre had opened). Bath B is contemporary with Taunton B style, and while it is possible that the Taunton B die-cutter had stopped working for a period of illness or some other reason, it is perhaps more likely that his workshop was not at Ilchester but at some other mint nearby. If so, Taunton is the most likely place. Of its 23 coins in our sample, 22 are of Taunton A or B style, and one (*SCBI* Copenhagen 3750) is struck from anomalous dies, which have a counter-part at Watchet (Hild. 3587), and were probably made locally early in the issue. The absence of dies from nearby Exeter appears deliberate, and brings to mind Shrewsbury's independence of dies from Chester. The situation in which a very productive mint obtains its dies from one that is less active has a parallel in Bristol obtaining its dies from Gloucester. But the attribution of these styles remains somewhat speculative, the more so if one considers the possibility that the die-cutters could have moved between mints making their dies.

Obverse legends commence: 12 o'clock
Ethnic: *Taun. A* ANGLORVM 5%; ANGLOR 84%; ANGLO 11%; stops (:) 16%; CNVD 53%
Taun. B ANGLORVM 26%; ANGLORVI 1%; ANGLORV 51%; ANGLOR 22%; stops (∵ , :, ·, or ÷) 16%
Reverse: ON, O, or nothing

Bath styles (Bath A and B)

The two remaining styles found at Somerset mints appear to be the work of different men, both probably operating from Bath. *Bath A* is a scarce short-lived style, belonging to the mid-issue. It has a delicate, carefully executed portrait with a small face, flowing drapery, and small fleurs on a straight crown band. The style is found on a handful of coins of Bath and Salisbury, and one obverse appears to have found its way to Northampton. *Bath B*, which is altogether cruder, was produced from the middle to the end of the issue. It is distinctive for its tall bust with a very thick neck and three or four parallel folds of drapery curling round behind the back. The quatrefoils are not well pronounced; on many dies the inner border is almost round. It is found at six mints, all in Somerset. The largest number of coins comes from Ilchester, but the dies probably emanated from Bath. Early in the issue Bath obtained all its dies from Winchester and Exeter, save for one pair (*SCBI* Copenhagen 19; Hild. 21) which was probably locally produced. In the mid weight range (1.05–1.19g) it used dies of Bath A and B styles, but it is not clear whether these were sequential or parallel. Its later, lighter coins are all of Bath B style.

Obverse legends commence: *Bath A* 9 or 12 o'clock; *Bath B* 12 o'clock
Ethnic: *Bath A* ANGLORVM 50%; ANGLORV 50%; stops (:) 33%
Bath B ANGLORVM 13%; ANGLORV 51%; ANGLORI 2%; ANGLOR 33%
Reverse: ON

Gloucester style (Gl. e and l)

This style encompasses two distinct groups of dies, one with crowned and the other with diademed busts, both apparently the work of the same die-cutter. They have in common the form of drapery (split at the front and with three folds radiating from the brooch), the presence of hatched lines representing the hair, the band of the crown or diadem turned down at each end, and the frequent use of a barred A. The obverse legend always begins at 11 or 12 o'clock and never ends with a space-filling I, although terminal stops are common. The *earlier dies* are those with a crowned bust, carefully executed. On the first of these the bust and epigraphy are larger and the quatrefoils deep; a few dies have a right-facing bust (Cricklade, Shrewsbury, and Winchcombe?). The style then settled down to uniform well-proportioned portraits, with smaller epigraphy, and looser quatrefoils. A number of dies have symbols before the bust; a sceptre or three pellets, a cross, omega, or a pellet. The *later dies* have a diademed bust (Hild. variety Ed). On some of these the diadem is so faint as to give the impression of a bare-headed bust. In other respects the portraiture and epigraphy of these later dies is similar to that of the earlier group, but the quatrefoils are very lax and there are occasional inaccuracies in the legends (e.g. CNCVT, CNT, CEVT, CNVTV, ANCOR, ANRELO, etc.). A diademed bust was occasionally employed at other centres (below, p. 252); the two obverse dies used at Bruton are slightly anomalous in style and may be local rather than Gloucester products.

The centre was active throughout the issue and appears to represent a continuation of Dolley's 'Western' style in *Last Small Cross*. The three main mints at which the style is found are Bristol, Gloucester, and Hereford. Bristol, a newly opened mint which grew dramatically during the issue, was the largest user of late dies of this style. However, since it received only a few earlier crowned bust dies and none of the earliest varieties, it can scarcely have been the site of their production. It is harder to choose between Gloucester and Hereford, both of which used dies exclusively of this style. Both were significant mints, but references to Gloucester in tenth-century sources suggest that it was a town of considerable importance and on balance we think it is the more likely site for a die-cutting centre.

Obverse legends commence: 11 or 12 o'clock
Ethnic: *Gl. e* ANGLORVM 8%; ANGLORV 10%; ANGLOR 33%; ANGLO 28%; ANGL 16%; ANG 4%; stops (∴, :, or ·) 59%

Gl. l ANGLORVM 2%; ANGLORV 33%; ANGLOR 43%; ANGLO 10%; ANGL 5%; irregular 7%; stops (∴, :, or ·) 57%
Reverse: ON or occasionally O

Worcester style (Worc.)

This small group of dies has a large face and a crown set low on the forehead, with large fleurs terminating in pellets. Little of the drapery is represented. The obverse legends begin variously between 6 and 12 o'clock. The lettering is irregular in size; the AS are usually unbarred. What is possibly the earliest die from this centre (*SCBI* Copenhagen 3978–9; Hild. 3640) is uncharacteristic in having an upright bust with hatched lines representing the hair. There is some risk of confusion with Shrewsbury dies, but the styles are distinct. One die probably of this style (pl. 13.9:18=Hild. 3703) has a diademed bust imitating Gl. l. The centre primarily served the Worcester mint – the large majority of its coins are of this style – but a few dies also occur at Warwick, Tamworth, Stafford, and London. It appears to have been in production throughout the issue, although the weight distribution of Worcester coins suggests that latterly the mint was not very active and may have had little need for new dies.

Obverse legends commence: between 6 and 12 o'clock
Ethnic: ANGLORVM 12%; ANGLORV 45%; ANGLOR 39%; ANGLO 6%; stops (: or ¨) 12%
Reverse: ON

Shrewsbury style (Shr.)

This style, found only at Shrewsbury, is represented by just a dozen or so dies. Evidently the die-cutter did not produce enough dies to develop great consistency, but certain features link them as a group. Although the portraits show considerable variation, they are generally composed of thick strokes and have a long face which has an element of caricature. The crown usually projects behind the head and the fleurs are poorly formed. The lettering, also composed of thick strokes, is uneven; the X in *rex* is often +. There is no regularity in either the positioning of the obverse legend or the form of its ending. There are also errors in the legends (e.g. CNAT, ANGLORVR, ZCROB, SCROC, etc.)

Initially, Shrewsbury moneyers obtained their dies from Gloucester or London, never Chester or Worcester, the two nearest die-cutting centres. Before long dies began to be cut locally, presumably produced occasionally when the moneyers required them. It is difficult to tell whether one or two anomalous Shrewsbury dies (e.g. *SCBI* Copenhagen 3378, 3383; Hild. 3127) are the work of the same hand at a different period or were produced by a different local craftsman.

Obverse legends commence: irregular
Ethnic: ANGLORVM 23%; ANGLORV 23%; ANGLOR 15%; ANGLO 8%; irregular 31%
Reverse: ON, O, or nothing

Chester style (Ch. e and l)

There is wide variation in the form and proportions of the bust, but the dies of this style are united by their similar composition – thin outlines with the face shown in light relief – characteristic lettering, and certain other common features. They have a generally untidy appearance. The brooch is normally positioned close to the chin, and the split in the drapery splays out in front of it. The crown is usually perched precariously on the head, often tipping forward; the centre of each fleur is formed by a wedge. The lettering is large and thin and somewhat irregular. The obverse legends begin at between 9 and 11 o'clock. The *early dies* usually have a larger face and ear. The profile of the back is normally represented by a single line, but on some dies the drapery curls round behind it. On about a third of the dies the

Plate 13.3 Gloucester, Worcester, Shrewsbury, and Chester styles (× 1·4).

obverse legend begins with a square G rather than C (confusion between these letters is found on a later reverse die reading CVNLEOF for *Gunleof*; Hild. 1326). A few early dies have one or three pellets in the obverse field. The *later dies*, a much larger group, have smaller faces, sometimes tall and thin, or sometimes squashed down upon the drapery. There are usually two lines to the back of the neck. The obverse legends tend to be more abbreviated than on the early dies. The reverses of both early and later dies have deep quatrefoils. Exceptionally for the later Anglo-Saxon coinage, some very late dies of Ætheric represented in the Bryn Maelgwyn hoard use a capital *thorn* rather than the usual *eth* in the moneyer's name.

The centre was active throughout the issue and was the exclusive supplier of dies to the Chester mint. Surprisingly, the dies were not distributed more widely in England, but one pair was cut at Chester for use in the Hiberno-Norse coinage of Dublin (Hild. Sihtric 101). The style should not be confused with a group of contemporary insular imitations mostly rendering the Chester mint-signature and the names of Chester moneyers.[15]

Obverse legends commence: 9–11 o'clock
Ethnic: *Ch. e* ANGLORVM 67%; ANGLORV 30%; ANGLOR 3%; stops (∵ or ·) 21%; GNVT 33%
Ch. l ANGLORVM 19%; ANGLORV 29%; ANGLOR 45%; ANGLO 6%; stops (∵, :, or ·) 7%; GNVT 5%
Reverse: ON or occasionally O

York style (York e and m)

This style is found virtually only at York. It is characterized by its drapery, consisting of three or four almost parallel folds coming from a simple Λ at the front, by its crown with deeply arched fleurs and the band turned down at each end, and by its face sculptured in relief. The reverse quatrefoils are rather square and remain fairly deep throughout the issue. The dies all appear to be the work of one hand, and while the earliest of them can readily be distinguished, we have been unable to find a satisfactory sub-division of the main group. The *early dies* have a taller, narrower bust with a crown snugly fitting the head. They have fuller obverse legends, and the quatrefoils on the reverse are fairly small, leaving a wide margin for the legend. The *main group* of dies has a squat bust, the face often too small for the drapery and the crown too big for the head, so that the crown band protrudes to the front and the rear. Within this main group there is a progression towards more abbreviated obverse legends, the latest, lightest coins usually being those with ANGLOR or shorter. On a number of dies there is a stop (:) preceding CNVT, and some have one or more stops (·) in the middle of the obverse legend.

Obverse legends commence: 5–7 o'clock
Ethnic: *York e* ANGLORVM 44%; ANGLORVI 4%; ANGLORV 52%; stops (:,∸ or ÷) 60%
York m ANGLORVM 13%; ANGLORVI 13%; ANGLORV 25%; ANGLORI 7%; ANGLOR 33%; ANGLOI 3%; ANGLO 5%; irregular 2%; stops (∴, :, or ·) 43%
Reverse: MO, M̄O, M:O, or O

Lincoln style (Lin. e, m, and l)

These dies are cleanly cut, using predominantly straight lines, and the epigraphy is uniform and clear, similar to that on York dies. The drapery consists of a simple Λ at the front, with usually three folds slanting at an angle across the shoulder. The brooch is often covered by the chin. A notable feature is the line representing the back, which starts at the centre of the ear and runs in a straight line until just before it meets the quatrefoil border where it curls inwards. The reverse quatrefoils tend to be rather square. A number of symbols are found in the obverse or reverse fields, including a sceptre, a cross, and a pellet, but these are often associated with a particular moneyer and their significance has not been fully explored.

15. See pp. 246–8 below.

York e

York m

Lin.e

Lin.m

Lin.l

Plate 13.4 York and Lincoln styles (× 1·4).

Once again the dies appear to be the work of one hand, but developments in the style enable us to distinguish three phases of die-cutting. The *early dies* have the best formed busts, with the three (or four) folds of drapery usually emanating from the vertical of the Λ, rather than radiating from the chin as on later dies. On the *middle dies*, the largest and most regular group, the bust is more stylized and the face smaller. This is carried a stage further on the *late dies*, where the back is more sloping and the crown extends well behind the head, giving the bust an appearance of leaning forward.

The centre supplied virtually all the dies used at Lincoln, Derby, Nottingham, and, until it produced its own dies, Stamford. They are also found at other mints in the Midlands and East Anglia: Torksey, Leicester, Warwick, Northampton, Huntingdon, Bedford, Cambridge, Ipswich, Thetford, and Norwich. The occasional die also reached London and York.

Obverse legends commence: 6 o'clock
Ethnic: *Lin. e.* ANGLORVM 50%; ANGLORVI 18%; ANGLORV 32%; stops (:) 14%
Lin. m. ANGLORVMI 1%; ANGLORVM 36%; ANGLORVI 23%; ANGLORV 39%; ANGLORI 1%; ANGLO 1%; stops (: or ·) 27%
Lin. l. ANGLORVMI 1%; ANGLORVM 20%; ANGLORVI 30%; ANGLORV 39%; ANGLORI 5%; ANGLOR 4%; stops (: or ·) 18%
Reverse: MO, M˙O, or M'O

Stamford styles (Stam. A and B)

This style was influenced by both Lincoln and London C dies. Two sub-styles, A and B, can be distinguished which appear to be the work of the same hand and were probably cut in the order A–B. Both resemble Lincoln dies in having a squarish face with a long nose and obverse legends commencing at 5 or 6 o'clock, but both borrow from London C its parallel horizontal folds of drapery and its sweeping line of the back. *Stamford A* has a straight band to the crown which often protrudes behind the head and has a single line to the back intersecting the curve of the ear as it does on Lincoln dies. The length of the crown band becomes progressively shorter until on *Stamford B* dies the fleurs are placed directly on the head and the back is given a double line which flows round the ear up to the forehead as on London C dies. The quatrefoils on the reverse are loose, almost round, and on several dies a wide bar has been gouged out of one quarter.

Most of the dies were used at Stamford, with just a few finding their way to Lincoln, Torksey, Norwich, Thetford, Huntingdon, Cambridge, and one pair apparently to Rochester.[16] The coins of this style are all light and thus late. Stamford moneyers first drew their dies from Lincoln, and the establishment of a local die-cutting centre seems to have coincided with an increase in activity at the mint during the latter part of the issue.

Obverse legends commence: 5 or 6 o'clock
Ethnic: *Stam. A.* ANGLORVM 29%; ANGLORVI 15%; ANGLORV 52%; ANGLOI 4%; stops (: or ·) 11%
Stam. B. ANGLORVM 50%; ANGLORVI 17%; ANGLORV 33%; stops, none
Reverse: MO, occasionally ON

16. The coin (Hild. 3070) is a puzzle. The reverse reads +ÆLFPOLD MO ROFCS, but both dies were undoubtedly cut at Stamford and the reverse has the typical wide bar in one quarter. The form of mint-signature is unusual, although an acceptable contraction of the normal *Rofecest*. Ælfwold is otherwise unknown at Rochester. He may be the Thetford moneyer of the same name, although what might have occasioned his obtaining local dies and travelling to Kent to strike coins is hard to imagine. Thus the possibility that these dies were produced for use at a short-lived mint in the Stamford region cannot be ruled out.

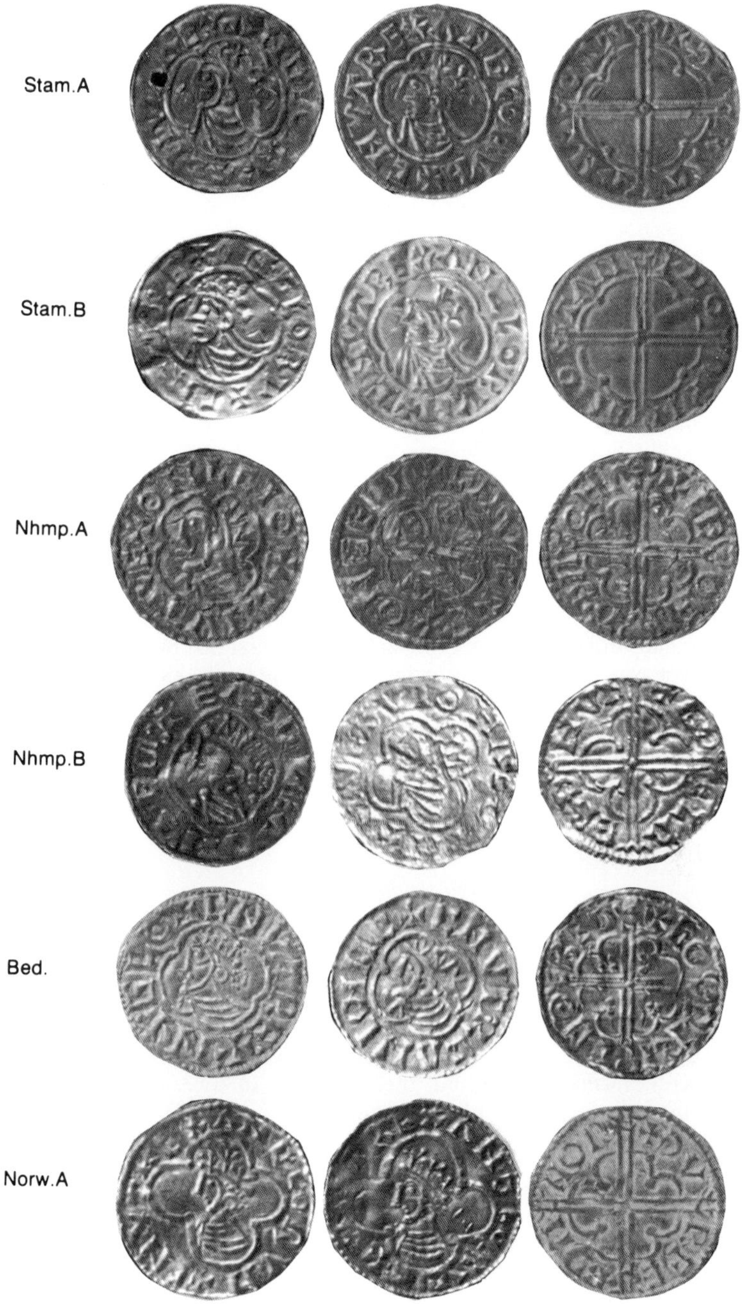

Plate 13.5 Stamford, Northampton, Bedford, and Norwich styles (× 1·4).

Northampton styles (Nhmp. A and B)

Two small groups of dies have distributions based on Northampton and Huntingdon, and although we have described them by the former, they could equally have been produced at the latter. The first, *Northampton A*, has a long face with a heavy jaw and three or four parallel folds of drapery. The crown runs almost vertically down behind the back. The obverse legends are distinctive for their combination of Latin and Old English; the five recorded obverse dies of this style read:

+CNVT RE+ ON ANGEL (2)
+CNVT RE+ ON GELI
+CNVT RE+ ON LGIO
+CNVT RE+ ON GLIORC (?)

The final element on the most literate dies is probably a contraction of OE *Angelcynne*, and the legend might be translated 'Cnut, king of England'.[17] From its rapid degeneration one suspects that the die-cutter was illiterate and was initially acting under someone else's instructions. These dies were used at Northampton (2), Huntingdon (2), and Leicester (1).

Of the second group, *Northampton B*, we know only four obverse dies, and they are the most barbarous and illiterate of the whole issue. The bust is crude and appears to be influenced by Lincoln or Stamford dies. The drapery radiates from the brooch and the crown extends behind the head at a 45° angle. The obverse legends are barbarous in the extreme: + CNVT RC ΛNLOINΛ, + EΛIGLEΛO+IREII:, + NVEBVTONΛEO + N, + ECTNOVN.TΛRN. Two dies were used at Northampton and two at Huntingdon.

Coins of both styles have in the past been described as 'not English'. However, their distribution between three neighbouring mints and the existence of die-links both between the two styles and with coins of late London C style suggest that they are official products.[18] The two styles may in fact be the work of the same die-cutter, produced at different times. The weight distributions suggest they both belong mid to late in the issue, though one cannot be sure since the Huntingdon mint, and possibly others in the region, maintained a heavier weight standard than, for example, London towards the end of the issue.

Obverse legends commence: irregular
Ethnic: see above
Reverse: MO or nothing

Bedford style (Bed.)

The die-cutting of this small group of coins is somewhat crude, the face is flat, and the crown leans back at a 45° angle. There is usually a + for the X in *rex*, but otherwise the obverse legends, with one exception (Hild. 62, 62A), are perfectly literate. This style is found primarily at Bedford, but some dies also reached Huntingdon, Northampton (?), Cambridge, Colchester, and London. The die-cutter appears to have been active in mid-issue. There are similarities with Northampton A, but the differences in style, literacy, and distribution suggest that they are the product of a different centre.

Obverse legends commence: irregular
Ethnic: ANGLOX 8%; ANGLORI 8%; ANGLOR 8%; ANGLO 23%; ANGL 23%; ANLOINC 31% (one die); stops (: or ·) 31%
Reverse: MO or nothing

17. We are grateful to Dr S. D. Keynes for advice on the form of this legend.
18. *SCBI* Copenhagen 1191 (Northampton A) is from the same reverse as *SCBI* Copenhagen 1189–90 (Northampton B). Hild. 1230 (Northampton B) is from the same reverse as *SCBI* Copenhagen 1271 (late London C).

Norfolk styles (Norw. A; Thet. A e, m, and l; Thet. B and C)

There are four separate styles which emanate from Norfolk. Two of them are contemporary and run from the beginning to the middle of the issue (one continuing slightly later than the other), another small group appears to be intermediate in date, and the fourth is entirely late. All four styles are mainly found at Thetford and Norwich, and we have sought to divide them between these two centres on the basis of their distributions. However, in view of the overlap in the distributions, it is possible that they are the product of different men or workshops in the same centre, each attracting a slightly different range of customers.

Outside Norfolk, all the styles except Thetford B are widely distributed throughout East Anglia. The earlier dies (Norwich A and early and middle Thetford A) are found at mints slightly further afield, the latter reaching as far west as Buckingham and as far south as London.

Norwich A dies have very deep quatrefoils on the obverse containing a tall bust with a small narrow face and drapery in three or more parallel but curved folds up to the chin. The reverse dies, with squarish quatrefoils, are very similar to those of Thetford A. The letters vary considerably in size even within one legend, and there are frequent spelling mistakes in both obverse and reverse legends. The dies belong early in the issue and are broadly contemporary with early and middle Thetford A dies. They are found predominantly at Norwich.

Obverse legends commence: 7 o'clock
Ethnic: ANGLORVMΩ 7%; ANGLORVM 46%; ANGLORM 4%; ANGLORVI 7%; ANGLORV 29%; ANGRORV 4%; ANGROXV 4%; stops, none
Reverse: MO, M, or nothing

Thetford A is the largest of the Norfolk groups. The bust has a prominent nose, a straight back, and drapery consisting of three or four folds of parallel or slightly radiating straight lines. The fleurs of the crown are somewhat irregular and the band often terminates in a pellet at the rear. The most distinctive feature of this style is the ending of *Anglorum* with a scribal contraction, ANGLORↀX or ANGLOROX, not found elsewhere in this issue. The style can be sub-divided into early, middle, and late. The *early* dies have large, well proportioned busts. On some there are pellets in the crown and representing hair below it. These pellets are more common in the *middle* group, where the bust is smaller and dumpier and the nose more prominent. The *late* dies have a still smaller bust, with a narrow neck, and the die-cutting is cruder and simpler; there are no pellets in the crown or hair and the drapery radiates from the brooch. The reverse dies have squarish quatrefoils, similar to those of Lincoln style but more crudely produced. On the latest dies the reverse quatrefoil is shallower.

The weight distributions of the coins in the Stockholm Systematic Collection and the Copenhagen collection suggest that although Thetford was more active than Norwich early in the issue, Norwich later became the more prolific mint. This may explain why early and middle Thetford A dies are more common at Thetford than Norwich, but for the late Thetford A dies the opposite is true. In addition, it appears that the Norwich A die-cutter ceased operating before the Thetford A die-cutter and that the latter then became the main source of dies for the Norwich mint. An inter-mint die-link (pl. 13.9:9–10) shows that at least one middle Thetford A die was transferred after some use from Thetford to Norwich (without an accompanying transfer of moneyer), which might indicate that Norwich moneyers were sending to Thetford for some of their dies.

Obverse legends commence: 11–12 o'clock
Ethnic: *Thet. Ae.* ANGLↀX 59%; ANGLOX 33%; ANGLↀVX 7% stops, none
Thet. Am. ANGLↀX 52%; ANGLOX 45%; ANGLORX 2%; ANGLO 2%; stops, none
Thet. Al. ANGLↀX 32%; ANGLOX 52%; ANGLↀ 6%; ANGLOI 2%; ANGLO 6%; ANGO 2%; stops, none
Reverse: MO or M

Thetford B is a small group of dies found almost only at Thetford. They have a narrow bust with drapery divided at the front and in two or three parallel folds. The lettering on most is thick but uniform. The reverse quatrefoils are squarish. The weight distribution suggests that they are roughly contemporary with late Thetford A dies.

Obverse legends commence: usually 10 o'clock
Ethnic: ANGLORVM 27%; ANGLORV 27%; ANGLOR 27%; ANGLO 18%; stops, none
Ethnic: MO, ON or O

Thetford C dies are composed of fine strokes. There is great variation in the form of the bust, but most imitate London C dies with fleurs springing directly from the head, with two lines for the back of the bust and, on some, double lines for the front of the drapery. A few dies imitate the Lincoln or Norwich A styles. The quatrefoils on the obverse and reverse are usually very shallow, almost circular, although on some reverses they are deeper, copying earlier London dies. There is no regularity in the position in which the obverse legend begins. The lettering is small and neat, but errors abound in both obverse and reverse legends (e.g. CNV, NVT, HCNTVI for 'Cnut'). A cross or pellet is sometimes found in the field of the obverse or reverse. Two Sudbury dies which have the bust dividing the legend (Hild. type Eb) are probably of this style.

These were the only dies produced in Norfolk late in the issue, and their attribution to a specific centre is difficult. They are more common at Norwich than Thetford, but this may be because of the higher mint activity there (cf. the high incidence of late Gloucester dies at the Bristol mint). We have suggested that Norwich only produced dies at the beginning of the issue, and on balance it would seem preferable to regard this group as a direct successor of the more important Thetford A style.

Obverse legends commence: irregular
Ethnic: ANGLORVM 9%; ANGLORVI 11%; ANGLORV 20%; ANGLOR 29% ANGLOI 2%; ANGLO 11%; ANGL 13%; ANGOR 2%; ANGLLOR 2%; stops (·) 7%
Reverse: usually ON or O

Lewes style (Lewes e and l)

Early dies of this style have narrow upright busts, with tall fleurs to the crown. The quatrefoils on obverse and reverse have deep but rounded lobes. One die has a right-facing bust (*SCBI* Copenhagen 1330–1). The coins are all heavy and this small group of dies appears to have been cut at the very inception of the issue.

A *later* phase of die-cutting apparently at the same centre could be the work of a different hand. The design is composed of much finer strokes. There are often four or five parallel folds of drapery, although a few dies have three radiating folds. The crown is set at an angle leaning backwards, and the fleurs are large and fine. The quatrefoils are pronounced and on the reverse the lobes are pointed. On some dies, obverse or reverse, there are four small pellets outside the quatrefoil border. The epigraphy varies in size and spacing appears to have caused the die-cutter some difficulty, for one obverse die ends ANGLORVMIIIIIIIIII.

The early dies are found at Lewes and Hastings, and while the later ones also occur most commonly at those mints, occasional dies reached Dover, Canterbury, and London. We cannot be certain from which of the two Sussex towns the die-cutter operated, but Lewes is perhaps the more likely, being marginally the more important mint and the dies being more frequently found there.

Obverse legends commence: *Lewes e.* 12 o'clock; *Lewes l.* irregular
Ethnic: *Lewes e.* ANGLORVI 17%; ANGLORV 67%; ANGL · 17%
Lewes l. ANGLORVMIIIIIIIIII 5%; ANGLORVMI 5%; ANGLORVMO 5%; ANGLORVMM

Thet.A e

Thet.A m

Thet.A l

Thet.B

Thet.C

Thet.C

Plate 13.6 Thetford styles (× 1·4).

5%; ANGLORVM 10%; ANLIORVM 5%; ANGLORV 25%; ANGLOR 5%; ANGLOII 5%; ANGLO 15%; ANGL 15%; stops (: or ·) 40%
Reverse: *Lewes e.* M; *Lewes l.* M, MM, MONE, ON, or nothing

London styles (Lon. A e, m, and l; Lon. B; Lon. C e, m, and l)

London was much the most important die-cutting centre in the country, initially operating with two ateliers but latterly with only one. During the early part of the issue two styles, London A and B, were produced in parallel in the ratio approximately 3:1. They both supplied dies to the moneyers of London and Southwark and to other mints within a radius of 50–70 miles, although London B has a more northerly bias than London A, being the main supplier to Hertford and absent from mints in Kent and Sussex. A few dies of both styles were sent to Shrewsbury. The third and most prolific style, London C, was probably the successor of London A, and it shows a similar, if slightly wider, distribution pattern. There is a notable absence of London C dies from Southwark, which is discussed below (p. 248). The high rate of production and large surviving sample of these dies has enabled us to sub-divide both London A and C styles into three chronological groups, providing a more detailed breakdown than for any other die-cutting centre.

London A dies are sharply cut. The crown has a straight band, occasionally projecting behind the head, with fleurs terminating either in wedges or pellets and latterly set on small stems. The back is formed by a single line which comes from a small crescent representing the ear. The drapery is divided at the front and consists of three or more parallel but curved lines. The obverse legend almost always begins at 7 or 8 o'clock. The NG in the ethnic is often ligatured, especially in short ethnics. The style can be divided into early, middle, and late. *Early dies* show a greater diversity in the form of the bust, but they generally have a larger face and the top left point of the quatrefoil is aligned somewhere between the tip of the nose and the front of the crown. The T tends to be rather large and the R frequently has a tail at the top projecting backwards, rarely found on middle and late dies. *Middle dies* are similar, but have either one, two, or three folds of the drapery projecting behind the line of the back. Some have a symbol, usually a group of three or four pellets, behind the head. On most dies the point of the quatrefoil touches the king's forehead. *Late dies* are the most common. The bust is still well formed, but the drapery no longer protrudes beyond the back and there are rarely symbols in the field. As on middle dies, the point of the quatrefoil generally meets the forehead. On a few late dies, which can be regarded as transitional with London C, the band of the crown follows the line of the hair, with occasionally a pair of ties at the rear.

London B, the smallest of the three groups, is contemporary with London A and may have continued for a while after the introduction of London C. The dies can be readily distinguished from those of London A by their obverse legends beginning at 11 or 12 o'clock and their drapery which radiates from the brooch. There are other differences in the treatment of the face and the crown which show that they are the work of another hand. The NG in the ethnic is never ligatured. The reverse dies cannot be satisfactorily distinguished from those of London A.

London C is the most common of all *Quatrefoil* styles and belongs broadly to the second half of the issue. The bust is aquiline, with a double line to the back and a double or treble line over the forehead upon which the fleurs are placed, thus there is no separate crown band. The front of the drapery is shown by double lines, and the folds are in parallel curves. The quatrefoil on the obverse is almost round, while on the reverse it becomes progressively looser until it too is virtually round. Like London A, the obverse legend begins at 7 or 8 o'clock. Again there are gradual changes in style which enable one to distinguish early, middle, and late dies, although the dividing lines, particularly between middle and late, are not well defined. The *early* dies are almost only found at the London mint and represent a short phase of die-cutting, perhaps of a few weeks. They are carefully executed and have a relatively large bust, with a large face.

Plate 13.7 Lewes and London styles (× 1·4).

Table 13.1. Obverse legends on *Quatrefoil* coins of London styles

	Ae %	Am %	Al %	Ce %	Cm %	Cl %	B %
ANGLORVM	2	3	31	16	–	–	1
ANGLORVI	2	3	5	–	–	–	3
ANGLORV	14	22	34	57	10	2	41
ANGLORI	–	3	2	–	–	–	1
ANGLOR	63	57	19	24	28	36	27
ANGLOI	4	1	1	–	4	10	1
ANGLO	14	2	7	3	53	44	16
ANGLI	–	–	–	–	–	1	–
ANGL	1	–	–	–	3	6	9
Other	–	7	2	–	2	2	–
Stops	30	12	22	19	14	22	9

On some there is a series of hatched lines shading the narrow area below the bottom fold of drapery. The *middle* group is the largest and reflects the greater stylization resulting from mass production. The dies are more crudely produced than the early ones with thicker strokes, the nose in particular being heavy and pointed. Within the middle group there is a progressive shortening of the legends, from ANGLORV/ANGLOR to ANGLOR/ANGLO, coins with the latter being struck to a distinctly lighter standard. The *late* dies are of similar composition, but executed in finer strokes with smaller lettering, and they show an improvement in style. There was some experimentation towards the end of the issue, some late dies, for example, having a pair of ties behind the crown as on a few of London A.

Although there are similarities between A and C styles, the differences in the design of the bust are marked and seem to be deliberate. The busts may be the work of different engravers, but continuity in the position and form of the obverse legend on late London A and early London C styles (see table 13.1) suggests that the same personnel were responsible for lettering the dies. The weight distributions discussed below indicate that these styles were successive. London C was imitated at other centres in eastern England, notably at Thetford, Stamford, and Northampton.

Obverse legends commence: *Lon. A* 7–8 o'clock; *Lon. B* 11–12 o'clock; *Lon. C* 7–8 o'clock
Ethnic: see table 13.1
Reverse: *Lon. A* MO, MON, ON or O, but usually nothing; *Lon. B* ON, O, or nothing; *Lon. C* ON, OON, O, or nothing.

Hiberno-Norse coins

The Hiberno-Norse coins of *Quatrefoil* type and another insular group imitating Chester coins will be the subject of a separate paper by one of us (MB), but they deserve brief notice here. Some of the Hiberno-Norse coins have the legend *Sihtric rex Dyflni*, but the majority copy the usual *Cnut rex Anglorum* and are distinguished from English coins by their characteristic style (pl. 13.8) and the presence of the Dublin mint-signature on the reverse. One pair of dies appears to have been commissioned from the Chester die-cutter, who used a mixture of Latin and Old English in the legend *Sihtric rex Irum* ('Sihtric king of [or among] the Irish').

Insular imitations of Chester coins

This group of light-weight imitations of uniform style (pl. 13.8) has recently been recognized as originating in the Irish Sea area, but not from Dublin. Their legends, which are often

Lon.C e

Lon.C m

Lon.C l

Hiberno-Norse

'Chester' imitations

Plate 13.8 London, Hiberno-Norse, and 'Chester' imitation styles (× 1·4).

blundered, copy Cnut's name and title and the names of Chester moneyers and the Chester mint-signature. They are distinguished by their style and weight. One specimen was present in the small hoard from Pant-yr-Eglwys at Great Orme, North Wales, to be published by Mr G. Boon.

Scandinavian imitations

A substantial number of imitations of *Quatrefoil* type were struck in southern Scandinavia, some belonging to complex imitative die-chains.[19] The local dies usually copy English legends with varying accuracy and they do not achieve a consistent style. A number of dies used in Scandinavia were official English ones which had been transported from mints or die-cutting centres in eastern England.[20] They include dies of York, Lincoln, Thetford, and London styles, and the Lincoln die-cutter even produced special dies with Cnut's Danish title.

The geographical pattern

Of the 19 die-cutting centres we have identified in the *Quatrefoil* issue, eight were major ones active throughout the issue: London, Winchester, Lincoln, York, Chester, Gloucester, Exeter, and Thetford. Five were minor centres active from the beginning of the issue: Lewes (or Hastings), Chichester, Bath, Worcester, and Norwich (probably closed in mid-issue). These centres are more or less the same as those found in the *Last Small Cross* type, but with Canterbury notably absent. In addition there were six new centres which opened during the course of the issue: Oxford, Taunton (or Ilchester), Shrewsbury, Stamford, Bedford, and Northampton (or Huntingdon).

Thus all the major mints, and many of the larger secondary ones, had their own die-cutter. There are five other 'second league' mints that might by virtue of their size have been expected to support a die-cutter – Bristol, Ilchester, Southwark, Canterbury, and Cambridge – but Bristol and Ilchester only grew in importance towards the end of the issue, and Southwark enjoyed a close relationship with the nearby London mint and seems to have been active for a relatively brief period. Its use of some 20 moneyers in this issue, mostly drawn from London, producing 10 per cent of the combined output of London and Southwark, was exceptional, for in other issues there were rarely more than three moneyers at Southwark producing 3 per cent of the combined output, *Crux* being the other exceptional type when 12 moneyers produced 32 per cent. However, the high production in *Quatrefoil* must have been limited to the first half of the issue, for there are no Southwark coins of London C style and the mint was presumably closed shortly before this style was introduced.[21] Southwark's output was volatile, and it appears to have been used to

19. C. S. S. Lyon, G. van der Meer, and R. H. M. Dolley, 'Some Scandinavian coins in the names of Æthelræd, Cnut, and Harthacnut attributed by Hildebrand to English mints', *BNJ 30* (1961), 235–51.
20. M. Blackburn, 'English dies used in the Scandinavian imitative coinages', in a forthcoming volume in honour of Professor Brita Malmer.
21. We considered and rejected the alternative explanation that Lon. A and B styles overlapped substantially with Lon. C style and that the A or B atelier was given exclusive rights to supply Southwark with dies. Although the weight distribution of Southwark coins lends some support to this, as it

supplement that of London in times of increased need, although why London moneyers should have needed to cross the Thames to strike additional coins is unclear, unless there were fiscal or administrative reasons for so doing.

The distribution of each of the styles between the various mints can be seen from Appendix 1. The regions supplied by each of the major die-cutting centres may give some indication of their economic or administrative links. London's influence extended over a wide area of eastern England from the south coast as far north as the Wash, while Winchester's was limited essentially to central Wessex. Lincoln-cut dies are found throughout the east Midlands and their frequent occurrence in East Anglia suggests that the Fens were not a major obstacle to communications. However, the distributions emphasize the political and physical isolation of York and Chester.

The number of instances in which dies are found at mints outside the centre's usual area of supply are few, but of some significance. A handful of early London style dies were used at Shrewsbury, possibly sent in a single urgent consignment for they include two that had previously been used by London moneyers.[22] Equally anomalous is a group of Winchester style dies used at Leicester, and some possibly at Northampton.[23] Occasionally an individual moneyer consistently obtained dies from a distant source with which he presumably had some special connection; thus Sæman at Salisbury took *Quatrefoil* dies from Exeter as he had done in the *Last Small Cross* issue, and Wulfric at Lincoln used some London style dies in both issues.As might be expected London attracted the greatest range of styles – including Win. m, Ox. l, Taun. A, Worc., Lin. e, m, and l, Bed., Thet. Ae, Thet C, and Lewes l – reflecting its central role in the English mint organization, although 95 per cent of its coins were struck from London-cut dies. Other exceptional occurrences of dies appear to be sporadic; Thet. Ae at Buckingham, Win. m and Gl. l at Exeter, Gl. l at Malmesbury, Gl. e and Bath A at Northampton, Win. e at Warwick, Gl. e at Winchester, and possibly Stam. A at Rochester. These exceptions only serve to

has a slightly lighter bias than London coins of Lon. A style, we consider it improbable that no Lon. C dies would have found their way to Southwark had Lon. C been current when the mint was open, in view of the general movement of moneyers and dies between these two mints.

22. See p. 250 below.
23. There are indications that the presence of the Winchester style – and even die-links with the Winchester mint – may not be as reliable a guide in distinguishing coins of Northampton and Southampton as had previously been supposed. Both used the mint-signature HAMTUN and their products have been distinguished mainly on the basis of their regional style and inter-mint die-links; see F. Elmore Jones, 'Southampton/Winchester die-links in Canute's *Quatrefoil* type', *BNJ 39* (1970), 6–11 and references there cited. If this test were strictly applied, all four Northampton moneyers (Eadwine, Leofnoth, Leofwine, and Leofwold – Eadwine so attributed on the basis of Hild. 1126 of Lon. Cl style) would have had colleagues with the same names at Southampton, a remarkable coincidence! Elmore-Jones attributed the unique Winchester style coin of Leofnoth (in the Bibliothèque Nationale) to Northampton, and it may be that the attribution of other 'Hamtun' coins should be reconsidered.

underline the otherwise consistent pattern found among the 3,000 or so coins we have studied.

INTER-MINT DIE-LINKS

A systematic search of the Stockholm Systematic Collection has thrown up a number of new inter-mint die-links, bringing the number recorded in the *Quatrefoil* type to 17 and these are listed below. They probably arose for a variety of reasons, many of which simply cannot be recognized today. One might have expected the transfer of moneyers between mints to have been a common cause, but in only three (nos. 8, 9, and 11) of the 17 cases does the same moneyer use the linking obverse die at both

1. Winchester, Ælfstan (Hild. 3677, 1.12g; 3678, 1.09g) – Southampton (?), Eadwine (Hild. 1125, 1.06g).Win. m style. Published *BNJ 39* (1970), 6–11 (illus.).
2. Winchester, Burwold (Hild. 3724, 0.99g) – Southampton (?), Leofwine (BM, *ex* Elmore-Jones lot 757, 0.79g chipped). Win. l style. Published *BNJ 39* (1970), 6–11 (illus.).
3. Winchester, Ladmær (Hild. 3763, 1.10g; 3764, 1.06g) – Southampton, Ælfsige (Hild. 1116, 0.87g). Win. m style. Published *BNJ 39* (1970), 6–11 (illus.).
4. Winchester, Wulfnoth (Hild. 3853, 1.15g) – Southampton, Siboda (Hild. 1149, 0.99g). Win. m style. Published *BNJ 39* (1970), 6–11 (illus.).
5. Shaftesbury, Æthelric (Hild. 3103, 0.82g) – Bristol, Wynsige (Hild. 94, 0.80g; 95, 0.77g). Win. m style. **Pl. 13.9:1–2** (Hild. 95).
6. Cissbury, Leofwine (Hild. 3194, 1.39g; *BMC* 514, 1.28g) – Chichester, Liofric (Hild. 209, 1.03g). Chi. style. *BNJ 28* (1956), 279–80 (illus).
7. Oxford, Godman (Hild. 3026, 0.84g pierced) – Cricklade, Toca (Hild. 258, 0.85g). Ox. l style. **pl. 13.9:3–4.**
8. 'Gothaburh', Carla (Hild. 999, 1.14g) – Exeter, Carla (Hild. 367, 1.02g chipped). Ex. style. Published *BNJ 28* (1956), 270–82 (illus.).
9. Ilchester, Ælfsige (Hild. 881, 0.89g) – Langport, Ælfsige (*SCBI* Copenhagen iiic 294, 0.91g). Taun. B style. Published *BNJ 29* (1958), 65–6 (illus.).
10. Ilchester, Ælfsige (Hild. 3589, 0.76g) – Lydford, Hunewine (Hild. 2509, fragment). Taun. B style. **Pl. 13.9:5–6.**
11. Bruton, Ælfelm (*BMC* 22, 1.16g) – Cadbury, Ælfelm (*BMC* 24, 1.01g). Bath l style. Published *BNJ 28* (1955), 99–105 (illus.).
12. Leicester, Wulfnoth (Hild. 1451, 1.44g) – London, Godwine (Hild. 2478, 1.01g). Lin. e style **Pl. 13.9:7–8.**
13. Thetford, Sumerleth (Hild. 3525, 1.28g; 3525 bis, 1.43g) – Norwich, Thurferth (Hild. 2993, 1.16g). Thet. Ae style. **Pl. 13.9:9** (Hild. 3525) – **10.**
14. London, Eadwi (Hild. 2175 bis, 1.03g) – Southwark, Ælfwerd (Hild. 3388, 0.94g). Lon. Al style. **Pl. 13.9:11–12.**
15. London, Eadwerd (Hild. 2157, 0.97g; 2272, 1.01g) – Shrewsbury, Godwine (Hild. 3137, 0.83g). Lon. B style. **Pl. 13.9:13** (Hild. 2157) – **14.**
16. London, Liofric (Hild. 2643, 1.34g) – Shrewsbury, Grim (Uddeby hoard, Varnum, Varmland, Sweden, SHM Inv. 6619, fragment). Lon. B style. **Pl. 13.9:15–16.**
17. London, Ealdred (*SCBI* Copenhagen iiib 2384, 1.06g) – Salisbury, Mani (C. E. Blunt col.). Lon. Al style. To be published by Blunt and Lyon in *Numismatiska meddelanden.*

Plate 13.9 1–16 Inter-mint die-links; 17–20 varieties.

mints. More often when the moneyer receiving the die had also worked at the mint of origin it had been used by a colleague (nos. 1–4 and 14) and there is no necessary connection with the moneyer's transfer or his contemporary activity at each mint. In eight cases (nos. 1–4, 13, and 14–16) the die seems to have been moved from the mint attached to the die-cutting centre which produced it to another mint normally supplied by that centre, and it is possible that moneyers ordering new dies were occasionally issued with ones which had been partially used. In one case (no. 6) a die appears to have been returned to the centre (Chichester) which originally supplied it. However, for five of the transfers (nos. 5, 7, 10, 12, and 17) there is no obvious explanation to account for them. The possibility that one of the moneyers was minting away from home cannot be ruled out.

Varieties

In this study we have concentrated on the centres of die-production and have not made a special analysis of those features of the design which appear to have been deliberately added or varied for administrative purposes. It is often difficult to tell which features were intended to have significance; a right-facing bust, for example, occurs so infrequently and randomly, and usually on very early dies, that one is inclined to view them as die-cutters' errors: Lewes (*SCBI* Copenhagen 1330–1 – Lewes e), London (*SCBI* Copenhagen 2707–Ox. e), Shrewsbury (Hild. 3129, 3135–Gl. e), Winchcombe (Hild. 3653–Gl. e). One coin of Exeter (**pl. 13.9:17**=Hild. 419), which appears to be transitional with the *Pointed Helmet* type, has been discussed above (p. 230). A number of apparent varieties can be shown merely to reflect differences in the styles of particular centres, some as radically different as the diademed bust of Gl. 1 dies (Hild. Ed; *BMC* viiid). A diademed bust occasionally occurs on dies from elsewhere – Bruton (*SCBI* Copenhagen 113–16 – possibly locally produced), London (Hild. 2723–4, 2729 – possibly Lon. C), Lincoln (Hild. 1646 – anomalous), Worcester (**pl. 13.9:18**=Hild. 3703 – Worc.) – but these are probably copying Gl. 1 dies, just as Win., Lin., and Lon. C influenced the products of other centres. The coins with a bust intruding into the obverse legend (Hild. Eb; *BMC* viiic), struck from only two dies, are an aberration of the Thet. C die-cutter, whose work generally was far from consistent.

There are some cases, on the other hand, where one can see that symbols were consciously added to differentiate the dies. At Lincoln, for example, most of the obverse dies used by Aslac have a sceptre in the field, while those of Iustan often have a cross in front of the bust and those of Sumerleth have a cross behind it. The same privy mark is found on many of Sumerleth's coins of *Long Cross*, *Helmet*, and *Last Small Cross* types, and it is probably indicative of some special status which he enjoyed. In the majority of cases the significance of added symbols is unknown. One of the more distinctive groups has trefoils on the four points of the reverse quatrefoil (**pl. 13.9:15**=Hild. 2643, and **19**=Hild. 349), and it occurs at such a wide range of mints, in several styles, that it may result from some central directive. On a number of dies there are diadem ties behind the crown, and while at Chichester this seems to have been a standard element of the design, at the London ateliers it appears to have been used only rarely but with some purpose (**pl. 13.9:20**=Hild. 190). This subject deserves further study generally, not limited to a single type.

METROLOGY OF THE ISSUE

In the periodic types which followed Edgar's reform the weight standard was progressively reduced during each issue and raised again at the beginning of the next. Multiple weight standards are evident from weight distributions and from the clustering of die-linked groups about certain weights, while their order – proceeding from heavy to light – can be discerned from hoards and other evidence such as a division between the three reigns spanned by the *Reform Small Cross* issue. It is clear from Petersson's analysis that there were multiple weight standards in the issues down to *Quatrefoil*,[24] and the major eighteenth-century hoard, possibly from Kingsholm, Glos., shows that the earliest *Quatrefoil* coins were heavy.[25] In most subsequent issues the weight range is more compact, resulting in histograms with a single prominent peak, but a study of die-linked groups in Mossop's Lincoln corpus shows that multiple standards continued to be employed at least until the end of Harthacnut's second reign and possibly later.[26] Although the general trend in each issue was downwards, at any particular time mints in different parts of the country did not necessarily apply the same standard,[27] and occasionally there was a reversion at some mints to a heavier standard before the end of the issue.[28]

A detailed analysis of die-cutting styles can provide us with a further means of sub-dividing an issue chronologically, and this may be used to study the pattern of weight changes on a broad statistical base.[29] In the *Quatrefoil* issue, seven of the major styles distinguished above have been sub-divided chronologically (Winchester, Gloucester, Chester, York, Lincoln, Thetford A, and London A/C), and a shift in the weight distribution is evident in each (see Appendix 2), showing that the general reduction in weight applied throughout the country. The distributions of most sub-styles

24. H. B. A. Petersson, *Anglo-Saxon Currency* (Lund, 1969), 179–85 and 202–15. Multiple weight standards had been identified in certain types by V. J. Butler, 'The metrology of the late Anglo-Saxon penny: the reign of Æthelræd II and Cnut', in *AS Coins*, 195–214; their chronological nature was further demonstrated in Lyon, 'Significance of the sack of Oxford', 34–5.
25. C. S. S. Lyon, 'Variations in currency in Late Anglo-Saxon England', in *Mints, Dies and Currency*, ed. R. A. G. Carson (1971), 101–20, at 111.
26. H. R. Mossop, *The Lincoln Mint c.890–1279* (1970). After 1042 the number of surviving coins is too few to make this approach useful, but the weight distribution of Edward's *Small Flan* issue displays three distinct peaks: Petersson, *op. cit.*, 189 and 225. On declining standards in the *Jewel Cross* issue, see Talvio, 'Harold I and Harthacnut's *Jewel Cross* type reconsidered', below.
27. Lyon, 'Variations in currency', 112; K. Jonsson, 'An example of regional weight variation in the coinage of Æthelred II: the Intermediate Small Cross/Crux mules and the Transitional Crux variety', *NC* 1977, 177–80.
28. Lyon, 'Variations in currency', 106–10.
29. This has been applied to York coins of the *Crux* type; Blackburn, 'A York die-cutting centre'.

include several standards. There are two reasons for this: first, because many of the sub-styles spanned one or more changes in standard, and a number of dies will have continued in use after the style had ceased to be produced; and secondly, because they may include coins from various mints which were striking to different standards.

If one takes the coins of a particular style just from the major mint at which it was used – which ought in general to have exhausted its dies more rapidly than its smaller neighbours – we find that the distributions are more sharply defined. Thus in Appendix 2 the coins of London, Winchester, and Lincoln have been listed separately, while both the Chester and York styles were effectively restricted to single mints anyway. These distributions provide us with an opportunity for identifying the specific standards that were used at each of the major mints. The evidence for London is the most detailed because the coins are very plentiful and they are divided into six chronological phases (fig. 13.2). Coins of the fourth phase, the short-lived early London C style, all appear to have been struck to a standard of c.1.05g, and they demonstrate how compact a distribution one can expect from coins of a single standard.[30] With this in mind, by comparing the distribution of each successive sub-style we have identified the following approximate standards:

London	c.1.40g, c.1.30g, c.1.15g, c.1.05g, c.1.00g
Winchester	c.1.50g, c.1.30g, c.1.20g, c.1.10g, c.1.00g
Lincoln	c.1.40g, c.1.30g, c.1.20g, c.1.10g, c.0.95g
York	c.1.40g, c.1.30g, c.1.10g, c.1.00g
Chester	c.1.40g, c.1.30g?, c.1.15g, c.1.10g, c.1.00g[31]

Five separate standards are apparent at four of the mints and there is a close correlation between them. Winchester started at a heavier standard than elsewhere (c.1.50g compared with c.1.40g), but thereafter each seems to have struck coins at standards of roughly c.1.30g, c.1.20g, c.1.10g, and c.1.00g. The second and third standards at London and the final one at Lincoln were perhaps a little lower. At York only four standards are evident, but it may be that a fifth one of c.1.20g was used but is poorly represented in our sample or is obscured by the preceding and succeeding standards. It is possible that at the end of the issue, when mint output was probably very low, there was an even lighter standard which is not apparent from the distributions. Mints in the south-west seem to have struck a substantial number of coins to a standard of c.0.90g (see the distributions of Ex., Taun. B, and Gl. l. styles in Appendix 2).

30. A comparable distribution is exhibited by the weights of 25 die-duplicates of *Long Cross* type by the moneyer Unbein of Lincoln (Mossop, *op. cit.*, pl. 15, no. 24) which are plotted as a histogram in M. Blackburn, 'A Scandinavian Crux/Intermediate Small Cross die-chain reappraised', in *Viking-Age Coinage in the Northern Lands*, ed. M. A. S. Blackburn and D. M. Metcalf (BAR Internat. Ser. 122, 1981), 425–47, at 432.

31. The existence of a c.1.00g standard at Chester is confirmed by the weight distribution of the coins in the Bryn Maelgwyn hoard, deposited at the very end of the *Quatrefoil* issue (the hoard contained one coin of *Pointed Helmet* type). We are grateful to Mr Boon for making a list of the coins available to us in advance of his publication of the hoard.

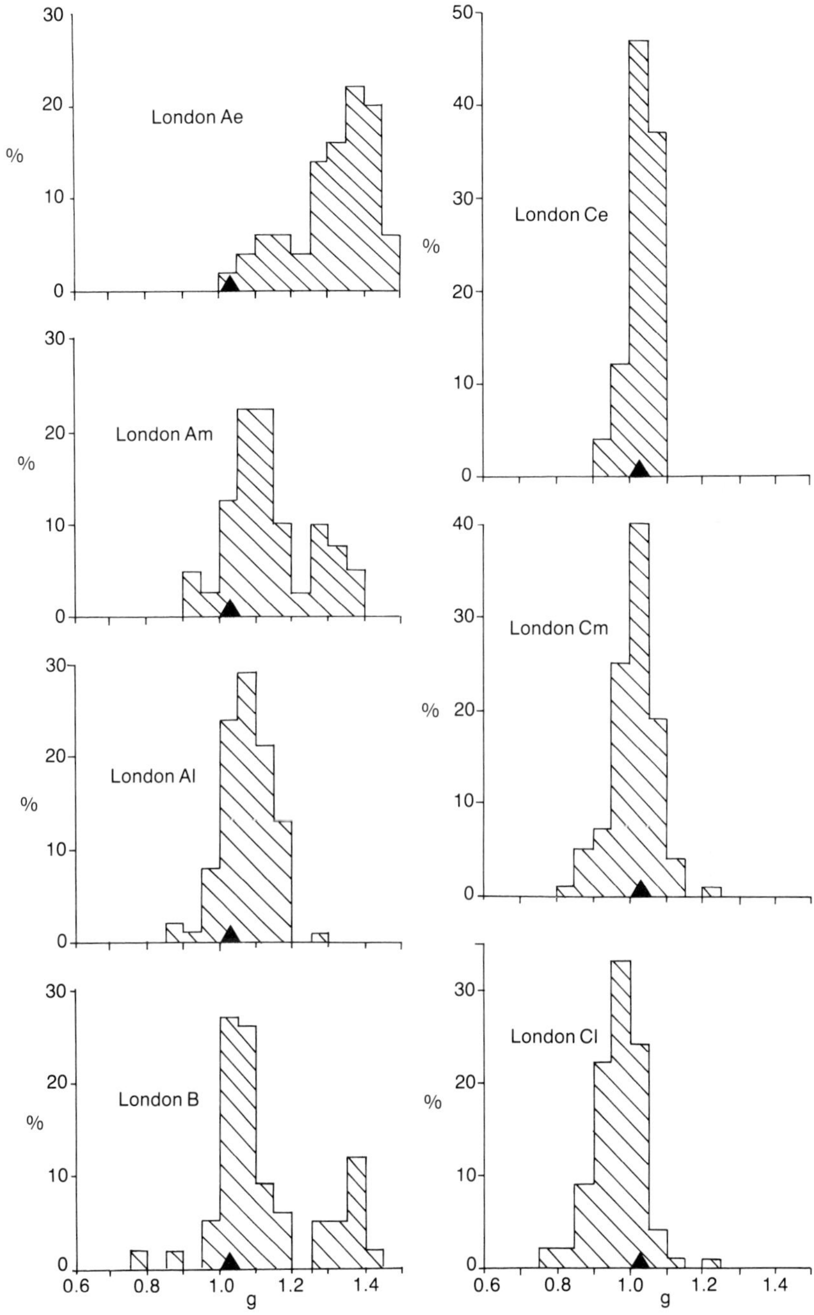

Fig. 13.2 Histograms of London style coins of the London mint (solid triangle shows median for issue).

There is no evidence for a late reversion to a higher weight standard in this issue,[32] but we have found some instances of different standards being applied concurrently at different mints. Dover, for example, maintained a higher weight standard than London towards the end of the issue (the weights of its coins of later styles are: Lon. Cm 1.13g, 1.13g, 1.12g, 1.11g, 1.10g; Lon. Cl 1.16g, 1.12g, 1.03g). Other provincial mints may have been slow to reduce their standards, cf. Lon. Cl coins of Hertford (*SCBI* Copenhagen 1225, 1.10g) and Norwich (Hild. 2913, 1.12g). On the other hand, mints in the south-west may have reduced their standards earlier and further.

The coinages struck to the four or five standards used at the major mints were not of equal size. If one looks at the surviving material for each of these mints in very broad terms, about 30 per cent of the coins were probably struck to the first three standards, about 40 per cent to the fourth standard (c.1.10g/c.1.05g) and about 30 per cent to the last standard (c.1.00g/c.0.95g). There is some variation between mints; Winchester may have struck a slightly higher proportion at the heavier standards and York a higher proportion at the lightest, but the overall pattern is much the same. Fortunately, the surviving material does not appear to be biased significantly in favour of any particular period. The standardized distribution set out in Appendix 3, adjusted with reference to the degree of reverse duplication among Lincoln coins, is very similar to the actual distribution (or, looked at another way, there is not a substantial variation in die survival as indicated by the die-survival ratio). We may therefore take the surviving *Quatrefoil* coins as reasonably representative of original mint output. However, we cannot make a direct correlation between the number of coins struck to a particular standard and its duration, since we do not know how the volume of coin production changed during the issue. It is likely that production was higher at the beginning than at the end, and therefore that the first two changes of weight standard occurred fairly early in the issue. But we should hesitate to infer that this was a result of some political or economic crisis, or even that it is an untypical pattern, for other issues have yet to be subjected to a similar analysis.

What has emerged from this study is evidence of some central co-ordination of the weight standards to be adopted at the mints, but with local variations as to timing and the precise weights used. Some of these variations appear to reflect a deliberate policy, such as the lower standards employed in the south-west, but others may represent a failure to implement instructions or technical differences in mint practice.

Dating of the Issue

Cnut struck three substantive issues, *Quatrefoil*, *Pointed Helmet*, and *Short Cross*. The Scandinavian hoard evidence places their relative chronology beyond doubt, but it is far more difficult to assign absolute dates to them. No compelling evidence

32. Other than two late London coins of anomalously high weight: Hild. 2223, 1.20g (Lon. Cm); and *SCBI* Copenhagen iiib 3032, 1.21g (Lon. Cl).

has yet been discovered by which to date the changes from *Quatrefoil* to *Pointed Helmet* or from *Pointed Helmet* to *Short Cross*. It is attractive to associate the Trondheim (Dronningensgate) hoard with the nearby battle of Stiklastad in July 1030,[33] implying an earlier date for the introduction of *Short Cross*, but the association cannot be proved. Nor are we happy with Malmer's suggestion that coins of a quasi-*Short Cross* type which give Cnut the title 'king of the Swedes' must be dated c.1027, implying an earlier date for the English type,[34] for as Lagerqvist has pointed out[35] we have no idea how long Cnut may have exercised authority over part of Sweden. There is nothing to suggest that any of the three issues was significantly longer or shorter than the others, and the best we can presently do is follow Dolley in assigning roughly equal periods to each. He originally dated them c.1017–23, c.1023–29, and c.1029–35, but in 1968 he modified this chronology moving each type forward by one year so that *Short Cross* extended beyond Cnut's death (12 November 1035) into 1036.[36] This last date seems preferable, for the *Jewel Cross* coins with the name 'Cnut' appear to have been struck under Harthacnut, and it also is consistent with the existence of a unique *Short Cross* coin of Harold I.[37] But the suggested postponement of the introduction of the *Quatrefoil* type from 1017 to 1018 deserves careful consideration.

Edmund Ironside died in November 1016. Cnut was accepted as king almost immediately and was crowned at St Paul's sometime in 1017.[38] It might be expected that one of his first priorities would have been the restoration of domestic and foreign trade to generate revenue for his court and the country, and this would have required

33. L. O. Lagerqvist and R. H. M. Dolley, 'The problem of the "Fleur-de-Lis" sceptre on the Sigtuna coins of Cnut', *BNJ* 30 (1961), 252–61, at 258–9; L. O. Lagerqvist, 'The coinage at Sigtuna in the names of Anund Jacob, Cnut the Great and Harthacnut', *Commentationes* II (1968), 383–413, at 388.
34. B. Malmer, *King Canute's Coinage in the Northern Countries* (The Dorothea Coke Memorial Lecture in Northern Studies delivered 30 May 1972 at University College, London; 1974), 19–20.
35. Lagerqvist, 'The coinage at Sigtuna', 409–10.
36. M. Dolley, 'A further die-link in the Scandinavian imitative series', *Fornvännen* 1968, 116–19, at 117.
37. A coin of the Bristol moneyer Leofwine in the Stockholm collection, without find provenance, to be published in T. Talvio's *SCBI* Stockholm, Harold I and Harthacnut (forthcoming), no. 1. A coin of similar type by the moneyer 'Leifine' of London (*BMC* Harold I, no. 65) is probably an imitation, for it is struck from the same reverse die as a coin from the Lübeck hoard with an irregular obverse legend (*SCBI* Copenhagen iiib 2688). *BMC* 65 had been purchased from Mr John Edwards in 1838, but Hawkins' assertion (*Silver Coins of England*, 3rd edn (1887), 157–8) that it was 'found in the Thames' seems to be an error based on the BM accessions register. On 1 January 1838 John Edwards sold the Museum 'Coin of Harold I (described in bill as Harold II)' and on 3 March 1838 a 'Coin? (found in the Thames)', but *BMC* 65 is presumably the first one.
38. For the date and place of Cnut's coronation see E. A. Freeman, *The History of the Norman Conquest of England*, I (1870), 673–7.

normal mint production. He must also have been concerned to see that the final tribute promised to the Danish army by Edmund shortly before his death was raised quickly and without recourse to the royal coffers. In fact the payment, the largest ever made, took almost two years to collect,[39] and it is hard to imagine that the mints were not in operation while this was being done. Only a small group of *Last Small Cross* coins with Cnut's name appear to be English,[40] so unless coins continued to be produced in the name of Æthelred II, which is unlikely, it is reasonable to suppose that he inaugurated the *Quatrefoil* type during 1017.

However, two points must be made. The first is that there is no evidence from the Scandinavian hoards that the tribute of 1018 was paid in early *Quatrefoil* coins. As indicated above (p. 256), the analysis of the surviving material based on the Lincoln corpus (see Appendix 3) suggests that *Quatrefoil* coins are fairly evenly represented throughout the issue, and that there is not the significant concentration of early coins that has been found, for example, in the *Long Cross* type.[41] But equally Æthelred's *Last Small Cross* type does not appear to show a bias in favour of later coins (Appendix 3), although this is more difficult to assess since the latest coins of an issue would normally be under-represented because they had less time in which to find their way to Scandinavia. One would wish to confirm these impressions with an analysis based on a non-Danelaw mint, but it would seem either that the tribute of 1018 was paid in a broad mixture of coin, or coin and bullion, or that a substantial proportion of it remained in England in the coffers of Cnut and other high-ranking Danes.[42]

Secondly, Cnut's earliest Danish coinage has some bearing on the English chronology. Coins of *Last Small Cross* type with the legend +CNUT REX DÆNOR are traditionally dated after 1018 when Cnut's elder brother Harold died and he became king of Denmark. It has not been sufficiently appreciated that some of these

39. Other tributes seem to have taken an appreciable time to collect, thus the tribute arranged late in 1006 was paid in 1007, and that arranged in 1011 was paid in 1012.
40. Struck at Norwich by the moneyer Oswold; see C. S. S. Lyon, 'Some problems in interpreting Anglo-Saxon coinage', *Anglo-Saxon England 5* (1976), 203, 223–4. Three of the 'Cnut' coins are known (Hild. 2971; *SCBI* Copenhagen iiic 3212; and *SCBI* East Anglian Museums 1249) and two of the Æthelred coins which die-link with them (Hild. 3183 and Elmore-Jones lot 622).
41. C. S. S. Lyon, 'The metrology of Æthelred's Long Cross type at Lincoln', in *Viking-Age Coinage in the Northern Lands* (n.30 above), 525–31. In that issue the die-survival ratio varies from 1.3 to 9.2 (Table A), compared with a range of 1.3 to 2.9 in *Quatrefoil* and 1.2 to 3.6 in *Last Small Cross* (Appendix 3 below).
42. That some geld was remitted to Scandinavia in this period is suggested by two rune stones in Uppland, Sweden which read: 'Ulv has in England taken three gelds. That was the first which Tosti paid. Then Thorkel paid. Then Cnut paid.' and 'Alle had this stone raised to his own memory. He took Cnut's payment in England. God help his soul.': S. B. F. Jansson, *Swedish Vikings in England. The Evidence of the Rune Stones* (The Dorothea Coke Memorial Lecture in Northern Studies delivered 11 March 1965 at University College, London; 1966), 12–14.

coins appear to have been struck before the introduction of *Quatrefoil* in England. One was present in the large Norwegian hoard from Slethei, which ends with some 530 *Last Small Cross* coins.[43] Furthermore, at least one of the dies appears to be the work of the Lincoln die-cutter late in the *Last Small Cross* issue.[44] However, it would be wrong to attach too much significance to the legends on one or two dies. The Scandinavian coinages of this period were not overtly regal issues. In the 990s they had borne the kings' names, but subsequent strikings had been entirely imitative, mostly copying English types and legends. The die(s) in question were supplied by the Lincoln die-cutter, who may have received inadequate instructions as to the legends he should engrave and may have been ignorant of Cnut's status in Denmark. More potent evidence is the Danish-cut dies with +CNVD REX IN DANORVM, but these are probably later and may post-date the introduction of the *Quatrefoil* type in England.

On balance, therefore, a date of c.1017 for the introduction of *Quatrefoil* seems preferable on the scanty evidence currently available.

Conclusions

When Cnut ordered his first coinage to be produced, he adopted without any significant change the network of mints and local die-cutting centres which had been operating at the end of Æthelred II's reign. During the course of the issue a number of smaller mints started cutting dies, principally for their own moneyers. There is a greater diversity of style in *Quatrefoil* than in any other issue, with some 19 centres producing dies. But any weakness this reflects was of a political rather than administrative nature; granting the privilege of die-cutting to a greater number of boroughs, or acquiescing in their assumption of it. Control of the mint organization remained as tight as ever. The number of dies which do not conform to one of the recognized styles is tiny; moneyers did not begin cutting their own dies, but continued to obtain them from established centres to which they presumably had to account for them.

This study has served to emphasize the sophistication of the late Saxon coinage, in both its administrative and economic aspects. The identification of a series of similar weight standards which applied at each of the country's major mints suggests that there was a centrally co-ordinated policy. Yet there are local and regional variations, the extent and significance of which have still to be determined.

43. C. I. Schive, 'Fortegnelse over Mynter fra Middelalderen . . .', *Forhandlinger i Videnskabs-Selskabet i Christiania* 1869, 87–106.
44. Blackburn, 'English dies used in Scandinavian imitative coinages'.

APPENDIX 1

Analysis of styles by mint (number of coins in the Stockholm Systematic and Copenhagen collections)

	Win. e	Win. m	Win. l	Chi	Ox. e	Ox. l	Ex.	Taun. A	Taun. B	Bath A	Bath B	Gl. e	Gl. l	Worc.	Shr.	Ch. e	Ch. m	York e	York m	Lin. e
Axbridge	–	–	–	–	–	–	–	–	1	–	4	–	–	–	–	–	–	–	–	–
Aylesbury	–	1	–	–	–	1	–	–	–	–	–	–	–	–	–	–	–	–	–	–
Barnstaple	–	–	–	–	–	–	8	–	–	–	–	–	–	–	–	–	–	–	–	–
Bath	5	2	–	–	–	–	2	–	–	6	13	–	–	–	–	–	–	–	–	–
Bedford	–	–	–	–	–	–	–	–	–	–	–	–	–	–	–	–	–	–	–	1
Bridport	1	–	–	–	–	–	–	–	–	–	–	–	–	–	–	–	–	–	–	–
Bristol	–	–	3	–	–	–	1	–	–	–	–	11	32	–	–	–	–	–	–	–
Bruton	1	–	–	–	–	–	–	–	–	–	6	–	4?	–	–	–	–	–	–	–
Buckingham	–	–	–	–	1	3	–	–	–	–	–	–	–	–	–	–	–	–	–	–
Cadbury	1	–	–	–	–	–	–	–	–	–	X	–	–	–	–	–	–	–	–	–
Caistor?	–	–	–	–	–	–	–	–	–	–	–	–	–	–	–	–	–	–	–	2
Cambridge	–	–	–	–	–	–	–	–	–	–	–	–	–	–	–	–	–	–	–	2
Canterbury	–	–	–	–	–	–	–	–	–	–	–	–	–	–	–	–	–	–	–	–
Chester	–	–	–	–	–	–	–	–	–	–	–	–	–	–	–	36	103	–	–	–
Chichester	–	–	–	20	–	–	–	–	–	–	–	–	–	–	–	–	–	–	–	–
Cissbury	–	–	–	1	–	–	–	–	–	–	–	–	–	–	–	–	–	–	–	–
Colchester	–	–	–	–	–	–	–	–	–	–	–	–	–	–	–	–	–	–	–	–
Crewkerne	–	–	–	–	–	–	10	–	–	–	–	–	–	–	–	–	–	–	–	–
Cricklade	2	13	–	–	–	1	–	–	–	–	–	2	3	–	–	–	–	–	–	–
Derby	–	–	–	–	–	–	–	–	–	–	–	–	–	–	–	–	–	–	–	2
Dover	–	–	–	–	–	–	–	–	–	–	–	–	–	–	–	–	–	–	–	–
'Eanbyri'	2	–	–	–	–	–	–	–	–	–	–	–	–	–	–	–	–	–	–	–
Exeter	–	X	–	–	–	–	50	1	–	–	–	–	2	–	–	–	–	–	–	–
Gloucester	–	–	–	–	–	–	–	–	–	–	–	31	8	–	–	–	–	–	–	–
'Gothabyrig'	–	–	–	–	–	–	8	–	–	–	–	–	–	–	–	–	–	–	–	–
Guildford	–	–	–	2	–	–	–	–	–	–	–	–	–	–	–	–	–	–	–	–
Hastings	–	–	–	–	–	–	–	–	–	–	–	–	–	–	–	–	–	–	–	–
Hereford	–	–	–	–	–	–	–	–	–	–	–	15	11	–	–	–	–	–	–	–
Hertford	–	–	–	–	–	–	–	–	–	–	–	–	–	–	–	–	–	–	–	–
Huntingdon	–	–	–	–	–	–	–	–	–	–	–	–	–	–	–	–	–	–	–	–
Ilchester	2	2	–	–	–	–	15	9	32	–	22	–	–	–	–	–	–	–	–	–
Ipswich	–	–	–	–	–	–	–	–	–	–	–	–	–	–	–	–	–	–	–	–
Langport	–	X	1	–	–	–	–	–	4	–	1	–	–	–	–	–	–	–	–	–
Leicester	–	11	1	–	–	–	–	–	–	–	–	–	–	–	–	–	–	–	–	4
Lewes	–	–	–	3	–	–	–	–	–	–	–	–	–	–	–	–	–	–	–	–

Note to Appendix 1. Certain styles have been noticed at mints only from coins in other collections (indicated by a cross): *Buckingham*, Lon. Ae (*BMC* 493, as Romney); *Cadbury*, Bath B (*BMC* 24); *Chichester*, Lon. Am (*CNS* 1.1.19.1550); *Exeter*, Win. m (*SCBI* Helsinki 617); *Langport*, Win m (*CNS* 1.1.19.1567); *Lincoln*, Norw. A? (Bryn Maelgwyn hoard), York m (*SCBI* Helsinki 633); *Malmesbury*, Gl. 1 (Karls hoard, *BNJ*

Lin. m	Lin. l	Stam. A	Stam. B	Nhmp. A	Nhmp. B	Bed.	Norw. A	Thet. Ae	Thet. Am	Thet. Al	Thet. B	Thet. C	Lewes e	Lewes l	Lon. Ae	Lon. Am	Lon. Al	Lon. B	Lon. Ce	Lon. Cm	Lon. Cl	Anomalous	Total
–	–	–	–	–	–	–	–	–	–	–	–	–	–	–	–	–	–	–	–	–	–	–	5
–	–	–	–	–	–	–	–	–	–	–	–	–	–	1	2	–	1	–	–	–	–	–	6
–	–	–	–	–	–	–	–	–	–	–	–	–	–	–	–	–	–	–	–	–	–	–	8
–	–	–	–	–	–	–	–	–	–	–	–	–	–	–	–	–	–	–	–	–	–	2	30
4	2	–	–	–	–	7	5	1	1	–	–	–	–	–	–	–	–	–	–	1	2	4	28
–	–	–	–	–	–	–	–	–	–	–	–	–	–	–	–	–	–	–	–	–	–	–	1
–	–	–	–	–	–	–	–	–	–	–	–	–	–	–	–	–	–	–	–	–	–	–	47
–	–	–	–	–	–	–	–	–	–	–	–	–	–	–	–	–	–	–	–	–	–	–	11
–	–	–	–	–	–	–	–	2	–	–	–	–	–	–	X	–	–	–	–	–	–	–	6
–	–	–	–	–	–	–	–	–	–	–	–	–	–	–	–	–	–	–	–	–	–	–	1
–	–	–	–	–	–	–	–	1	–	–	–	–	–	–	–	–	–	–	–	–	–	–	3
4	–	1	1	–	–	1	3	–	10	8	4	4	–	–	–	–	17	2	–	11	23	–	91
–	–	–	–	–	–	–	–	–	–	–	–	–	–	1	6	5	17	1?	2	8	–	–	40
–	–	–	–	–	–	–	–	–	–	–	–	–	–	–	–	–	–	–	–	–	–	–	139
–	–	–	–	–	–	–	–	–	–	–	–	–	–	–	–	X	–	–	–	–	–	–	20
–	–	–	–	–	–	–	–	–	–	–	–	–	–	–	–	–	–	–	–	–	–	–	1
–	–	–	–	–	–	1	–	–	6	17	–	2	–	–	–	–	–	–	–	6	7	–	39
–	–	–	–	–	–	–	–	–	–	–	–	–	–	–	–	–	–	–	–	–	–	–	10
–	–	–	–	–	–	–	–	–	–	–	–	–	–	–	–	–	–	–	–	–	–	1	22
2	1	–	–	–	–	–	–	–	–	–	–	–	–	–	–	–	–	–	–	–	–	–	5
–	–	–	–	–	–	–	–	–	–	–	–	–	–	2	4	2	4	–	–	6	4	–	22
–	–	–	–	–	–	–	–	–	–	–	–	–	–	–	–	–	–	–	–	–	–	–	2
–	–	–	–	–	–	–	–	–	–	–	–	–	–	–	–	–	–	–	–	–	–	–	53
–	–	–	–	–	–	–	–	–	–	–	–	–	–	–	–	–	–	–	–	–	–	–	39
–	–	–	–	–	–	–	–	–	–	–	–	–	–	–	–	–	–	–	–	–	–	–	8
–	–	–	–	–	–	–	–	–	–	–	–	–	–	–	–	–	–	1	–	–	–	–	3
–	–	–	–	–	–	–	–	–	–	–	–	–	1	5	–	–	–	–	–	–	3	–	9
–	–	–	–	–	–	–	–	–	–	–	–	–	–	–	–	–	–	–	–	–	–	–	26
–	–	–	–	–	–	–	–	1	1	–	–	–	–	–	1	1	–	10	–	6	14	–	34
4	1	2	–	2	3	1	–	1	3	1	–	–	–	–	–	–	1	–	–	2	6	1	28
–	–	–	–	–	–	–	–	–	–	–	–	–	–	–	–	–	–	–	–	–	–	1	83
2	1	–	–	–	–	–	6	1	7	11	–	8	–	–	–	–	2	–	–	–	2	1	41
–	–	–	–	–	–	–	–	–	–	–	–	–	–	–	–	–	–	–	–	–	–	–	6
2	1	–	–	1	–	–	–	–	–	–	–	–	–	–	–	–	–	–	–	–	–	1	21
–	–	–	–	–	–	–	–	–	–	–	–	–	4	10	–	7	1	–	–	4	2	–	31

36 (1967), pl. 9, no. 48); *Northampton*, Win. m (see n.23 above); *Tamworth*, Worc. (*CNS* 1.4.18.1946 and SHM Inv. 14565–89); *Torksey*, Lin. l (Lockett (Glendining 26.4.1960), lot 3755); *Wareham*, Win. m (*CNS* 1.1.9.553); *Watchet*, Ex. (Elmore Jones (Glendining, 12 May 1971) lot 895).

Uncertain mints not shown in Appendix 1 include: *BR*, Stam. B. (*CNS* 1.1.19.1541);

	Win. e	Win. m	Win. l	Chi	Ox. e	Ox. l	Ex.	Taun. A	Taun. B	Bath A	Bath B	Gl. e	Gl. l	Worc.	Shr.	Ch. e	Ch. m	York e	York m	Lin. e
Lincoln	–	–	–	–	–	–	–	–	–	–	–	–	–	–	–	–	–	–	X	47
London	–	1	–	–	–	1?	–	1	–	–	–	–	–	2	–	–	–	–	–	1
Lydford	–	–	–	–	–	–	4	–	9	–	–	–	–	–	–	–	–	–	–	–
Lympne	–	–	–	–	–	–	–	–	–	–	–	–	–	–	–	–	–	–	–	–
Maldon	–	–	–	–	–	–	–	–	–	–	–	–	–	–	–	–	–	–	–	–
Malmesbury	1	5	2	–	–	–	–	–	–	–	–	–	X	–	–	–	–	–	–	–
Northampton	–	X	–	–	1	–	–	–	–	5?	–	3	–	–	–	–	–	–	–	1
Norwich	–	–	–	–	–	–	–	–	–	–	–	–	–	–	–	–	–	–	–	–
Nottingham	–	–	–	–	–	–	–	–	–	–	–	–	–	–	–	–	–	–	–	3
Oxford	20	4	–	–	13	16	–	–	–	–	–	–	–	–	–	–	–	–	–	–
Rochester	–	–	–	–	–	–	–	–	–	–	–	–	–	–	–	–	–	–	–	–
Romney	–	–	–	–	–	–	–	–	–	–	–	–	–	–	–	–	–	–	–	–
Salisbury	3	12	1	–	–	–	6	–	–	1	–	–	–	–	–	–	–	–	–	–
Shaftesbury	8	12	5	–	–	–	–	–	–	–	–	–	–	–	–	–	–	–	–	–
Shrewsbury	–	–	–	–	–	–	–	–	–	–	–	7	–	–	16	–	–	–	–	–
Southampton	–	18	6	–	–	–	–	–	–	–	–	–	–	–	–	–	–	–	–	–
Southwark	–	–	–	–	–	–	–	–	–	–	–	–	–	–	–	–	–	–	–	–
Stafford	–	–	–	–	–	–	–	–	–	–	–	–	–	1	–	–	–	–	–	–
Stamford	–	–	–	–	–	–	–	–	–	–	–	–	–	–	–	–	–	–	–	7
Sudbury	–	–	–	–	–	–	–	–	–	–	–	–	–	–	–	–	–	–	–	–
Tamworth	–	–	–	–	–	–	–	–	–	–	–	–	–	X	–	–	–	–	–	–
Taunton	–	–	–	–	–	–	–	4	18	–	–	–	–	–	–	–	–	–	–	–
Thetford	–	–	–	–	–	–	–	–	–	–	–	–	–	–	–	–	–	–	–	5
Torksey	–	–	–	–	–	–	–	–	–	–	–	–	–	–	–	–	–	–	–	–
Totnes	–	–	–	–	–	–	11	–	–	–	–	–	–	–	–	–	–	–	–	–
Wallingford	9	10	2	–	–	–	–	–	–	–	–	–	–	–	–	–	–	–	–	–
Wareham	–	X	–	–	–	–	–	–	–	–	–	–	–	–	–	–	–	–	–	–
Warwick	1	–	–	–	–	–	–	–	–	–	–	–	–	1	–	–	–	–	–	3
Watchet	–	–	–	–	–	–	X	4	2	–	–	–	–	–	–	–	–	–	–	–
Wilton	2	2	–	–	–	–	–	–	–	–	–	–	–	–	–	–	–	–	–	–
Winchcombe	–	–	–	–	2	–	–	–	–	–	–	3	–	–	–	–	–	–	–	–
Winchester	54	92	32	2	–	–	–	–	–	–	–	1	–	–	–	–	–	–	–	–
Worcester	–	–	–	–	–	–	–	–	–	–	–	2	–	15	–	–	–	–	–	–
York	–	–	–	–	–	–	–	–	–	–	–	–	–	–	–	–	–	25	243	1
Total	112	185	53	28	17	22	115	19	66	12	46	75	60	19	16	36	103	25	243	79

PEP, Taun. B (*CNS* 1.1.6.1010, attributed to Petherton, but the mint is not otherwise recorded before Edward the Confessor's reign); *PERHAI*, Lin. l (*SCBI* Copenhagen 3949, attributed to Wareham, but the style makes this improbable); . .*RCOB(?)*, Bath B (*SCBI* Copenhagen 3371, attributed to Shrewsbury, but more probably a Somerset mint – the moneyer is recorded at Bruton).

Lin. m	Lin. l	Stam. A	Stam. B	Nhmp. A	Nhamp. B	Bed.	Norw. A	Thet. Ae	Thet. Am	Thet. Al	Thet. B	Thet. C	Lewes e	Lewes l	Lon. Ae	Lon. Am	Lon. Al	Lon. B	Lon. Ce	Lon. Cm	Lon. Cl	Anomalous	Total
115	72	1	–	–	–	–	X?	–	–	–	–	–	–	–	–	–	1	–	–	–	–	6	242
2	1	–	–	–	–	3	–	2	–	–	–	3	–	1	51	42	87	65	53	208	96	13	633
–	–	–	–	–	–	–	–	–	–	–	–	–	–	–	–	–	–	–	–	–	–	–	13
–	–	–	–	–	–	–	–	–	–	–	–	–	–	–	–	–	–	–	–	2	–	–	2
–	–	–	–	–	–	–	–	1	1	2	–	–	–	–	–	–	6	–	–	1	9	–	20
–	–	–	–	–	–	–	–	–	–	–	–	–	–	–	–	–	–	–	–	–	–	–	8
–	–	–	–	5	6	1?	–	–	–	–	–	–	–	–	–	–	2	1	–	4	6	–	35
11	1	2	–	–	–	–	10	3	15	18	–	16	–	–	–	–	–	–	1	4	3	–	84
2	2	–	–	–	–	–	–	–	–	–	–	–	–	–	–	–	–	–	–	–	–	–	7
–	–	–	–	–	–	–	–	–	–	–	–	–	–	–	–	2	–	–	–	–	–	–	55
–	–	1?	–	–	–	–	–	–	–	–	–	–	–	–	4	1	1	–	–	2	–	–	9
–	–	–	–	–	–	–	–	–	–	–	–	–	–	–	1	2	1	1	–	1	1	–	7
–	–	–	–	–	–	–	–	–	–	–	–	–	–	–	–	–	–	–	–	–	–	1	24
–	–	–	–	–	–	–	–	–	–	–	–	–	–	–	–	–	–	–	–	–	–	–	25
–	–	–	–	–	–	–	–	–	–	–	–	–	–	–	–	1	5	5	–	–	–	3	37
–	–	–	–	–	–	–	–	–	–	–	–	–	–	–	–	–	–	–	–	–	–	–	24
–	–	–	–	–	–	–	–	–	–	–	–	–	–	–	15	7	32	14	–	–	–	3	71
–	–	–	–	–	–	–	–	–	–	–	–	–	–	–	–	–	–	–	–	–	–	–	1
20	15	15	11	–	–	–	–	–	–	–	–	3	–	–	–	–	–	–	–	–	–	6	77
–	–	–	–	–	–	–	3	–	–	–	–	5	–	–	–	–	–	–	–	–	6	–	14
–	–	–	–	–	–	–	–	–	–	–	–	–	–	–	–	–	–	–	–	–	–	–	–
–	–	–	–	–	–	–	–	–	–	–	–	–	–	–	–	–	–	–	–	–	–	1	23
21	5	1	–	–	–	–	3	15	19	9	7	8	–	–	–	–	–	–	–	–	–	–	93
–	X	1	–	–	–	–	–	–	–	–	–	–	–	–	–	–	–	–	–	–	–	–	1
–	–	–	–	–	–	–	–	–	–	–	–	–	–	–	–	–	–	–	–	–	–	–	11
–	–	–	–	–	–	–	–	–	–	–	–	–	–	–	–	–	–	–	–	–	–	–	21
–	–	–	–	–	–	–	–	–	–	–	–	–	–	–	–	–	–	–	–	–	–	–	–
1	1	–	–	–	–	–	–	–	–	–	–	–	–	–	–	–	–	–	–	–	–	3	10
–	–	–	–	–	–	–	–	–	–	–	–	–	–	–	–	–	–	–	–	–	–	1	7
–	–	–	–	–	–	–	–	–	–	–	–	–	–	–	–	–	–	–	–	–	–	–	4
–	–	–	–	–	–	–	–	–	–	–	–	–	–	–	–	–	–	–	–	–	–	–	5
–	–	–	–	–	–	–	–	–	–	–	–	–	–	–	–	–	–	–	–	–	–	–	181
–	–	–	–	–	–	–	–	–	–	–	–	–	–	–	–	–	–	–	–	–	–	–	17
–	–	–	–	–	–	–	–	–	–	–	–	–	–	–	–	–	–	–	–	–	–	1	270
190	103	24	12	8	9	14	30	28	63	66	11	49	5	20	84	70	178	100	56	266	184	49	2,950

APPENDIX 2

Weight distributions of the *Quatrefoil* styles, based on the Stockholm Systematic and Copenhagen collections (omitting fragments and damaged coins)

Weight g	All mints Win. e	Win. m	Win. l	Win. mint Win. e	Win. m	Win. l	Chi.	Ox. e	Ox. l	Ex. (all mints)	Ex. (Exeter mint)	Taun. A	Taun. B
Over	9	–	–	4	–	–	1	–	–	–	–	–	–
1.45–.49	16	–	–	7	–	–	–	–	–	1	1	–	–
1.40–.44	3	–	–	–	–	–	–	–	–	4	3	–	–
1.35–.39	7	–	–	1	–	–	1	–	–	–	–	–	–
1.30–.34	11	1	–	4	–	–	–	–	–	2	1	–	–
1.25–.29	21	1	–	16	1	–	–	–	–	1	1	–	–
1.20–.24	6	4	–	5	3	–	–	1	–	3	–	–	–
1.15–.19	9	26	1	4	12	–	3	5	2	7	3	–	–
1.10–.14	13	60	7	5	40	4	6	8	7	12	5	3	1
1.05–.09	11	37	6	4	18	6	2	3	2	9	4	5	6
1.00–.04	1	18	6	1	6	4	5	–	2	12	6	6	8
0.95–.99	2	16	7	2	7	3	6	–	3	21	10	1	4
0.90–.94	–	8	7	–	3	4	1	–	3	12	4	2	23
0.85–.89	–	7	11	–	2	7	2	–	1	14	4	–	11
0.80–.84	–	1	4	–	–	2	–	–	1	4	1	–	6
0.75–.79	–	2	2	–	–	–	–	–	–	3	2	–	2
0.70–.74	–	–	–	–	–	–	–	–	–	2	–	–	–
less	–	–	–	–	–	–	–	–	–	–	–	–	1
no. of coins	109	181	51	53	92	30	27	17	21	107	45	17	62

Weight g	Lin. mint Lin. e	Lin. m	Lin. l	Stam. A	Stam. B	Nhmp. A	Nhmp. B	Bed.	Norw. A	Thet. Ae	Thet. Am	Thet. Al	Thet. B	The C
Over	1	–	–	–	–	–	–	–	–	1	–	–	–	–
1.45–.49	–	–	–	–	–	–	–	–	4	1	3	1	–	–
1.40–.44	9	–	–	–	–	–	–	–	2	1	5	–	–	–
1.35–.39	5	–	–	–	–	–	–	–	4	5	1	–	–	–
1.30–.34	7	–	–	–	–	–	–	–	3	5	2	1	–	–
1.25–.29	9	6	–	–	–	–	–	1	5	8	16	5	–	–
1.20–.24	2	1	–	–	–	1	–	–	4	4	8	7	1	–
1.15–.19	3	3	–	–	–	–	1	1	3	1	3	2	1	–
1.10–.14	2	10	1	–	–	–	–	–	–	–	4	3	3	–
1.05–.09	6	25	11	–	–	4	3	2	2	–	4	9	1	–
1.00–.04	1	20	9	2	–	2	1	8	2	1	9	12	3	7
0.95–.99	–	27	12	6	4	1	2	2	–	–	5	11	2	6
0.90–.94	1	13	20	4	2	–	2	–	1	–	1	10	–	12
0.85–.89	–	3	12	5	5	–	–	–	–	–	–	2	–	11
0.80–.84	–	1	1	5	–	–	–	–	–	–	–	2	–	7
0.75–.79	–	–	1	1	1	–	–	–	–	–	–	–	–	5
0.70–.74	–	–	2	–	–	–	–	–	–	–	–	–	–	1
less	–	–	–	–	–	–	–	–	–	–	–	–	–	–
no. of coins	46	109	69	23	12	8	9	14	30	27	61	65	11	49

										All mints		
Bath A	Bath B	Gl. e	Gl. l	Worc.	Shr.	Ch. e	Ch. m	York e	York m	Lin. e	Lin. m	Lin. l
–	–	3	–	1	–	1	–	–	–	1	–	–
–	–	–	–	1	–	–	–	1	–	2	–	–
–	–	3	–	–	–	–	–	2	–	10	–	–
–	–	1	–	–	–	6	–	3	1	7	1	–
–	–	–	–	1	–	3	–	4	4	8	–	–
–	–	3	–	2	–	5	–	8	13	12	8	–
–	–	3	–	–	–	2	–	3	10	6	1	–
–	3	9	2	4	5	1	–	2	4	5	4	1
3	6	26	4	–	2	9	1	–	12	3	16	2
4	3	8	2	4	2	3	28	–	61	10	45	13
–	1	5	4	3	1	2	39	1	76	7	39	14
–	2	4	13	1	1	–	18	–	39	–	40	17
–	10	1	17	–	2	2	10	–	10	1	17	28
–	8	–	5	1	1	–	4	–	4	–	7	19
–	7	–	2	–	–	–	1	–	1	1	5	2
–	6	–	1	–	–	–	–	–	1	–	–	1
–	–	–	3	–	–	–	–	–	–	–	1	3
–	–	–	4	–	–	–	–	–	–	–	–	–
7	46	66	57	18	14	34	101	24	236	73	184	100

		All mints							Lon. mint						
Lewes e	Lewes l	Lon. Ae	Lon. Am	Lon. Al	Lon. B	Lon. Ce	Lon. Cm	Lon. Cl	Lon. Ae	Lon. Am	Lon. Al	Lon. B	Lon. Ce	Lon. Cm	Lon. Cl
1	–	–	–	–	–	–	–	–	–	–	–	–	–	–	–
2	–	5	–	–	–	–	–	–	3	–	–	–	–	–	–
–	–	14	1	–	1	–	–	–	10	–	–	1	–	–	–
1	–	16	3	–	8	–	–	–	11	2	–	8	–	–	–
1	–	14	4	–	3	–	–	–	8	3	–	3	–	–	–
–	–	11	7	1	3	–	–	–	7	4	1	3	–	–	–
–	–	6	3	–	6	–	1	1	2	1	–	–	–	1	1
–	2	6	5	17	6	1	–	1	3	4	11	4	–	–	–
–	5	5	12	31	11	1	10	4	3	9	18	6	–	7	1
–	5	3	12	36	22	19	39	4	2	9	25	17	19	38	4
–	2	2	8	48	23	24	89	26	1	5	20	18	24	78	22
–	3	–	4	21	8	6	55	42	–	1	7	3	6	48	30
–	3	–	3	9	2	3	29	32	–	2	1	–	2	13	20
–	–	–	2	6	3	–	23	37	–	–	2	1	–	9	8
–	–	–	–	4	3	–	3	27	–	–	–	–	–	1	2
–	–	–	–	1	1	–	1	4	–	–	–	1	–	–	2
–	–	–	–	–	–	–	2	4	–	–	–	–	–	–	–
–	–	–	–	–	–	–	–	–	–	–	–	–	–	–	–
5	20	82	64	174	100	54	252	182	50	40	85	65	51	195	90

APPENDIX 3

Actual and standardized weight distributions of Lincoln coins of *Quatrefoil* and *Last Small Cross* types

Based on the method described in Lyon, 'The metrology of Æthelred's Long Cross type' (n. 41 above).

Quatrefoil

Weight g	No. of specimens (n) arranged acccording to the degree of rev. die duplication (r)							Total (a)	Standardized total (b) ($\Sigma\frac{n}{r}$)	Die-survival ratio ($\frac{a}{b}$)
	1	2	3	4	5	6	7			
1.75–1.79	–	–	–	–	–	–	–	–	–	–
1.70–1.74	–	–	–	–	–	–	–	–	–	–
1.65–1.69	–	–	–	–	–	–	–	–	–	–
1.60–1.64	–	–	–	–	–	–	–	–	–	–
1.55–1.59	1	–	1	–	–	–	–	2	1.3	1.5
1.50–1.54	–	–	–	–	–	–	–	–	–	–
1.45–1.49	–	3	1	–	–	1	–	5	2.0	2.5
1.40–1.44	4	2	3	–	–	–	–	9	6.0	1.5
1.35–1.39	5	7	4	–	2	–	–	18	10.2	1.8
1.30–1.34	6	4	7	–	–	2	–	19	10.7	1.8
1.25–1.29	–	5	8	–	1	1	2	17	5.8	2.9
1.20–1.24	1	1	–	–	2	1	1	6	2.2	2.7
1.15–1.19	4	3	1	3	–	–	–	11	6.6	1.6
1.10–1.14	9	11	3	9	2	–	2	36	18.4	2.0
1.05–1.09	18	16	18	13	8	–	5	78	37.6	2.1
1.00–1.04	20	25	17	17	10	2	1	92	44.9	2.0
0.95–0.99	18	23	11	13	3	1	1	70	37.3	1.9
0.90–0.94	23	16	10	9	2	–	–	60	37.0	1.6
0.85–0.89	9	6	2	5	1	2	–	25	14.4	1.7
0.80–0.84	6	1	–	3	1	–	–	11	7.5	1.5
0.75–0.79	1	–	–	3	–	–	–	4	1.8	2.3
0.70–0.74	2	–	–	1	–	–	–	3	2.3	1.3
0.65–0.69	1	–	–	–	–	–	–	1	1.0	1.0
w.n.r./frag.	9	11	13	8	3	2	2	48	22.1	2.2
Total coins	137	134	99	84	35	12	14	515	269	1.9
Total dies	137	67	33	21	7	2	2	269		

Quatrefoil (continued)		*Last Small Cross*		
Actual distribution (*a* %)	Standardized distribution (*b* %)	Die-survival ratio	Actual distribution	Standardized distribution
–	–	2.7	0.3%	0.3%
–	–	3.0	0.2%	0.1%
–	–	3.6	1.7%	1.0%
–	–	3.4	7.9%	5.0%
0.4%	0.5%	3.5	3.6%	2.2%
–	–	2.2	2.2%	2.1%
1.0%	0.7%	3.6	3.4%	2.1%
1.7%	2.2%	2.5	11.0%	9.3%
3.5%	3.7%	3.1	7.9%	5.5%
3.7%	3.8%	2.2	9.8%	9.7%
3.3%	2.2%	2.4	8.2%	7.3%
1.2%	0.8%	1.8	9.5%	11.0%
2.1%	2.5%	1.6	6.5%	8.8%
7.0%	6.8%	1.5	6.9%	9.6%
15.1%	14.0%	1.7	3.6%	4.6%
17.9%	16.7%	1.7	3.3%	4.2%
13.6%	13.9%	1.5	1.0%	1.5%
11.7%	13.9%	1.4	0.9%	1.4%
4.9%	5.3%	1.2	1.0%	1.9%
2.1%	2.8%	–	–	–
0.8%	0.5%	–	–	–
0.6%	0.8%	–	–	–
0.2%	0.4%	–	–	–
9.3%	8.2%	1.9	11.0%	12.3%
100.1%	99.7%	2.2	99.9%	99.9%

APPENDIX 4

Styles of the coins in the Stockholm Systematic and Copenhagen collections

Winchester e

Hild. 34, 44–5, 45A, 111, 118–19, 248, 896, 920, 2943, 3007, 3010, 3017, 3020, 3025, 3027, 3029, 3045, 3054, 3096, 3096A, 3101, 3105–6, 3114, 3173–4, 3199, 3600, 3601, 3606, 3609, 3622, 3649, 3664, 3666A, 3667, 3681, 3683–4, 3716–17, 3720–1, 3728, 3731, 3782, 3784, 3791, 3799A, 3804, 3806, 3806A, 3808, 3810, 3813, 3817, 3828–9, 3835, 3840, 3850, 3852. *SCBI* Copenhagen 47, 290, 415, 3129, 3245, 3258, 3260–1, 3268, 3287–9, 3293, 3356, 3361, 3460, 3898, 3933, 3934, 3944–5, 3983, 4006, 4011, 4018, 4070–1, 4123, 4126–7, 4131–2, 4136–8, 4146–7, 4151, 4153, 4155, 4160, 4167–8, 4174, 4177–8, 4236.

Winchester m

Hild. 3, 182–3, 245–7, 256–7, 260, 875, 892, 1108, 1116, 1117, 1119, 1122–3, 1125, 1142A, 1148–9, 1442, 1445, 2889, 3056, 3095, 3098, 3102–4, 3109, 3115, 3154, 3157, 3160, 3172, 3181, 3186, 3582, 3604–5, 3605A, 3607–8, 3610, 3619, 3644–5, 3666, 3668–9, 3677–8, 3680, 3682, 3690–1, 3702, 3718, 3722A, 3726–7, 3729–30, 3735, 3746, 3763–4, 3781, 3786–8, 3792, 3795, 3803, 3805, 3809, 3811–12, 3814–15, 3819–20, 3823–7, 3836, 3838–9, 3841–2, 3847, 3849, 3853, 3857. *SCBI* Copenhagen 17, 18, 286–9, 295–6, 1171–4, 1187–8, 1200–1, 1207–8, 1479, 1482–4, 1489, 1493–4, 2149?, 3128, 3130–2, 3291, 3300–1, 3345–6, 3352, 3355, 3367, 3415?, 3426, 3441–2, 3452, 3459, 3936, 3946–7, 4007, 4010, 4012–13, 4015, 4016–17, 4027, 4029, 4031, 4043, 4058, 4062, 4068, 4072, 4075–6, 4125, 4129–30, 4135, 4142–5, 4148–50, 4152, 4154, 4156, 4158, 4161–3, 4165–6, 4173, 4175–6, 4179, 4188–9, 4192–3, 4196, 4198.

Winchester l

Hild. 94–5, 1118, 1120, 1142, 1309, 1455, 2889A, 2890, 3097, 3187, 3665, 3679, 3696–7, 3704, 3722, 3724, 3732–4, 3736, 3798, 3800, 3807, 3816, 3821–2, 3848, 3851, 3858–60. *SCBI* Copenhagen 1175–6, 1297, 3351, 3353–4, 3935, 4009, 4014, 4030, 4039, 4040–1, 4063, 4073–4, 4157, 4159, 4197, 4415.

Chichester

Hild. 199–203, 209, 209A, 210, 1084, 1278, 3194, 3783. *SCBI* Copenhagen 224–30, 230A, 235, 240–2, 1132, 1324, 1333, 4069.

Oxford e

Hild. 1128, 3006, 3009, 3013–14, 3028, 3030, 3651. *SCBI* Copenhagen 2707, 3241–2, 3244, 3257, 3270, 3298–9, 3991.

Oxford l

Hild. 115, 258, 361, 3003, 3008, 3016, 3018–19, 3019A, 3024, 3026, 3046–7, 3055. *SCBI* Copenhagen 121, 2322, 3243, 3246–7, 3255–6, 3269, 3290, 3292, 4235.

Exeter

Hild. 7, 7A, 10, 12, 13, 36, 96, 263–7, 267A, 268, 367, 388, 388A, 389, 389A, 390, 396–9, 404–8, 417–24, 424A, 884, 886, 888, 894, 897–8, 912, 915, 921, 921A, 922–3, 999, 1001–3, 1003A, 2860–1, 3183, 3183A, 3184, 3559–64. *SCBI* Copenhagen 7, 8, 12, 30, 299–301, 426–8, 431, 441–2, 450–4, 459, 461, 463–5, 470–2, 483–7, 944, 946, 970, 1059, 1062–3, 3102–3, 3259, 3453, 3455–6, 3891–5.

Taunton A

Hild. 369, 904, 911, 916, 960, 3436, 3436A, 3441?, 3586, 3586A. *SCBI* Copenhagen 935, 940, 956, 961, 967, 2606, 3751?, 3917–18.

Taunton B

Hild. 876, 876A, 881, 883, 883A, 887, 893, 900, 905–8, 917–19, 1288–9, 1289A, 2509, 2862–5, 2879, 3433, 3433A, 3434, 3434A,

3435, 3437, 3437A, 3438, 3438A, 3439–40, 3585, 3588–9. *SCBI* Copenhagen 2, 936, 939, 941–2, 958–9, 962, 964–6, 968–9, 1294, 3104–7, 3747–9, 3752–5, 3915–16.

Bath A

Hild. 37, 43, 1132?, 1132A? *SCBI* Copenhagen 32–3, 44–5, 1183–5?, 3454.

Bath B

Hild. 5, 5A, 20?, 21, 36, 41–2, 44A, 44B, 101–2, 106, 110, 878–80, 880A, 882, 903, 909, 909A, 910, 913A, 914, 914A, 1014. *SCBI* Copenhagen 1, 3, 16, 19, 28–9, 31, 42–3, 46, 112, 937–8, 943, 945, 953–5, 957, 960, 963, 1293, 3371.

Gloucester e

Hild. 69, 70, 75–6, 82, 259, 961–2, 965, 973–6, 982–5, 986A, 987–9, 1133, 1143, 1180, 1182–4, 1189, 1196–1200, 3129, 3135, 3642, 3652, 3653? *SCBI* Copenhagen 74, 76, 80–3, 297, 1013, 1027–32, 1036–9, 1043–6, 1202, 1231–3, 1239?, 1240, 3374, 3384, 3390, 3404–5, 3980, 4028.

Gloucester l

Hild. 69A, 71–2, 77–80, 83, 87–9, 93, 97–8, 98A, 99, 255, 370, 813A, 966, 977–8, 1187, 1201–3, 1208, 1216–17. *SCBI* Copenhagen 73, 75, 78–9, 84–6, 88–9, 92, 99–104, 112–16, 294, 429, 1018–20, 1040, 1047, 1235, 1248–9, 1257.

Worcester

Hild. 2434, 3580, 3631, 3633, 3640–1, 3701, 3703, 3741. *SCBI* Copenhagen 2607, 3490, 3955–6, 3968–9, 3976–9.

Shrewsbury

Hild. 3122, 3124, 3126, 3127?, 3128, 3136, 3152. *SCBI* Copenhagen 3376–7, 3379–82, 3383?, 3391, 3411.

Chester e

Hild. 1291, 1301, 1312–13, 1315, 1319, 1327, 1330, 1351, 1357, 1359, 1361, 1368, 1378, 1380–2, 1382A, 1388, 1425. *SCBI* Copenhagen 1357, 1359, 1401, 1406, 1408, 1410, 1427–8, 1435, 1456–7, 1463, 1465, 1469–70.

Chester l

Hild. 271, 1297–1300, 1314, 1316–18, 1322, 1326, 1328–9, 1340–4, 1347, 1352–4, 1356, 1357A, 1358, 1360, 1362–3, 1372–3, 1383, 1383A, 1398–1403, 1405–9, 1414–16, 1416A, 1417–18, 1423–4, 1430–1, 1431A, 1432, 1436–9. *SCBI* Copenhagen 1338, 1346, 1358, 1360–1, 1363–7, 1373–4, 1377, 1379, 1388–90, 1392, 1399–1400, 1402, 1405, 1407, 1409, 1411–13, 1420–1, 1436, 1446–9, 1454–5, 1459–60, 1462, 1466–8, 1472–3.

York e

Hild. 452, 466, 477, 501, 505, 551, 551A, 558, 645, 722, 724, 754, 776. *SCBI* Copenhagen 540–1, 566–7, 613, 707, 713, 792, 817, 835–6, 890.

York m

Hild. 450–1, 451A, 453–5, 463, 465, 468–9, 476, 484A, 488–9, 489A, 491, 491A, 492–3, 496A, 497–9, 502–4, 506–7, 515–24, 556–7, 565–6, 566A, 582–5, 638, 640–4, 646, 646A, 647–8, 664, 679–80, 690–1, 695–701, 701A, 702, 702A, 703, 703A, 704–7, 709, 720, 720A, 721, 723, 725, 739–44, 744A, 745, 745A, 746–7, 749–53, 755–6, 758, 767–73, 773A, 774–5, 788–90, 796, 796A, 797–801, 813, 828, 830–1, 831A, 832–6, 866–7. *SCBI* Copenhagen 521–3, 530, 539, 550–4, 558–61, 564–5, 568, 576–83, 605, 610–12, 619–21, 641–5, 704–5, 708–12, 714–16, 750, 757–61, 764–9, 774, 789–91, 793, 805–16, 818, 830–4, 845–6, 854–9, 872, 891–7, 919–21, 1504.

Lincoln e

Hild. 59, 125, 193, 354A, 356, 827, 1048, 1135, 1443, 1451, 1488, 1496, 1499, 1554, 1556–8, 1607, 1615, 1617, 1649, 1661, 1670, 1676, 1688–9, 1717, 1717A, 1742, 1777–9, 1781, 1822, 1826–7, 1829, 2478, 3210, 3260, 3271, 3304, 3368, 3467, 3469, 3502, 3509, 3527, 3572. *SCBI*

Copenhagen 214, 1081, 1480, 1543, 1545, 1575–6, 1578, 1608, 1675, 1688, 1694–5, 1757, 1780, 1806, 1813, 1834, 1882–3, 1923–4, 1928, 3476, 3482, 3555, 3592, 3911–12.

Lincoln m

Hild. 57, 354, 927, 1022–3, 1228–9, 1235, 1444, 1470, 1473, 1481, 1486, 1489, 1493, 1495, 1502–3, 1518, 1520, 1555, 1558, 1583, 1602, 1614, 1616, 1616A, 1647–8, 1659, 1668, 1671, 1675, 1681, 1691–2, 1719, 1722–3, 1725, 1733, 1738–40, 1742A, 1772, 1780, 1806, 1818–21, 1823–4, 1828, 1865, 2476, 2924, 2929, 2941–2, 2987–8, 2992, 3207–8, 3227–8, 3233–4, 3245, 3252, 3259, 3261, 3270, 3273, 3462, 3475, 3510, 3512, 3519, 3523, 3526, 3526A. *SCBI* Copenhagen 59, 63–4, 414, 975, 1078, 1091, 1272, 1492, 1513–16, 1528–9, 1531–2, 1540–2, 1549–50, 1553–5, 1577, 1579–80, 1607, 1611, 1614, 1630–1, 1642, 1654–9, 1678–9, 1690–3, 1733–6, 1753, 1768–9, 1783, 1805, 1810, 1814–18, 1828–9, 1832– 3, 1866, 1884, 1906–8, 1920–2, 1926–7, 2240?, 3162, 3169–70, 3184, 3499–500, 3508, 3510–11, 3540, 3554, 3593–4, 3657, 3762, 3805, 3808, 3830, 3835–6, 3843, 3847, 3849–50, 3875, 3899, 4220, 4421.

Lincoln l

Hild. 56, 56A, 355, 940, 1242, 1468–9, 1471, 1487, 1497–8, 1504–5, 1519, 1520A, 1521–2, 1541, 1559, 1579–82, 1601, 1603, 1609, 1611–13, 1660, 1662, 1669, 1670A, 1672–4, 1687, 1690, 1721, 1724, 1732, 1748, 1763, 1783, 1796, 1804, 1807–8, 1825, 2383, 2384?, 3209?, 3232, 3241, 3258, 3306, 3323–4, 3345, 3474, 3522, 3535, 3547, 3573. *SCBI* Copenhagen 1481, 1530, 1544, 1551–2, 1556, 1605?, 1633?, 1680–2, 1696, 1752, 1754–6, 1758–67, 1781–2, 1811–12, 1842, 2773?, 2995, 3225, 3475, 3520, 3528, 3536–8, 3541, 3556, 3597, 3801, 3858, 3900, 3949.

Stamford A

Hild. 1026, 1227?, 1238, 1482, 3070, 3231, 3240, 3269, 3272, 3274, 3325, 3342, 3347–9, 3517, 3553. *SCBI* Copenhagen 3185, 3193, 3513?, 3519, 3552, 3557, 3654, 3881.

Stamford B

Hild. 3282, 3326–7. *SCBI* Copenhagen 1106, 3505–7, 3509, 3514, 3516, 3612, 3625.

Northampton A

Hild. 1129, 1144, 1236–7. *SCBI* Copenhagen 1178–9, 1191, 1485.

Northampton B

Hild. 1130, 1130A, 1136, 1230. *SCBI* Copenhagen 1180, 1189–90, 4262–3.

Bedford

Hild. 55, 60, 62, 62A, 220, 1222, 2365, 2479. *SCBI* Copenhagen 62, 65–6, 1186?, 2528.

Norwich A

Hild. 58, 61, 61A, 936, 945, 957, 1046, 2917, 2920, 2938, 2972, 2972A, 2975, 2991, 3395, 3489. *SCBI* Copenhagen 60–1, 997, 1001, 1002?, 1079, 1089, 3158, 3160, 3180, 3713, 3718, 3820–1.

Thetford Ae

Hild. 114, 194?, 928, 1173, 1225, 2065, 2349, 2869, 2927A, 2993, 3446, 3461, 3476, 3484, 3485, 3485A, 3488, 3506, 3525, 3525A, 3549. *SCBI* Copenhagen 58, 120, 3222, 3799, 3832, 3877–8.

Thetford Am

Hild. 211–12, 221, 901, 901A, 941, 947, 956, 1009–11, 1024, 1037, 1047, 1047A, 1223–4, 1226, 2899, 2901, 2928, 3470, 3476A, 3478, 3499–501, 3505, 3507, 3529, 3529A. *SCBI* Copenhagen 57, 243, 245–6, 976, 999, 1070–1, 1117, 1228, 3113, 3140–2, 3156–7, 3166–8, 3214–15, 3223, 3228, 3758, 3788–9, 3809, 3818, 3828, 3848, 3851–2.

Thetford Al

Hild. 218, 221A, 232–3, 929–30, 933–4, 946, 1062–3, 1073, 2878, 2900, 2914–15,

2921–2, 2939, 2949, 2973–4, 2990, 3443, 3468, 3477, 3490, 3524, 3528, 3536. *SCBI* Copenhagen 244, 253–5, 257–61, 270–1, 983–6, 996, 1009, 1074, 1090, 1099–1101, 1270, 3120, 3190, 3213, 3226–7, 3806–7, 3831, 3859.

Thetford B

Hild. 1021, 1044–5, 3486–7, 3491, 3511. *SCBI* Copenhagen 1088, 3819, 3823, 3837.

Thetford C

Hild. 234, 931, 937, 1052, 1072, 1510, 2367?, 2663, 2918, 2925, 2933, 2950–1, 2985–6?, 2996, 3268?, 3373, 3420, 3479, 3498, 3548. *SCBI* Copenhagen 272, 977–82, 1115–16, 1998, 3148, 3159, 3163, 3177, 3191–2, 3217, 3224, 3539, 3732, 3790, 3810–11, 3822, 3876, 3551?

Lewes e

Hild. 1110, 1260. *SCBI* Copenhagen 1330–2.

Lewes l

Hild. 2, 155, 336, 1091, 1091A, 1092, 1111, 1256, 1266, 1279, 1281, 1285, 1307, 1339, 2644. *SCBI* Copenhagen 378, 1164, 1327–9.

London Ae

Hild. 4, 135, 139, 304, 332–3, 1179, 1915, 1925, 1961, 1965, 2005, 2023, 2070–1, 2153, 2225, 2345, 2348, 2366, 2386, 2477, 2540, 2542, 2569, 2570, 2572, 2572A, 2573, 2671, 2681–2, 2692, 2746, 2750–1, 2755, 2762, 2762A, 2767, 2767A, 3068, 3071, 3073, 3084?, 3377, 3389, 3403, 3407, 3407A, 3427–8, 3431, 3431A. *SCBI* Copenhagen 138, 144–5, 202, 375, 1387, 2097, 2238, 2360–2, 2516, 2529, 2612, 2727–9, 2758, 2767, 2887, 2890, 2898, 2934, 2960, 2967, 3302, 3698–9, 3726, 3743–5.

London Am

Hild. 166, 235, 349, 1284, 1364, 1387, 1439A, 1834, 1852, 1916, 2006, 2022, 2068, 2101, 2119, 2125, 2147, 2149, 2151, 2151A, 2161, 2213, 2382, 2538, 2539, 2672, 2702, 2752, 2763–4, 2782, 3048, 3048A, 3080, 3141, 3391, 3400, 3404–5, 3409. *SCBI* Copenhagen 405, 1103–5, 1110, 1325, 1334, 1336, 2150, 2153–4, 2237, 2269, 2285, 2323–4, 2505, 2580, 2680, 2766, 2871, 2957, 2968, 2993, 3092, 3308, 3320, 3703, 3725.

London Al

Hild. 124, 127, 136, 140, 140A, 154?, 154A?, 154B?, 165, 165A, 169, 175, 191–2, 292, 302, 305, 311, 794, 935, 935A, 954, 1005, 1015, 1016, 1016A, 1017?, 1056, 1070, 1137, 1924, 1926, 1928, 1964, 2047, 2048, 2948A, 2100, 2163, 2169, 2172, 2175, 2175A, 2191, 2214–16, 2368, 2385, 2414, 2421, 2438–40, 2442, 2445, 2474, 2481, 2543, 2574, 2578, 2655, 2660, 2670?, 2695, 2703, 2718, 2720, 2728, 2778, 2786, 2791, 2808, 2811, 2868, 2872, 2876, 3058, 3075, 3123, 3148–9, 3385–8, 3398–9, 3401, 3410, 3412, 3415–17, 3426, 3432, 3789. *SCBI* Copenhagen 6, 128–9, 142, 157–8, 170, 213, 1064–7, 1072–3, 1077, 1094, 1109, 1111, 1113, 1269, 1305, 1929, 2042, 2044, 2046, 2049?, 2208, 2232, 2236, 2239, 2339, 2345, 2347, 2384, 2442, 2466, 2530, 2532, 2546, 2579, 2587, 2589, 2613–14, 2616, 2619, 2642–3, 2646–7, 2693–4, 2771, 2881–2, 2888, 2900, 2955–6, 2983, 2986–7, 2997–8, 3003, 3029–30, 3110–12, 3321, 3402–3, 3695–7, 3706, 3711–12, 3714–17, 3724, 3729–30, 3733, 3739–41, 3746.

London B

Hild. 1004, 1085, 1146, 1167–8, 1178, 1835, 1847, 1852A, 2016, 2046, 2069, 2157, 2168, 2179, 2179A, 2190, 2192, 2195, 2272, 2324, 2324A, 2364, 2410, 2436, 2615, 2636–8, 2640, 2640A, 2642–3, 2678, 2685, 2691, 2691A, 2753, 2783, 2816, 3057, 3059, 3137, 3142, 3393, 3396, 3397, 3406, 3406A, 3414, 3418, 3424, 3429, 3430, 3430A. *SCBI* Copenhagen 174?, 1108, 1223, 1227, 1506–8, 2045, 2052, 2118? 2171, 2199, 2200, 2201?, 2235?, 2271?, 2335, 2358?, 2359?, 2363–4, 2444, 2493, 2575–6, 2608–9, 2831?, 2835,

2862, 2865–6, 2892–3, 2896–7, 2959, 2994, 3326, 3395–6, 3401, 3707, 3719?, 3723, 3742.

London Ce

Hild. 2029, 2051, 2121, 2144–5, 2162, 2166, 2186, 2199, 2347, 2420, 2423, 2441, 2443–4, 2576–7, 2639, 2659, 2676–7, 2684, 2689, 2727, 2781A, 2792, 2794, 2819, 2842. *SCBI* Copenhagen 200–1, 2102, 2175, 2181–2, 2270, 2315–18, 2338, 2342, 2353, 2367, 2495, 2520, 2531, 2588, 2617–18, 2769–70, 2772, 2774, 3033, 3161.

London Cm

Hild. 54, 145, 145A, 213, 217, 231, 301, 301A, 303, 309, 348, 1053, 1055, 1057–8, 1060–1, 1066, 1066A, 1069, 1071, 1074, 1147, 1162–3, 1166, 1174–6, 1231, 1231A, 1265, 1265A, 1365, 1462, 1863, 1864, 1909, 1923, 1927?, 1929–31, 1935, 1962–3, 1966, 1968, 1980, 1998, 2000, 2014, 2026–8, 2033, 2102, 2102A, 2103, 2120, 2129, 2132, 2135, 2144A, 2146, 2152, 2158–60, 2160A, 2164, 2164A, 2165, 2171, 2173, 2180A, 2181–2, 2184–5, 2193–4, 2196–8, 2198A, 2223–4, 2273–4, 2276, 2300–1, 2321–3, 2325A, 2327, 2331–2, 2333?, 2333A?, 2346, 2351–2, 2411, 2411A, 2412, 2415, 2415A, 2417–18, 2418A, 2419, 2422, 2422A, 2435, 2437A, 2457, 2496, 2575, 2576A, 2579, 2587, 2641, 2651–3, 2657–8, 2661–2, 2664, 2667–8, 2679–80, 2683, 2683A, 2686, 2688, 2688A, 2690, 2717, 2722, 2725–6, 2756–8, 2760, 2765, 2768, 2777, 2779, 2779A, 2780–1, 2784, 2784A, 2785, 2787–90, 2793, 2793A, 2809, 2812, 2818, 2820, 2871, 2873–4, 2916A, 2923, 2989, 2995. *SCBI* Copenhagen 141, 146?, 147?, 171, 187, 247, 251, 269, 394, 1112, 1192–3, 1205, 1309, 1335, 1503, 2047, 2100, 2119, 2139–40, 2151–2, 2174?, 2178?, 2179?, 2272, 2295, 2300–2, 2305, 2307, 2336–7, 2340–1, 2343–4, 2349, 2352, 2365–6, 2385, 2386–7, 2389–91, 2443, 2464–5, 2467–8, 2489–92, 2494, 2498, 2503–4, 2515, 2517–19, 2521, 2533, 2577–8, 2581–6, 2610–11, 2615, 2790, 2864, 2870, 2883–5, 2889, 2891, 2895, 2935–7, 2961?, 2962–3, 2964?, 2965, 2984–5, 2990–1, 2996, 2999, 3000–2, 3004, 3026–7, 3031, 3065, 3090, 3100, 3100A, 3307, 3315.

London Cl

Hild. 65. 139A, 190, 216, 219, 222, 335, 925–6, 932, 1012–13, 1020, 1025, 1029, 1030, 1040–3, 1054, 1059, 1064, 1067–8, 1094, 1126, 1134, 1145, 1154, 1158–61, 1170–2, 1177, 1249, 1249A, 1277, 1908, 1932, 1967, 1969, 1997, 2015, 2030, 2031, 2122, 2129A, 2130, 2132–3, 2133A, 2134, 2136, 2167, 2170, 2174, 2176–8, 2183, 2218–21, 2221A, 2222, 2224, 2226, 2235, 2330, 2350, 2416, 2433, 2480, 2616, 2656, 2665–6, 2669, 2687, 2719, 2721, 2759, 2810, 2813–14, 2817, 2841, 2875, 2877, 2883–4, 2913, 2916, 2919, 3074, 3083, 3419, 3421–2. *SCBI* Copenhagen 55, 248–50, 256, 348, 376–7, 987, 1080, 1087, 1095, 1098, 1102, 1107, 1114, 1118, 1141, 1153, 1203–4, 1206, 1212, 1221, 1224–6, 1266, 1271, 1281, 1283, 1288, 1326, 1505, 1971, 2018–20, 2043, 2048, 2050–1, 2054, 2096, 2098–9, 2101, 2169–70, 2176?, 2177, 2180, 2183–4, 2303, 2308, 2346, 2348, 2350–1, 2388, 2402, 2645, 2768, 2791, 2855, 2876–7, 2880, 2894, 2907–8, 2975, 2988–9, 2992, 3005–6, 3032, 3116–19, 3121, 3734–6.

Anomalous

Hild. 21, 63–4, 64A, 205, 1253, 1286, 1450, 1494, 1646, 2334, 2343–4, 2413, 2522, 2632, 2723–4, 2729, 3117, 3239, 3402, 3408, 3425, 3581, 3587, 3903. *SCBI* Copenhagen 19, 291, 951, 1539, 1632, 1925, 2325, 2863, 2938–9, 3025, 3369–70, 3378, 3440, 3515, 3549–50, 3652–3, 3750, 3913.

Note. Scandinavian imitations have been omitted so far as possible, even where struck from a transported English obverse or reverse die.

14 Harold I and Harthacnut's *Jewel Cross* type reconsidered

Tuukka Talvio

One of Michael Dolley's earlier contributions to Anglo-Saxon numismatics was his paper 'The "Jewel Cross" coinage of Ælfgifu-Emma, Harthacnut, and Harold I', which was read at the numismatic congress in Paris in 1953.[1] He intended to return to the problems of the *Jewel Cross* type, but other work always occupied his time. In 1977 he suggested to me that I should begin to study the coinages of Harold I and Harthacnut, and a part of that work is presented here. Some of my conclusions differ from those of Dolley, but it will be obvious to all who know the subject how much I am indebted to him, both to his published work and to his personal encouragement.

Although *Jewel Cross* was one of the shorter-lived of the late Anglo-Saxon coin types, it is also one of the most interesting, for it offers a rare opportunity to catch a glimpse of the political developments between Cnut's death in the autumn of 1035 and Harold's acquisition of sole power early in 1037. The historical significance of the coins of that period has long been recognized. It was first noted by H. A. Parsons in 1915, discussed again by Dolley in 1953, and it has recently been commented on by David Hill in his *Atlas of Anglo-Saxon England*.[2] Their attention has been mainly focused on the geographical distribution of Harthacnut's mints. This paper seeks to review the issue generally by examining the internal chronology of the type and its pattern of die-production.

Acknowledgments This study has come about in connection with a planned *Sylloge* publication of the coins of Harold I and Harthacnut in the Stockholm collection. My thanks are due to the authorities of the Royal Coin Cabinet, which has made the material available to me, and to the Sven Svensson Foundation which has given me two generous grants for working in Stockholm. As an E. S. G. Robinson visiting scholar, and enjoying the hospitality of Wolfson College as a C. M. Kraay visitor, I had in 1982 the opportunity to spend a month in Oxford, where Dr Michael Metcalf and his staff gave me genial working conditions in the Heberden Coin Room. In preparing the final typescript I have been helped in many ways by Mark Blackburn, whose efficiency and kind criticism have been invaluable to me.

1. *Congrès International de Numismatique, Paris, 6–11 juillet 1953* (2 vols., Paris, 1953 and 1957), II, 324–34. Hereafter reference is made to the revised version in *BNJ* 27 (1952–4), 266–75.
2. D. Hill, *An Atlas of Anglo-Saxon England* (1981), 95.

In the first edition of his *Anglosachsiska mynt i Svenska Kongliga Myntkabinettet – Monnaies anglosaxonnes du cabinet royal de Stockholm* (1846),[3] Bror Emil Hildebrand published 237 coins with the name of Harold I and 31 with the name of Harthacnut. His classification of the coins of both rulers into two main types is still valid, but the following names are now generally used in English publications:[4]

Harold I
Hildebrand A (Brooke[5] 1: *BMC* i) = *Jewel Cross*
Hildebrand B (Brooke 2: *BMC* v, vi) = *Fleur-de-Lys*

Harthacnut
Hildebrand A (Brooke 1: *BMC* i, cf. Cnut xx) = *Jewel Cross*
Hildebrand B (Brooke 2: *BMC* ii, cf. Cnut xvii) = *Arm-and-Sceptre*

Hildebrand also referred to several other types, especially with the name of Harthacnut, which he considered 'undoubtedly' Danish, although he did not deny that a few unusual pieces may also have been struck by English mints.[6] Without apparently changing this opinion he formulated it more cautiously in the second (1881) edition of the work, where besides the 'completely normal English types' (A and B) he listed three other types for Harold (C-E) and no less than seven for Harthacnut (C-I). With the exception of Harthacnut's type I, which is a mule between *Arm-and-Sceptre* and Edward the Confessor's first or *Pacx* type, these additional types are now all regarded as Scandinavian.[7] The main difference in the second edition is that it contains almost five times as much material for these kings as the first: 1,050 coins with Harold's name and 216 coins with Harthacnut's. This is due to the very large hoard found in 1880 at Äspinge in Hurva parish, Scania.[8]

In England, the second volume of the *Catalogue of English Coins in the British Museum, Anglo-Saxon Series*, was published in 1893 by C. F. Keary and H. A. Grueber. Six main types are listed for Harold I and nine for Harthacnut, all of which the authors considered English;[9] six of the latter we would now regard as Danish. However, all the 115 coins of Harold and 25 of Harthacnut then in the collection belong in fact to English types, with the exception of a coin of Harthacnut from Lund in Scania wrongly attributed to Harold and London.[10]

The first numismatist to devote a special study to the period was Harry Alexander Parsons who published a paper on the coins of Harthacnut in the 1915 volume of *BNJ*.[11] A similar treatise on the coins of Harold I appeared in *BNJ* for 1919–

3. The 2nd edn (Stockholm, 1881) has the English parallel title *Anglosaxon Coins in the Royal Swedish Cabinet of Medals at Stockholm*.
4. See G. van der Meer, 'Some corrections to and comments on B. E. Hildebrand's catalogue of the Anglo-Saxon coins in the Swedish Royal Coin Cabinet', *AS Coins*, 169–87, at 196.
5. G. C. Brooke, *English Coins* (3rd edn, 1950), 69.
6. Hildebrand, *op. cit.*, (1846), 248.
7. Van der Meer, *op. cit.*, 184–5.
8. The hoard is said to have included 1,049 coins of Harold I and 173 of Harthacnut. See *SCBI 4*, Copenhagen i, p. 37.
9. *BMC* pp. xcii, 304–6, and 321–4.
10. *BMC* Harold 64. See also p. 287 below.
11. H. A. Parsons, 'The Anglo-Saxon coins of Harthacnut', *BNJ 11* (1915), 21–55.

20.[12] Both papers consist of a discussion of the types and their chronology, followed by a listing of the coins according to their legends. Parsons came to the same conclusion as Hildebrand – although expressed more categorically – that the number of main English types of each ruler should be reduced to two.

In dating the coin types Parsons was less successful, as was demonstrated by Dolley in 1953. The arguments used by Dolley did not essentially differ from those of Parsons, but he presented a more critical approach tempered by his work with the Scandinavian hoard material. In his postscript to the paper he mentioned a forthcoming study by Peter Seaby, in which the chronology was to be further modified. This paper, 'The sequence of Anglo-Saxon coin types, 1030–1050', was published in *BNJ* for 1955–7.[13]

The chronology suggested by Dolley and Seaby can be summarized as follows:[14]

November 1035-Spring 1036. *Jewel Cross* coins with the name 'Cnut' and (left-facing busts) with the name of Harthacnut (figs. 14.2:4–6).
Spring 1036–Autumn 1037. *Jewel Cross* coins with the name of Harold and (right-facing busts) with the name of Harthacnut (figs. 14.1:1–3; 14.2:7–10; 14.3:11–13).
Autumn 1037-March 1040. *Fleur-de-Lys* coins of Harold.
March 1040-June 1040. *Fleur-de-Lys* coins of Harthacnut.
June 1040-June 1042. *Arm-and-Sceptre* coins of Harthacnut (including those with the name 'Cnut').

In 1968 Dolley revised his chronology of the coins of Cnut, allowing *Short Cross* to continue beyond Michaelmas (25 September) 1035, but without committing himself as to how soon after Cnut's death the *Jewel Cross* type was introduced.[15]

A few comments are here necessary. The possibility of a slightly later date for the introduction of *Jewel Cross* would accord well with the existence of a few *Short Cross* coins in the name of Harold. These can hardly represent a substantial issue, and the same is true of the *Fleur-de-Lys* coins with Harthacnut's name. The *Fleur-de-Lys* type was thus practically confined to Harold's sole reign.

A post-1035 dating for the *Jewel Cross* type is, of course, only possible if the coins with Cnut's name can be shown to be posthumous. It was Dolley who first noted that these coins appear to be associated with the coins of Harthacnut,[16] and the analysis presented below agrees with his theory. We know for certain that the *Arm-and-Sceptre* coins of 'Cnut' belong to Harthacnut's sole reign, and there seems to be no reason why he should not have used Cnut as a short form of his name earlier.

12. *Idem*, 'The coins of Harold I', *BNJ 15* (1919–20), 1–48.
13. *BNJ 28* (1955–7), 111–46.
14. Cf. J. J. North, *English Hammered Coinage*, I (2nd edn, 1980), 132–3.
15. M. Dolley, 'A further link in the Scandinavian imitative series', *Fornvännen* 1968, 118–19, at 117 n.5. This revised chronology has not been acknowledged in all quarters.
16. M. Dolley, 'The "Jewel Cross" coinage of Ælfgifu-Emma, Harthacnut and Harold I', 269–70.

The material

There are over 3,000 coins of Harold I and Harthacnut today in public collections. As can be seen from table 14.1, the museums of Stockholm, Copenhagen, and London are incomparably the richest. The number of coins in private collections and in public collections not mentioned in the table can be assumed to be small.[17]

The *Jewel Cross* coins included in the material presented in table 14.1 are subdivided in table 14.2. Detailed information of the material in the museums of the Soviet Union was not available.

The stylistic analysis undertaken in the present study is based on the Stockholm material, of which the author has a photographic record, and on the material published in volumes 1–30 of the *Sylloge of Coins of the British Isles* (including the Copenhagen collection). The two large Scandinavian collections constitute 82 per cent of the material in table 14.2.

As regards the representativeness of the material, it can be noted that of the 105 different die-combinations of *Jewel Cross* type published in H. R. Mossop's corpus of the Lincoln coins, no less than 95 (90.5 per cent) can be found in the Stockholm and Copenhagen collections alone.[18] There is reason to believe that the situation concerning the other mints is not essentially different.[19]

Types, varieties, and styles

One of the typical features of the late Anglo-Saxon monetary system was the successive recoinages. The coins normally had the royal bust – a representation of the king, not an attempt at true portraiture[20] – on the obverse, and on the reverse there was an ornamental motif (most often in the form of a cross), and both were different in sequential types. When a new type was issued, the engravers apparently were provided with officially approved models in order to ensure a coinage of reasonably homogeneous appearance, but for different reasons the degree of uniformity could vary. The variation could be intentional, or it could simply result from the idiosyncrasies of the individuals involved with the production of the dies.

In this paper, the word 'variety' is used to denote such differences within a coin type which seem intentional. The *Jewel Cross* coins of Harold can thus be divided

17. The figures for the Soviet Union in table 14.1 are based on find statistics published in V. M. Potin, *Drevnjaja Rus' i evropejskie gosudarstva v X-XIII vv.* (Leningrad, 1968), 110; the number of coins in Russian and Baltic museums is, however, likely to be higher. As regards private collections it can be noted that less than 40 coins of Harold I and Harthacnut were offered for sale in *NCirc* during the 12 years 1971–82.
18. H. R. Mossop, *The Lincoln Mint c.890–1279* (1970), pls. LVII-X, LXIII.
19. Cf. M. A. S. Blackburn and D. M. Metcalf, 'Five-finger exercises on the List hoard', in *Viking-Age Coinage in the Northern Lands*, ed. Blackburn and Metcalf (BAR Internat. Ser. 122; 1981), II, 495–524, at 508.
20. Although this may seem self-evident, it is not exceptional to see the 'determined chin' etc. of a tenth-century coin portrait commented on in a popular history book.

Table 14.1. Coins of Harold I and Harthacnut in public collections

	1	2	3	4	5	6	7	8	Total
Jewel Cross	110	82	679	342	17	46	12	6	1,294
Fleur-de-Lys	175	126	700	307	25	35	20	13	1,401
Arm-and-Sceptre	50	50	292	134	15	17	3	5	566
	335	258	1,671	783	57	98	35	24	3,261

Key to columns:
1. London, British Museum
2. Other collections in England, as published in *SCBI 1–29*
3. Stockholm, Royal Cabinet
4. Copenhagen, Royal Collection (*SCBI 18*)
5. Other collections in Scandinavia: Oslo, University Cabinet; Bergen, Historical Museum; Helsinki, National Museum (*SCBI 25*)
6. Collections in Soviet Union (see n.17 above)
7. Berlin, DDR State Museum
8. Collections in U.S.A., as published in *SCBI 16* and *30*

Table 14.2. *Jewel Cross* coins in public collections

	1	2	3	4	5	7	8	Total
Harthacnut								
right-facing	14	6	74	28	1	–	1	124
left-facing	2	1	15	10	–	–	–	28
'Cnut'	2	1	18	10	–	–	–	31
Harold	92	74	572	294	16	12	5	1,065
	110	82	679	342	17	12	6	1,248

Key to columns: as for table 14.1 (material in Soviet Union not included)

into two varieties on the basis of the form of the diadem. Other divisions could perhaps be made on other criteria, but the form of the diadem has chronological significance: as will be shown below, the coins with a simpler type of diadem are later. The new type may have been initiated by an individual engraver, but it was also adopted by his colleagues, and for this reason it can be called a variety rather than a style.

'Style' is used here to mean a complex of features which distinguish the products of one die-cutter or workshop from those of others. While the classification of varieties must be based on unambiguous definitions, a degree of subjectivity can be difficult to avoid when discussing the styles. After all, the engravers and their assistants were obliged to copy a given model as faithfully as possible, and even if they failed to do so, the picture may be far from clear. Sometimes the differences between various ateliers were very notable (for example in the *Last Small Cross* type of Æthelred II), but in some types (as in Æthelred's *Crux*) local styles have been identified only recently.[21] In so far as can be seen, there were few engravers at work in the *Jewel Cross* type, and their dies can in most cases be identified by letter forms. A few other characteristics will also be listed, and these together with the epigraphic criteria make it possible to divide the coins into stylistic groups, leaving aside only a small number of coins of anomalous style.

THE MAIN CHARACTERISTICS OF THE JEWEL CROSS TYPE

The name 'Jewel Cross' is obviously based on the reverse motif, which consists of four ovals in the form of a cross. Hildebrand saw them as 'shields',[22] Brooke as 'jewels',[23] and the latter appellation has since then been generally adopted. There is no factual evidence for this identification, and as an easily memorized name for an ornamental pattern it does not necessarily need further justification. It can be noted, however, that in an apparently early variety (Harthacnut's coins with right-facing bust, variety R below; fig. 14.1:1) the 'jewels' are usually more or less circular, and a reverse design containing similar elements had been used in Cnut's *Pointed Helmet* type. The reverses of late Anglo-Saxon coin types often repeat details of the obverse, and on the obverse of *Pointed Helmet* there is a round brooch or jewel which resembles the circles on the reverse.

The obverse of the *Jewel Cross* type has a diademed profile bust without sceptre. On most coins the diadem has a crescent on the forehead, representing a jewel seen in profile, and there are even a few coins with the jewel shown as a full circle enclosing a pellet.[24] Similar diadems are found on late Roman coins, and it is noteworthy that the upturned head on variety R also has late Roman prototypes.[25]

In the following discussion of the varieties, the division of the coins with left-facing busts into two groups, L1 and L2, is mainly based on the form of the diadem, which can be depicted either with two lines or one. The reverses of all the three varieties – R, L1, L2 – are similar, with the exception of what has been said above of variety R.

Variety R (right-facing, ornamental diadem)

This variety represents all the coins with right-facing busts and is identical with Hildebrand Harthacnut *Aa*. All other *Jewel Cross* coins, whether in the name of Harthacnut, 'Cnut', or Harold, have left-facing busts. Characteristic features of the obverse of this variety are a slightly upturned face – as if the king were looking for divine guidance – and a diadem formed of two bands, normally with a row of pellets between them or coinciding with the upper band. The ornamented strip coming down from the left shoulder always overlaps the right-hand one, and on the latter the uppermost pellet is larger than the others. The stylistical unity is such that there is no doubt about all or practically all the dies having been produced by one atelier, and it

21. M. Blackburn, 'A York die-cutting centre in the Crux issue of Æthelræd II', *NCirc* (1982), 336–8.
22. Hildebrand, *op. cit.*, 69.
23. Brooke, *op. cit.*, 69.
24. E.g. Hild. 955 and *SCBI 15*, 561 (same dies).
25. For the influence of Roman coins on Anglo-Saxon coin types see J. P. C. Kent, 'From Roman Britain to Saxon

Fig. 14.1 1–3 Variety R. Harthacnut, Winchester style (1,2); Harthacnut, anomalous style (3) (scale × 1½).

is even possible to attribute to this workshop two coins of variety L1 (with left-facing busts) of Winchester and Exeter which share the same obverse die.[26] As we shall see, the most likely location for this workshop is Winchester.

The workmanship is generally coarse, but on some of the obverses the details are sharper than on others and, interestingly, the 'jewels' on the reverse of these coins are markedly elongated in contrast to the round ones found on many of the coins. The variation in the form of the 'jewels' is not, however, capable of straightforward classification: regardless of the mint and of whether the coin is heavy or light, round and oval as well as intermediate forms are found. Apparently this detail was not stabilized during the short duration of the issue. It can be noted that the characteristic round 'jewels' are usual at Canterbury and Oxford but not at Winchester; there is insufficient material from other mints for comparison.

As can be seen from table 14.2, this variety constitutes 10 per cent of the surviving *Jewel Cross* coins. Parsons was the first to note that among its mints, those situated to the south of the Thames strongly predominate,[27] a question which is discussed in more detail below.

Variety L1 (left-facing, ornamental diadem)

Most of the coins have Harold's name, but the names of Harthacnut and 'Cnut' are also found. Except for the bust being left-facing, there is a general similarity with the preceding variety. The diadem is formed of two bands, often with a row of pellets between them or coinciding with the upper band.

Three styles can be discerned in this variety. One of them is clearly local and two have a national distribution. (We have already also mentioned one die with a left-

England', *AS Coins*, 1–17.

26. Hild. 38 (Exeter) and 206 (Winchester). For another Exeter-Winchester obverse link see *SCBI 18*, 626 and 724.

27. Parsons, 'Coins of Harthacnut', 42–3.

Fig. 14.2 4–10 Variety L1. Harthacnut, 'National A' style (4,5); 'Cnut', 'National A' style (6); Harold, 'National A' style (7,8); Harold, 'National B' style (9); Harold, Lincoln style (10) (scale × $1\frac{1}{2}$).

facing bust which is of the Winchester style of variety R.) Of the two national styles the more common, here called 'National A' (figs. 14.2:4–8), has the following distinctive features:

- letter A without bar
- hair on forehead marked with vertical hatching
- neatly formed head with close-fitting diadem
- with name of Harold, Harthacnut, or 'Cnut'

Fig. 14.3 11–13 Variety L2. Harold, 'National A' style (11); Harold, 'National B' style (12); Harold, Lincoln style (13) (scale × $1\frac{1}{2}$).

The drapery of variety L1 has usually two overlapping ornamental strips, but on a number of coins of 'National A' style only one such strip is shown. This type of drapery is in most cases found together with a diadem without pellets. The same kind of drapery is typical for coins of 'National A' style in variety L2 (fig. 14.3:11), which can be shown to be later than variety L1. Thus the simplified drapery must also be later than the type with two strips.

'National B' style can be particularized as follows:

- letter A normally with bar
- hair marked with horizontal hatching
- the head tends to have drooping chin; diadem formed of long lines extending outside the contours of the head
- with name of Harold only

The reverse dies of the two styles cannot be distinguished with certainty if the letter A is not included in the legend, and obverse and reverse dies of different styles – including the Lincoln style described below – are frequently found combined on the same coin. 'National A' can be seen as a continuation of the uniform style of the bulk of the coins of Cnut's last type, *Short Cross*, but the engraver responsible for 'National B' dies likewise seems to have begun his career under Cnut.[28]

The third style is mainly found in Lincoln and is so easily recognizable that instead of a verbal definition, reference to fig. 14.2:10 should be sufficient. The style is recognizable on both obverse and reverse. A few coins of this style are known from Derby, Nottingham, Stamford, and London, and in variety L2 (fig. 14.3:13) even from some other mints.

28. For a *Short Cross* coin of 'National B' style see e.g. *SCBI 9*, 727.

Variety L2 (left-facing, simple diadem)

This variety has a left-facing bust with a diadem formed of one band. All coins have Harold's name. The same three styles occur as in variety L1, and we can suppose that the same engravers were at work. What has been said above of the epigraphical criteria and the bust of styles 'National A' and 'National B' is also relevant here, with the following modifications concerning 'National A': the diadem curves over the head without any ornament on the forehead (as in the *Short Cross* type of Cnut), and only one ornamented strip is normally shown on the bosom. In coins of the Lincoln style the difference between varieties L1 (fig. 14.2:10) and L2 (fig. 14.3:13) is also visible, although less clearly. Besides Lincoln, this style is now found sporadically in coins from Cambridge, Northampton, Thetford, and York.

THE MINTS

Jewel Cross coins are known from nearly 60 mints. Table 14.3 shows the distribution of the different varieties and styles between the mints, and in order to carry on the discussion begun by Parsons and Dolley the mints have been divided into three groups according to their location in relation to the Thames. The figures give the numbers of determinable obverse dies in the Stockholm and Copenhagen collections; in the few cases where the picture has been completed with material from other collections the symbol + has been used.

Reading table 14.3 from left to right, we first note the well-known fact that Harthacnut's coinage was mainly struck by the mints to the south of and on the Thames. Not only is the number of northern mints striking for him small, but their coins are rare – with the exception of Gloucester, a mint which seems to have sided with Harthacnut's party. The single coin known from Lincoln (fig. 14.1:3) has the same obverse as one of the two Stamford coins, and this obverse is also known with a reverse reading +LEOFRIC ON DENM.[29] The identity of this presumably northern mint cannot at present be solved. The obverse in question is of peculiar style, but it is in fact quite carefully executed. It is very possibly the work of one of Harold's engravers, who was not used to producing right-facing busts. The York coin published by Hildebrand appears to belong to Hertford, but there is in the British Museum a coin of the right-facing variety by the York moneyer Wither(w)ine.[30]

Harthacnut's coins with left-facing busts are totally lacking in the north, and they are distinctly rare even in the south. The same is true of the coins with Cnut's name, of which one is known, however, from Cambridge.[31] Interestingly, London is the

29. Hild. 92 (= Mossop, *op. cit.*, pl. LXIII, 23) and 175; Stockholm, Royal Coin Cabinet, Inv. 16181/1045. The Lincoln coin has been suspected of being an imitation (M. Blackburn, C. Colyer, and M. Dolley, *Early Medieval Coins from Lincoln and its Shire c.770–1100* (1983), 23) but as such it would be no less difficult to explain.

30. Hild. 42. The BM coin was acquired from the Montagu sale (16 November 1897, lot 40). I am indebted to Miss Marion Archibald, who has kindly sent me a photograph of it.

31. *Fitzwilliam Museum, Cambridge. The Annual Reports of the Syndicate and of the Friends of the Fitzwilliam*, 1978, 20 and pl. IV, 1; S. Keynes and M.

main mint for the left-facing coins of Harthacnut and Cnut – a situation contrary to that of the right-facing variety, in which London coins account for less than 5 per cent of the obverses known.

When we move to the coins with Harold's name, we find another remarkable feature: while variety L2 was struck in the whole of England, coins of variety L1 are practically only known from mints to the north of and on the Thames. There are a few exceptions, a coin of Warminster and another of Hastings belonging to variety L1. The latter is die-linked with London[32] and may thus have been struck by a London moneyer moving south after Harold's acquisition of sole power. It must also be noted that one of the unlocated mints, 'Landcaster', is represented in variety L1.

There can hardly be any doubt that varieties R and L1 were parallel issues. Coins of both varieties were struck for Harthacnut in southern England, while Harold struck variety L1 in the north. London and three other mints on the Thames worked for both rulers, and a few northern mints occasionally struck coins in the name of Harthacnut. Coins with Cnut's name side regionally with those of Harthacnut of the same variety, L1. What is interesting is the way in which one London workshop ('National A') supplied southern mints with dies bearing the name Harthacnut/ Cnut, while at the same time supplying northern mints with dies in Harold's name. The division of minting at this period thus appears to be the result of a formal agreement recognized on both sides rather than *de facto* control of different parts of the country.

The dating of variety L2 also seems clear: against the background of Harold's growing power, a variety which was struck by all mints must be later than one which is not found on the southern side of the Thames. The somewhat simplified type of the obverse is consistent with a later date, especially in view of the increase in the die-cutters' work.

During the first phase of the issue, Winchester produced the larger proportion of Harthacnut's dies, but the 'National A' workshop also supplied dies with the name of Harthacnut or 'Cnut' to a number of mints on or south of the Thames, including Winchester. When the Winchester die-cutting centre closed at the end of variety L1, the 'National A' workshop became virtually the sole supplier of dies to mints in the south. The style is prominent at London and it also occurs extensively at mints north of the Thames. The attribution of the 'National A' style to a workshop in London seems certain. In variety L1, 'National A' and 'National B' styles were of comparable importance (116:103 dies, from table 14.3), but in variety L2 the relative output of 'National B' declined (164:70 dies). 'National B' is best represented in the north, but it is also common at London. There is no major mint to which it was the dominant or exclusive supplier in both varieties, and the location of the workshop must be left open for the present. However, it can hardly have been situated south of the Thames and it is possible that as in the *Quatrefoil* issue there were two workshops operating concurrently in London.

Blackburn, *Anglo-Saxon Coins* (1985), 40, no. 81.

32. Hild. 274 (Hastings) and 698 (London).

Table 14.3. The mints of *Jewel Cross*
(Numbers of obverse dies in the Stockholm and Copenhagen collections)

	Harthacnut		'Cnut'	Harold I					
	R	LlA	LlA	LlA	LlB	LlL	L2A	L2B	L2L
South of Thames									
Axbridge	2	–	–	–	–	–	–	–	–
Bath	1	1	–	–	–	–	3	–	–
Bridport	1	–	–	–	–	–	–	–	–
Bristol	+	–	1	–	–	–	5	1	–
Bruton	1	–	–	–	–	–	–	–	–
Canterbury	4	–	–	–	–	–	11	3	–
Chichester	2	–	–	–	–	–	2	–	–
Crewkerne	–	–	–	–	–	–	1	–	–
Cricklade	1	–	–	–	–	–	1	–	–
Dorchester	2	–	–	–	–	–	2	–	–
Dover	2	2	2	–	–	–	7	1	–
Exeter	4	2	1	–	–	–	8	2	–
Guildford	1	–	–	–	–	–	–	–	–
Hastings	1	–	–	1	–	–	3	–	–
Ilchester	3	–	–	–	–	–	1	–	–
Langport	1	–	–	–	–	–	2	–	–
Lewes	2	1	–	–	–	–	3	–	–
Lydford	–	–	+	–	–	–	1	–	–
Malmesbury	1	–	–	–	–	–	1	1	–
Rochester	2	–	–	–	–	–	1	–	–
Romney	2	–	–	–	–	–	1	–	–
Salisbury	2	–	1	–	–	–	4	–	–
Shaftesbury	1	–	–	–	–	–	1	–	–
Steyning	1	–	–	–	–	–	–	–	–
Taunton	+	–	–	–	–	–	–	–	–
Totnes	–	–	1	–	–	–	–	–	–
Warminster	–	–	–	–	1	–	–	1	–
Watchet	1	–	–	–	–	–	1	–	–
Wilton	–	–	–	–	–	–	2	–	–
Winchester	9	2	–	–	–	–	14	1	–
	49	8	7	1	1	–	75	10	–
On the Thames									
London	3	8	6	36	22	1	33	16	–
Oxford	5	–	–	–	2	–	3	1	–
Southwark	2	–	1	2	1	–	3	1	–
Wallingford	–	1	2	–	–	–	2	–	–
	10	9	9	38	25	1	41	18	–

Table 14.3. continued

	Harthacnut		'Cnut'	Harold I					
	R	L1A	L1A	L1A	L1B	L1L	L2A	L2B	L2L
North of Thames									
Bedford	–	–	–	–	1	–	1	–	–
Buckingham	–	–	–	1	–	–	–	–	–
Cambridge	–	–	+	–	2	–	–	1	1
Chester	–	–	–	3	6	–	5	3	–
Colchester	–	–	–	1	2	–	–	–	–
Derby	–	–	–	1	4	2	1	–	1
Gloucester	6	–	–	–	–	–	1	–	–
Hereford	–	–	–	–	7	–	–	–	–
Hertford	1	–	–	–	–	–	–	–	–
Huntingdon	–	–	–	–	1	–	–	–	–
Ipswich	–	–	–	2	–	–	1	1	–
Leicester	–	–	–	2	–	–	–	–	–
Lincoln	1[a]	–	–	6	20	14	13	12	10
Maldon	–	–	–	1	–	–	–	–	–
Northampton	–	–	–	2	–	–	1	–	–
Norwich	–	–	–	1	9	–	–	–	–
Nottingham	–	–	–	1	–	1	1	–	1
Shrewsbury	–	–	–	–	4	–	1	1	–
Stamford	2[a]	–	–	8	6	1	4	11	–
Thetford	–	–	–	4	3	1	2	–	1
Warwick	2	–	–	1	–	–	2	–	–
Worcester	–	–	–	5	–	–	2	–	–
York	+	–	–	4	12	1	13	13	1
	13	–	1	43	77	20	48	42	15
Uncertain									
'DENM'	1[a]	–	–	–	–	–	–	–	–
'GOÐAB'	–	–	–	–	–	–	–	2	–
'LANDC'	–	–	–	1	–	–	2	–	–
Total	73	17	17	83	103	21	166	72	15

[a] The same obverse die, of irregular style, was used to strike the unique coins of Lincoln and 'DENM' and one of the two Stamford coins.

THE WEIGHTS

In a recent paper, Michael Metcalf writes: 'The coins of Harthacnut, type Aa (the variety with right-facing bust), are nearly all heavy and on a closely-controlled weight-standard . . ., presenting a sharp contrast with Harold's coins, which range over several weight-standards.'[33] Without aiming at a detailed metrology of the *Jewel Cross* type, this section attempts to clarify at least in some degree the picture presented by Dr Metcalf.

We may first note that the differences between the coins of Harthacnut of both varieties and of 'Cnut' are small. The material in Stockholm and Copenhagen gives the following average weights (the numbers of specimens in brackets):

	All mints	Winchester	London
Harthacnut, R	1.10g (84)	1.11g (14)	1.08g (8)
Harthacnut, L1	1.08g (17)	1.12g (2)	1.09g (10)
'Cnut', L1	1.09g (21)	– (–)	1.09g (11)

The Winchester coins are generally heavier than those of London, and a similar situation has been observed in other types.[34] The lower average weights of variety L1 can thus at least partially be explained by the fact that more than half of the coins were struck at London.

Harold's coins are less rare than those of Harthacnut/Cnut, and the following figures are based on the Copenhagen material only. We may note, however, that the average weight of the 159 determinable whole coins in Copenhagen is the same – 1.07g – as that of the 946 coins studied by Bertil Petersson.[35]

When divided into two varieties, L1 and L2, the coins show different average weights:

	All mints	Winchester	London
Harold I, L1	1.08g (143)	– (–)	1.08g (35)
Harold I, L2	1.05g (116)	1.11g (5)	1.01g (28)[36]

It can be seen that Winchester maintained its own high weight standard (1.11–1.12g) throughout the issue.[37] At London, coins of variety L1 in Harold's name have the same average weights (1.08–1.09g) as those with the names of Harthacnut or 'Cnut', but later during variety L2 the standard declined, resulting in an average weight of 1.01g. The same pattern is observed when all the mints are taken together (the average weights decline from 1.08–1.09g to 1.05g), although differences in contemporary standards can be observed from mint to mint. Thus York coins are heavier than the national average (1.10g declining to 1.08g), while those of Lincoln and Stamford are lighter (1.05g declining to 0.98g at Lincoln, and 1.07g declining to 1.00g at Stamford).

While average weights cannot be used to determine individual standards, of which there may have been several in succession, these figures suggest that *Jewel Cross* conforms to the pattern of previous issues in which, although contemporary

33. D. M. Metcalf, 'Continuity and change in English monetary history c.973–1086', pt. 2, *BNJ 51* (1981), 52–90, at 61.
34. H. B. A. Petersson, *Anglo-Saxon Currency* (Lund, 1969), 244–7.
35. *Ibid.*, 219.
36. One exceptionally light (0.59g) London coin has been excluded from the material.
37. That the high average weight of L2 coins of Winchester in the Copenhagen collection is not accidental is shown by the 21 specimens in Stockholm, which have an average weight of 1.12g.

standards often differed from mint to mint, at most mints there were one or more reductions during the type.[38] Winchester and other mints in the heart of Wessex often struck to a heavier standard which they maintained throughout the issue. This probably explains the slightly heavier average weight of variety R (1.10g) compared with L1 (1.09–1.08g), which it has been suggested above was a parallel issue. At London where both varieties were struck, their average weights were virtually the same (1.08g and 1.08–1.09g). Thus the coin weights support the conclusions of the stylistic analysis that varieties R and L1 belong together and L2 follows after them.

THE INTRODUCTION AND DURATION OF THE TYPE

As noted above, Dolley in his later writings considered that the currency of *Short Cross* continued beyond Cnut's death (12 November 1035), though how much longer is a question which he left open. There is in Stockholm a *Short Cross* penny with Harold's name, struck in Bristol;[39] another from London in the British Museum may be imitative.[40] If this is all that survives from the intermediate coinage before *Jewel Cross*, the period cannot have been long. It is probable, however, that in the political hiatus of the months following Cnut's death the mints would have continued to issue coins in Cnut's name in anticipation of an impending recoinage. After the 970s there is no certain case of an Anglo-Saxon king continuing the coin type of his predecessor for more than a short transitory period.

In this situation, both contendants naturally would have had a strong political motivation for having their own names placed on the coinage. Yet the numismatic analysis suggests that there was unity in the issue from its start and that it was the result of an agreement between the two parties – it would have been extremely difficult for either party to implement a recoinage in only a part of the country. That there was an agreement is further suggested by the way in which a London atelier ('National A') supplied dies with the name of Harthacnut to southern mints, with the name of Harold to northern mints, and with either name to the border mints on the Thames. This agreement concerning the recoinage was probably made at the *witan* of Oxford or some other central meeting early in 1036.

As can be seen from table 14.2, the coins of Harthacnut (including those with 'Cnut') account for no more than some 15 per cent of the whole material. Considering that these 200 or so coins were struck by at least 39 mints the figure is low, and it seems indisputable that the minting in Harthacnut's name did not last long. The total number of *Jewel Cross* coins, on the other hand, is relatively high compared with the two following types, even if we look only at the English collections (table 14.1:1–2) and disregard the large Scandinavian collections (table 14.1:3–4) which may not be representative. If introduced at the earliest possible dates, the *Fleur-de-Lys* and the *Arm-and-Sceptre* types can have had circulation periods of three and a half and two years respectively (early 1037 to mid-1040 to mid-

38. For example in the *Quatrefoil* type, see M. Blackburn and S. Lyon, 'Regional die-production in Cnut's *Quatrefoil* issue', at pp. 253–6 above.

39. Royal Coin Cabinet, without provenance (group 'U').

40. *BMC* Harold 65; see Blackburn and Lyon, p. 257 n. 37 above.

1042). This would not leave more than a year or so for *Jewel Cross*. Although calculations based on statistics such as these can be misleading,[41] the figures in table 14.1 make it difficult to believe that the circulation period of *Jewel Cross* should have been essentially shorter than those of the two following types. Probably Harold continued to strike variety L2 of *Jewel Cross* for several months after being recognized as sole ruler.[42]

Conclusions

The *witan* of Oxford resulted, according to the *Anglo-Saxon Chronicle*, in Harold being elected regent of all England early in 1036 while the queen-mother Emma was allowed to hold Winchester by means of Harthacnut's housecarles. Florence of Worcester, on the other hand, says that after Harold had reigned for a short time 'as if the legitimate heir', the kingdom was divided 'by lot'. Both Florence and the *Chronicle* agree, however, in recording that by the next year Harold was elected king everywhere and Emma was expelled and deprived of her treasures.[43]

Dolley, in accordance with F. M. Stenton, relies mainly on the *Chronicle* in his interpretation of the transfer of power.[44] Parsons and Hill lay stress on the division of the country, connecting the distribution of Harthacnut's mints with Florence's account of the events.[45] Dolley, too, noted the geographical pattern of Harthacnut's minting, but he stressed the unity of the country.

As we have seen, the unity of the coinage speaks in itself for at least a formal agreement between the co-claimants, while the division of the mints appears to have been more drastic than even Parsons realized. A cautious interpretation of the numismatic evidence presented in this paper can perhaps be formulated as follows.

At the beginning of the issue Harthacnut's party, grouped around Emma and her court in Winchester, struck coins at the mints of southern England, and small numbers of coins with the name of Harthacnut or Cnut were also struck by some of

41. Cf. M. Dolley and B. Grover, 'The 1981 Chelsea Reach (London) find of Second Hand pennies of Æthelræd II', *Numismatiska Meddelanden 33*, (1983), 85–99, *passim*.
42. There are five mules between *Jewel Cross* obverses and *Fleur-de-Lys* reverses in Stockholm and one in Copenhagen. One of these (Hild. 116) has an L1 *obv.* with Harthacnut's name (possibly used in error because of indistinct lettering in the royal name), another (Hild. 799) belongs to the same variety with Harold's name. The remaining four (Hild. 54a, 61, 63; *SCBI 18*, 369) have obverses belonging to variety L2. There is in Stockholm also a *Short Cross*/*Jewel Cross* mule (Hild. 440) with somewhat unusual style on the *obv*. Another mule, with Harthacnut *Jewel Cross obv.* and *Short Cross rev.* mentioned by Dolley ('The "Jewel Cross" coinage', 270) with reference to the fourth Lawrence sale (Glendining, 28 November 1951, lot 1397, not illustrated) has not been seen by the present author.
43. D. Whitelock (ed.) *EHD* I (2nd edn, 1979), 256–7, 315.
44. Dolley, 'The "Jewel Cross' coinage', *passim*; F. M. Stenton, *Anglo-Saxon England* (3rd edn, 1971), 419–20.
45. Parsons, 'Coins of Harthacnut', 39–43; Hill, *op. cit.*, 95.

the northern mints. Most of the coins were struck with dies produced by a single atelier, probably situated in Winchester, but some were struck with dies engraved by a workshop in London ('National A') which worked mainly for Harold. It is not clear why the dies produced by Harthacnut's Winchester workshop should have right-facing busts, while those from Harold's workshops (including the dies in the names of Harthacnut and 'Cnut') should have left-facing busts, but the fact that the distinction was connected with workshops rather than rulers may mean that it was of secondary importance.

While Harthacnut's supporters controlled the mints to the south of the Thames, Harold struck coins in the north. It is noteworthy that whereas there are coins in the name of Harthacnut from northern mints, including Stamford, Lincoln, and York, the Thames seems to have formed an effective southern border for Harold's minting (for the few exceptions see p. 283 above). Clearly Harthacnut's party had real power over their territory – but this cannot have lasted long, to judge from the scarcity of their coins.

The statement by Florence of Worcester that England was divided 'by lot' may have a different meaning from what is conveyed by the word today. In any case it must retain a memory of an actual division of the country, such as is attested by the division of the mints. How the situation developed we do not know in detail, but the written sources tell that Harold soon resorted to drastic measures against Queen Emma. He possessed himself of Winchester, and this must have been the end, or the beginning of the end, of the coinage in Harthacnut's name. Harold now had all the mints under his control. To this time apparently belongs the introduction of a modified design for the coin portrait, here called variety L2. The new design has no parallel in the coins with Harthacnut's or Cnut's name. It was used until the *Fleur-de-Lys* type was introduced, probably late in 1037 or early 1038.[46]

APPENDIX

In the following list an attempt is made to classify the *Jewel Cross* coins in the Danish Royal Collection in Copenhagen according to the stylistic analysis presented in this paper. The figures refer to *SCBI 18* (Harold and Harthacnut) and *SCBI 13–15* (coins with the name 'Cnut').

Variety R: 614–15, 615A, 616–17, 620, 627, 630, 635, 638, 647, 665–6, 671–2, 694, 697–8, 700–1, 704, 710–11, 715, 719, 723, 725, 727

Variety L1

'National A', Harthacnut: 626, 648, 667–9, 678, 680, 684, 720, 724

'National A', 'Cnut': 91, 374, 393, 2292–3, 2440, 3019–20, 3890

'National A', Harold: 17, 45, 69–70, 85, 109, 118, 137, 197, 200, 204–5, 235, 289, 295, 297, 312–13, 325, 327–8,

46. The illustrated coins, enlarged ×$1\frac{1}{2}$, are: 1. Exeter, *Edmær*, Hild. 216; 2. Winchester, *Godwine*, Hild. 205; 3. Lincoln, *Hildulf*, Hild. 92; 4. Bath, *Wædel*, Hild. 2; 5. London, *Leofred*, Hild. 124; 6. London, *Brunman*, Hild. 2117; 7. London, *Wynsiige*, Hild. 758; 8. London, *Godmon*, Hild. 615; 9. Norwich, *Æficc*, Hild. 766; 10. Lincoln, *Thurstan*, Hild. 477; 11. London, *Edræd*, Hild. 576; 12. London, *Cinewold*, Hild. 548; 13. Northampton, *Ælfwine*, Hild. 279.

335, 337, 360–1, 364, 366, 379, 380, 410, 413, 437, 519, 530, 532, 534, 540, 542, 553, 561, 566, 579–80

'National B', Harold: 28–9, 32, 35, 38–9, 83, 87, 90, 110, 112, 123, 131, 142, 160, 166, 171, 174–7, 189, 207, 214, 216–17, 221–4, 229, 233, 235–7, 240–1, 248, 261, 275, 285, 331, 338, 359, 363, 365, 372, 378, 395, 400, 435, 438, 440–1, 452–6, 458–60, 467–8, 472, 477, 483, 486, 508–9, 520, 524–7, 538–9, 550–1, 554, 606

Lincoln, Harold: 37, 65, 209, 211, 213, 220, 225, 232, 259–60, 262–3, 270, 549

Variety L2

'National A', Harold: 1, 14, 34, 49, 56–7, 59–61, 72, 78–81, 92–4, 108, 111, 117, 119, 122, 133, 149–51, 181–3, 187, 191, 194, 238, 242, 255, 283–4, 290–2, 298, 329, 334, 336, 369, 382, 392, 394, 399, 401–2, 411–12, 414, 421, 428–9, 432, 436, 443, 476, 478–9, 485, 487–8, 497, 535, 541, 560, 571, 582, 585, 588, 591–2

'National B', Harold: 18, 46, 71, 73, 81, 84, 91, 95, 99–101, 103, 106–7, 114–16, 132, 144, 190, 196, 210, 212, 267–9, 271, 273–4, 293, 296, 299, 330, 339, 371, 425, 430, 450–1, 473, 480, 482, 514–15, 517, 521–2, 531, 536, 597

Lincoln, Harold: 36, 143, 215, 249, 272, 286–8, 552

Unclassified because of style: Harold/ Harthacnut, 43–4, 442, 457, 602–5; Cnut, 3368

Unclassified because of condition: Harold/ Harthacnut, 64, 234, 362, 409, 431, 439, 502, 541

Coins probably of Scandinavian origin have not been included.

15 A revised check-list of coin hoards from the British Isles, c.500–1100

Mark Blackburn and Hugh Pagan

This check-list is a revision of the 'Provisional Listing of Viking-Age hoards from Great Britain and Ireland (c.795–1105)' published by Michael Dolley in his *SCBI* volume on *The Hiberno-Norse Coins in the British Museum* (1966), 47–54. That listing, which summarized a decade of intensive research primarily by Dolley himself, provided an authoritative guide to the hoards, and this has been for the last 20 years the basic tool for all numismatists, archaeologists, and historians interested in the hoard evidence. The purpose of this revision, in essentially the same format, is to give the listing a new lease of life so that the evidence brought together by Dolley may continue to be widely used and built upon.

Some 75 post-795 hoards have been added to the basic 1966 listing, 28 of them subsequent discoveries and the remainder older forgotten finds. Eleven hoards have been deleted or amalgamated with others (nos. 18, 20–1, 24, 29–30, 36, 61, 64, 130, and 197 in the original listing), while one (no. 26) is now regarded as two separate finds. A few hoards listed by Dolley for which the evidence now seems insufficient to support an approximate dating have been extracted from the main body of the list and placed in the group of uncertain hoards at the end. The descriptions of the content and date of deposit of various of the hoards have been modified as a result of further archival work or in the light of current research, but the essential validity of Dolley's original compilation remains unimpeached. We have followed the scheme of the original listing in citing only the principal modern references for the hoards, i.e. the sources cited by Dolley, unless they have been superseded, and any relevant post-1966 literature where it adds significantly to these or provides a convenient summary.

We have, however, departed from Dolley's arrangement of the material in three respects. First, we have included coin hoards of the sixth to eighth centuries. Secondly, because of uncertainties as to their dating, we have listed the ninth-century hoards with Northumbrian coins under a separate heading, positioned between the earlier hoards and those with ninth-century silver pennies. Thirdly, we have distinguished by an asterisk those finds consisting solely of two or three associated coins; the evidential value of any hoard varies according to its size and nature, and although small groups of coins such as these are of less value to scholars than larger ones, even the smallest group of associated coins can provide relevant information provided it is handled with care.

In preparing this revised list, M.A.S.B. has been responsible for the periods c.500–800 and c.975–1100, and H.E.P. for the period c.800–975. We are very grateful for information and comments received from C. E. Blunt, Mrs S. E. Chadwick Hawkes, J. A. Graham-Campbell, and M. Kenny.

Note on arrangement

Column 1
  running number
Column 2
  findspot, county (old), and year of discovery
Column 3
  region:
  E = England; M = Isle of Man
  NWE = N.W. England; S = Scotland
  I = Ireland; W = Wales
Column 4
  size:
    ⋆ = 2–3 associated coins
    X = hoard with less than 20 coins
    XX = 20–119 coins
    XXX = 120–1,199 coins
    XXXX = 1,200 or more coins
Column 5
  classes of coin represented:
    A/B = Ancient-British
    A/S = Anglo-Saxon
    B = Byzantine
    C = Continental
    H/M = Hiberno-Manx
    H/N = Hiberno-Norse
    K = Kufic
    N = Norman
    V = Vikings of East Anglia and Northumbria
Column 6
  + = coins accompanied by metal objects other than containers
Column 7
  containers:
    b = bone or horn; p = pottery
    c = cloth; s = stone
    l = leather; w = wood
    m = metal
Column 8
  approximate date of deposit (not *terminus post quem*)

THE CHECK-LIST

1	Kingston-on-Thames, Surrey, 1848	E	X	C	–	–	c.530?
2	Chatham Lines, Kent, 1779	E	X	C	+	–	c.530/40
3	Canterbury (St Martin's), Kent, c.1840	E	X	A/S, C	+	–	c.590
4	Faversham, Kent, c.1800	E	X	C	–	–	c.600
5	Sarre, Kent, 1860	E	X	C	–	–	c.620
6	Sutton Hoo, Suff., 1939	E	XX	C	+	m	c.625
7	Crondall, Hants., 1882	E	XX	A/S, B, C	+	–	c.645
8	Sibertswold Down, Kent, 1772	E	X	C	+	–	c.650
9	York, pre-1846	E	⋆	A/S	–	–	c.660
10	Finglesham (no.1), Kent, 1959	E	X	A/S, C	+	–	c.670
11	Dover, Kent, 1952	E	⋆	A/S	–	–	c.680
12	Mucking, Essex, 1976	E	⋆	A/S	–	–	c.685
13	Hougham, Kent, c.1780	E	XXX	A/S	–	–	c.690
14	Milton Regis, Kent, 1916	E	XX	A/S	+	–	c.690
15	Finglesham (no.2), Kent, 1965	E	X	A/S	–	–	c.695
16	Broadstairs, Kent, 1911	E	X	A/S	+	–	c.695
17	Barham, Kent, 1841	E	X	A/S	+	–	c.695
18	Southend, Essex, 1929	E	X	A/S	–	–	c.700

19 Birchington, Kent, pre-1848	E	X	A/B?, A/S, C	–	–	c.700
20 Ozengell, near Ramsgate, Kent, 1846	E	⋆	A/S, C	–	?	c.700
21 Aston Rowant, Oxon., 1971/4	E	XXX	A/S, C	–	–	c.710
22 Royston, near, Cambs., 1985	E	⋆	A/S	–	–	c.710
23 Garton-on-the-Wolds, Yorks., 1959	E	X	A/S	–	w?	c.725
24 Southampton (no.1), Hants., pre-1864	E	X	A/S	–	w?	c.725?
25 Southampton (no.2, Kingsland), Hants., 1947	E	XX	A/S	–	–	c.730
26 Wrotham, Kent, pre-1958	E	⋆	A/S	–	–	c.735
27 Cambridge, near, pre-1894	E	X	A/S	–	–	c.735
28 London (Thames bank), 1860	E	X	A/S	–	–	c.740
29 Manchester (Campfield), Lancs., 1821	NWE	X	A/S or C	–	–	c.720/50
30 Middle Harling, Norf., 1981/3	E	XX	A/S	–	–	c.760

Hoards containing pre-867 Northumbrian coins only

31 York ('railway'), 1840	E	XX		–	–	*temp.* Eanred or Æthelred II (first reign)?
32 York (St Leonards Place, no.1), 1833	E	XX		–	–	*temp.* Æthelred II (first reign) or later
33 York (City Art Gallery), 1879	E	XXX		–	–	,,
34 Colonsay (Kiloran Bay), Argyll, 1882–3	S	⋆		+	–	,,
35 Grange-over-Sands, Lancs., 1765	NWE	XX?		–	–	,,
36 Lancaster, 1914	NWE	XX?		–	–	,,
37 Paisley, Renf., 1782	S	XX?		–	–	,,
38 Hexham, Northumb., 1832/1841	E	XXXX		–	m	*temp.* Æthelred II (second reign)
39 Grange-over-Sands, Lancs., 1892	NWE	X		–	–	*temp.* Æthelred II (second reign) or later
40 Ripon, Yorks., 1695/1846	E	XXX?		–	–	*temp.* Osberht
41 Kirkoswald, Cumb., 1808	NWE	XXX		+	p?	,,
42 York (St Leonards Place, no.2), 1842	E	XXXX		–	–	,,
43 Bolton Percy, Yorks., 1847/1967	E	XXXX		–	c/p	,,
44 Beverley, Yorks., 1981	E	XX		–	–	,,

Hoards containing pre-867 Northumbrian coins together with other coins

45 York (Coney Street), c.1760	E	XXX?	(with C)	–	c?	c.865?
46 Talnotrie, Kirkc., 1912	S	X	(with A/S, C, K)	+	–	c.875?

Other post-800 hoards from the British Isles

47	Blandford (area), Dorset, c.1912	E	X	A/S	–	–	c.827
48	Delgany, Co. Wicklow, 1874	I	XXX	A/S, C	–	–	c.830
49	Suffolk (NE corner), c.1827	E	XX	A/S	–	–	c.835
50	London (Middle Temple), 1893	E	XXX	A/S, C	–	–	c.842
51	Croy, Inv., 1875	S	⋆	A/S	+	–	c.845?
52	Hampshire (no.2), 1837	E	X	A/S	–	–	c.845?
53	Mullaghboden, Coghlanstown West, Co. Kild., 1871	I	X	C	?	–	c.847
54	Sevington, Wilts., 1834	E	XX	A/S	+	w?	c.850
55	Penard, Glam., 1948	W	⋆	A/S, C	–	–	c.850
56	Cushendall (near Red Bay), Co. Antrim, 1849	I	⋆	A/S	–	–	c.850?
57	Croydon (Old Palace), Surrey c.1907	E	X	A/S	–	–	c.857
58	Dorking, Surrey, 1817	E	XXX	A/S, C	–	w	c.862
59	Trewhiddle, Corn., 1774	E	XX	A/S, C	+	–	c.868
60	Hampshire (no.1), 1836	E	XX?	A/S	–	–	c.870
61	Reading, Berks., 1839	E	X	A/S	–	–	c.870
62	Hitchin (village north of), Herts., 1895	E	X	A/S	–	–	c.870
63	Great Casterton, Rut., 1955	E	⋆	A/S	–	–	c.870
64	Gravesend, Kent, 1838	E	XXX	A/S, C	+	–	c.871
65	London (Waterloo Bridge), c.1883	E	XX	A/S	–	–	c.872
66	Leckhampton, Glos., 1924	E	X	A/S	–	–	c.872?
67	Croydon (Whitehorse), Surrey, 1862	E	XXX	A/S, C, K	+	c	c.872
68	London (Westminster Bridge), c.1895	E	XX?	A/S	–	–	c.872
69	Wandsworth, Surrey, pre-1913	E	X	A/S	–	–	c.873
70	Repton (no.1), Derby, 1982	E	X	A/S	–	–	c.873
71	Repton (no.2), Derby, 1985	E	X	A/S	+	–	c.874
72	Ireland?, pre-1886?	I	X	A/S	–	–	c.875
73	Beeston Tor, Staffs., 1924	E	XX	A/S	+	l?	c.875
74	Dunsforth, Yorks., c.1873	E	X	A/S	–	–	c.875
75	Hook Norton, Oxon., 1848	E	X	A/S	–	–	c.875
76	Gainford, Durham, 1864	E	X	A/S	–	–	c.875
77	Laxfield, Suff., 1819	E	X	A/S?, C	–	–	c.875?
78	Satley, Durham, c.1874	E	X	A/S	–	–	c.875?
79	Washington, Sussex, 1904	E	X	A/S	–	–	c.882
80	St Albans (Abbey Orchard), Herts., 1968	E	XX	A/S	–	–	c.873/88
81	London (Bucklersbury), 1872	E	XX	A/S	–	p	c.890
82	Erith (near), Kent, c.1840	E	X	A/S	–	–	c.890
83	Leigh-on-Sea, Essex, 1892 or 1893	E	XX	A/S	–	–	c.895
84	Ashdon (Steventon End), Essex, 1984	E	XX	A/S, V, C	–	–	c.895
85	Stamford, Lincs., 1902	E	XX	A/S, V, C	–	–	c.895
86	Cambridge (Castle Hill), 1968	E	⋆	V	–	–	c.905
87	Cuerdale, Lancs., 1840	NWE	XXXX	A/S, V, C, K, B	+	m	c.905

88	Drogheda, Co. Louth, 1846	I	XXXX?	V, K	–	–	c.905
89	Shrewsbury, Shrops., 1936	E	XXX?	A/S	–	–	c.910
90	Co. Londonderry, pre-1804	I	XXX?	K	–	m	c.910?
91	Magheralagan, Co. Down, 1835	I	X?	K	+	–	c.910?
92	Harkirk, Little Crosby, Lancs., 1611	NWE	XXX	A/S, V, C, K	+	–	c.910
93	Dysart Island (no.4), Lough Ennell, Co. Westmeath, 1980	I	XX	A/S, V, C, K	+	–	c.910
94	York (Walmgate), 1856	E	XX	V	–	–	c.915
95	Dean, Cumb., pre-1790	NWE	XX	A/S, V, C, K	–	m	c.915
96	Lancashire, 1734	NWE	XX	V	–	–	c.915
97	Leggagh, Nobber, Co. Meath, 1843	I	X	A/S, V, K	–	–	c.915
98	Anglesey?, 1696	W	X	A/S, V	–	–	c.915
99	Chester (St John's), 1862	NWE	X	A/S, V	–	–	c.917
100	Northampton, Northants., pre-1882	E	X	A/S	–	–	c.920
101	Goldsborough, Yorks., 1858	E	XX	A/S, K	+	p	c.920
102	Nottingham, Notts., 1693	E	XX?	A/S	–	–	c.920
103	Castle Bellingham, Co. Louth, pre-1907	I	*	A/S	–	–	c.920?
104	Amesbury, Wilts., 1853	E	*	A/S	–	–	c.920?
105	Geashill, Co. Offaly, c.1862	I	X	V, C	–	–	c.922
106	Bangor (Midland Bank), Caer., 1894	W	X	A/S, V, K	+	–	c.925
107	Morley St Peter, Norf., 1958	E	XXX	A/S, V	–	p	c.925
108	Bossall/Flaxton, Yorks., 1807	E	XXX	A/S, V, K	+	m	c.925
109	Northampton, near, 1984	E	*	A/S	–	–	c.925
110	Glasnevin, Co. Dublin, 1838	I	X	A/S, V, K	–	–	c.927
111	Dunmore Cave, Co. Kilk., 1973	I	X	A/S, V, K	+	–	c.928
112	Whippendell Woods, Watford, Herts., 1980–1	E	X	A/S	–	–	c.930
113	Tywardreath, Corn., 1953	E	X	A/S	–	–	c.930
114	Co. Kildare, 1840	I	X	A/S, K	–	–	c.935
115	Scotby, Cumb., 1855	NWE	XX	A/S, V?	+	–	c.935
116	Skye (Storr Rock), Inv., 1891	S	XX	A/S, V, K	+	–	c.935
117	Co. Dublin, 1883	I	XX	A/S, V	+	–	c.935
118	Oxford, 1896	E	X	A/S	–	–	c.935?
119	Ireland, pre-1726	I	XX?	A/S	–	–	c.935?
120	Deptford, near, Kent, pre-1860?	E	*?	A/S	+	–	c.935?
121	York (Coppergate), 1980	E	X	A/S, V	–	–	c.940
122	Durrow, Co. Offaly, c.1850	I	X	A/S, V	–	–	c.940
123	Cockburnspath (St Helen's), Ber., c.1842	S	XX?	A/S	+?	–	c.940?
124	Glendalough (no.2), Co. Wick., pre-1822	I	XX	A/S	–	–	c.942
125	Co. Tipperary, 1843?	I	X	A/S	–	–	c.942
126	London (Threadneedle Street), pre-1924	E	X	A/S	–	–	c.945

127 Castle Freke, Rathbarry, Co. Cork, 1799	I	X	A/S	–	l?	c.945
128 Fennor, Co. Meath, pre-1870	I	⋆	A/S	–	–	c.945?
129 Skaill, Sandwick, Orkney, 1858	S	XX	A/S, V, K	+	–	c.950
130 Knowth, Co. Meath, 1969	I	⋆	A/S	–	–	c.950?
131 Newtownlow, Kilbeggan, Co. Westmeath, 1982	I	X	A/S	–	–	c.953
132 Macroom, Co. Cork, c.1840?	I	XX?	A/S	–	–	c.953
133 Hundon, Suff., 1687	E	XXX?	A/S	–	c	c.953
134 Monasterboice, Co. Louth, 1746	I	XX?	A/S	+	–	c.953
135 Mungret, Co. Lim., c.1842	I	X	A/S, V	+	–	c.953
136 Bath (Abbey), Som., 1755	E	XX	A/S	–	w	c.955
137 Kirtling, Cambs., 1847	E	⋆	A/S, V	–	–	c.955?
138 Killyon Manor, Hill of Down, Co. Meath, 1876	I	XX	A/S, V	–	–	c.955
139 Oldcastle, Co. Meath, pre-1900	I	X	A/S, V	–	–	c.958
140 Kintbury, Berks., 1761	E	XX	A/S	–	–	c.960
141 Tetney, Lincs., 1945	E	XXX	A/S, V	+	s	c.963
142 Ballitore (near), Co. Kild., 1837	I	XX	A/S, V	–	–	c.965
143 Ballaqueeney, Port St Mary, 1874	M	XX	A/S, V, C	–	–	c.965
144 Chester (Castle Esplanade), 1950	NWE	XXX	A/S, V, C	+	p	c.965
145 Ireland, 1862	I	XX	A/S, V	–	–	c.965
146 Lough Lene, Co. Westmeath, 1843	I	XX	A/S, V, C	–	–	c.965
147 Smarmore, Ardee, Co. Louth, 1929	I	XX	A/S, V	–	–	c.965
148 York (Pavement), 1951	E	⋆	A/S	–	–	c.965?
149 Armagh (near), 1831	I	X?	A/S, V	–	–	c.965?
150 Bangor (Vicars Garden), Caer., 1845 or 1846	W	⋆	A/S	–	–	c.965?
151 Kent, c.1858	E	X?	A/S	–	–	c.965?
152 Burt (Carrowen), Co. Don., 1863 or 1864	I	X	A/S	–	–	c.970
153 Chester (Eastgate Street), 1857	NWE	XX	A/S	–	–	c.970
154 Killincoole, Co. Louth, 1864	I	XX	A/S	+	–	c.970
155 Kirk Andreas, 1866 or 1867	M	XX	A/S	–	–	c.970
156 Co. Meath, 1845	I	X	A/S, K	–	–	c.970
157 Rahan (no.1), Co. Offaly, c.1820	I	XX?	A/S	–	–	c.970?
158 Rahan (no.2), Co. Offaly, 1828	I	XX?	A/S	+	–	c.970?
159 Ballakilpheric, pre-c.1885	M	XX?	A/S	–	–	c.970?
160 Bullock (no.1), Co. Dublin, 1838	I	⋆	A/S	–	–	c.970?
161 Bullock (no.2), Co. Dublin, 1840?	I	XX	A/S	–	–	c.970
162 Skye (no.2), 1850	S	XX	A/S	+	–	c.970?
163 Dalkey, Co. Dublin, c.1840	I	XX	A/S	–	–	c.970
164 Derrykeighan, Co. Antrim, 1843	I	XXX	A/S, V, C	–	–	c.970
165 Ballaquayle (Douglas), 1894	M	XXX	A/S, V	+	p	c.970
166 Glendalough (no.3), Co. Wick., c.1835	I	X	A/S	–	–	c.970
167 Ballycastle (Trench Farm, no.2), Co. Antrim, c.1890	I	XX?	A/S	–	–	c.970?
168 Islay (Machrie), 1850	S	XX	A/S, V, K, C	+	–	c.970

169	Port Glasgow, Renf., pre-1705	S	XX?	A/S	+	–	c.970
170	Co. Kilkenny (west), pre-1824	I	XX	A/S	+	–	c.970
171	Tiree, Argyll, 1782	S	XXX	A/S	+	–	c.970
172	Laugharne, Carm., c.1930	W	XX	A/S	–	–	c.975
173	Welwyn, Herts., 1912	E	X	A/S	–	–	c.978
174	Chester (Pemberton's Parlour), 1914	NWE	XXX	A/S	–	–	c.980
175	Oakham, near, Rut., 1749	E	XXX	A/S	+	p	c.980
176	Spettisbury Ring, Dorset, c.1790	E	*	A/S	–	–	c.980?
177	North Uist, pre-1780	S	XX	A/S	–	–	c.985?
178	Ipswich (Butter Market), Suff., 1863	E	XXX	A/S	–	–	c.985
179	Mullingar (no.1) ('Marl Valley'), Co. Westmeath, 1841	I	XXX	A/S	+	–	c.986
180	Iona Abbey, Argyll, 1950	S	XXX	A/S, V, C	+	–	c.986
181	London (Chelsea Reach), 1981	E	X	A/S	–	–	c.988
182	Ecton, Northants., 1762	E	X?	A/S	–	–	c.990?
183	Kildare, near, 1923	I	XX	A/S	–	–	c.991
184	Isleworth, Middx., 1886	E	XX	A/S	–	–	c.991
185	Bury St Edmunds, near, Suff., pre-1873	E	*	A/S	–	–	c.995
186	Bradda Head, c.1848	M	XXX	A/S	–	–	c.995
187	Dundalk, Co. Louth, 1980	I	X	A/S, H/N	–	–	c.995
188	Clondalkin (no.2), Co. Dublin, c.1830	I	XXX	H/N	–	–	c.997
189	Welbourn, Lincs., 1980–2	E	XX?	A/S	–	–	c.1000?
190	Tarbat, Ross, 1889	S	X	A/S, C	+	–	c.1000
191	Kilmartin, Argyll, pre-1845	S	X	A/S	–	–	c.1000?
192	Quendale (Garthsbanks), Shetland, 1830	S	XX?	A/S	+	b	c.1000
193	Burray, Orkney, 1889	S	X	A/S, C	+	w	c.1000
194	Inchkenneth, Argyll, c.1830	S	XX	A/S, V, H/N, C	+	–	c.1000
195	Knockmaon, Co. Wat., 1912	I	XX?	A/S, H/N, C	–	–	c.1000
196	Derrymore, Co. Westmeath, 1872	I	X	A/S, H/N	–	–	c.1000
197	Great Barton, Suff., c.1850	E	XX	A/S	–	–	c.1000
198	Harting Beacon, Sussex, 1892	E	X	A/S	–	–	c.1000
199	London (Honey Lane Market), 1837	E	X	A/S	+	–	c.1000
200	Shaftesbury, Dorset, 1940	E	XX	A/S	–	–	c.1000
201	York (Micklegate), 1882	E	X	A/S	–	–	c.1000
202	Co. Westmeath, 1984	I	X	A/S, H/N	–	–	c.1005
203	Penrice, Glam., c.1830	W	XX	A/S	–	w	c.1008
204	London (St Martin's-le-Grand), pre-1870	E	XX	A/S	–	–	c.1015
205	Constantine, Cornwall, c.1690	E	XX?	A/S	–	c	c.1020?
206	Kingsholm, Glos., c.1780	E	XXX?	A/S	–	–	c.1020?
207	Pant-yr-Eglwys, Great Orme, Caer., 1981	W	X	A/S	–	–	c.1023
208	Bryn Maelgwyn, near Llandudno, Caer., 1979	W	XXX	A/S, H/N	–	–	c.1024

209	Jedburgh (Bongate), Rox., c.1827	S	XX?	A/S	–	–	c.1025?
210	Barrowby, Lincs., 1871/2	E	XXX?	A/S	–	b	c.1025?
211	Rougham, Suff., c.1850	E	X?	A/S	–	–	c.1025?
212	Halton Moor, Lancs., 1815	NWE	XXX	A/S, C	+	m	c.1025
213	Southampton (no. 3), Hants., 1967	E	XX	C	–	–	c.1030
214	Manchester (Castle Hill), Lancs., 1849	NWE	*	A/S, C	–	–	c.1030
215	Drwsdangoed, Caer., pre-1850	W	X	A/S	–	–	c.1030?
216	Parkhill, Lindores, Fife, 1814	S	XX?	A/S, H/N? or C?	+	p	c.1030?
217	Fourknocks, Co. Meath, 1951	I	XX	A/S, H/N	+	l	c.1030
218	Ballycastle (Trench Farm, no.1), Co. Antrim, 1890	I	XXX	A/S, H/N	–	–	c.1030
219	Park Llewellyn, Kirk Maughold, 1835	M	XX?	A/S, H/N, H/M	–	b	c.1030
220	Bottisham, Cambs., 1982	E	*	A/S	–	–	c.1035
221	Caldale, Orkney, 1774	S	XXX	A/S	+	b	c.1035
222	Tonyowen, near Finnea, Co. Westmeath, 1977	I	*	H/N	–	–	c.1035
223	Ballacannell?, Kirk Lonan, 1786	M	XXX	A/S, H/N?, C?	–	–	c.1020s/30s
224	Stafford, 1800	E	XXX	A/S	–	p	c.1040?
225	Titchmarsh, Northants., 1979/82	E	X	A/S	–	–	c.1040
226	Kilkenny, near, 1792	I	XXX?	A/S, H/N	–	–	c.1040
227	River Liffey, Co. Dublin, c.1940	I	X	H/N	–	–	c.1040
228	Ballaberna, Kirk Maughold, 1834	M	X?	H/N	–	p	c.1040
229	Wedmore, Som., 1853	E	XXX	A/S	–	p	c.1043
230	Kirk Andreas Churchyard (no.2), 1874	M	XX	A/S, H/N, H/M	+	–	c.1045
231	West Nappin, pre-1900	M	X	A/S, H/N, H/M	+	–	c.1045
232	Thwaite, Suff., 1832	E	XXX	A/S	–	m	c.1048
233	Mullingar (no.2), Co. Westmeath, 1856	I	X	A/S, H/N	–	–	mid 11th c
234	Rathlin Island, Co. Antrim, 1916	I	X	H/N?	–	–	mid 11th c
235	Adare, Co. Limerick, 1834	I	XX?	A/S, H/N	–	–	mid 11th c
236	Ballylynan, Co. Laois, 1786	I	XXX	A/S, H/N	–	p	c.1050
237	Dunbrody, Co. Wexford, 1836	I	XXXX	A/S, H/N	–	–	c.1050
238	Baltinglass, Co. Wicklow, pre-1882	I	XX	H/N	–	–	c.1050
239	Peel Castle, St Patrick's Isle, 1982	M	XX	H/N	–	–	c.1050
240	Milton Street, near Alfriston, Sussex, 1830/43	E	XX	A/S	–	–	c.1055
241	Nottingham (Sherwood Forest), 1789	E	X	A/S	–	–	c.1058
242	Nottingham (Barkergate), 1786	E	X	A/S	–	–	c.1058
243	Mayfield, Staffs., pre-1844	E	XX?	A/S	–	–	c.1060?
244	London (Gracechurch Street), c.1850?	E	XX?	A/S	–	–	c.1062?
245	Dunrossness, Shetland, c.1844	S	X	C	+	–	c.1065?

246 Clondalkin (no.1), Co. Dublin, 1816	I	XX?	H/N	–	–	c.1065
247 Limerick, 1833	I	XX	H/N	–	–	c.1065
248 Kirk Michael Churchyard (no.2), 1972/5	M	XX	A/S, H/N, H/M, C	+	c	c.1065
249 Ballaugh, 1772	M	XX	A/S?, H/N?	–	–	c.1065?
250 Salisbury Plain, Wilts., pre-1855	E	X	A/S, C	–	–	c.1065
251 Stockbridge Down, Hants., 1935	E	X	A/S	–	–	c.1065
252 Harewood, Yorks., 1895	E	XX	A/S	–	–	c.1065
253 York (Bishophill, no.1), 1882	E	XXX	A/S	–	p	c.1065
254 Sedlescombe, near Battle, Sussex, 1876	E	XXXX	A/S	–	w/m	c.1064/66
255 Chancton Upper Farm, Sussex, 1866	E	XXXX	A/S	–	p	c.1066
256 Ashdown Forest (Camp Hill), Sussex, 1822?	E	XX?	A/S	–	–	c.1066?
257 Offham, near Arundel, Sussex, 1796	E	XX	A/S	–	–	c.1066
258 Arundel Castle, Sussex, pre-1899	E	?	A/S	–	–	c.1066?
259 Oving, Sussex, 1789	E	XX	A/S	+	p	c.1066
260 Castor, Northants., 1759	E	XXX	A/S	–	–	c.1066
261 London (Queen Victoria Street; 'Walbrook'), 1872	E	XXXX	A/S, B, C	+	p	c.1066/74
262 Rotherham, Yorks., 1939	E	XX	A/S, N	–	–	c.1068
263 Soberton, near, Hants., c.1850	E	XXX	A/S, N	+	p	c.1068
264 Norwich (Garlands), Norfolk, 1972	E	X	N	–	–	c.1068
265 Denge Marsh, Kent, 1739	E	XXX	A/S, N	–	?	c.1068
266 Oulton, Staffs., 1795	E	XXX	A/S, N	+	–	c.1069
267 Bierley, Yorks., pre-1741	E	X?	N	–	–	c.1069?
268 Bramham Moor, Yorks., pre-1816	E	X?	N	–	–	c.1069?
269 Middleham, Yorks., pre-1898	E	X?	N	–	–	c.1069
270 York (Baile Hill), 1802	E	XX	N	–	–	c.1069
271 York (Jubbergate, no.1), 1845	E	XXX	N	–	–	c.1069
272 York (High Ousegate), 1704	E	XXX	N	–	w	c.1069
273 York (Bishophill, no.2), 1882	E	XX	N	–	–	c.1069
274 Betham, Westmor., 1834	NWE	XX	A/S, N	–	–	c.1070?
275 Bury St Edmunds (Mill Lane), Suff., 1851	E	XX?	N	–	–	c.1070?
276 Sutton (Isle of Ely), Cambs., 1694	E	XX	N	+	m	c.1070?
277 Colsterworth, near Grantham, Lincs., pre-1735	E	X	N	–	–	c.1070?
278 Laxey neighbourhood?, Kirk Lonan, pre-1950	M	X	H/N	–	–	c.1070
279 Whitchurch, Oxon., pre-1900	E	XX?	A/S, N	–	–	c.1072
280 Beddington Park, Croydon, Surrey, 1978	E	X	N	–	–	c.1074
281 Malmesbury, Wilts., 1826	E	X	N	–	–	c.1074
282 London (St Mary Hill), 1774	E	XXX	A/S, N	+	p	c.1074
283 Kirk Michael Churchyard (no.1), 1834	M	XXX?	H/N, H/M	–	–	c.1075
284 Scaldwell, Northants., 1914	E	XXX	N	–	–	c.1080

285	York (Monkgate), 1851	E	XX	N	–	–	c.1080
286	York (Jubbergate, no.2/Peterlane), 1847	E	X	N	–	–	c.1086
287	Beauworth, Hants., 1833	E	XXXX	N	–	m	c.1086
288	Tamworth, Staffs., 1877	E	XXX	N	–	m	c.1090
289	Clonmacnoise, Co. Offaly, 1979	I	XX	H/N	+	–	c.1090
290	Co. Meath, 1786/7	I	XX?	H/N	–	–	c.1090
291	Dunamase, Co. Laois, pre-1758	I	XXX	H/N	–	–	c.1090
292	Glendalough (no.1), Co. Wick., 1639	I	XX?	H/N	–	–	c.1090
293	Armagh (Cathedral), pre-1834	I	*?	H/N	–	–	c.1100 or
294	Dublin (Christchurch Cathedral), c.1870	I	X	H/N	–	–	,,
295	Donaghenry, Co. Tyrone, 1823	I	XXX?	H/N	–	m	,,

Uncertain hoards

296	Ireland?, pre-1940	I	X?	A/S	–	–	c.978
297	England, pre-1835	E	XX?	A/S, C	–	–	mid 11th
298	Unknown findspot, pre-1853	E	X	A/S, N	–	–	c.1067
299	Kilcullen, Co. Kildare, 1305	I	XXX?	H/N?	–	–	11th/12th
300	'Buttack' (Outlack?), Co. Armagh, 1847	I	X	H/N?	–	–	11th/12th
301	Kilmainham, Co. Dublin, c.1800	I	X?	H/N	–	–	11th/12th
302	Fife, 1832	S	X?	H/N?	–	–	11th/12th
303	Jedburgh (Abbey Bridge), Rox., c.1834	S	?	A/S?	–	–	?
304	Otterspool, Lancs., 1863	NWE	?	?	–	–	?
305	Stretford, Lancs., 1774	NWE	?	A/S	–	–	?
306	Rushall Hall, Staffs., pre-1887	E	?	A/S	–	–	?
307	York (Layerthorpe Bridge), 1829	E	X?	A/S	–	–	?

Principal modern references

In general, only the principal modern references for the numismatic content of each find are cited, i.e. Thompson's *Inventory of British Coin Hoards A.D. 600–1500* (1956) and subsequent publications. The number in Dolley's 1966 hoard listing ('D.') is given first, followed by that in the *Inventory* ('*Inv.*'). Articles by Dolley are cited by reference to the numbered bibliography of his works at the end of this volume, while those by other authors are listed after these notes.

1 *Inv.* –; Rigold 1975, 665, nos. 3–12.

2 *Inv.* –; Rigold 1975, 667, no. 43a. Three fifth-century silver coins and a Roman bronze coin, pierced for suspension as ornaments, were found in a grave dated by Mrs Sonia Chadwick Hawkes (pers. comm.) c.530/40.

3 *Inv.* –; Grierson 1952; Hawkes, Merrick, and Metcalf 1966, 104–6; *SCBI* Merseyside, nos. 5–10; Rigold 1975, nos. 16, 46, 65, 73, 77, 115.

4 *Inv.* –; Rigold 1975, 668–71, nos. 47?, 48–9, 51, 66, 69, 78.

5 *Inv.* –; Rigold 1975, 688, nos. 54, 56, 58–9.

6 *Inv.* 347; Kent 1975 (superseding previous accounts); Brown 1981.

7 *Inv.* 106; Sutherland 1948; additions and corrections in Grierson 1953 and Grierson 1970.
8 *Inv.* –; Hawkes, Merrick, and Metcalf 1966, 111–13; Rigold 1975, 672–3, nos. 85, 98; *SCBI* Merseyside, nos. 17–18.
9 *Inv.* –; Sutherland 1948, 94, nos. 75a–c; Grierson 1962.
10 *Inv.* –; Hawkes, Merrick, and Metcalf 1966, 115–16; Rigold 1975, 669, 676, nos. 62, 132.
11–30 See relevant entry in Rigold and Metcalf 1984. The dating is that proposed in Blackburn 1984.
12 *Inv.* –; Rigold 1977.
13 *Inv.* –; Blunt 1979a.
19 *Inv.* 43. Possibly a group of single-finds rather than a hoard, although chronologically they are reasonably compact.
22 Rigold and Metcalf 1984 –. Two coins of Series J (Rigold BIIIA) adhering to one another; to be published by Blackburn and Bonser.
29 D.28–9; *Inv.* –; Metcalf 1969, 92; Richardson 1984, showing that this was a single hoard of 'sceattas', not two of 'stycas'.
30 Rogerson 1982; to be published by Miss M. M. Archibald.
31–46 Problems in dating the Northumbrian coinage are considered in Pagan 1969, though the scheme there proposed is open to criticism. The contents of these hoards are summarized by Pirie, pp. 67–90 above.
31 D. –; *Inv.* –; *SCBI* Yorkshire pt.i, xxxi.
32 D. –; *Inv.* –; *SCBI* Yorkshire pt.i, xxxi.
33 D. 19; *Inv.* –; *SCBI* Yorkshire pt.i, xxxii.
34 D. 31; *Inv.* 96; *SCBI* Edinburgh, xx.
35 D. 32; *Inv.* –; Metcalf 1960, 93–4.
36 D. 35; *Inv.* –; Metcalf 1960, 96.
37 D. 38; *Inv.* 302; Metcalf 1960, 98; *SCBI* Edinburgh, viii, xxii. The association with this find of parcels of 'stycas' given to the Society of Antiquaries of Scotland by Alexander Copland in 1782 and by Selkirk Stewart in 1783 is, as indicated *SCBI loc. cit.*, 'at best a possibility'; Copland was a landowner in Dumfriesshire and Kirkcudbrightshire, not in Renfrewshire, and it is conceivable, despite the apparent difference in the metal of the coins concerned, that his gift derived from the 'leather bag, containing silver coins of the Saxon heptarchy, and a silver crucifix' allegedly found in Lochar Moss, outside Dumfries, around 1770 (Walker 1803, 16).
38 D. 13; *Inv.* 188; Bailey 1974; Pagan 1974b; Sugden and Warhurst 1979; Pirie 1981, 44; Pirie 1982a, 3, 6; Pagan 1982b. See also *SCBI* Mack, x.
39 D. 33; *Inv.* –; Metcalf 1960, 94.
40 D. 17/18; *Inv.* 317; Metcalf 1960, 99; Pirie 1982b.
41 D. 34; *Inv.* 225; Wilson 1964, 139–40; Pirie 1982a, 2–3, 5.
42 D. 15; *Inv.* 391; Pirie 1981, 44–6.
43 D. 14 (1847 parcel); *Inv.* 364 (1847 parcel); Pagan 1973a (1967 parcel); Pirie 1981 (1847 parcel).
44 D. –; *Inv.* –; *CH* 7 (1985), no. 535; to be published by Miss E. J. E. Pirie.
45 D. 12/20; *Inv.* –; Metcalf 1957, 199–201; Dolley (418) 1966; *SCBI* Yorkshire pt.i, xxxi, xxxiii. The association by Dolley of some individual Carolingian coins in the former Winchester Cathedral collection with this hoard is open to question.
46 D. 49; *Inv.* 349; Dolley and Morrison (350) 1963, 78; *SCBI* Edinburgh, xii-xiii, xxiii; Graham-Campbell 1976b, 118, 127.
47 D. 1; *Inv.* 125; *SCBI* BM H/N, 20 n. 9.
48 D. 4; *Inv.* 117; Pagan and Rhodes 1962; Dolley and Morrison (350) 1963, 77.
49 D. 2; *Inv.* –; Blunt, Lyon, and Stewart 1963, 43–5; Pagan 1977.

50 D. 5; *Inv.* 366; Dolley (715) 1976; *CH* 4 (1978), 104, no. 342.
51 D. 9; *Inv.* 109; *SCBI* Edinburgh, xix; Graham-Campbell 1976b, 117–18, 127.
52 Cf. D. 26; cf. *Inv.* 182; Dolley and Skaare (272) 1961, 66; Blunt 1972a, 9 n.1.
53 D. 6; *Inv.* 276: Dolley (277) 1961; Dolley and Morrison (350) 1963, 78; Hall 1974, 71.
54 D. 7; *Inv.* 328; Dolley and Skaare (272) 1961, 64; Wilson 1964, 167–71; Blunt 1972a.
55 D. 3; *Inv.* 305; Dolley and Morrison (350) 1963, 78; Dykes 1976, 27, no. 1.
56 D. 8; *Inv.* –; Seaby 1959, 250–1; Hall 1974, 73; Graham-Campbell 1976a, 61–2.
57 D. 10; *Inv.* 110; Dolley and Skaare (272) 1961, 65.
58 D. 11; *Inv.* 123; Dolley and Skaare (272) 1961, 65–6; Dolley and Morrison (350) 1963, 78; Blunt 1972b; Pagan 1982a, 55 n.6.
59 D. 50; *Inv.* 362; Wilson and Blunt 1961; Wilson 1964, 179–91; Pagan, pp. 61–2 above.
60 Cf. D. 26; cf. *Inv.* 182. The manuscript letter referred to by Dolley (*SCBI* H/N, 21 n.20) is one dated 10 Nov. 1836 from Richard Sainthill to the Very Rev. H. R. Dawson.
61 D. 25; *Inv.* 315; Sherlock 1956.
62 D. 23; *Inv.* 190.
63 D. 22; *Inv.* –; Dolley (310) 1961.
64 D. 43; *Inv.* 176; Blunt and Dolley (214) 1959, 221; Wilson 1964, 134–5; Pagan 1982a, 56 n.8.
65 D. 47; *Inv.* 256; Blunt and Dolley (214) 1959, 221; Dolley (265) 1960, 4.
66 D. 46; *Inv.* 82; Blunt and Dolley (214) 1959, 221.
67 D. 40; *Inv.* 111; Blunt and Dolley (214) 1959, 222–34; Spufford 1961, 214–15; Brooks and Graham-Campbell, pp. 91–110 above.
68 D. –; *Inv.* –; Pagan 1965, 24. One further coin from this hoard is in the Hugh Goodacre collection on loan to the Ashmolean Museum.
69 D. 27; *Inv.* –; Dolley (265) 1960, 7.
70 D. –; *Inv.* –; Biddle *et al.*, pp. 111–24 above. The coins were found among disarticulated bones in a mass burial. While it is not certain that they constitute a single hoard, they appear at least to have been lost or deposited on the same occasion.
71 D. –; *Inv.* –; cf. pp. 114–15 above; to be published by Pagan.
72 D. –; *Inv.* –; Dolley (430) 1967; Hall 1974, 73.
73 D. 39; *Inv.* 40; Blunt and Dolley (214) 1959, 220; Wilson 1964, 119–22; *SCBI* Midlands, xx (an additional coin).
74 D. 41; *Inv.* 146; Blunt and Dolley (214) 1959, 221; *SCBI* Mack, xii.
75 D. 44; *Inv.* –; Blunt and Dolley (214) 1959, 221.
76 D. 42; *Inv.* 167; Blunt and Dolley (214) 1959, 221; Pagan 1966.
77 D. 45; *Inv.* –; *SCBI* BM H/N, 21 n.23.
78 D. 48; *Inv.* –; Metcalf 1960, 99.
79 D. 51; *Inv.* –; Blunt and Dolley (214) 1959, 234; Dolley (351) 1963.
80 D. –; *Inv.* –; Lyon 1969, 225; the coins will be included in *SCBI* South East (forthcoming).
81 D. 52; *Inv.* –; Blunt and Dolley (214) 1959, 234; Dolley (265) 1960, 5; Pagan 1983.
82 D. 53; *Inv.* –; Grierson 1957; Blunt and Dolley (214) 1959, 235; Dolley (265) 1960, 7.
83 D. 54; cf. *Inv.* 197; Blunt and Dolley (214) 1959, 235–8. The coins were found 'in the hollow of the left shoulder of a skeleton that had been buried with horse and sword' (Brooke 1930, 283 n.1).
84 D. –; *Inv.* –; Blackburn 1985.
85 D. 55; *Inv.* 339; Grierson 1957; Blunt and Dolley (214) 1959, 239; Dolley and Morrison (350) 1963, 79.
86 D. –; *Inv.* –; Grierson and Blackburn 1986, nos. 1395A–B.
87 D. 56; *Inv.* 112; Blunt and Dolley

(214) 1959, 240–6; Lyon and Stewart 1961; Dolley and Morrison (350) 1963, 80; Pagan 1972; Dolley and Talvio (643) 1974; Lowick 1976; Sugden and Warhurst 1978; Talvio 1980; Dolley and Shiel (839) 1982; Dhénin and Leclercq 1982; Blunt 1983; Archibald 1985a.

88 D. 57; *Inv.* 129; Hall 1974, 73; Graham-Campbell 1976a, 48, 63.

89 D. –; *Inv.* –; Robinson 1983.

90 D. –; *Inv.* –; Hall 1974, 83; Graham-Campbell 1976a, 62. The dating of this hoard and the next is uncertain, but if they contained Kufic coins a date in the early tenth century seems appropriate.

91 D. –; *Inv.* –; Briggs and Graham-Campbell 1976; Briggs 1978.

92 D. 60; *Inv.* 184; Dolley (113) 1955; Blunt and Dolley (214) 1959, 247; Dolley and Morrison (350) 1963, 82.

93 D. –; *Inv.* –; Ryan *et al.* 1984 (the discussion of the coins is by M. Kenny and N. M. Lowick).

94 D. 59; *Inv.* 392; *SCBI* Yorkshire pt.i, xxxiii.

95 D. 63; *Inv.* –; Strudwick 1955a; Blunt and Dolley (214) 1959, 247; Dolley and Morrison (350) 1963, 82.

96 D. –; *Inv.* –; Blunt 1979b, 14–5; Blunt and Stewart 1983, 161 n.38.

97 D. 65; *Inv.* 263; Dolley (583) 1972; Hall 1974, 73; Graham-Campbell 1976a, 63, 67.

98 D. –; *Inv.* –; Nichols 1809, 54–6 (letter of 25 Jan. 1696/7 about the hoard from William Nicolson to Edward Lhwyd). The original of Nicolson's letter survives in Lhwyd's correspondence in the Bodleian Library, Oxford.

99 D. 62; *Inv.* 83; Mack 1967a; *SCBI* Mack, x, xii.

100 Cf. D. 58; *Inv.* –. Dolley relied on three St Edmund Memorial coins published in Rigold 1958, 189, but it is not clear that they were associated finds. However, a group of Edward the Elder coins, adhering to each other, from the same excavations has since come to light (*SCBI* Midlands, xviii).

101 D. 67; *Inv.* 175.

102 D. 68; *Inv.* 293.

103 D. –; *Inv.* –; Dolley (489) 1969, 20; Hall 1974, 73.

104 D. –; *Inv.* –; Robinson 1984.

105 D. 66; *Inv.* –; Dolley (172) 1957; Hall 1974, 73. The coin supposed by Dolley to carry on the obverse the dispersed inscription SCI PETRI MO has since been identified by Miss M. M. Archibald as an imitation of a coin of Dorestad reading DORESTATVS.

106 D. 70; *Inv.* 32; Blunt 1954; Dykes 1976, 27, no. 2.

107 D. 69; *Inv.* –; *SCBI* East Anglia, pp. 1–45 and plates I–XXII.

108 D. 71; *Inv.* 162; Blunt and Stewart 1983.

109 D. –; *Inv.* –; Blackburn and Bonser 1985, nos. 49–50.

110 D. 72; *Inv.* 89; *SCBI* BM H/N, 28 n.9; Hall 1974, 73.

111 D. –; *Inv.* –; Hall 1974, 73; Dolley (680) 1975; Graham-Campbell 1976a, 63.

112 D. –; *Inv.* –; Poole 1983.

113 D. 73; *Inv.* –; Dolley (112) 1955.

114 D. 78; *Inv.* 205; *SCBI* BM H/N, 28 n.12; Hall 1974, 74.

115 D. 79; *Inv.* 324; Blunt 1974, 156–8 (Appendix II, 'The Scotby hoard').

116 D. 80; *Inv.* 312; *SCBI* Edinburgh, xiii, xxiii; Graham-Campbell 1976b, 119, 127.

117 D. 77; *Inv.* 133; Dolley (320) 1962; Hall 1974, 73; Graham-Campbell 1976a, 49, 62, 66.

118 D. 74; *Inv.* 300; *SCBI* Oxford, pl. xiii and facing text.

119 D. 'uncertain hoards (b)'; *Inv.* –; Hall 1974, 74. The letter cited by Dolley is in the British Library, not the National Library of Ireland; the relevant passage reads: 'a few years since many Saxon coins of King Aethelstan's were dug up in Ireland'.

120 D. –; *Inv.* –; Graham-Campbell 1976a, 49, 65, 68 (as 'found in Ireland'), but in a forthcoming note

he shows that it was 'found in the Thames, near Deptford', citing the sale catalogue of the collection of the 1st Baron Londesborough (d.1860), Christie, 4 July 1888, lot 885.

121 D. –; *Inv.* –; publication by Miss E. J. E. Pirie in *Archaeology of York* 8.1 (forthcoming).

122 D. –; *Inv.* –; Dolley (599) 1973; Hall 1974, 74.

123 D. 75; *Inv.* –; *SCBI* Edinburgh, xiii; Graham-Campbell 1976b, 118, 127.

124 D. 81; *Inv.* –; Dolley and Pagan (380) 1964; Hall 1974, 74.

125 D. 82; *Inv.* 356; Dolley (325) 1962; Hall 1974, 74.

126 D. 83; *Inv.* –; Dolley (265) 1960, 5.

127 D. 76; *Inv.* –; Hall 1974, 74; Pagan 1974a; McCarthy and Dolley (751) 1977.

128 D. –; *Inv.* –; Dolley (489) 1969, 20.

129 D. 84; *Inv.* 322; *SCBI* Edinburgh, xiv, xxii; Graham-Campbell 1976b, 119–21, 127; Graham-Campbell 1984.

130 D. –; *Inv.* –; Dolley (489) 1969; Hall 1974, 75.

131 D. –; *Inv.* –; Kenny 1984.

132 D. 86; *Inv.* –; Dolley and Ingold (276) 1961, 242; Dolley (542) 1970; Hall 1974, 75.

133 D. 85; *Inv.* –; Strudwick 1955b; Metcalf 1957, 194–5; Blunt and Pagan 1975, 28.

134 D. 87; *Inv.* –; Metcalf 1957, 195; Hall 1974, 75; Graham-Campbell 1976a, 63, 67.

135 D. 88; *Inv.* 277; Dolley (256) 1960; Hall 1974, 75; Graham-Campbell 1976a, 63, 67; McShane 1980.

136 D. 93; *Inv.* –; Metcalf 1958, 77–9; Blunt and Pagan 1975.

137 D. –; *Inv.* –; British Museum, Dept of Coins and Medals, Accessions Register.

138 D. 89; *Inv.* 215; Pagan and Rhodes 1962, 23–5; Hall 1974, 75.

139 D. 91; *Inv.* 298; Seaby 1959, 253–4; Hall 1974, 75–6.

140 D. 90; *Inv.* 220; Blunt and Pagan 1975.

141 D. 108; *Inv.* 355; *SCBI* Lincolnshire pls. 57–60.

142 D. 94; *Inv.* 29; Dolley (327) 1962; Hall 1974, 76.

143 D. 92; *Inv.* 34; Dolley (676) 1975, 190–1; Dolley (683) 1975, no. 3; Dolley (807) 1979; Graham-Campbell 1983, 56–7.

144 D. 102; *Inv.* 86; Blunt and Dolley (43) 1953; Archibald 1967; *CH* 2 (1976), no. 444.

145 D. 95; *Inv.* –; Hall 1974, 76.

146 D. 96; *Inv.* 260; Dolley (442) 1967; Hall 1974, 76.

147 D. 107; *Inv.* 333; Blunt 1953; Hall 1974, 77.

148 D. 109; *Inv.* –; Dolley (29) 1952; *SCBI* Yorkshire pt.i, xxxix.

149 D. 98; *Inv.* 13; *SCBI* BM H/N 32 n.13; Hall 1974, 76. A newspaper cutting from the *Newry Examiner* of 2 June 1831 indicates that the coin of Athelstan cited by Lindsay was of *Circumscription Cross* type, London mint, moneyer Ellaf (and not of *Two-line* type as might be deduced from the Lindsay reference). The date of deposit of the hoard is somewhat more uncertain than Dolley's readers might suppose.

150 D. 99; *Inv.* –; Dolley (235) 1959; Dykes 1976, 27, no. 3.

151 D. –; *Inv.* –; Christmas 1861.

152 D. 100; *Inv.* 75/261; Seaby 1959, 249; Dolley (242) 1959; Hall 1974, 76.

153 D. 101; *Inv.* 84.

154 D. 103; *Inv.* 212; Hall 1974, 77; Graham-Campbell 1976a, 63, 67.

155 D. 97; *Inv.* 8; Dolley (676) 1975; Dolley (683) 1975, no. 4; Dolley (811) 1979.

156 D. 104; *Inv.* –; Dolley (252) 1960; Hall 1974, 77; Graham-Campbell 1976a, 63.

157 D. 105; *Inv.* –; Dolley (320) 1962; Hall 1974, 77.

158 D. 106; *Inv.* –; Dolley (320) 1962; Hall 1974, 77; Graham-Campbell 1976a, 63, 67.

159 D. –; *Inv.* –; Dolley (807) 1979, 124; Graham-Campbell 1983, 57.

160 D. –; *Inv.* –; Dolley (655) 1974; Hall 1974, 77.
161 D. –; *Inv.* –; Briggs and Dolley (615) 1973; Dolley (655) 1974; Hall 1974, 77.
162 D. –; *Inv.* –; Graham-Campbell 1982b.
163 D. 110; *Inv.* 115; Dolley (290) 1961; Dolley (655) 1974; Hall 1974, 77.
164 D. 111; *Inv.* 119; Dolley (385) 1965; Hall 1974, 78.
165 D. 112; *Inv.* 127; Blunt 1966; Dolley (500) 1969; Dolley (676) 1975; Dolley (683) 1975, no. 5; Pagan 1980.
166 D. 113; *Inv.* 174: Dolley (252) 1960; Hall 1974, 78.
167 D. –; *Inv.* –; Warner 1975. A second find(?) from the same site as no. 218.
168 D. 114; *Inv.* 201; *SCBI* Edinburgh, xxi. The 'Knowe, Islay' parcel (*Inv.* 202) is probably from this hoard.
169 D. 115; *Inv.* –; *SCBI* Edinburgh, xv, xxii.
170 D. 116; *Inv.* 207; Dolley and Martin (226) 1959; Hall 1974, 78.
171 D. 119; *Inv.* 357; *SCBI* Edinburgh, xxiii; Graham-Campbell 1976b, 128. Dumas (1979, no. 38) dismisses, on chronological grounds, the attribution of four Normandy deniers in the Edinburgh collection to this hoard.
172 D. 117; *Inv.* –; Dolley (215) 1959; Dykes 1976, 27 no. 4.
173 D. –; *Inv.* –; Dolley (492) 1969.
174 D. 120; *Inv.* 85; Dolley and Pirie (370) 1964.
175 D. 24, 121, 'uncertain (c)'; *Inv.* –; Blunt and Lyon 1979. Unpublished evidence among the Ruding MSS in the British Library suggests that the hoard may have contained some *First Hand* pennies of Æthelred II.
176 D. –; *Inv.* –; Metcalf and Jonsson 1980.
177 D. 122; *Inv.* –; Dolley (236) 1959; *SCBI* Edinburgh, xxii.
178 D. 125; *Inv.* 199; Dolley (369) 1964; Sadler 1981.
179 D. 123; *Inv.* 265; *SCBI* BM H/N, 33 n. 2; Hall, 1974, 78; Graham-Campbell 1976a, 61.
180 D. 124; *Inv.* 198; Dolley and Morrison (350) 1963, no. 21; *SCBI* Edinburgh, xx; Dumas 1979, no. 7.
181 D. –; *Inv.* –; Dolley and Grover (848) 1983.
182 D. 126; *Inv.* –; *SCBI* BM H/N, 34 n.12.
183 D. 127; *Inv.* 134; *SCBI* BM H/N, 33 n.3; Hall 1974, 79.
184 D. 128; *Inv.* 203.
185 D. –; *Inv.* –; Spufford 1961, 215–16.
186 D. 129; *Inv.* 320; Dolley (683) 1975, no. 6; Dolley (821) 1980.
187 D. –; *Inv.* –; Kenny 1985.
188 D. 131; *Inv.* 91; *SCBI* BM H/M, 55–6; Hall 1974, 79.
189 D. –; *Inv.* –; Blackburn, Collyer, and Dolley 1983, 39 no. 3; Blackburn 1985b.
190 D. 118; *Inv.* 351; Dolley and Morrison (350) 1963, no. 20; *SCBI* Edinburgh, xxiii; Dumas 1971, 117 n. 3; Pagan 1973b (redating the hoard on the basis of the Continental element).
191 D. –; *Inv.* –; *SCBI* Edinburgh, xx.
192 D. 130 and 136; *Inv.* 144 and 161; *SCBI* Glasgow, xii; *SCBI* Edinburgh, xix; Graham-Campbell 1976b, 128–9.
193 D. 132; *Inv.* 61; Dolley and Morrison (350) 1963, no. 22; *SCBI* Edinburgh, xviii.
194 D. 133; *Inv.* 196; Dolley and Morrison (350) 1963, no. 24; *SCBI* BM H/N, 58; *SCBI* Edinburgh, xix; Dumas 1979, no. 26.
195 D. 135; *Inv.* –; Dolley and Morrison (350) 1963, no. 23; *SCBI* BM H/N, 57; Hall 1974, 79; Dumas 1979, no. 3; Blackburn 1981, 53–4.
196 D. 137; *Inv.* –; Dolley and Ingold (276) 1961, 246–50; *SCBI* BM H/N, 58–9.
197 D. 138; *Inv.* –; Dolley (198) 1958. Dolley associated hoard nos. 197–201 with the St Brice's Day Massacre of 1002; *SCBI* BM H/N, 39.
198 D. 139; *Inv.* –; Dolley (198) 1958.
199 D. 140; *Inv.* –; Dolley (198) 1958; Wilson 1964, 150–1.
200 D. 141; *Inv.* –; Dolley (144) 1956.

201 D. 142; *Inv.* –; *SCBI* Yorkshire pt.i, xxxiii.
202 D. –; *Inv.* –; to be published by M. Kenny.
203 D. 143; *Inv.* –; Dolley (228) 1959, 187–8; Dykes 1976, 27 no. 5.
204 D. 144; *Inv.* 249; Butler and Dolley (217) 1959; *SCBI* South East (forthcoming).
205 D. 145; *Inv.* –; Dolley and Metcalf (274) 1961, 164; cf. Dolley and Metcalf (193) 1958, 71. The source for this find is *Magna Britannia* I (1720), 310, the relevant passage of which reads: 'about 30 years since, near the church, in a place where once stood a cross, (as is said) was found a buff bag full of silver pieces, some of King Arthur's coin, and some of King Canute's, of which this is the figure, the reverse not so perfect as to be read.'

This appears to be a *Quatrefoil* coin of Cnut (?depicting the obverse legend and reverse design), and those of 'King Arthur' were probably ones of Æthelred II.
206 D. 146; *Inv.* –; Metcalf 1958, 82–3; Dolley and Metcalf (193) 1958, associating a large group of early *Quatrefoil* coins mainly from western mints with a recorded find of unspecified Anglo-Saxon coins from Kingsholm. The coherence of the group is generally supported by their heavy weights (Lyon 1971), though some of the lighter coins are unlikely to belong to the hoard.
207 D. –; *Inv.* –; *CH* 7 (1985), no. 544; publication by G. Boon forthcoming.
208 D. –; *Inv.* –; *CH* 6 (1981), no. 372; publication by G. Boon forthcoming.
209 D. 147; *Inv.* 46; *SCBI* Edinburgh, xx.
210 D. 148; *Inv.* 35; Dolley (790) 1978.
211 D. 150; *Inv.* –; *SCBI* BM H/N, 40 n.4, on the authority of 'Mrs J. S. Martin who cites *Notes and Queries* i, p. 347'. However, this reference is an error and we have been unable to find Mrs Martin's source for the find.
212 D. 151; *Inv.* 181; Dolley (224) 1959; Dolley and Morrison (350) 1963, no. 25; Dumas 1979, no. 25.
213 D. –; *Inv.* –; Dolley (662) 1975, 321, 326–8; Dumas 1979, no. 36.
214 D. –; *Inv.* –; *SCBI* Merseyside, xx; Dumas 1979, no. 32.
215 D. 153; *Inv.* 131 and 306; Dykes 1976, 27 no. 6.
216 D. 149; *Inv.* 234; Butler and Dolley (297) 1961; *SCBI* Edinburgh, xxii. See note to no. 302 below.
217 D. 154; *Inv.* –; Dolley and Ingold (276) 1961, 250–5; *SCBI* BM H/N, 63–4; O'Sullivan 1971; Hall 1974, 80.
218 D. 155; *Inv.* –; Dolley and Ingold (276) 1961, 255–7; Dolley (657) 1974; Warner 1975.
219 D. 134; *Inv.* 222; Dolley (683) 1975, no. 7; Dolley (701) 1976.
220 D. –; *Inv.* –; Blackburn 1983.
221 D. 152; *Inv.* 66; Dolley and Strudwick (97) 1955, 52; *SCBI* Edinburgh, xviii.
222 D. –; *Inv.* –; Hall 1974, –; Dolley (753) 1977.
223 D. –; *Inv.* –; Wilson 1974, 36–7, 46; Dolley (683) 1975, no. 8; Graham-Campbell 1983, 58.
224 D. 158; *Inv.* 338; Robinson 1969.
225 D. –; *Inv.* –; Archibald 1985b.
226 D. 156; *Inv.* –; *SCBI* BM H/N, 64; Hall 1974, 80.
227 D. –; *Inv.* –; Hall 1974, 80, citing a letter from I. Stewart to M. Dolley, the contents of which were never published and cannot now be recalled by Dr Stewart.
228 D. –; *Inv.* –; Dolley (701) 1976; Dolley (802) 1979.
229 D. 157; *Inv.* 374; Seaby 1955, 124–5; Dolley and Strudwick (97) 1955, 35–6, 54; *SCBI* West Country 574, doubtfully a stray.
230 D. 161; *Inv.* 9; *SCBI* BM H/N, 56;

Dolley (683) 1975, no. 9; Dolley (823) 1980; Graham-Campbell 1983, 60.
231 D. -; *Inv.* –; Dolley (652) 1974; Dolley (683) 1975, no. 10; Graham-Campbell 1983, 58.
232 D. 160; *Inv.* 69 and 360; Martin 1956; *SCBI* Oxford pt.i, xiv. Parcels from this hoard, similar to those in the Ashmolean and British Museums, were presented by Mrs R. Wilson (7 coins?) and by Rev. Greville J. Chester (2 coins) to the Fitzwilliam Museum, though the coins cannot now be individually identified.
233 D. -; *Inv.* –; Hall 1974, 79.
234 D. –; *Inv.* –; Dolley (654) 1974; Hall 1974, 80.
235 D. 162; *Inv.* 6; *SCBI* BM H/N, 69.
236 D. 163; *Inv.* –; Metcalf 1957, 183–5; *SCBI* BM H/N, 65; Hall 1974, 80.
237 D. 164; *Inv.* –; *SCBI* BM H/N, 67–8; Dolley (417) 1966. Probable parcels from this hoard are published in Stewart 1971; Blackburn and Seaby 1976.
238 D. 165; *Inv.* 30; *SCBI* BM H/N, 69; Hall 1974, 80–1.
239 D. –; *Inv.* –; information W. A. Seaby, publication in preparation.
240 D. 166; *Inv.* 270; Fearon 1971.
241 D. 167; *Inv.* –; Dolley and Strudwick (147) 1956, 297.
242 D. 168; *Inv.* 294; Dolley and Strudwick (147) 1956, 295–6.
243 D. –; *Inv.* –; Robinson 1970.
244 D. 169; *Inv.* 244; Dolley (47) 1953.
245 D. –; *Inv.* –; Dolley and Skaare (602) 1973; Graham-Campbell 1976b, 128.
246 D. 170; *Inv.* –; *SCBI* BM H/N, 70; Hall 1974, 81.
247 D. 171; *Inv.* 233; *SCBI* BM H/N, 70; Hall 1974, 81.
248 D. –; *Inv.* –; Dumas 1979, no. 51; Cubbon and Dolley (820) 1980.
249 D. –; *Inv.* –; Dolley (683) 1975, no. 12; Graham-Campbell 1983, 60.
250 D. 172; *Inv.* –; Dolley (171) 1957.
251 D. 173; *Inv.* –; Dolley (135) 1956.
252 D. 174; *Inv.* –; Dolley (313) 1961; *SCBI* Yorkshire pt.i, xli.
253 D. 175; *Inv.* 386; Dolley (546) 1971; Pirie 1972; *SCBI* Yorkshire pt.i, xxxiii.
254 D. 176; *Inv.* 327; Dolley (251) 1960; *CH* 5 (1979), no. 275. Although the hoard ends with Edward the Confessor's penultimate issue, its deposit may have been occasioned by the Norman conquest of 1066. An unpublished note (in the possession of one of the writers) by the late G. C. Dunning, F.S.A., who had inspected the iron remains of the container, suggests that it may have been an iron-bound wooden box, rather than the fragmentary iron pot and leather bag of the original account.
255 D. 177; *Inv.* 81 and 345; Sugden 1979; Knowles 1981; Holden 1982.
256 D. –; *Inv.* –. An unpublished addendum in J. D. A. Thompson's card index of hoards (Ashmolean Museum, Oxford) cites *Sussex Archaeol. Collections 14* (1862), 36–7, and *Sussex Notes and Queries 3* (1930), 101, for this find. These refer to some 20 coins 'of the Saxon dynasty' purchased c.1820 by Gideon Mantell, the Lewes surgeon and geologist, and said to have been found while cutting peat near the bend of a stream on the northern slopes of Camp Hill, between Nutley and Crowborough, and near Duddleswell. These may perhaps be the same find as that from Sussex referred to in the papers of the Lincoln antiquarian E. J. Willson, which illustrate and describe a coin of Harold II 'found last summer 1822, with a hoarde of Saxon coins' (Blunt 1981, 6, fig. 17; Blackburn, Colyer, and Dolley (845) 1983, 20).
257 D. 179; *Inv.* 297.
258 D. –; *Inv.* –; Pagan, forthcoming.
259 D. 180; *Inv.* –; Metcalf 1957, 198.
260 D. 159; *Inv.* –; Dolley (261) 1960; Pagan 1984.
261 D. 178; *Inv.* 225; Dolley (265) 1960, 4; Whitting 1961, 33; Burrows 1977. Also known as the 'City hoard'. Doubt exists over the date of deposition, since although the bulk of

the hoard has a *terminus* of c.1066, both Willett and Evans recorded a few coins of William I, types i-iv. Dolley considered these interlopers from a second hoard listed in 1966:
197. London (Walbrook, no. 2), 1872 E X N + – c.1075.

262 D. 186; *Inv.* 318.

263 D. 187; *Inv.* 334; Pagan, forthcoming.

264 D. –; *Inv.* –; Clough 1973; *SCBI* East Anglia, nos. 1348–54.

265 D. 183; *Inv.* –; Metcalf 1957, 186–90; *SCBI* Oxford pt.i, xi.

266 D. 185; *Inv.* –; Robinson 1969; Robinson 1979.

267 D. 181; *Inv.* –; *SCBI* BM H/N, 44 n.8., but ref. is in 2nd edn (1816) of Thorseby. Coins in possession of Dr R. Richardson (1663–1741).

268 D. 182; *Inv.* –; *SCBI* BM H/N, 44 n.9., but ref. in 2nd edn (1816) of Thorseby as 'lately discovered'.

269 D. 184; *Inv.* –; *SCBI* BM H/N, 44 n.3.

270 D. 188; *Inv.* –; *SCBI* Yorkshire pt.i, xxxv.

271 D. 189; *Inv.* 388; Pirie 1972; *SCBI* Yorkshire pt.i, xxv.

272 D. 190; *Inv.* 387; *SCBI* Yorkshire pt.i, xxxiv.

273 D. –; *Inv.* –; Dolley (546) 1971; Pirie 1972; *SCBI* Yorkshire pt.i, xxxvi.

274 D. 191; *Inv.* –; Dolley and Metcalf (274) 1961, 165. Unpublished notes in J. D. A. Thompson's card index cites, in addition, *Procs. Soc. of Antiquaries 2* (1849–51), 166, and Lewis 1845, I, 195, referring to 'upwards of 100 coins chiefly of the reigns of William the Conqueror and his son William Rufus, with a few of Edward the Confessor and Canute the Dane . . . in a fine state of preservation' found while digging a grave in the nave of the church.

275 D. 192; *Inv.* 62; *SCBI* BM H/N, 44 n.13.

276 D. 193; *Inv.* 346; Wilson 1964, 174–7.

277 D. –; *Inv.* –; *J. Brit. Archaeol. Ass.*[2] 5 (1899), 148, reproducing minutes of the Peterborough Gentlemen's Society: 'June 11, 1735 – Rev. Mr Mason, Rector of Cotesworth, near Grantham . . . presents a "Peter's peny" found with several others of the same sort in digging a grave in his churchyard. It is a coin of Wm. the Conqueror.'

278 D. –; *Inv.* –; Dolley (683) 1975, no. 13 (7 coins formerly the property of a Laxey resident).

279 D. 195; *Inv.* 376.

280 D. –; *Inv.* –; *CH* 5 (1979), no. 278.

281 D. 196; *Inv.* 264.

282 D. 198; *Inv.* 250; Dolley (265) 1960, 3. Dolley associated this hoard with the troubles of 1075.

283 D. 194; *Inv.* 224; *SCBI* BM H/N, 71–2; Dolley (604) 1973; Dolley (683) 1975, no. 14; Dolley (819) 1980.

284 D. 199; *Inv.* 323; Dolley (164) 1957; *SCMB* 1979, 373–4; *CH* 6 (1981), no. 375.

285 D. 200; *Inv.* 390; *SCBI* BM H/N, 44 n.19; *SCBI* Yorkshire pt.i, xxxvi.

286 D. 201; *Inv.* –; *SCBI* Yorkshire pt.i, xxxvii.

287 D. 202; *Inv.* 37; Mack 1967b.

288 D. 203; *Inv.* 350.

289 D. –; *Inv.* –; Kenny 1983.

290 D. –; *Inv.* –; Dolley (681) 1975.

291 D. 204; *Inv.* –; Metcalf 1958, 81; *SCBI* BM H/N, 72–5; Hall 1974, 81.

292 D. 205; *Inv.* 173; *SCBI* BM H/N, 75–6; Hall 1974, 81; Dolley (826) 1981; *SCBI* Belfast pt.ii, 5.

293 D. 207; *Inv.* –; *SCBI* BM H/N, 77; Hall 1974, 81.

294 D. 208; *Inv.* –; *SCBI* BM H/N, 78–9 and 231 pl.C; Hall 1974, 81; *SCBI* Belfast pt.ii, 6 and nos. 361–7.

295 D. 209; *Inv.* 122; *SCBI* BM H/N, 79–80; Graham-Campbell 1976a, 63–4; *SCBI* Belfast pt.ii, 6–7.

296 D. –; *Inv.* –; Hall 1974, 78.

297 D. 'uncertain (f)'; *Inv.* –; Lindsay 1849, 4; Dolley and Morrison (350) 1963, no. 26. Normandy deniers

'found in some part of England with a parcel of the Confessor's'. The deniers illustrated by Lindsay (pl.1, nos. 2–10) belong to Dumas's group A, which she dates to the first third of the 11th cent. (Dumas 1979).

298 D. –; *Inv.* –; Blunt 1976. A parcel of some 16 coins of Harold II and 2 of William I, type i.

299 D. 206; *Inv.* 213; *SCBI* BM H/N, 76–7; Hall 1974, 81. Based on an inference as to their weight, Dolley considered these likely to have been Hiberno-Norse coins of the late 11th or early 12th cent.

300 D. 210; *Inv.* –; *SCBI* BM H/N, 80; Hall 1974, 81. Dolley thought these likely to have been crude coins of the late 11th or early 12th cent., but their illegibility was apparently due to their poor condition.

301 D. –; *Inv.* –; Hall 1974, 83–4; Graham-Campbell 1976a, 62, 64.

302 D. –; *Inv.* –. Sotheby, 1 Nov. 1920 (property of a 'baronet'), lot 369: 'Hiberno-Danish pennies (10), rude helmeted head, blundered inscriptions, and three others, all very fine . . . The former are from a find in Fifeshire in 1832.'

This description suggests that they were Hiberno-Norse derivatives of the *Long Cross* type; they cannot have been Hiberno-Manx as insufficient coins without provenance survive, nor is it likely that they were Scandinavian imitations which only occur in mixed hoards with other European coins. Hiberno-Norse coins are not otherwise recorded from mainland Scotland and the reported provenance should therefore be treated with reserve. However, the 'baronet' also had some coins from the 12th-cent. Outchester, Northumb. (1817) hoard, which suggests that he was a northern, rather than an Irish, collector. It is possible that they were a parcel from the 1814 Parkhill find (no. 216), and that the indecipherable coins which made up the bulk of that hoard were in fact Hiberno-Norse pennies of Phase II or III.

303 D. 16; *Inv.* –; *SCBI* Edinburgh, xx. Descriptions of this hoard are conflicting.

304 D. 37; *Inv.* –; Metcalf 1960, 97. It remains to be established that this was a hoard of the Anglo-Saxon period.

305 D. 'uncertain (e)'; *Inv.* –; Dolley and Metcalf (193) 1958, 77, referring to research of Mrs J. S. Martin, but her source is not cited.

306 D. –; *Inv.* –; Robinson 1970.

307 D. –; *Inv.* 389; *SCBI* Yorkshire pt.i, xxxiv.

Omissions

The following hoards listed by Dolley have been omitted from the revised check-list.

D.21 Barking, 1724. It has not been established that the coin of Burgred exhibited to a meeting of the Society of Antiquaries on 28 April 1725 derived from the grave find of 10 October 1724 cited by Metcalf (1958, 76), and there is no evidence that the 'several Saxon coins' found in Barking in the early 18th cent. were found together.

D.30 Castleton, 1814. See Metcalf 1960, 121, where he expresses the view that 'the coins were probably not a hoard'.

D.36 Meols, pre-1823. See Dolley (312) 1961, 198, where he concludes that on balance the coins were not found together.

D.61 Boxmoor, pre-1863. See Blunt 1979b, 14, doubting the existence of this hoard.

D.64 Derbyshire, c.1860. See Blunt 1979b, 12–14, doubting the existence of this hoard.

Bibliography

Archibald, M. M., 1967. 'Disposition of the Chester (1950) hoard', *BNJ 36* (1967), 189.

— 1985a. 'A Scandinavian coin of

Carolingian type from the Cuerdale hoard', *Hikuin 11* (1985), 79–82.

— 1985b. 'The Titchmarsh (Northants.) hoard of Harold I pennies *c.*1040', *CH 6* (1985), 375–8.

Bailey, R. N., 1974. 'The Anglo-Saxon metalwork from Hexham', in *Saint Wilfrid at Hexham*, ed. D. P. Kirby (1974), 141–67.

Blackburn, M. A. S., 1981. 'An imitative workshop active during Æthelræd II's *Long Cross* issue', in *Studies in Northern Coinages of the Eleventh Century*, ed. C. J. Becker (Copenhagen, 1981), 29–88.

— 1983. 'A penny of Coenwulf and a small hoard of Cnut from Bottisham, Cambridgeshire', *BNJ* 53 (1983), 176–7.

— 1984. 'A chronology for the sceattas', in Hill and Metcalf 1984, 165–74.

— 1985a. 'A preliminary account of the 9th-century coins in the Ashdon (Steventon End) hoard 1984', *NCirc* 1985, 43–4.

—1985b. 'The Welbourn, Lincs. hoard 1980/82 of Æthelred II coins', *BNJ 55* (1985).

Blackburn, M. A. S., and M. J. Bonser, 1985. 'Anglo-Saxon and Norman single-finds – 2', *BNJ 55* (1985).

Blackburn, M. A. S., and W. A. Seaby, 1976. 'The "Francis" and "Brand" parcels of Hiberno-Norse coins', *BNJ 46* (1976), 29–38.

Blunt, C. E., 1953. 'The Smarmore hoard of tenth-century pennies', *BNJ 27* (1953), 161–6.

— 1954. 'Saxon coins from Southampton and Bangor', *BNJ 27* (1954), 256–62.

— 1966. 'A new parcel from the Douglas, I.O.M., 1894 hoard (?)', *BNJ 35* (1966), 7–11.

— 1972a. 'The Sevington hoard of 1834', *BNJ 41* (1972), 7–13.

— 1972b. 'A small parcel from the Dorking (1817) hoard', *BNJ 41* (1972), 179.

— 1974. 'The coinage of Athelstan, 924–939. A survey', *BNJ 42* (special vol.; 1974), 35–158.

— 1976. 'Grangerized copies of Ruding's Annals', *NCirc* 1976, 226–7.

— 1979a. 'The Hougham hoard of sceattas c.1780', *NC* 1979, 108–10.

— 1979b. 'Some doubtful St. Peter hoards', *BNJ 49* (1979), 12–16.

— 1981. *The Lincoln and Stamford Mints in the Tenth and Eleventh Centuries* (Lincolnshire Museums Information Sheet no. 5).

— 1983. 'The composition of the Cuerdale hoard', *BNJ 53* (1983), 1–6.

Blunt, C. E., and C. S. S. Lyon, 1979. 'The Oakham hoard of 1749, deposited c.980', *NC* 1979, 111–21.

Blunt, C. E., C. S. S. Lyon, and B. H. I. H. Stewart, 1963. 'The coinage of southern England 796–840', *BNJ 32* (1963), 1–74.

Blunt, C. E., and H. E. Pagan, 1975. 'Three tenth-century hoards: Bath (1755), Kintbury (1761), Threadneedle Street (before 1924)', *BNJ 45* (1975), 19–32.

Blunt, C. E., and B. H. I. H. Stewart, 1983. 'The coinage of Regnald I of York and the Bossall hoard', *NC* 1983, 146–63.

Briggs, C. S., 1978. 'The Magheralagan hoard: an additional note', *UJA 41* (1978), 102.

Briggs, C. S., and J. A. Graham-Campbell, 1976. 'A lost hoard of Viking-age silver from Magheralagan, County Down', *UJA 39* (1976), 20–4.

Brooke, G. C., 1930. 'Treasure trove', *BNJ 20* (1930), 279–89.

Brown, D., 1981. 'The dating of the Sutton Hoo coins', *Anglo-Saxon Studies in Archaeology and History* 2 (BAR British Series 92; 1981), 71–86.

Burrows, O., 1977. 'An unnoticed parcel from the 1872 Queen Victoria Street hoard', *BNJ 47* (1977), 66–76.

Christmas, H., 1861. 'Unpublished English and Anglo-Gallic coins', *NC*^{2} *1* (1861), 17–31.

Clough, T. H. McK., 1973. 'A small hoard of William I type i pennies from Norwich', *BNJ 43* (1973), 142–3.

Dhénin, M., and P. Leclercq, 1982. 'The

coins of Quentovic from the Cuerdale hoard in the museum of Boulogne-sur-Mer', *BNJ 52* (1982), 104–7.
Dumas, F., 1979. 'Les monnaies normandes (Xe-XIIe siècles) avec un répertoire des trouvailles', *Revue Numismatique* 1979, 84–140.
Dykes, D. W., 1976. *Anglo-Saxon Coins in the National Museum of Wales* (1976).
Fearon, D., 1971. 'The re-discovery of a group of fifteen pence from the Milton Street hoard', *NCirc* 1971, 54–6.
Graham-Campbell, J. A., 1976a. 'The Viking-age silver hoards of Ireland', *Procs. of the Seventh Viking Congress*, ed. B. Almqvist and D. Greene (Dublin, 1976), 39–74.
— 1976b. 'The Viking-age silver and gold hoards of Scandinavian character from Scotland', *PSAS 107* (1975–6), 114–35.
— 1982a. 'The Viking silver hoards: an introduction', in *The Vikings*, ed. R. T. Farrell (1982), 32–41.
— 1982b. 'An unpublished gold finger-ring of Viking-age date from the Isle of Skye, and new light on the 1850 Skye hoard', *PSAS 112* (1982), 568–70.
— 1983. 'The Viking-age silver hoards of the Isle of Man', in *The Viking Age in the Isle of Man*, ed. C. Fell *et al.* (1983), 53–80.
— 1984. 'Two Viking-age silver brooch fragments believed to be from the 1858 Skaill (Orkney) hoard', *PSAS 114* (1984), 289–301.
Grierson, P., 1952. 'The Canterbury (St Martin's) hoard of Frankish and Anglo-Saxon coin-ornaments', *BNJ 27* (1952), 39–51.
— 1953. 'A stray from the Crondall hoard', *NC* 1953, 148–9.
— 1957. 'Halfpennies and third pennies of King Alfred', *BNJ 28* (1957), 477–93.
— 1962. 'The authenticity of the York "thrymsas" ', *BNJ 31* (1962), 8–10.
— 1970. 'The purpose of the Sutton Hoo coins', *Antiquity 44* (1970), 14–18.
Grierson, P., and M. Blackburn, 1986. *Medieval European Coinage* 1. *The Early Middle Ages (5th–10th centuries)* (1986).
Hall, R. A., 1974. 'A check-list of Viking-age coin finds from Ireland', *UJA 36–7* (1973–4), 71–86.
Hawkes, S. C., J. M. Merrick, and D. M. Metcalf, 1966. 'X-ray fluorescent analysis of some Dark Age coins and jewellery', *Archaeometry 9* (1966), 98–138.
Hill, D., and D. M. Metcalf (eds.), 1984. *Sceattas in England and on the Continent* (BAR British Series 128; 1984).
Holden, E. W., 1982. 'The Chancton hoard of Anglo-Saxon pennies', *Sussex Archaeol. Collections 120* (1982), 214–15.
Inv. J. D. A. Thompson, *Inventory of British Coin Hoards A.D.600–1500* (1956).
Kenny, M., 1983. 'A hoard of Hiberno-Norse coins from Clonmacnoise, Co. Offaly', *Numismatic Soc. of Ireland Occasional Papers 24–8* (1983), no. 25.
— 1984. 'Find of Anglo-Saxon pennies from Newtownlow, Co. Westmeath', *Riocht na Midhe* 7 (1984), 37–43.
— 1985. 'A small hoard of Anglo-Saxon and Hiberno-Norse coins from Co. Louth', *SCMB* 1985, 201–4.
Kent, J. P. C., 1975. 'The date of the Sutton Hoo hoard' and 'Catalogue of the Sutton Hoo coins, blanks and billets', *The Sutton Hoo Ship Burial* I, ed. R. L. S. Bruce-Mitford (1975), 588–647.
Knowles, L., 1981. 'Seven Anglo-Saxon pennies from the Chancton (Sussex) hoard', *Sussex Archaeol. Collections 119* (1981), 216–17.
Lewis, S., 1845. *A Topographical Dictionary of England* (5th edn, 1845).
Lindsay, J., 1849. *Notices of Remarkable Medieval Coins etc.* (Cork, 1849).
Lowick, N., 1976. 'The Kufic coins from Cuerdale', *BNJ 46* (1976), 19–28.
Lyon, C. S. S., 1969. 'The presidential review of the year', *BNJ 38* (1969), 223–5.
— 1971. 'Variations in currency in late Anglo-Saxon England', in *Mints, Dies and Currency*, ed. R. A. G. Carson (1971), 101–20.
Lyon, C. S. S., and B. H. I. H. Stewart,

1961. 'The Northumbrian Viking coins in the Cuerdale hoard', *A-S Coins*, 96–121.

Mack, R. P., 1967a. 'St John's Church, Chester, hoard of 1862', *BNJ 36* (1967), 36–9.

— 1967b. 'Beauworth 1833', *BNJ 36* (1967), 192.

McShane, J., 1980. 'Viking ingots found at Mungret Co. Limerick', *IN* 1980, 164–5.

Martin, J. S., 1956. 'The supposed finds at Thwaite and Campsey Ash, 1832', *BNJ 28* (1956), 414–16.

Metcalf, D. M., 1957. 'Find-records of medieval coins from Gough's Camden's *Britannia*', *NC* 1957, 181–207.

— 1958. 'Eighteenth-century finds of medieval coins from the records of the Society of Antiquaries', *NC* 1958, 73–96.

— 1960. 'Some finds of medieval coins from Scotland and the north of England', *BNJ 30* (1960), 88–123.

Metcalf, D. M., and K. Jonsson, 1980. 'A hoard from early in the reign of Æthelred II found at Spettisbury Rings Hill Fort, Dorset', *BNJ 50* (1980), 132–3.

Nichols, J. (ed.), 1809. *Letters on Various Subjects . . . to and from William Nicholson, D.D.* (1809).

O'Sullivan, W., 1971. 'Report on a hoard of Hiberno-Norse coins from site II', in P. J. Harknett, 'The excavation of two tumuli at Fourknocks (sites II and III), Co. Meath', *PRIA*, Section C, *71* (1971), 35–89, at 82–9 [O'Sullivan's report written 1951].

Pagan, H. E., 1965. 'Coinage in the age of Burgred', *BNJ 34* (1965), 11–27.

— 1966. 'The Gainford hoard', *BNJ 35* (1966), 190–1.

— 1969. 'Northumbrian numismatic chronology in the ninth century', *BNJ 38* (1969), 1–15.

— 1972. 'An unpublished fragment of a coin of Ceolwulf II', *BNJ 41* (1972), 14–20.

— 1973a. 'The Bolton Percy hoard of 1967', *BNJ 43* (1973), 1–44.

— 1973b. 'A cross-channel view of the Fécamp hoard', *NCirc* 1973, 96–7.

— 1974a. 'An Anglo-Saxon coin hoard from the west of Country Cork', *Cork Hist. and Archaeol. Soc. 79* (1974), 62–3.

— 1974b. 'Anglo-Saxon coins found at Hexham', in *Saint Wilfrid at Hexham*, ed. D. P. Kirby (1972), 185–90.

— 1977. 'The "Suffolk" find of ninth-century Anglo-Saxon pence: a further note', *BNJ 47* (1977), 128–30.

— 1980. 'The 1894 Ballaquayle hoard: five further parcels of coins Æthelstan–Eadgar', *BNJ 50* (1980), 12–19.

— 1982a. 'The coinage of the East Anglian kingdom from 825–870', *BNJ 52* (1982), 41–83.

— 1982b. Review of Pirie 1982a, *BNJ 52* (1982), 253–4.

— 1983. 'Two groups of coins of Aelfred with the London Monogram', *NCirc* 1983, 121.

— 1984. 'The Castor hoard of mid-eleventh century pence', *BNJ 54* (1984), 289–90.

—, forthcoming. 'The coinage of Harold II', *Numismatiska Meddelanden.*

Pagan, H. E., and N. G. Rhodes, 1962. 'Anglo-Saxon coins in the Westminster School collection', *BNJ 31* (1962), 11–26.

Pirie, E. J. E., 1971. 'A further note on the Bishopshill (York) find of 1882', *Annual Rep. Yorkshire Philosophical Soc.* 1971, 101–2.

— 1972. 'Early Norman coins in the Yorkshire Museum', *Annual Rep. Yorkshire Philosophical Soc.* 1972, 33–8.

— 1981. 'Early Northumbrian coins at auction, 1981', *BNJ 51* (1981), 32–51.

— 1982a. *Catalogue of the Early Northumbrian Coins in the Museum of Antiquities, Newcastle upon Tyne* (1982).

— 1982b. 'The Ripon hoard, 1695: contemporary and current interest', *BNJ 52* (1982), 84–103.

Poole, H., 1983. 'An important coin find', *Hertfordshire's Past 15* (Autumn 1983), 27–9 [Whippendell Woods, Watford, hoard].

Richardson, T., 1984. 'The Manchester hoard of sceattas and a group of sceattas from Manchester City Art Gallery', in Hill and Metcalf 1984, 217–21.

Rigold, S. E., 1958. 'Finds of St Edmund Memorial and other Anglo-Saxon coins from excavations at Thetford', *BNJ 29* (1958), 189–91.

— 1975. 'The Sutton Hoo coins in the light of the contemporary background of coinage in England', *The Sutton Hoo Ship Burial* I, ed. R. L. S. Bruce-Mitford (1975), 653–77.

— 1977. 'A group of three sceattas from excavations at Mucking, Essex', *BNJ 47* (1977), 127–8.

Rigold, S. E., and D. M. Metcalf, 1984. 'A revised check-list of English finds of sceattas', in Hill and Metcalf 1984, 245–68.

Robinson, P. H., 1969. 'The Stafford (1800) and Oulton (1795) hoards', *BNJ 38* (1969), 22–30.

— 1970. 'On a possible late Anglo-Saxon hoard from Mayfield, Staffs.', *NCirc* 1970, 384–5.

— 1979. 'A further small parcel of coins from the Oulton hoard (1795)', *BNJ 49* (1979), 125–7.

— 1983. 'The Shrewsbury hoard (1936) of pennies of Edward the Elder', *BNJ 53* (1983), 7–13.

— 1984. 'Saxon coins of Edward the Elder from St. Mary's Churchyard, Amesbury', *NC* 1984, 198–201.

Rogerson, A., 1982. 'Saxon coin hoard from Middle Harling', *SCMB* 1982, 81–2.

Ryan, M., *et al.*, 1984. 'Six silver finds of the Viking period from the vicinity of Lough Ennell, Co. Westmeath', *Peritia 3* (1984), 334–81.

Sadler, J. C., 1981. 'Some contemporary literary sources relating to the 1863 Ipswich Buttermarket hoard', *SCMB* 1981, 220–3.

Seaby, W. A., 1959. 'Anglo-Saxon hoards and coin finds in the north of Ireland', *BNJ 29* (1959), 248–54.

Sherlock, R. J., 1956. 'A nineteenth-century manuscript book on coins', *BNJ 28* (1956), 394–9.

Spufford, P., 1961. 'Some hoard evidence from a nineteenth-century collection', *BNJ 30* (1961), 213–16.

Stewart, I., 1971. 'A group of Hiberno-Norse pennies', *NCirc* 1971, 405–8.

Strudwick, J. S., 1955a. 'Saxon and Arabic coins found at Dean, Cumberland', *BNJ 28* (1955), 177–80.

— 1955b. 'An account of some coins found at Honedon, near Clare, Suffolk, 1687', *BNJ 28* (1955), 180–2.

Sugden, K. F., 1979. 'Coins from the Chancton find', *NCirc* 1979, 336.

Sugden, K. F., and M. Warhurst, 1978. 'A Cuerdale parcel rediscovered', *BNJ 48* (1978), 107–9.

— 1979. 'An unrecorded parcel from the Hexham hoard of 1832', *NC*[7] *19* (1979), 212–17.

Sutherland, C. H. V., 1948. *Anglo-Saxon Gold Coinage in the Light of the Crondall Hoard* (1948).

Talvio, T., 1980. 'A parcel of coins from Cuerdale in the Reichel collection', *NC* 1980, 188–91.

Walker, J., 1803. 'An essay on peat', *Prize Essays and Trans. of the Highland Soc. of Scotland* 2 (1803), 1–163.

Warner, R. B., 1974. 'The re-provenancing of two important penannular brooches of the Viking period', *UJA 36–7* (1973–4), 58–70.

— 1975. 'The coin-hoard from Ballycastle and a reprovenanced tortoise brooch from the River Bann', *UJA 38* (1975), 89–90.

Whitting, P. D., 1961. 'The Byzantine empire and the coinage of the Anglo-Saxons', *A-S Coins*, 23–38.

Wilson, D. M., 1964. *Anglo-Saxon Ornamental Metalwork 700–1100 in the British Museum* (1964).

— 1974. *The Viking Age in the Isle of Man: The Archaeological Evidence* (Odense, 1974).

Wilson, D. M., and C. E. Blunt, 1961. 'The Trewhiddle hoard', *Archaeologia 48* (1961), 75–122.

16 The published writings of Michael Dolley, 1944–1983

Compiled by R. H. Thompson

Michael Dolley was an exceedingly prolific writer. He had himself forgotten a significant proportion of what he had published, and it cannot be hoped that there are no omissions from this bibliography. In particular, a spoof criticism of T. S. Eliot's 'Macavity', and a history of the Cistercians in Ireland (Portglenone brochure), have not been traced. It was not possible to follow up the references in all his publications, let alone check the files of all the journals to which he contributed. It is understood that he published a number of pieces in his youth, but there is nothing here earlier than 1944. (The 1944–5 publications, having been found at a late stage, are identified by letters.)

The following have been deliberately omitted: insubstantial letters (in *IN*, *Manxman*, *NCirc*); contributions of a purely editorial character (in *BNJ* and *SCBI* volumes); uninformative reports of papers read (including that in the *Atti* of the International Numismatic Congress, Rome, 1961), and reports superseded by later publication; insubstantial reports of exhibitions (in *BNJ* and *NC*).

Arrangement is chronological by date of publication, or by titular date in the case of periodicals (the last year where a volume covers more than one); at the end there is a group of forthcoming publications, and another of manuscripts; there follows a synopsis of subjects and an index of collaborators and persons honoured by a *Festschrift*. Under each year, books are placed first; then contributions to other works, in alphabetical order of the titles of the periodicals or other volumes in which they appear; and finally, reviews. A superscript numeral following the title of a periodical identifies a numbered series of that periodical. The name *Ríocht na Midhe* has been used in place of the Irish characters of that journal's title. Asterisked items have not been examined by the compiler; certain others have been seen in the form of offprints or photocopies only.

Michael Dolley was baptized 'Reginald Hugh', and confirmed 'Michael'. He had been born with dual nationality, British and Irish, but in 1966 publicly divested himself of the former. As far as the Irish State was concerned he was legally Michael Dolley = Micheál Ó Dathlaoich.

From 1944 to 1952 his publications are signed 'Reginald Hugh Dolley' (in full or abbreviated), a form of name which continues on a few publications of 1953–4, and also on items 123*bis* and 195. From 1953 to 1966 the majority of his publications are signed 'R. H. M. Dolley', but he used 'Michael Dolley' (or 'M. D.') on items 90, 93,

128–9, 142, 168–9, 171, 197, 224, 255, 264, 292, 308–9, 323, 328, 356, 363, 367, 384, 391, 393, 399–401, 407, 418, and 424–8. Item 271 is signed 'Michael', and item 253 'Micheál Maolmuire Ó Dathlaoich' (the second name, which he also spelled *Maolmhuire*, means 'devotee of Mary'). From 1967 the form of signature is normally 'Michael Dolley' ('Dolly' [sic] on 498), but 'R. H. M. Dolley' occurs on items 455, 482–3, 496, 730, and 813–14. Item 524*bis* uses the names 'Seán Óg Ó Fearghail' and 'Micheál Ó Dathlaoich'; item 551, 'Merus Hibernicus'; and item 591*bis*, 'Seamus MacMuiris'.

1944

a. Hellas, 480 BC–AD 1944. *Hellas: national Greek weekly* no. 98, 28 Jan. 1944, 3. [Poetry].

b. March 25, 1944. *Ibid.* no. 106, 24 Mar. 1944, 3. [Poetry, on the anniversary of Greek independence day].

c. Stanley Casson (killed on active service, April 1944). *Ibid.* no. 111, 28 Apr. 1944, 4. [Poetry, signed 'R. H. D.'; translation into classical Greek by John L. Myres, *ibid.* no. 113, 12 May 1944, 6].

d. Krete. *Ibid.* no. 117, 9 June 1944, 4. [Poetry].

e. The new Helen. *Ibid.* no. 127, 18 Aug. 1944, 3. [Poetry].

f. Athens. *Ibid.* no. 137, 27 Oct. 1944, 3. [Poetry].

1945

g. Four Roman philhellenes. *Hellas: national Greek weekly* no. 184, 21 Sept. 1945, 4. [Scipio Aemilianus Africanus; Sulla; Nero; Hadrian].

h. Constantine VII – scholar and emperor. *Ibid.* no. 190, 2 Nov. 1945, 3.

1948

1. A forgotten Byzantine conquest of Kypros. *Bulletin de la Classe des lettres et des sciences morales et politiques – Académie royale de Belgique,*[5] *34*(5), 1948, 209–24.
2. The warships of the Later Roman Empire. *J. Roman Studies 38*(1/2), 1948, 47–53, pl. v.

1949

3. Oleg's mythical campaign against Constantinople. *Bulletin de la Classe des lettres et des sciences morales et politiques – Académie royale de Belgique,*[5] *35*(2), 1949, 106–30.
4. The historical significance of the translation of St Lazaros from Kypros to Byzantion. *Byzantion 19*: Actes du VIIe Congrès des études byzantines, Bruxelles 1948 (i), 1949, 59–71.
5. Angleterre. In *Dix années d'Etudes byzantines: bibliographie internationale, 1939–1948* [éditée par l'] Association internationale des Études byzantines, Paris 1949, 23–32.
6. The rig of early medieval warships. *Mariner's Mirror 35*(1), Jan. 1949, 51–5. [Note by R. LeB. Bowen, *36*(1), January 1950, 88–9; *see also* items 10, 79].
7. The origin of the ram. *Ibid. 35*(2), April 1949, 152. [Note by J. E. de Courcy Ireland, *36*(1), January 1950, 89–90; *see also* item 9.]

1950

8. The date of the St Mokios attempt on the life of the Emperor Leon VI. *Annuaire de l'Institut de Philologie et d'Histoire Orientales et Slaves – Université Libre de Bruxelles, 10*: ΠΑΓΚΑΡΠΕΙΑ: mélanges Henri Grégoire [ii], 1950, 231–8.
9. Origin of the ram. *Mariner's Mirror 36*(2), April 1950, 157–8. [*See also* item 7.]
10. The rig of early medieval warships. *Ibid.*, 158–60. [*See also* items 6, 79.]

Reviews

11. Louis Bréhier, *Les Institutions de l'empire byzantin*, livre III, ch. VI, 404–29: *La Marine impériale*. *Byzantion 20*: Actes du VIIe Congrès des études byzantines, Bruxelles 1948 (ii), 1950, 375–7.
12. Paul-Marie Duval, 'La forme des navires romains d'après la mosaïque d'Althiburus'. *Mariner's Mirror 36*(3), July 1950, 272–3.

1951

13. Six coins of Henry I, class XIV from an uncertain hoard. *BNJ 26*(3), 1951, 345–6; *27*(1), 1952, pl. vi.
14. Meteorology in the Byzantine navy. *Mariner's Mirror 37*(1), Jan. 1951, 5–16.
15. A Byzantine analogy with English nautical idiom. *Ibid. 37*(3), July 1951, 245–6.
16. Haselbury Plucknett treasure trove. *NC*^{6} *11*, 1951, 134–5. [20th-cent.]

Reviews

17. G. C. Brooke, *English Coins*, 3rd edn. *Ibid.*, 150–1.

1952

18. Maidstone treasure-trove, by R. H. Dolley and E. J. Winstanley; a note on the Maidstone pot [by] A. Warhurst. *BNJ 27*(1), 1952, 58–65. [16th-cent.]
19. A small find of Anglo-Saxon pennies from Roncesvalles. F. Mateu y Llopis, R. H. Dolley. *Ibid.*, 89–91. [10th-cent.]
20. A find of Edward pence at Chester. R. H. Dolley, F. Elmore Jones, Graham Webster. *Ibid.*, 91–2.
21. An 1895 find of Elizabethan silver coins. R. H. Dolley, Graham Webster. *Ibid.*, 93–4. [Mickle Trafford find].
22. Gads. *Mariner's Mirror 38*(1), Feb. 1952, 68.
23. An early form of sea-anchor. *Ibid.*, 68–9.
24. Richard Wright, marine painter. *Ibid.*, *38*(2), May 1952, 142.
25. 'Nefs' or 'corbitae'? *Ibid.*, 143–4, pl. 2.
26. The 'nef' ships of the Ravenna mosaics. *Ibid 38*(4), Nov. 1952, 315–18, pl. 1. [Reply by R. LeB. Bowen, *39*(3), Aug. 1953, 224–7.]
27. Skeletons at Sheerness. *Ibid.*, 329.
28. Two coins of Edgar recently discovered at York. *NC*^{6} *12*, 1952, 118.
29. Orston treasure trove. *Ibid.*, 118–22. [17th-cent.]
30. Gloucester treasure trove. *Ibid.*, 122–4. [17th-cent.]
31. Axminster treasure trove. *Ibid.*, 124. [19th-cent.]
32. Aylesbury treasure trove. *Ibid.*, 125. [15th-cent.]
33. Coin finds: the Orston treasure trove; Maidstone treasure trove. *NCirc 60*(5), May 1952, cols. 257–8. [Also published as 'Notes on finds', *SCMB* no. 408, May 1952, 208–9].
34. [The Queen's name on the new coinage]. *SCMB* no. 417, Feb. 1953, 63–4. [Repr. from the *Daily Telegraph*, 9 Dec. 1952.]
35. Pseudo-Symeon (pp. 705–7) and the Oleg controversy. *Slavonic and East European Rev. 30*(75), June 1952, 551–5.

Reviews

36. Pierre Paris, 'Note sur deux passages de Strabon et de Pline dont l'intérêt n'est pas seulement nautique'. *Mariner's Mirror 38*(1), Feb. 1952, 74.
37. Henri Seyrig, 'Antiquités de Beth-Maré'. *Ibid. 38*(3), Aug. 1952, 246–7.
38. R. C. Anderson, *Naval Wars in the Levant, 1559–1853*. *Ibid. 38*(4), Nov. 1952, 333–4.
39. V. Laurent, *Documents de Sigillographie, I: La collection C. Orghidan*. *NC*^{6} *12*, 1952, 164–6.

1953

39*bis*. *Kings & queens*, AD *653–1953: [catalogue of an exhibition]*, Diploma Gallery, Royal Academy of Arts, London. [1953]. xii, 73pp. ['3rd edition' examined; 'the catalogue entries . . . for coins, medals and seals [were written] by Mr R. H. Dolley' – preface; 'Explanatory note on the coins, medals, dies, and seals' by R. H. Dolley, pp. 66–71.]

40. The 'Jewel-Cross' coinage of Ælfgifu Emma, Harthacnut, and Harold I. In *Actes – Congrès international de Numismatique, Paris . . . 1953*, Paris 1957, 325–34. [*See also* item 72].

41. A Saxon treasure hoard found at Chester, 1950: a note on the coins. *AntJ 33*(1/2), Jan./Apr. 1953, 29–31. [Principal author G. Webster].

42. English coins. *BMQ 18*(2), 1953, 54–5, pl. xv.

43. The Chester (1950) hoard, by C. E. Blunt and R. H. M. Dolley. *BNJ 27*(2), 1953, 125–60, pls. i-v.

44. The significance of die-axis in the context of the later Anglo-Saxon coinage. *Ibid.*, 167–72.

45. A piedfort lead trial-piece of Edward the Confessor. *Ibid.*, 175–8, pl. vi. [A coin-weight.]

46. A contemporary forgery of a William III crown, by R. H. M. Dolley, G. F. Howell, and H. G. Stride. *Ibid.*, 204–10, pl. vii.

47. Two unpublished hoards of late Saxon pence in the Guildhall Museum. *Ibid.*, 212–13. [London, St Martin-le-Grand and Gracechurch Street finds; *see also* item 217].

48. A late-nineteenth-century find of Edward pence from Falhills Wood in Scotland. *Ibid.*, 215–18, pl. viii. [Penicuik find.]

49. Painswick treasure trove (1941). D. F. A[llen] and R. H. M. D[olley]. *Ibid.*, 219–20. [17th-cent.]

50. An unrecorded variety of the countermarked dollar. *Ibid.*, 220–1, pl. viii.

51. The type sequence of Æthelred II and Cnut: [report]. *Ibid.*, 231–2.

52. Venetian manuscripts. *Mariner's Mirror 39*(1), Feb. 1953, 67–8. [The locations of two MSS.]

53. Beulah Hill treasure trove, 1953: Edward I–III, 138 coins, c.1364. *NC*^{6} *13*, 1953, 115–22.

54. Wimbledon Common find (1953) of Roman coins. *Ibid.*, 143–4.

55. Farmborough treasure trove: 503 coins, Edward VI to Charles I, c.1640. *Ibid.*, 150–3. [*See also* item 83.]

56. An unrecorded Civil War hoard: 480 coins, Mary to Charles I, deposit c.1646. *Ibid.*, 153–5. ['West Country' hoard.]

57. Kirkby treasure trove (modern English coins). *Ibid.*, 155–6.

58. Market Rasen treasure trove (Queen Anne). *Ibid.*, 156.

59. A hoard of medieval silver coins of the Two Sicilies. *Ibid.*, 156–8. [13th to 14th-cent., found ?Italy.]

60. A presumed hoard of Lusignan deniers from Cyprus. *Ibid.*, 158–61. [Repr. in *Num. Report – Cyprus Num. Soc. 4*, 1973, 37–9].

61. Coin-portraits of some English kings and queens: [report]. *Ibid.*, vi-vii.

62. Naval tactics in the heyday of the Byzantine thalassocracy. *Studi Bizantini e Neoellenici* 7: Atti dello VIII Congresso Internazionale di Studi Bizantini, Palermo . . . 1951 (i), 1953, 324–39.

63. The Lord High Admiral Eustathios Argyros and the betrayal of Taormina to the African Arabs in 902. *Ibid.*, 340–53.

Reviews

64. Henri Seyrig, 'Le phare de Laodicée'. *Mariner's Mirror 39*(3), August 1953, 238. [The attribution of a new Septimius Severus coin to Laodicea = Latakieh.]

65. Sir John Craig, *The Mint*. *NC*[6] *13*, 1953, 180–2.
66. H. G. Stride, *The Royal Mint: an outline history*, 2nd edn. *Ibid.*, 182–3.
67. Torgny Lindgren, *Sveriges Mynt, 1719–1776*. *Ibid.*, 185–6.

1954

68. A numismatic postscript on Bryan Faussett's sculpture of 'King Canute' [sketches by Mrs J. S. Strudwick]. *Archæologia Cantiana 68*, 1954, 217–19.
69. Some late Anglo-Saxon pence. *BMQ 19*(3), Sept. 1954, 59–64, pl. xxiv.
70. The Cotton collection of Anglo-Saxon coins. *Ibid. 19*(4), 1954, 75–81.
71. A new Anglo-Saxon mint: Medeshamstede. *BNJ 27*(3), 1954, 263–5, pl. ii.
72. The 'Jewel-Cross' coinage of Ælfgifu Emma, Harthacnut, and Harold I. *Ibid.*, 266–75, pls. ii-iii. [*See also* item 40].
73. The 1953 Bootham treasure trove, by R. H. M. Dolley and I. H. Stewart; note on the bronze container of the Bootham coin hoard by G. F. Willmot. *Ibid.*, 281–93. [14th-cent.]
74. An early seventeenth-century collection of Anglo-Saxon coins, by R. H. M. Dolley and Mrs J. S. Strudwick. *Ibid.*, 302–12. [Cotton collection.]
75. The gold coinage of the mythical King Lucius. *Ibid.*, 354–8. [An Andecavic stater.]
76. A small parcel from the great find at Eccles. *Ibid.*, 358–9. [13th-cent.]
77. A little-known Swedish publication of an important find of thirteenth-century English pence. *Ibid.*, 359–61. [Norrbys (Follingbo) find.]
78. Godsfield Row (Alresford) find, 1871. *Ibid.*, 361. [17th-cent.]
79. The rig of early medieval warships. *Mariner's Mirror, 40*(1), 1954, 76–7. [*See also* items 6, 10; reply by R. LeB. Bowen, *40*(4), 1954, 315–20.]
80. A piece of medallic evidence for a shift of emphasis in the Roman concept of thalassocracy. *Ibid. 40*(4), 1954, 312–13, pl. ii. [Medallions of Commodus and Diocletian.]
81. The sack of Wilton in 1003 and the chronology of the 'Long Cross' and 'Helmet' types of Æthelræd II. *NNUM* no. 5, May 1954, 152–6. ['Till Nils Ludvig Rasmussons femtioårsdag'.]
82. The so-called piedforts of Alfred the Great. *NC*[6] *14*, 1954, 76–92, pl. vi.
83. Farmborough treasure trove: addenda. R. H. M. Dolley and P. Spufford. *Ibid.*, 218–19. [Addenda to item 55.]
84. Nils Ludvig Rasmusson jubilee. *NCirc 62*(6), June 1954, cols. 238–9.
85. A note on the mint at Wareham under Cnut. *Procs. Dorset Nat. Hist. and Archaeol. Soc. 76*, 1954, 56–7.
86. The Early Iron Age treasure from Snettisham, Norfolk. Appendix: The speculum ('tin') coins in hoard C. *Procs. Prehistoric Soc. 20*(1), 1954, 72–86, pl. xix. [Principal author R. R. Clarke.]

87–9. Your questions answered: [Crescent-shaped nicks in Anglo-Saxon pence]; [Crinkling of flans]; [and, Methods of cutting the blanks]. *SCMB* no. 431, Apr. 1954, 153.

90. Peter's Pence: Anglo-Saxon evidence of devotion to the Holy See. *The Tablet 203*(5953), 26 June 1954, 612–13.
91. The Crewkerne mint. In *Years Beyond Memory: the story of a south Somerset village in its wider setting*, by Edward J. King, 1954, 125–6, plate.

Reviews

92. F. C. Thompson and A. K. Chatterjee, 'The age-embrittlement of silver coins'. *NCirc 62*(10), Oct. 1954, col. 404.
93. Michael Grant, *Roman Imperial Money*. *The Tablet, 203*(5946), 8 May 1954, 454.

1955

94. The 1955 Dover treasure trove. *Archæologia Cantiana 69*, 1955, 62–8, pl. i. [13th-cent.]
95. Three Merovingian tremisses. *BMQ 20*(1), 1955, 13–15, pl. vi.
96. A neglected but vital Yorkshire hoard. *BNJ 28*(1), 1955, 11–17. [Bossall hoard, 10th-cent.]
97–98. The provenances of the Anglo-Saxon coins recorded in the two volumes of the British Museum catalogue, by R. H. M. Dolley and Mrs J. S. Strudwick; appendix A: Some corrigenda to the two volumes of the British Museum catalogue of Anglo-Saxon coins, [by] C. E. B[lunt], R. H. M. D[olley], F. E[lmore] J[ones]. *Ibid.*, 26–59.
99. An Intermediate Small Cross issue of Æthelræd II and some late varieties of the Crux type, by R. H. M. Dolley and F. Elmore Jones. *Ibid.*, 75–87, pl. iv. [*See also* item 216].
100–2. Three late Anglo-Saxon notes: A new Anglo-Saxon mint; A probable new mint in Shropshire; [and], The emergency mint of Cadbury. *Ibid.*, 88–105, pl. v. [100, Caistor; 101, BRYGIN].
103. The Dover hoard: the first English hoard with groats of Edward I, by R. H. M. Dolley; Scotland by Ian Halley Stewart; the container [by] P. E. Lasko. *Ibid.*, 147–68, pls. viii-xii.
104. Two tremisses of the Merovingian mint of Quentovic. R. H. M. Dolley and R. G. Hughes. *Ibid.*, 176–7, pl. xiv.
105. A new type for the halfpenny of Eadred. *Ibid.*, 182–4, pl. xiv.
106. Contemporary forgeries of late Saxon pence. *Ibid.*, 185–9, pl. xiv.
107. A new irregular penny of Stephen. *Ibid.*, 195–6.
108. A nineteenth-century Scottish hoard of Edward pence: 807 coins, deposit c.1345? *Ibid.*, 196–201, pl. xiv.
109. Dodford (Northants.) treasure trove. *Ibid.*, 201–2, pl. xv. [15th-cent.]
110. The Anglo-Saxon farthing; [sketch by Mrs J. S. Strudwick]. In *The Church of St Bertelin at Stafford and its cross: excavation report*, edited by Adrian Oswald [1955], 28–9.
111. The mint of Chester. Part I: Edward the Elder to Eadgar. *J. Chester and North Wales Architectural, Archaeol. and Hist. Soc. 42*, 1955, 1–20, pls. i-ii.
112. The Tywardreath (Fowey) treasure trove: 17 AR, Edward the Elder and Æthelstan, deposit c.929. *NC*[6] *15*, 1955, 5–9, pl. ii.
113. A further note on the Harkirke find. *Ibid.*, 189–93. [10th-cent.]
114. Grimsby treasure trove (1954): 4 AV 'Morinic', c.70BC. *Ibid.*, 242–3.
115. A seventeenth-century hoard from Carrigtwohill (Cork): 58 coins AR, Elizabeth I – Charles I. *Ibid.*, 247–9.
116. Some new light on the later Anglo-Saxon coinage: [report]. *Ibid.*, xx.
117. A 1798 United States dollar with the George III octagonal countermark. *NCirc 63*(2), Feb. 1955, cols. 59–60.
118. The mints of Northampton, Southampton and Hamwich: a provisional note. *Ibid. 63*(4), Apr. 1955, cols. 159–61. [*See also* item 411.]
119. A curious numismatic superstition. *Ibid. 63*(9), Sept. 1955, col. 378. [On the burying of coins beneath walnut trees.]
120. A note on the mythical mint of Dunwich. *Ibid. 63*(11), Nov. 1955, col. 470. [Æthelred II *First Small Cross*, Eadsige, is reattributed to London; *see also* item 208.]
121. A 'new type' for Æthelræd II. *Ibid.* 63(12), Dec. 1955, cols. 529–30. [A lead medallion.]
122. An important unpublished coin of the Dorchester mint. *Procs Dorset Nat. Hist. and Archaeol. Soc. 77*, 1955, 155–6.
123. A penny of Edward the Elder from

Lansdown, Bath, by J. W. Gardner; [incorporating a report by R. H. M. Dolley.] *Procs. Somersetshire Archaeol. and Nat. Hist. Soc. 99/100*, 1954/5, 105, 112.

123*bis*. Byzantine coin found at Ipswich. *Procs. Suffolk Institute of Archaeology 26*, 1955, 60–1. [11th-cent.: Alexius Comnenus, anonymous class VIII.]

Reviews

124. Helmer Salmo, *Ett par västfinska silverdepåfynd från 1000-talet. BNJ 28*(1), 1955, 207.
125. H. V. Mansfeld-Büllner, *Afbildninger af samtlige hidtil kjendte danske Mønter fra tidsrummet 1241–1377*, new and rev. edn. *NCirc 63*(2), Feb. 1955, cols. 65–6.
126. *English Historical Documents*, I (c.500–1042), ed. Dorothy Whitelock. *Ibid. 63*(4), Apr. 1955, cols. 171–3.
127. Howard W. A. Linecar, *Coins. Ibid. 63*(9), Sept. 1955, cols. 381–2.
128. C. H. V. Sutherland, *Art in Coinage . . . The Oxford Mag. 73*(18), 5 May 1955, 314.
129. Ethelbert Stauffer, *Christ and the Caesars. The Tablet 205*(6000), 21 May 1955, 500–1.

1956

130. A notable gift of Anglo-Saxon coins by the Pilgrim Trust. *BMQ 20*(3), 1955/6, 66–71, pls. xxi-xxii.
131. The Lockett gift of Anglo-Saxon coins. *Ibid. 20*(4), 1956, 84–7, pl. xxix.
132. A new type and moneyer for Eadbearht 'Præn'. *BNJ 28*(2), 1956, 243–8, pl. xxv.
133. A note on the mints of Sudbury and Southwark at the end of the reign of Æthelræd II. *Ibid.*, 264–9.
134. The mints 'æt Gothabyrig' and 'æt Sith(m)estebyrig', by R. H. M. Dolley and F. Elmore Jones, with a philological and topographical note on Cissbury by M. Daunt. *Ibid.*, 270–82, pls. xxii-xxiii.
135. The Stockbridge Down find of Anglo-Saxon coins. *Ibid.*, 283–7. [11th-cent.]
136. A find of pence of Edward I and II at Neath Abbey. *Ibid.*, 294–8, pl. xxv.
137. A surface find of three silver coins of the Dobuni. *Ibid.*, 403, pl. xxv. [Colerne find.]
138. A suspect 'Tower' type penny of King Edward the Elder [incorporating a report by A. Dunning]. *Ibid.*, 408–11, pl. xxv.
139. An alleged *Agnus Dei* penny of the Wareham mint. *Ibid.*, 412–14.
140. The heavy Calais quarter-noble of Henry IV. *Ibid.*, 416, pl. xxv.
141. New light on a Hertfordshire token [entries from Tring parish registers by Miss E. Grosstephan]. *Ibid.*, 420–1.
142. A note on the dating of Bohemian coins by alleged English prototypes. *HBN 3*(9/10), 1955/6, 159–62.
143. The Anglo-Saxon mint at Newark; in memoriam Hans Holst. *NNUM*, Nov. 1956, 215–19.
144. The Shaftesbury hoard of pence of Æthelræd II. *NC*^{6} *16*, 1956, 267–80, pls. xix-xx.
145. A small find of fourteenth-century groats from Flanders. *Ibid.*, 281–3, pl. xxi.
146. A provisional note on the origins of the Leicester mint. *Ibid.*, 285–91. [*See also* item 368.]
147. A note on the mint of Torksey and on some early finds of English coins from Nottinghamshire. R. H. M. Dolley, J. S. Strudwick. *Ibid.*, 293–302.
148. A preliminary note on an Intermediate Small Cross type of Æthelræd II in relation to late varieties of Crux, by R. H. M. Dolley and F. Elmore Jones. *NCirc 64*(1), Jan. 1956, cols. 5–8.
149. Bror Emil Hildebrand, 22 ii 1806–30 viii 1884. *Ibid. 64*(2), Feb. 1956, cols. 65–8.
150. The regional distribution of dies in

the West Country, c.1017–1023. *Ibid.* *64*(7/8), July/Aug. 1956, cols. 321–5; *64*(9), Sept. 1956, cols. 373–6.

151. Two Anglo-Saxon myths. *Ibid.* *64*(11), Nov. 1956, cols. 469–71. [(1) That coins of Æthelræd II are not found in England; (2) that Maldon was the only battle against the Vikings.]

152. In memoriam: Hans Holst, † 23:ix:56. *Ibid.*, cols. 485–6. [Unsigned.]

Reviews

153. M. Dreijer, 'Die Ziernadal [i.e. Ziernadel] von Syllöda'. *BNJ* *28*(2), 1956, 426. [Finds included an Athelstan.]

154. H. T. Wallinga, *The Boarding-Bridge of the Romans*. *Mariner's Mirror* *42*(4), 1956, 350–1.

1957

155. A new coin of the Kentish rebel Eadbearht Præn. *Archæologia Cantiana* *71*, 1957, 162–6, pl. i.

156. A note on the Anglo-Saxon and Norman mint at Guildford. In *The Borough of Guildford, 1257–1957: catalogue of an exhibition of the borough plate and the borough records at the Guildhall, June 29th–July 6th, 1957* [compiled by E. M. Dance], [1957], 32–3.

157. More English acquisitions from the Lockett collection. *BMQ* *21*(1), Mar. 1957, 15–18, pl. iii.

158. Medieval gold coins from the Lockett collection. *Ibid.* *21*(2), July 1957, 41–4, pl. xii.

159. The Anglo-Saxon coins in the Vatican Library, by C. E. Blunt and R. H. M. Dolley. *BNJ* *28*(3), 1957, 449–58, pl. xxvi.

160. Two stray finds from St Albans of coins of Offa and of Charlemagne, by R. H. M. Dolley and D. M. Metcalf. *Ibid.*, 459–66. [Includes 8th to 9th-cent. finds from southern England.]

161–2. Two Anglo-Saxon notes: An enigmatic penny of Edward the Martyr; [and], The mysterious mint of 'FRO'. *Ibid.*, 499–508.

163. A further find of Edward pennies at Neath Abbey. *Ibid.*, 555–9.

164. The find-spot of the 'War Area' hoard of pence of William I. *Ibid.*, 650–1. [Scaldwell.]

165. An interesting new variety of the late thirteenth-century sterling of Namur. *Ibid.*, 654–5, pl. xxxvii.

166. An unpublished seventeenth-century token halfpenny of London. *Ibid.*, 659–61, pl. xxxvii.

167. A group of medieval and modern coins from a site in Malvern. *Ibid.*, 662–5.

168. En vikingatida silverskatt från Gandarve i Alva på Gotland: de engelska mynten. *Gotländskt Arkiv* 1957, 29–30, 42–50.

169. Three pennies of Regensburg found at Smyrna. *HBN* *3*(11), 1957, 463–5, pl. 24. [11th-cent.]

170. Een munt van Bisschop Bernoldus, gevonden in Engeland. R. H. M. Dolley, G. van der Meer. *JMP* *44*, 1957, 54–6, pl. i; summary, 'A coin of Bishop Bernoldus [of Utrecht] found in England', 56. [Old Sarum find.]

171. En penning fra Magnus den Gode fundet i England. *NNUM*, Nov. 1957, 253–6. [Salisbury Plain find.]

172. An unpublished Irish hoard of 'St Peter' pence. *NC*^{6} *17*, 1957, 123–32, pl. xvi. [Geashill hoard.]

173. A small find of medieval Swiss coins. *Ibid.*, 133–5, pl. xvi.

174. An eleventh-century hoard from the Danzig area. Peter Berghaus, R. H. M. Dolley. *Ibid.*, 209–17, pls. xx-xxi. [Orunia hoard.]

175. A Spanish dirham found in England. *Ibid.*, 242–3. [11th-cent., found at Cerne Abbas.]

176. An unpublished minor variety of a penny of Edward I. *Ibid.*, 244–5.

177. An unpublished variant of the Crux type of Æthelræd II from the H. W.

Taffs collection, by R. H. M. Dolley and F. Elmore Jones. *NCirc 65*(2), Feb. 1957, cols. 57–8.

178. A note on the date of the so-called 'Raven' pence of Anlaf Guthfrithsson. *Ibid. 65*(5), May 1957, cols. 189–94.

179. A mythical moneyer of Maldon. *Ibid. 65*(12), Dec. 1957, cols. 535–6. [Cnut *Quatrefoil*, reattributed to Ilchester.]

Reviews

180. *The* De Moneta *of Nicholas Oresme and English Mint Documents*, trans. from the Latin with introduction and notes by Charles Johnson. *NCirc 65*(1), Jan. 1957, cols. 13–16.

181. Carlo M. Cipolla, *Money, Prices and Civilization in the Mediterranean, fifth to seventeenth century. Ibid.* 65(7/8), July-Aug. 1957, cols. 311–13.

182. Wilfrid Bonser, *An Anglo-Saxon and Celtic Bibliography (450–1087). Ibid.* 65(10), Oct. 1957, cols. 421–3.

183. B. Richmond, *Time Measurement and Calendar Construction. Ibid.* 65(11), Nov. 1957, col. 487.

1958

184. *Some Reflections on Hildebrand type A of Æthelræd II*. Stockholm 1958. 41pp. (Kungl. Vitterhets Historie och Antikvitetsakademien. Antikvarist arkiv 9.)

185. The Morley St Peter hoard: (b) the significance of the find. *Antiquity 32*, 1958, 102–3, pl. xi. [Principal author R. R. Clarke.]

186. An important group of tenth-century pence. *BMQ 21*(3), June 1958, 74–6, pl. xxiii. [From the Hon. R. W. H. Erskine.]

187–9. Three more late Saxon notes: A possible sixth Anglo-Saxon mint in Lincolnshire; An Æthelræd II die-link between London and Hertford; [and], The mythical mint of Totleigh [i.e. Totley]. *BNJ 29*(1), 1958, 51–60. [187: Horncastle; 188: Æthelred II *Helmet*; 189: Cnut *Pointed Helmet*, reattributed to Totnes.]

190–2. Three West Country notes: The coinage of Milborne Port; The identity of the mint of 'LA(N)G'; [and], An unpublished Cnut moneyer of Lydford. *Ibid.*, 61–8, pl. iv. [191: Langport; 192 Huwine, reattributed from London.]

193. Cnut's Quatrefoil type in English cabinets of the eighteenth century, by R. H. M. Dolley and D. M. Metcalf. *Ibid.*, 69–81.

194. A parcel of Cross-and-Crosslets pence from Tealby find, by R. H. M. Dolley and F. Elmore Jones. *Ibid.*, 82–6, pl. v.

195. Coinage. In *Medieval England*, new edn, . . . ed. Austin Lane Poole, I, 1958, 264–99, pls. 27–36.

196. The post-Brunanburh Viking coinage of York, with some remarks on the Viking coinages which preceded the same. *NNÅ* 1957/8, 13–85; sammanfattning, 86–8.

197. Det första myntet från en Gotländsk skatt som nådde en engelsk samling. *NNUM* no. 4, Apr. 1958, 83–7.

198. Three forgotten English finds of pence of Æthelræd II. *NC*[6] *18*, 1958, 97–107, pl. viii. [London, Honey Lane Market; Great Barton (Suffolk); Harting Beacon (Sussex).]

199. The 1958 Coventry treasure trove of Long Cross pence of Henry III. *Ibid.*, 109–22, pl. viii.

200. A group of Anglo-Saxon pence at Sudeley Castle. R. H. M. Dolley, Gay van der Meer. *Ibid.*, 123–9, pl. ix.

201. Modern forgeries of the post-Brunanburh Viking coins of York and Derby. *Ibid.*, 131–4, pl. ix.

202. A mythical moneyer of Worcester. *NCirc 66*(2), Feb. 1958, 35; *66*(3), Mar. 1958, 64. [Æthelræd II *Last Small Cross*: Æthelwig, reattributed to Leicester.]

203. The John Natt token of

Charterhouse. *Ibid.* *66*(3), Mar. 1958, 64.

204. Lincoln or London: one problem resolved. *Ibid.* *66*(4), Apr. 1958, 90–1. [Cnut *Quatrefoil*: Wulfwine, reattributed to London.]

205. The Morley St Peter treasure trove. *Ibid.* 66(5), May 1958, 113–14.

206. The last coins of the mint at Lydford. *Ibid.* *66*(7/8), July/Aug. 1958, 161–2. [Edward the Confessor *Small Flan*, reattributed from London.]

207. A mythical moneyer of the Leicester mint. *Ibid.* *66*(9), Sept. 1958, 183. [Edward Confessor *Sovereign/Eagles*: Leofwine, reattributed to Canterbury.]

208. A further note on the mythical mint of Dunwich. *Ibid.* *66*(11), Nov. 1958, 229–30. [Further to item 120.]

209. An illusory coin of Ilchester, by R. H. M. Dolley and G. van der Meer. *Ibid.* *66*(12), Dec. 1958, 253–4. [Edward Confessor *Trefoil Quadrilateral*; Leofwine, reattributed to Aylesbury.]

210. A non-existent link between the Oxford and Cricklade mints. *Oxoniensia 23*, 1958, 142–3.

Reviews

211. Archibald R. Lewis, *The Northern Seas*. *NCirc* *66*(12), Dec. 1958, 255.

1959

212. Some new light on the Trewhiddle hoard. *BMQ 21*(4), Oct. 1959, 94–7. [Manuscripts of Jonathan and Philip Rashleigh.]

213. An Icenian coin hoard from Lakenheath, Suffolk: B. The coins: (b) Ancient British coins. *BNJ* *29*(2), 1959, 218–19.

214. The hoard evidence for the coins of Alfred, by C. E. Blunt and R. H. M. Dolley [incorporating a report by D. M. Wilson]. *Ibid.*, 220–47, pl. xvi.

215. A hoard of pennies of Eadgar from Laugharne churchyard in South Wales. *Ibid.*, 255–8.

216. Some further remarks on the Transitional Crux issue of Æthelræd II. *Ibid.*, 259–64. [*Further to* item 99.]

217. New light on the nineteenth-century find of pence of Æthelræd II from St Martin's-le-Grand, by V. J. Butler and R. H. M. Dolley. *Ibid.*, 265–74. [*See also* item 47.]

218. The myth of a coinage of the Ostmen of Dublin in the name of Tymme Sjællandsfar. *Ibid.*, 275–88, pls. xvii-xviii.

219. New light on the order of the early issues of Edward the Confessor. *Ibid.*, 289–92.

220. A note on the chronology of some published and unpublished 'Short Cross' finds from the British Isles. *Ibid.*, 297–321.

221. A die-link between the mints of Dover and London at the end of the reign of Æthelræd II. R. H. M. Dolley, G. van der Meer. *Ibid.*, 416–17.

222. New light on the 1864 hoard from Kinghorn. *Ibid.*, 419–21. [Otherwise Abden hoard, 13th to 14th-cent.; transcribes a letter by J. M. Lornie.]

223. Myntfynden i Hornborga Kyrkoruin i Västergötland, av Lars O. Lagerqvist och R. H. M. Dolley. *Fornvännen* h.2/3, 1959, 113–35; summary, 'Coin-finds from the ruined church at Hornborga in Västergötland', 135–6.

224. The Continental coins in the Halton Moor find and other Norman deniers found in the British Isles. *HBN 4*(12/13), 1958/9, 53–7, pl. 2. [11th-cent.]

225. The Kensington stone. *Mariner's Mirror 45*(2), 1959, 167.

226. New light on a tenth-century find from the west of the County Kilkenny. R. H. M. Dolley, J. S. Martin. *NC*[6] *19*, 1959, 175–82. [Co. Kilkenny hoard.]

227. The earliest penny of the Bruton mint. *Ibid.*, 183–5.
228. Two unpublished English finds of eleventh-century pence. *Ibid.*, 187–92, pl. xviii. [Penrice (Glam.); unknown site (S. Midlands?).]
229. An apparently mythical type of Cnut. *Ibid.*, 193–7.
230. A small find of late thirteenth-century pence from Skipton Castle. *Ibid.*, 199–200.
231. A small find of Scottish billon coins of the sixteenth century. *Ibid.*, 201–2. [Baldock parcel.]
232. An enigmatic penny of Cnut's first issue. *NCirc* 67(1), Jan. 1959, 4. [*Quatrefoil*: Leofwi, reattributed from Wareham to Warwick.]
233. The mysterious mint of 'TON'. *Ibid.* 67(2), Feb. 1959, 26. [Æthelred II, *Helmet*, identified as Totnes.]
234. A mythical Æthelræd II moneyer of Leicester. *Ibid.* 67(3), Mar. 1959, 53. [*Long Cross*: Wulfric reattributed to Worcester, but *see also* item 301.]
235. A note on the Mercian coinage of Eadgar. *Ibid.* 67(4), Apr. 1959, 76. [Includes the Bangor find.]
236. A query concerning the 1782 find of Anglo-Saxon coins on Tiree. *Ibid.* 67(9), Sept. 1959, 159.
237. The Eadgar millennium, Oct. 1st 959 – Oct. 1st, 1959. *Ibid.* 67(10), Oct. 1959, 177–8.
238. Three Long Cross pennies of Æthelræd II, c.1000, misattributed to the mint of Winchester. *Ibid.* 67(11), Nov. 1959, 200–1. [Reattributed to Lincoln, Dublin, and London respectively. *See also* item 334.]
239. A further die-link within the York mint in the so-called 'Paxs' type of William I. *Ibid.* 67(12), Dec. 1959, 227.
240. A penny of Æthelræd II from the Isle of Wight: description of the coin and commentary. *Procs. Isle of Wight Nat. Hist. and Archaeol. Soc.* 5(4), 1959, 158–9. [Carisbrooke find; principal author J. D. Jones.]
241. A penny of Cnut found in the churchyard at Colesbourne. *Trans. Bristol and Glos. Archaeol. Soc. 78*, 1959, 92–5, pl. iii.
242. A neglected tenth-century coin-hoard from Donegal. *Ulster J. of Archaeology 22*, 1959, 56–8. [Burt hoard.]

Reviews

243. *The Map of Great Britain circa* AD *1360 Known as the Gough Map. . .*, introduction by E. J. S. Parsons. *NCirc* 67(4), Apr. 1959, 77.
244. Carlo M. Cipolla, *Le avventure della lira*. *Ibid.* 67(5), May 1959, 97.
245. Georg Galster, *Coins and History*. *Ibid.* 67(6), June 1959, 120. [Review bears the title 'Coins and history'; unsigned.]

1960

246. The Taffs memorial gift of Anglo-Saxon coins. *BMQ 22*, 1960, 24–5, pl. v.
247. A further gift of medieval coins by the Lockett family. *Ibid.*, 25–6, pl. v.
248. Two die-links relative to the Anglo-Saxon mint at Northampton, by V. J. Butler and R. H. M. Dolley. *BNJ 30*(1), 1960, 54–6.
249. The mythical 'Helmet'/'Long Cross' mules of Æthelræd II. *Ibid.*, 57–60, pl. v. [Scandinavian imitations.]
250. A note on the Anglo-Saxon mint of Reading. *Ibid.*, 70–5.
251. A small parcel of pennies of the Confessor from the Sedlescombe find. *Ibid.*, 76–81, pl. vii.
252. A hoard of tenth-century Anglo-Saxon coins from Glendalough. *JRSAI 90*(1), 1960, 41–7.
253.* Was there a mint at Limerick 900 years ago? by Micheál Maolmuire Ó Dathlaoich [i.e. Michael Dolley]; [illustrated by] J. S. M[artin]. *Limerick Leader*, 20 Feb. 1960, 9. [Hiberno-Norse, Phase IV.]
254. Wrecks off Hayling Island.

Mariner's Mirror 46(3), 1960, 233.

255. Nytt lys over Skandinavias nordligste skattefun med angelsaksiske og kufiske mynter, av Michael Dolley og Kolbjørn Skaare. *NNÅ* 1960, 5–23; summary, 'New light on the coins of the most northerly tenth-century hoard', 23–4. [Rønvik.]
256. Some new light on the Viking-Age silver hoard from Mungret. *North Munster Ant. J. 8*(3), 1960, 116–33.
257. Some remarks on *BMC* type VII var. *B* of Edward the Confessor. R. H. M. Dolley, F. Elmore Jones. NC^6 *20*, 1960, 183–90, pls. xiv-xv.
258. An unpublished Chester penny of Harthacnut found at Caerwent. *Ibid.*, 191–3.
259. Another mythical coin of the Leicester mint. *NCirc 68*(3), March 1960, 50. [Edward the Confessor *Pointed Helmet*, reattributed to Chester.]
260. Another illusory penny of the Ilchester mint. *Ibid. 68*(6), June 1960, 131. [Æthelred II *Crux*, reattributed to Colchester.]
261. A note on some early sources for the coins of Edward the Confessor. *Ibid. 68*(9), Sept. 1960, 183–4; *68*(10), Oct. 1960, 211–12. [Two pre-1783 York hoards; 1774 St Mary Hill; 1759 Caistor hoards.]
262. A new late Saxon mint in Suffolk. *Ibid. 68*(11), Nov. 1960, 236. [The mint of 'DYR'.]
263. A misattributed portrait penny of Æthelstan. *Ibid. 68*(12), Dec. 1960, 262. [*BMC* 146, reattributed from Winchester to Wallingford.]
264. Nieznany dotychczas pens mennicy w Southampton znaleziony w skarbie polskim [= An unpublished penny of the Southampton mint from a Polish hoard]. *Prace i Materiały Muzeum Archeologicznego i Etnograficznego w Łodzi, seria archeologiczna 5*, 1960, 79–90; text in English, 91–8. [Cnut, *Quatrefoil.*]
265. Coin hoards from the London area as evidence for the pre-eminence of London in the Later Saxon period. *Trans. London and Middx Archaeol. Soc. 20*(2), 1960, 37–50.

Reviews

266. George Slocombe, *William the Conqueror: a new biography. NCirc 68*(3), Mar. 1960, 53.
267. Marjorie and C. H. B. Quennell, *Everyday Life in Roman and Anglo-Saxon Times. Ibid.*
268. Francis Wormald, *The Benedictional of St Ethelwold. Ibid.*
269. Eilert Ekwall, *The Concise Oxford Dictionary of English Place-Names*, 4th edn. *Ibid. 68*(5), May 1960, 104–5.

1961

270. *Anglo-Saxon Coins: studies presented to F. M. Stenton on the occasion of his 80th birthday, 17 May 1960*, ed. R. H. M. Dolley. 1961. iii-xv, 296 pp., front., [2], xvi pls.
271. Preface [Michael scripsit]. *AS Coins*, 1961, ix-x.
272. The coinage of Æthelwulf, King of the West Saxons, 839–58, by R. H. M. Dolley and K. Skaare. *Ibid.*, 63–76, pl. viii.
273. The chronology of the coins of Ælfred the Great, 871–99, by R. H. M. Dolley and C. E. Blunt. *Ibid.*, 77–95, pls. ix-x.
274. The reform of the English coinage under Eadgar, by R. H. M. Dolley and D. M. Metcalf. *Ibid.*, 136–68, pls. xiii-xiv.
275. A new suggestion concerning the so-called 'martlets' in the 'Arms of St Edward', by R. H. M. Dolley and F. Elmore Jones. *Ibid.*, 215–26, pl. xv. [Eagles.]
276. Viking Age coin-hoards from Ireland and their relevance to Anglo-Saxon studies, by R. H. M. Dolley and J. Ingold. *Ibid.*, 241–65, pl. xvi.
277. The 1871 Viking-Age find of silver

coins from Mullaghboden as a reflection of Westfalding intervention in Ireland. *Årbok – Universitetets oldsaksamling (Oslo)*, 1960/1, 49–62.

278. Hiberno-Norse coins from the Lockett collection. *BMQ 23*(2), Jan. 1961, 45–8, pl. xxi.

279. Some 'Northern' variants, etc., of the 'Crux' issue of Æthelræd II, by R. H. M. Dolley and V. J. Butler. *BNJ, 30*(2), 1961, 217–20, pl. xviii. [Scandinavian imitations.]

280. An apparently unrecorded class of Hiberno-Norse imitation of the coinage of Æthelræd II. *Ibid.*, 227–30. [*Helmet* with pseudo-English legends.]

281. Some further critical die-links in the Hiberno-Norse series. *Ibid.*, 231–4. [Phase I.]

282. Some Scandinavian coins in the names of Æthelræd, Cnut, and Harthacnut attributed by Hildebrand to English mints, by C. S. S. Lyon, G. van der Meer, and R. H. M. Dolley. *Ibid.*, 235–51, pls. xii-xiv. [*See also* items 470, 606.]

283. The problem of the 'Fleur-de-Lis' sceptre on the Sigtuna coins of Cnut, by L. O. Lagerqvist and R. H. M. Dolley. *Ibid.*, 252–61.

284. Coins at Nostell Priory, Yorkshire. C. E. Blunt, R. H. M. Dolley. *Ibid.*, 360–1, pl. xxiii. [Archbishop Jænberht and five St Peter coins ?from Bossall hoard.]

285. A late noble of Henry V recently found in Yorkshire. *Ibid.*, 365, pl. xxiii. [Barmby on the Moor find.]

286. Series summary index: [*BNJ*]vols. *21–30* (1931–1961) [compiled by R. H. M. Dolley]. *Ibid.*, 396–417.

287. The relevance of obverse die-links to some problems of the later Anglo-Saxon coinage. In *Commentationes I*, redaktion N. L. Rasmusson, L. O. Lagerqvist, Stockholm 1961, 153–72.

288. The transition between the 'Hand of Providence' and 'Crux' types of Æthelræd II, by R. H. M. Dolley and F. Elmore Jones. *Ibid.*, 173–86.

289. Some thoughts on the engraving of the dies for the English coinage c.1025, by R. H. M. Dolley and J. Ingold. *Ibid.*, 187–222, vi pls.

290. The 'lost' hoard of tenth-century Anglo-Saxon silver coins from Dalkey. *JRSAI 91*(1), 1961, 1–18, pls. i-ii.

291. Tre engelska mynt funna på Gotland, av R. H. M. Dolley och Veronica J. Butler. *NNUM*, Jan. 1961, 1–4. [Edgar, Harthacnut, and William II.]

292. Knud den Stores apokryfe jordiske rester; veritas temporis filia. *Ibid.*, Apr. 1961, 67–72. [*See also* item 299.]

293. A small find of fourteenth-century coins from West Limerick. *North Munster Ant. J. 8*(4), 1961, 157–67; corrigenda, 205. [Knocknasna, corrected to Athea.]

294. A hoard of Anglo-Saxon pennies from Sicily. *NC*[7] *1*, 1961, 151–61, pls. xx-xxi. [Catania neighbourhood.]

295. The personal name 'L(O)C(I)' on eleventh-century English coins. *Ibid.*, 163–8.

296. A small find of continental sterlings from Aberdeenshire. *Ibid.*, 169–70. [Fyvie find.]

297. A note on the Viking-Age hoard from Lindores and on some other finds from the British Isles which are alleged to have contained coins of Ecgbeorht. Veronica J. Butler and R. H. M. Dolley. *Ibid.*, 171–4.

298. A recent find of Long Cross pennies of Henry III from Winchester. *Ibid.*, 185–9, pl. xxiv.

299. An apocryphal corpse of Canute, or, Early and not-so-early instances of the abuse of numismatic evidence; veritas temporis filia. *NCirc 69*(1), Jan. 1961, 9–10. [Unsigned; *see also* item 292; the coin found was a Nuremberg jetton.]

300. A 'pseudo-*orans*' on a Hiberno-Norse penny of the Dublin mint. *Ibid. 69*(2), Feb. 1961, 32–3. [Phase V.]
301. More light on a mythical moneyer of the Leicester mint, by V. J. Butler and R. H. M. Dolley. *Ibid. 69*(3), Mar. 1961, 59. [Reattributing the coin discussed in item 234 to Hiberno-Norse series.]
302. A bastard penny of Bath, by V. J. Butler and R. H. M. Dolley. *Ibid.*, 60. [Æthelred *Last Small Cross*, reattributed to Hiberno-Norse series.]
303. An unpublished Norman penny of the Winchester mint. *Ibid. 69*(4), Apr. 1961, 91.
304. A note on the Anglo-Saxon mint of Petherton. *Ibid. 69*(7/8), July/August 1961, 167.
305. A Spanish dinero found at Verulamium in 1959. *Ibid. 69*(9), Sept. 1961, 186. [11th-cent.]
306. The degree of contraction of the ethnic as an index of relative date in the case of 'Long Cross' pennies of Æthelræd II. *Ibid. 69*(11), Nov. 1961, 240–1.
307. The mythical leather currency of King Eadgar. *Quarterly Mag. – International Banknote Soc.*, Christmas 1961, 29–33.
308. Progress in mediaeval numismatics (1952–59). In *Relazioni – Congresso internazionale di Numismatica, Roma, . . . 1961*, Rome, 1961, 211–12.
309. Great Britain and Ireland [cards prepared by H. S. A. Copinger]. *Ibid.*, 359–73.
310. Saxon coins. In *The Roman Town and Villa at Great Casterton, Rutland: third report for the years 1954–1958*, by members of the [University of Nottingham] Summer School in Romano-British Archaeology held at Great Casterton 1954–8, ed. the late Philip Corder, 1961, 88, pl. xvii. [Two Burgred pennies.]
311. A note on the Anglo-Saxon mint at Berkeley. *Trans. Bristol and Glos. Archaeol. Soc. 80*, 1961, 80–9, pl. xii.
312. The Anglo-Saxon coins from Meols Sands. *Trans. Historic Soc. of Lancs. and Cheshire 113*, 1961, 197–201.
313. The unpublished 1895 find of coins of Edward the Confessor from Harewood. *Yearbook of the Brit. Assoc. of Num. Societies* no.7, 1961, 17–25.

Reviews

314. Lord Twining, *A History of the Crown Jewels of Europe. NCirc 69*(1), Jan. 1961, 16–17.
315. L. O. Lagerqvist and E. Nathorst-Böös, *Mynt och medaljer. Ibid. 69*(12), Dec. 1961, 268.

1962

316–17. Two Anglo-Saxon notes: A Cnut die-link between the mints of Salisbury and Wilton; [and], A probable reattribution from Lincoln to Langport. *BNJ 31*, 1962, 53–6. [316: *Short Cross*; 317: Harthacnut *Jewel Cross*.]
318. The 1962 Llantrithyd treasure trove, and some thoughts on the first Norman coinage of Wales. *Ibid.* 74–9, pl. iv. [*See also* item 375.]
319. A small find of Stephen pennies from Berkshire. *Ibid.*, 162–4. [Henley-on-Thames, Park Place find.]
320. A note on the find-spots and probable composition of two Viking-Age coin-hoards from the County Offaly. *Bull. – Num. Soc. of Ireland* no. 5, 1962, 1–4.
321. A note on the 1883 Viking-Age silver hoard from Co. Dublin. *Ibid.* no.6, Aug. 1962, 2–5.
322. En ny Karl XII-medalj, av Lars O. Lagerqvist och R. H. M. Dolley. *Fornvännen* h.2/3, 1962, 165–71; summary, 'An unknown medal of Charles XII of Sweden', 171–2.
323. Some Temple-type coins found in

Great Britain. *HBN* 5(16), 1962, 321–4, pl. 16.

324. Beal Boru, Co. Clare. Appendix IV: The coins from Beal Boru. *J. Cork Hist. and Archaeol. Soc.* 67(205), Jan./June 1962, 18–27, pl. vii. [Principal author M. J. O'Kelly.]
325. The 1843(?) find of Viking-Age silver coins from Co. Tipperary. *Ibid.*, 41–7, pl. viii.
326. A mythical west Cork find of a gold coin of the Spanish Umayyads. *Ibid.*, 51–3. [*Recte* 13th-cent.]
327. New light on the 1837 Viking-Age coin-hoard from Ballitore. *JRSAI* 92(2), 1962, 175–86.
328. Sven Estridsen-mønt fundet i London 1872. *NNUM*, Sept. 1962, 133–5. [Walbrook hoard.]
329. A penny of Coenwulf of Mercia found at Yaxham, Norfolk. *Norfolk Archaeology* 33(1), 1962, 43–4, plate.
330. A note on four 'type immobilisé' coins of Melle from British finds, by R. H. M. Dolley and K. F. Morrison, NC^7 2, 1962, 157–60.
331. The 1961 Beachy Head (Bullock Down) hoard of third-century coins of the Central and Gallic empires, by R. H. M. Dolley and Miss M. A. O'Donovan. *Ibid.*, 163–88.
332. An unpublished London moneyer of Eadgar. *Ibid.*, 189–94.
333. A West Country grouping of pennies of Eadwig and Eadgar. *Ibid.*, 195–202.
334. Significant new die-links in the Hiberno-Norse coinage of Dublin. *NCirc* 70(1), Jan. 1962, 6. [Die-links with coin discussed in item 238.]
335. A Dublin link with Devonshire. *Ibid.* 70(2), Feb. 1962, 26.[Sihtric *Long Cross*, pseudo-Totnes coin]
336. A neglected early fourteenth-century hoard of silver coins from Berwickshire. *Ibid.* 70(4), Apr. 1962, 80. [Cockburnspath.]
337. Stafford, Stamford or Steyning? *Ibid.* 70(5), May 1962, 106–7. [Edward the Confessor *Pyramids*, attributed to Stafford; 1795 Oulton hoard discussed.]
338. An enigmatic First Hand penny of Æthelræd II. *Ibid.* 70(6), June 1962, 130–2. ['-luthey' mint.]
339. A coin certainly of Leicester but with a mint-signature of Chester, by R. H. M. Dolley and E. J. E. Pirie. *Ibid.* 70(9), Sept. 1962, 182–3. [Edward the Confessor *Hammer Cross.*]
340. A new class of Scandinavian imitation? *Ibid.* 70(12), Dec. 1962, 245–6. [Of Æthelred II *Long Cross*, Shrewsbury, but possibly copied from Hiberno-Norse imitation.]
341. The date of the medieval coin-hoard from Tom a'Bhuraich in Aberdeenshire. *PSAS* 95, 1961/2, 241–8. [13th-cent.]
342. The Viking-Age coin-hoard from Ballycastle in Co. Antrim. *Ulster J. of Archaeology* 24/25, 1961/2, 88–90.

Reviews

343. Graham Teasdill, *Coin Finds of the Huddersfield District. NCirc* 70(1), Jan. 1962, 9.
344. Christopher Brooke, *From Alfred to Henry III, 871–1272. Ibid.* 70(2), Feb. 1962, 33.
345. Sir F. Maurice Powicke and E. B. Fryde, *Handbook of British Chronology*, 2nd edn. *Ibid.* 70(3), Mar. 1962, 58–9.
346. C. R. Josset, *Money in Britain. Ibid.* 70(5), May 1962, 111.
347. Hope Mirrlees, *A Fly in Amber, being an extravagant biography of the romantic antiquary Sir Robert Bruce Cotton. Ibid.*
348. *Proceedings of the International Congress of Celtic Studies held in Dublin . . . 1959*, ed. Brian O Cúiv. *Ibid.* 70(9), Sept. 1962, 189.

1963

349. The 1958 Whittonstall treasure trove (1,206 AR, principally Edw. I and II, dep. c.1311?). R. H. M. Dolley and G. L. V. Tatler.

Archaeologia Aeliana[4] *41*, 1963, 65–83.

350. Finds of Carolingian coins from Great Britain and Ireland. R. H. M. Dolley and K. F. Morrison. *BNJ 32*, 1963, 75–87.
351. An unpublished hoard-provenance for a penny of Ceolwulf II of Mercia. *Ibid.*, 88–90, pl. viii. [Washington (Sussex); lists known coins of Ceolwulf II.]
352. Two 'new' Yorkshire hoards of Short Cross pennies. J. D. Brand and R. H. M. Dolley. *Ibid.*, 94–8. [York Minster; Barnsley neighbourhood.]
353. The Irish coinage of Henry III, Appendix I: The hoard evidence. *Ibid.*, 112–14. [Principal author D. W. Dykes.]
354. An early nineteenth-century discovery of Edward pennies at Knaresborough Priory. R. H. M. Dolley and H. E. Pagan. *Ibid.*, 117–26.
355. Two 'unique' Plantagenet pennies from Midlands mints [line drawings prepared by E. Hart]. *Cunobelin* no.9, 1963, 29–36. [*Short Cross* pennies of 'Oxford' and 'Lichfield'.]
356. Two unpublished letters of a distinguished Cork antiquary. *J. Cork Hist. and Archaeol. Soc. 68*(207 & 208), Jan./Dec. 1963, 55–65. [Letters of Richard Sainthill.]
357. The Dublin pennies in the name of Sihtric Silkbeard in the Hermitage Museum at Leningrad. *JRSAI 93*(1), 1963, 1–8, pls. i-iii.
358. An unpublished variety of the Short Cross penny of King Cnut. *NC*[7] *3*, 1963, 93–5, pl. vii.
359. The fifteenth-century coinage of Ireland: [report]. R. H. M. Dolley and D. W. Dykes. *Ibid.* 5–6 (Procs of the Royal Numismatic Society).
360. A fictitious First Hand moneyer of Lydford. *NCirc 71*(1), Jan. 1963, 1–2. [Reattributed to London.]
361. A mythical moneyer of the Bristol mint. *Ibid. 71*(2), Feb. 1963, 22. [Cnut *Short Cross*, Ælric, reattributed to Winchester.]
362. Witham, Worcester or Bath? *Ibid. 71*(3), Mar. 1963, 45. [Harthacnut *Jewel Cross*, reattributed to Bath.]
363. 'Plumbei Angliae': a find of sixteenth-century(?) lead tokens from Huntingdon, by Michael Dolley and Anthony Hocking. *Ibid. 71*(10), Oct. 1963, 206–7.
364. The sequence of moneyers at Rhuddlan in the Short-Cross period. *Ibid. 71*(11), Nov. 1963, 226–7.
365. Two mythical moneyers of Exeter and of Lincoln. *Ibid. 71*(12), Dec. 1963, 248. [Harold I *Fleur-de-Lis*, reattributed to Malmesbury.]
366. Excavations at Cox Lane (1958) and at the Town Defences, Shire Hall yard, Ipswich (1959): the coins. *Procs Suffolk Inst. of Archaeology 29*(3), 1963, 286–91, pl. xxxvii. [Principal author S. E. West.]

1964

367. *Anglo-Saxon Pennies*. Trustees of the British Museum, 1964. 32pp., front., xvi pls.
368. A probable fourth Kentish mint of Æthelstan. *BNJ 33*, 1964, 30–3. [Lympne, to which Torhtelm is reattributed from Leicester (cf. item 146.]
369. A small parcel of First Hand pennies of Æthelræd II from the 1863 Ipswich hoard. *Ibid.* 34–8, pl. i. [*See also* item 415.]
370. The repercussions on Chester's prosperity of the Viking descent on Cheshire in 980, by R. H. M. Dolley and Miss E. J. E. Pirie. *Ibid.* 39–44, pl. viii.
371. Some mis-attributed Fleur-de-lis coins of Harold I. *Ibid.*, 45–7, pl. ix.
372. The 1961 find of fourteenth-century silver coins from Mareham-le-Fen in Lincolnshire. *Ibid.*, 83–9, pls. iii-iv.
373. Two neglected Northumbrian hoards of late 14th-century gold coins. *Ibid.*, 90–3, pl. ii. [Fenwick

(including a David II); Brinkburn Priory.]
374. The Witchingham, Norfolk, XV-XVI c. hoard (1805), by C. E. Blunt and R. H. M. Dolley. *Ibid.*, 107–9.
375. Two further coins of Henry I from Llantrithyd. *Ibid.*, 169–71. [*See also* item 318.]
376. Obituary: John Walker . . . *Ibid.*, 181–2.
377. An example of the relevance to numismatics of an early nineteenth-century local history. *Cunobelin*, no.10, 1964, 26–9. [On an Exeter find of a Limerick penny of John.]
378.* And would not stay for an answer: when were the Casement diaries found? *The New Nation 1*(7), Aug./Sept. 1964, 6–8. [An independent journal for social, cultural, and political comment on Irish affairs, published by Irish Unity.]
379.* When we are free: Education. *Ibid. 1*(8), Oct. 1964, 7–10. [Educational policy in Northern Ireland.]
380. A half-forgotten Viking-Age coin-hoard from Glendalough, by R. H. M. Dolley and H. E. Pagan. *NCirc 72*(1), Jan. 1964, 1–2.
381. The Roycc collection at Stow-on-the-World: the coins: Anglo-Saxon coins. *Trans. Bristol and Glos. Archaeol. Soc. 83*, 1964, 17–19, pl. ii.
382. A supposititious gold coin of 'Sithric' from near Hull. *Trans. Yorkshire Num. Soc.*,[2] *2*(1), 1964, 18–19. [Corrected to a Merovingian tremissis of Rodez.]

Reviews
383. Sir Geoffrey Duveen and H. G. Stride, *The History of the Gold Sovereign*. *EHR 79*(311), Apr. 1964, 407–8.

1965
384. *Viking Coins of the Danelaw and of Dublin*. Trustees of the British Museum, 1965. 32pp., xvi pls.
385. New light on the 1843 Viking-Age coin-hoard from Derrykeighan near Dervock in Co. Antrim. *BNJ 34*, 1965, 32–6.
386. The Buckingham mint, by R. H. M. Dolley, D. J. Elliott and F. Elmore Jones. *Ibid.*, 46–52, pl. iv. [Late 10th/11th-cent.]
387. The Corofin (Co. Clare) hoard, late 12th-early 13th centuries, by R. H. M. Dolley and William O'Sullivan. *Ibid.*, 98–103.
388. A parcel of Long-Cross coins –? from the 1869 Tower Hill hoard, by R. H. M. Dolley and W. A. Seaby. *Ibid.*, 104–8, pl. xiii.
389. The authenticity of the Palatina obolus of Lothaire II found at Litton Cheney in Dorset; [incorporating a report by A. E. Werner and R. M. Organ]. *Ibid.*, 167–8.
390. A note on the Belfast issuers of two of the advertisement imitations of 'spade' guineas. *Ibid.*, 170–2.
391. The earliest German imitations of Anglo-Irish coins. In *Dona numismatica, Walter Hävernick zum 23. Januar 1965 dargebracht*, herausgegeben von Peter Berghaus und Gert Hatz, Hamburg 1965, 213–18, pl. xviii.
392. The 1834 Bantry find and the Battle of Callann. *J. Cork Hist. and Archaeol. Soc. 70*, 1965, 135–9. [13th-cent.]
393. A seventeenth-century coin-find from Galway City. *J. Galway Archaeol. and Hist. Soc. 31*(1/2), 1964/5, 5–7.
394. A spurious hoard of Northumbrian copper coins from Bath. *NC*[7] *5*, 1965, 197–200, pl. xx.
395. Master Percival de Porche of 'Luk' – Italian or Liégeois? *Ibid.*, 201–3.
396. Bek, Beaumont, Bury, and Hatfield: some neglected hoard-evidence. *NCirc 73*(2), Feb. 1965, 35–6.
397. Christoba Columbus! *Ibid. 73*(4), Apr. 1965, 81–2. ['Christoba' as the name of a Ceolwulf moneyer.]
398. Two problematical pennies of

Harold I. *Ibid. 73*(7/8), Jul/Aug. 1965, 154–5. [*Jewel Cross*, Exeter and Derby.]

399. [The term 'crozier']. *Ibid. 73*(9), Sept. 1965, 183 (Correspondence).

400. Odium numismaticum: two Ultonian manifestations. *Ibid.*, 183–4.

401. Tre kronor = Trí choróin: a note on the date of the 'three-crown' coinage of Ireland. *Numismatiska Meddelanden 30*, 1965, 103–12. ['Till Nils Ludvig Rasmusson'.]

402. A largely forgotten 17th-century coin-hoard from the south-east of Co. Donegal. *Ulster J. of Archaeology*[3] *28*, 1965, 117–21. [Lough Derg hoard.]

Reviews

403. Georg Galster, 'Møntfundet fra Kongsø Plantage'. *BNJ 34*, 1965, 181–3.

404. John Porteous, *Coins*. *Ibid.*, 184–6.

405. Ludwig Bieler, *Ireland: Harbinger of the Middle Ages*. *J. Ecclesiastical History 16*(1), Apr. 1965, 98.

1966

406. *The Carolingian Coins in the British Museum*, by R. H. M. Dolley and K. F. Morrison. Trustees of the British Museum, 1966. ix, 46pp., xii pls.

407. *The Norman Conquest and the English Coinage*. 1966. 40pp.

408. *Sylloge of Coins of the British Isles, [8]: The Hiberno-Norse Coins in the British Museum*. Trustees of the British Museum, 1966. xi, 234pp., viii pls. [Includes Viking-Age coin-hoards from Great Britain and Ireland, pp. 47–91, maps.]

409. New light on the Mullingar find of Hand pence of Æthelræd II. *BNJ 35*, 1966, 12–21.

410. An unpublished link between the First and Second Hand types of Æthelræd II. *Ibid.*, 22–4. [Canterbury, altered dies.]

411. Further Southampton/Winchester die-links in the reign of Æthelræd II. *Ibid.*, 25–33. [*Further to* item 118.]

412. A small find of twelfth- and thirteenth-century pennies from Tullintowell. *Ibid.*, 113–15.

413. An eighteenth-century forgery of an Anglo-Irish groat or half groat of Edward IV. *Ibid.*, 148–51.

414. A note on the weight and fineness of the 1646 Ormonde 'pistole'. *Ibid.*, 152–4.

415. The left-facing First Hand pennies of Æthelræd II: two additions. *Ibid.*, 191–2. [*Additions to* item 369.]

416. A die-link between 'Chester' and 'Lydford' in the Hiberno-Norse coinage of Dublin. *Ibid.*, 192–3.

417. An important unpublished penny of the Confessor from an Irish hoard. *Ibid.*, 193–4. [*Radiate/Small Cross*, Hereford mint.]

418. New light on the pre-1760 Coney Street (York) find of coins of the Duurstede mint. *JMP 52/53*(1), 1965/6, 1–7; samenvatting, 7.

419. Some unpublished variants of the Pacx type of Edward the Confessor. *NC*[7] 6, 1966, 207–16, pls. xvii-xviii. [*See also* item 750.]

420. Two neglected finds of coins of Henry VIII from Co. Down, by R. H. M. Dolley and W. A. Seaby. *Ibid.*, 217–19. [Downpatrick; Ballynahinch; 'Co. Down'; Ballyholme.]

421. The Continental hoard-evidence for the chronology of the Anglo-Irish pence of John. *NCirc 74*(2), Feb. 1966, 30–2.

422. The 'Ireland' find (c.1842) of Profile halfpence of John. *Ibid. 74*(3), Mar. 1966, 66–7.

423. Dr George Petrie's hoard of Anglo-Irish coins of King John. *Ibid. 74*(5), May 1966, 127–9.

424. A note on some toponymics occurring among the personnel of the Long-Cross coinage of Henry III. *Ibid. 74*(6), June 1966, 150–2.

425. A mythical Second Hand/First

Hand mule of Æthelræd II. *Ibid.* *74*(10), Oct. 1966, 236. [Transitional *First Hand* coin of Ipswich; *see also* item 779.]

426. The metrology of the English coins in the 1911 Glemminge hoard from southern Sweden. *Ibid.* *74*(11), Nov. 1966, 276–7. [Æthelred II *Hand* and *Crux* types.]

427. Four neglected Irish finds of Anglo-Irish coins of John. *Ulster J. of Archaeology*[3] *29*, 1966, 130–7, pl. xix. ['Leinster'; Loughlinstown; Arklow; 'Poer Trench'.]

Reviews

428. B. Malmer, *Olof Skötkonungs mynt och andra Ethelred-imitationer några svensk-engelska myntproblem.* *NC*[7] *6*, 1966, 366–9.

1967

429. On an alleged penny of Ludica, King of Mercia 825–7, by C. E. Blunt and Michael Dolley. *BNJ 36*, 1967, 29–31.

430. A fourth find of ninth-century coins from Ireland? *Ibid.*, 32–5.

431. OE *Christðegn – an unsuspected instance of Early Middle Irish influence on English name-giving. *Ibid.*, 40–5, pl. ii.

432. A parcel of Reform-Type pence of Eadgar and his successors, by Michael Dolley and C. E. Blunt. *Ibid.*, 55–8, pl. ii. [Willes parcel = 1749 Oakham hoard.]

433. Additional evidence for the sequence of types early in the reign of Edward the Confessor, by Michael Dolley and Stewart Lyon. *Ibid.*, 59–61.

434. A preliminary account of the Anglo-Saxon element in the 1966 find from Tingstäde parish on Gotland, by Michael Dolley, Lillemor Lundström, and Gay van der Meer. *Ibid.*, 62–80, pls. viii-ix.

435. The Anglo-Saxon element in the 1967 Burge hoard from Lummelunda parish, Gotland, by Michael Dolley, with C. E. Blunt and Miss G. van der Meer. *Ibid.*, 81–5.

436. Some unpublished early nineteenth-century Irish finds, by Michael Dolley and W. A. Seaby. *Ibid.*, 96–105.

437. 'Le money del Oraylly' (O'Reilly's money), by Michael Dolley and W. A. Seaby. *Ibid.*, 114–17, pl. xiv. [Plated copies of clipped English groats.]

438. Elizabethan *bungal(l)* – a contribution to Anglo-Irish lexicography. *Ibid.*, 118–21.

439. A rediscovered 'new' moneyer for Eadgar. *Ibid.*, 191, pl. xv. [Etfer(n).]

440. An unpublished London find of early thirteenth-century pennies. *Ibid.*, 193–5.

441. Obituary: Charles Wilson Peck . . . *Ibid.*, 203–7.

442. Lough Lene find of 1843. *Coins and Medals 4*(6), June 1967, 336–9, 355, 357.

443. 'There is only one thing in life that matters, and that is the truth'; Nevill Boyd Maunsell interviews Michael Dolley. *Coins, Medals & Currency 1*(20), 15 Sept. 1967, 7–8.

444. [see 497*bis*].

445. The historical background to the 1580 map of Smerwick. *Mariner's Mirror 53*(1), Feb. 1967, 74–5. [Reply by T. Glasgow, 75–6.]

446. An early sixteenth-century coin-hoard from the eastern slopes of Mount Brandon. *North Munster Ant. J. 10*(2), 1967, 223–5. [Cloonsharragh hoard.]

447. The chronology of the first Anglo-Irish coinage. Michael Dolley and William O'Sullivan. In *North Munster studies: essays in commemoration of Monsignor Michael Moloney*, ed. Etienne Rynne, Limerick 1967, 437–78.

448. The identity of the 'Dominick grote'. *NC*[7] 7, 1967, 163–6. [*See also* item 697.]

449. A mythical Æthelræd II moneyer of the Romney mint. *NCirc 75*(1), Jan. 1967, 1. [*Last Small Cross*, Manna reattributed to Norwich.]
450. Æthelræd's Rochester ravaging of 986: an intriguing numismatic sidelight. *Ibid. 75*(2), Feb. 1967, 33–4.
451. Obituaries: Carsten Svarstad. *Ibid. 75*(6), June 1967, 170.
452. A Snelling non-bicentenary. *Ibid. 75*(7/8), July/Aug. 1967, 201.
453. Recent progress in Anglo-Irish numismatics, c.1200–c.1600. *SCMB* no.591, Nov. 1967, 416–20.
453*bis*. Some coin-names in *Ceart Uí Néill*. Michael Dolley and Gearóid Mac Niocaill. *Studia Celtica 2*, 1967, 119–24, plate. [The text is sixteenth-century.]
454. Great Britain & Ireland, by Michael Dolley and Hugh Pagan. In *A Survey of Numismatic Research, 1960–1965. II: Medieval and oriental numismatics*, ed. Kolbjørn Skaare and George C. Miles [for the] International Numismatic Commission, Copenhagen 1967, 174–202.
455. A Hiberno-Norse penny of Dublin found in Wigtownshire, by R. H. M. Dolley and W. F. Cormack. *Trans. Dumfriesshire and Galloway Nat. Hist. and Ant. Soc.*[3] *44*, 1967, 122–5, pl. xii. [Whithorn find.]
456. Three unpublished nineteenth-century Irish finds of coins, by Michael Dolley, Noel Nesbitt, and David Rebbeck. *Ulster J. of Archaeology*[3] *30*, 1967, 89–94. [Longford; Ballymahon; Oldcastle.]

Reviews

457. Philip Grierson, *Bibliographie numismatique*. *EconHR*[2] *20*(3), 1967, 579–80.
458. Brita Malmer, *Nordiska mynt före åar 1000*. *Fornvännen 62*(4), 1967, 274–8.
459. *Venice and History: the collected papers of Frederic C. Lane . . . Mariner's Mirror 53*(2), May 1967, 202–4.
460. *Sefunim*, no.1, 1966 (Bulletin of the Haifa Maritime Museum). *Ibid.*, 204.
461. *The Course of Irish History*, ed. T. W. Moody and F. X. Martin. *NCirc 75*(4), Apr. 1967, 102.

1968

462. *Sylloge of Coins of the British Isles, [10]: Ulster Museum, Belfast, Part I: Anglo-Irish coins: John-Edward III*, by Michael Dolley and Wilfred Seaby. British Academy and the Trustees of the Ulster Museum, 1968. lvii, 33pp., xvi pls. [Includes 12th- to 14th-cent. hoards from Ireland, Great Britain, and the Continent, pp. xlviii-lv.]
463. A fourteenth-century coin-find from County Cavan, by Michael Dolley and Colm Gallagher. *Bréifne 3*(11), 1968, 387–9. [Annagh hoard.]
464. A parcel of late eleventh-century Hiberno-Norse coins found in Northern Italy, by Michael Dolley and S. N. Lane. *BNJ 37*, 1968, 25–8, pl. xxi.
465. The Anglo-Norman coins in the Uppsala University Cabinet. *Ibid.*, 29–34.
466. The sixteenth-century coin-hoard from Moig South, Askeaton, Co. Limerick, by Michael Dolley, Colm Gallagher, and W. A. Seaby. *Ibid.*, 85–92, pls. viii-xi.
467. A hitherto unconfirmed class of Irish petty paper-money. Michael Dolley and W. A. Seaby. *Ibid.*, 196–8.
468. The date of some glosses on *Bretha Déin Chécht*. *Celtica 8*, 1968, 167–73. [*Screpal*, *pinginn*, *lethpinginn*, and *crosóc* as values in tables of compensation; late 13th/14th-cent.]
469. Trí hórmharg. Michael Dolley, Gearóid Mac Niocaill. *Éigse: a journal of Irish studies 12*(3), 1968, 173–6. [The phrase 'three gold marks' in a 15th-cent. text.]

470. A further die-link in the Scandinavian imitative series. *Fornvännen 63*(2), 1968, 116–19. [Redating of Cnut's issues proposed.]
471. A further unpublished letter of a distinguished Cork antiquary. *J. Cork Hist. and Archaeol. Soc. 73*(217), Jan./June 1968, 31–9. [A letter from Richard Sainthill.]
472–3. Two numismatic notes. i: Some Hiberno-Norse coins of Dublin recently discovered on the Baltic island of Gotland; ii: The mythical Roman coin-hoard from Tara. *JRSAI 98*, 1968, 57–65, pls. 5–6. [(i) Karls (Tingstäde parish) hoard.]
474. The Hiberno-Norse coins in the 1967 find from Lummelunda parish, Gotland. *Ibid.*, 197–9, pl. 11. [Burge hoard.]
475. New light on the 1872 find of coins from Ballykinvarga (Kilfenora), Co. Clare. *North Munster Ant. J. 11*, 1968, 22–6. [14th-cent.]
476. A very late 14th- or early 15th-century coin-hoard from near Roscrea. Michael Dolley and W. A. Seaby. *Ibid.*, 71–3.
477. The first treasure trove inquest in Ireland? *Northern Ireland Legal Quarterly 19*(2), June 1968, 182–8.
478. A gold coin of the time of Offa, by C. E. Blunt and Michael Dolley; scientific report . . .[by] A. E. Werner, Robert M. Organ. NC^7 *8*, 1968, 151–60, pl. xv.
479. A case of die-theft at or about the Millennium. *NCirc 76*(2), Feb. 1968, 36. [Æthelred II *Long Cross*, die of Worcester used in Hiberno-Norse series; *see also* item 510.]
480. A note on the attribution of the regally anonymous 'Three-Crown' coinage given by Smith and Coffey to Edward IV. *Ibid. 76*(4), Apr. 1968, 118.
481. Saxon Southampton: a review of the evidence. Part I: History, location, date and character of the town. P. V. Addyman and D. H. Hill [with contributions by Michael Dolley]. *Procs. Hants. Field Club 25*, 1968, 61–93, pl. ii.
482. Excavations at Dalkey Island, Co. Dublin, 1956–1959. Appendix 4: Medieval coins and jettons. *PRIA*, Section C, *66*(2), 1967/8, 179–82. [Principal author G. D. Liversage.]
483. The Irish mints of Edward I in the light of the coin-hoards from Ireland and Great Britain. *Ibid. 66*(3), Jan. 1968, 235–97.
484. A Viking-Age coin of Norway discovered in Shetland. *PSAS 100*, 1967/8, 193–5, pl. 23. [Jarlshof(?) find.]
485. A parcel of Edwardian sterlings in the Ulster Museum, by Michael Dolley and Wilfred Seaby. *SCMB* no.597, May 1968, 161–6. [Ulster(?) hoard, 14th-cent.]

1969

486–7. *Sylloge of Coins of the British Isles, [11]: University Collection, Reading: Anglo-Saxon and Norman coins* [by C. E. Blunt and Michael Dolley]; [*and*], *Royal Coin Cabinet, Stockholm: Anglo-Norman pennies* [by Michael Dolley, with F. Elmore Jones and C. S. S. Lyon]. British Academy and Kungl. Vitterhets Historie och Antikvitets Akademien, 1969. [4], 87pp., viii, xii pls.
488. The ruined church of Stone-by-Faversham: the sceatta (pl. lviiia). *AntJ 49*(2), 1969, 290–2. [Principal authors Sir E. Fletcher and G. W. Meates.]
489. The Anglo-Saxon pennies from the 'upper souterrain' at Knowth. *BNJ 38*, 1969, 16–21.
490. The coinages for Ireland of Henry VIII. Michael Dolley and W. D. Hackmann. *Ibid.*, 84–108. [Dolley contributed to pp. 84–97, 100–8.]
491. The Cloncreen Bog (Clonbulloge) find of Elizabethan coins from the Co. Offaly. Michael Dolley and A. Gunstone. *Ibid.*, 109–12, pls. iv-v.
492. The 1912 Welwyn find of pence of

Eadgar and of Edward the Martyr. *Ibid.*, 183–5.
493.* An Eleven Years' War coin-hoard from County Monaghan, by Michael Dolley and Colm Gallagher. *Clogher Record* 7(1), 1969, 105–7.
494.* An Eleven Years' War find from the south of Co. Donegal. Michael Dolley and David Rebbeck. *Donegal Annual 8*(1), 1969, 106–8. [Ardara hoard.]
495. Some neglected evidence from Irish chronicles concerning the alleged poisoning of Pope Clement II. *Frühmittelalterliche Studien 3*, 1969, 343–6.
496. Gotlands största silverskatt, funnen vid Burge i Lummelunda: mynten: England och Irland. *Gotländskt Arkiv 41*, 1969, 54–8.
497. Foreword. In *The Guide Book to the Coinage of Ireland* . . ., by Anthony Dowle and Patrick Finn . . ., 1969, 4–5.
497*bis*. Anglo-Irish monetary policies, 1172–1637. In *Historical Studies: papers read before the Irish Conference of Historians*, 7: [8th conference, Belfast, 1967], ed. J. C. Beckett, 1969, 45–64.
498. The Normans – a lasting impact. *Ireland of the Welcomes 18*(1), May/June 1969, 36–9.
499. 400 years of coin collecting in Ireland. *IN 2*(10), July/Aug. 1969, 196–9. [Previously published in the First Ulster Coin Fair brochure.]
500. New light on the 1894 Douglas hoard. *J. Manx Museum* 7(85), 1969, 121–4, pl. 32.
501. The two Viking ages of Britain [by P. H. Sawyer]: an Irish comment. *MScand 2*, 1969, 179–85.
502. The mediaeval coin-hoards of Thomond. *North Munster Ant. J. 12*, 1969, 23–34.
503. The Roman coin-hoard from Timberland (Lincs.): a revision, by Michael Dolley and Malcolm Todd. *NC*^{7} 9, 1969, 107–12.
504–7. Four notes on unpublished Irish finds of the sixteenth and seventeenth centuries. 1: An early sixteenth-century coin-find from north Connacht; 2: Two finds of coins of Henry VIII; 3: A late Tudor coin-hoard from Co. Mayo; 4: An Eleven Years' War coin-hoard from the right bank of the Shannon, by Michael Dolley and Colm Gallagher. *Ibid.*, 219–33. [(1) Dromod; (2) Rossinver and unknown site; (3) Ballysakeery; (4) Meelick. (1) and (4) are by Dolley alone.]
508. The coinage of Lambert Simnel: [report]. *Ibid.*, xii-xiii. [Also reported in *NCirc* 77(6), June 1969, 207, and *SCMB* no. 610, June 1969, 202.]
509. Random sampling. *NCirc* 77(2), Feb. 1969, 45. [The case of the Fishpool hoard.]
510. Some remarks on the identity of the Worcester moneyer Wulfric. *Ibid.* 77(4), Apr. 1969, 126–8. [A reply to a critic of item 479.]
511. Was there an Anglo-Irish coinage in the name of Edward VI? *Ibid.* 77(9), Sept. 1969, 274–5.
512. The sequence and chronology of the 'Portrait' Anglo-Irish groats of Henry VII. *Ibid.* 77(11), Nov. 1969, 370–4.
513. Two crannog finds of fire-damaged coins of the Tudors. In *Occasional Papers – Num. Soc. of Ireland* nos. 5–9, Mar. 1969, 1–3, pl. i. [Magheracloone; Lough Ackrick; *see also* item 690.]
514. Excavations at Mellifont Abbey, Co. Louth. Appendix C: The thirteenth-century coin-hoard. *PRIA*, Section C, *68*(2), 1969, 160–4, pl. xliii. [Principal author L. de Paor.]
515. More thoughts on the Winchester mint under William II. *SCMB* no. 605, Jan. 1969, 11–15.
516. Simnel and Warbeck: some recent misconceptions. *Ibid.*, no. 616, Dec. 1969, 424–5.
517. A twentieth-century paper money

hoard from East Belfast, by Michael Dolley and David Rebbeck. *Ulster J. of Archaeology*,[3] *32*, 1969, 105–8. [Strandtown hoard.]

518. Medieval British and Irish coins as dating evidence for the archaeologist. *World Archaeology 1*(2), Oct. 1969, 200–7.

Reviews

519. L. R. Laing, *Coins and Archaeology*. *Coins, Medals & Currency 3*(33), 13 Dec. 1969, 6–7, 10.

520–1. R. P. C. Hanson, *St Patrick: his origins and career*; [and], Brendan Lehane, *The Quest of Three Abbots: pioneers of Ireland's Golden Age*. *J. Ecclesiastical History 20*(1), Apr. 1969, 121–3.

522.* K. H. Connell, *Irish Peasant Society: four historical essays*. *Newman Rev. 1*(1), 1969, 48–50.

523. G. A. Hayes-McCoy, *Irish Battles*. *Ulster J. of Archaeology*[3] *32*, 1969, 118–19.

524. E. M. Johnston, *Irish History: a select bibliography*. *Ibid.*, 122–3.

1970

524*bis*.* *Law(?) and Orders: the Belfast 'curfew' of 3–5 July 1970*, by Seán Óg Ó Fearghail; [preface by Micheál Ó Dathlaoich, i.e. Michael Dolley]. [Belfast] (printed Dundalk): Central Citizens' Defence Committee, 1970. 45pp., 16pls.

525. Some single finds of tenth- and eleventh-century English coins from Wales, by M. Dolley and J. K. Knight. *Archaeologia Cambrensis 119*, 1970, 75–82, pl. xx.

526. An early fourteenth-century coin hoard from the Co. Roscommon. Michael Dolley and Michael K. Murphy. *BNJ 39*, 1970, 84–90. [Carns hoard.]

527. A pattern shilling Irish of Mary Tudor. *Ibid.*, 98–110.

528.* Mediaeval coin-hoards from the Ulster mearing. *Clogher Record* 7(2), 1970, 204–20.

529. Irish numismatics and the 1970s. *Irish Numismatics 3*(14), Mar./Apr. 1970, 87–91. [Repr. from the programme of the 1st Irish International Coin Fair, Dublin, 1970.]

530. The 1846 find of English gold coins from Seneschal Lane, Douglas, by Michael Dolley and A. M. Cubbon. *J. Manx Museum* 7(86), 1970, 140–3, pl. 34. [Deposited 1505.]

531. The King John portion of the Anglo-Irish element in the 1908 Brussels hoard. *JRSAI 100*, 1970, 67–70, pl. 17.

532. Introduction. In *The Lincoln Mint, c.890–1279*, by H. R. Mossop . . ., 1970, 9–10.

533. The origin, purpose and date of pilaster-strips in Anglo-Saxon architecture. Appendix II: The numismatic evidence. *North Staffordshire J. Field Studies 10*, 1970, 42–3. [Edward the Elder's Tower type; principal author H. M. Taylor.]

534. A critical unpublished penny Irish of Elizabeth. *NCirc 78*(5: special Irish number), May 1970, 190–1.

535. An Anglo-Irish hybrid forgery from the 1280s. *Ibid. 78*(7/8), July-Aug. 1970, 286. [Obv. as Edward I, rev. as Henry III.]

536. A small find of 'Dominick Grotes' from the Co. Donegal. *Ibid. 78*(9), Sept. 1970, 330. [Rossnowlagh find.]

537. The harp on Anglo-Irish coins: a preliminary exposition. In *Occasional Papers – Num. Soc. of Ireland* nos. 10–14, Jan. 1970, 1–10, pls. i-ii.

538. A parcel of Three-Crown groats probably from a find of 1838. Michael Dolley and Stuart N. Lane. *Ibid.*, 11–14, pl. iii. [Co. Meath find.]

539. A parcel of Irish 'white money' from (?) Co. Tipperary. Gerard Brady and Michael Dolley. *Ibid.*, 15–19, pl. iii.

540. The location of the pre-Ælfredian mint(s) of Wessex. *Procs. Hampshire Field Club and Archaeol. Soc. 27*, 1970, 57–61.
541. Irish hoards with thirteenth- and fourteenth-century Scottish coins. *SCMB* no. 617, Jan. 1970, 4–10.
542. A supplementary note on the Macroom find of tenth-century English pence. *Ibid.*, no. 622, June 1970, 199–200.
543. St Patrick: the myth and the man. *The Tablet 224*(6776), 11 Apr. 1970, 352–3.
544. The pattern of Elizabethan coin-hoards from Ireland. *Ulster J. of Archaeology*,[3] *33*, 1970, 77–88.

1971

545. *A Bibliography of Coin Hoards of Great Britain and Ireland, 1500–1967*. I. D. Brown and Michael Dolley. 1971. 88pp. (Royal Numismatic Society. Special publication, no. 6). [Part II: Ireland, pp. 61–82, is by Dolley; *see also* items 677–9.]
546. The mythical Norman element in the 1882 Bishophill (York) find of Anglo-Saxon coins. *Annual Report – Yorkshire Philosophical Soc.* 1971, 88–101.
547. Hope or LSD?: part of a lecture delivered at Benburb Priory [i.e. Servite Priory, Benburb, Co. Tyrone], autumn 1970. *Aquarius, formerly Everyman: an annual religio-cultural review* no. 4, 1971, 138–44.
548. A group of tenth-century coins found at Mont Saint-Michel. Michael Dolley and Jacques Yvon. *BNJ 40*, 1971, 1–16, pl. vi.
549. A third type for the Cardiff mint under Henry I. George C. Boon and Michael Dolley. *Ibid.*, 172–3.
550. A neglected medieval sidelight on the Greek trireme. *Classical Quarterly*, n.s., *21*(1), May 1971, 285–7.
551. 'Anglo-Irish' or 'Irish'?: a plea for reasoned numismatic nomenclature, by Merus Hibernicus [i.e. Michael Dolley]. *Coins, Medals & Currency 4*(40), 13 Feb. 1971, 4–5.
552. The nummular brooch from Sulgrave. In *England before the Conquest: studies in primary sources presented to Dorothy Whitelock*, ed. Peter Clemoes and Kathleen Hughes, 1971, 333–49, pl. viii. [The brooch is of *Agnus Dei* design; comments on *Agnus Dei* coinage of Æthelred II.]
553. A note on the obverse and the reverse types of the 'St Patrick' coinage. *IN 4*(22), July/Aug. 1971, 142–4.
554. Anglo-Norman coins found in Ireland. *Ibid.*, 155. [A Stephen, and a reproduction.]
555. A series of advertisement reproductions of early coins, by M. Dolley and W. A. Seaby. *Ibid. 4*(23), Sept./Oct. 1971, 200–2.
556. A small find of nineteenth-century coins from Kanturk. *J. Cork Hist. and Archaeol. Soc. 76*(224), 1971, 150–1.
557. An English halfpenny of Edward I from Cronk ny Merriu. *J. Manx Museum* 7(87), 1971, 175–6, pl. 43.
558. The mints of Northampton and Southampton up to the time of Edgar's Reform, by C. E. Blunt and Michael Dolley. In *Mints, Dies and Currency: essays dedicated to the memory of Albert Baldwin*, ed. R. A. G. Carson, 1971, 91–100, pl. x.
559. The anomalous Long-Cross coins in the Anglo-Irish portion of the Brussels hoard, by Michael Dolley and W. A. Seaby. *Ibid.*, 291–317, pls. xx-xxi.
560. A nineteenth-century discovery of Elizabethan coins in Co. Clare. *North Munster Ant. J. 14*, 1971, 46–8. [Sixmilebridge find.]
561. The weight-standard of the later seventeenth-century copper halfpenny Irish. *NCirc 79*(5), May 1971, 198–200.
562. A neglected 14th-century coin-hoard from Co. Antrim. *Ibid. 79*(7/8),

July/Aug. 1971, 278. [Ballyclare hoard.]

563. A find of thirteenth-century pewter tokens from the National Museum excavations at Winetavern Street, Dublin, by Michael Dolley and W. A. Seaby. *Ibid. 79*(12), Dec. 1971, 446–8.

564. The A. N. spellings 'Stifne', 'Stefne', and 'Stiefne' found in the obverse legends of English coins of Stephen's first substantive type, by Michael Dolley and K. A. Goddard. *PRIA*, Section C, *71*(2), 1971, 19–34.

565. An early seventeenth-century coin-find from the Co. Donegal. *SCMB* no. 632, Apr. 1971, 134–6. [Ballyshannon find.]

Reviews

566. L. O. Lagerqvist, *Svenska mynt under Vikingatid och Medeltid. NCirc 79*(3), Mar. 1971, 105–6.

1972

567. *Anglo-Norman Ireland, c.1100–1318.* Dublin [1972]. [14], 210pp. (The Gill History of Ireland, 3.)

568. *Medieval Anglo-Irish coins.* 1972. x, 90pp. [Includes medieval Irish coin-hoards, pp. 57–71, 83; treasure trove, pp. 72–4; *see also* item 679.]

569.* A George II silver basket associated with Bishop Clayton of Clogher, by Michael Dolley and Erina George. *Clogher Record* 7(3), 1971/2, 447–8.

570. A critical and unpublished Hiberno-Norse penny. *Coins & Antiquities Ltd. [Coin List]* no. 5/6, 1972, [2–3], plate. [Phase I, *Helmet* type.]

571. A small find of Edwardian sterlings from the County Clare, by Michael Dolley and W. A. Seaby. *IN 5*(27), May/June 1972, 107–9. [Barnatick find.]

572. A small parcel of silver coins from an apparently unrecorded English find of the 14th century, by Stuart N. Lane and Michael Dolley. *Ibid.* 5(29), Sept./Oct. 1972, 201–2.

573. A provisional note on some Kilkenny halfpence. *Ibid.* 5(30), Nov./Dec. 1972, 243–5.

574. Four Carolingian coins found at Wijk-bij-Duurstede and now in the Royal Coin Cabinet at Stockholm, by Michael Dolley and Tamás Sárkány. *JMP 58/59*, 1971/2, 5–9, pl. i.

575. Four unpublished letters from Aquilla Smith to the Cork numismatist Richard Sainthill. *J. Cork Hist. and Archaeol. Soc. 77*, 1972, 28–38.

576. A find of fifteenth-century English groats from Co. Dublin. Michael Dolley and Stuart N. Lane. *JRSAI 102*(2), 1972, 143–50, pls. 22–23. [Portmarnock find.]

577. An unexpected Irish dimension of the Anglo-Saxon coinage of Winchester. *NNÅ* 1972, 27–47; sammanfattning, 48.

578. A neglected Scillonian circulation of Wood's Halfpence. *NC^7 12*, 1972, 217–19.

579. A parcel of fourth-century Roman coins from north-western Asia Minor, by Michael Dolley and W. A. Seaby. *NCirc 80*(4), Apr. 1972, 137–8.

580. Some Danish evidence for the commencement of imitation of imitation in the Hiberno-Norse series. *Ibid. 80*(10), Oct. 1972, 358.

581. The newest find with Anglo-Saxon coins from Gotland. *Ibid. 80*(12), Dec. 1972, 450. [Burge hoard.]

582. George Petrie and a century of Irish numismatics. *PRIA*, Section C, *72*(8), 1972, 165–93, pl. iv (Aspects of George Petrie, III.)

583. The c.1843 Leggagh (Nobber) coin-hoard reconsidered. *Ríocht na Midhe: records of Meath Archaeol. and Hist. Soc.* 5(2), 1972, 14–21.

584. A neglected early Tudor coin-hoard from County Tyrone, by C. S. Briggs and Michael Dolley. *SCMB* no. 646, June 1972, 222–4. [Omagh hoard.]

585. Some new light on the early twelfth-

century coinage of Dublin. *Ibid.*, no. 650, Oct. 1972, 404–6.

586. Editors' note. C. E. B[lunt], M. D[olley]. In *Sylloge of Coins of the British Isles, 18: Royal Collection of Coins and Medals, National Museum, Copenhagen, Part IV: Anglo-Saxon coins from Harold I, and Anglo-Norman coins*, by Georg Galster, 1972, ix-x.

Reviews

587. Roald Morcken, 'Old Norse nautical distance tables in the Mediterranean Sea'. *Mariner's Mirror 58*(4), Nov. 1972, 482.

1973

588. *Sylloge of Coins of the British Isles, 19: Bristol and Gloucester museums: Ancient British coins and coins of the Bristol and Gloucestershire mints*, by L. V. Grinsell, C. E. Blunt, and Michael Dolley. British Academy, 1973. 142pp., table, xviii, ix pls. [Includes C. E. Blunt and Michael Dolley on the mints of Gloucester, Winchcombe, Berkeley, and ?Cirencester, pp. 95–112, table.]

589. Some Irish evidence for the date of the *Crux* coins of Æthelred II. *ASE 2*, 1973, 145–54.

590. Some reflections on the English coinages of Sihtric Caoch, King of Dublin and of York. Michael Dolley and C. N. Moore. *BNJ 43*, 1973, 45–59.

591. Concerning the function of certain incuse countermarks. *Bull. – Token Corresponding Soc. 1*(9), Mar. 1973, 191–2.

591*bis*. Anglo-Irish tokens. Seamus MacMuiris [i.e. Michael Dolley]. *Coins 10*(12), Dec. 1973, 37. [A letter commenting on 'Mid 18th-century Irish trade tokens' by Arthur E. J. Went, *ibid. 10*(7), July 1973, 28–31.]

592. The Viking-Age coins of Irish provenance in the Royal Coin Collection at Copenhagen. *IN 6*(31), Jan./Feb. 1973, 21–2. [Hiberno-Norse, *ex* J. J. A. Worsaae.]

593. Some remarks on Thomas Wyon's 1813 pattern pennies Irish, by Michael Dolley and W. A. Seaby. *Ibid.* 6(32), Mar./Apr. 1973, 46–50.

594. The hoard-provenances of the Hiberno-Norse coins in Finnish collections. *Ibid.* 6(33), May/June 1973, 122–3.

595. A provisional note on the 1804 Bank of Ireland token for six shillings Irish. *Ibid.* 6(35), Sept./Oct. 1973, 208–16.

596. A Scandinavian reverberation from the Boyne. *Ibid.* 6(36), Nov./Dec. 1973, 243–5. [Gun Money.]

597. Some preliminary observations on the pennies Irish of 1822 and 1823; photographs by W. A. Seaby. *Ibid.* 6(36), Nov./Dec. 1973, 253–64.

598. A nineteenth-century find of fifteenth-century coins from Caherciveen. *J. Kerry Archaeol. and Hist. Soc.* no. 6, 1972/3, 195–7.

599. A forgotten find of tenth-century English coins from Durrow. *J. Old Athlone Soc. 1*(3), 1972/3, 140–2, pl. 10.

600. The thirteenth-century Anglo-Irish coins in the Kirial find from Denmark. Michael Dolley and W. A. Seaby. *JRSAI 103*, 1973, 86–92, pls. 11–12.

601. Nogle danske(?) efterligninger af irsk-nordiske penninge. *NNUM* no. 4, Apr. 1973, 93–9. ['Some Danish(?) imitations of Hiberno-Norse pennies'.]

602. To penninger fra Harald Hardråde funnet på Vesterhavsøyene. Michael Dolley, Kolbjørn Skaare. *NNUM* nr. 8, Oct. 1973, 221–6; summary, 227. [Two coins of Harold Hardrada, found in the Shetlands and in Ireland.]

603. A parcel of later Anglo-Saxon pennies with a putative Finnish hoard-provenance. Michael Dolley and Elsa Lindberger. *NC*[7] *13*, 1973, 126–33, pl. 7.

604. A Hiberno-Norse penny misattributed to the 1834 hoard from Kirk Michael. *NCirc 81*(1), Jan. 1973, 2.
605. An unexpected 'mint' in the Hiberno-Norse imitative series. *Ibid. 81*(2), Feb. 1973, 44. ['Ipswich', *Helmet* type.]
606. A further die-link in the Anglo-Scandinavian imitative series, by Michael Dolley and Tuukka Talvio. *Ibid. 81*(4), Apr. 1973, 138. [Further to item 282.]
607. A new C-R-V-X penny of Edward the Confessor. *Ibid.*, 152.
608. A 'new' moneyer for 'Winchester' in the Hiberno-Norse imitative series. *Ibid. 81*(5), May 1973, 186. [Phase I, *Long Cross* type.]
609. A sesquicentennial note on some official restrikes of the British Colonial 1/50 and 1/100 dollar patterns dated 1823. *Ibid. 81*(7), July/Aug. 1973, 290–1.
610. A parcel of countermarked early nineteenth-century farthings Irish. In *Occasional Papers – Num. Soc. of Ireland* nos. 15–16, Oct. 1973, 1–4, pl. i.
611. The forms of the proper names appearing on the earliest coins struck in Ireland. In *Otium et negotium: studies in onomatology and library science presented to Olof von Feilitzen*, ed. Folke Sandgren, Stockholm 1973, 49–65. [Includes a corpus of Hiberno-Norse *Crux* coins.]
612. Late Saxon settlements in the St Neots area. III: The village or township at St Neots: the finds: metal objects: silver coin: note. *Procs. Cambridge Ant. Soc. 64*, 1972/3, 96. [Harthacnut, Stamford mint; principal author P. V. Addyman.]
613. A note on the seventeenth-century tokens of the Ó'Melaghlins of Mullingar. *Ríocht na Midhe* 5(3), 1973, 46–8.
614. An unusual find of nineteenth-century coins from Rathkenny (Wilkinstown). *Ibid.*, 56–62.
615. An unpublished hoard from north County Dublin with pennies of Eadgar, by C. S. Briggs and Michael Dolley. *SCMB* no. 654, Feb. 1973, 47–50. [Bullock hoard; *see also* item 655].
616. The Eadgar millenary: a note on the Bath mint. *Ibid.* no. 657, May 1973, 156–9.
617. The reverse legend of Mary Tudor's gold: a neglected numismatic innuendo. *Ibid.*, no. 659, July 1973, 244–5.
618. A note on the earliest Finnish coin hoard with Anglo-Saxon pennies. Michael Dolley and Tuukka Talvio. *Suomen Museo* 1973, 25–8. [Piikkiö hoard.]
619. Seventh report of excavations at Tamworth, Staffs. . . . Appendix: the Anglo-Saxon coin. *Trans. – South Staffs. Archaeol. and Hist. Soc. 14*, 1972/3, 42–4, pl. i. [Edward the Martyr cut halfpenny; principal author K. Sheridan.]

1974

620. Towards a revision of the internal chronology of the coinages of Edward the Elder and Plegmund. *ASE 3*, 1974, 175–7.
621. The 1969 Colchester hoard: editorial note [by Michael Dolley, H. E. Pagan, and M. Delmé-Radcliffe]. *BNJ 44*, 1974, 39–40.
622. Coins found at Kells Priory . . . *Ibid.*, 95–6.
623.* Coin club or national society? *Bull. Num. Soc. of Ireland* no. 20, 1974, 1–12.
624. Some thoughts on the manner of publication of coins found in the course of archaeological excavations. In *Coins and the Archaeologist*, ed. John Casey and Richard Reece, 1974 (BAR 4), 224–33.
625. En gotländsk silverskatt med en grupp av pseudo-iriska mynt påträffad vid 1800-talets början;

översättning Ragnar Engeström. *Fornvännen 69*(1), 1974, 30–3; summary, 'A group of pseudo-Irish coins from an early nineteenth-century find from Gotland', 34. [*Long Cross* type, from Myrungs hoard.]

626. The mediaeval coins from the 1973 season of excavations at Muckamore Priory, County Antrim. *Irish Archaeol. Research Forum 1*(1), Apr. 1974, 25–31.
627. Nineteenth-century coin finds in Co. Wexford: a comment. *IN* 7(37), Jan./Feb. 1974, 25–6.
628. The most obvious criterion of the proof of the 1806 farthing Irish; photographs by W. A. Seaby. *Ibid.*, 29–32.
629. The Anglo-Irish coins in the Systematic Collections of the Royal Coin Cabinet at Stockholm. *Ibid.* 7(38), Mar./Apr. 1974, 57–62. [Includes tokens.]
630. An American interpretation of early Irish numismatic history. *Ibid.*, 75–7.
631. A parcel of Edwardian sterlings of uncertain provenance, by Michael Dolley and Stuart N. Lane. *Ibid.*, 79–80. [Probably of Irish provenance: 13th to 14th-cent. and an Edward the Confessor.]
632. The Anglo-Irish coins in the Hermitage Museum at Leningrad. *Ibid.* 7(39), May/June 1974, 111–14.
633. Some specimen-strikings of Matthew Boulton's Cronebane and Enniscorthy token halfpence of 1789 and 1800. *Ibid.* 7(40), July/Aug. 1974, 142–3.
634. An English sixpence of Elizabeth I found at Newry. *Ibid.*, 153.
635. An 'Irish' provenance for the so-called Tribute Penny. *Ibid.*, 158–9.
636. The Anglo-Irish coins at Borgå Lyceum, Porvoo. *Ibid.* 7(41), Sept./Oct. 1974, 185–6. [*See also* item 818.]
637. The Anglo-Irish coins in the Lincoln City and County Museum. *Ibid.* 7(42), Nov./Dec. 1974, 222–3.
638. A later nineteenth-century Kerry forger's mould from Lispole. Michael K. Murphy and Michael Dolley. *J. Kerry Archaeol. and Hist. Soc.* no. 7, 1974, 139–42, pls. 2–3.
639. A hoard of the so-called 'gun-money' from Causeway. *Ibid.*, 146–8.
640. Dansk efterligning af en samtidig irsk gengivelse af en engelsk penning fra Knud den Store. *NNUM* no. 5, May 1974, 138–42. [Danish imitation of a contemporary Irish copy of an English penny of Cnut the Great.]
641. Tre engelska mynt från 1100-talet funna i Finland. *Ibid.* no. 8, Oct. 1974, 221–3. [Two coins of Stephen and one of Henry II found in Finland.]
642. Rahat propaganda-aseina Pohjois-Irlannissa [trans. Tuukka Talvio]. *Numismaatikko* no. 2, 1974, 12–13. [Propagandist coinage in Northern Ireland; 20th-cent. countermarked coins.]
643. An unpublished hoard-provenance for the ninth-century coinage of Hedeby. Michael Dolley and Tuukka Talvio. *NC*[7] *14*, 1974, 190–2, pl. 16. [Cuerdale hoard.]
644. Odium numismaticum: some more recent Ulidian manifestations *NCirc 82*(2), Feb. 1974, 58–60.
645. Dr Nils Ludvig Rasmusson (1904–1973): an appreciation. *Ibid. 82*(3), Mar. 1974, 103–5.
646. The Anglo-Irish coins in the Helsinki University Cabinet, by Michael Dolley and Tuukka Talvio. *Ibid. 82*(4), Apr. 1974, 138–40.
647. [The KAI countermark]. *Ibid. 82*(5), May 1974, 194 (Correspondence).
648. Two anomalous *Pacx* pennies attributed to Edward the Confessor. *Ibid. 82*(6), June 1974, 239. [Scandinavian imitations.]
649. A parcel of forged nineteenth-

century pence and halfpence Irish. *Ibid. 82*(7/8), July/Aug. 1974, 282–3.

650. Some further instances of Ulidian odium numismaticum. *Ibid. 82*(10), Oct. 1974, 381–3.

651. A neglected nineteenth-century coin-hoard from Ramsey (I.o.M.). *Ibid. 82*(12), Dec. 1974, 478.

652. The 'forgotten' Viking-Age silver hoard from the West Nappin, Jurby. *Procs. – Isle of Man Nat. Hist. and Ant. Soc.*, n.s., *8*(1), 1972/4, 54–64, [2] pls.

653.* An Edward III hoard, found in the Victorian epoch, from Scarden, Corbetstown, Co. Westmeath. Michael Dolley and W. A. Seaby. *Ríocht na Midhe* 5(4), 1974, 78–86.

654. A forgotten Hiberno-Norse find from Rathlin Island. *SCMB* no. 666, Feb. 1974, 39–40.

655. Further light on early nineteenth-century finds of Eadgar pennies from Co. Dublin. *Ibid.* no. 669, May 1974, 145–8. [*Further to* item 615.]

656. Some reflections on the volume of the 'Brass Money' of James II. *Ibid.*, no. 676, Dec. 1974, 377–83.

657. Some further light on the 1891 Viking-Age coin-hoard from Ballycastle. *Ulster J. of Archaeology*[3] *36/37*, 1973/4, 87–9.

Reviews

658. Francois Dumas-Dubourg, *Le Trésor de Fécamp et le monnayage en Francie occidentale pendant la seconde moitié du Xe siècle. Cahiers de civilisation médiévale 17*(3), July/Sept. 1974, 257–9.

1975

659. *Corpus nummorum saeculorum IX-XI qui in Suecia reperti sunt . . . 1: Gotland. [1]: Akebäck–Atlingbo*, ediderunt Brita Malmer, Nils Ludvig Rasmusson; cooperantibus Peter Berghaus, Michael Dolley, . . . et aliis. Stockholm: Kungl. Vitterhets Historie och Antikvitets Akademien, 1975. xxviii, 200pp., 27 pls.

660. *Sylloge of Coins of the British Isles, 22: Royal Collection of Coins and Medals, National Museum, Copenhagen, Part 5: Hiberno-Norse and Anglo-Irish coins*, by Georg Galster, with Michael Dolley and Jørgen Steen Jensen. British Academy, 1975. xxx, [47]pp., 22 pls. [Includes finds with Irish coins from Denmark etc., pp. xvi-xxiii.]

661. The small finds: the coin-weight. In *Excavations in Medieval Southampton, 1953–1969*, ed. Colin Platt and Richard Coleman-Smith with . . . [others], II, 1975, 250, 252.

662. The coins and jettons. *Ibid.*, 315–30, pls. 133–7.

663. The Anglo-Irish coins and tokens in the University Coin-Cabinet at Oslo. *IN 8*(43), Jan./Feb. 1975, 9–12.

664. An unusual provenance for the IN MEMORY OF THE GOOD OLD DAYS counter, by Michael Dolley and J. McGrath. *Ibid. 8*(44), Mar./Apr. 1975, 47. [Harare find.]

665. A neglected minor parcel of 'brass money' shillings and sixpences of James II. *Ibid.*, 53–4.

666. The Anglo-Irish coins in the Cabinet des Médailles at the Bibliothèque Nationale, Paris. *Ibid. 8*(45), May/June 1975, 83–7.

667. A find of early 19th-century silver tokens from near Killala, Co. Mayo. *Ibid. 8*(46), July/Aug. 1975, 119–23. [Doonadoba (Ballycastle) find.]

668. Some preliminary observations on the supply of specie to Ireland under the Union. *Ibid. 8*(47), Sept./Oct. 1975, 174–8.

669. The display of coins in the new County Museum at Monaghan. *Ibid. 8*(48), Nov./Dec. 1975, 215–18.

670. A neglected sidelight on the last years of Ardfert corporation. *J. Kerry Archaeol. and Hist. Soc.* no. 8,

1975, 178–81. [On R. Sainthill, *Olla Podrida, 1*, 1844, 257–63.]
671. An early nineteenth-century forger's run from the Co. Offaly. *J. Old Athlone Society 1*(4), 1974/5, 271–2, pl. 18.
672. A further note on the fourteenth-century armorial of Ireland. *North Munster Ant. J. 17*, 1975, 31–3. ['Féilsgríbhinn Éamoinn mhic Giolla Iasachta', i.e. special volume to honour Edward A. MacLysaght.]
673. Some 18th-century fabrications of the 'brass money' of James II. *NCirc 83*(1), Jan. 1975, 6–8.
674. A neglected nineteenth-century find from the Co. Laois. *Ibid. 83*(2), Feb. 1975, 60–1. [Sleaty find.]
675. A find of eighteenth-century copper coins from Ramsey (I.o.M.). *Ibid. 83*(3), Mar. 1975, 102.
676. Some preliminary observations on three Manx coin-hoards appearing to end with pennies of Eadgar. *Ibid. 83*(4), Apr. 1975, 146–7; *83*(5), May 1975, 190–2. [Kirk Andreas, Ballaqueeney, and Ballaquayle hoards; *see also* items 807, 811.]
677. Two Irish addenda to the Bibliography of Coin Hoards of Great Britain and Ireland, 1500–1967. *Ibid. 83*(6), June 1975, 240. [*Addenda to* item 545.]
678. A Co. Cork omission from the Bibliography of Coin Hoards of Great Britain and Ireland. *Ibid. 83*(10), Oct. 1975, 381. [*Omitted from* item 545; 17th-cent. 'Co. Cork' find.]
679. Some more omissions from recent listings of Irish coin-hoards. *Ibid. 83*(11), Nov. 1975, 425–6. [*Omissions from* items 545 and 568.]
680. The 1973 Viking-Age coin-find from Dunmore Cave. *Old Kilkenny Rev.: journal of the Kilkenny Archaeological Society*, n.s., *1*(2), 1975, 70–9.
681. A forgotten eighteenth-century discovery of Hiberno-Norse coins in the County Meath. *Ríocht na Midhe 6*(1), 1975, 55–8. ['Co. Meath' find.]
682. A mythical parcel from the 1894 Ballaquayle (Douglas) hoard. *SCMB* no. 679, Mar. 1975, 76–7.
683. The pattern of Viking-Age coin-hoards from the Isle of Man. *Ibid.*, no. 685, Sept. 1975, 296–302; no. 686, Oct. 1975, 337–40.
684. Excavation in the Franciscan Friary Church, Armagh. Appendix IV: The coins, by Donal Bateson and Michael Dolley. *Ulster J. of Archaeology[3] 38*, 1975, 78–80. [Principal author C. J. Lynn.]

1976

685. *Some Irish dimensions to Manx history: an inaugural lecture delivered before the Queen's University of Belfast on 28 January 1976*. [1976]. 23pp. (New lecture series, no. 92.)
686. The thirteenth-century trebuchet-type coin balance . . ., by M. Dolley and L. Ketteringham. In *Alsted: excavation of a thirteenth-fourteenth century sub-manor house with its ironworks in Netherne Wood, Merstham, Surrey*, by Lesley L. Ketteringham, 1976, 61–3, pl. xiii.
687. A medieval house at 13 and 13A Old Street, St Helier: the finds: the coins. *Annual Bulletin – Société Jersiaise 21*(4), 1976, 489. [12th-cent., English and French; principal author M. B. Finlaison.]
688. The coins. In *The Archaeology of Anglo-Saxon England*, ed. David M. Wilson, 1976, 349–72; list of sources, 463–511.
689. Découverte en France d'un groat anglo-irlandais du XVe siecle; traduction . . . *Bulletin – Le Club francais de la Médaille*, n° 51/52, 1976, 144–50. [Beaulieu (Corrèze) find.]
690.* A further find of fused coins from Rahans Lough, Magheracloone. *Clogher Record 9*(1), 1976, 76–7. [16th-cent.; *see also* item 513.]
691. A significant findspot for a penny of Harold I. *Durobrivae: a review of Nene Valley archaeology* no. 4, 1976,

20–1. [Southwick (Northants.) find; *Fleur-de-lis* type, Stamford.]

692. A prize-medal in gold awarded to Richard Brinsley Sheridan's cousin. In *Essays Presented to Michael Roberts*, ed. J. Bossy and P. Jupp, 1976, 70–9, plate. [Awarded by the Constitutional Free Debating Society in 1771 to Richard Sheridan (c.1745–1793) for supporting the law of the land against the House of Commons.]
693. The first coin from Ireland to reach the continent of Europe. In *Festoen, opgedragen aan A. N. Zadoks-Josephus Jitta bij haar zeventigste verjaardag*, redactie J. S. Boersma . . . [*et al*], Groningen; Bussum [1976], 223–6. [Hiberno-Norse, *Crux* type, from the Le Puy hoard; and, St Dympna.]
694. A provisional note on the incidence of coin-hoarding in Viking-Age Ireland. Michael Dolley and Christopher Lynn. *Irish Archaeol. Research Forum 3*(2), 1976, 1–6.
695. A rare variety of the Charles II halfpenny Irish with the date 1682, by Michael Dolley and K. W. H. Glass. *IN* 9(49), Jan./Feb. 1976, 7–9.
696. Some remarks on the 'pewter' (tin) petty coinage of March/April 1690, by Donal Bateson and Michael Dolley. *Ibid.* 9(50), Mar./Apr. 1976, 44–9.
697. Further evidence concerning the identity of the 'Dominick grote', by Michael Dolley and S. G. Ellis. *Ibid.* 9(51), May/June 1976, 93–4. [*Further to* item 448.]
698. An Anglo-Saxon penny found on the outskirts of modern Dublin. *Ibid.* 9(52), July/Aug. 1976, 132–4. [Edgar, *Two-Line* type.]
699. A medallic memorial of an Irish patriot malgré lui. *Ibid.* 9(53), Sept./Oct. 1976, 179–84. [On Roger O'Connor.]
700. A numismatic sidelight on a Manx parallel for an Irish popular devotional practice. *Ibid.* 9(54), Nov./Dec. 1976, 220–8. [On well-offerings.]
701. The two near-contemporary findings of Hiberno-Norse coins from Maughold. *J. Manx Museum* 7(88), 1976, 236–40, pl. 61.
702. Fourteen pence to a shilling. *Manxman* no. 3, 1975/6, 24–6.
703. The first Manx coins. *Ibid.*, no. 4, 1976, 57–8.
704. A late seventeenth-century instance of Irish and Scottish money being legal tender on Man. *Ibid.*, no. 5, 1976, 26–7.
705. A page of history in a penny. *Ibid.*, no. 6, 1976, 42–4. [An Edgar penny, perhaps from Ballaquayle.]
706. To mynter fra en norsk konge funnet på Isle of Man. *NNF-Nytt: meddelelser fra Norsk Numismatisk Forening* no. 1, Jan. 1976, 3–6. [Two coins of Eric Bloodaxe found on the Isle of Man.]
707. En 'ny' norrøn utmyntning fra De vestlige øyer; oversatt J. H. N[ordbø]. *Ibid.*, no. 2, May 1976, [15–17]. [Hiberno-Manx.]
708. The Irish coinage, 1534–1691. In *A New History of Ireland*, ed. T. W. Moody . . . [*et al.*], III, 1976, 408–19, 683–4.
709. A Hiberno-Manx coinage of the eleventh century. *NC 136*, 1976, 75–84, pl. 13.
710. An altered early nineteenth-century Manx token halfpenny in the Ulster Museum, by Donal Bateson and Michael Dolley. *NCirc 84*(2), Feb. 1976, 50.
711. A further parcel of Reform-Type pence from an eighteenth-century find from N. E. England [i.e. N.-E. Midlands]. *Ibid. 84*(4), Apr. 1976, 141. [Oakham hoard.]
712. An abortive if apparently official attempt at 'improvement' of the latinity of the Manx national motto. *Ibid. 84*(5), May 1976, 182–4.
713. A nineteenth-century concealment of English silver coins. *Ibid. 84*(6),

June 1976, 228–31. [Douglas, North Quay, find.]

714. The mint of [i.e. or] mints of BMC Type XIV of Edward the Elder. *Ibid. 84*(7/8), July/Aug. 1976, 276–7.

715. A note on the circumstances of the finding of the Middle Temple hoard. *Ibid. 84*(9), Sept. 1976, 316–17.

716. A mythical Manx coinage of the tenth century. *Ibid. 84*(11), Nov. 1976, 410.

717. A modern forgery of a Limerick brass- ('gun'-) money shilling of James II, by Michael Dolley and Patrick Finn. *Ibid. 84*(12), Dec. 1976, 463.

718. Excavations at Clontuskert Priory, Co. Galway. Appendix 1: The coins from Clontuskert. *PRIA*, Section C, 76(5), 1976, 163–9, pl. xxvii. [Principal author T. Fanning.]

719. Roman coins from Ireland and the date of St Patrick. *Ibid. 76*(7), 1976, 181–90. [Presented to a Colloquium on Hiberno-Roman Relations and Material Remains, Dublin, 1974.]

720. A neglected minor find of later fourteenth-century Scottish silver coins from the Isle of Man. *SCMB* no. 690, Feb. 1976, 43–5. [Castletown, Strandhall, find.]

721. Some neglected Scandinavian evidence for the ordering of the early types of Edward the Confessor. *Ibid.*, no. 693, May 1976, 154–8.

722. The identity of the 'seuadoore' of a 1696(?) petition to Lord Derby by the Manx Keys. *Ibid.*, no. 694, June 1976, 196.

723. Show me the colour of your money, by Michael Dolley and L. S. Garrad. *Ibid.*, no. 696, Aug. 1976, 312–17. [On the description of patination colours.]

724. A note on the Edward the Confessor element in the 1880 Espinge hoard. *Ibid.*, no. 700, Dec. 1976, 461–4.

725. The site of the Bishop's Court, Mullynure, Co. Armagh. Appendix: A note on the coins. *Seanchas Ard Mhacha: journal of the Armagh Diocesan Hist. Soc. 8*(1), 1975/6, 132. [Principal author C. J. Lynn.]

Reviews

726. *Ships and Parts of Ships on Coins*, ed. A. L. Ben-Eli. *Mariner's Mirror 62*(2), May 1976, 198.

727. Herbert Ewe, *Schiffe auf Siegeln*. *Ibid. 62*(3), Aug. 1976, 299–300.

1977

728. *Corpus nummorum saeculorum IX-XI qui in Suecia reperti sunt . . . 1: Gotland. 2: Bäl –Buttle*, . . . edidit Brita Malmer; cooperantibus Peter Berghaus, Michael Dolley, . . . et aliis. Stockholm: Kungl. Vitterhets Historie och Antikvitets Akademien, 1977. xxxiv, 341pp., 52 pls.

729. Treasure trove: a note on Manx law and practice. *Antiquity 51*(202), July 1977, 137–9.

730. Patricius, Auxilius, Isserninus. In *The Bishops' Synod ('The First Synod of St Patrick'): [proceedings of] a symposium, with text, translation, and commentary*, ed. M. J. Faris, 1977, 28–9. [On Corpus Christi College, Cambridge, MS 279.]

731. The regional pattern of die-cutting exhibited by the First Hand pennies of Æthelræd II preserved in the British Museum. Michael Dolley and Tuukka Talvio. *BNJ 47*, 1977, 53–65.

732. The twelfth of the Agnus Dei pennies of Æthelræd II. Michael Dolley and Tuukka Talvio. *Ibid.*, 131–3. [*See also* item 797.]

733. Coins from the Winchester excavations, 1961–1973. Michael Dolley and C. E. Blunt. *Ibid.*, 135–8, pl. iv.

734. The Norwegian hoard-evidence for the chronology of the Dublin coinages of the eleventh century. *IN 10*(55), Jan./Feb. 1977, 15–17.

735. A Waterford penny of Edward I found in England. *Ibid. 10*(56),

Mar./Apr. 1977, 37, 54–5. [Moulsecoombe (Brighton) find.]

736. The Armagh County Museum, by D. Bateson and M. Dolley. *Ibid.* *10*(58), July/Aug. 1977, 120–3.

737. New evidence for the date of the so-called 'St Patrick's' halfpence and farthings, by Michael Dolley and Margaret Warhurst. *Ibid.* *10*(59), Sept./Oct. 1977, 161–3. [Finds from the *Mary* wreck.]

738. The date of the Ballinrees ('Coleraine') hoard. *Ibid.* *10*(60), Nov./Dec. 1977, 223–4.

739. The coins. In *Llantrithyd: a ringwork in South Glamorgan*, [by a sub-group of the] Cardiff Archaeological Society, 1977, 52–6.

740. A note on Man's 'Brummagem' coinage. *Manxman* no. 7, 1976/7, 16, 18. [The Manx coins and tokens in Lund; the striking of the 1758 coinage in Birmingham by Florry.]

741. A false planchet coin in the modern Anglo-Manx series. *Ibid.*, no. 8, 1977, 19.

742. The Yorkshire influence. *Ibid.*, no. 9, 1977, 44–5. [The family and political connections behind the Manx appointments of Sir Wadsworth Busk, William Frankland, and Cornelius Smelt.]

743. Den atlantiske omkrets: noen upåaktede sammentreff fra de to siste tiår av det 12. århundre; [trans. J. H. Nordbø]. *NNF-Nytt* no. 1, Jan. 1977, 19–25. ['The Atlantic circumference: some unnoticed coincidences (in the coinages of Scandinavia and the British Isles), 1180–1200'.]

744. En kommentar till sigillmatriserna som nyligen hänförts till Olof Skötkonungs tid; översatt av Tuukka Talvio. *NNUM* no. 9, Nov. 1977, 161–6. ['A commentary on the seal recently attributed to the time of Olof Skötkonung'.]

745. The Anglo-Manx coins and tokens in the university collections at Helsinki and Oslo. *NCirc* *85*(2), Feb. 1977, 48.

746. A dubious Edward the Confessor moneyer of Dover, by Miss F. E. Colman and Michael Dolley. *Ibid.*, 56. [*Radiate/Small Cross*, Ælfwine, reattributed to York.]

747. The Anglo-Manx coins and tokens in the Royal Coin and Medal Collection in Copenhagen. *Ibid.* *85*(4), Apr. 1977, 147–8.

748. The eighteenth- and nineteenth-century Anglo-Manx coins in the Royal Coin Cabinet, Stockholm. *Ibid.* *85*(5), May 1977, 200.

749. Ten additional Anglo-Irish coins in the Helsinki collection. *Ibid.* *85*(7/8), July/Aug. 1977, 308–9.

750. A further note on certain unpublished variants of the *Pacx* type of Edward the Confessor. *Ibid.* *85*(9), Sept. 1977, 357–8. [*Further to* item 419.]

751. The Castle Freke (Rathbarry, Co. Cork) find of tenth-century Anglo-Saxon coins, by J. P. McCarthy and Michael Dolley. *Ibid.* *85*(11), Nov. 1977, 488–90.

752. A little-known contribution to Hiberno-Norse numismatics of Otto Alcenius (1838–1913), by Michael Dolley and Tuukka Talvio. *PRIA*, Section C, 77(5), 1977, 213–21.

753. An *ex voto* of eleventh-century silver coins from Co. Westmeath. *Ríocht na Midhe* 6(3), 1977, 19–22.

754. The last(?) Coroner's treasure trove inquest to be held on the Isle of Man. *SCMB* no. 705, May 1977, 177–81. [Castletown(?) find.]

755. The two Viking-Age coins recently found at Abbey Street, Armagh. *Seanchas Ard Mhacha* 8(2), 1977, 281–3, plate. [Eadwig, *Two-Line* type; Hiberno-Norse, Phase III.]

Reviews

756. James A. Mackay, *The Pobjoy Encyclopaedia of Isle of Man Coins and Tokens*. *BNJ* *47*, 1977, 150–2.

757. R. H. Kinvig, *The Isle of Man: a*

social, cultural and political history [3rd edn]. *J. Hist. Geography 3*(1), 1977, 76–7.

758. Kolbjørn Skaare, *Coins and Coinage in Viking-Age Norway*. *NCirc 85*(5), May 1977, 207–9.

759. James A. Mackay, *The Pobjoy Encyclopaedia of Isle of Man Coins and Tokens*. *Ibid. 85*(10), Oct. 1977, 430–1.

1978

760. The Hiberno-Norse coins in Gotlands Fornsal, Visby. *BNJ 48*, 1978, 20–34. [Appendix: The Anglo-Saxon coins in Gotlands Fornsal from the former Visby High School collection. Lists 423 coins.]

761.* A Byzantine copper coin of the twelfth century from the churchyard at Tydavnet, Co. Monaghan. *Clogher Record 9*(3), 1978, 374–6.

762. The Hiberno-Norse element in the 1924 Igelösa hoard from Skåne. *Coin Hoards 4*, 1978, 157–9.

763. An introduction to the coinage of Æthelræd II. In *Ethelred the Unready: papers from the Millenary conference*, ed. David Hill, 1978 (BAR 59), 115–33.

764. The Anglo-Irish coins in the University Collection at Bergen. *IN 11*(61), Jan./Feb. 1978, 15.

765. 'St Patrick' half-groats and pennies? *Ibid.*, 39.

766. The Anglo-Irish coins and tokens in the University Coin Cabinet at Lund. *Ibid. 11*(62), Mar./Apr. 1978, 59–60.

767. A post-Easter-Rising coin-hoard from the Co. Fermanagh. *Ibid. 11*(63), May/June 1978, 124–5. [Derryad (Lisnaskea) find.]

768. A spurious hoard of Greek coins from Ireland, by D. Bateson and M. Dolley. *Ibid. 11*(64), July/Aug. 1978, 159.

769. The Anglo-Irish tokens and tickets in the Royal Coin and Medal Collection at Copenhagen. *Ibid.*, 177–9.

770. The Hiberno-Norse coins without hoard-provenance in the University Coin-Cabinet at Lund. *Ibid. 11*(65), Sept./Oct. 1978, 207–9.

771. Neglected evidence from Ireland for periodicity of type in the English coinage of Æthelræd II. *Ibid. 11*(66), Nov./Dec. 1978, 278–81.

772. A paranumismatic sidelight on several centuries of Manx history: the wreck of the *Lucy* (1702). In *Man and Environment in the Isle of Man*, ed. Peter Davey, II, 1978 (BAR 54(ii)), 373–400.

773. Lady Isabella's rival? *Manxman* no. 12, 1978, 9–13. [The mill-wheel at Lummelunda on Gotland.]

774. Things are not always what they seem. . .! Michael Dolley and Hilary Guard. *Ibid.*, no. 13, 1978, 36–8. [A 1758 Manx penny struck on an Anglo-Irish halfpenny of 1769.]

775. En ny penny från Olof den Helige av Norge i Gotlands Fornsal. *Meddelande från Klinte Hembygdsförening* (Klintehamn), 1978, [2–6].

776. Sveriges första import av irländska mynt; övers. T. L[indgren] och L. L[agerqvis]t. *Myntkontakt* no. 4, Apr. 1978, 102–3, 119. ['The first Swedish import of Irish coins'; finds of Hiberno-Norse, *Crux* type.]

777. En ny engelsk funn-proveniens for en Eirik Blodøks-mynt; oversatt J. H. N[ordbø]. *NNF-Nytt* no. 2, Sept. 1978, 12–14. [A new English hoard-provenance (Chester) for a coin of Eric Bloodaxe.]

778. Et glemt funn av 1600-talls engelske mynter fra Stavanger Domkirke; [oversatt J. H. Nordbø]. *Ibid.* no. 3, Dec. 1978, 19–20.

779. An illusory Ipswich mule! *NCirc 86*(3), Mar. 1978, 130. [Æthelred II, transitional *First Hand* type; *see also* item 425.]

780. The Anglo-Manx coins and tokens in the university collections at Bergen and Trondheim. *Ibid. 86*(4), Apr. 1978, 180.

781. Some additional light on Callister's Ramsey (I.o.M) token of 1831, by Michael Dolley and Frank Cowin. *Ibid. 86*(5), May 1978, 245–8.
782. Three Scots countermarked Spanish dollars in the Royal Coin and Medal Collection at Copenhagen. *Ibid. 86*(7/8), July/Aug. 1978, 362.
783. The Churchill portrait brouhaha: a similar incident involving a nineteenth-century Finnish numismatist, by Michael Dolley and Tuukka Talvio. *Ibid. 86*(9), Sept. 1978, 418. [On H. F. Antell (1847–1893).]
784. A Lincolnshire provenance for an 'Ælfred' penny in the British Museum. *Ibid. 86*(12), Dec. 1978, 587–8.
785. Archaeological excavations at Trim Castle, Co. Meath, 1971–74. Appendix III: Report on numismatic material. *PRIA*, Section C, *78*(6), 1978, 193–8, pl. xvii. [Principal author P. D. Sweetman.]
786. A note on the insular element in the 1934 Ludwiszcze hoard. *SCMB* no. 713, Jan. 1978, 8–9. [10th to 11th-cent.]
787. A 'Canterbury' coin of Æthelræd II's Helmet type in the National Museum at Helsinki, by Michael Dolley and Tuukka Talvio. *Ibid.*, no. 718, June 1978, 170–2. [Scandinavian imitation.]
788. The identity of the 'levadoon' appearing in a Manx document of 1693. *Ibid.*, no. 720, Aug. 1978, 241–2. [*Leuadoor* or *Louis d'or*.]
789. An unpublished Edward the Confessor moneyer of Norwich. *Ibid.*, no. 721, Sept. 1978, 268–70. [*Facing Small Cross* type, Godeverd.]
790. A note on the 1871/1872 Barrowby (Grantham, Lincs.) find of later Anglo-Saxon pennies. *Ibid.*, no. 723, Nov. 1978, 343–5.
791. The Anglo-Danish and Anglo-Norse coinages of York. In *Viking-Age York and the North*, ed. R. A. Hall, 1978, 26–31.

Reviews

792. Philip Grierson, *Monnaies du Moyen Âge*. *EHR 93*(366), Jan. 1978, 153–4.
793. Niall Fallon, *The Armada in Ireland*. *Mariner's Mirror 64*(4), Nov. 1978, 380–1.
794. J. D. Bateson, *Coins and Medals: a guide to the numismatic collections in the Ulster Museum, Belfast*. *NCirc 86*(12), Dec. 1978, 586–7.

1979

795. Roger of Wendover's date for Eadgar's coinage reform. *BNJ 49*, 1979, 1–11.
796. The Hiberno-Norse element of the List hoard from Sylt. Mark Blackburn and Michael Dolley. *Ibid.*, 17–25, pl. i.
797. A thirteenth *Agnus Dei* penny of Æthelræd II. Michael Dolley and Tuukka Talvio. *Ibid.*, 122–5.
798. The last(?) Hiberno-Norse penny to reach the U.S.S.R. *IN 12*(67), Jan./Feb. 1979, 22–5. [Juura find.]
799. An unlooked-for Manx sidelight on the Irish token coinage of the later eighteenth century. *Ibid. 12*(68), Mar./Apr. 1979, 79–84. [On J. H. Kyan of Camac, Kyan & Camac.]
800. An unpublished(?) medal of Feargus O'Connor. *Ibid. 12*(70), July/Aug. 1979, 191–5.
801. The Irish coins in the Dresden Coin-Cabinet. *Ibid. 12*(71), Sept./Oct. 1979, 229–30.
802. An eleventh-century Dublin penny found on the Isle of Man. *Ibid. 12*(72), Nov./Dec. 1979, 289–91. [From the Ballaberna (Kirk Maughold) hoard.]
803. En gotländsk nyckel till den engelska myntningens rätta gruppering under 1040-talet; [översättningen Ragnar Engeström]. *Myntkontakt* no. 9/10, Dec. 1979, 186–7; summary, 'A Gotland clue to

the proper ordering of the English coinage of the early 1040s', 187. [Stora Sojdeby find.]

804. Det første autentiske funn av en norsk vikingtidsmynt i Nordamerika = The first authentic finding of a Norwegian Viking-Age coin in continental America. *NNF-Nytt*, no. 2, May 1979, 18–28. [English text, pp. 23–7. Olaf Kyrre; Maine, Hancock Co., Blue Hill Bay find.]
805. Et nyt eksemplar af Svend Tveskægs mønt, af Mark Blackburn, Michael Dolley og Kenneth Jonsson; oversat J. S[teen] J[ensen]. *NNUM* no. 4, May 1979, 61–5. [Lists all coins of Sweyn Forkbeard; *see also* items 822, 849. Special issue for G. Galster's 90th birthday.]
806. The Hiberno-Norse coins in the University Coin-Cabinet at Uppsala. *NC 139*, 1979, 225–9, pl. 33.
807. A supplementary note on the 1874 Ballaqueeney find from the Isle of Man. *NCirc 87*(3), Mar. 1979, 123–4. [*Supplements* item 676.]
808. A mythical numismatic tour-de-force. *Ibid. 87*(6), June 1979, 285–6. [On John Ives (1751–1776).]
809. The murky career of 'Major Medallion' (James Mudie, 1779–1852). *Ibid. 87*(7/8), July/Aug. 1979, 337–9.
810. An unpublished letter of Irish interest from a neglected nineteenth-century English clerical collector. *Ibid. 87*(10), Oct. 1979, 446–8; *87*(11), Nov. 1979, 501–2. [A letter from Rev. Joseph William Martin to Aquilla Smith about Edward IV, etc.]
811. Promised further light on the 1866 Kirk Andreas find. *Ibid. 87*(12), Dec. 1979, 548–9. [*Further to* item 676.]
812. A page of Shannon's history in a silver penny. *The Other Clare (Shannon Archaeol. and Hist. Soc.) 3*, Apr. 1979, 5–6. [A 14th-cent. Canterbury sterling found in Tullyglass townland.]
813. Silver Saxon and medieval coins . . . In *The Saxon and medieval palaces at Cheddar: excavations 1960–62*, [by] Philip Rahtz . . ., 1979 (BAR 65), 291–5, 367, pl. xviii.
814. The tokens, jettons and a medalet . . . *Ibid.*, 296–7, 367.
815. The 'Armstrong and Legge' (*recte* 'Knox'?) halfpence Irish with dates 1680/1/2/3/4. *SCMB* no. 728, Apr. 1979, 118–20.
816. A sliver of silver speaks. *U.N.E. Convocation Bulletin and Alumni News – University of New England*, no. 45, Mar. 1979, 8–9. [On the Olaf Kyrre penny from America.]

1980

817. A Carolingian *denarius* with a Devonshire provenance. Michael Dolley and Norman Shiel. *BNJ 50*, 1980, 7–11. [Culm Davy find.]
818. Five further Anglo-Irish pieces with a Porvoo (Borgå) provenance. *IN 13*(73), Jan./Feb. 1980, 9–11. [*Further to* item 636.]
819. Additional light on the 1834 coin-hoard from Kirk Michael (Isle of Man). *Ibid. 13*(74), Mar./Apr. 1980, 82–4.
820. The 1972 Kirk Michael Viking treasure trove: the numismatic element of the hoard, and a possible historical context. *J. Manx Museum 8*(89), 1980, 11–20. [Principal author A. M. Cubbon.]
821. Skatten fra Bradda Mountain [på] Man fra 1848: en oversett norsk tilknytning = The neglected Norwegian dimension to the 1848 coin-hoard from Bradda Mountain (Isle of Man). *NNF-Nytt* no. 2, Sept. 1980, 7–24. [Text in English, pp. 15–22; evidence that Olaf Tryggvason was present in the Irish Sea after winter 994/5.]
822. Proveniensen för Svend Tveskægs mynt, af Michael Dolley, Mark Blackburn, Kenneth Jonsson. *NNUM* no. 3, Apr. 1980, 57. [*See also* item 805; the provenance

(Gotland, Hellviparish, Kännungs) of a Sweyn Forkbeard coin.]

823. Some Insular(?) imitations from the 1030s of contemporary English pence of Cnut. *NCirc 88*(3), Mar. 1980, 86–8. [Hiberno-Manx.]

824. The minimal English content of the 1973 Dorow find (Mecklenburg/Pommern). *SCMB* no. 739, Mar. 1980, 82–4. [10th-cent.]

825. Ephippiorum Artifex vindicatus. *Ibid.*, no. 740, Apr. 1980, 107. [An illustration of a Gloucester coin of Cnut incorrectly engraved as Ipswich.]

1981

826. The 1639 coin-hoard from near Glendalough (Co. Wicklow) as a case-study in the 'improvement' of seventeenth-century and later line illustrations of coins. *IN 14*(79), Jan./Feb. 1981, 8–15.

827. [The excavations at Fishamble Street, Dublin]. *Ibid. 14*(81), May/June 1981, 151. (Letters to the editor.)

828. 'Men mange som er de første, skal bli de siste . . .' (Matt. XIX.30) = 'Many who are first will be last . . .' (Matthew XIX.30); norsk oversettelse J. H. N[ordbø]. *NNF-Nytt* no. 1, Mar. 1981, 54–8; English text, 58–63. [Tenth anniversary issue, and celebration of Kolbjørn Skaare's 50th birthday. On the paradox that Norsemen were present in the coin-using British Isles from the 8th-cent., but did not strike coins in Norway until the end of the 10th-cent.]

829. [Historical numismatics, etc.] *NC 141*, 1981, xiii-xvi. [Address delivered upon receiving the Royal Numismatic Society's medal for 1981.]

830. The palimpsest of Viking settlement on Man. In *Proceedings of the eighth Viking Congress, Århus . . . 1977*, ed. Hans Bekker-Nielsen . . . [*et al.*], Odense 1981, 173–81. [The pattern of coin-finds.]

831. Imitation and imitation of imitation: some problems posed by the non-English *Helmet* pennies with the name of Æthelræd II. In *Studies in Northern Coinages of the Eleventh Century*, ed. C. J. Becker, Copenhagen 1981 (Danske Videnskabernes Selskab. Historisk-filosofiske Skrifter, 9(4)), 89–111.

832. Imitative anticipation: yet another dimension to the problem of Scandinavian imitation of Anglo-Saxon coins, by Michael Dolley and Kenneth Jonsson. *Ibid.*, 113–18.

833. A summing-up. In *Viking-Age coinage in the Northern Lands: [proceedings of] the sixth Oxford symposium on coinage and monetary history*, ed. M. A. S. Blackburn and D. M. Metcalf, II, 1981 (BAR S-122(ii)), 533–52.

Reviews

834. *Danefæ*, ed. P. V. Glob. *NCirc 89*(2), Feb. 1981, 44.

1982

835. *Corpus nummorum saeculorum IX-XI qui in Suecia reperti sunt . . . 1: Gotland. 3: Dalhem–Etelhem*, edidit Brita Malmer; cooperantibus Peter Berghaus, Michael Dolley . . . et aliis. Stockholm: Kungl. Vitterhets Historie och Antikvitets Akademien, 1982. xxxiv, 323pp., 17 pls.

836. *Corpus nummorum saeculorum IX-XI qui in Suecia reperti sunt . . . 1: Gotland. 4: Fardhem–Fröjel*, edidit Brita Malmer; cooperantibus . . . aliis. Stockholm: Kungl. Myntkabinettet; Kungl. Vitterhets Historie och Antikvitets Akademien, 1982. xxvii, 303pp. ['The following have taken part in the preparation . . . Irish coins: Michael Dolley, Brita Malmer' – p. xi.]

837. Two Scandinavian coins found in Lincoln. Mark Blackburn, Michael Dolley. In *Archaeology in Lincoln*,

1981–82: tenth annual report of Lincoln Archaeological Trust, 1982, 33–5. [Magnus the Good; Olaf Kyrre.]

838. Dateringen af de seneste St Peters-mønter fra York. *NNUM* no. 5, Sept. 1982, 82–90; bemærkninger fra Kirsten Bendixen, 90; afsluttende svar fra Michael Dolley, 91. [The date of the latest St Peter coins from York.]

839. A hitherto unsuspected oriental element in the 1840 Cuerdale hoard. Michael Dolley and Norman Shiel. *NC 142*, 1982, 155–6.

840. The Anglo-Saxon and Anglo-Norman coins at Dresden, by Mark Blackburn and Michael Dolley. *NCirc 90*(2), Mar. 1982, 47–9; *90*(3), Apr. 1982, 85–6. [Lists 372 coins.]

841. Obituaries: 'F.E.J.'. *Ibid. 90*(2), Mar. 1982, 52. [Francis Elmore Jones.]

Reviews

842. Thomas A. Schweich, 'Clue to a puzzling period: the mystery of Late Anglo-Saxon coinage'. *Ibid. 90*(8), Oct. 1982, 274.

843. *Viking-Age Coinage in the Northern lands . . .*, ed. M. A. S. Blackburn and D. M. Metcalf. *SCMB* no. 763, Mar. 1982, 96–7.

844. *The Vikings in England*, ed. E. Roesdahl. *Ibid.*, no. 769, Sept. 1982, 288–90.

1983

845. *Early Medieval Coins from Lincoln and its Shire, c.770–1100*. Mark Blackburn, Christina Colyer, and Michael Dolley . . . Council for British Archaeology for the Lincoln Archaeological Trust, 1983. [2], 46pp. (The Archaeology of Lincoln, vol. VI-1). [Includes 'The Danish descent(s) on Lindsey in 841', by Michael Dolley, pp. 40–2.]

846. The jettons from the excavations . . . In *Excavations in Christchurch, 1969–1980*, [by] Keith S. Jarvis . . . 1983 (Dorset Natural History and Archaeol. Soc. Monograph series, no. 5), 82–3.

847. The identity of the second(?) Hiberno-Norse mint in Ireland. *IN 16*(94), July/Aug. 1983, 121–4. [Phase IV, ?Waterford.]

848. The 1981 Chelsea Reach (London) find of Second Hand pennies of Æthelræd II, by Michael Dolley and Brian Grover [with a note by Mark Blackburn]; in memoriam Dorotheae Whitelock. *Numismatiska Meddelanden 33*, 1983, 85–99; sammanfattning, 99.

849. A new specimen of Svend Tveskæg's coinage. Mark Blackburn, Michael Dolley, and Kenneth Jonsson. *SCMB* no. 775, Mar. 1983, 60–4. [*A slightly revised version of* item 805.]

850. Ælfred the Great's abandonment of the concept of periodic coinage. In *Studies in Numismatic Method Presented to Philip Grierson*, ed. C. N. L. Brooke . . . [*et al.*], 1983, 153–60.

Forthcoming publications

851. Gunmoney, by Michael Dolley and Fr. G. Rice. For the Belfast Branch, Numismatic Society of Ireland.

852. High Street and Winetavern Street, Dublin, excavations: the coin finds. For the National Museum of Ireland.

853. The *Liber Assedationis* (1510/1514) and the pattern of Scandinavian settlement on the Isle of Man. For *Nomina*.

854. *R. v. Heywood* (1786): the leading case in the history of the Manx law of treasure trove.

855. St Patrick's Isle (I.o.M.) hoard of Hiberno-Norse coins.

856. Sylloge of Coins of the British Isles: Manx Museum, Douglas: Anglo-Saxon and Hiberno-Norse coins, by Michael Dolley, Mark Blackburn, and Christopher Blunt.

857. Sylloge of Coins of the British Isles: Royal Coin Cabinet, Stockholm: Edward the Confessor and Harold II, by Frances E. Colman and Michael Dolley.
858. Sylloge of Coins of the British Isles: Royal Coin Cabinet, Stockholm: Hiberno-Norse coins, by Michael Dolley and Mark Blackburn.
859. Nummular brooches, by Michael Dolley and Melinda Mays. For *The Crafts and Industries of Medieval Winchester*, ed. Martin Biddle (Winchester Studies 7.ii).
860. Disc and rectangular brooches: note. *Ibid.* [Principal author D. A. Hinton.]
861. The (?)seal trial-piece, by Michael Dolley and Melinda Mays. For *The Winchester Mint and Other Numismatic Studies*, by Yvonne Harvey *et al.* (Winchester Studies 8).
862. Coins from the Winchester excavations of 1961–71, by C. E. Blunt and Michael Dolley. *Ibid.*
863. Wood Quay, Dublin, excavations: the coin finds. For the National Museum of Ireland.
864. The scandal of Deemster Gawne, 1823.

Manuscripts

1.* Naumachia, or, The principles of naval warfare, by Leo VI, Philosophus, Emperor of the Romans; translated, with notes, sketches and plans, from the Greek text of M. Alphonse Dian (Collection Budé 1943), by R. H. Dolley [c.1950.] 31pp. Typescript.
2. Undersökning av 43 förfalskade engelska guldsovereigns med George V:s bild, baserad på uppgifter av Sveriges Riksbank och Kungl. Mynt- och Justeringsverket samt utförd av Kungl. Myntkabinettet, genom R. H. M. Dolley och Lars O. Lagerqvist. [1957]. 8 leaves. Typescript; in British Museum, Department of Coins and Medals; binding title 'Yemen sovereigns'.
3.* The *Agnus Dei* pennies of Æthelræd II. [c.1960.] 160pp. Typescript.
4.* The Canadian tokens alleged to read 'Vexator Canadiensis'. R. H. M. Dolley and J. P. C. Kent. 1963.

SYNOPSIS OF SUBJECTS

Note Autobiographical contributions may be found under 'Numismatists'.

INDEX OF COLLABORATORS AND OF PERSONS HONOURED BY A *FESTSCHRIFT*

Index

This index does not include detailed references to the lists of finds in Chapters 5 and 15 or to Michael Dolley's bibliography. For the latter, a 'Synopsis of subjects' and an 'Index of collaborators and persons honoured by a *Festschrift*' appear on pp. 353–60.
Unless otherwise indicated, 'king' signifies 'king of the English'.